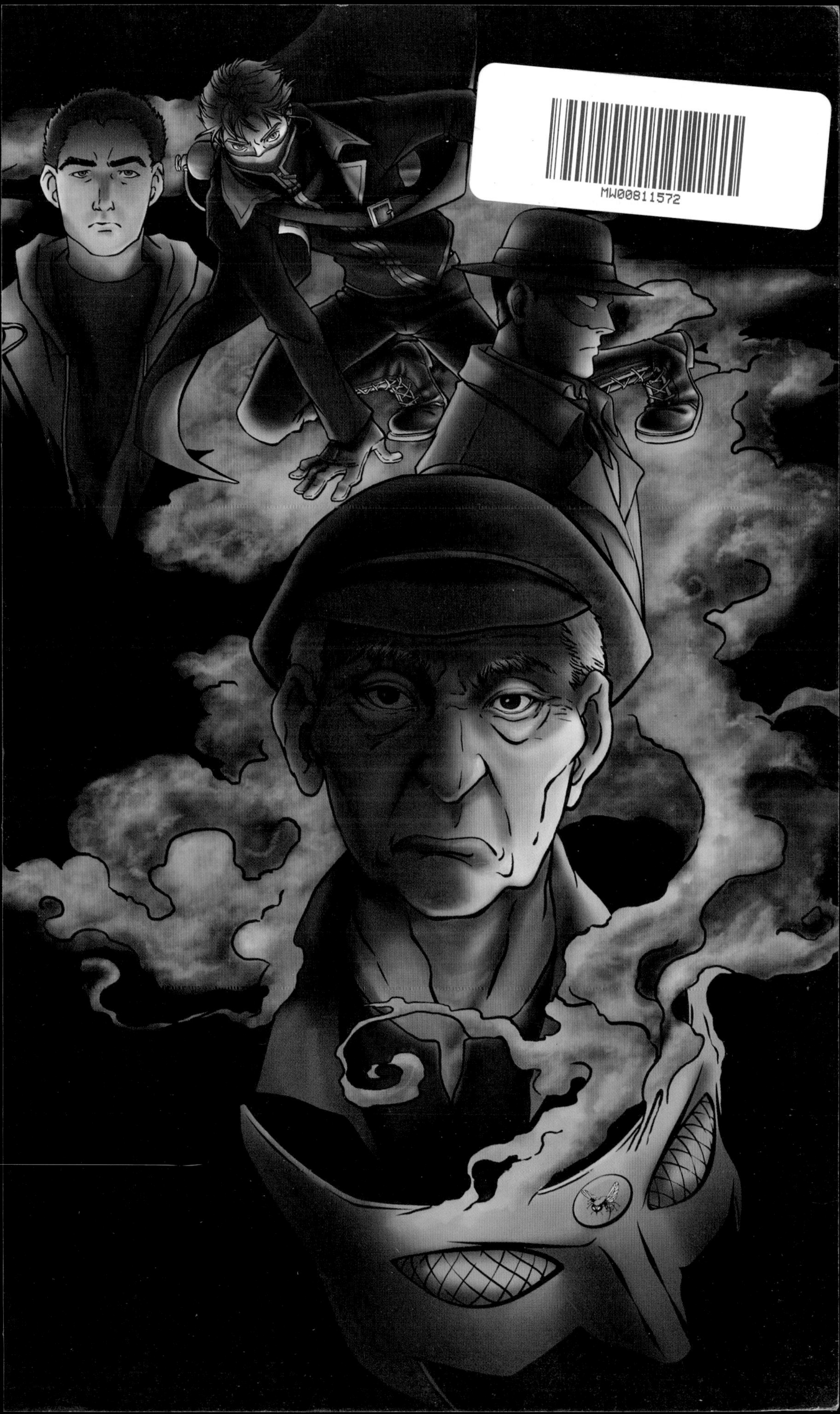

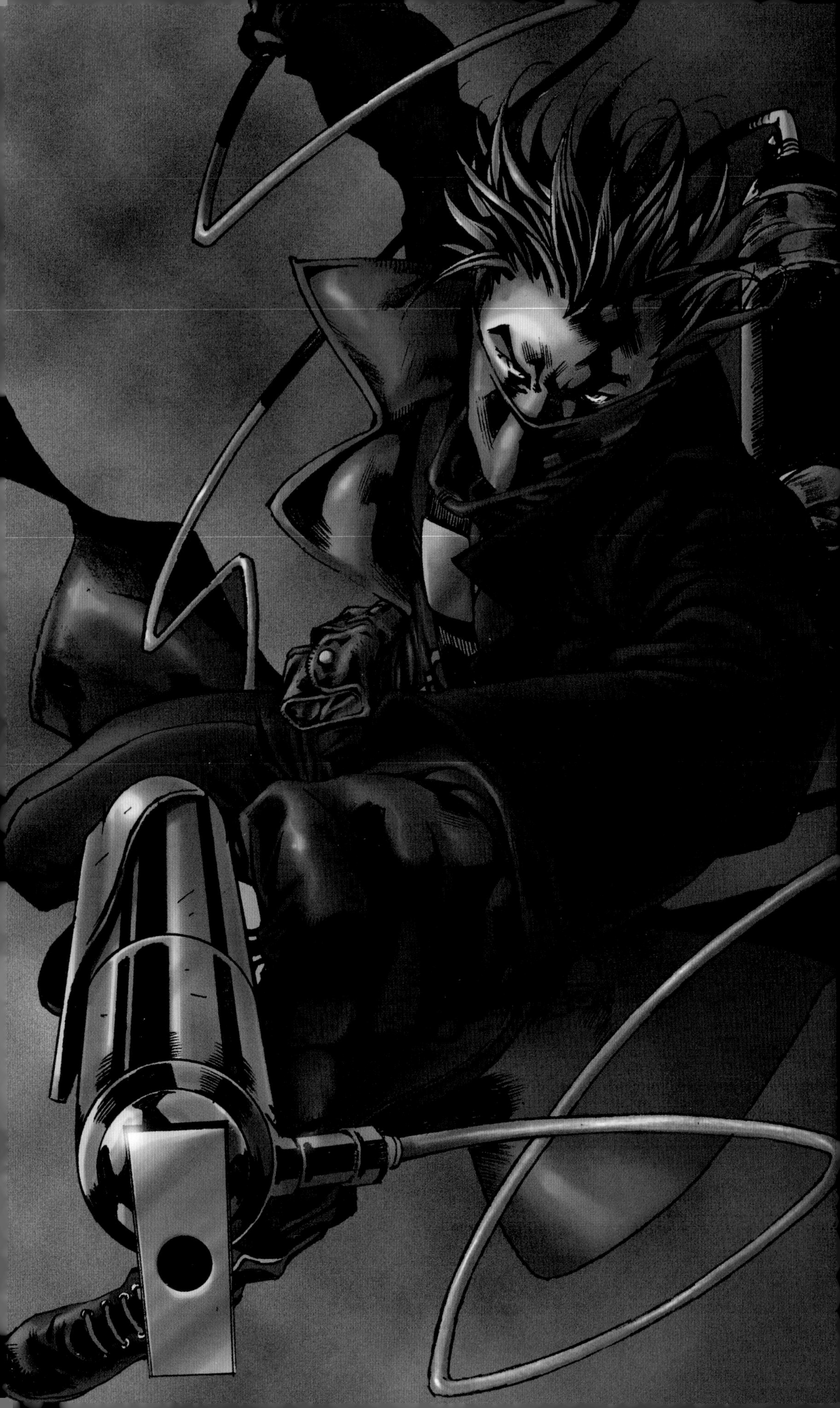

THE GREEN HORNET STRIKES!

Written by
BRETT MATTHEWS

Art by
ARIEL PADILLA (issues 1-9)
DAN BORGONOS (issue 10)

Colors by
GIOVANNA GUIMARAES (issues 1-4)
MARCELO PINTO (issues 5-10)

Letters by
SIMON BOWLAND

Collection cover by
JOHN CASSADAY

Special thanks to DAVID GRACE at Green Hornet Inc.

This volume collects issues 1-10
of The Green Hornet Strikes! by Dynamite Entertainment

DYNAMITE®

:k Barrucci, CEO / Publisher
an Collado, President / COO
:h Young, Director Business Development
ith Davidsen, Marketing Manager

e Rybandt, Senior Editor
rah Litt, Digital Editor
sh Green, Traffic Coordinator
)lly Mahan, Assistant Editor

sh Johnson, Art Director
son Ullmeyer, Senior Graphic Designer
tie Hidalgo, Graphic Designer
ris Caniano, Production Assistant

ISBN-10: 1-60690-156-7
ISBN-13: 978-1-60690-156-4
First Printing
10 9 8 7 6 5 4 3 2 1

 Visit us online at **www.DYNAMITE.com**
Follow us on Twitter **@dynamitecomics**
Like us on Facebook **/Dynamitecomics**
Watch us on YouTube **/Dynamitecomics**

For information regarding press, media rights, foreign rights, licensing, promotions, and advertising e-mail:
marketing@dynamite.com

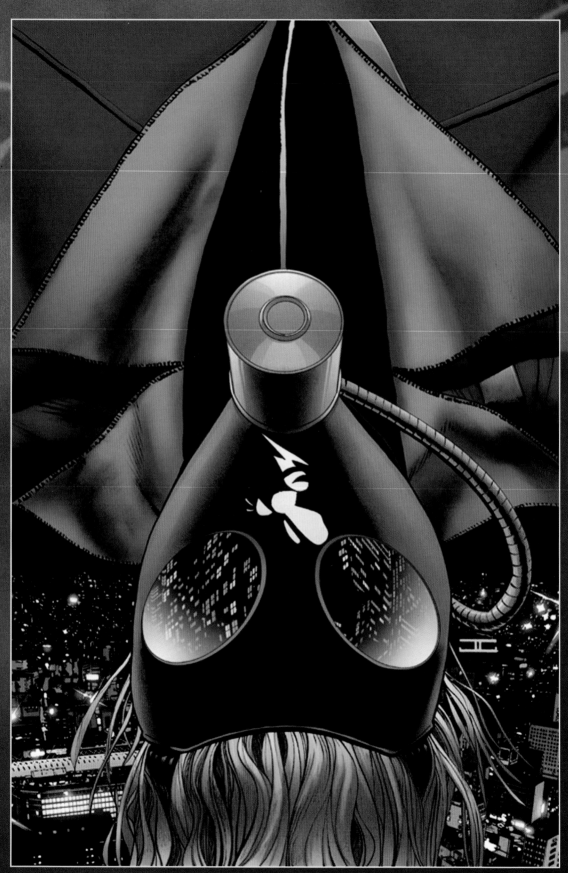

Issue #1 cover by JOHN CASSADAY

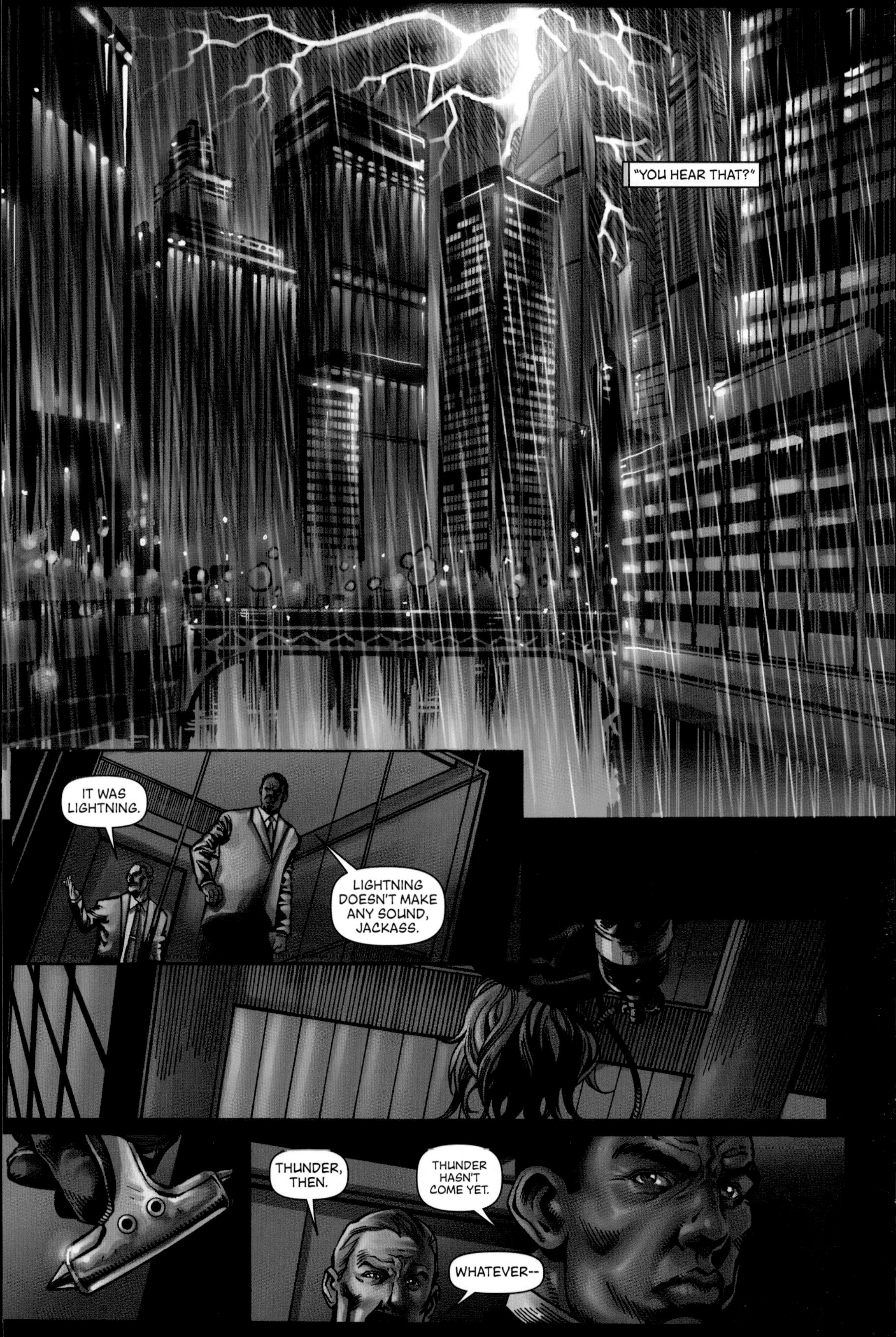
"YOU HEAR THAT?"
IT WAS LIGHTNING.
LIGHTNING DOESN'T MAKE ANY SOUND, JACKASS.
THUNDER, THEN.
THUNDER HASN'T COME YET.
WHATEVER--

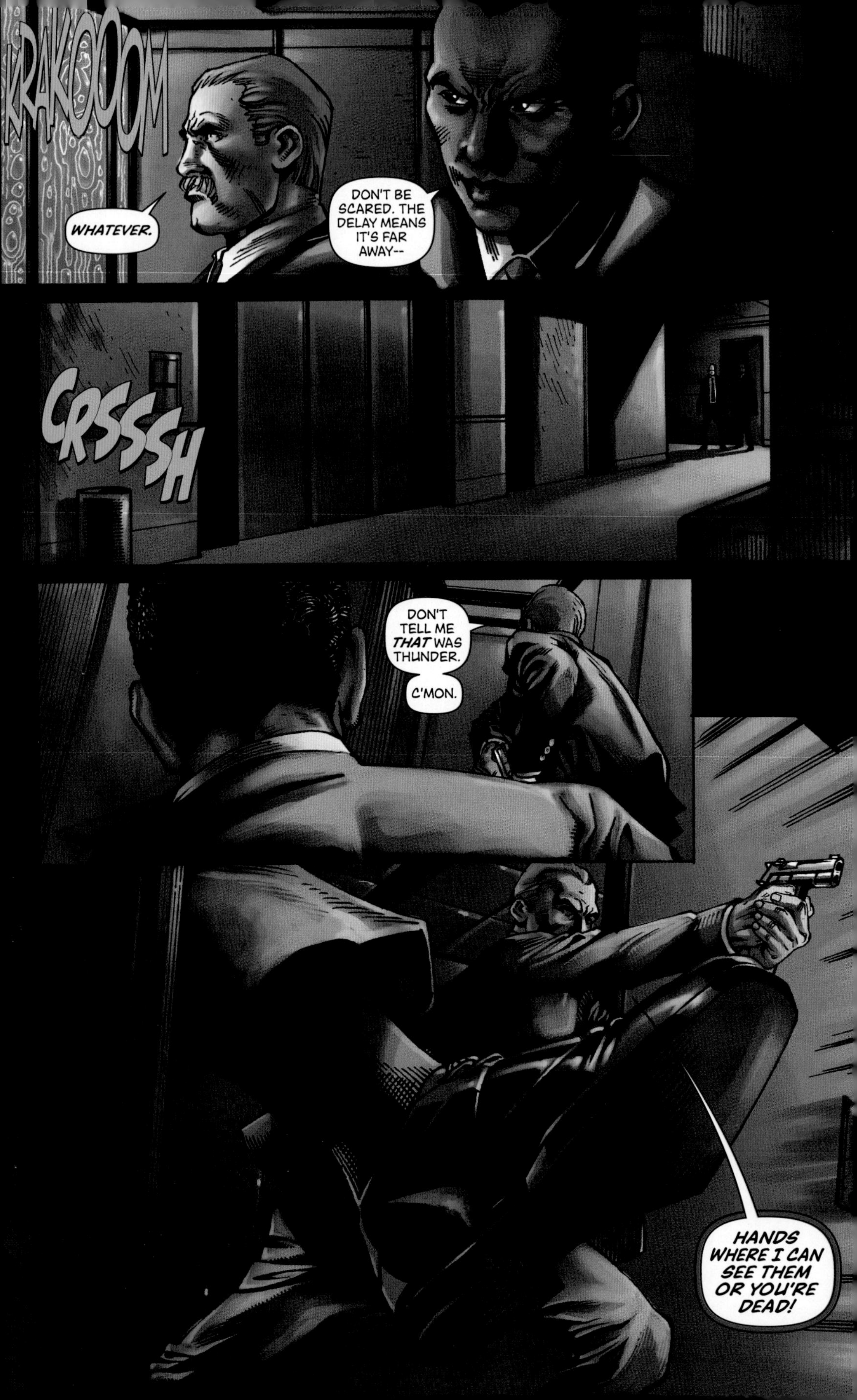
KRAKOOOM
WHATEVER.
DON'T BE SCARED. THE DELAY MEANS IT'S FAR AWAY--
CRSSSH
DON'T TELL ME THAT WAS THUNDER.
C'MON.
HANDS WHERE I CAN SEE THEM OR YOU'RE DEAD!

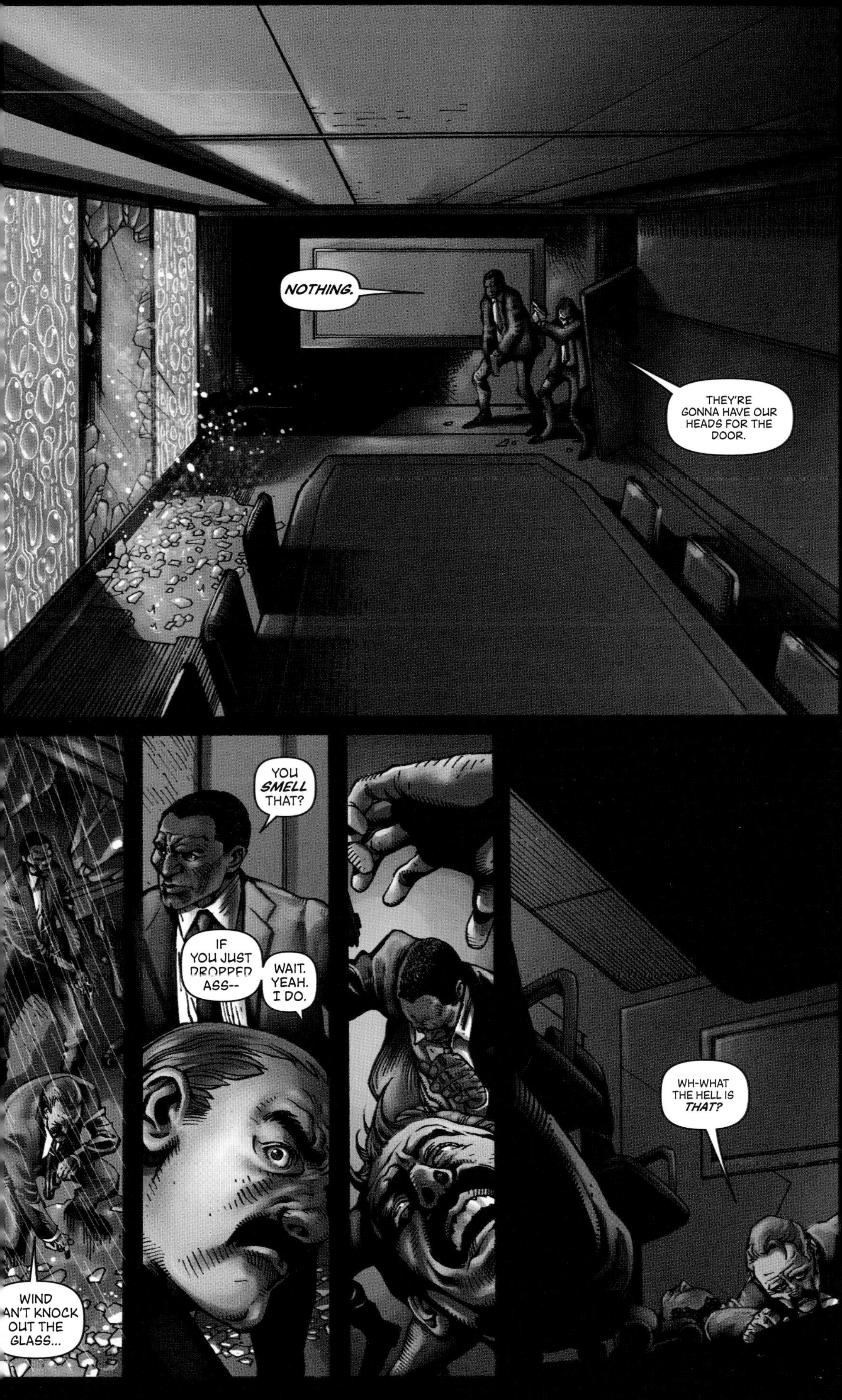
NOTHING.
THEY'RE GONNA HAVE OUR HEADS FOR THE DOOR.
WIND AN'T KNOCK OUT THE GLASS...
YOU SMELL THAT?
IF YOU JUST DROPPED ASS--
WAIT. YEAH. I DO.
WH-WHAT THE HELL IS THAT?

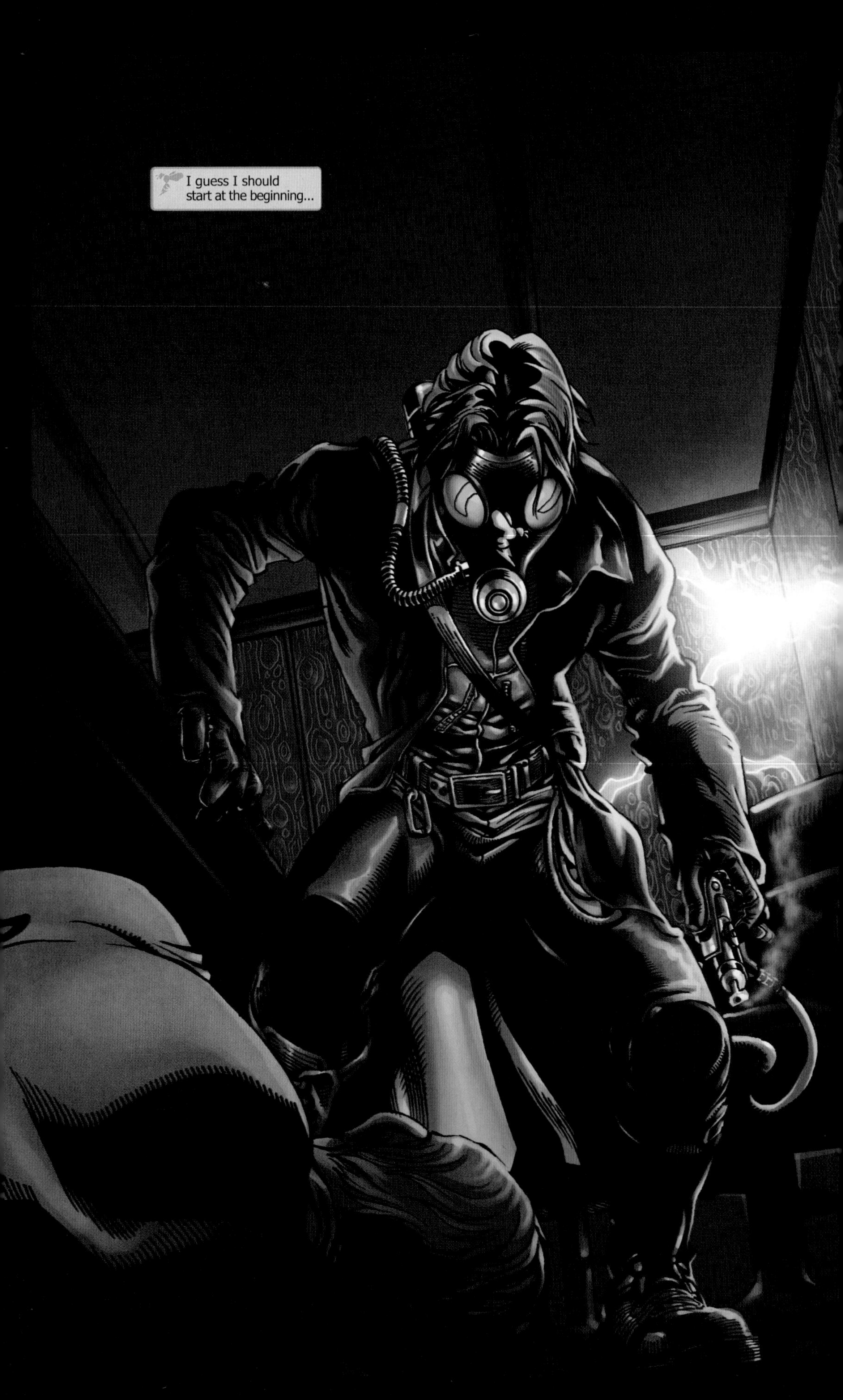
I guess I should start at the beginning...

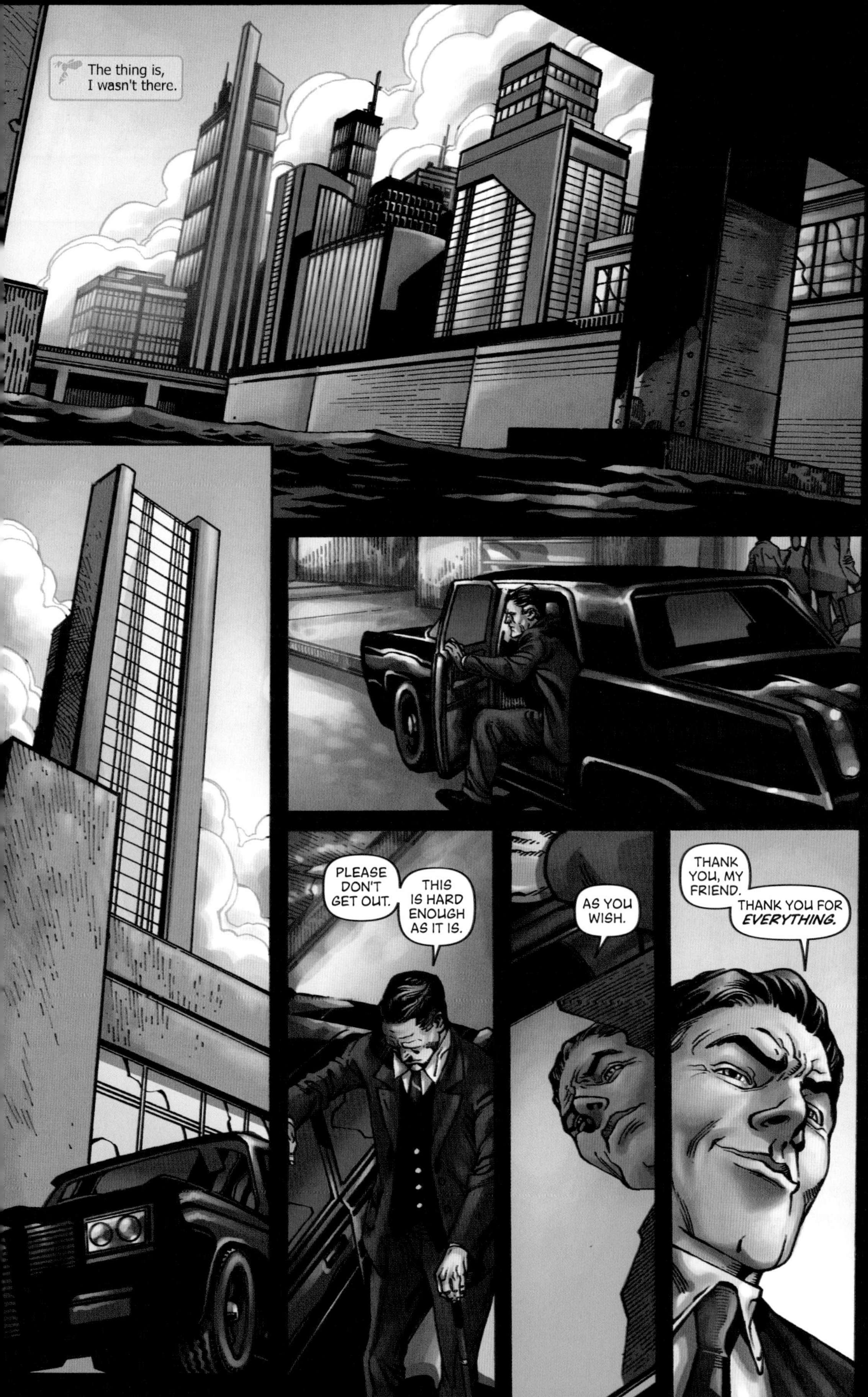
The thing is, I wasn't there.
PLEASE DON'T GET OUT.
THIS IS HARD ENOUGH AS IT IS.
AS YOU WISH.
THANK YOU, MY FRIEND.
THANK YOU FOR *EVERYTHING.*

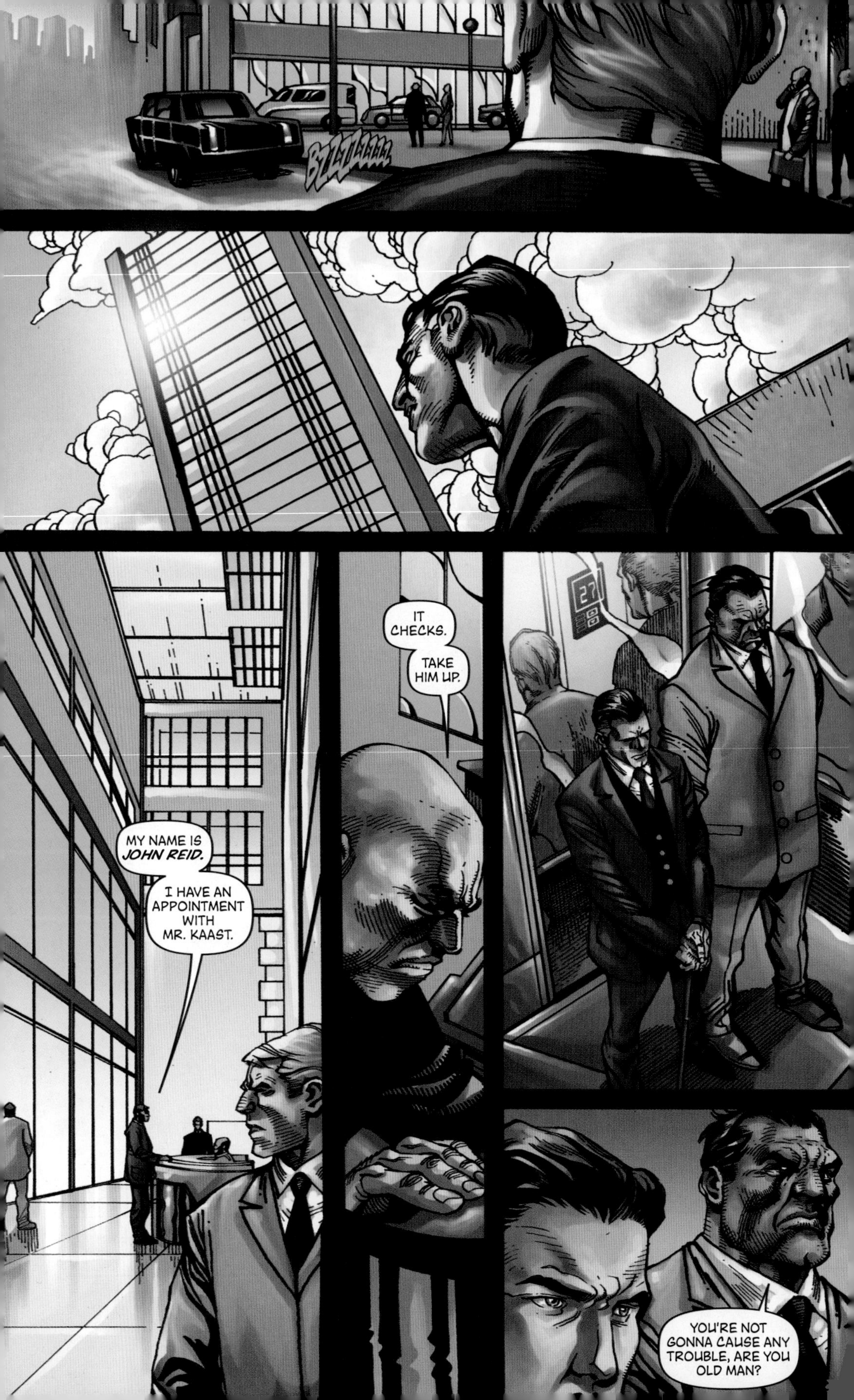

MY NAME IS *JOHN REID.*
I HAVE AN APPOINTMENT WITH MR. KAAST.
IT CHECKS.
TAKE HIM UP.
YOU'RE NOT GONNA CAUSE ANY TROUBLE, ARE YOU OLD MAN?

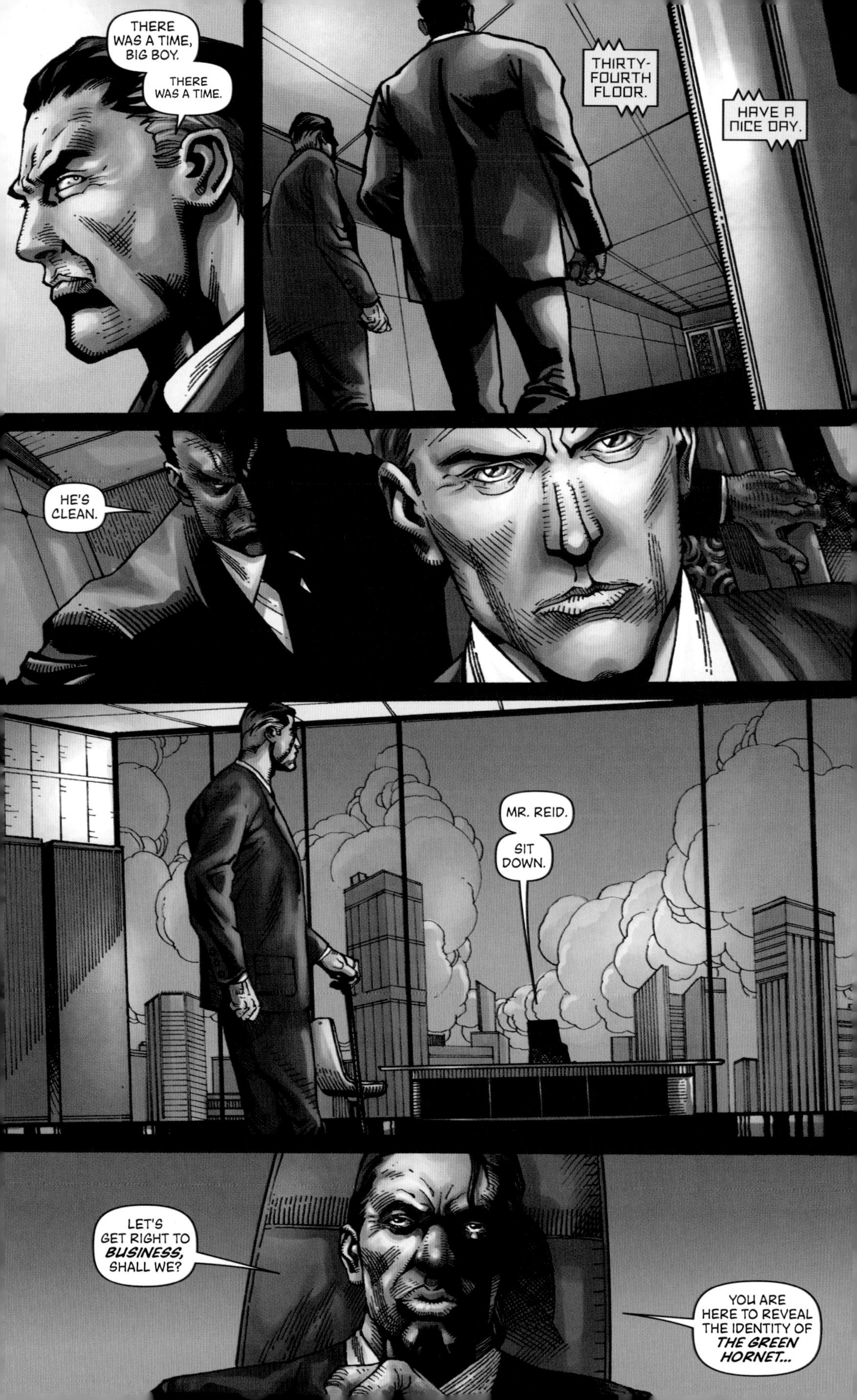
THERE WAS A TIME, BIG BOY.
THERE WAS A TIME.
THIRTY-FOURTH FLOOR.
HAVE A NICE DAY.
HE'S CLEAN.
MR. REID.
SIT DOWN.
LET'S GET RIGHT TO *BUSINESS*, SHALL WE?
YOU ARE HERE TO REVEAL THE IDENTITY OF *THE GREEN HORNET...*

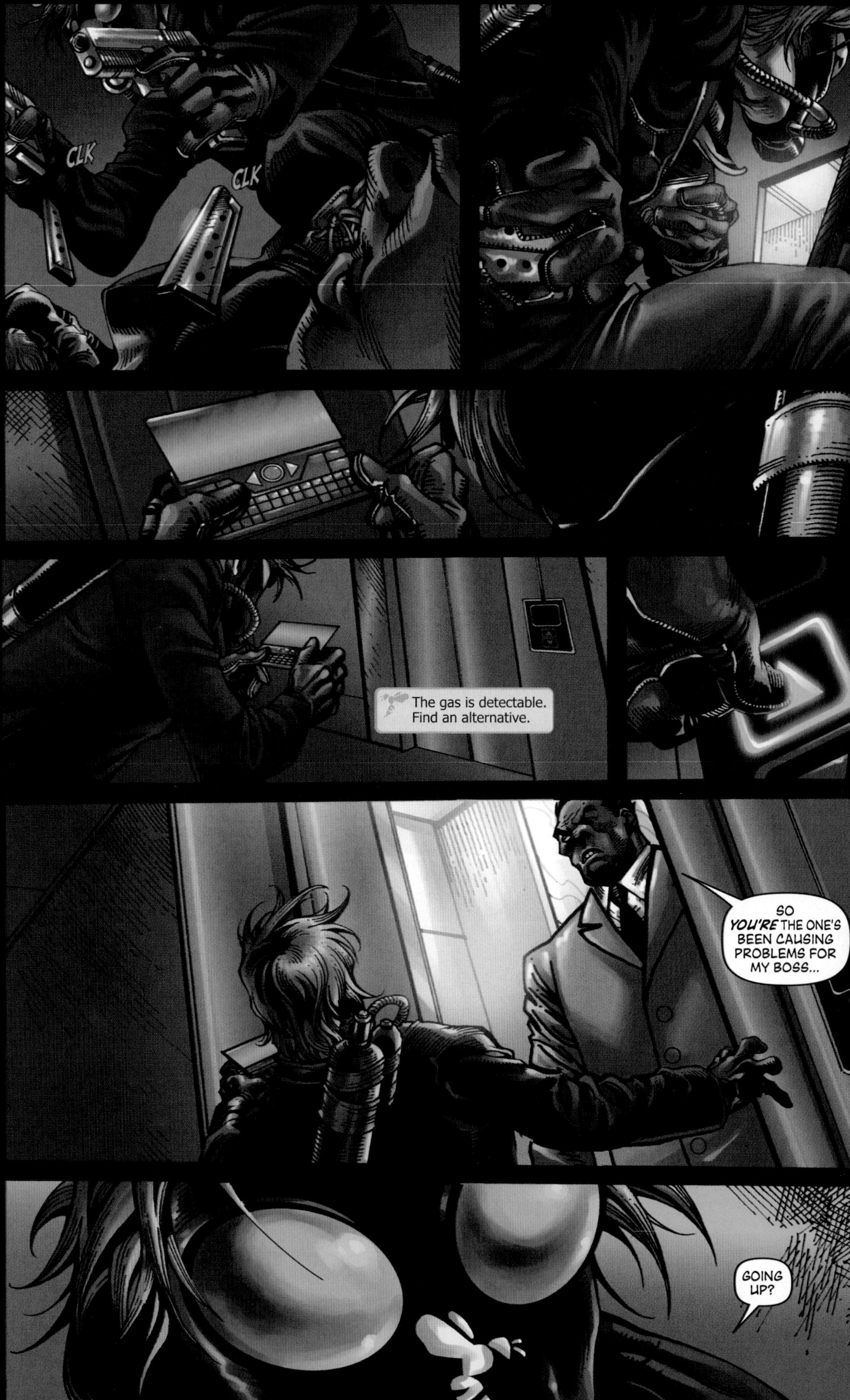
CLK
CLK
The gas is detectable. Find an alternative.
SO *YOU'RE* THE ONE'S BEEN CAUSING PROBLEMS FOR MY BOSS...
GOING UP?

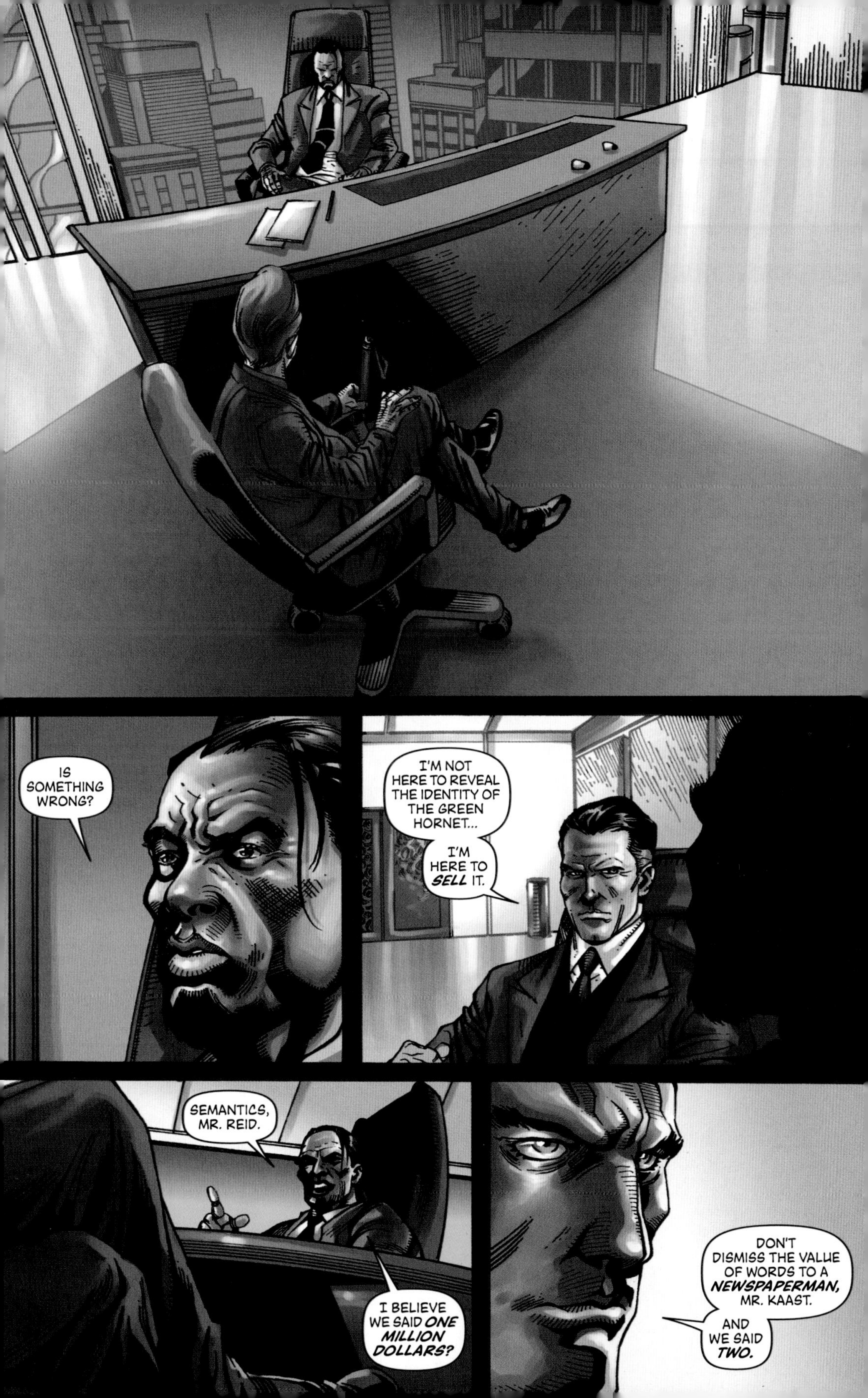
IS SOMETHING WRONG?
I'M NOT HERE TO REVEAL THE IDENTITY OF THE GREEN HORNET...
I'M HERE TO SELL IT.
SEMANTICS, MR. REID.
I BELIEVE WE SAID ONE MILLION DOLLARS?
DON'T DISMISS THE VALUE OF WORDS TO A NEWSPAPERMAN, MR. KAAST.
AND WE SAID TWO.

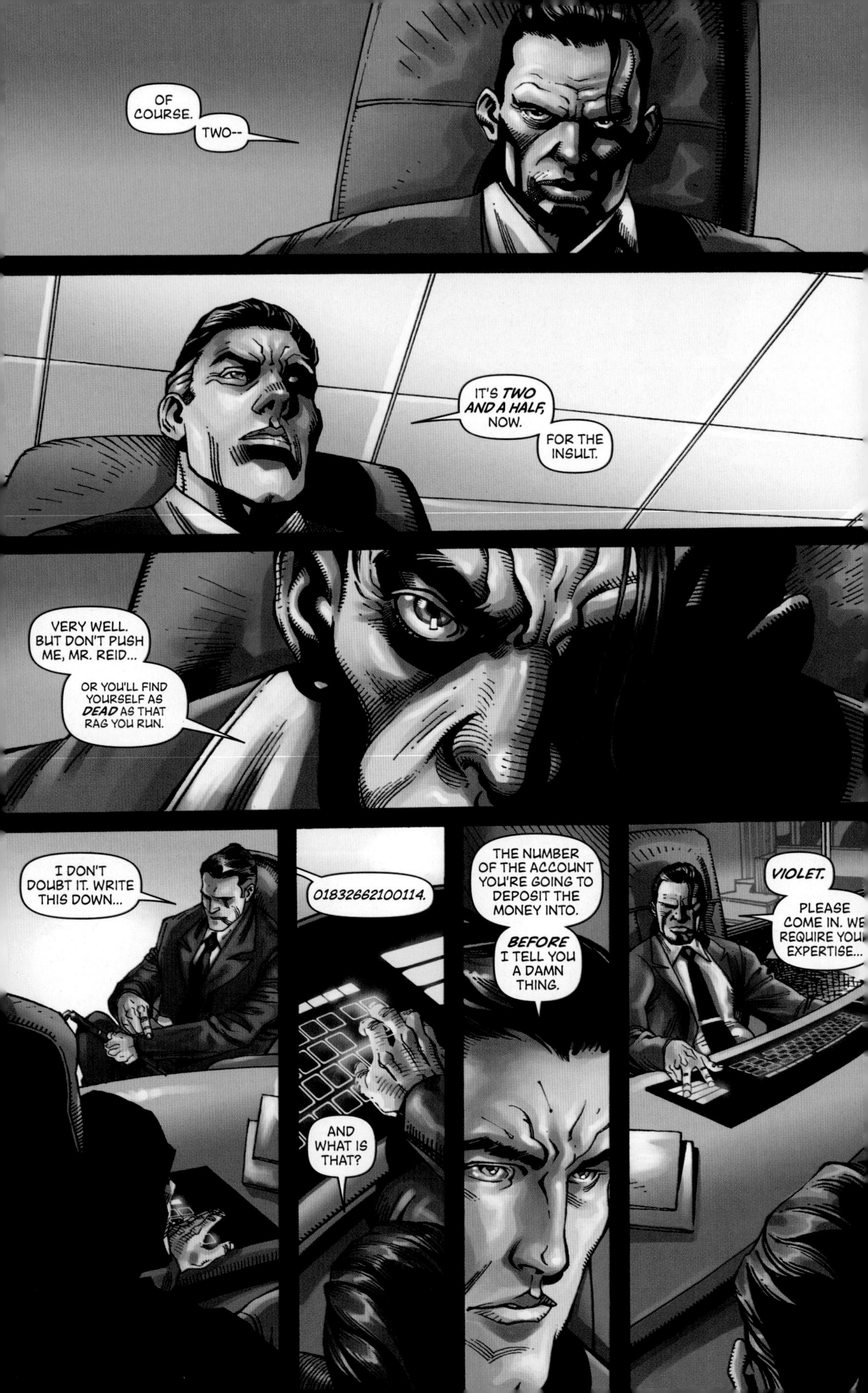
OF COURSE.
TWO--
IT'S *TWO AND A HALF,* NOW.
FOR THE INSULT.
VERY WELL. BUT DON'T PUSH ME, MR. REID...
OR YOU'LL FIND YOURSELF AS *DEAD* AS THAT RAG YOU RUN.
I DON'T DOUBT IT. WRITE THIS DOWN...
01832662100114.
AND WHAT IS THAT?
THE NUMBER OF THE ACCOUNT YOU'RE GOING TO DEPOSIT THE MONEY INTO.
BEFORE I TELL YOU A DAMN THING.
VIOLET.
PLEASE COME IN. WE REQUIRE YOUR EXPERTISE...

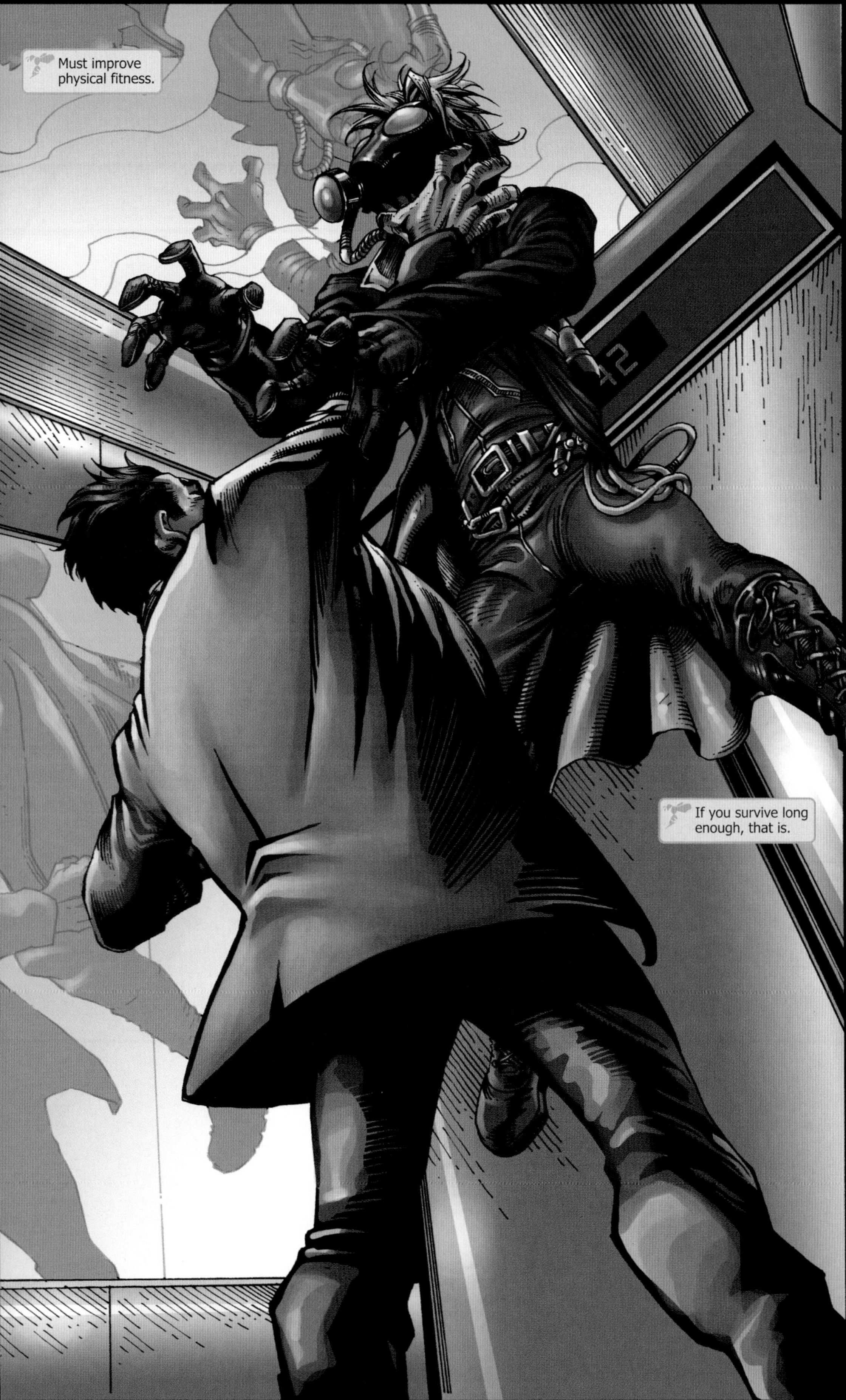
Must improve physical fitness.
If you survive long enough, that is.
42

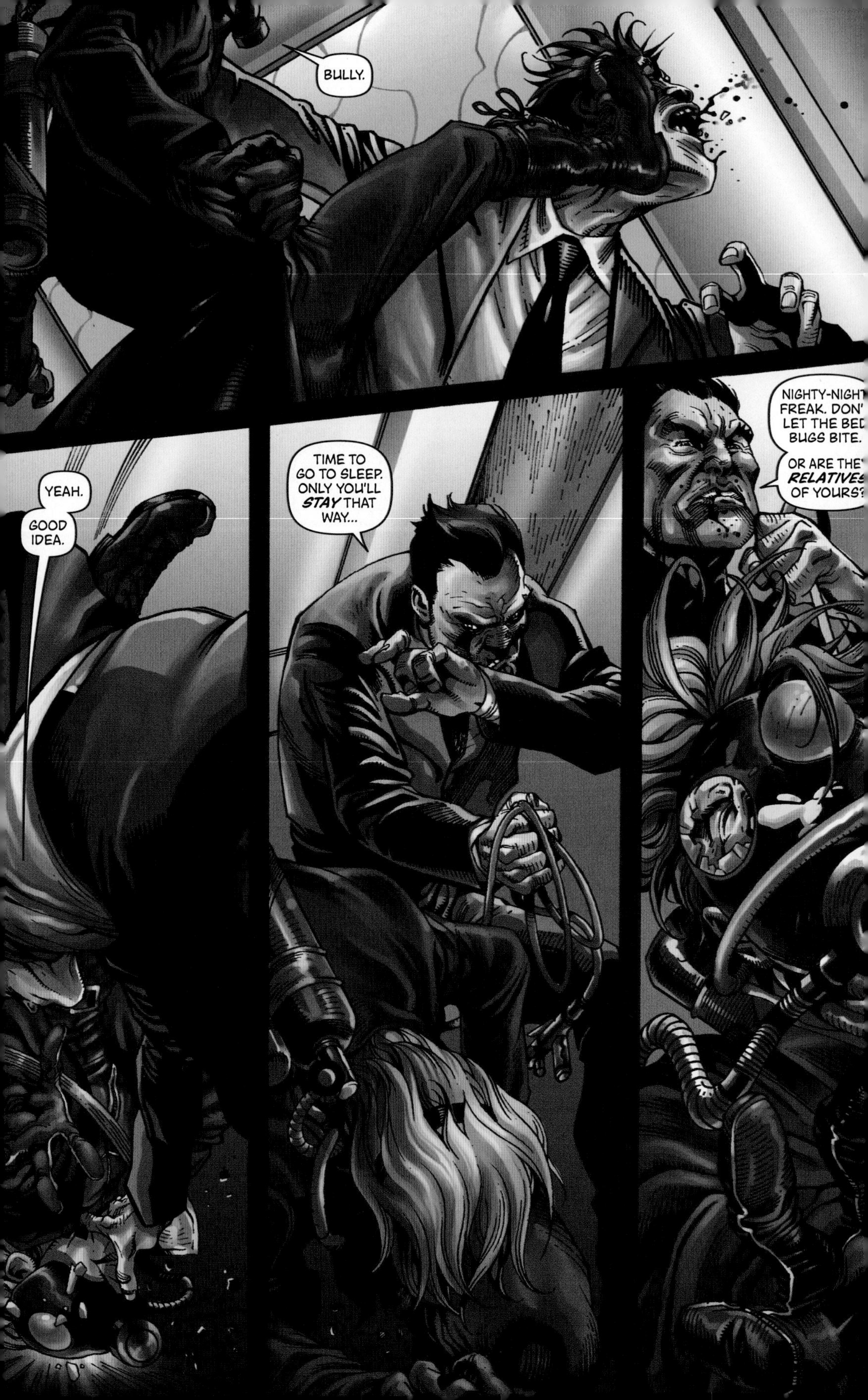
BULLY.
YEAH.
GOOD IDEA.
TIME TO GO TO SLEEP. ONLY YOU'LL STAY THAT WAY...
NIGHTY-NIGHT FREAK. DON' LET THE BED BUGS BITE.
OR ARE THE' RELATIVES OF YOURS?

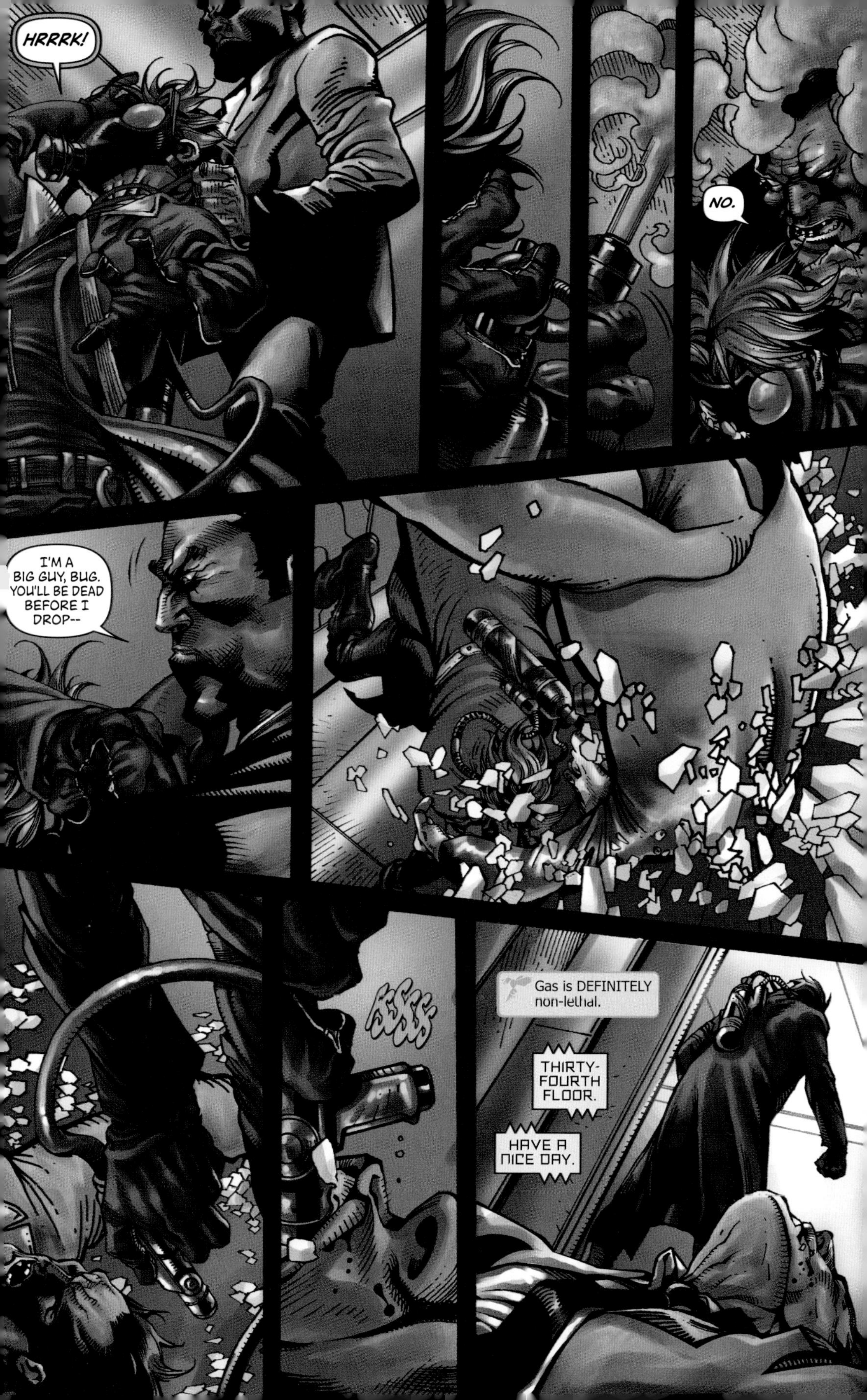
HRRRK!
NO.
I'M A BIG GUY, BUG. YOU'LL BE DEAD BEFORE I DROP--
FSSSS
Gas is DEFINITELY non-lethal.
THIRTY-FOURTH FLOOR.
HAVE A NICE DAY.

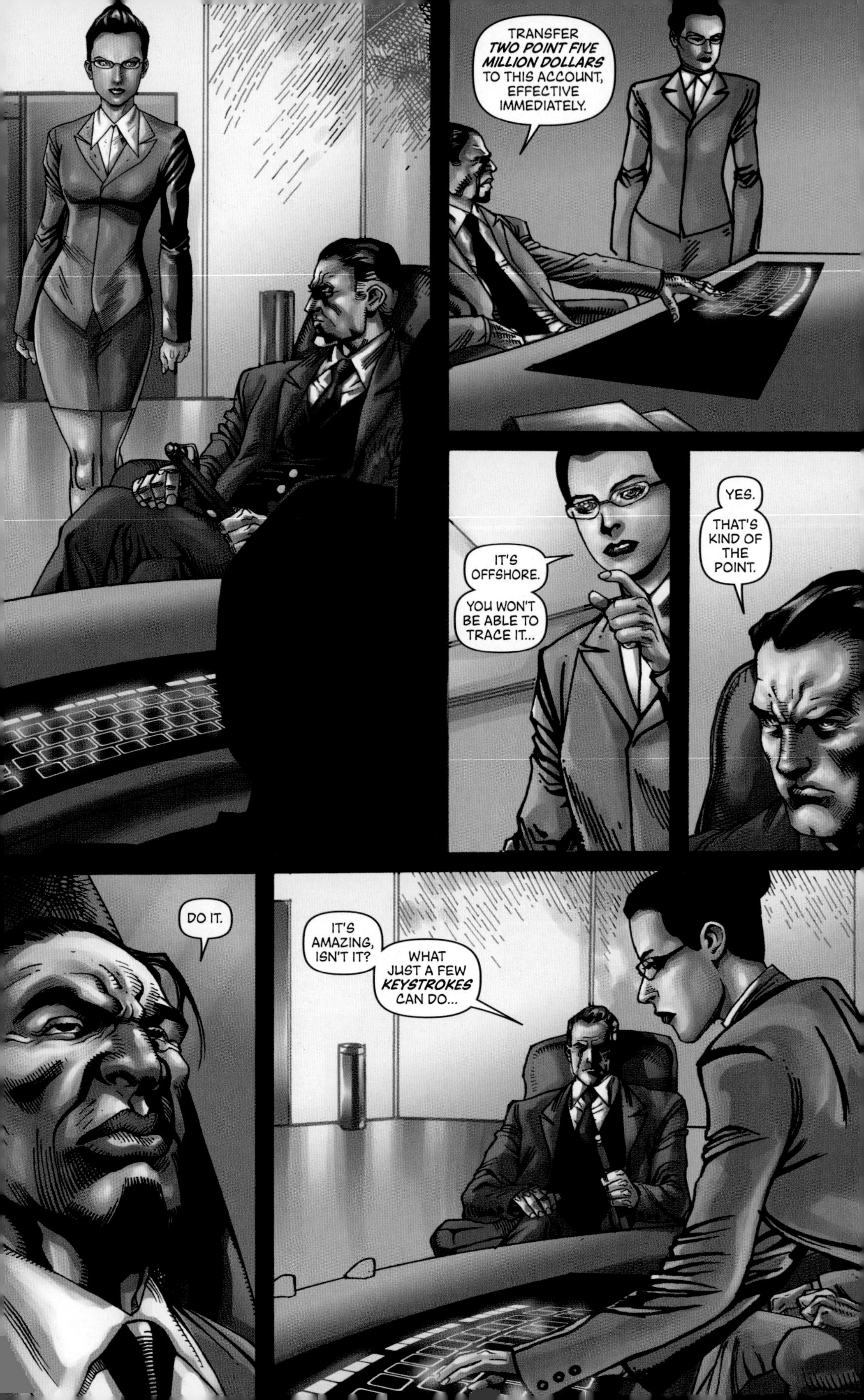
TRANSFER TWO POINT FIVE MILLION DOLLARS TO THIS ACCOUNT, EFFECTIVE IMMEDIATELY.
IT'S OFFSHORE.
YOU WON'T BE ABLE TO TRACE IT...
YES.
THAT'S KIND OF THE POINT.
DO IT.
IT'S AMAZING, ISN'T IT?
WHAT JUST A FEW KEYSTROKES CAN DO...

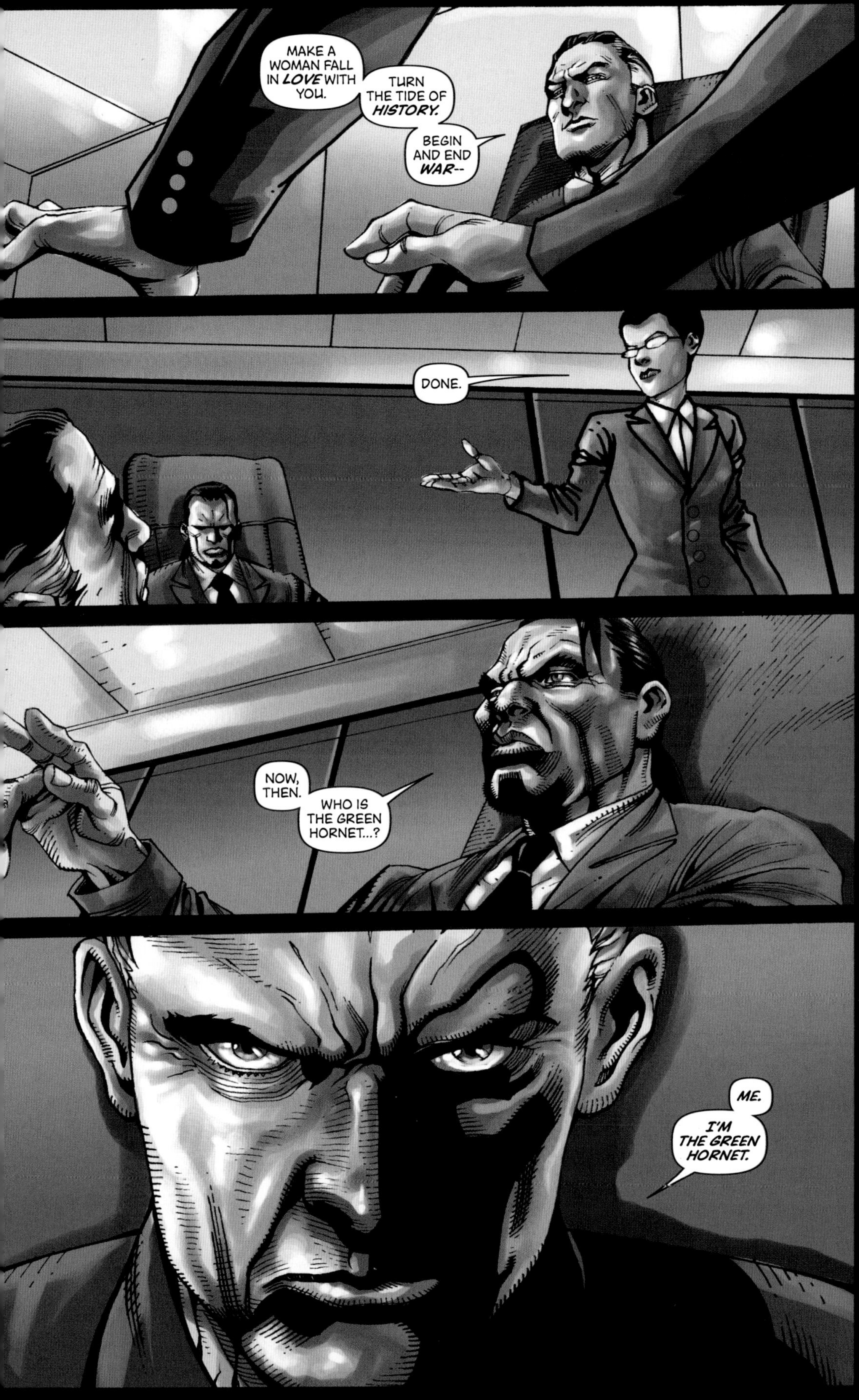
MAKE A WOMAN FALL IN *LOVE* WITH YOU.
TURN THE TIDE OF *HISTORY.*
BEGIN AND END *WAR*--
DONE.
NOW, THEN.
WHO IS THE GREEN HORNET...?
ME.
I'M THE GREEN HORNET.

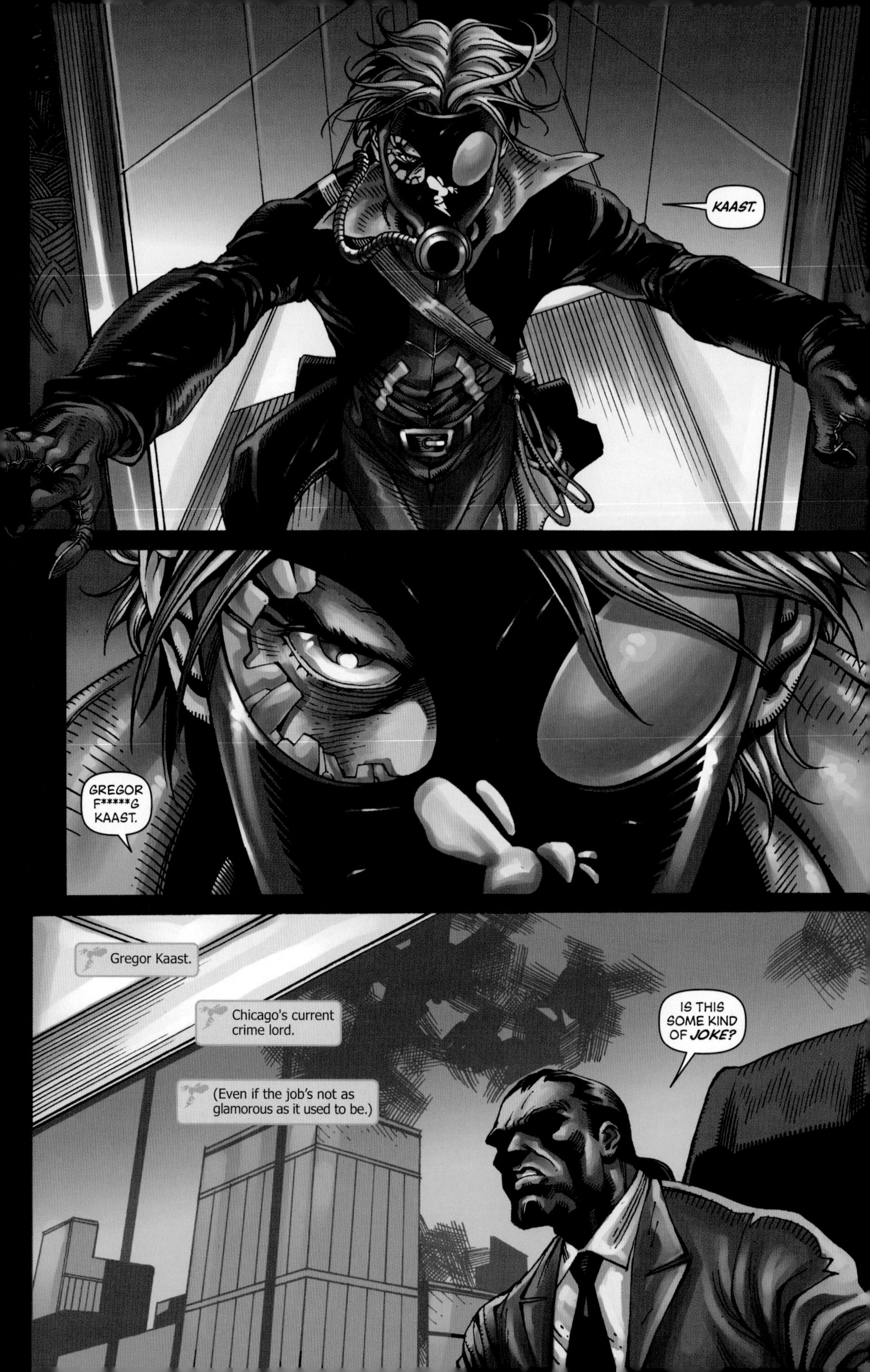
KAAST.
GREGOR F*****G KAAST.
Gregor Kaast.
Chicago's current crime lord.
(Even if the job's not as glamorous as it used to be.)
IS THIS SOME KIND OF JOKE?

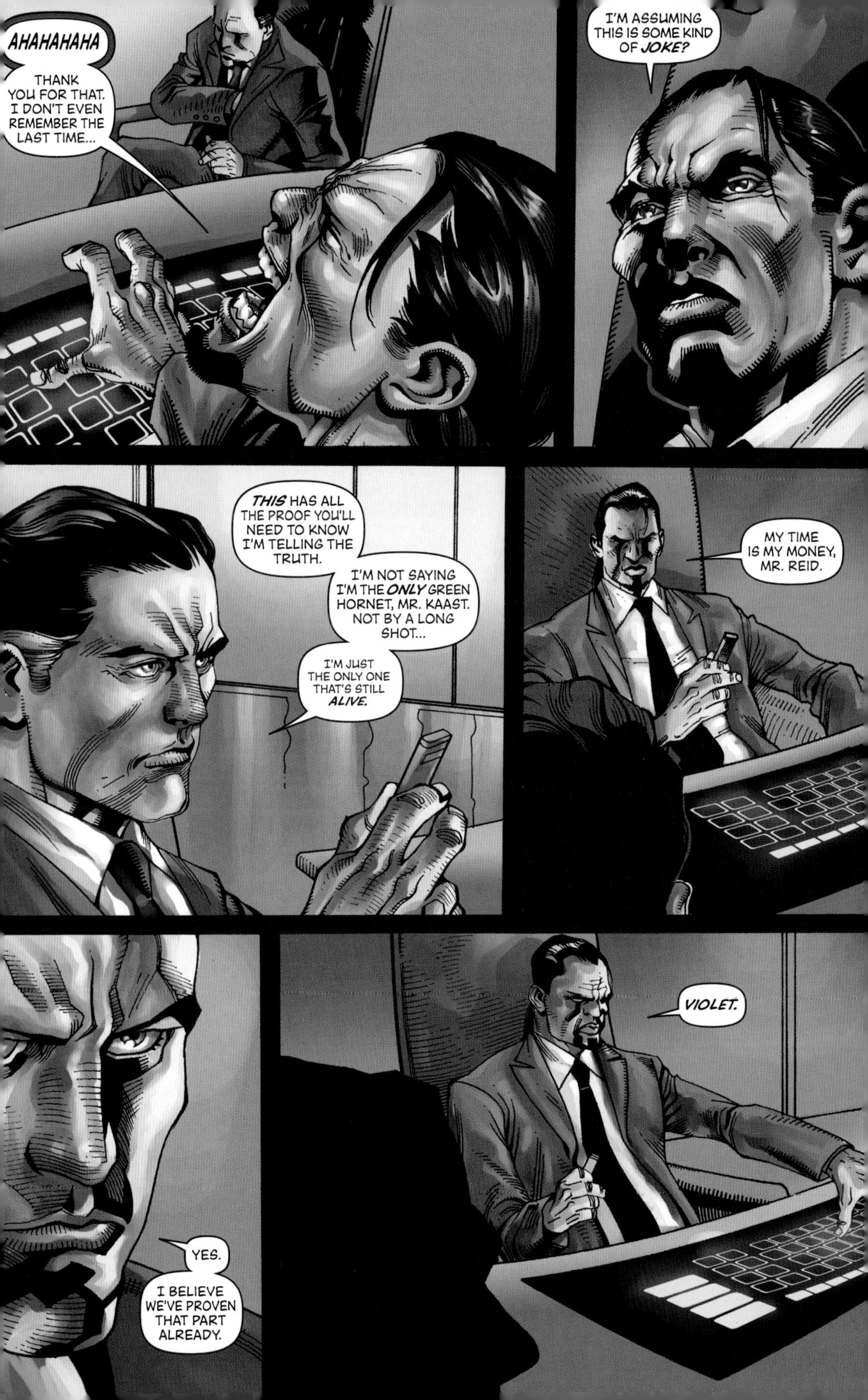

AHAHAHAHA
THANK YOU FOR THAT. I DON'T EVEN REMEMBER THE LAST TIME...
I'M ASSUMING THIS IS SOME KIND OF JOKE?
THIS HAS ALL THE PROOF YOU'LL NEED TO KNOW I'M TELLING THE TRUTH.
I'M NOT SAYING I'M THE ONLY GREEN HORNET, MR. KAAST. NOT BY A LONG SHOT...
I'M JUST THE ONLY ONE THAT'S STILL ALIVE.
MY TIME IS MY MONEY, MR. REID.
YES.
I BELIEVE WE'VE PROVEN THAT PART ALREADY.
VIOLET.

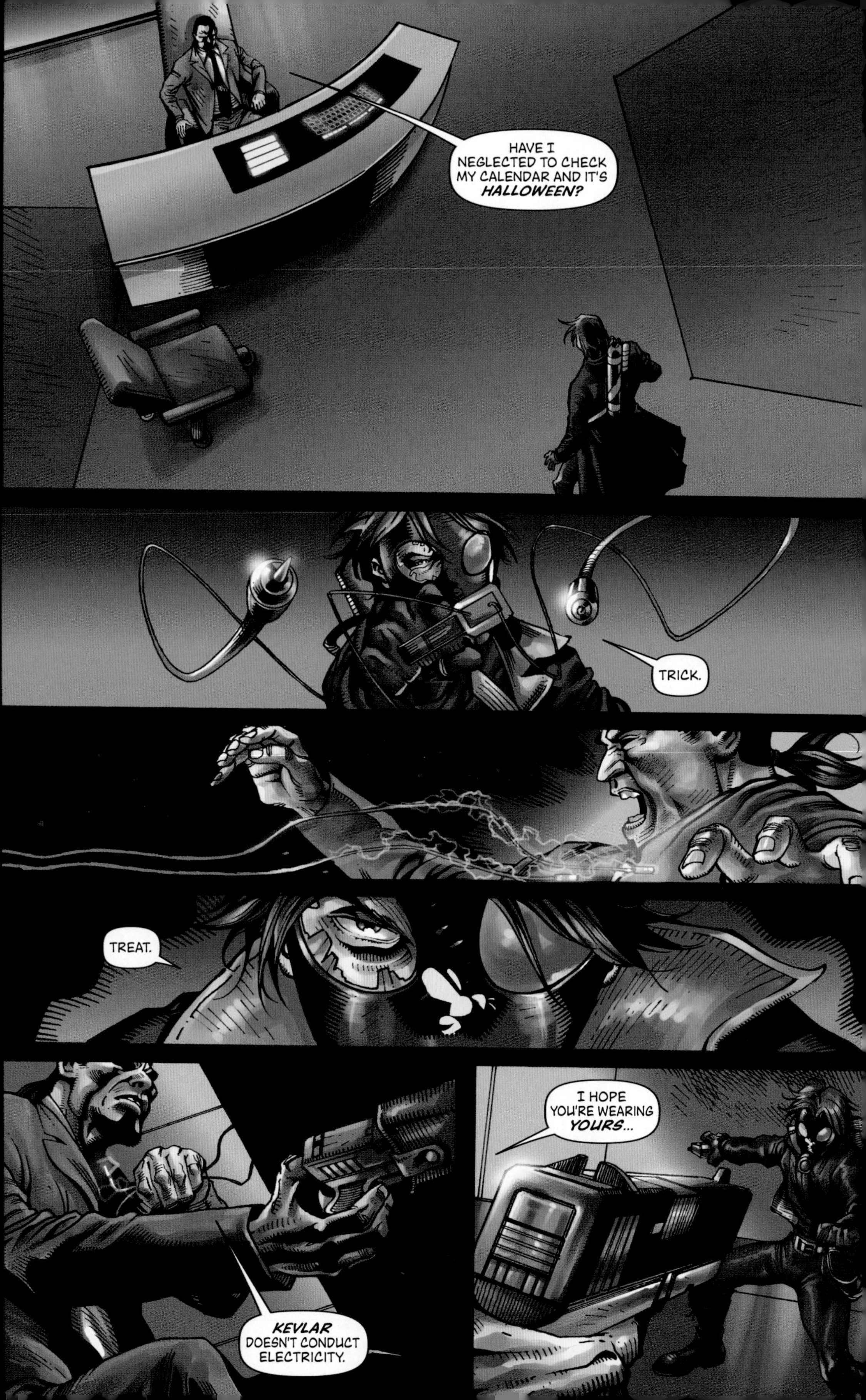
HAVE I NEGLECTED TO CHECK MY CALENDAR AND IT'S *HALLOWEEN?*
TRICK.
TREAT.
KEVLAR DOESN'T CONDUCT ELECTRICITY.
I HOPE YOU'RE WEARING *YOURS*...

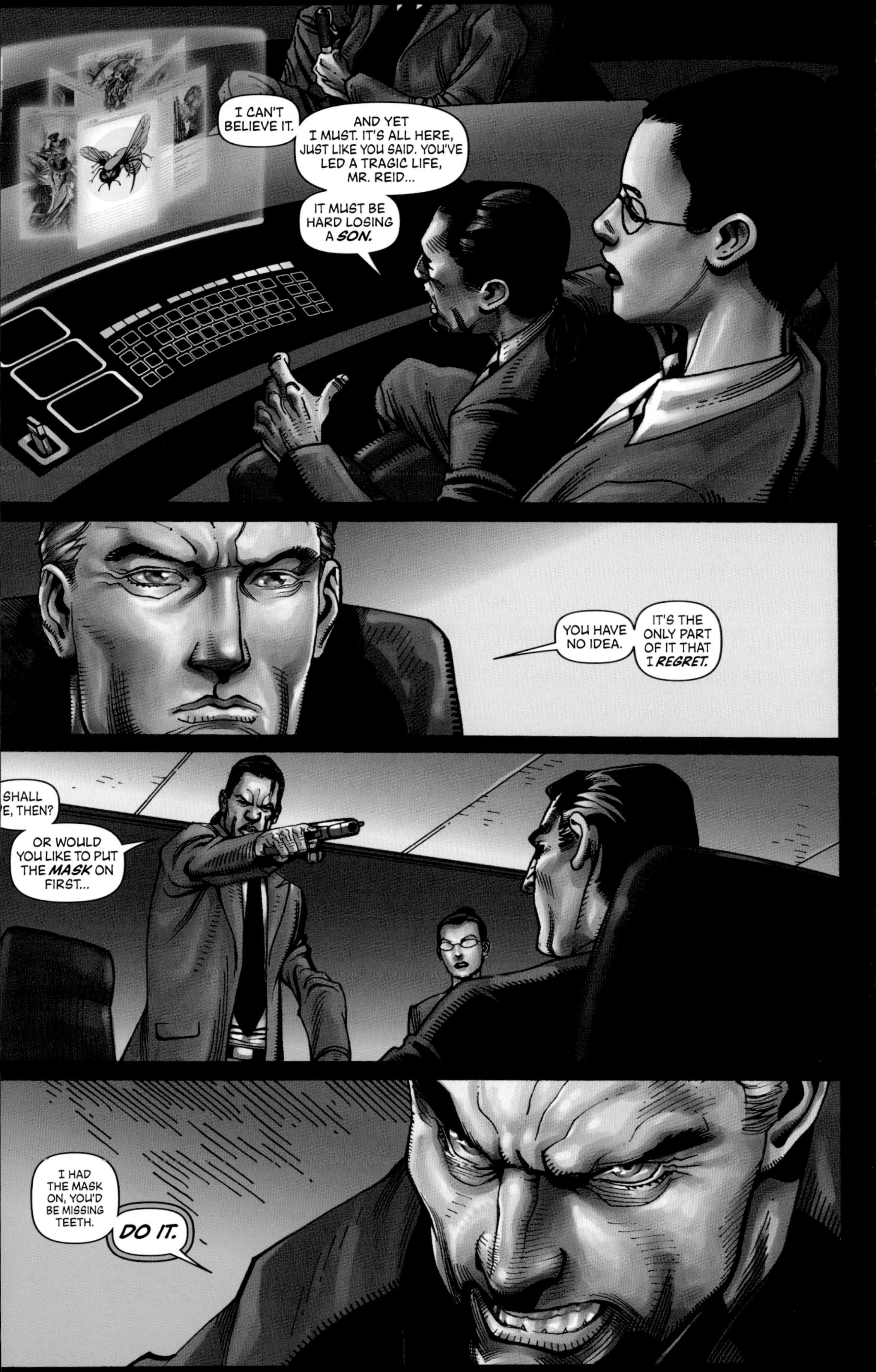
I CAN'T BELIEVE IT.
AND YET I MUST. IT'S ALL HERE, JUST LIKE YOU SAID. YOU'VE LED A TRAGIC LIFE, MR. REID...
IT MUST BE HARD LOSING A SON.
YOU HAVE NO IDEA.
IT'S THE ONLY PART OF IT THAT I REGRET.
SHALL E, THEN?
OR WOULD YOU LIKE TO PUT THE MASK ON FIRST...
I HAD THE MASK ON, YOU'D BE MISSING TEETH.
DO IT.

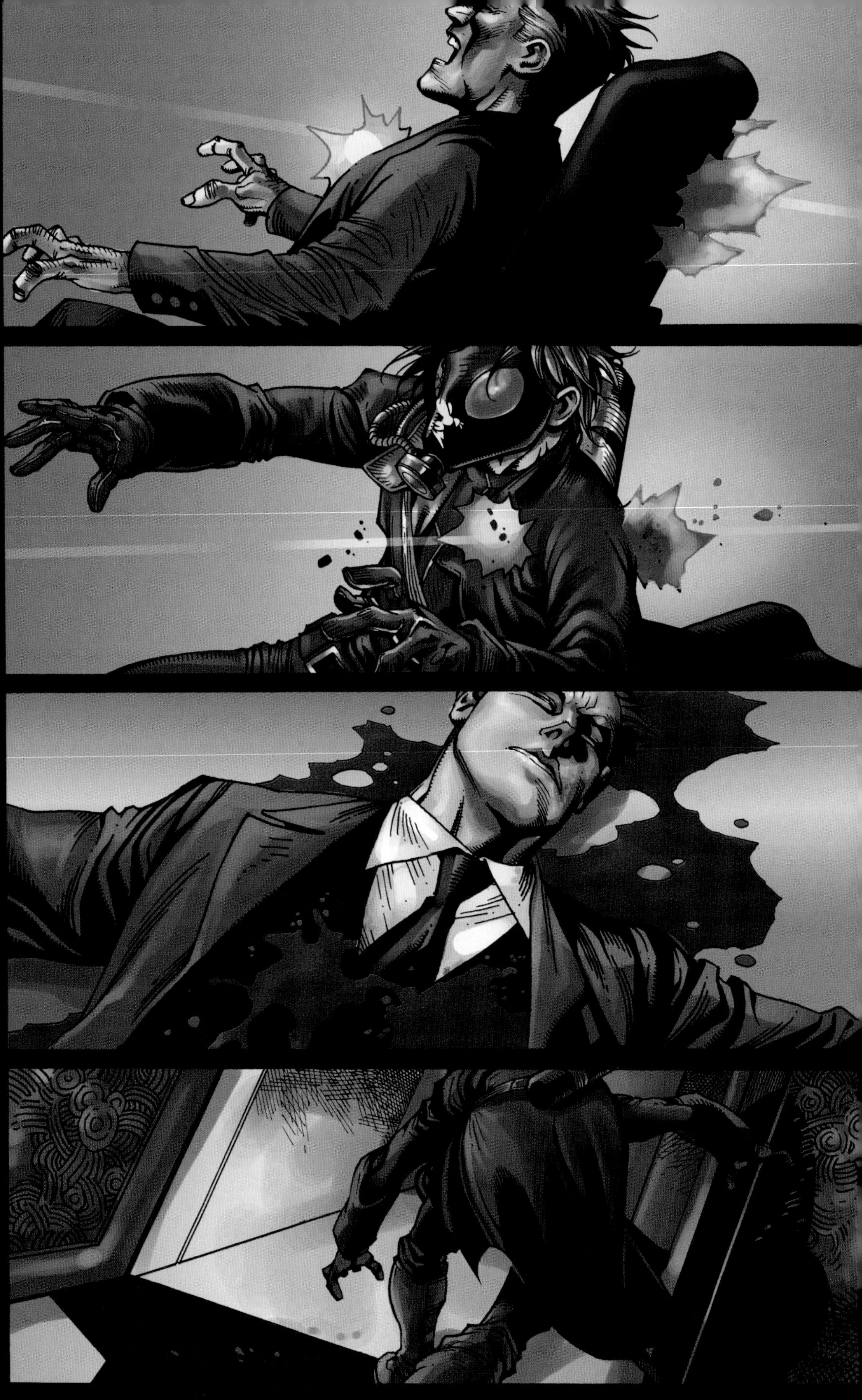

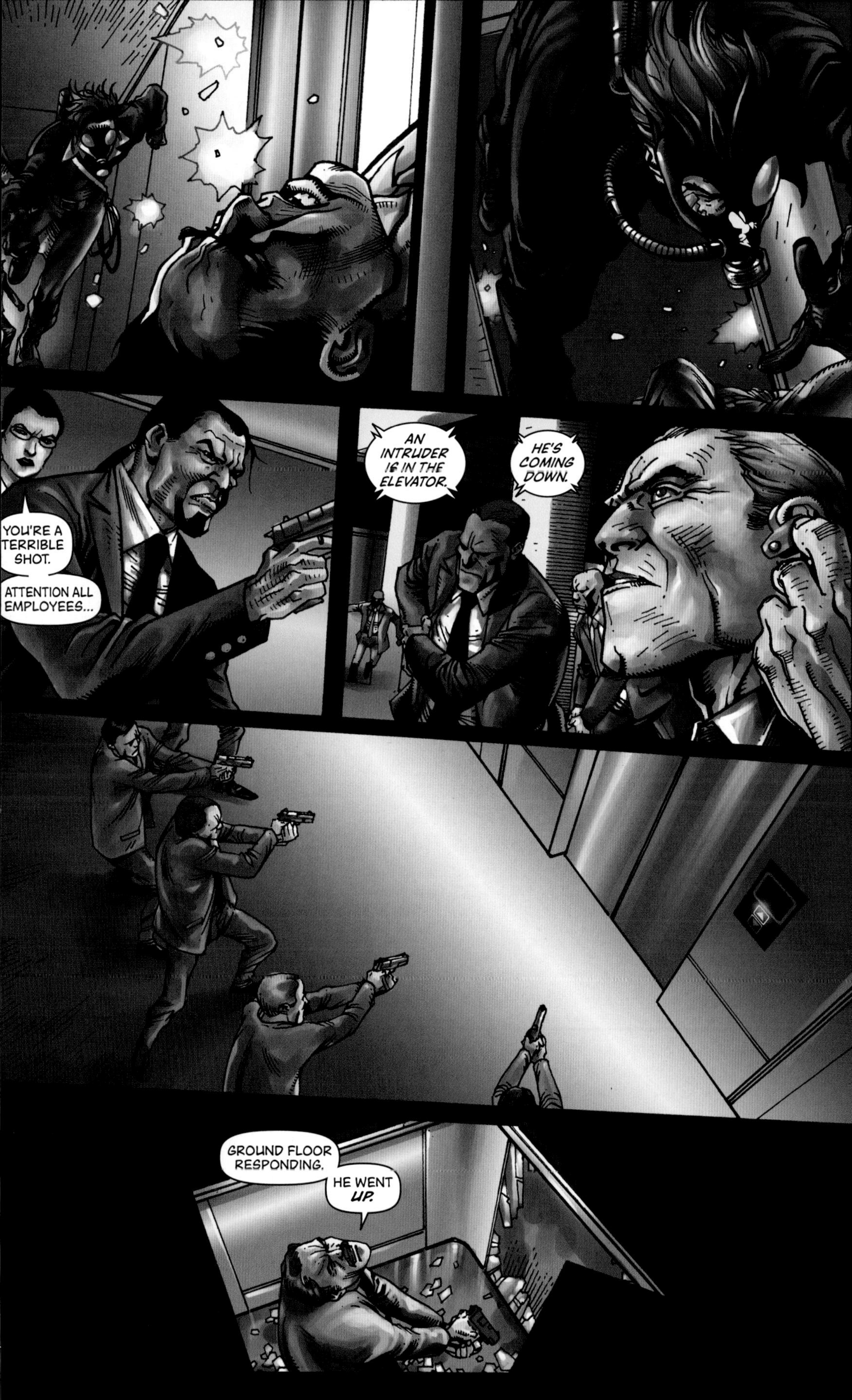
YOU'RE A TERRIBLE SHOT.
ATTENTION ALL EMPLOYEES...
AN INTRUDER IS IN THE ELEVATOR.
HE'S COMING DOWN.
GROUND FLOOR RESPONDING.
HE WENT UP.

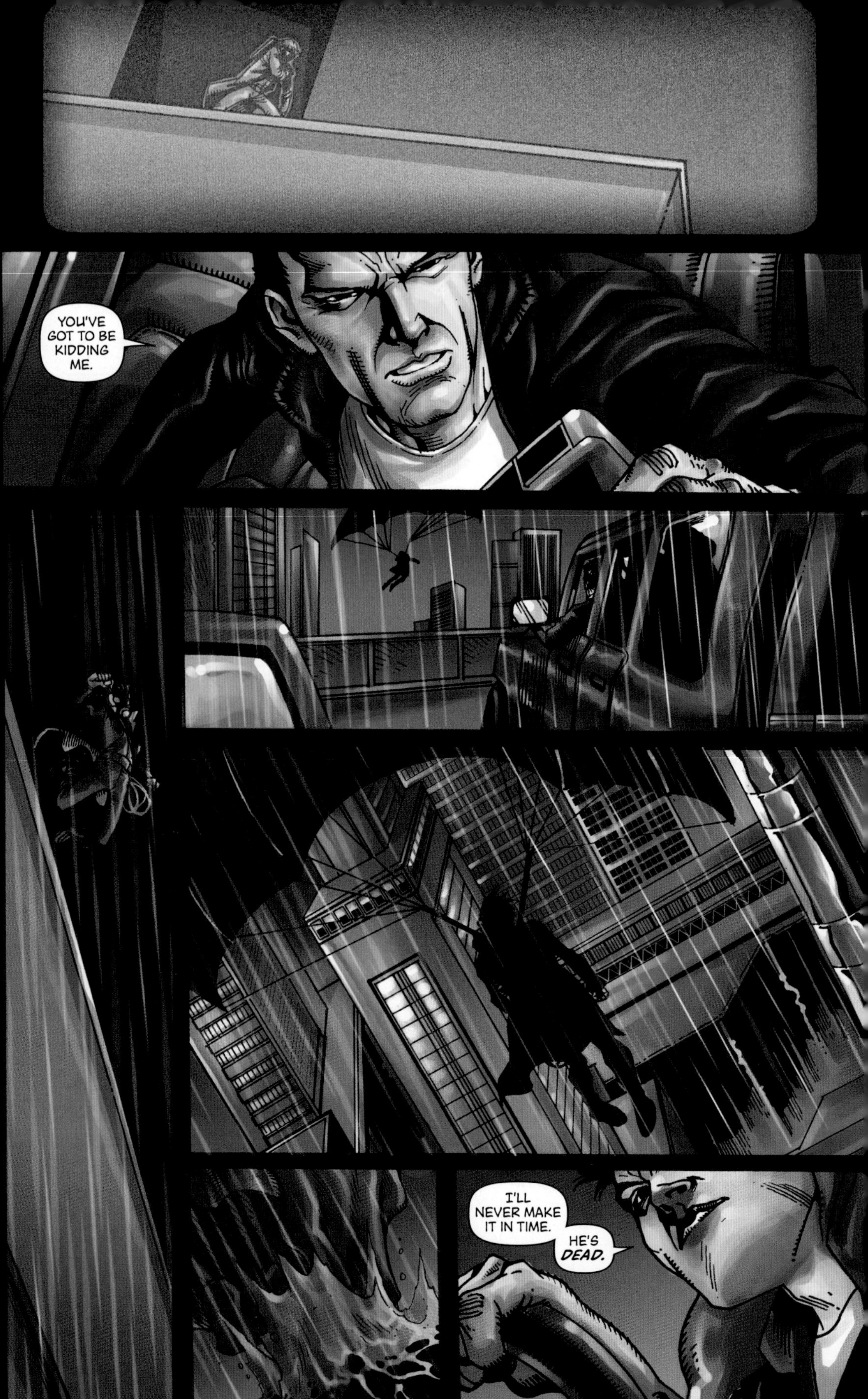
YOU'VE GOT TO BE KIDDING ME.
I'LL NEVER MAKE IT IN TIME.
HE'S *DEAD.*

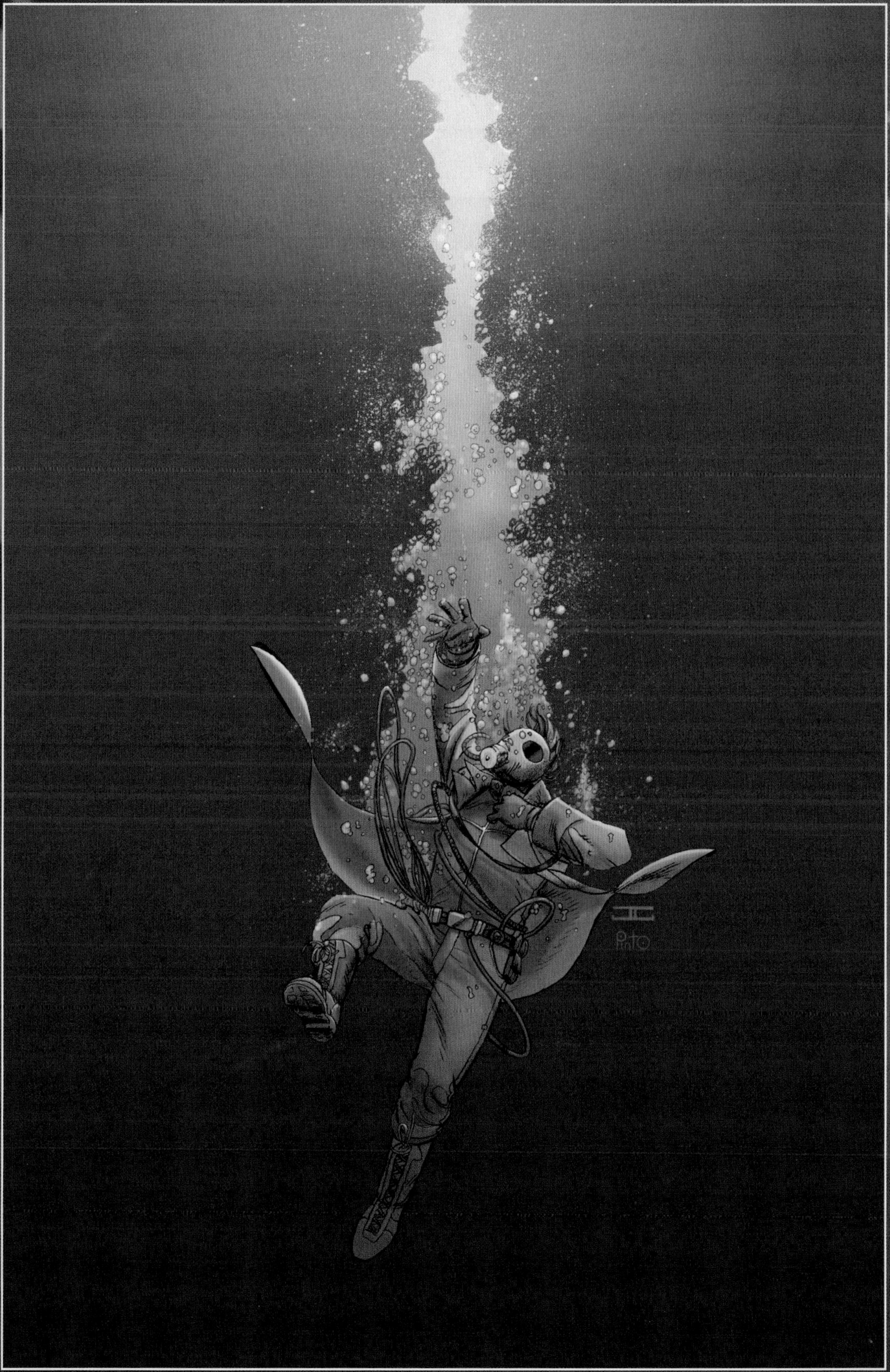

Issue #2 cover by JOHN CASSADAY

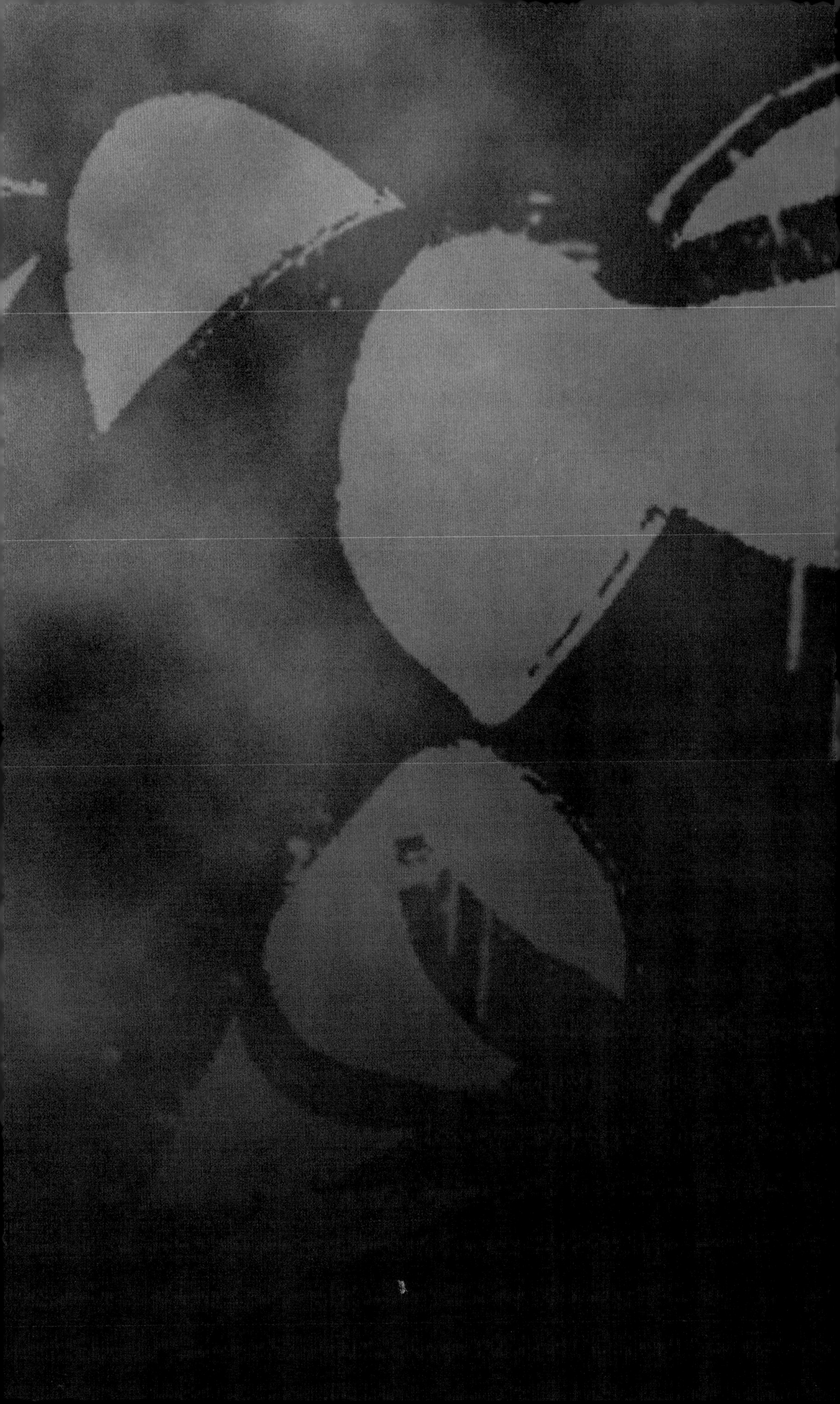

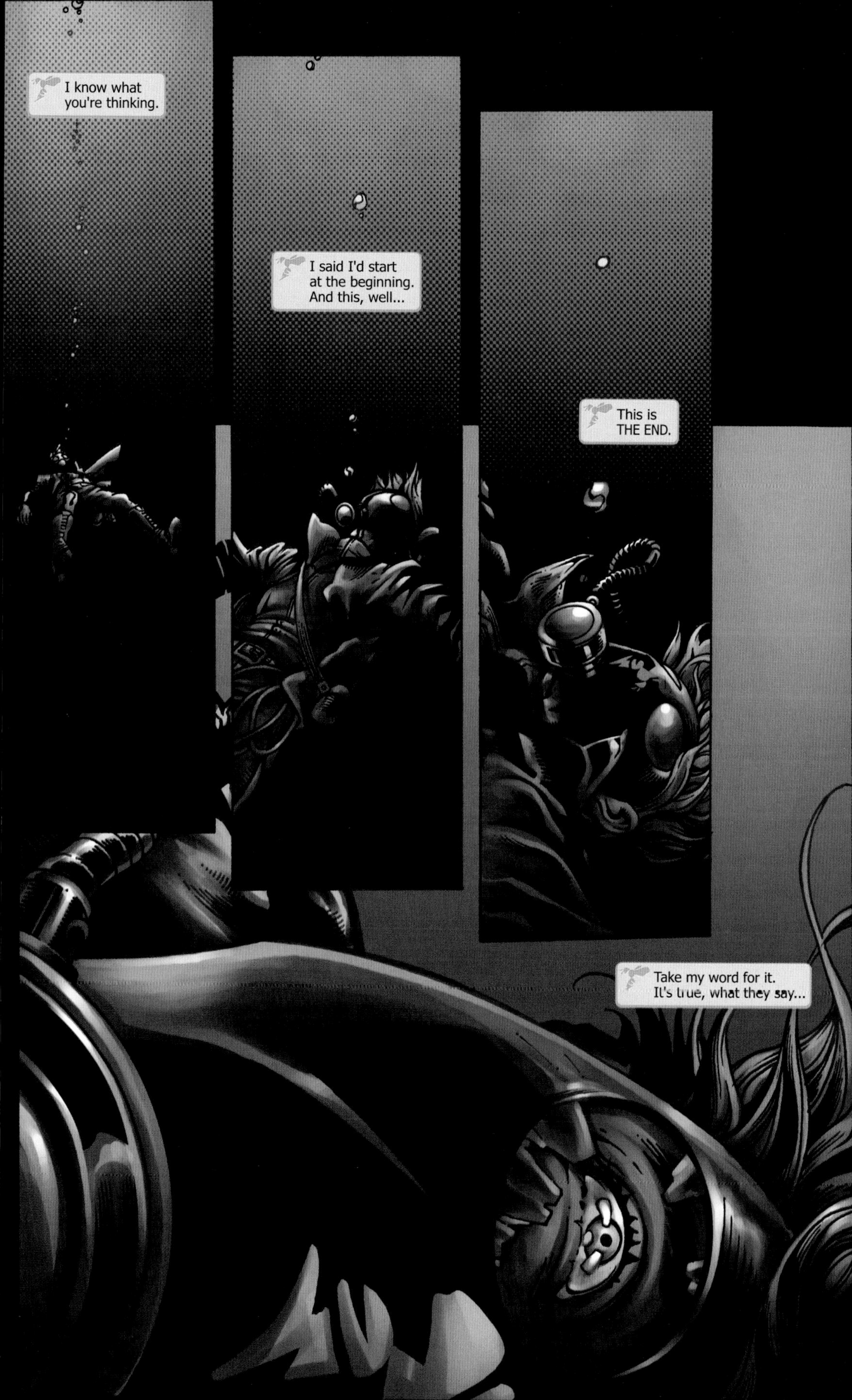
I know what you're thinking.
I said I'd start at the beginning. And this, well...
This is THE END.
Take my word for it. It's true, what they say...

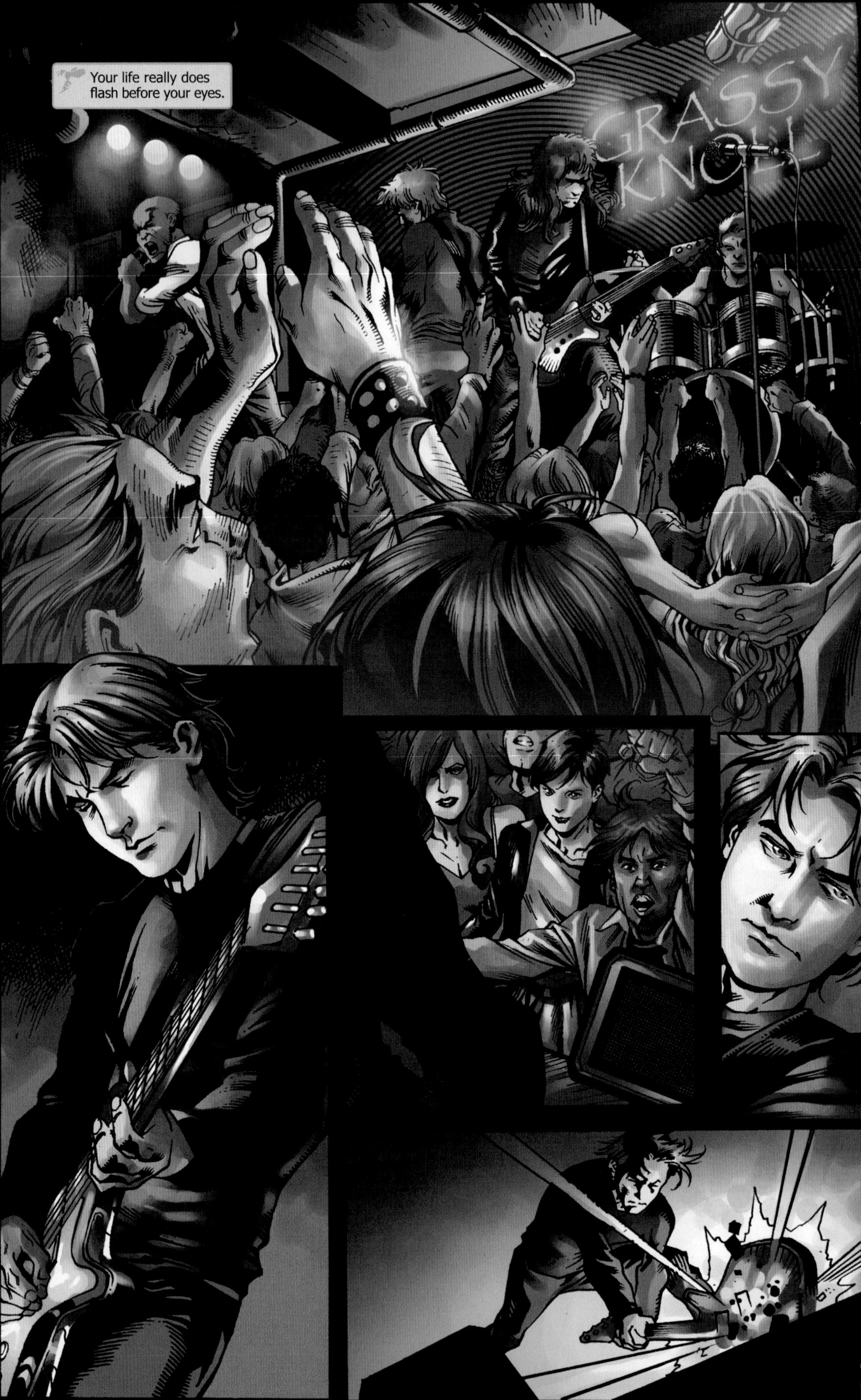
Your life really does flash before your eyes.
GRASSY KNOLL

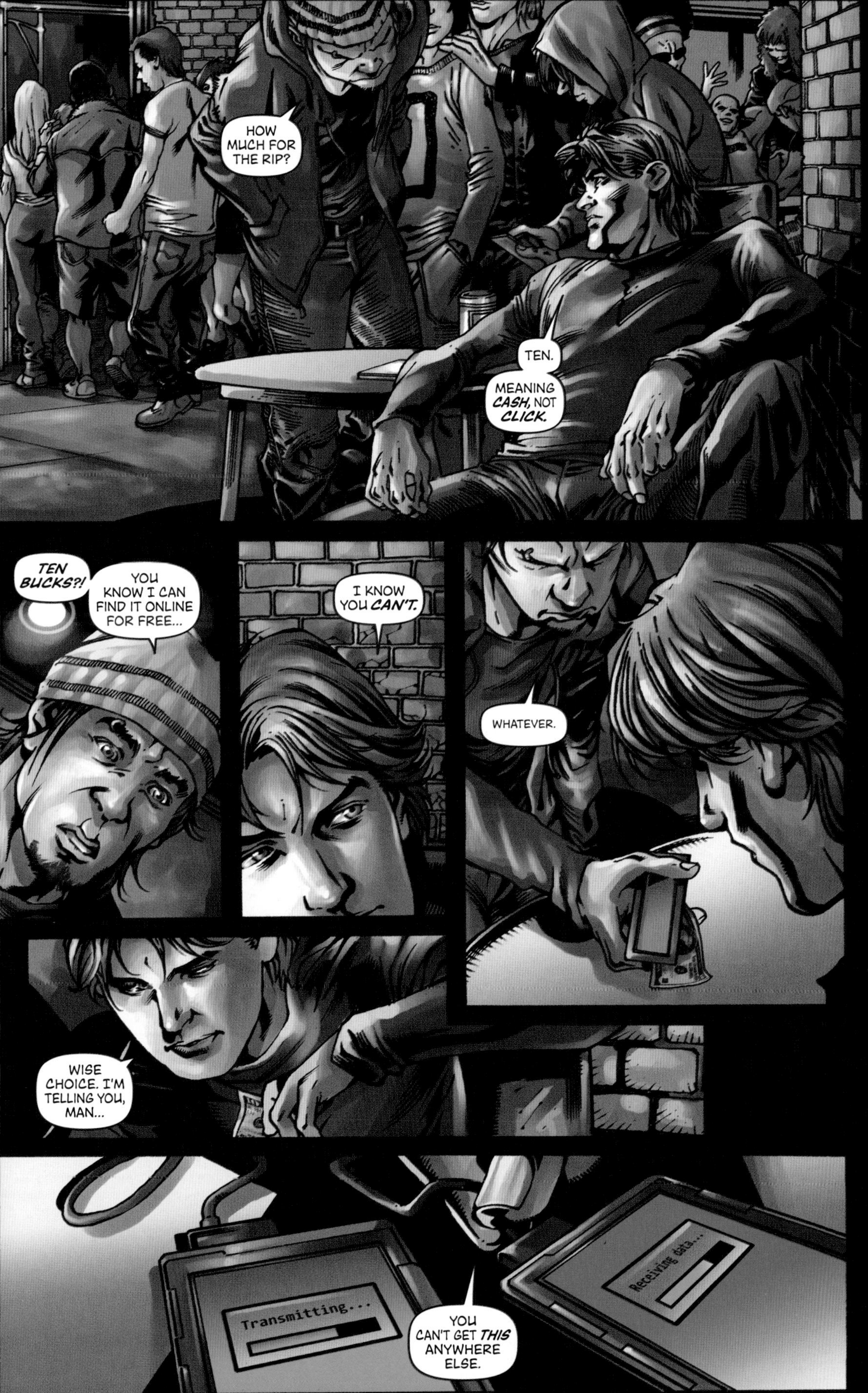
HOW MUCH FOR THE RIP?
TEN.
MEANING CASH, NOT CLICK.
TEN BUCKS?!
YOU KNOW I CAN FIND IT ONLINE FOR FREE...
I KNOW YOU CAN'T.
WHATEVER.
WISE CHOICE. I'M TELLING YOU, MAN...
Transmitting...
Receiving data...
YOU CAN'T GET THIS ANYWHERE ELSE.

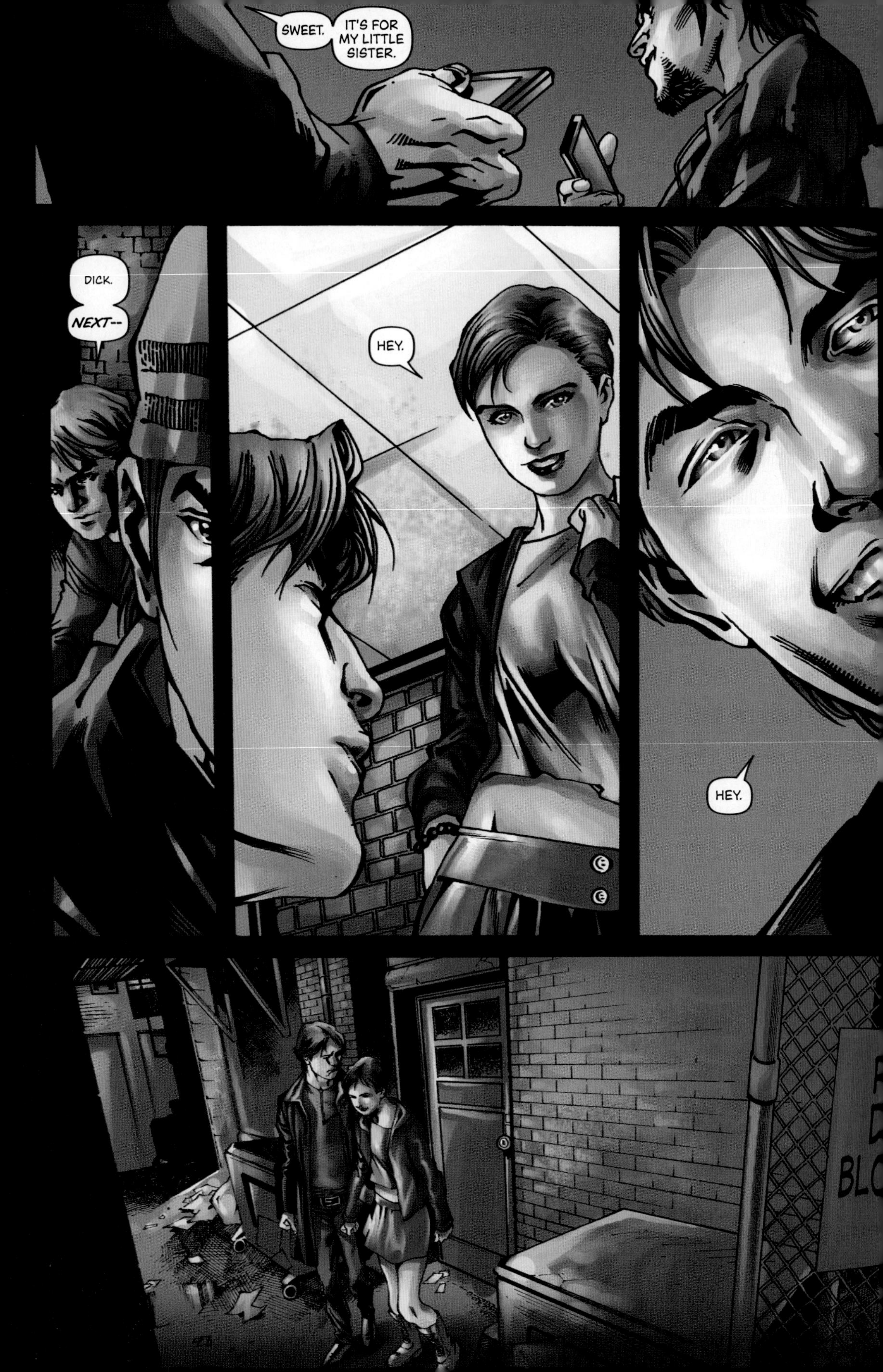
SWEET.
IT'S FOR MY LITTLE SISTER.
DICK.
NEXT--
HEY.
HEY.

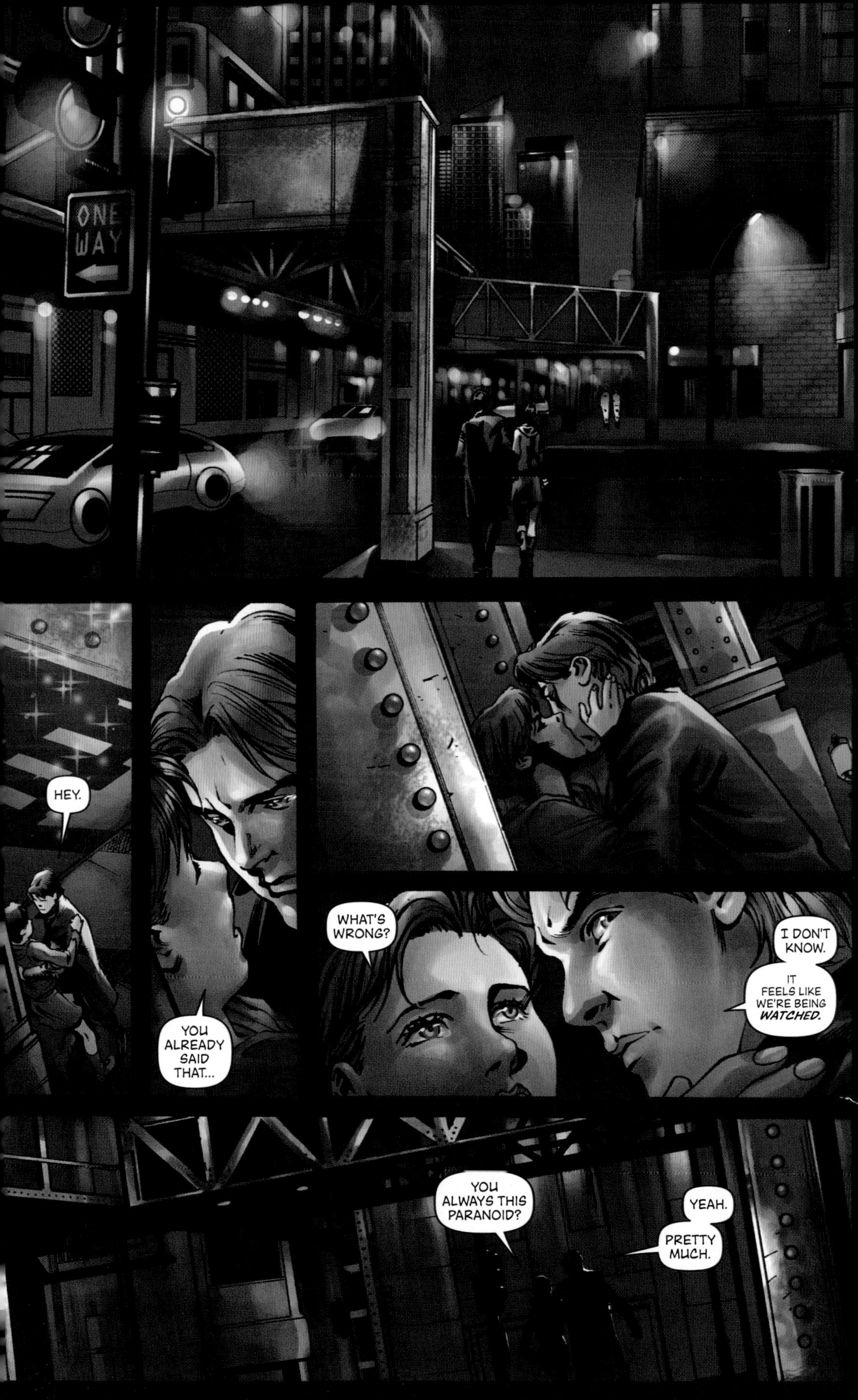
ONE WAY
HEY.
YOU ALREADY SAID THAT...
WHAT'S WRONG?
I DON'T KNOW.
IT FEELS LIKE WE'RE BEING ***WATCHED.***
YOU ALWAYS THIS PARANOID?
YEAH.
PRETTY MUCH.

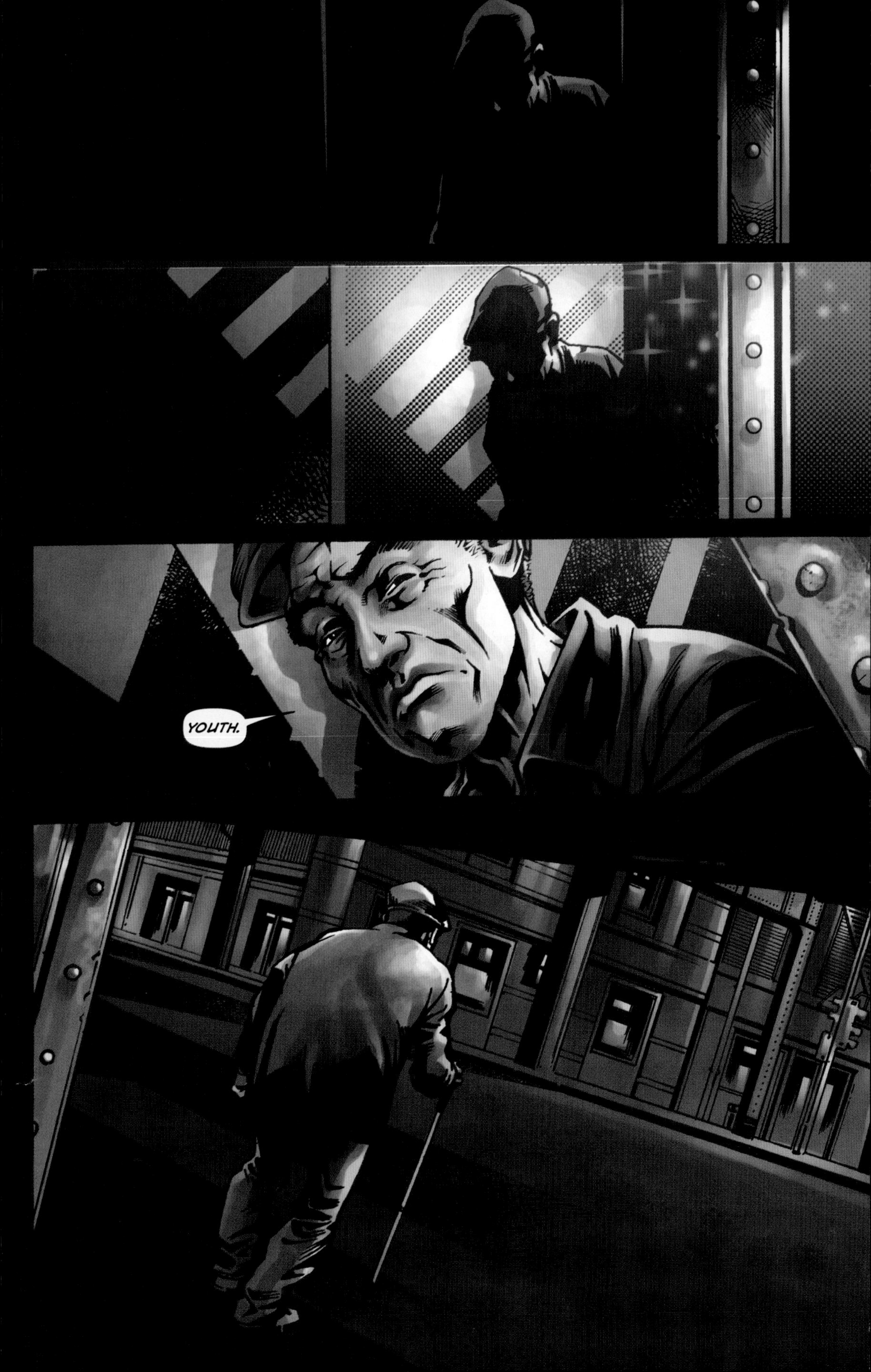
YOUTH.

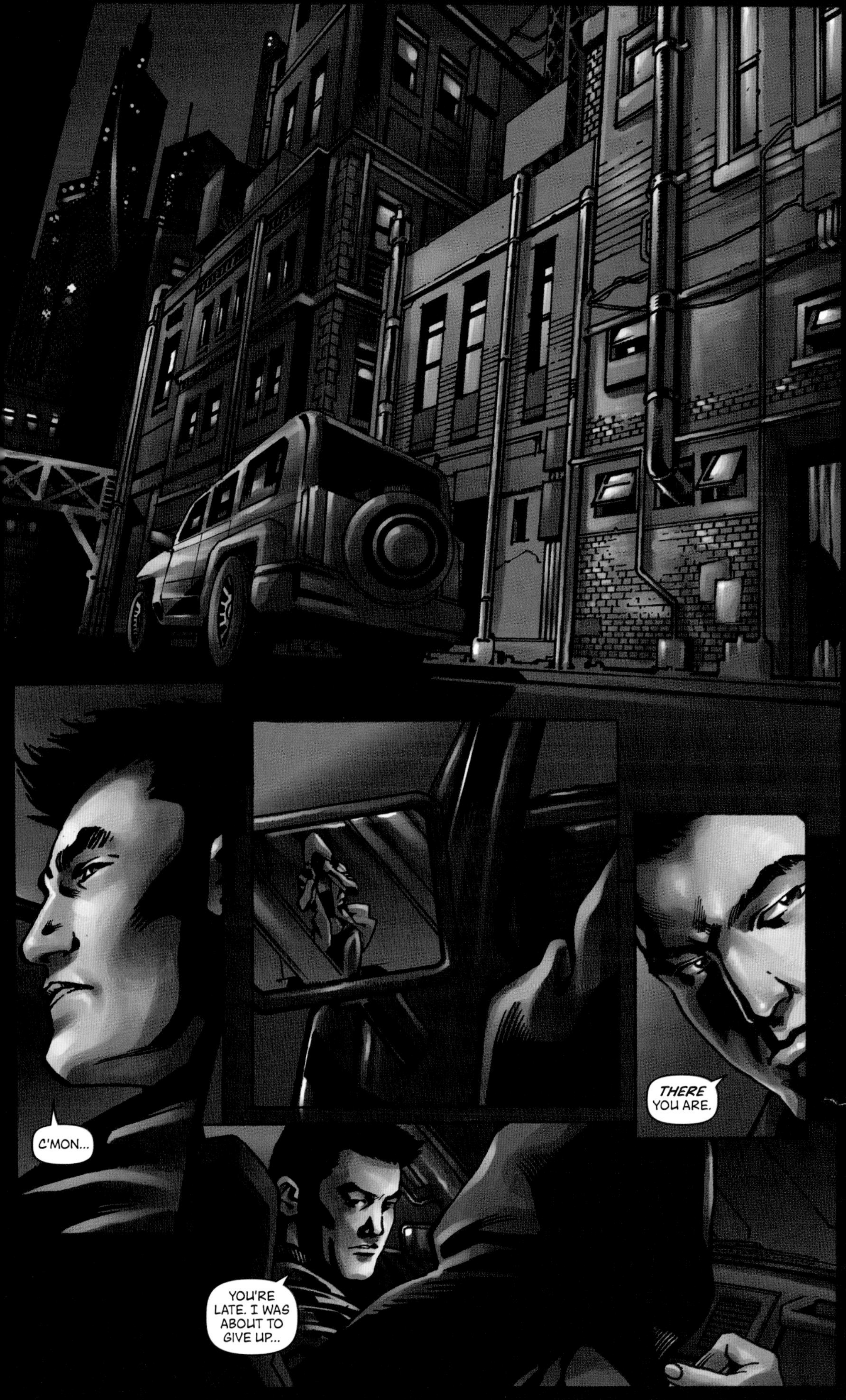
C'MON...
THERE YOU ARE.
YOU'RE LATE. I WAS ABOUT TO GIVE UP...

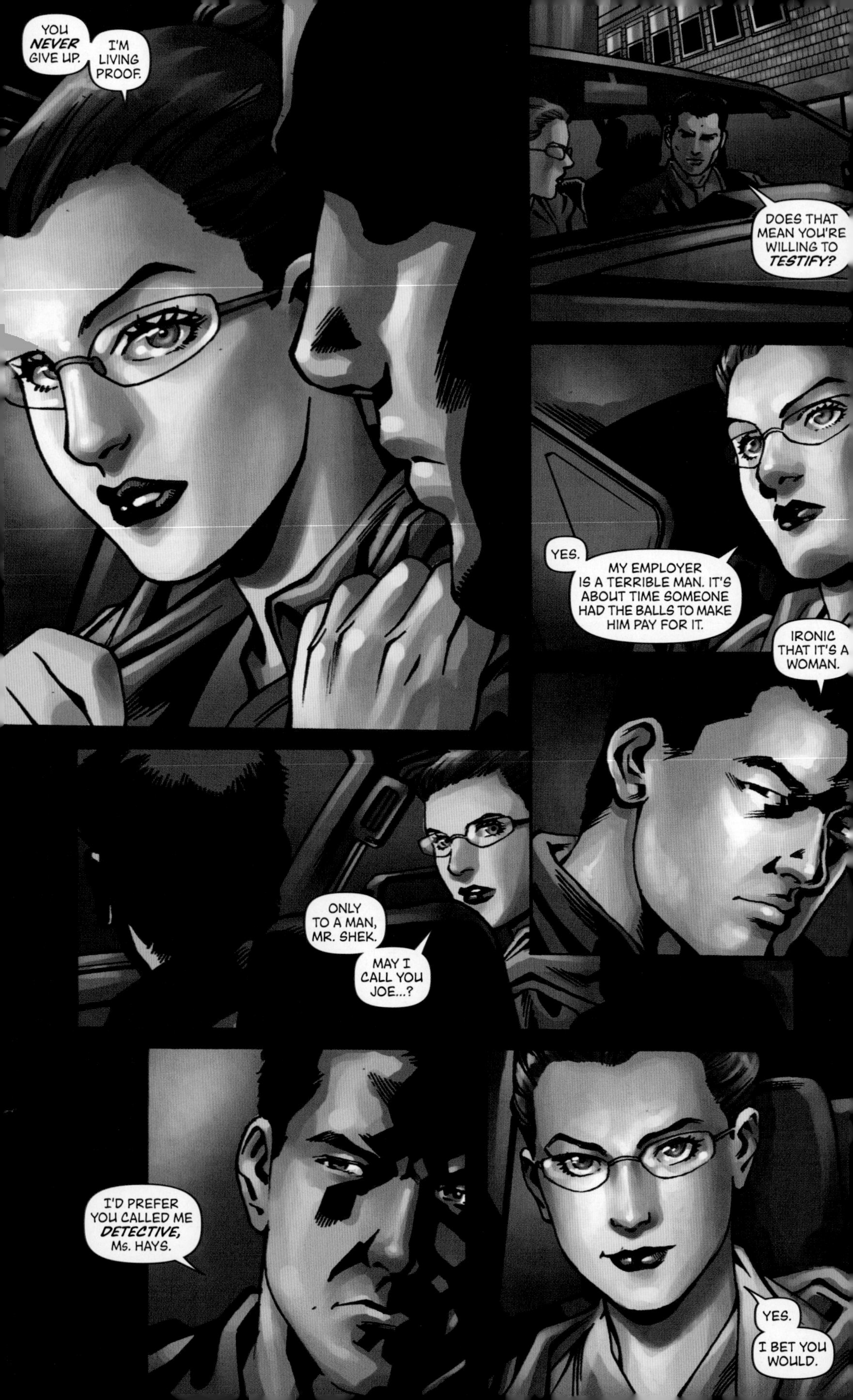
YOU NEVER GIVE UP.
I'M LIVING PROOF.
DOES THAT MEAN YOU'RE WILLING TO TESTIFY?
YES.
MY EMPLOYER IS A TERRIBLE MAN. IT'S ABOUT TIME SOMEONE HAD THE BALLS TO MAKE HIM PAY FOR IT.
IRONIC THAT IT'S A WOMAN.
ONLY TO A MAN, MR. SHEK.
MAY I CALL YOU JOE...?
I'D PREFER YOU CALLED ME DETECTIVE, Ms. HAYS.
YES.
I BET YOU WOULD.

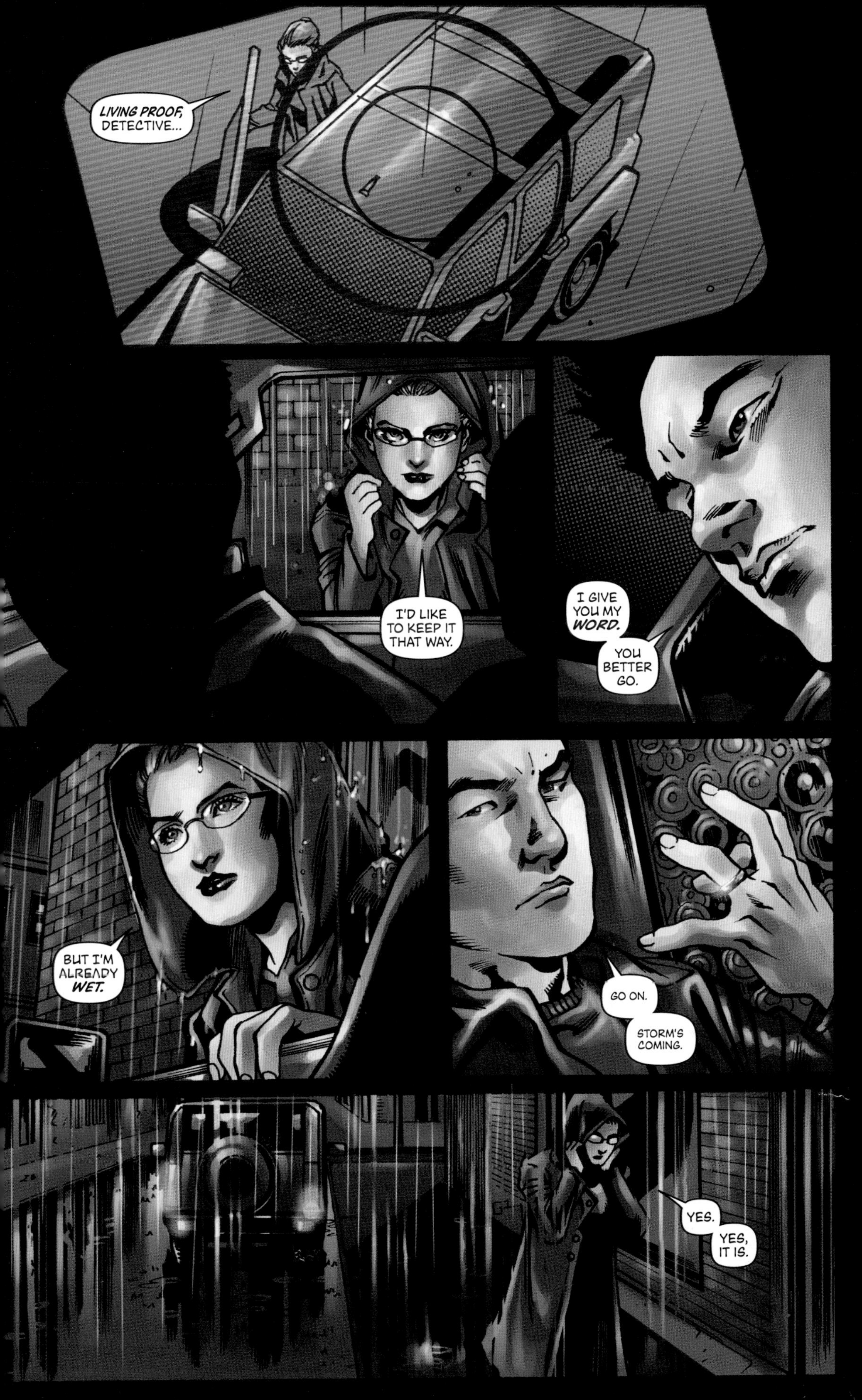
LIVING PROOF, DETECTIVE...
I'D LIKE TO KEEP IT THAT WAY.
I GIVE YOU MY WORD.
YOU BETTER GO.
BUT I'M ALREADY WET.
GO ON.
STORM'S COMING.
YES.
YES, IT IS.

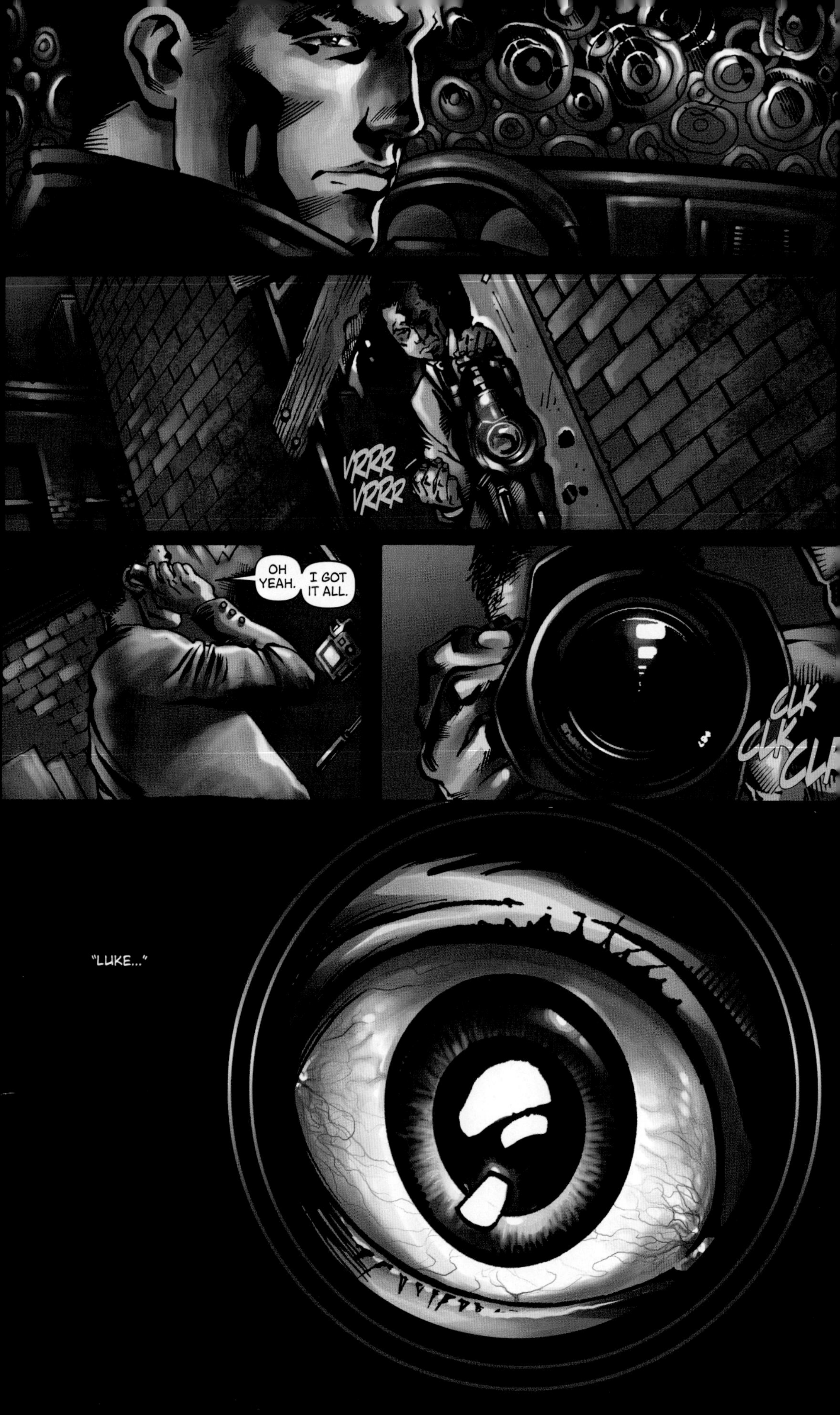
VRRR VRRR
OH YEAH.
I GOT IT ALL.
CLK CLK CLK
"LUKE..."

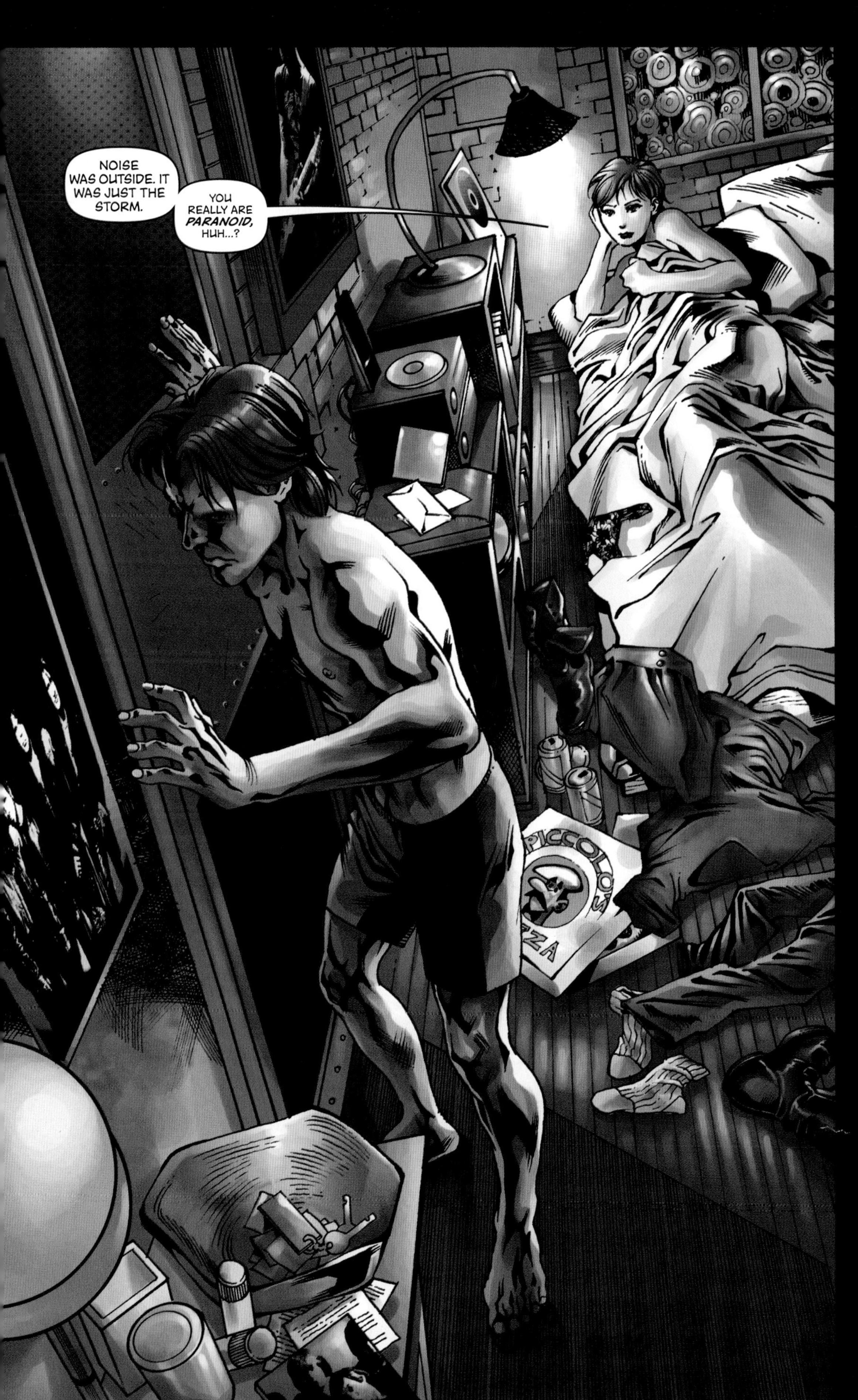

NOISE WAS OUTSIDE. IT WAS JUST THE STORM.
YOU REALLY ARE *PARANOID,* HUH...?
PICCOLO'S
ZA

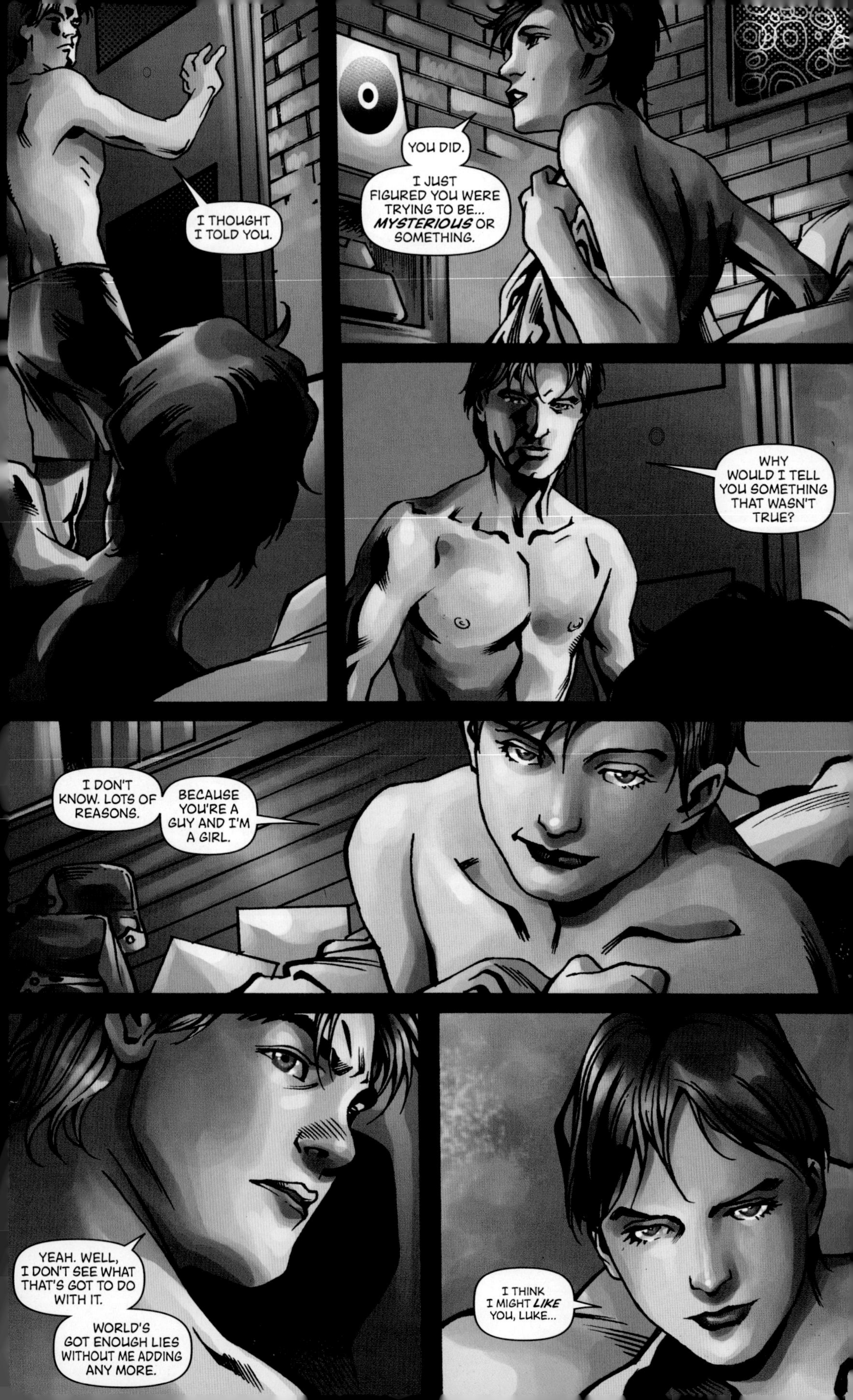
I THOUGHT I TOLD YOU.
YOU DID.
I JUST FIGURED YOU WERE TRYING TO BE... MYSTERIOUS OR SOMETHING.
WHY WOULD I TELL YOU SOMETHING THAT WASN'T TRUE?
BECAUSE YOU'RE A GUY AND I'M A GIRL.
I DON'T KNOW. LOTS OF REASONS.
YEAH. WELL, I DON'T SEE WHAT THAT'S GOT TO DO WITH IT.
WORLD'S GOT ENOUGH LIES WITHOUT ME ADDING ANY MORE.
I THINK I MIGHT LIKE YOU, LUKE...

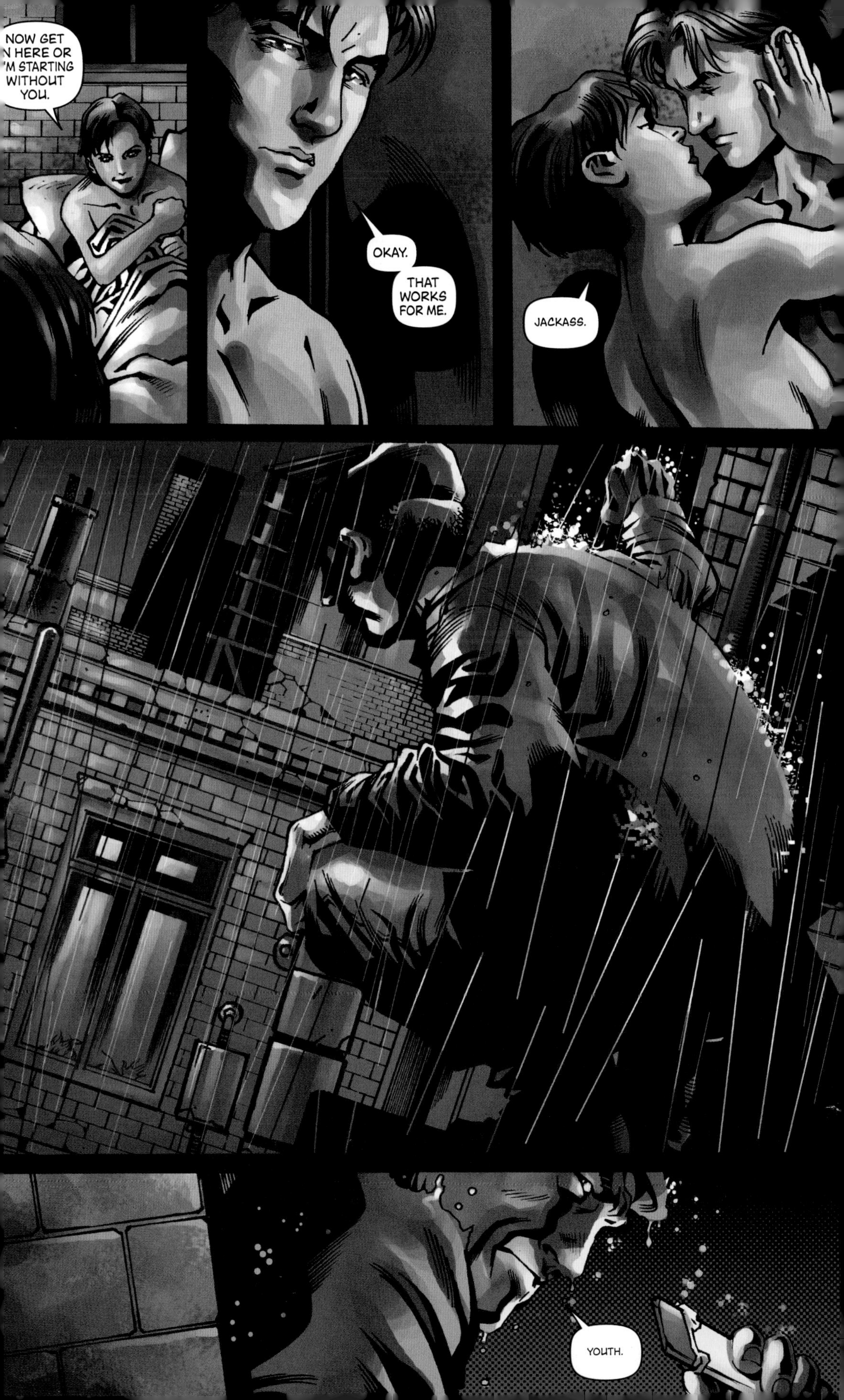
NOW GET
N HERE OR
'M STARTING
WITHOUT
YOU.
OKAY.
THAT
WORKS
FOR ME.
JACKASS.
YOUTH.

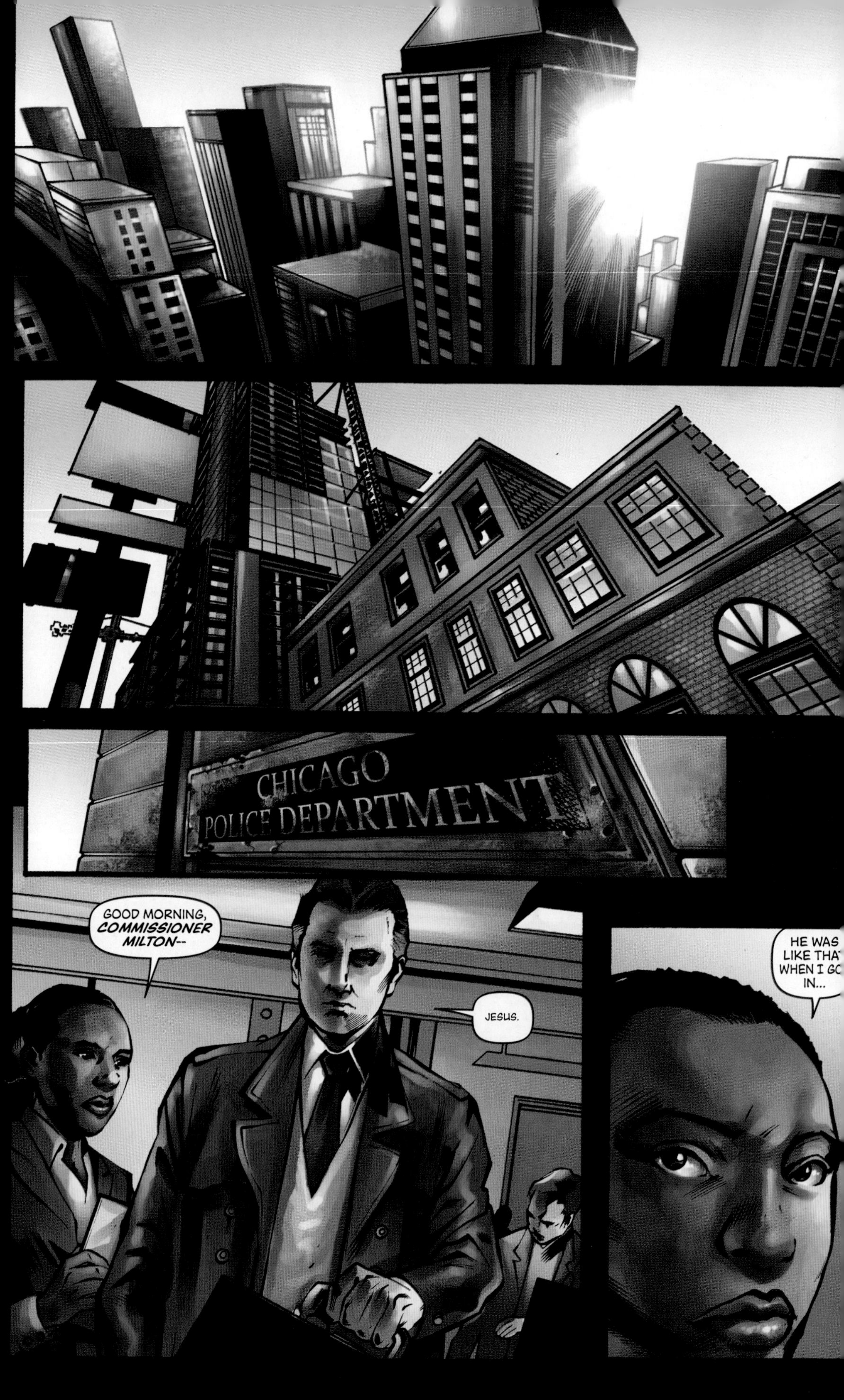
CHICAGO
POLICE DEPARTMENT
GOOD MORNING, COMMISSIONER MILTON--
JESUS.
HE WAS LIKE THAT WHEN I GO IN...

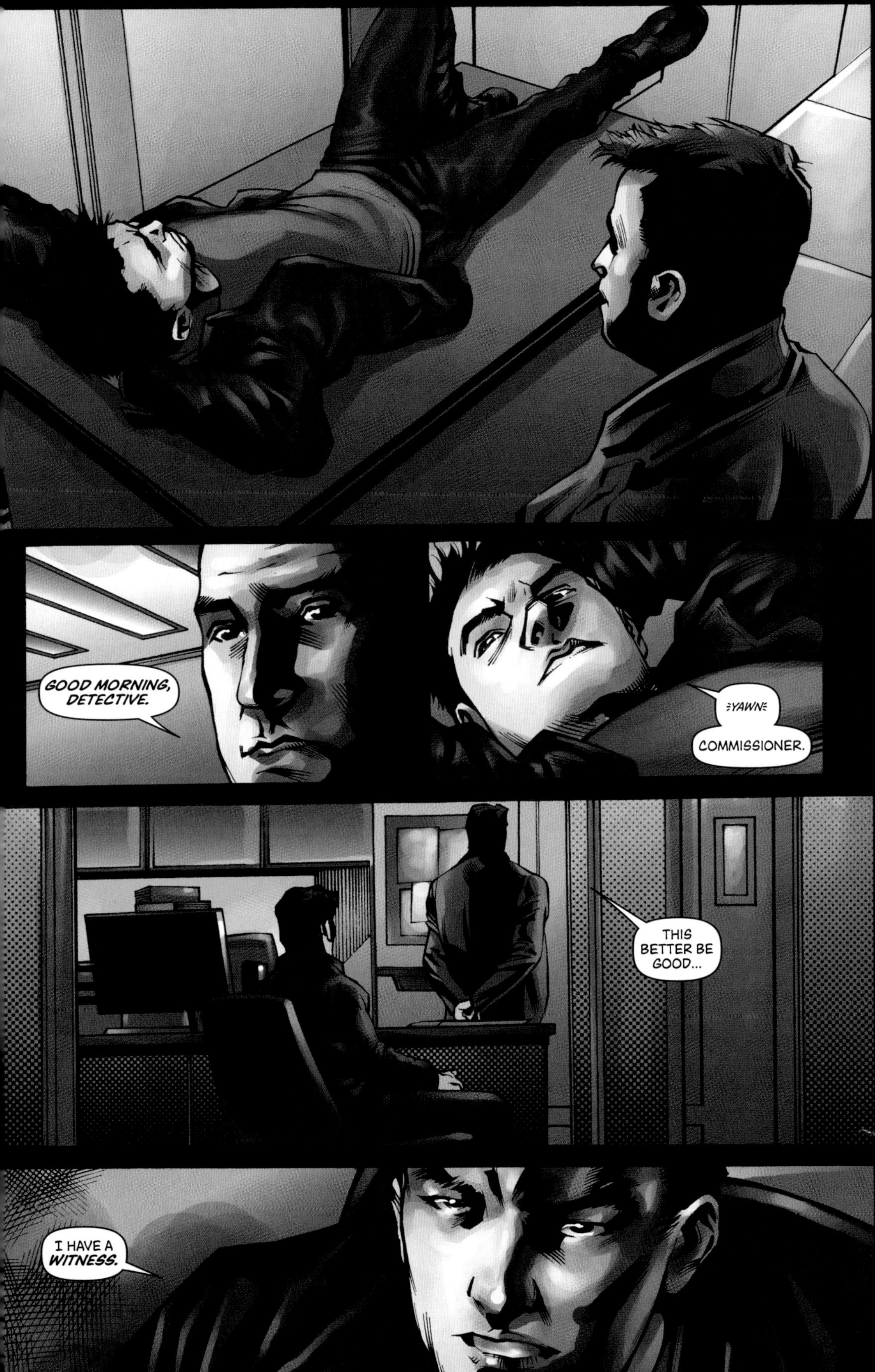
GOOD MORNING, DETECTIVE.
YAWN
COMMISSIONER.
THIS BETTER BE GOOD...
I HAVE A WITNESS.

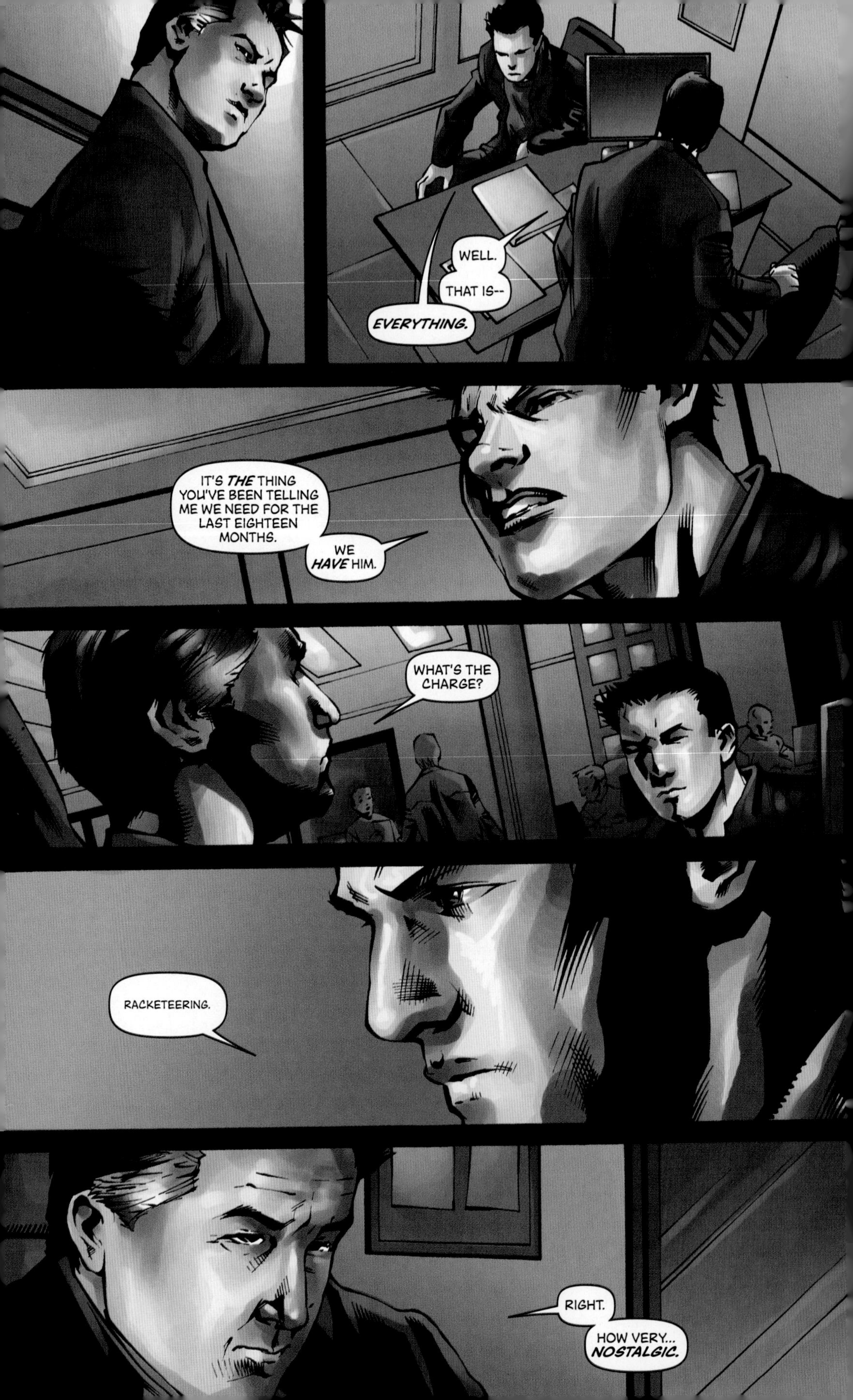
WELL.
THAT IS--
EVERYTHING.
IT'S THE THING YOU'VE BEEN TELLING ME WE NEED FOR THE LAST EIGHTEEN MONTHS.
WE HAVE HIM.
WHAT'S THE CHARGE?
RACKETEERING.
RIGHT.
HOW VERY... NOSTALGIC.

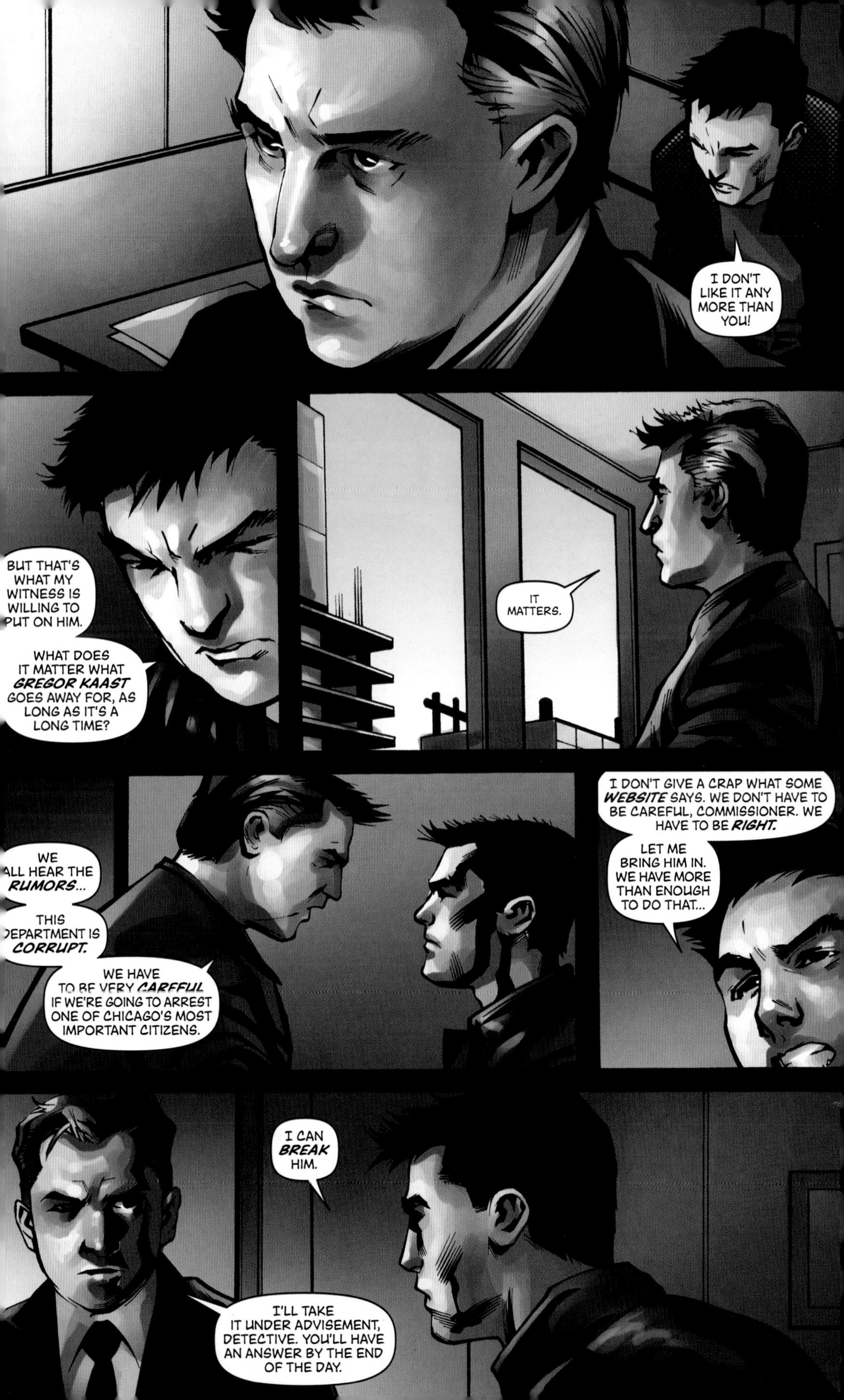

I DON'T LIKE IT ANY MORE THAN YOU!
BUT THAT'S WHAT MY WITNESS IS WILLING TO PUT ON HIM.
WHAT DOES IT MATTER WHAT GREGOR KAAST GOES AWAY FOR, AS LONG AS IT'S A LONG TIME?
IT MATTERS.
WE ALL HEAR THE RUMORS...
THIS DEPARTMENT IS CORRUPT.
WE HAVE TO BE VERY CAREFUL IF WE'RE GOING TO ARREST ONE OF CHICAGO'S MOST IMPORTANT CITIZENS.
I DON'T GIVE A CRAP WHAT SOME WEBSITE SAYS. WE DON'T HAVE TO BE CAREFUL, COMMISSIONER. WE HAVE TO BE RIGHT.
LET ME BRING HIM IN. WE HAVE MORE THAN ENOUGH TO DO THAT...
I CAN BREAK HIM.
I'LL TAKE IT UNDER ADVISEMENT, DETECTIVE. YOU'LL HAVE AN ANSWER BY THE END OF THE DAY.

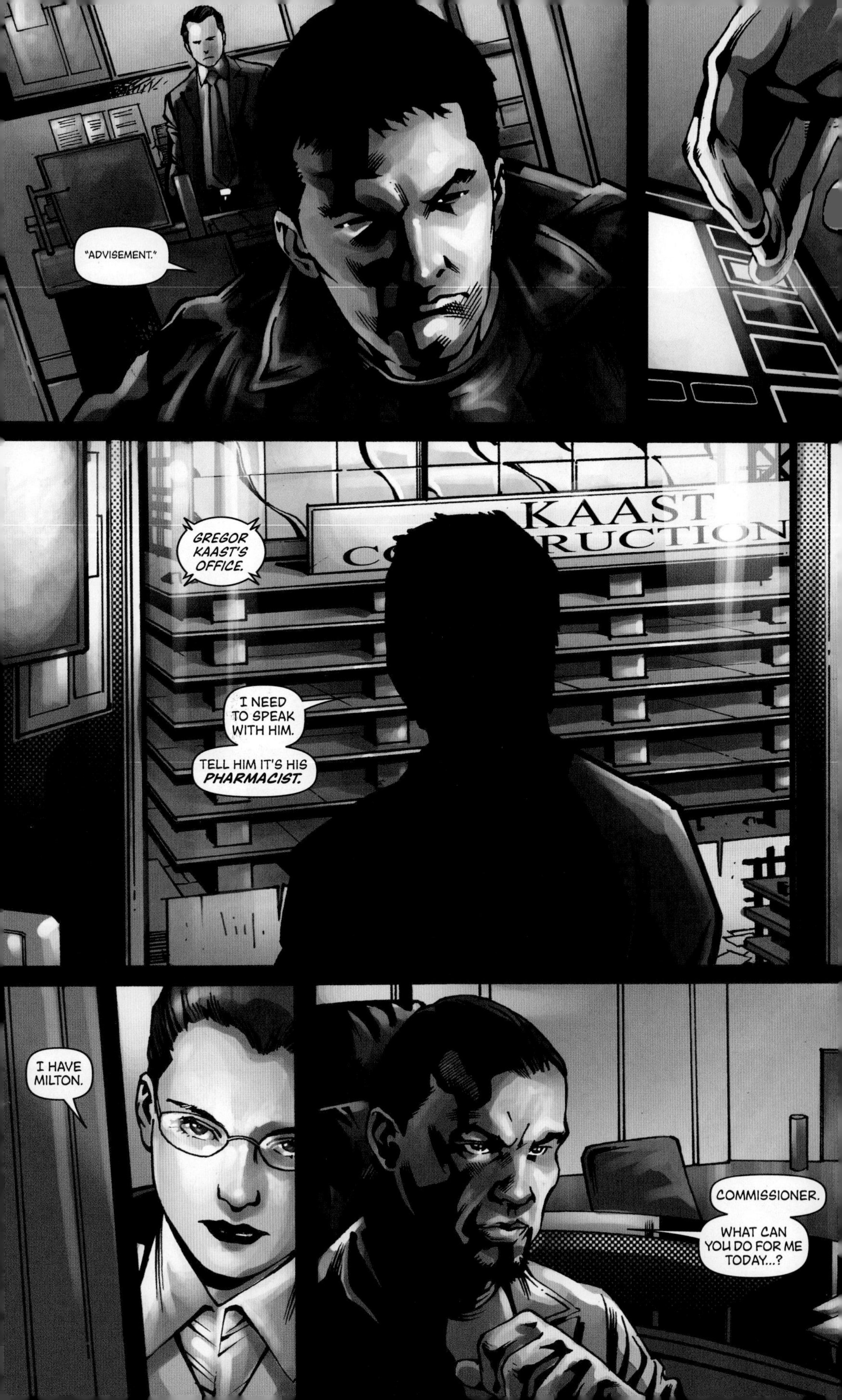
"ADVISEMENT."
KAAST CO...RUCTION
GREGOR KAAST'S OFFICE.
I NEED TO SPEAK WITH HIM.
TELL HIM IT'S HIS *PHARMACIST.*
I HAVE MILTON.
COMMISSIONER.
WHAT CAN YOU DO FOR ME TODAY...?

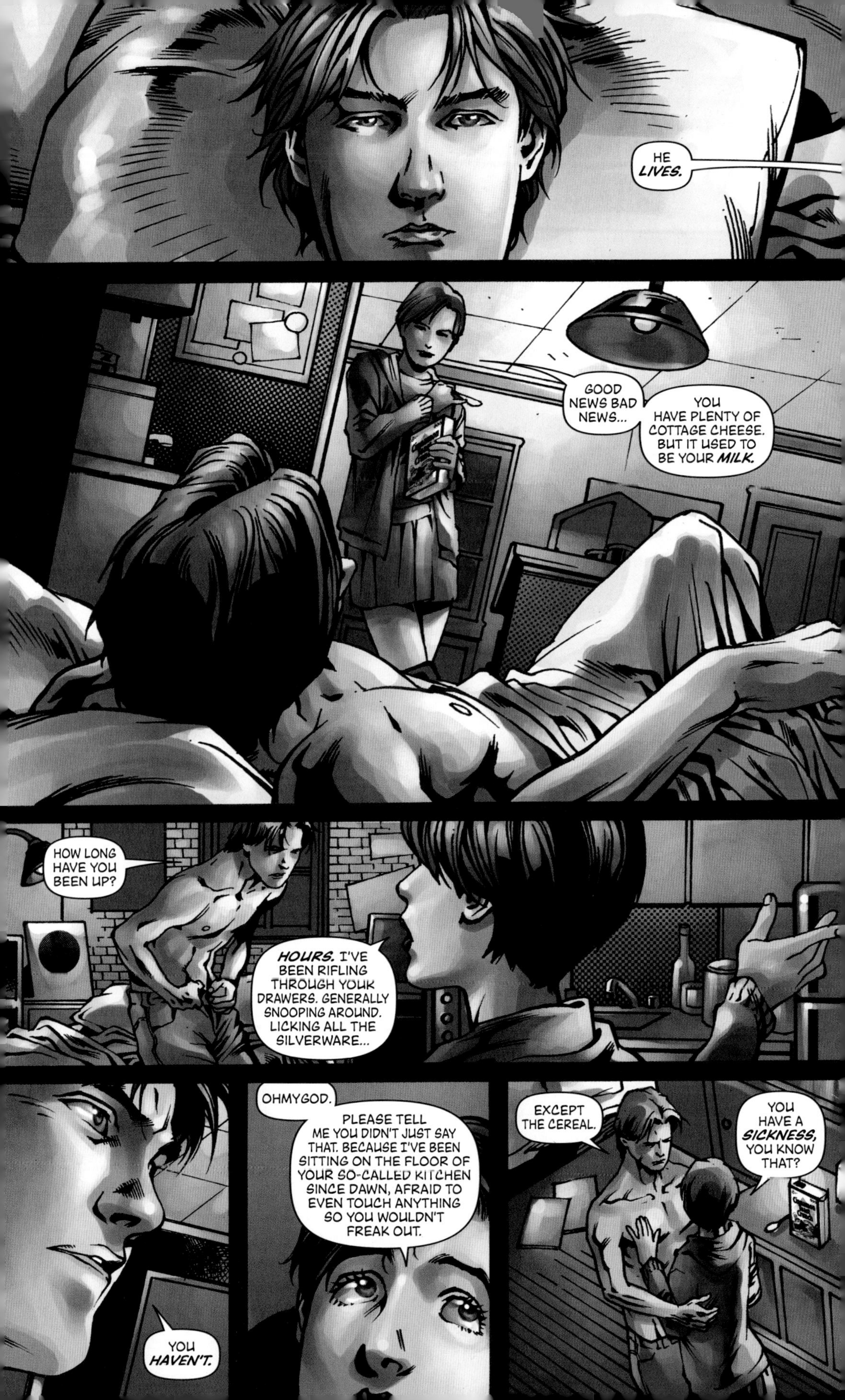
HE LIVES.
GOOD NEWS BAD NEWS...
YOU HAVE PLENTY OF COTTAGE CHEESE. BUT IT USED TO BE YOUR MILK.
HOW LONG HAVE YOU BEEN UP?
HOURS. I'VE BEEN RIFLING THROUGH YOUR DRAWERS. GENERALLY SNOOPING AROUND. LICKING ALL THE SILVERWARE...
YOU HAVEN'T.
OHMYGOD.
PLEASE TELL ME YOU DIDN'T JUST SAY THAT. BECAUSE I'VE BEEN SITTING ON THE FLOOR OF YOUR SO-CALLED KITCHEN SINCE DAWN, AFRAID TO EVEN TOUCH ANYTHING SO YOU WOULDN'T FREAK OUT.
EXCEPT THE CEREAL.
YOU HAVE A SICKNESS, YOU KNOW THAT?

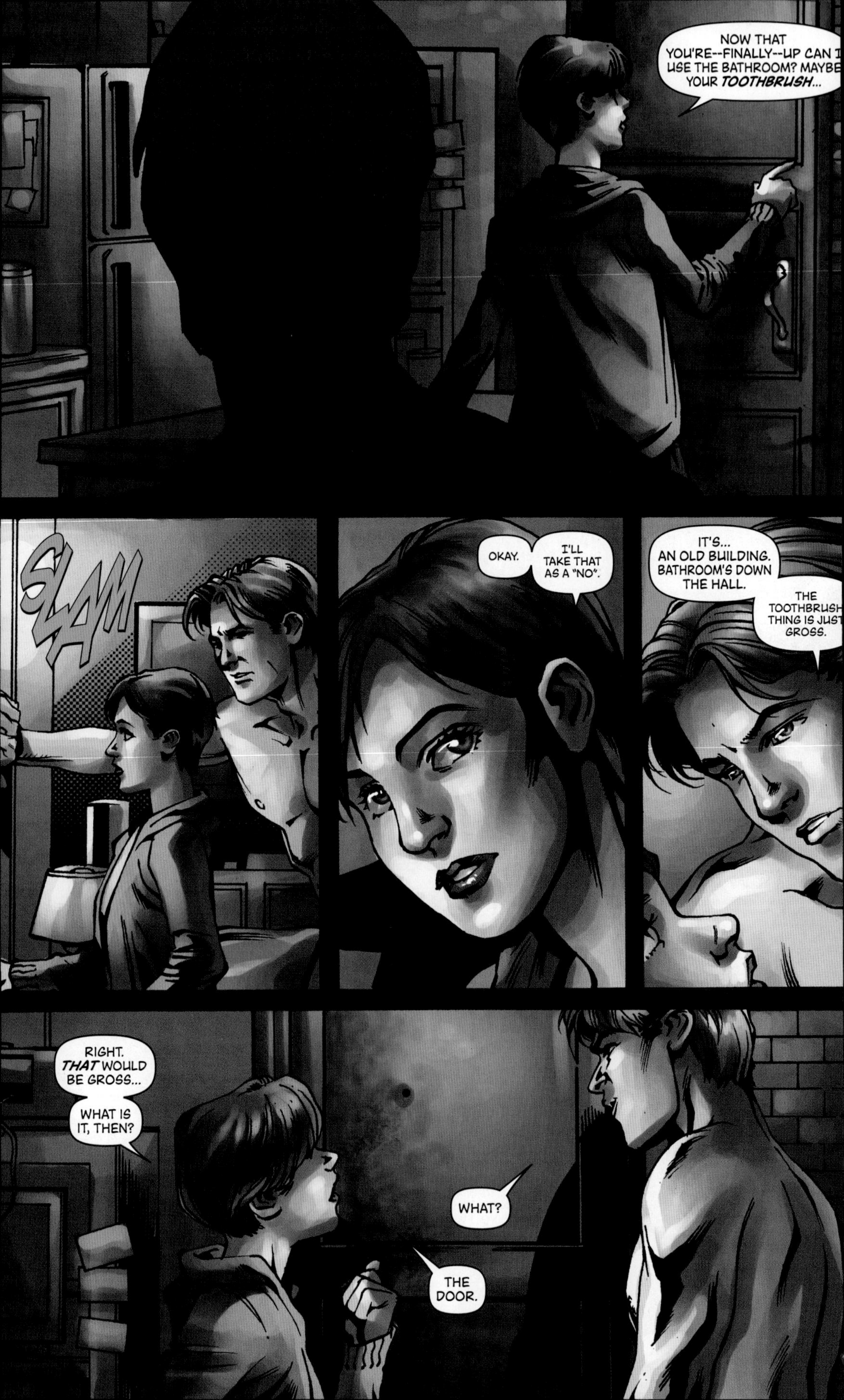
NOW THAT YOU'RE--FINALLY--UP CAN I USE THE BATHROOM? MAYBE YOUR TOOTHBRUSH...
SLAM
OKAY.
I'LL TAKE THAT AS A "NO".
IT'S... AN OLD BUILDING. BATHROOM'S DOWN THE HALL.
THE TOOTHBRUSH THING IS JUST GROSS.
RIGHT. THAT WOULD BE GROSS...
WHAT IS IT, THEN?
WHAT?
THE DOOR.

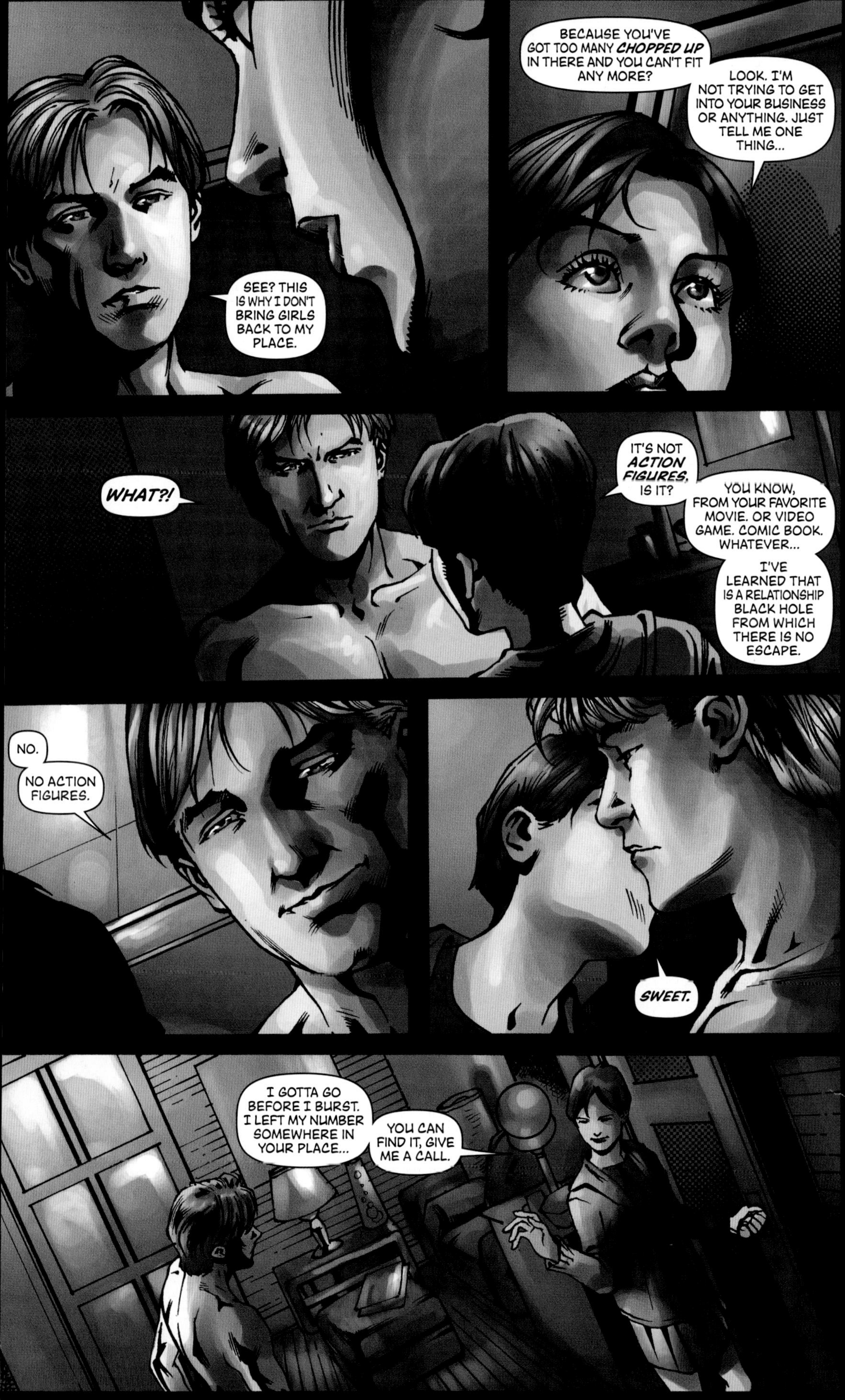

SEE? THIS IS WHY I DON'T BRING GIRLS BACK TO MY PLACE.
BECAUSE YOU'VE GOT TOO MANY CHOPPED UP IN THERE AND YOU CAN'T FIT ANY MORE?
LOOK. I'M NOT TRYING TO GET INTO YOUR BUSINESS OR ANYTHING. JUST TELL ME ONE THING...
WHAT?!
IT'S NOT ACTION FIGURES, IS IT?
YOU KNOW, FROM YOUR FAVORITE MOVIE. OR VIDEO GAME. COMIC BOOK. WHATEVER...
I'VE LEARNED THAT IS A RELATIONSHIP BLACK HOLE FROM WHICH THERE IS NO ESCAPE.
NO.
NO ACTION FIGURES.
SWEET.
I GOTTA GO BEFORE I BURST. I LEFT MY NUMBER SOMEWHERE IN YOUR PLACE...
YOU CAN FIND IT, GIVE ME A CALL.

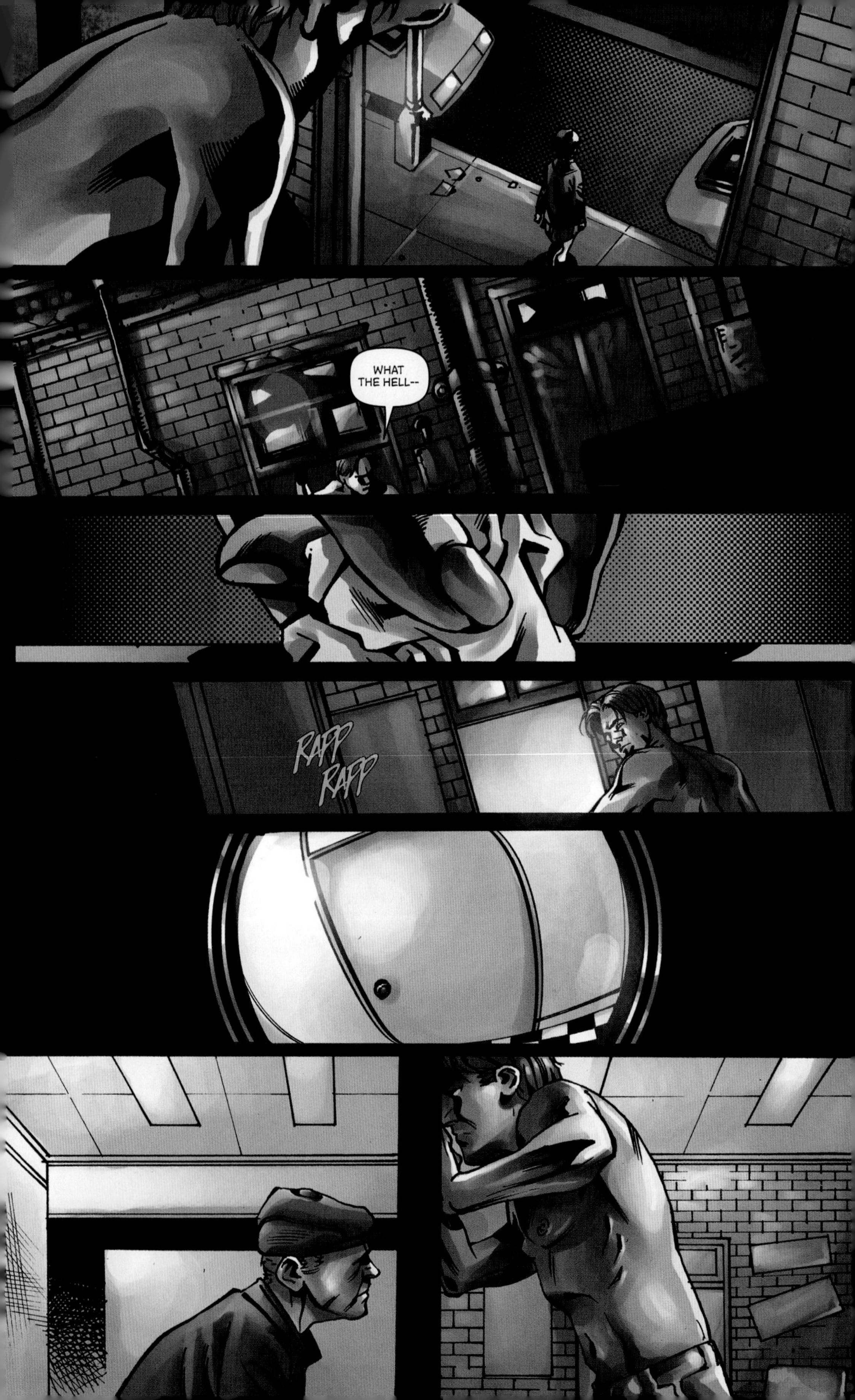
WHAT THE HELL--
RAPP RAPP

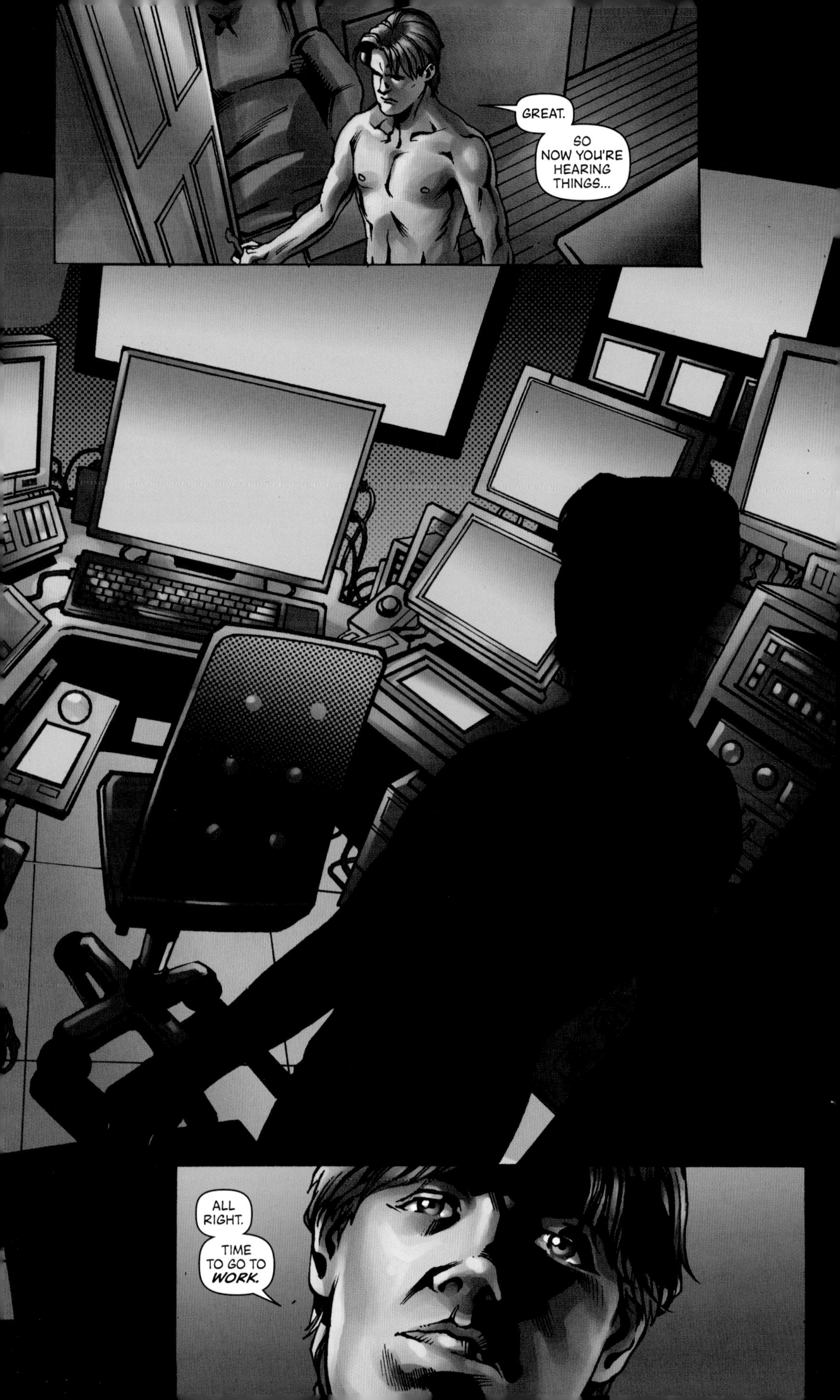
GREAT.
SO NOW YOU'RE HEARING THINGS...
ALL RIGHT.
TIME TO GO TO *WORK.*

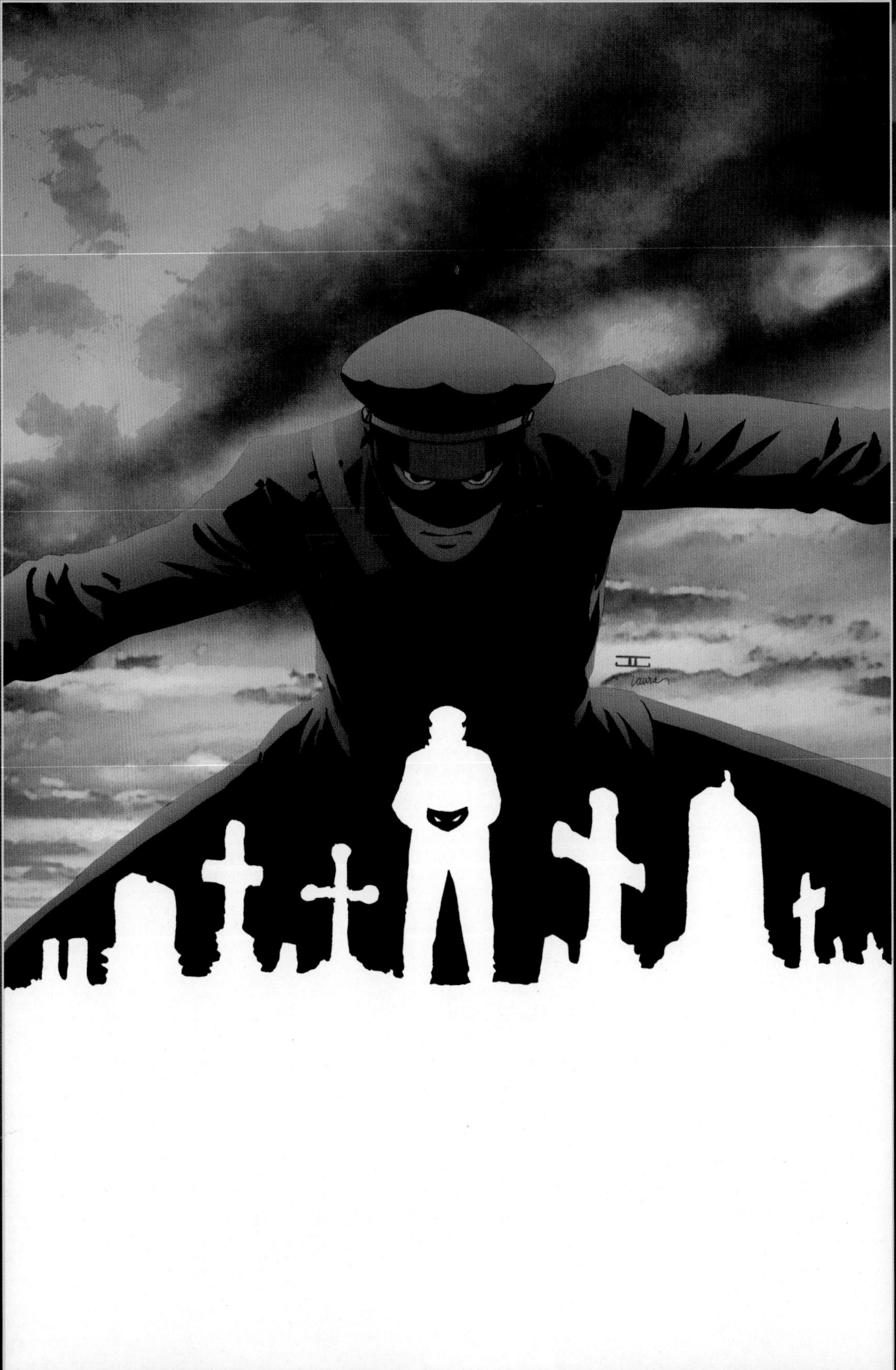

Issue #3 cover by JOHN CASSADAY

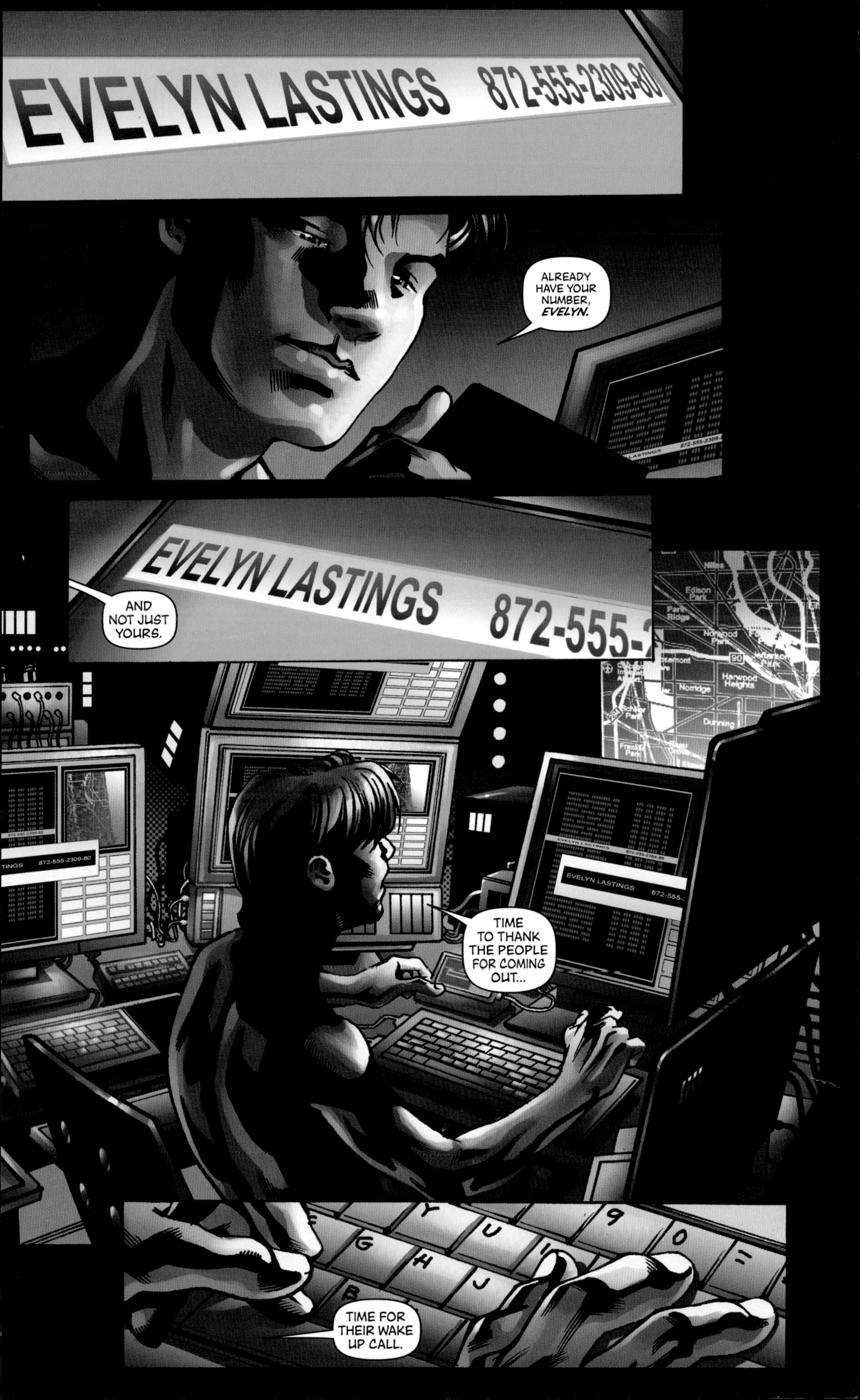
EVELYN LASTINGS 872-555-2309-80
ALREADY HAVE YOUR NUMBER, *EVELYN.*
EVELYN LASTINGS 872-555-2
AND NOT JUST YOURS.
EVELYN LASTINGS 872-555-
TIME TO THANK THE PEOPLE FOR COMING OUT...
TIME FOR THEIR WAKE UP CALL.

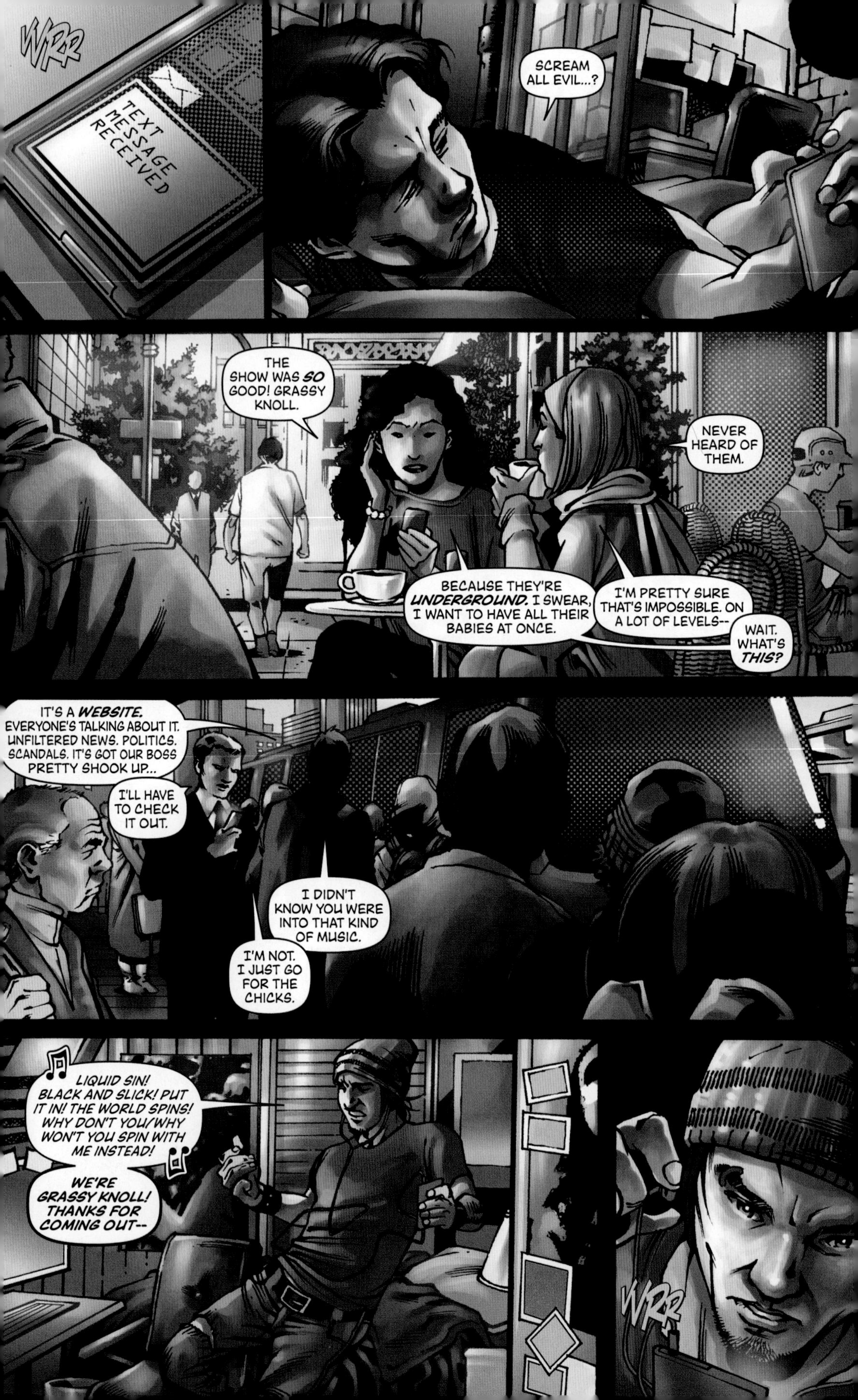

WRR
TEXT MESSAGE RECEIVED
SCREAM ALL EVIL...?
THE SHOW WAS SO GOOD! GRASSY KNOLL.
NEVER HEARD OF THEM.
BECAUSE THEY'RE UNDERGROUND. I SWEAR, I WANT TO HAVE ALL THEIR BABIES AT ONCE.
I'M PRETTY SURE THAT'S IMPOSSIBLE. ON A LOT OF LEVELS--
WAIT. WHAT'S THIS?
IT'S A WEBSITE. EVERYONE'S TALKING ABOUT IT. UNFILTERED NEWS. POLITICS. SCANDALS. IT'S GOT OUR BOSS PRETTY SHOOK UP...
I'LL HAVE TO CHECK IT OUT.
I DIDN'T KNOW YOU WERE INTO THAT KIND OF MUSIC.
I'M NOT. I JUST GO FOR THE CHICKS.
LIQUID SIN! BLACK AND SLICK! PUT IT IN! THE WORLD SPINS! WHY DON'T YOU/WHY WON'T YOU SPIN WITH ME INSTEAD!
WE'RE GRASSY KNOLL! THANKS FOR COMING OUT--
WRR

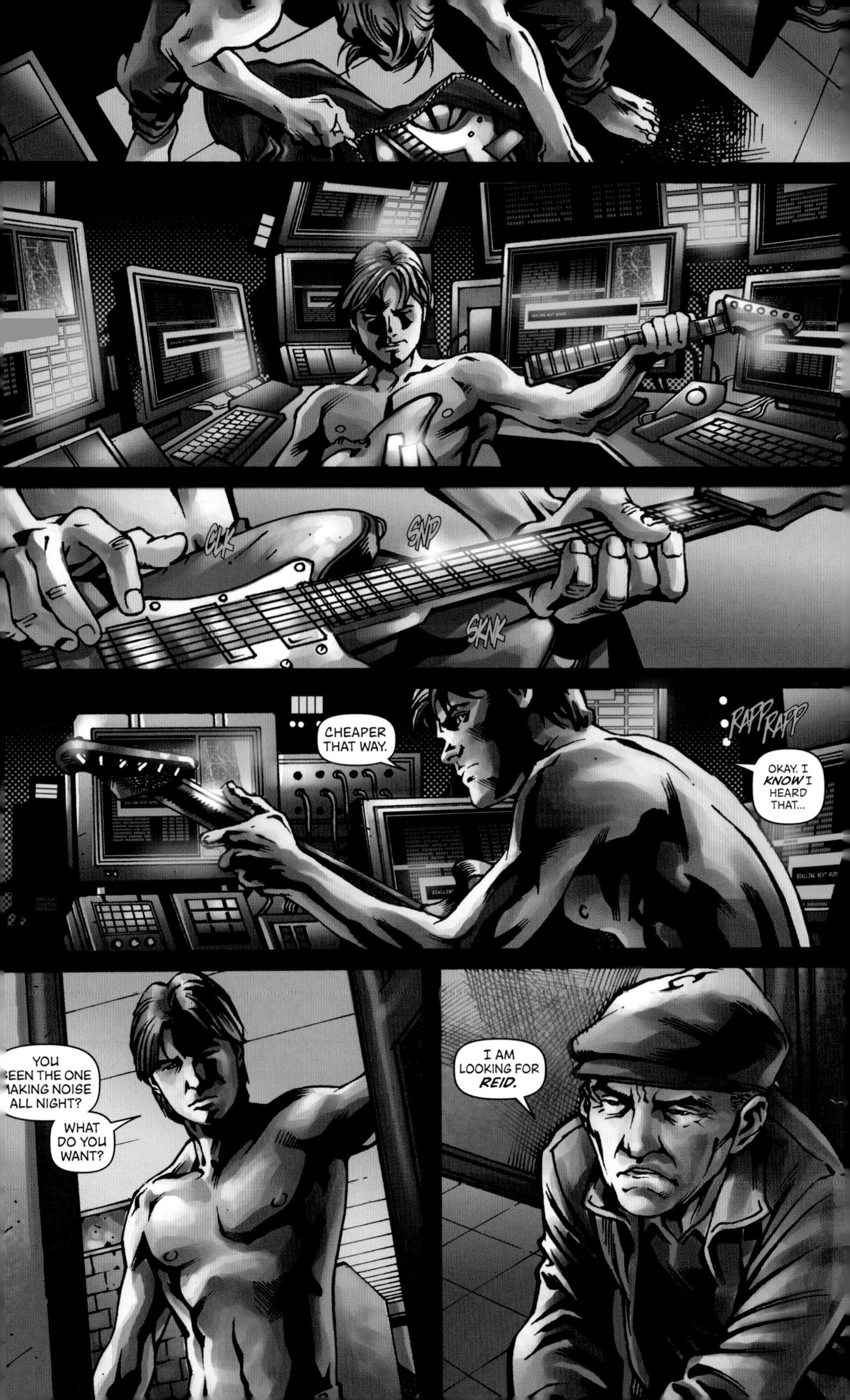
CLK
SNP
SKNK
CHEAPER THAT WAY.
RAPP RAPP
OKAY. I *KNOW* I HEARD THAT...
I AM LOOKING FOR *REID.*
YOU BEEN THE ONE MAKING NOISE ALL NIGHT?
WHAT DO YOU WANT?

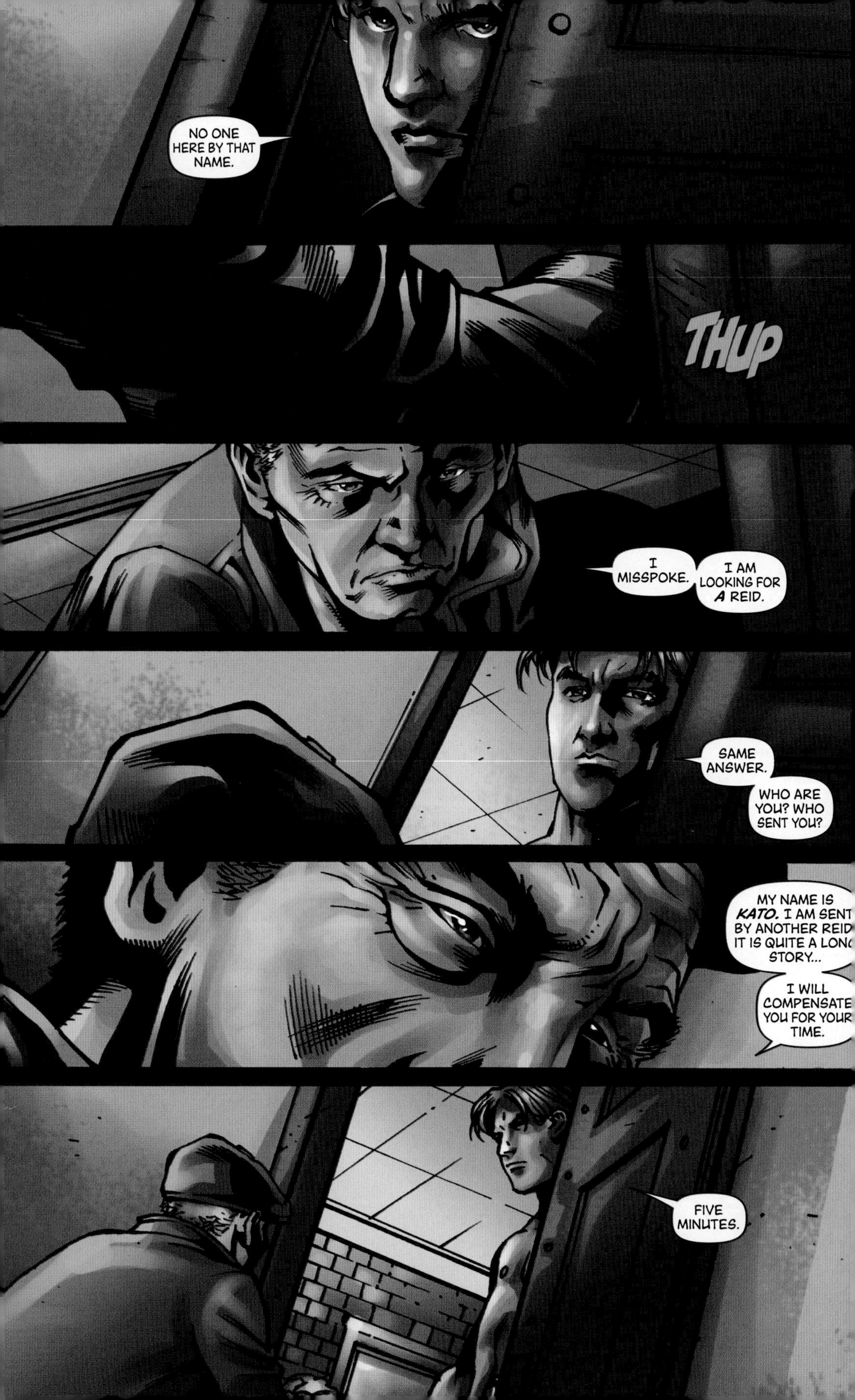
NO ONE HERE BY THAT NAME.
THUP
I MISSPOKE.
I AM LOOKING FOR *A* REID.
SAME ANSWER.
WHO ARE YOU? WHO SENT YOU?
MY NAME IS *KATO.* I AM SENT BY ANOTHER REID. IT IS QUITE A LONG STORY...
I WILL COMPENSATE YOU FOR YOUR TIME.
FIVE MINUTES.

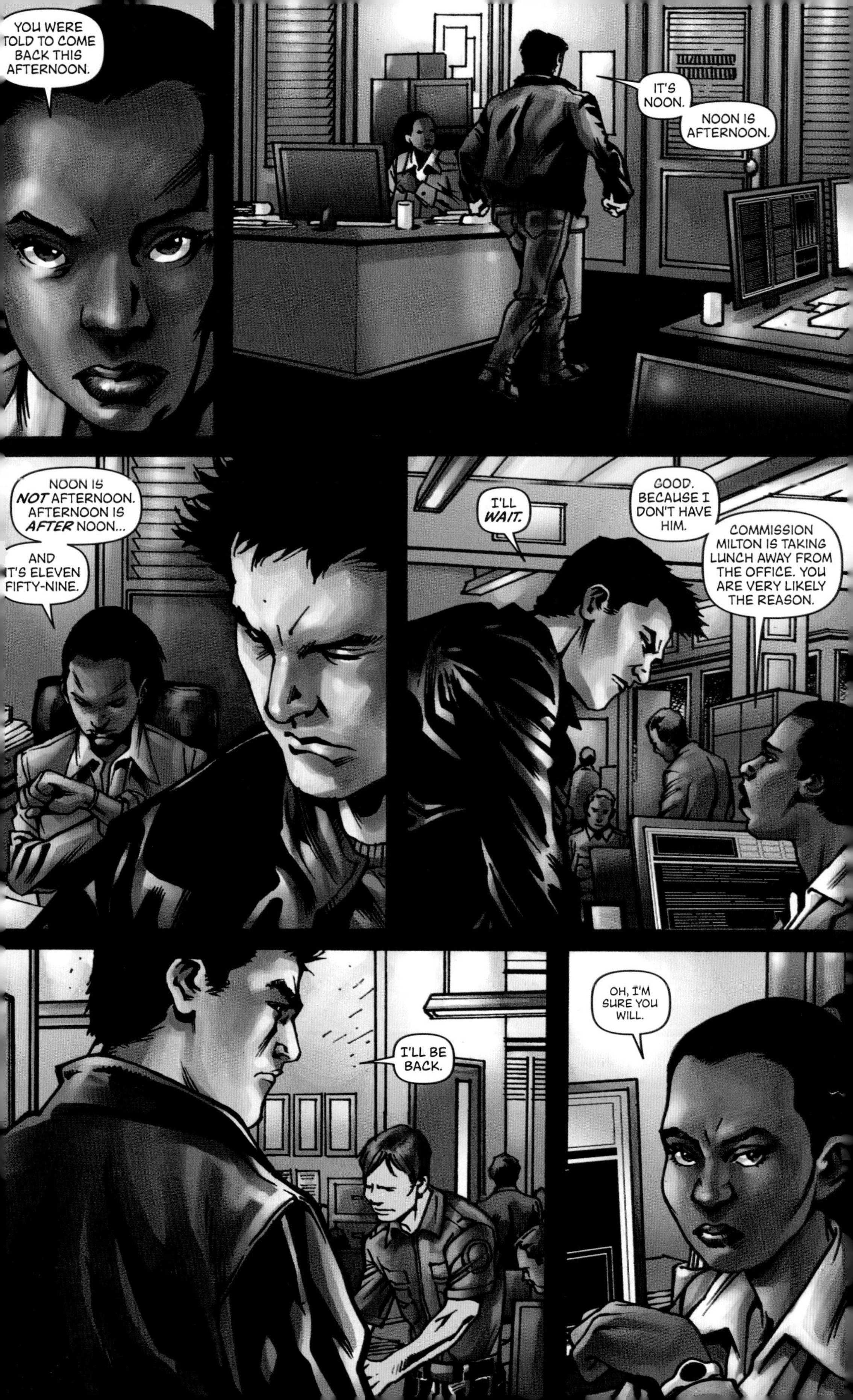
YOU WERE TOLD TO COME BACK THIS AFTERNOON.
IT'S NOON.
NOON IS AFTERNOON.
NOON IS *NOT* AFTERNOON. AFTERNOON IS *AFTER* NOON...
AND IT'S ELEVEN FIFTY-NINE.
I'LL *WAIT.*
GOOD. BECAUSE I DON'T HAVE HIM.
COMMISSION MILTON IS TAKING LUNCH AWAY FROM THE OFFICE. YOU ARE VERY LIKELY THE REASON.
I'LL BE BACK.
OH, I'M SURE YOU WILL.

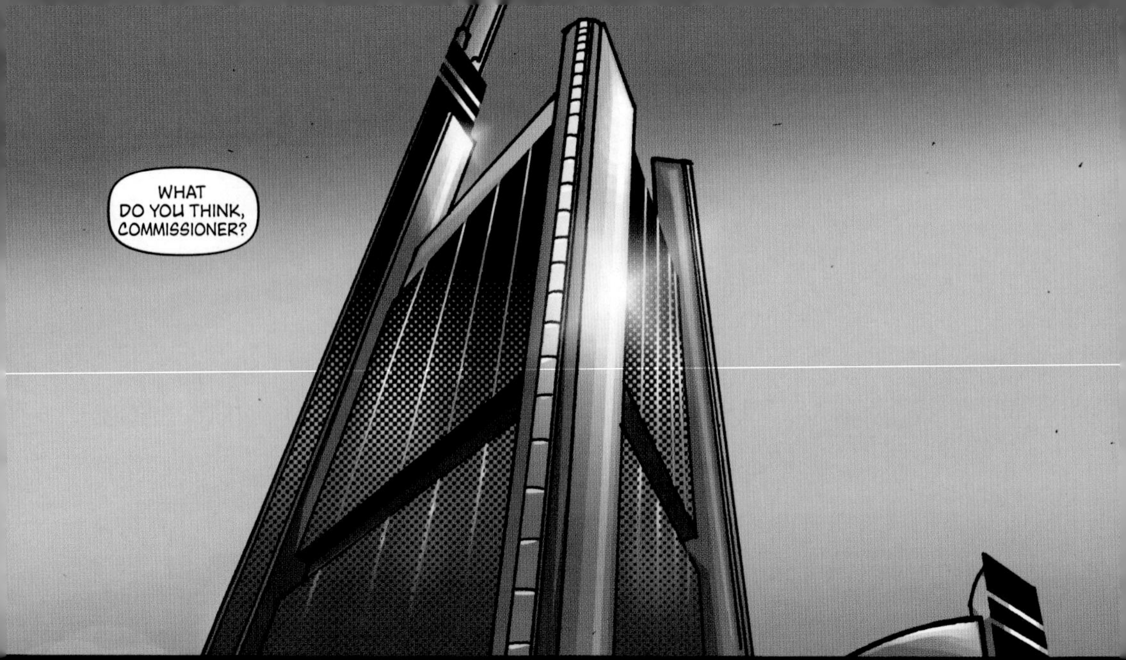
WHAT DO YOU THINK, COMMISSIONER?

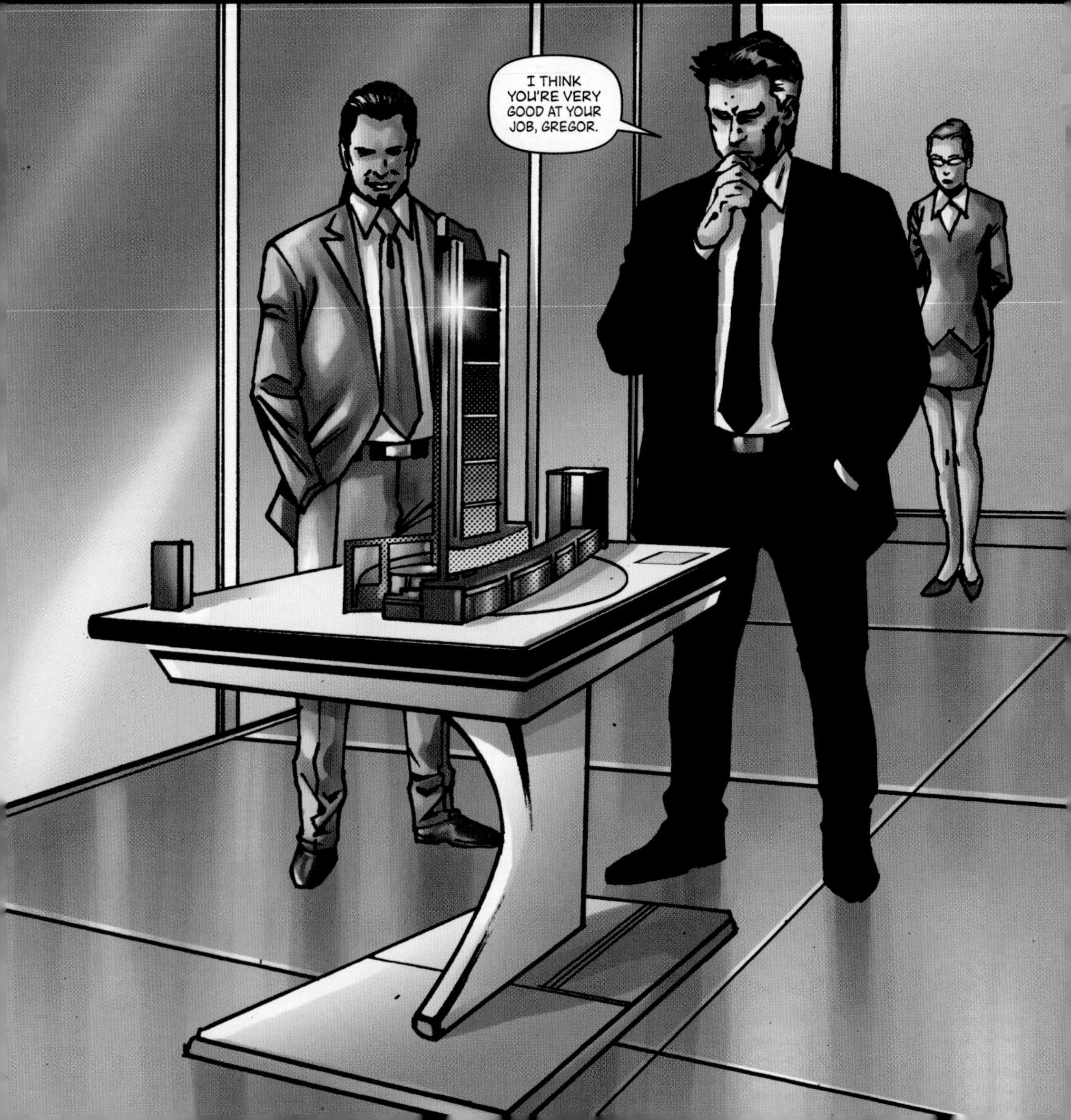
I THINK YOU'RE VERY GOOD AT YOUR JOB, GREGOR.

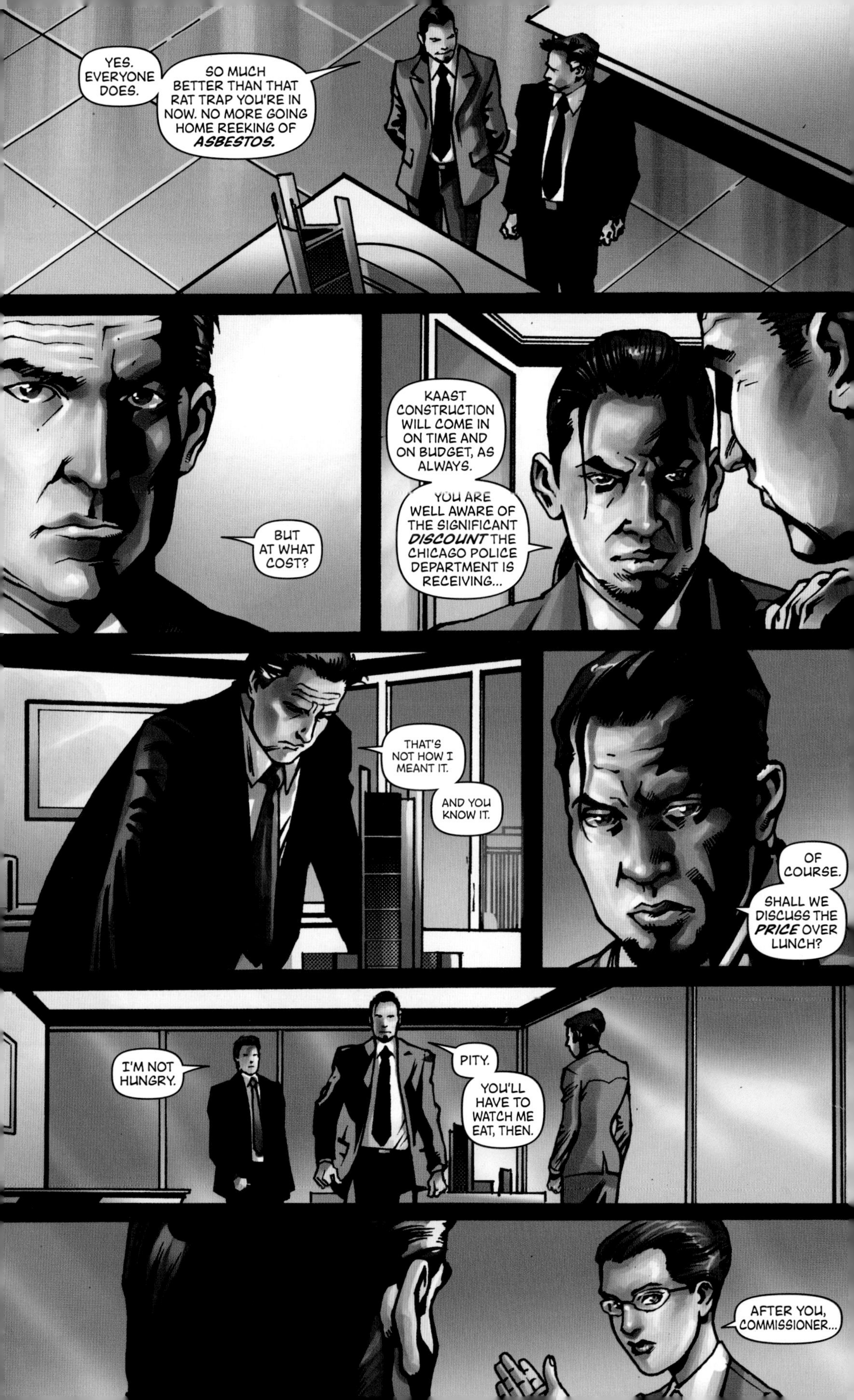
YES. EVERYONE DOES.
SO MUCH BETTER THAN THAT RAT TRAP YOU'RE IN NOW. NO MORE GOING HOME REEKING OF ASBESTOS.
BUT AT WHAT COST?
KAAST CONSTRUCTION WILL COME IN ON TIME AND ON BUDGET, AS ALWAYS.
YOU ARE WELL AWARE OF THE SIGNIFICANT DISCOUNT THE CHICAGO POLICE DEPARTMENT IS RECEIVING...
THAT'S NOT HOW I MEANT IT.
AND YOU KNOW IT.
OF COURSE.
SHALL WE DISCUSS THE PRICE OVER LUNCH?
I'M NOT HUNGRY.
PITY.
YOU'LL HAVE TO WATCH ME EAT, THEN.
AFTER YOU, COMMISSIONER...

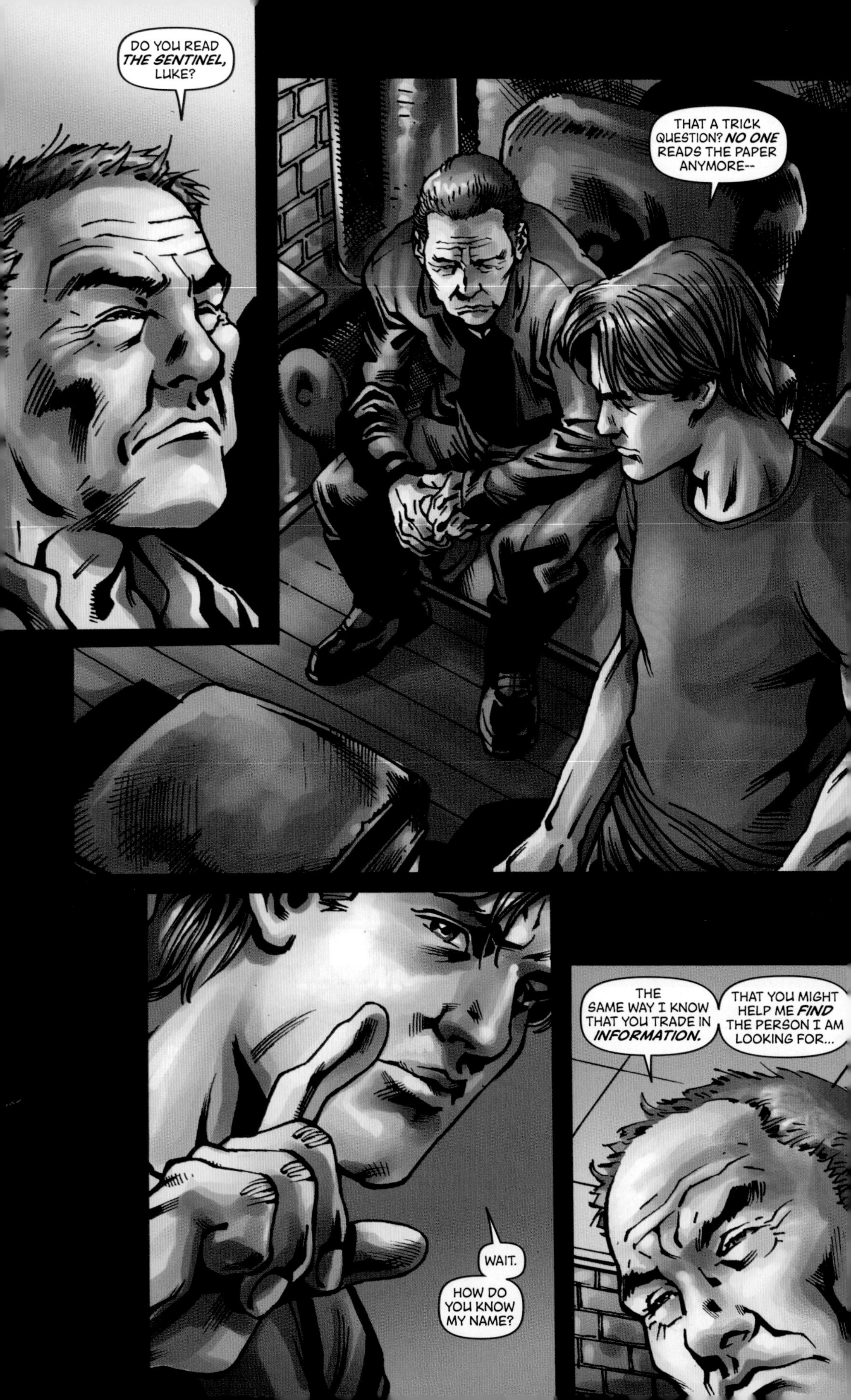
DO YOU READ *THE SENTINEL,* LUKE?
THAT A TRICK QUESTION? *NO ONE* READS THE PAPER ANYMORE--
WAIT.
HOW DO YOU KNOW MY NAME?
THE SAME WAY I KNOW THAT YOU TRADE IN *INFORMATION.*
THAT YOU MIGHT HELP ME *FIND* THE PERSON I AM LOOKING FOR...

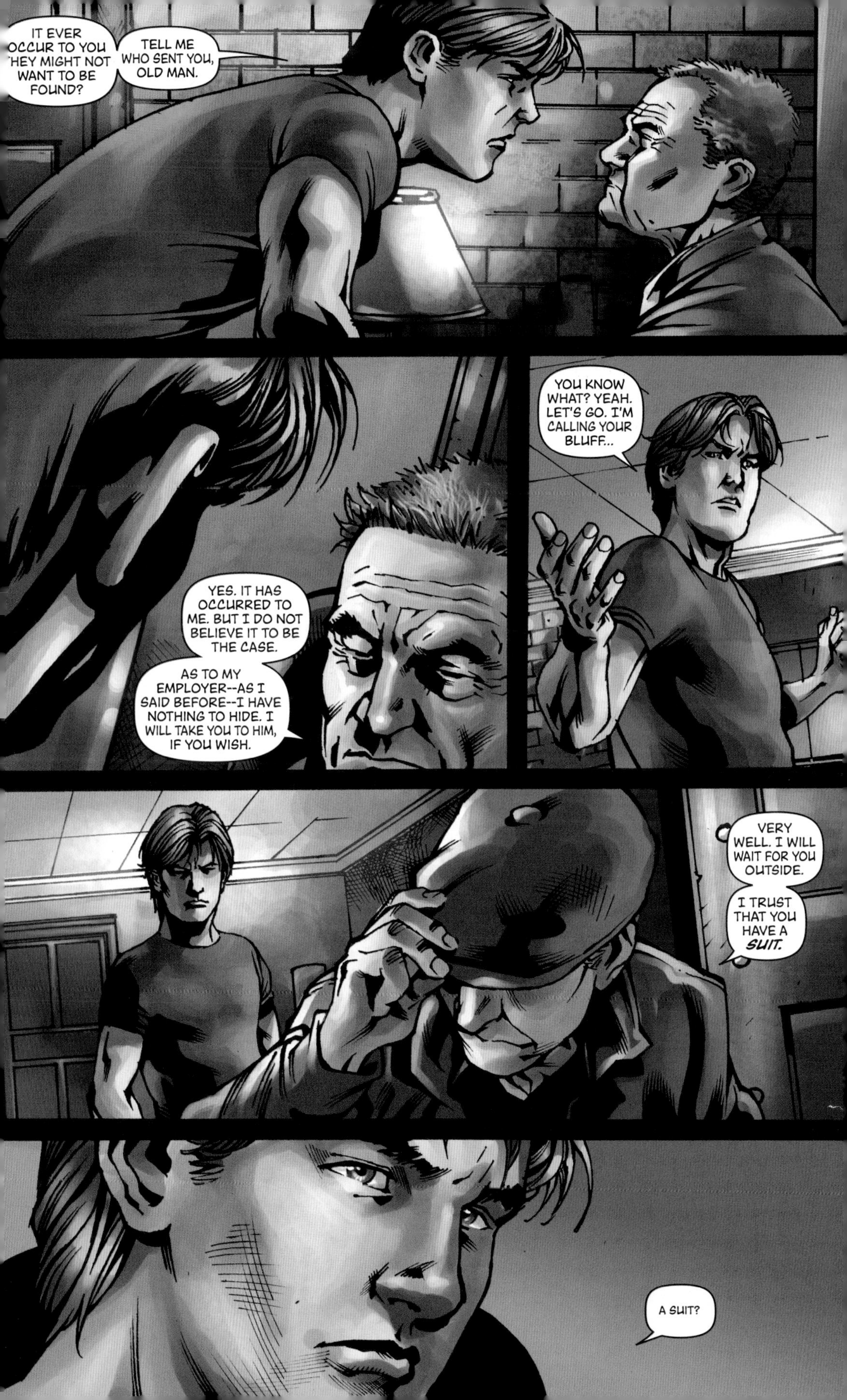
IT EVER OCCUR TO YOU THEY MIGHT NOT WANT TO BE FOUND?
TELL ME WHO SENT YOU, OLD MAN.
YES. IT HAS OCCURRED TO ME. BUT I DO NOT BELIEVE IT TO BE THE CASE.
AS TO MY EMPLOYER--AS I SAID BEFORE--I HAVE NOTHING TO HIDE. I WILL TAKE YOU TO HIM, IF YOU WISH.
YOU KNOW WHAT? YEAH. LET'S GO. I'M CALLING YOUR BLUFF...
VERY WELL. I WILL WAIT FOR YOU OUTSIDE.
I TRUST THAT YOU HAVE A ***SUIT.***
A SUIT?

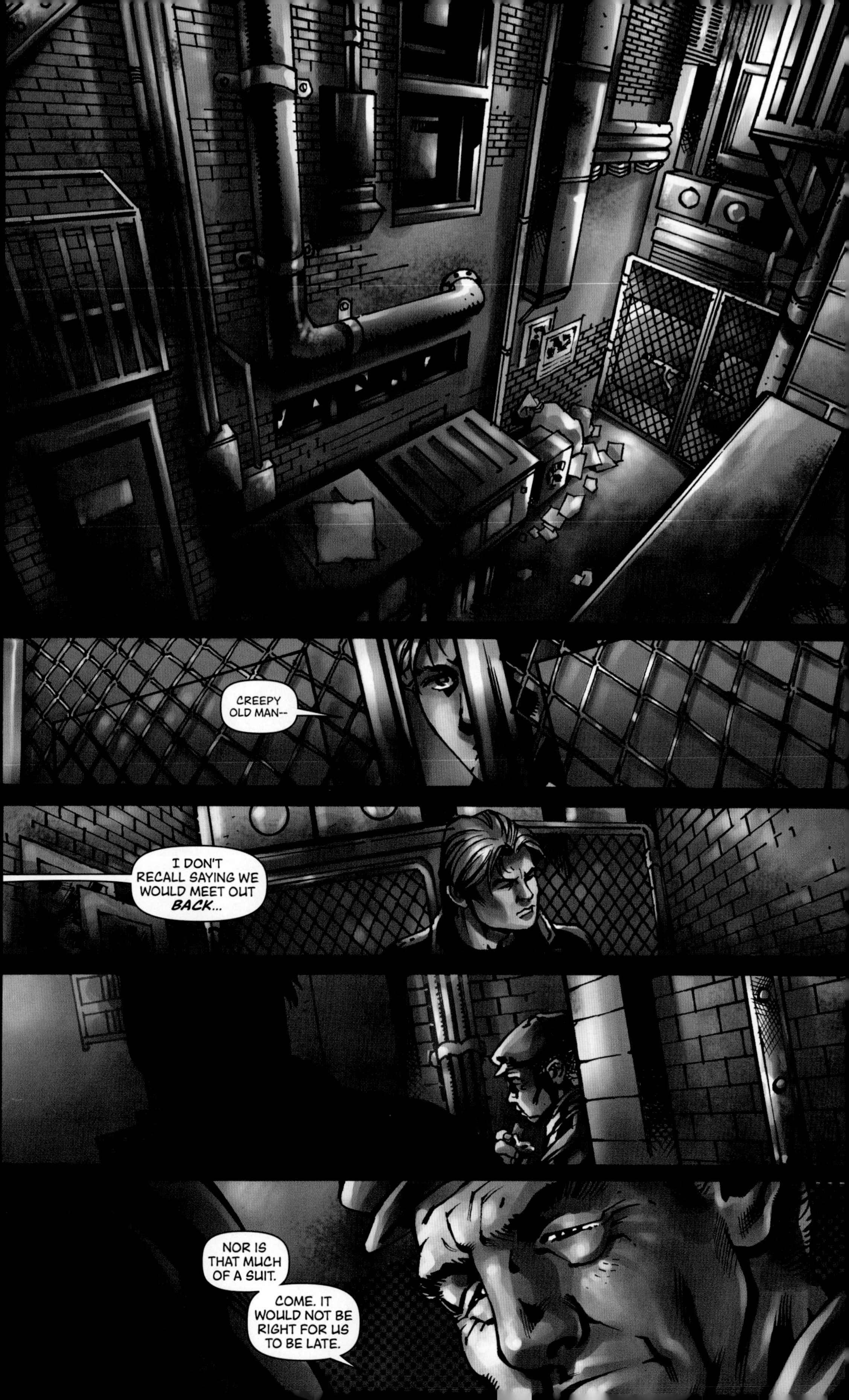
CREEPY OLD MAN--
I DON'T RECALL SAYING WE WOULD MEET OUT BACK...
NOR IS THAT MUCH OF A SUIT.
COME. IT WOULD NOT BE RIGHT FOR US TO BE LATE.

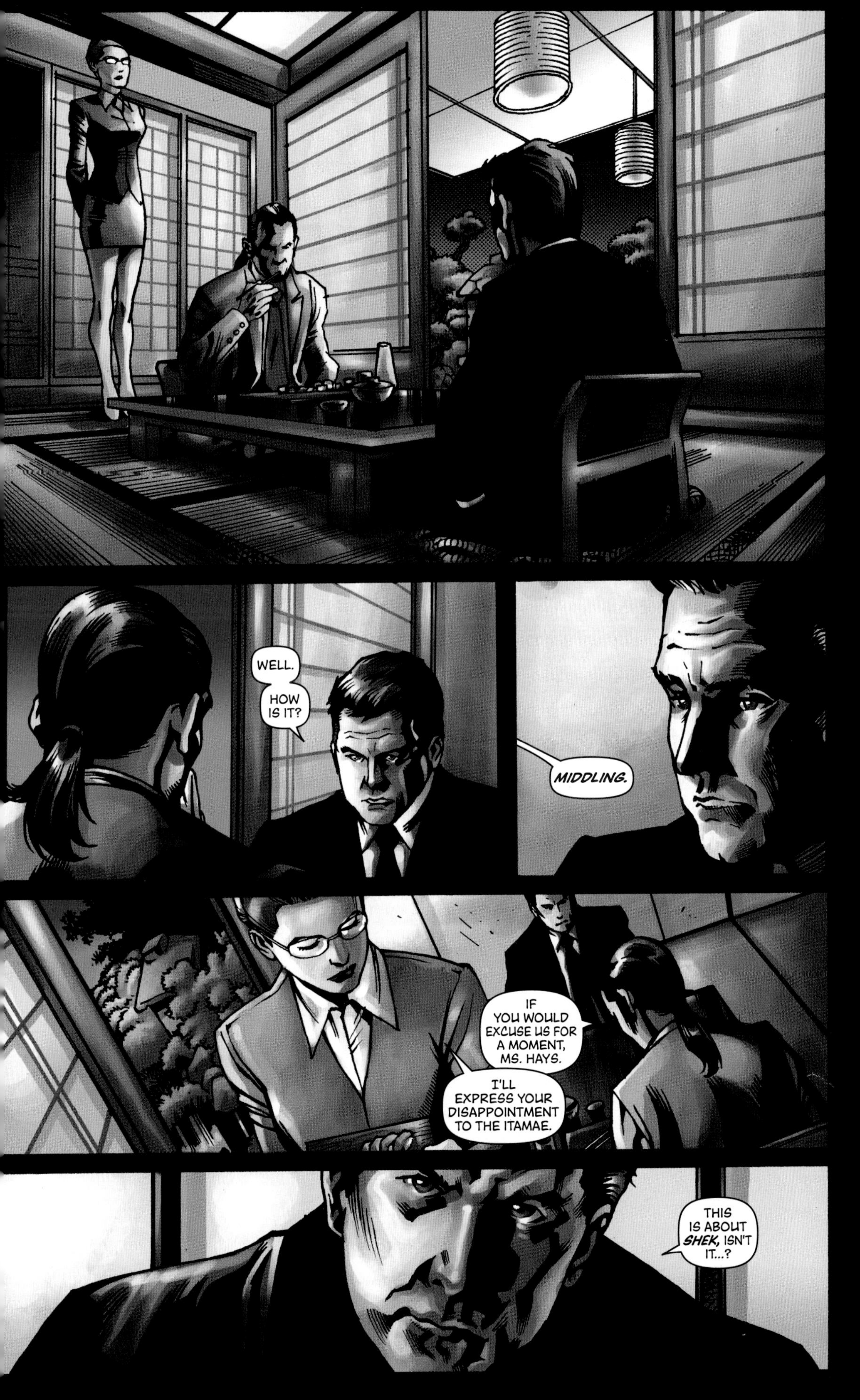
WELL.
HOW IS IT?
MIDDLING.
IF YOU WOULD EXCUSE US FOR A MOMENT, MS. HAYS.
I'LL EXPRESS YOUR DISAPPOINTMENT TO THE ITAMAE.
THIS IS ABOUT SHEK, ISN'T IT...?

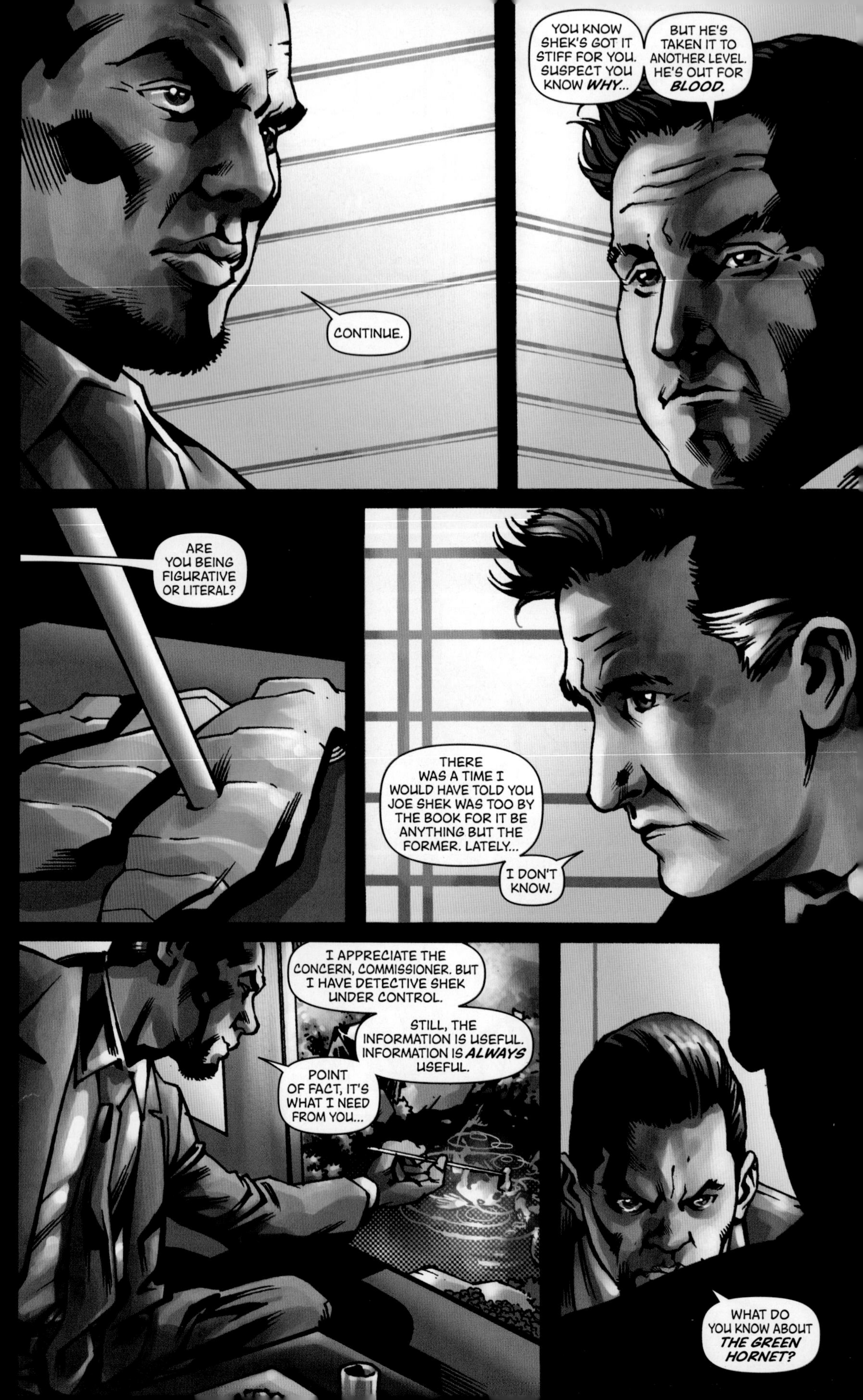
YOU KNOW SHEK'S GOT IT STIFF FOR YOU. SUSPECT YOU KNOW *WHY*...
BUT HE'S TAKEN IT TO ANOTHER LEVEL. HE'S OUT FOR ***BLOOD.***
CONTINUE.
ARE YOU BEING FIGURATIVE OR LITERAL?
THERE WAS A TIME I WOULD HAVE TOLD YOU JOE SHEK WAS TOO BY THE BOOK FOR IT BE ANYTHING BUT THE FORMER. LATELY...
I DON'T KNOW.
I APPRECIATE THE CONCERN, COMMISSIONER. BUT I HAVE DETECTIVE SHEK UNDER CONTROL.
STILL, THE INFORMATION IS USEFUL. INFORMATION IS ***ALWAYS*** USEFUL.
POINT OF FACT, IT'S WHAT I NEED FROM YOU...
WHAT DO YOU KNOW ABOUT ***THE GREEN HORNET?***

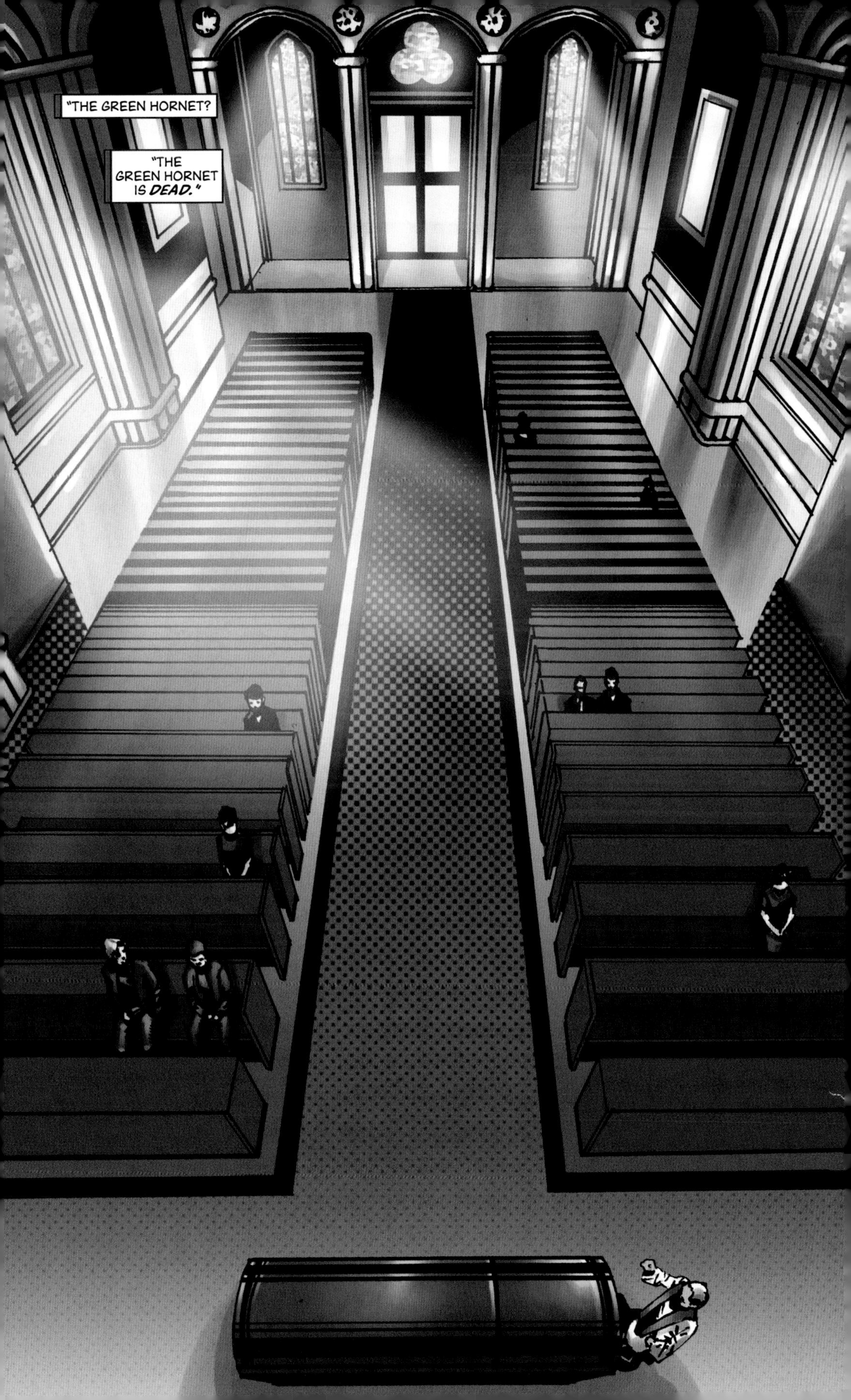
"THE GREEN HORNET?
"THE GREEN HORNET IS DEAD."

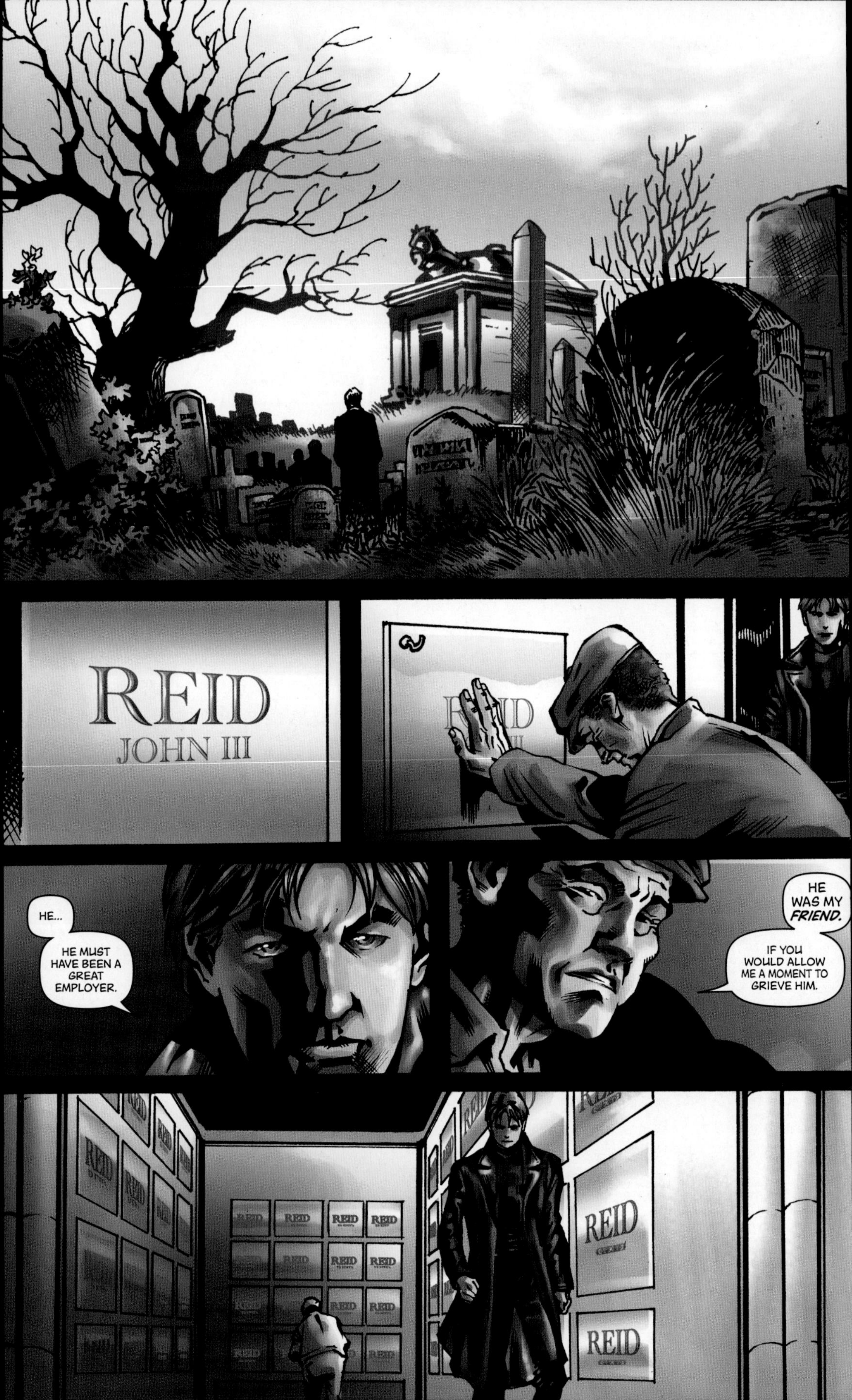
REID
JOHN III
HE...
HE MUST HAVE BEEN A GREAT EMPLOYER.
HE WAS MY FRIEND.
IF YOU WOULD ALLOW ME A MOMENT TO GRIEVE HIM.
REID
REID

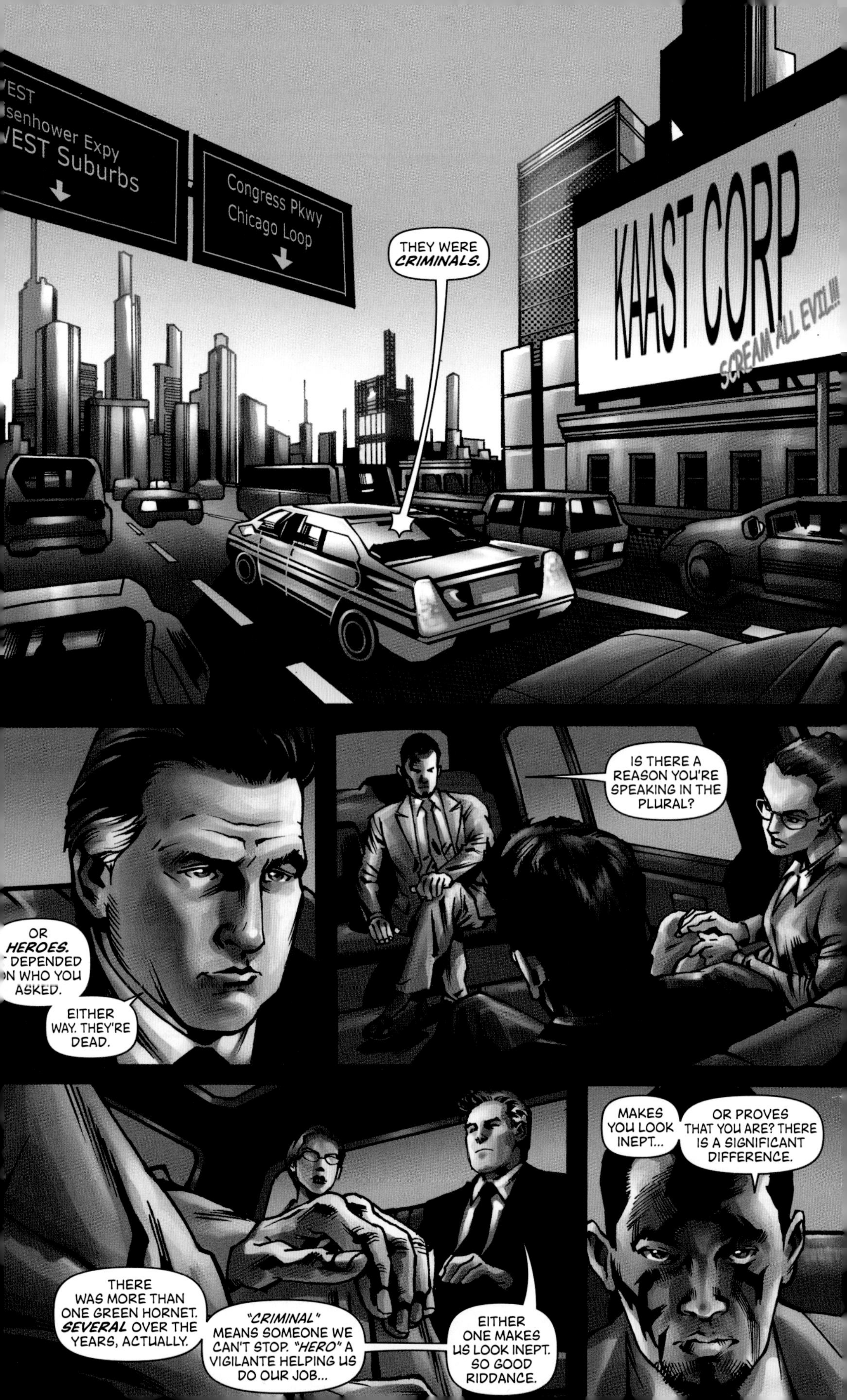

EST
senhower Expy
EST Suburbs
Congress Pkwy
Chicago Loop
KAAST CORP
SCREAM ALL EVIL!!!
THEY WERE *CRIMINALS.*
OR *HEROES.* DEPENDED ON WHO YOU ASKED.
EITHER WAY. THEY'RE DEAD.
IS THERE A REASON YOU'RE SPEAKING IN THE PLURAL?
THERE WAS MORE THAN ONE GREEN HORNET. *SEVERAL* OVER THE YEARS, ACTUALLY.
"CRIMINAL" MEANS SOMEONE WE CAN'T STOP. *"HERO"* A VIGILANTE HELPING US DO OUR JOB...
EITHER ONE MAKES US LOOK INEPT. SO GOOD RIDDANCE.
MAKES YOU LOOK INEPT...
OR PROVES THAT YOU ARE? THERE IS A SIGNIFICANT DIFFERENCE.

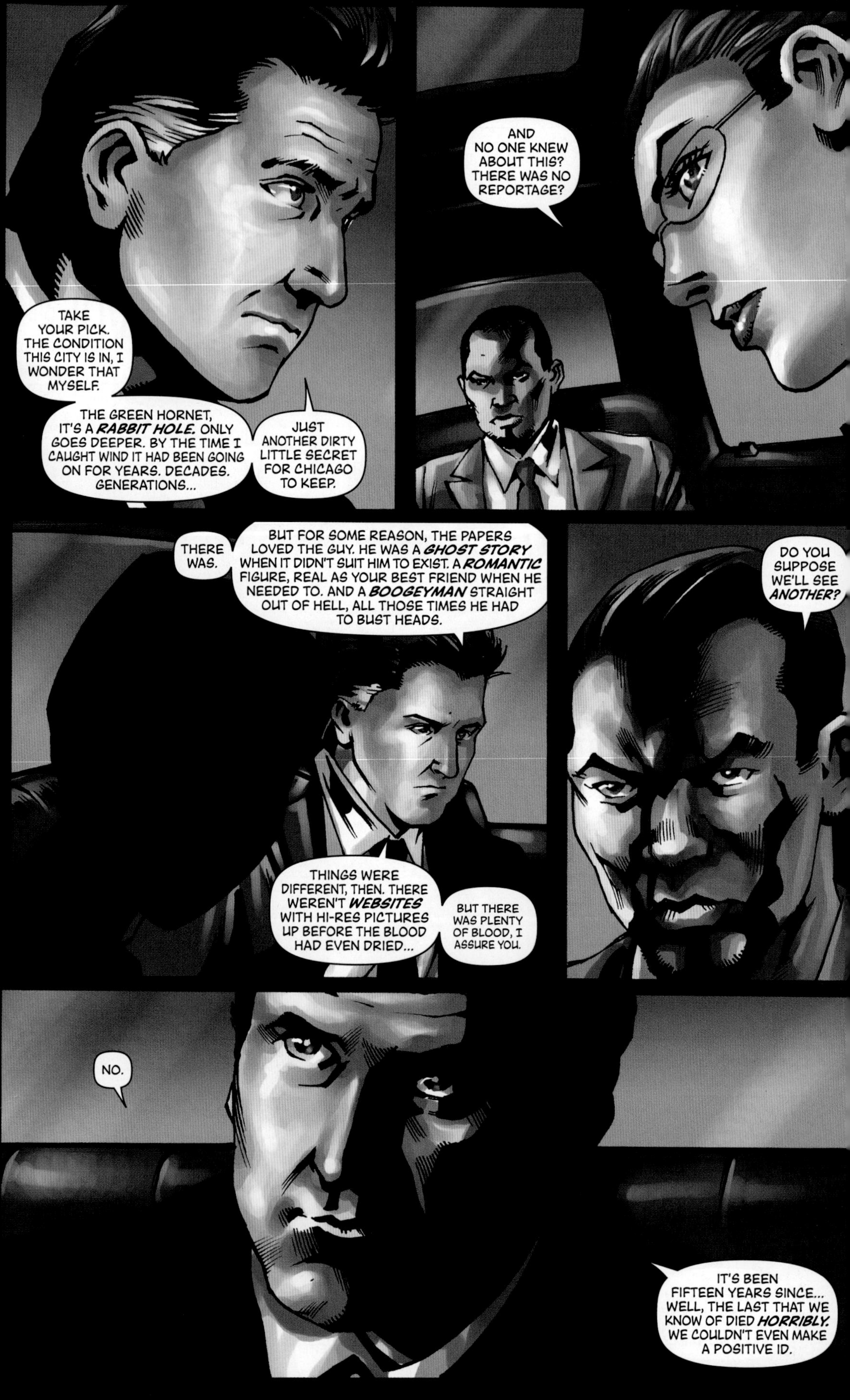
TAKE YOUR PICK. THE CONDITION THIS CITY IS IN, I WONDER THAT MYSELF.
THE GREEN HORNET, IT'S A *RABBIT HOLE.* ONLY GOES DEEPER. BY THE TIME I CAUGHT WIND IT HAD BEEN GOING ON FOR YEARS. DECADES. GENERATIONS...
JUST ANOTHER DIRTY LITTLE SECRET FOR CHICAGO TO KEEP.
AND NO ONE KNEW ABOUT THIS? THERE WAS NO REPORTAGE?
THERE WAS.
BUT FOR SOME REASON, THE PAPERS LOVED THE GUY. HE WAS A *GHOST STORY* WHEN IT DIDN'T SUIT HIM TO EXIST. A *ROMANTIC* FIGURE, REAL AS YOUR BEST FRIEND WHEN HE NEEDED TO. AND A *BOOGEYMAN* STRAIGHT OUT OF HELL, ALL THOSE TIMES HE HAD TO BUST HEADS.
THINGS WERE DIFFERENT, THEN. THERE WEREN'T *WEBSITES* WITH HI-RES PICTURES UP BEFORE THE BLOOD HAD EVEN DRIED...
BUT THERE WAS PLENTY OF BLOOD, I ASSURE YOU.
DO YOU SUPPOSE WE'LL SEE *ANOTHER?*
NO.
IT'S BEEN FIFTEEN YEARS SINCE... WELL, THE LAST THAT WE KNOW OF DIED *HORRIBLY.* WE COULDN'T EVEN MAKE A POSITIVE ID.

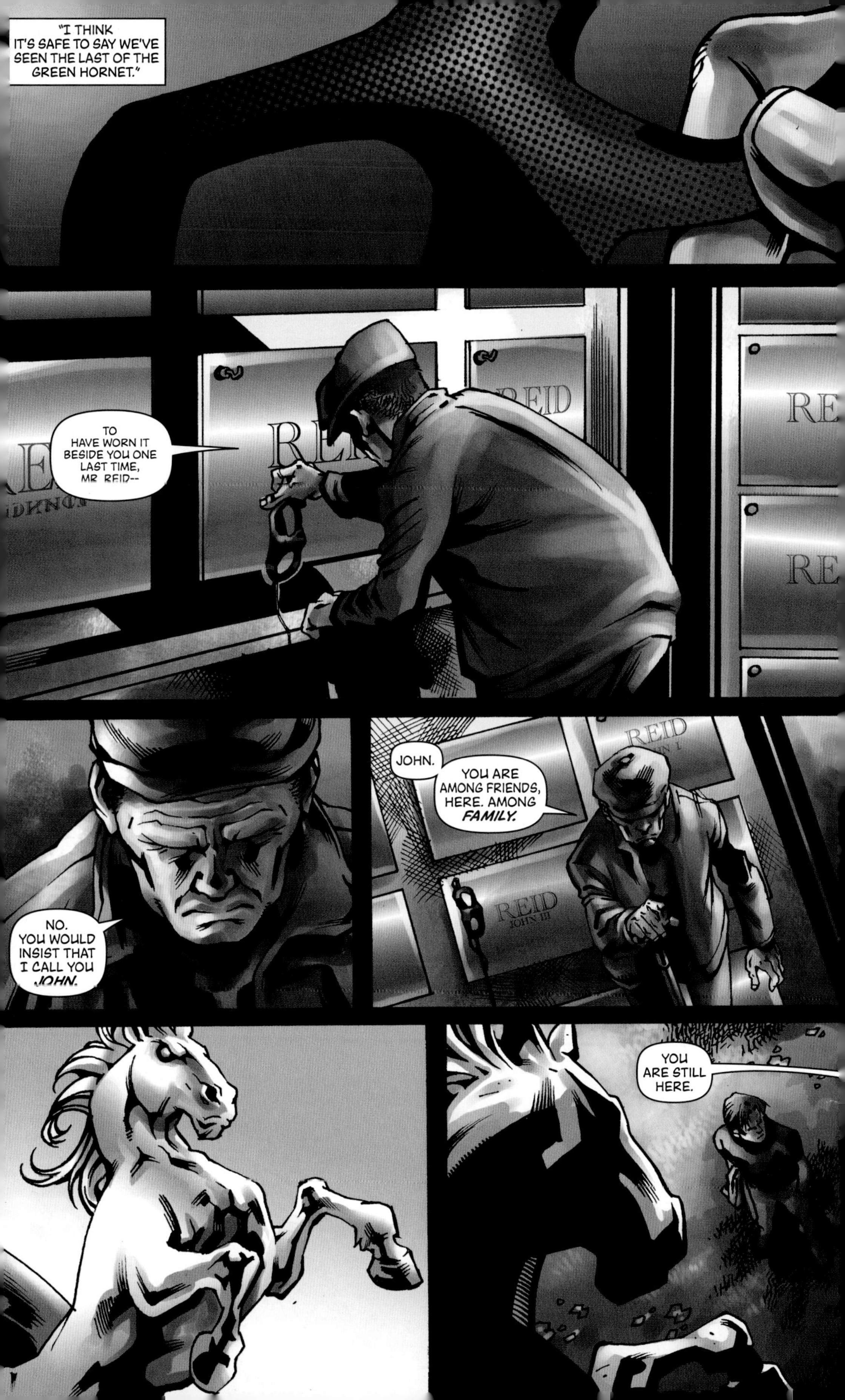
"I THINK IT'S SAFE TO SAY WE'VE SEEN THE LAST OF THE GREEN HORNET."
REID
REID
TO HAVE WORN IT BESIDE YOU ONE LAST TIME, MR. REID--
NO. YOU WOULD INSIST THAT I CALL YOU *JOHN.*
JOHN.
YOU ARE AMONG FRIENDS, HERE. AMONG *FAMILY.*
REID
REID
JOHN III
YOU ARE STILL HERE.

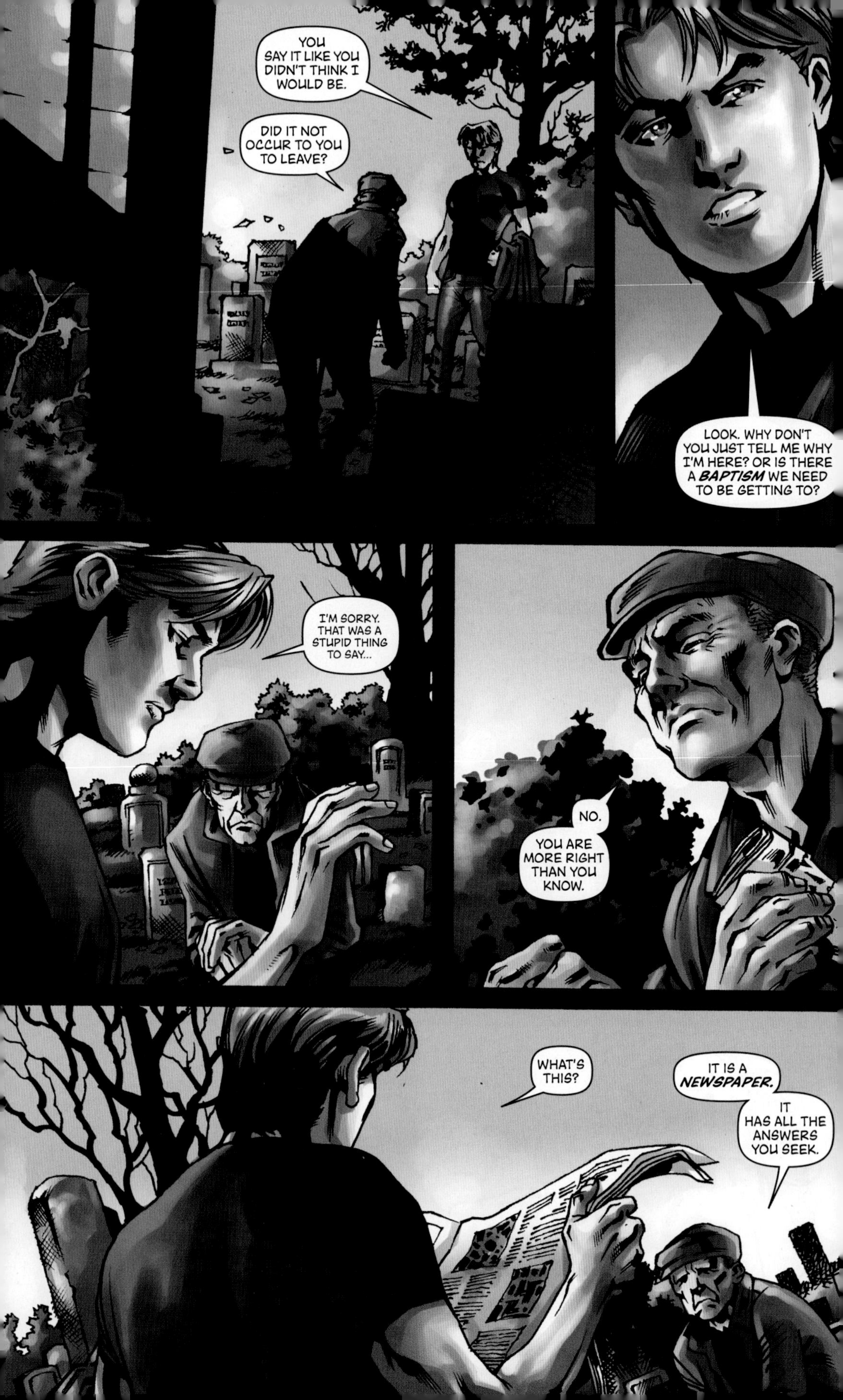
YOU SAY IT LIKE YOU DIDN'T THINK I WOULD BE.
DID IT NOT OCCUR TO YOU TO LEAVE?
LOOK. WHY DON'T YOU JUST TELL ME WHY I'M HERE? OR IS THERE A BAPTISM WE NEED TO BE GETTING TO?
I'M SORRY. THAT WAS A STUPID THING TO SAY...
NO.
YOU ARE MORE RIGHT THAN YOU KNOW.
WHAT'S THIS?
IT IS A NEWSPAPER.
IT HAS ALL THE ANSWERS YOU SEEK.

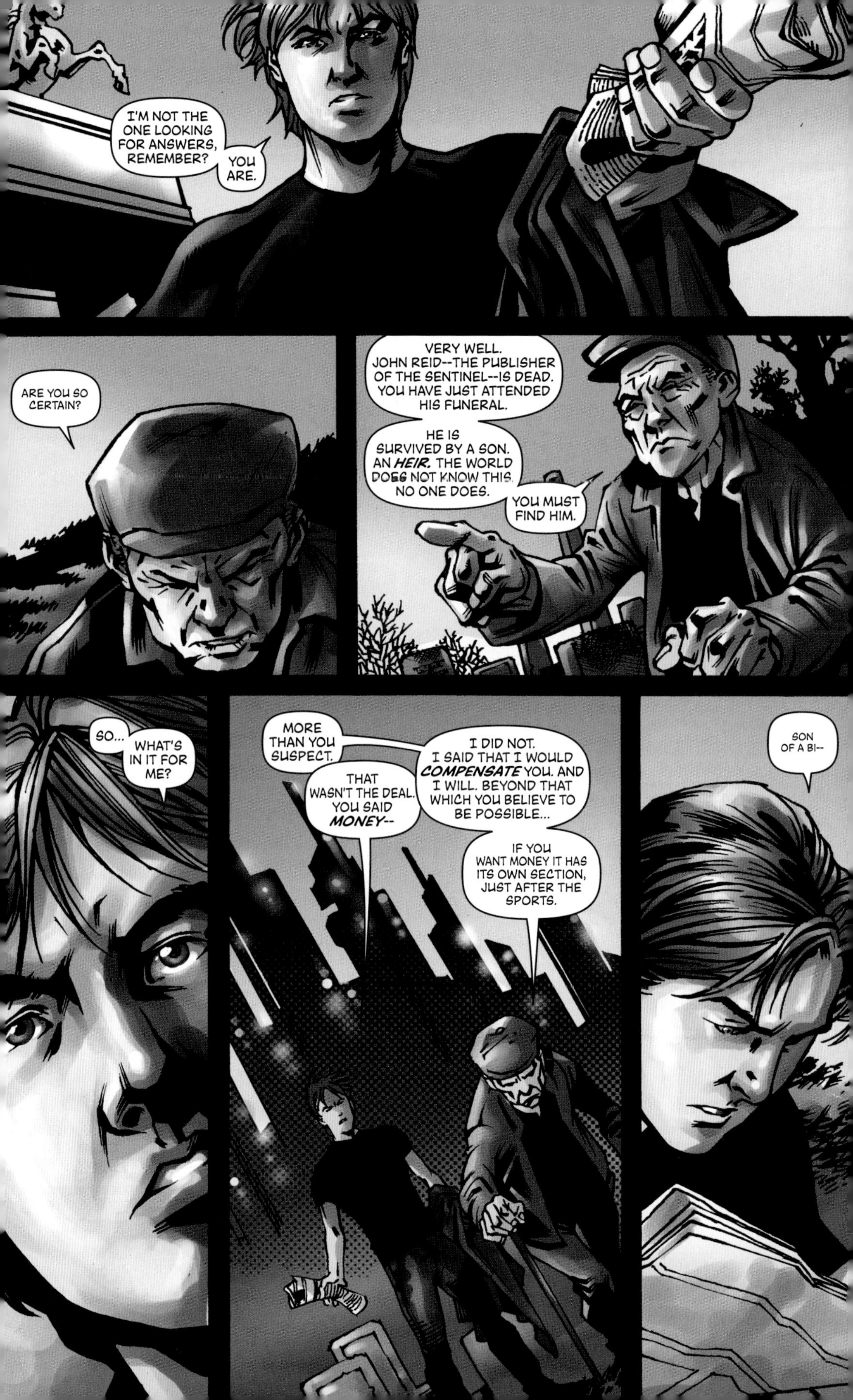
I'M NOT THE ONE LOOKING FOR ANSWERS, REMEMBER?
YOU ARE.
ARE YOU SO CERTAIN?
VERY WELL. JOHN REID--THE PUBLISHER OF THE SENTINEL--IS DEAD. YOU HAVE JUST ATTENDED HIS FUNERAL.
HE IS SURVIVED BY A SON. AN HEIR. THE WORLD DOES NOT KNOW THIS. NO ONE DOES.
YOU MUST FIND HIM.
SO...
WHAT'S IN IT FOR ME?
MORE THAN YOU SUSPECT.
THAT WASN'T THE DEAL. YOU SAID MONEY--
I DID NOT. I SAID THAT I WOULD COMPENSATE YOU. AND I WILL. BEYOND THAT WHICH YOU BELIEVE TO BE POSSIBLE...
IF YOU WANT MONEY IT HAS ITS OWN SECTION, JUST AFTER THE SPORTS.
SON OF A BI--

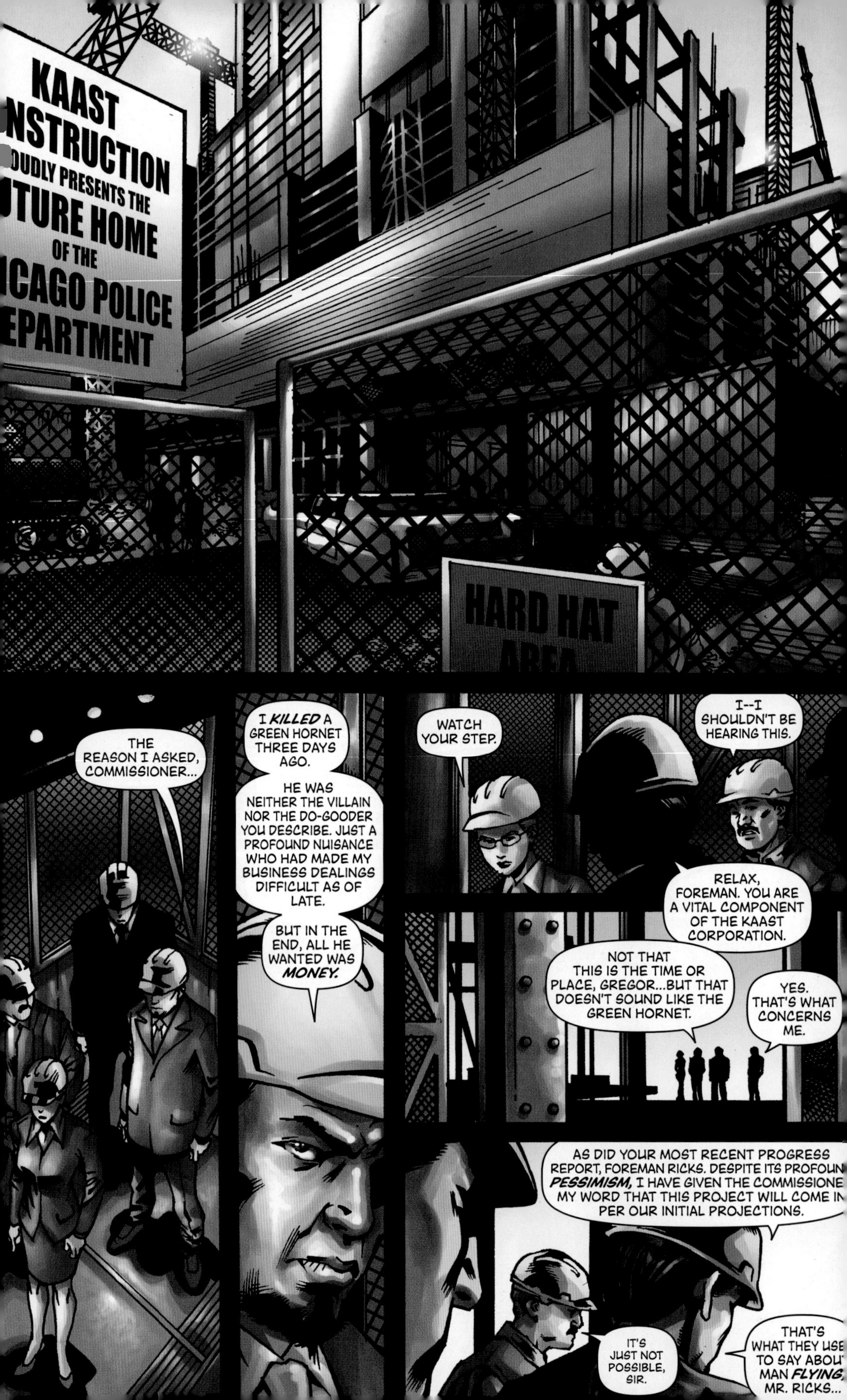
KAAST
NSTRUCTION
OUDLY PRESENTS THE
UTURE HOME
OF THE
ICAGO POLICE
EPARTMENT
HARD HAT
THE REASON I ASKED, COMMISSIONER...
I KILLED A GREEN HORNET THREE DAYS AGO.
HE WAS NEITHER THE VILLAIN NOR THE DO-GOODER YOU DESCRIBE. JUST A PROFOUND NUISANCE WHO HAD MADE MY BUSINESS DEALINGS DIFFICULT AS OF LATE.
BUT IN THE END, ALL HE WANTED WAS MONEY.
WATCH YOUR STEP.
I--I SHOULDN'T BE HEARING THIS.
RELAX, FOREMAN. YOU ARE A VITAL COMPONENT OF THE KAAST CORPORATION.
NOT THAT THIS IS THE TIME OR PLACE, GREGOR...BUT THAT DOESN'T SOUND LIKE THE GREEN HORNET.
YES. THAT'S WHAT CONCERNS ME.
AS DID YOUR MOST RECENT PROGRESS REPORT, FOREMAN RICKS. DESPITE ITS PROFOUN PESSIMISM, I HAVE GIVEN THE COMMISSIONE MY WORD THAT THIS PROJECT WILL COME IN PER OUR INITIAL PROJECTIONS.
IT'S JUST NOT POSSIBLE, SIR.
THAT'S WHAT THEY USE TO SAY ABOU MAN FLYING, MR. RICKS...

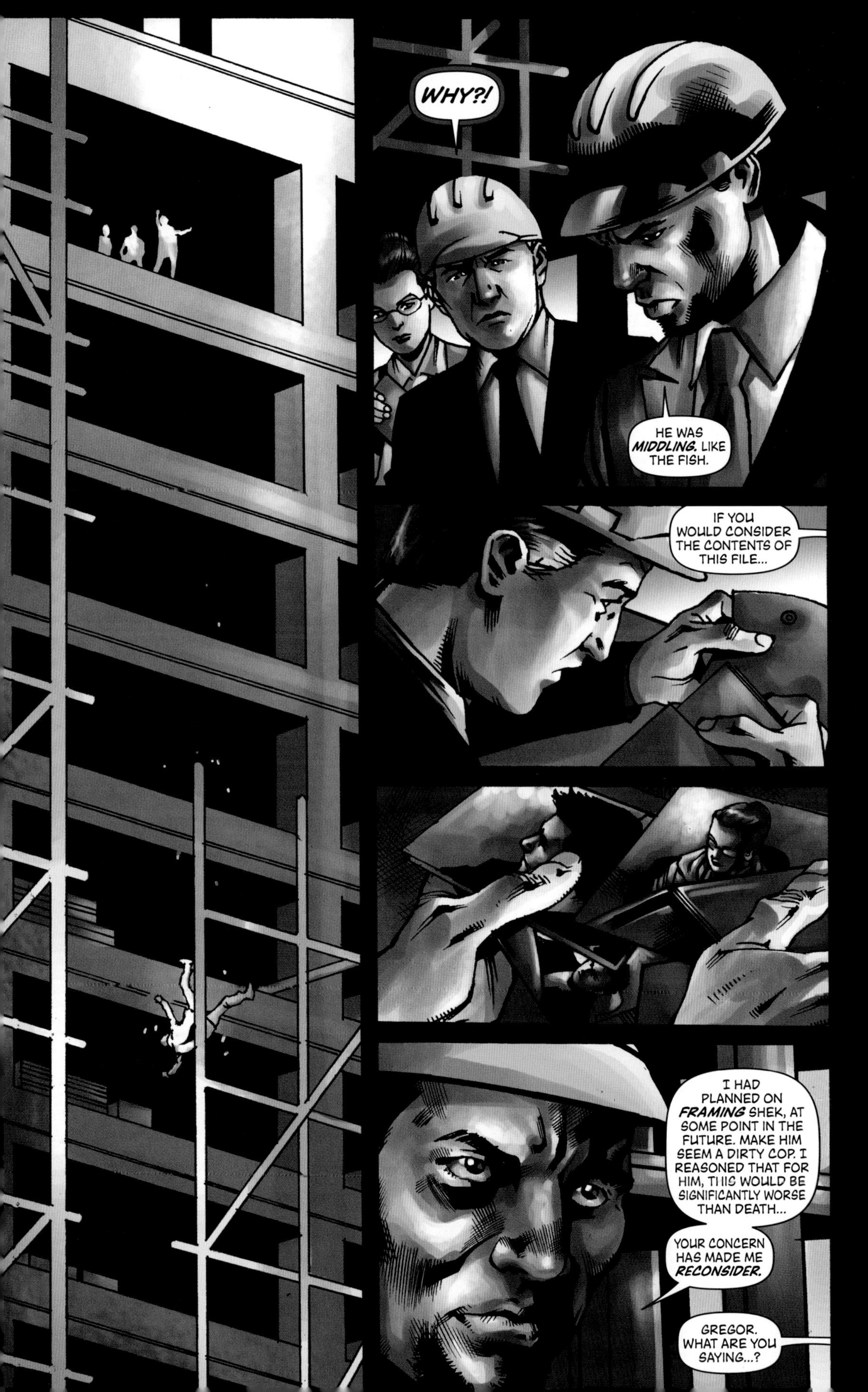
WHY?!
HE WAS MIDDLING. LIKE THE FISH.
IF YOU WOULD CONSIDER THE CONTENTS OF THIS FILE...
I HAD PLANNED ON FRAMING SHEK, AT SOME POINT IN THE FUTURE. MAKE HIM SEEM A DIRTY COP. I REASONED THAT FOR HIM, THIS WOULD BE SIGNIFICANTLY WORSE THAN DEATH...
YOUR CONCERN HAS MADE ME RECONSIDER.
GREGOR. WHAT ARE YOU SAYING...?

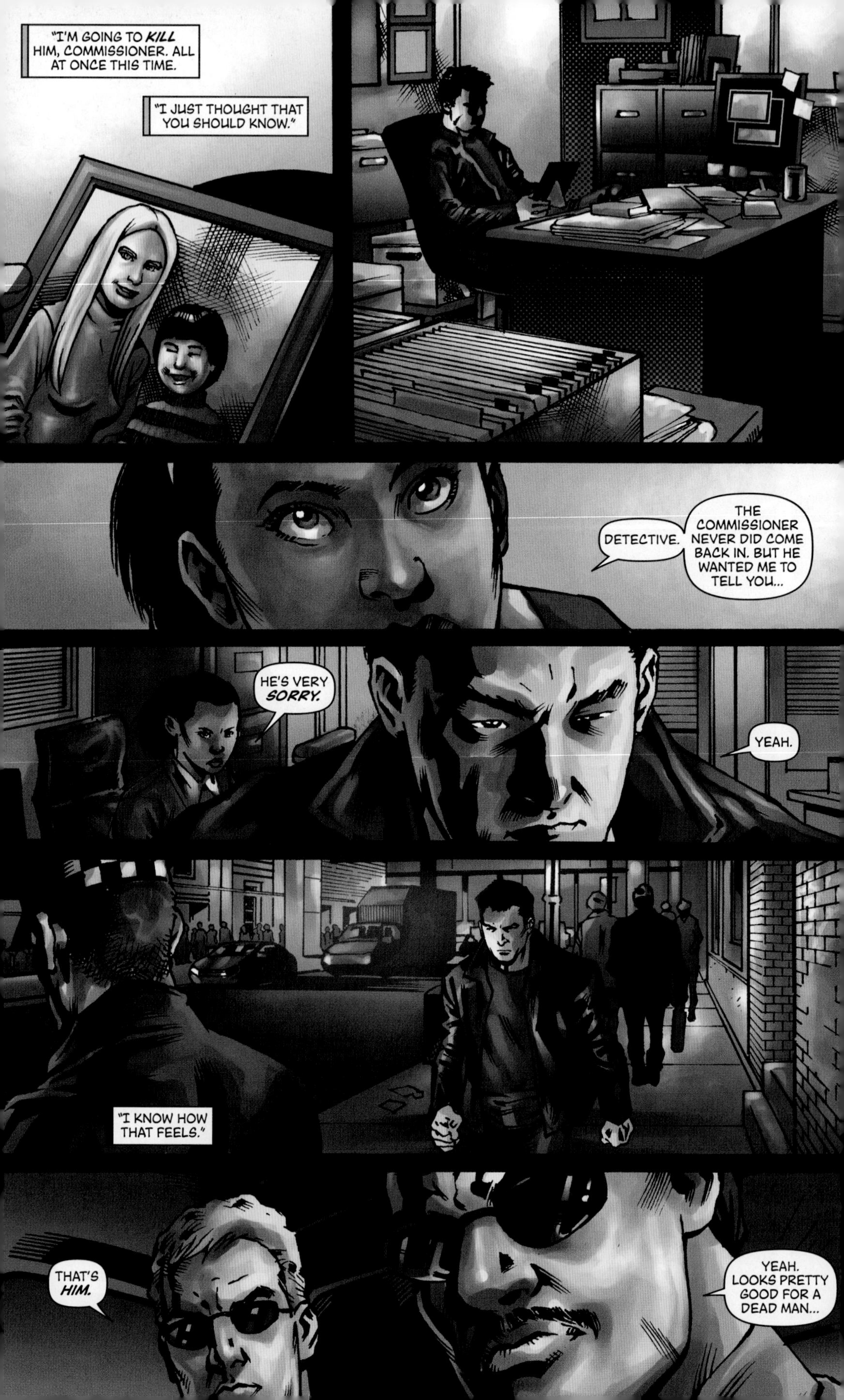
"I'M GOING TO KILL HIM, COMMISSIONER. ALL AT ONCE THIS TIME.
"I JUST THOUGHT THAT YOU SHOULD KNOW."
DETECTIVE.
THE COMMISSIONER NEVER DID COME BACK IN. BUT HE WANTED ME TO TELL YOU...
HE'S VERY SORRY.
YEAH.
"I KNOW HOW THAT FEELS."
THAT'S HIM.
YEAH. LOOKS PRETTY GOOD FOR A DEAD MAN...

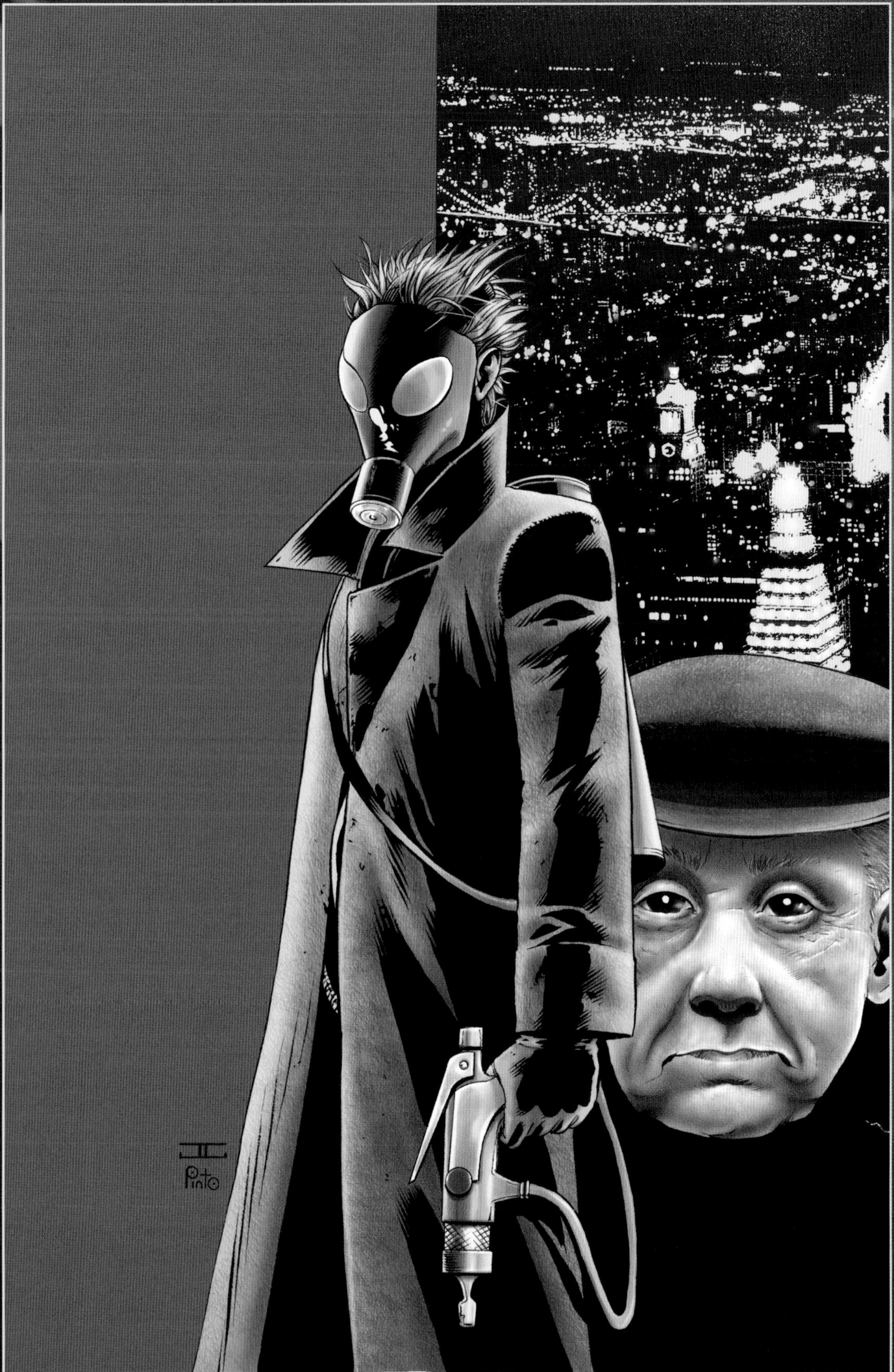

Issue #4 cover by JOHN CASSADAY

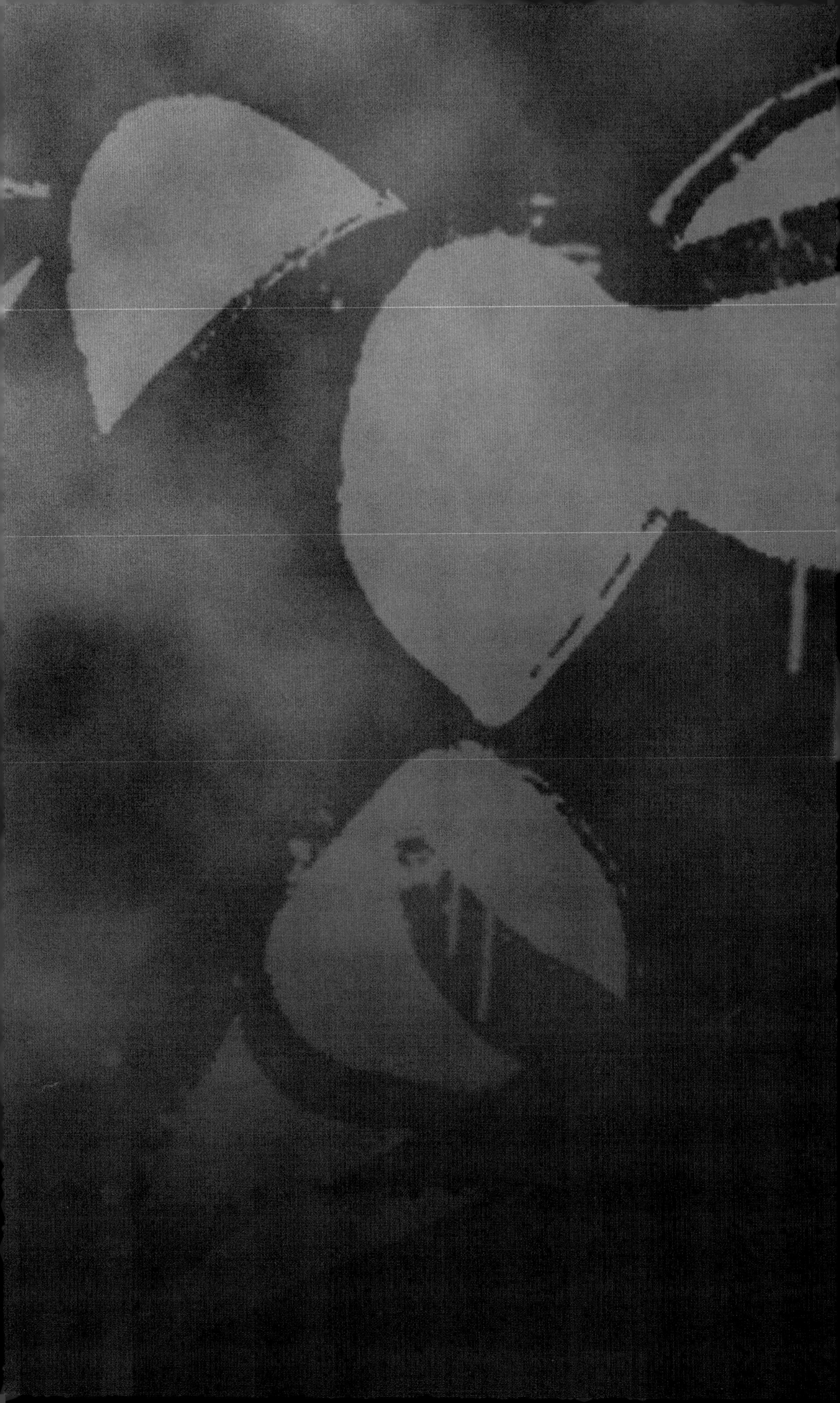

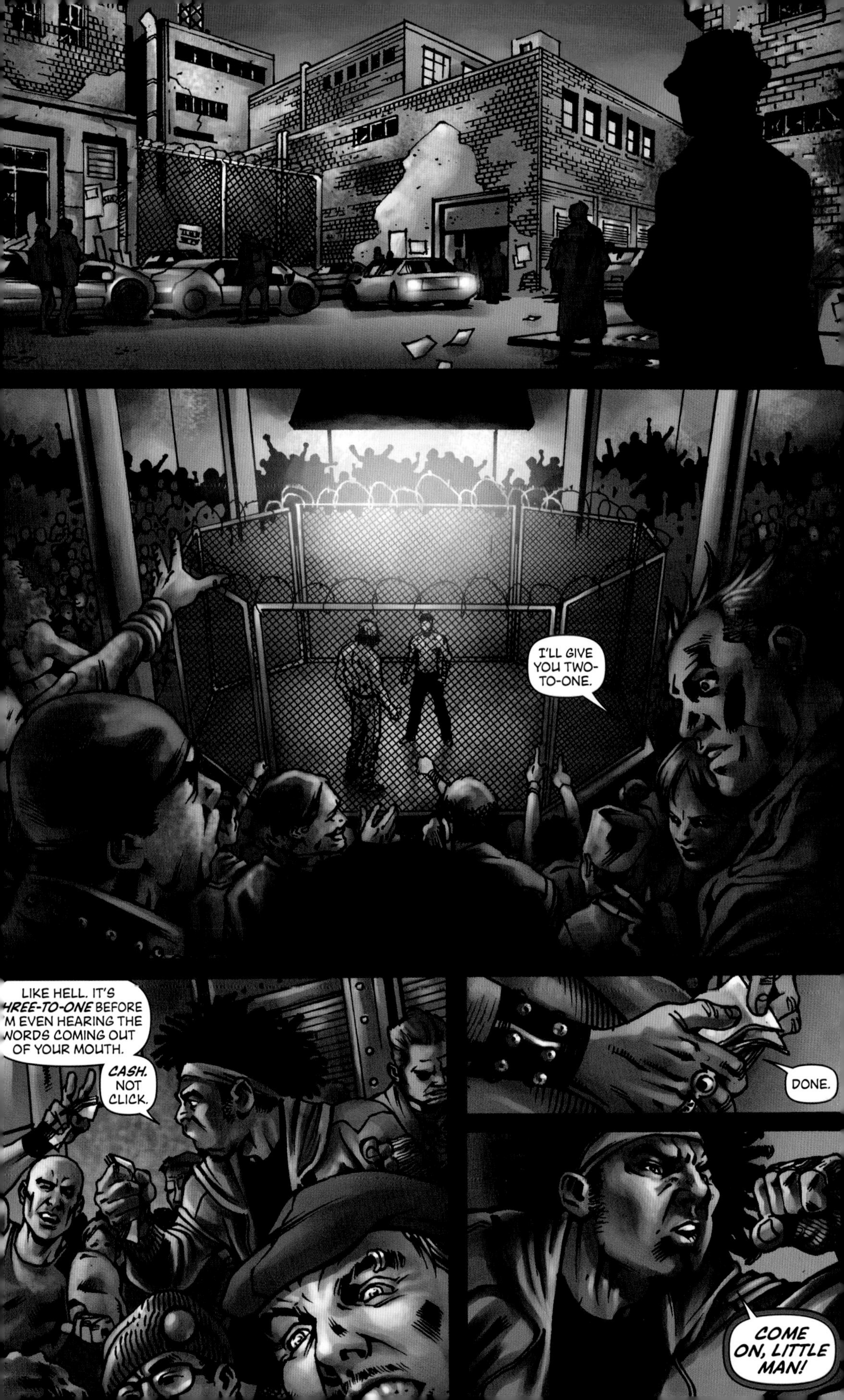
I'LL GIVE YOU TWO-TO-ONE.
LIKE HELL. IT'S HREE-TO-ONE BEFORE 'M EVEN HEARING THE WORDS COMING OUT OF YOUR MOUTH.
CASH. NOT CLICK.
DONE.
COME ON, LITTLE MAN!

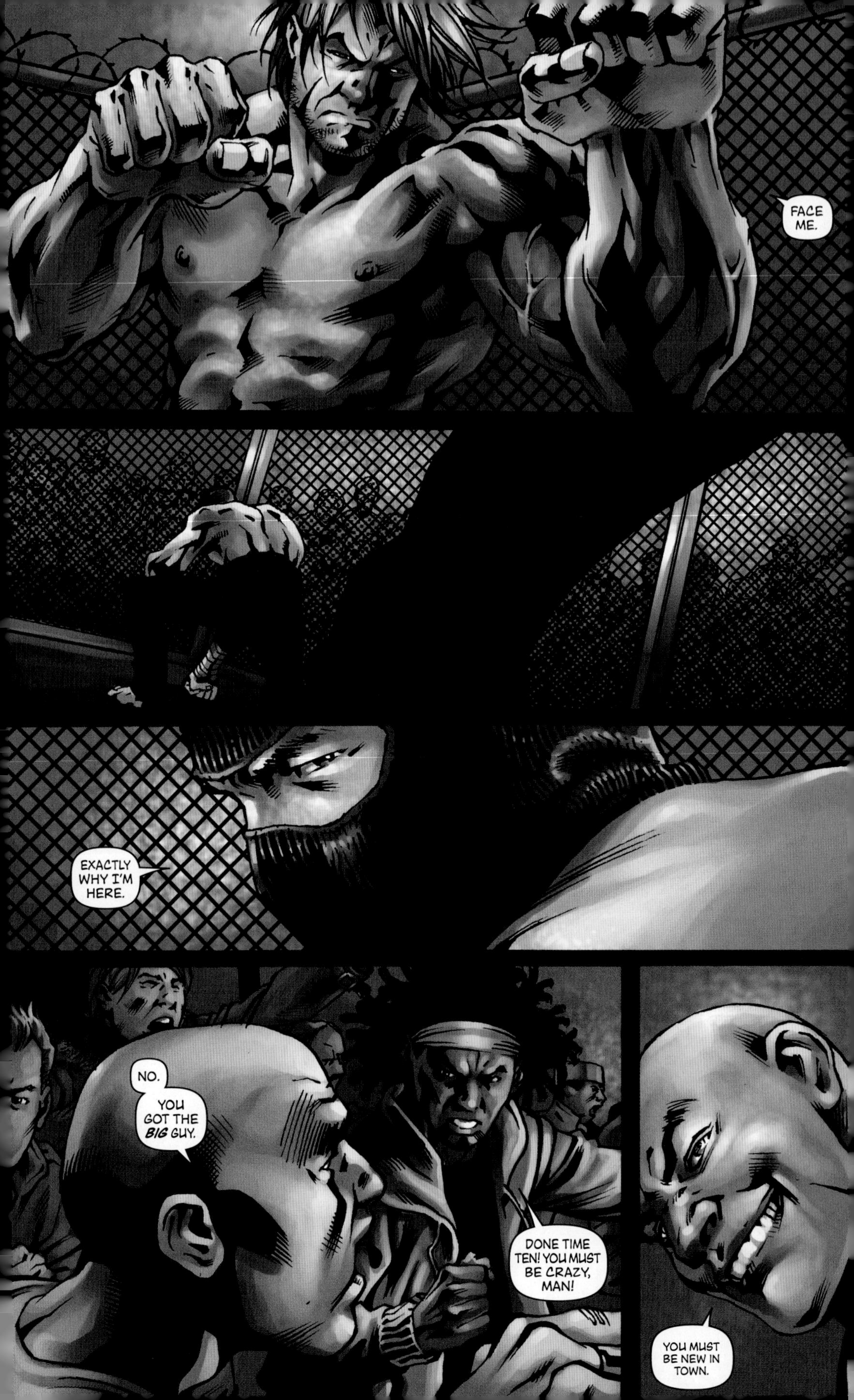
FACE ME.
EXACTLY WHY I'M HERE.
NO.
YOU GOT THE *BIG* GUY.
DONE TIME TEN! YOU MUST BE CRAZY, MAN!
YOU MUST BE NEW IN TOWN.

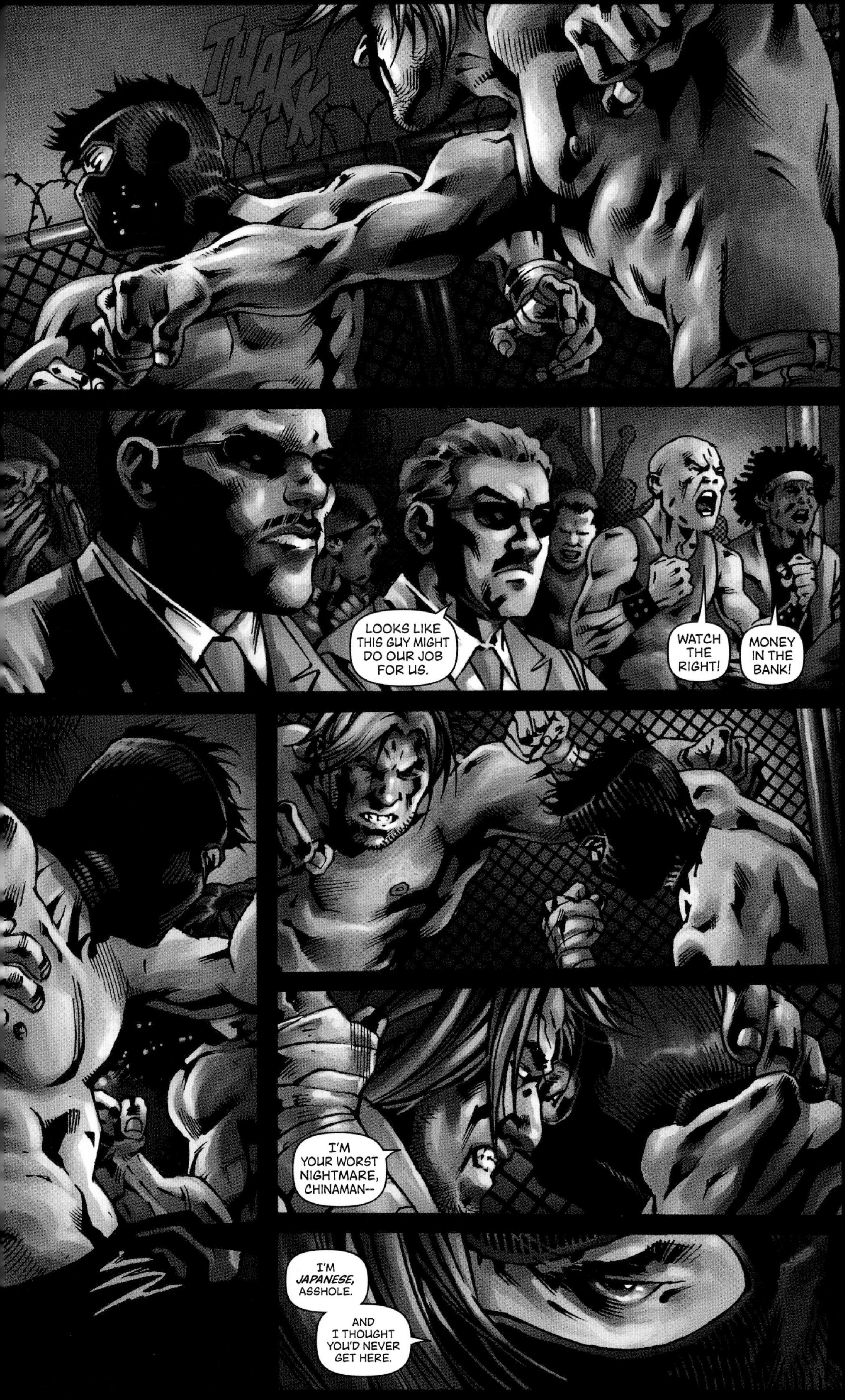
THAKK
LOOKS LIKE THIS GUY MIGHT DO OUR JOB FOR US.
WATCH THE RIGHT!
MONEY IN THE BANK!
I'M YOUR WORST NIGHTMARE, CHINAMAN--
I'M *JAPANESE,* ASSHOLE.
AND I THOUGHT YOU'D NEVER GET HERE.

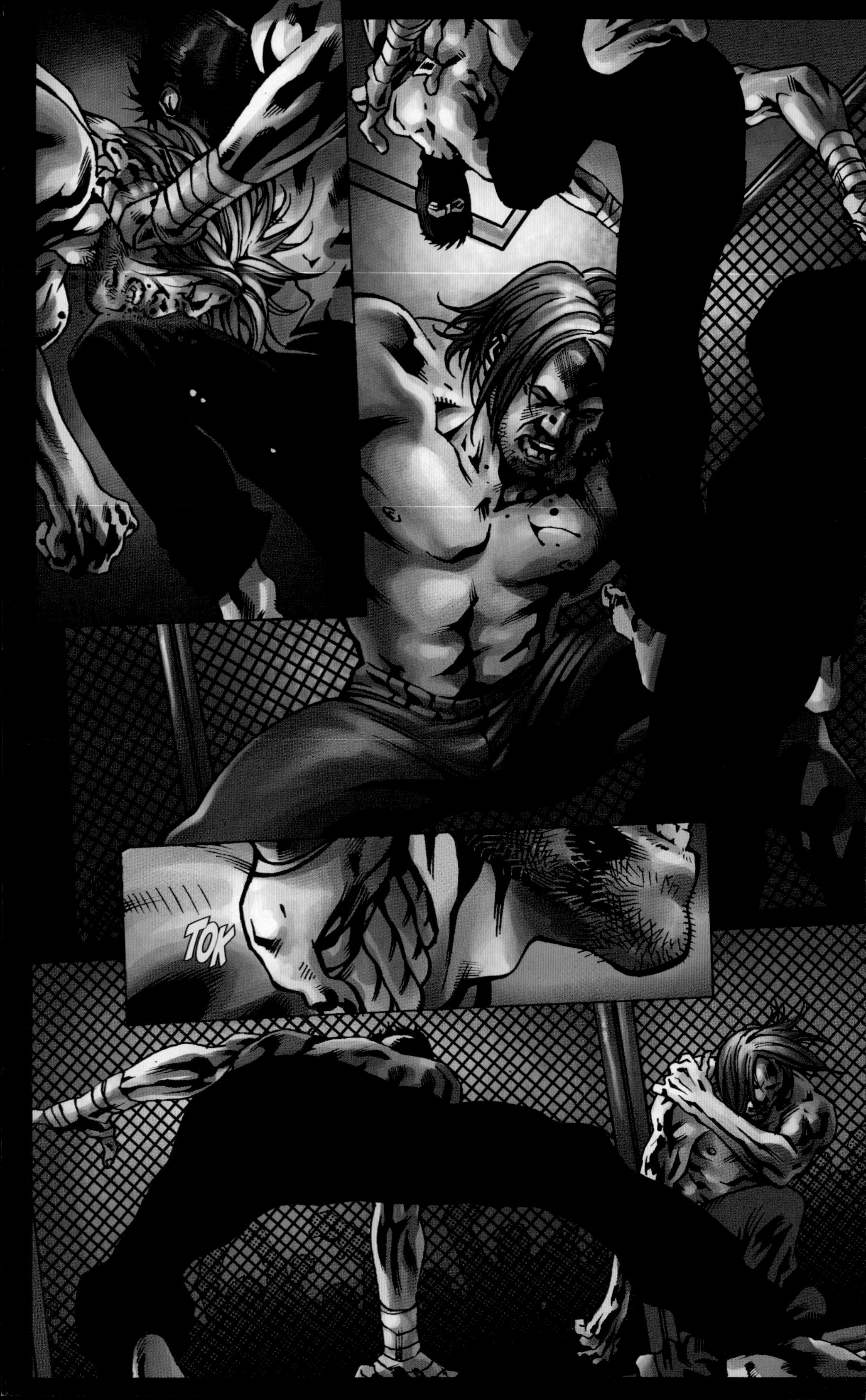
TOK

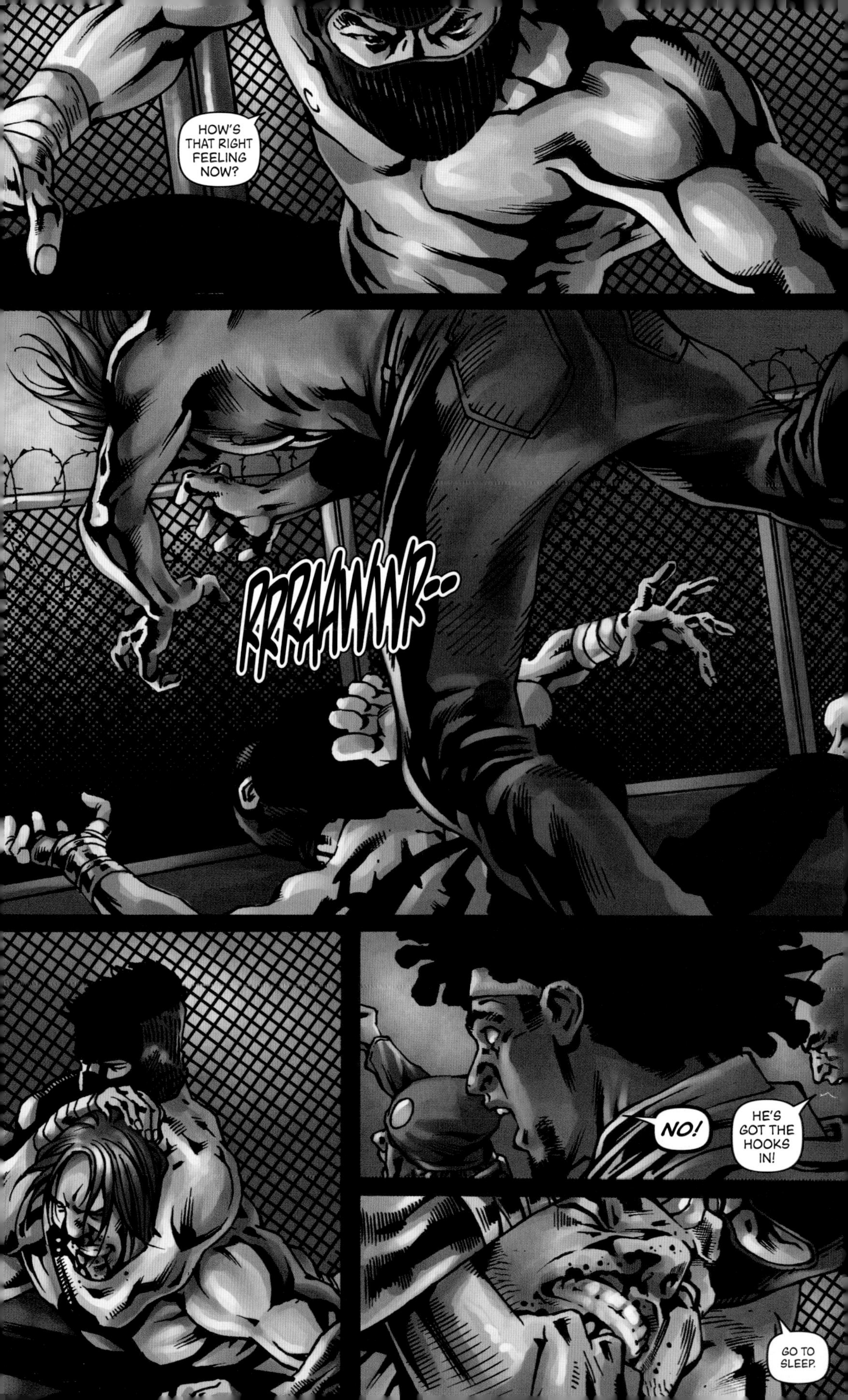
HOW'S THAT RIGHT FEELING NOW?
RRRAAWWR--
NO!
HE'S GOT THE HOOKS IN!
GO TO SLEEP.

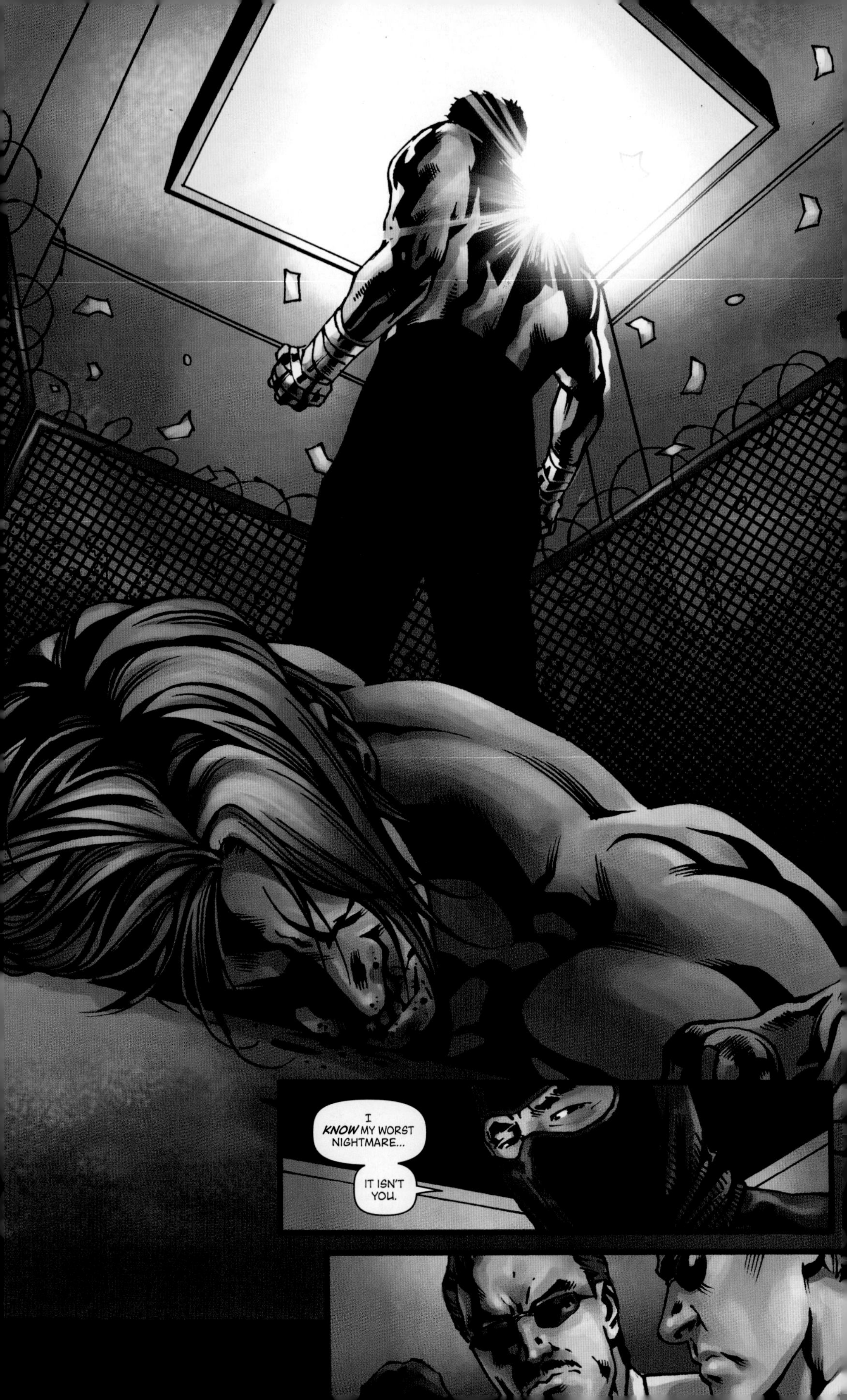
I *KNOW* MY WORST NIGHTMARE...
IT ISN'T YOU.

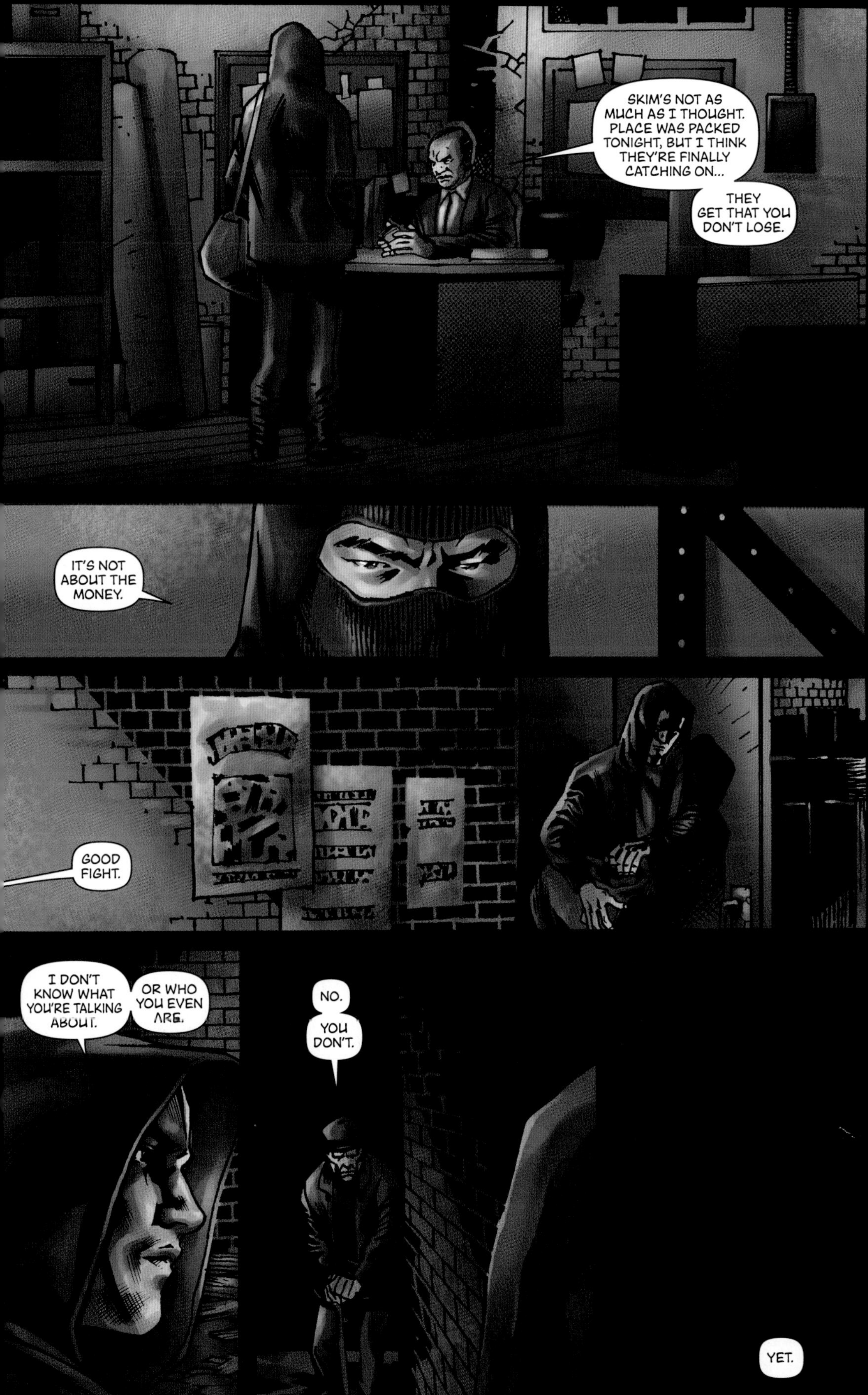
SKIM'S NOT AS MUCH AS I THOUGHT. PLACE WAS PACKED TONIGHT, BUT I THINK THEY'RE FINALLY CATCHING ON...
THEY GET THAT YOU DON'T LOSE.
IT'S NOT ABOUT THE MONEY.
GOOD FIGHT.
I DON'T KNOW WHAT YOU'RE TALKING ABOUT.
OR WHO YOU EVEN ARE.
NO.
YOU DON'T.
YET.

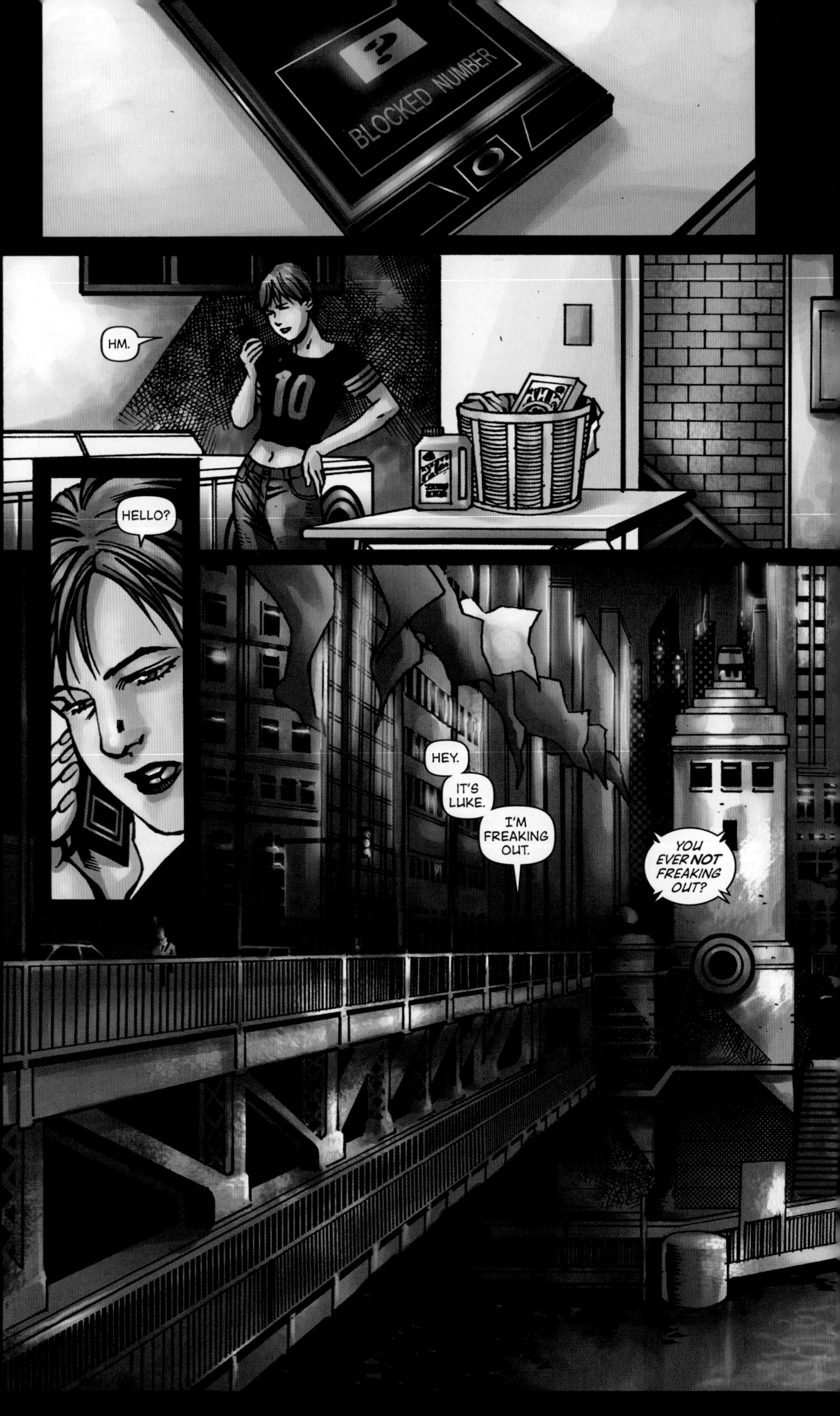
BLOCKED NUMBER
HM.
HELLO?
HEY.
IT'S LUKE.
I'M FREAKING OUT.
YOU EVER NOT FREAKING OUT?

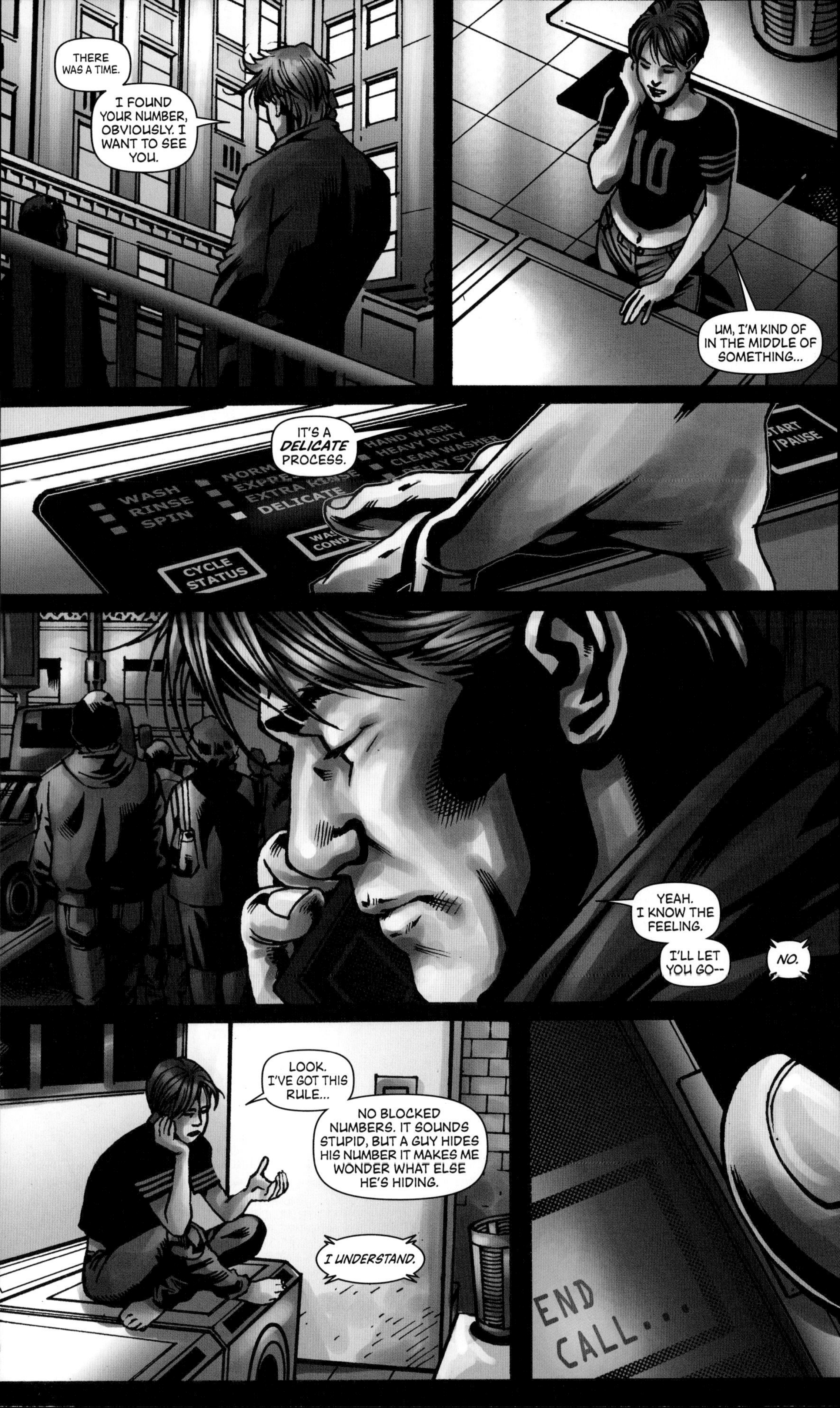
THERE WAS A TIME.
I FOUND YOUR NUMBER, OBVIOUSLY. I WANT TO SEE YOU.
UM, I'M KIND OF IN THE MIDDLE OF SOMETHING...
IT'S A *DELICATE* PROCESS.
WASH
RINSE
SPIN
DELICATE
EXTRA RINSE
HAND WASH
HEAVY DUTY
CLEAN WASHER
START /PAUSE
CYCLE STATUS
YEAH. I KNOW THE FEELING.
I'LL LET YOU GO--
NO.
LOOK. I'VE GOT THIS RULE...
NO BLOCKED NUMBERS. IT SOUNDS STUPID, BUT A GUY HIDES HIS NUMBER IT MAKES ME WONDER WHAT ELSE HE'S HIDING.
I UNDERSTAND.
END CALL...

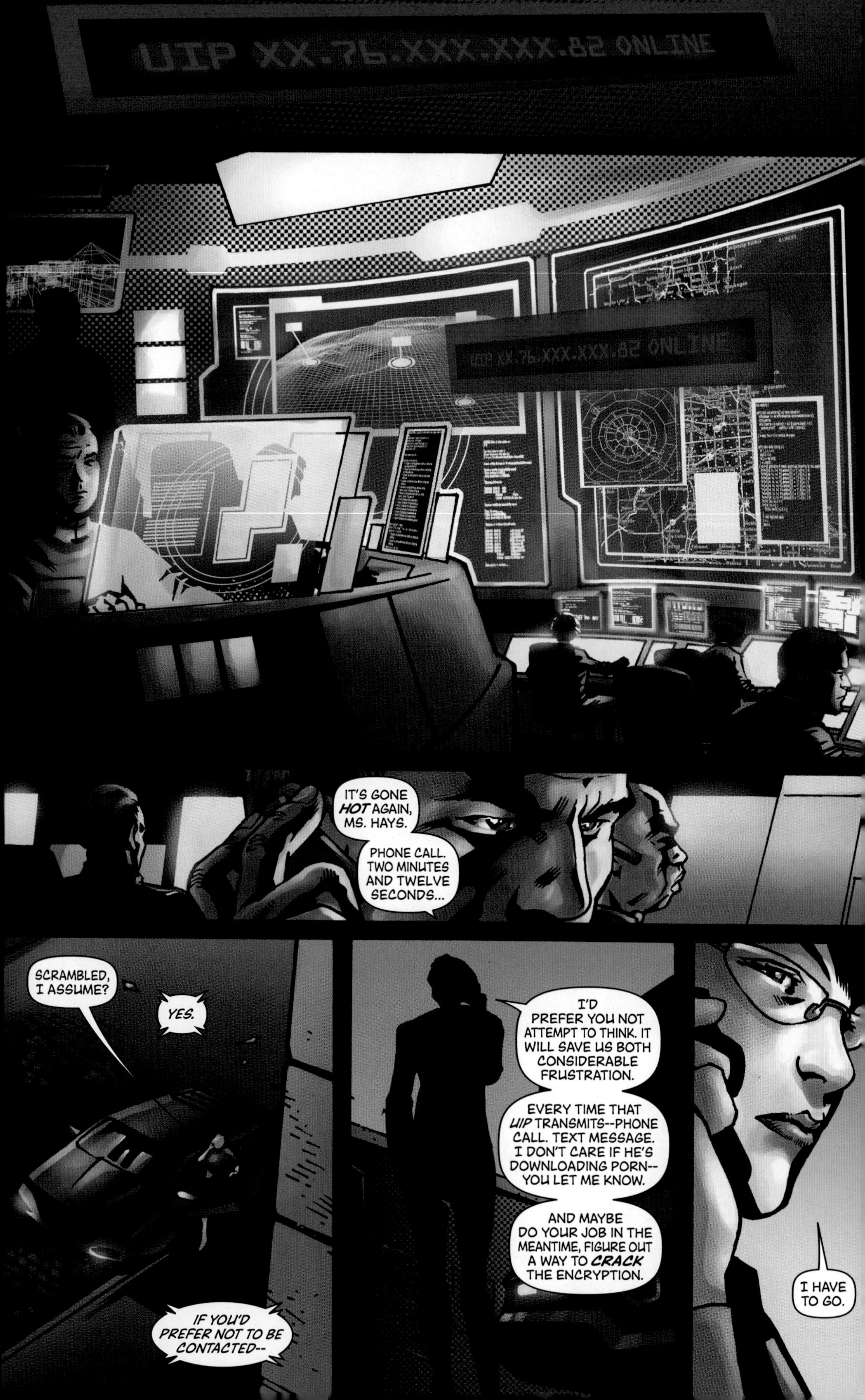
UIP XX.76.XXX.XXX.82 ONLINE
UIP XX.76.XXX.XXX.82 ONLINE
IT'S GONE HOT AGAIN, MS. HAYS.
PHONE CALL. TWO MINUTES AND TWELVE SECONDS...
SCRAMBLED, I ASSUME?
YES.
IF YOU'D PREFER NOT TO BE CONTACTED--
I'D PREFER YOU NOT ATTEMPT TO THINK. IT WILL SAVE US BOTH CONSIDERABLE FRUSTRATION.
EVERY TIME THAT UIP TRANSMITS--PHONE CALL. TEXT MESSAGE. I DON'T CARE IF HE'S DOWNLOADING PORN--YOU LET ME KNOW.
AND MAYBE DO YOUR JOB IN THE MEANTIME, FIGURE OUT A WAY TO CRACK THE ENCRYPTION.
I HAVE TO GO.

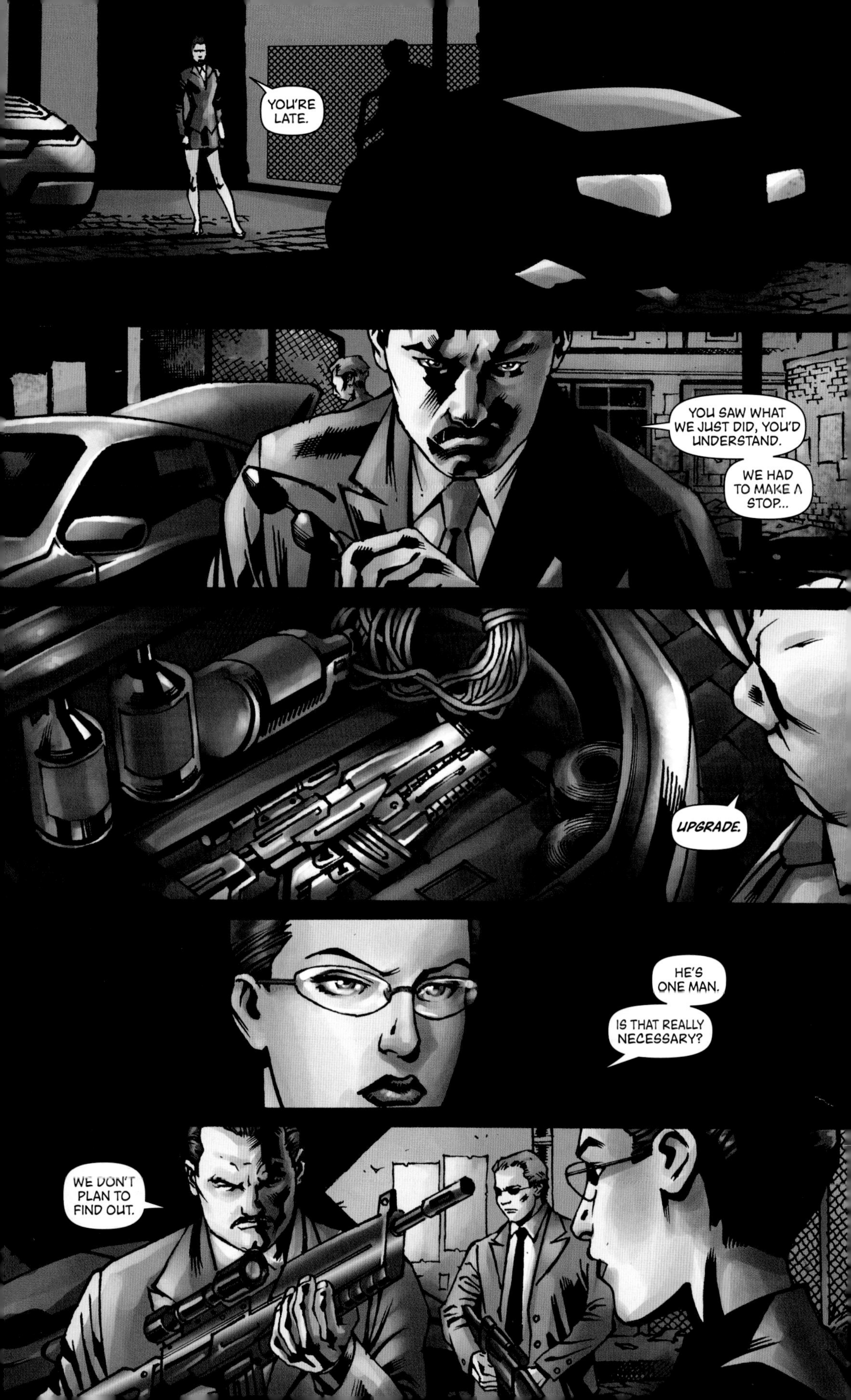

YOU'RE LATE.
YOU SAW WHAT WE JUST DID, YOU'D UNDERSTAND.
WE HAD TO MAKE A STOP...
UPGRADE.
HE'S ONE MAN.
IS THAT REALLY NECESSARY?
WE DON'T PLAN TO FIND OUT.

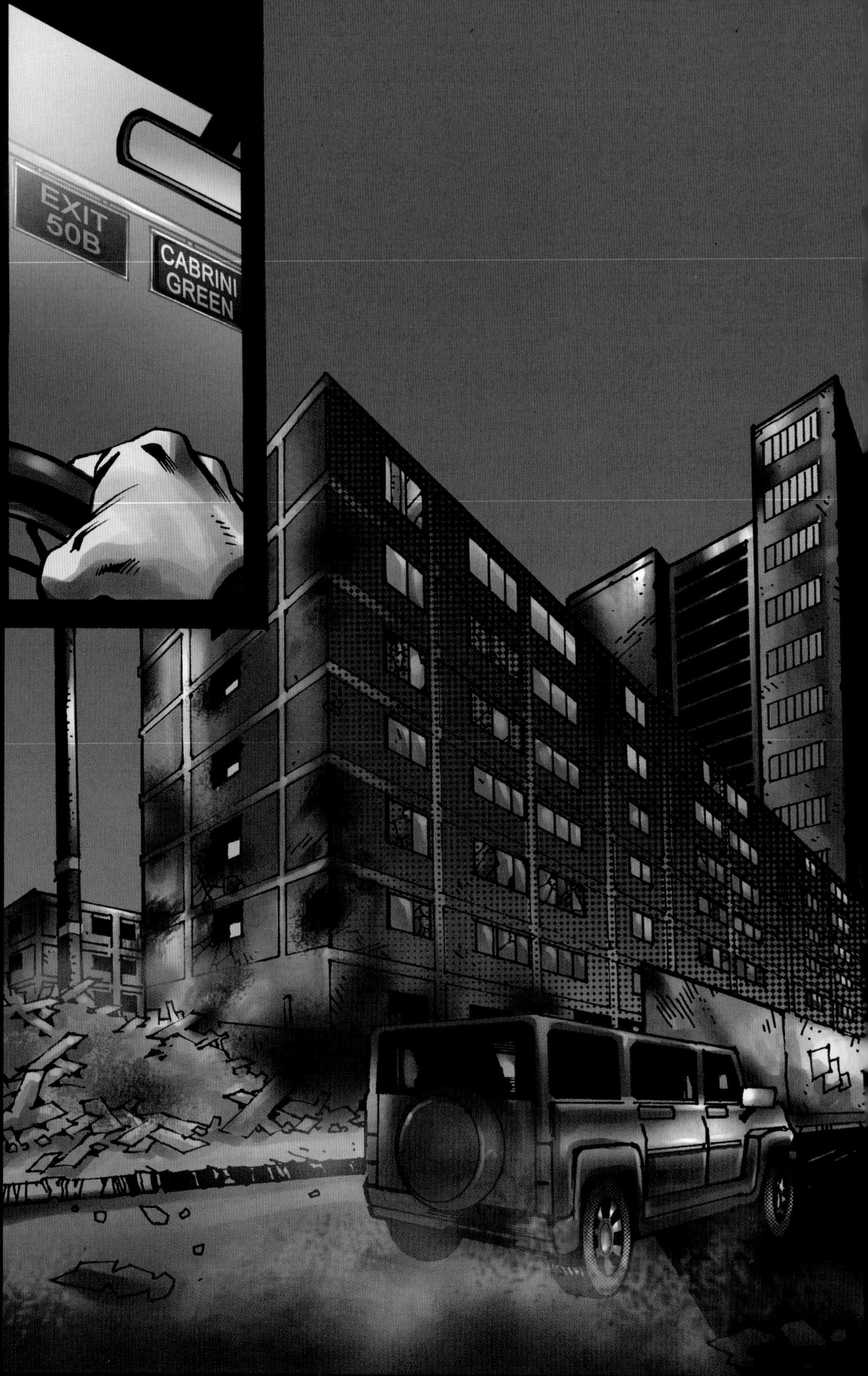
EXIT
50B
CABRINI
GREEN

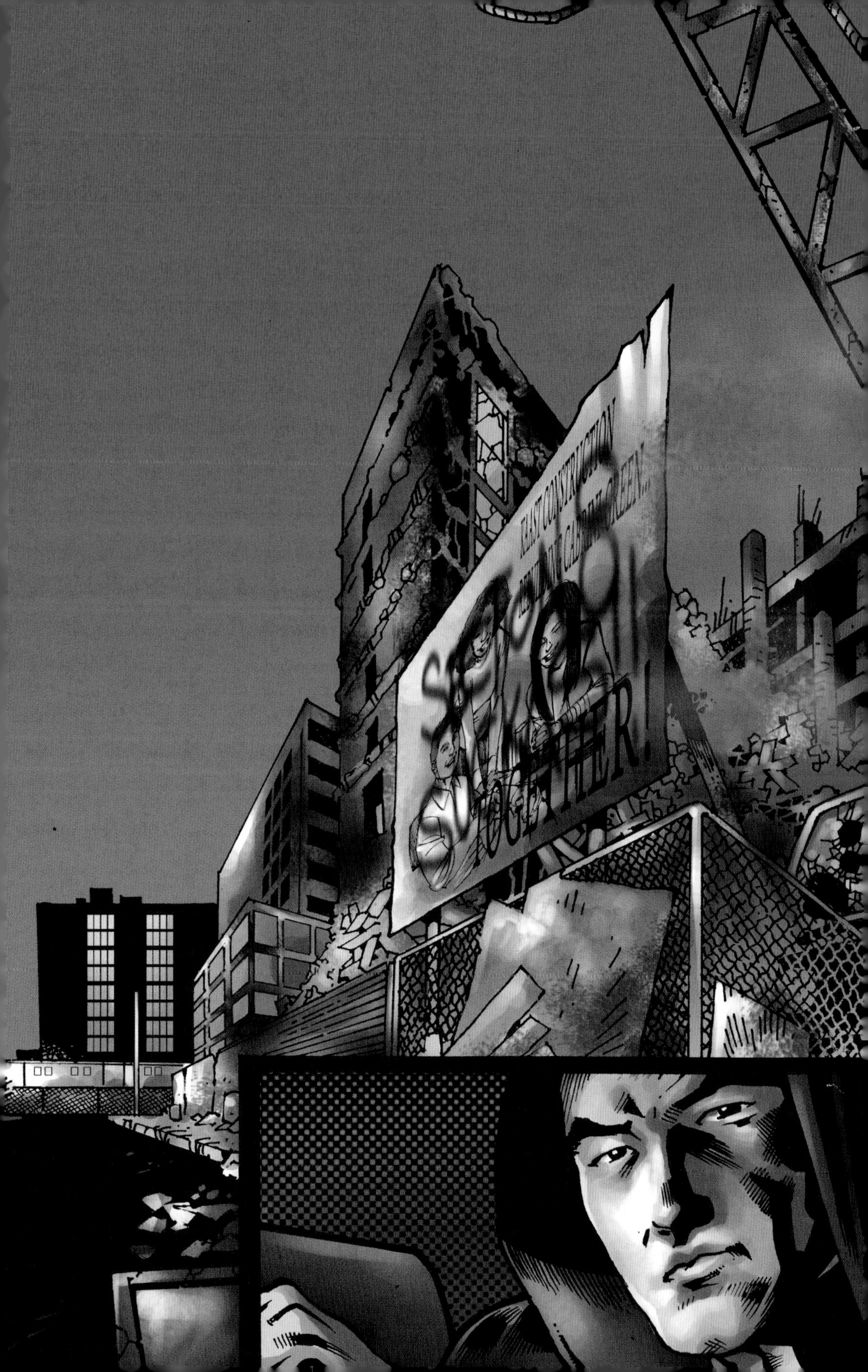
KRAST CONSTRUCTION
TOGETHER!

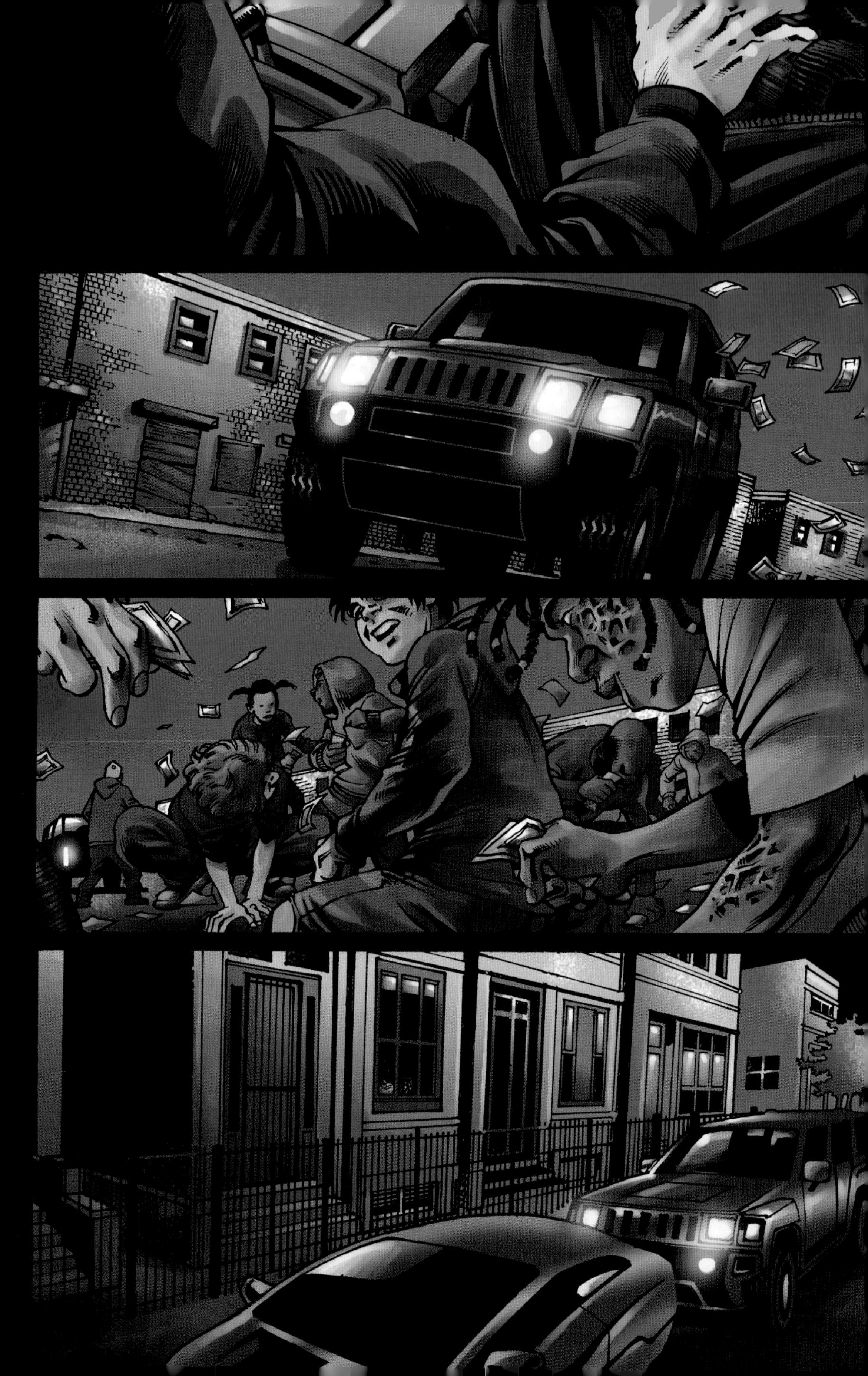

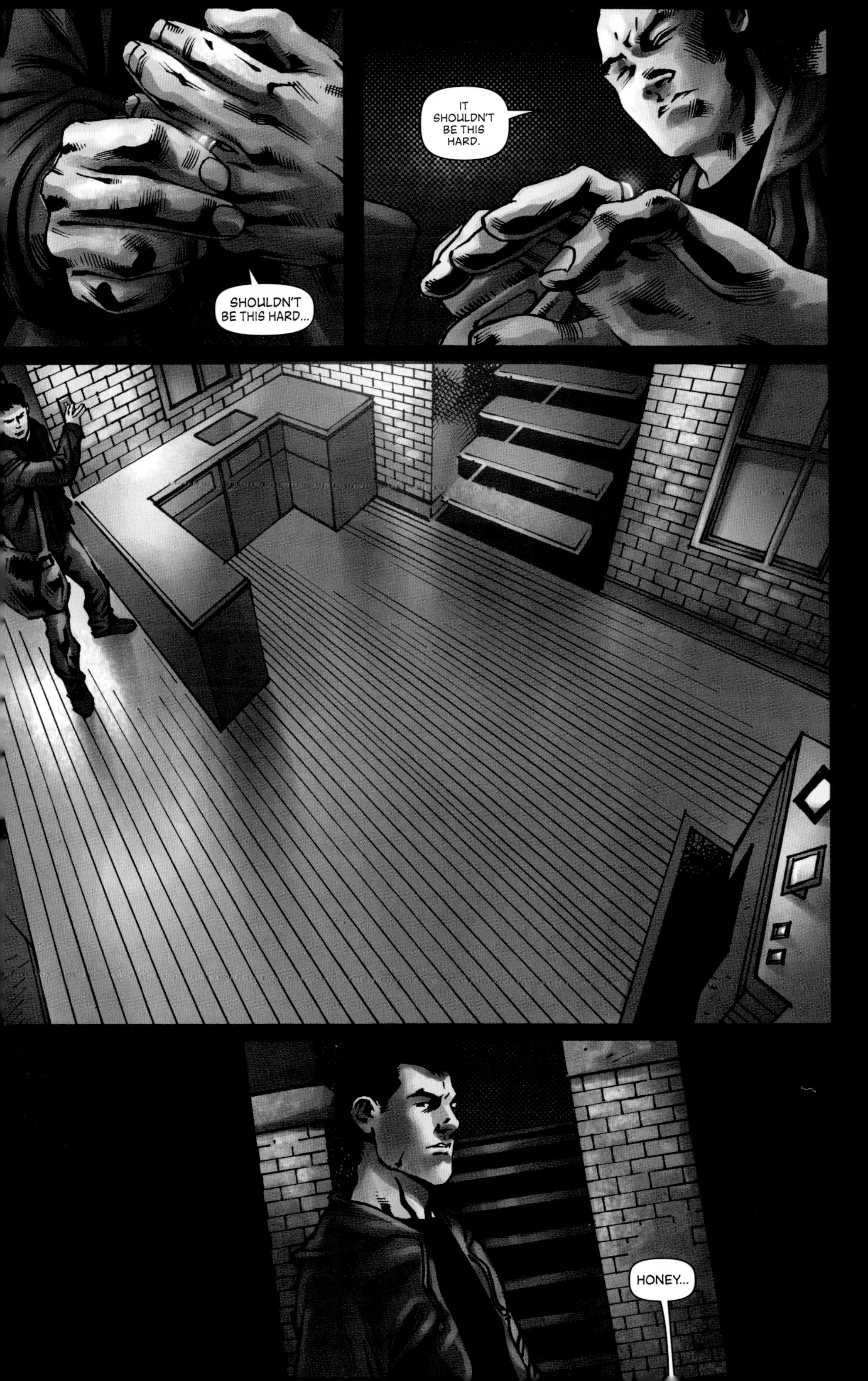
SHOULDN'T BE THIS HARD...
IT SHOULDN'T BE THIS HARD.
HONEY...

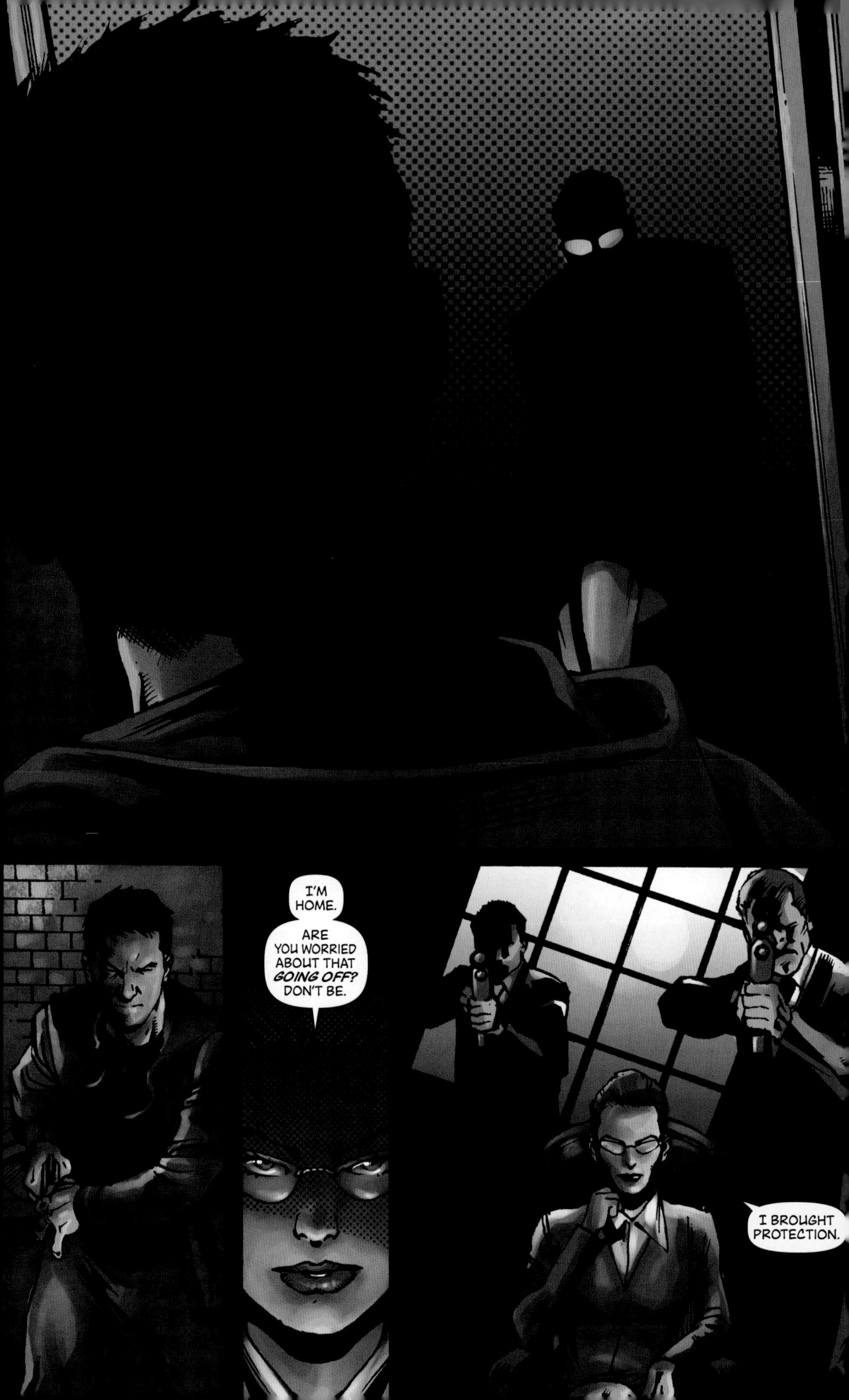

I'M HOME.
ARE YOU WORRIED ABOUT THAT *GOING OFF?* DON'T BE.
I BROUGHT PROTECTION.

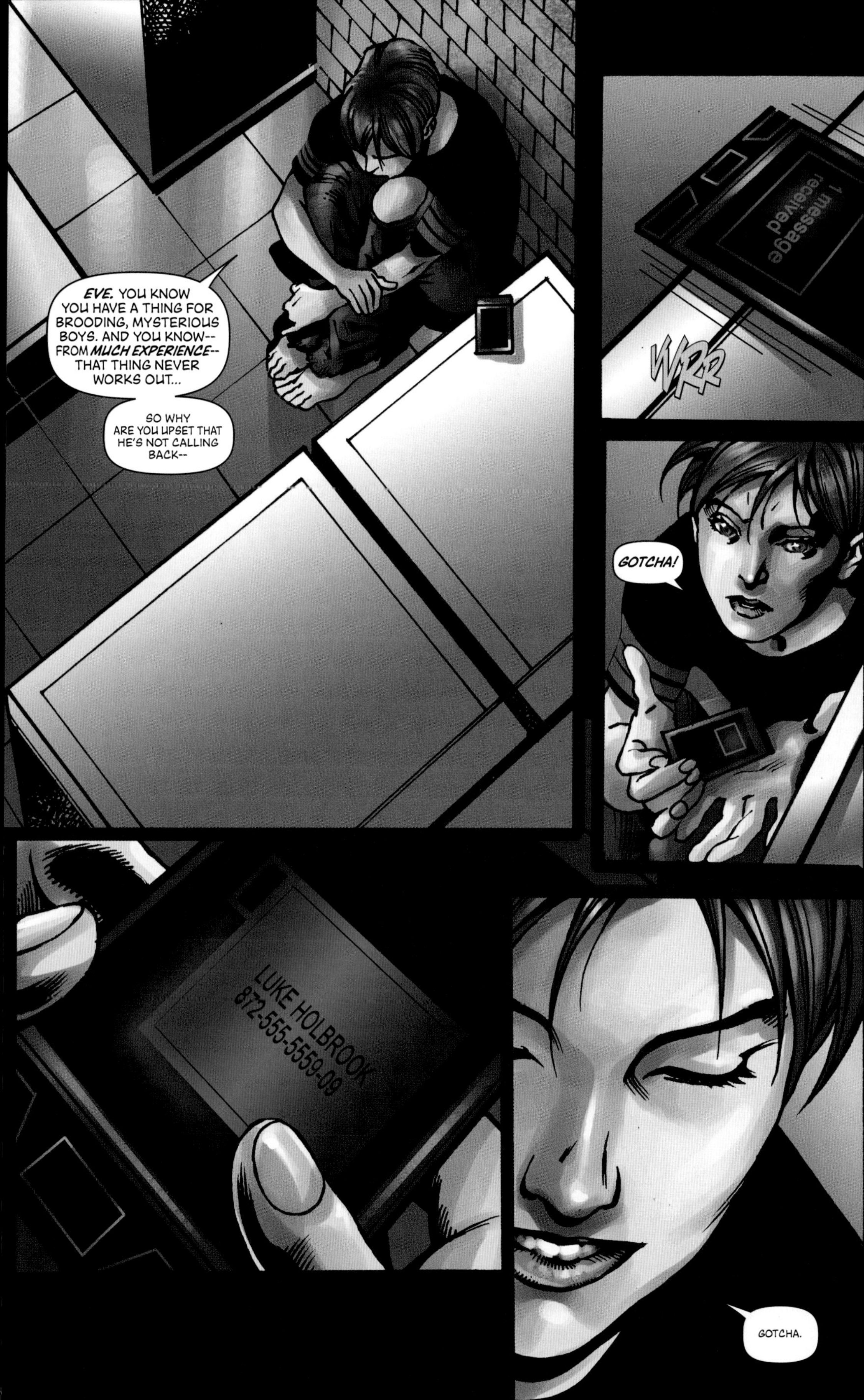
EVE. YOU KNOW YOU HAVE A THING FOR BROODING, MYSTERIOUS BOYS. AND YOU KNOW-- FROM MUCH EXPERIENCE-- THAT THING NEVER WORKS OUT...
SO WHY ARE YOU UPSET THAT HE'S NOT CALLING BACK--
1 message received
WRRR
GOTCHA!
LUKE HOLBROOK 872-555-5559-09
GOTCHA.

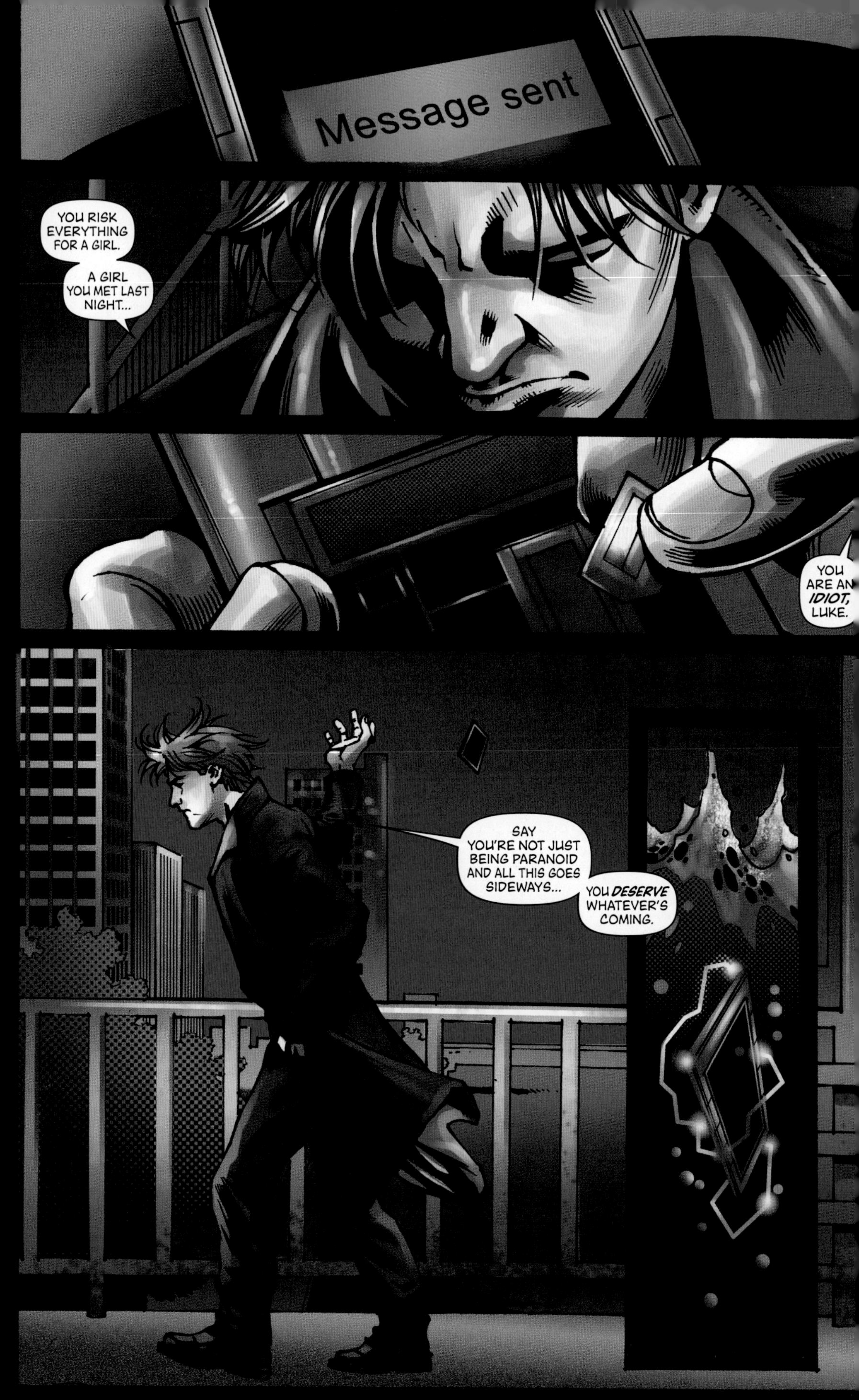
Message sent
YOU RISK EVERYTHING FOR A GIRL.
A GIRL YOU MET LAST NIGHT...
YOU ARE AN *IDIOT,* LUKE.
SAY YOU'RE NOT JUST BEING PARANOID AND ALL THIS GOES SIDEWAYS...
YOU *DESERVE* WHATEVER'S COMING.

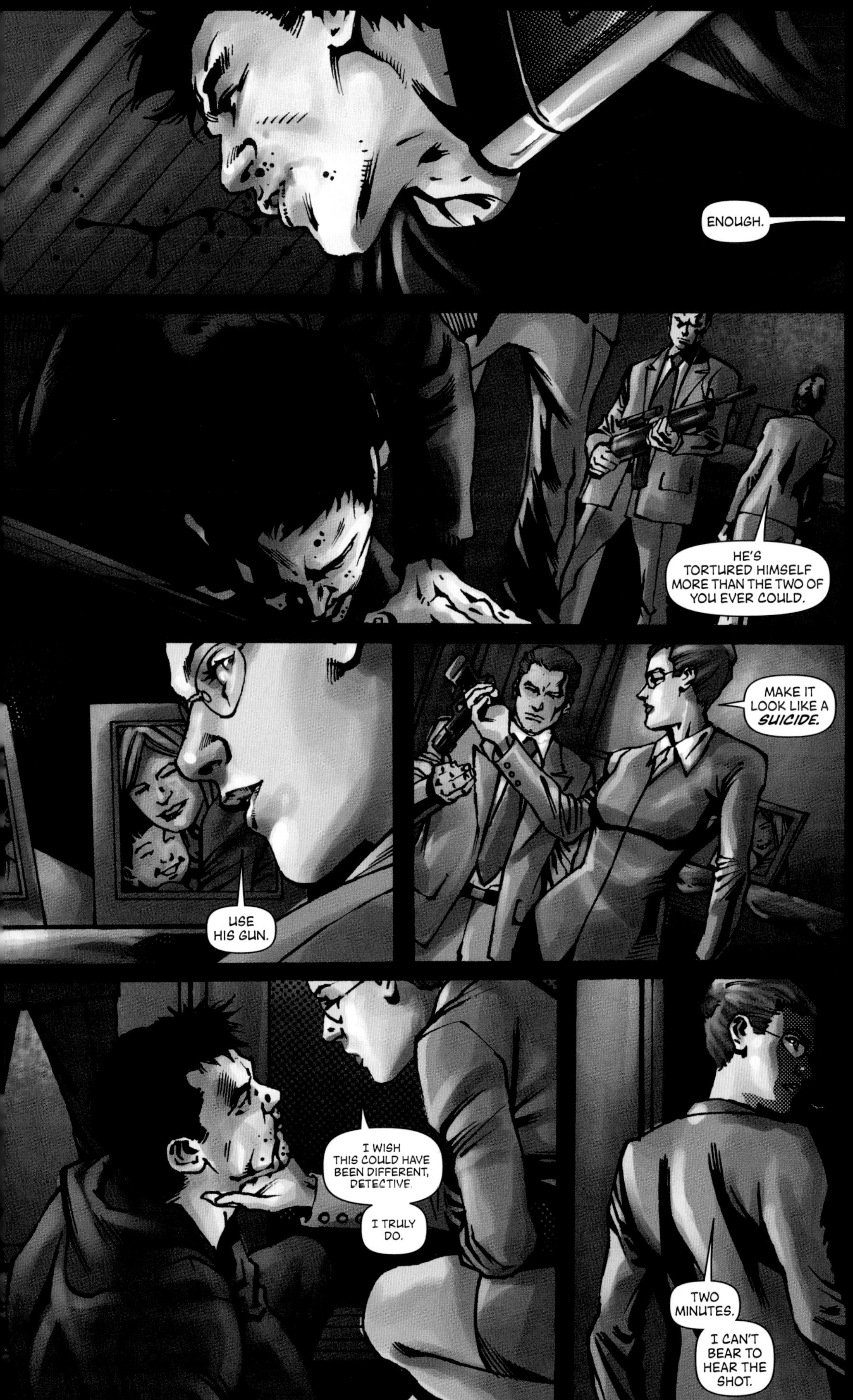

ENOUGH.
HE'S TORTURED HIMSELF MORE THAN THE TWO OF YOU EVER COULD.
USE HIS GUN.
MAKE IT LOOK LIKE A ***SUICIDE.***
I WISH THIS COULD HAVE BEEN DIFFERENT, DETECTIVE.
I TRULY DO.
TWO MINUTES.
I CAN'T BEAR TO HEAR THE SHOT.

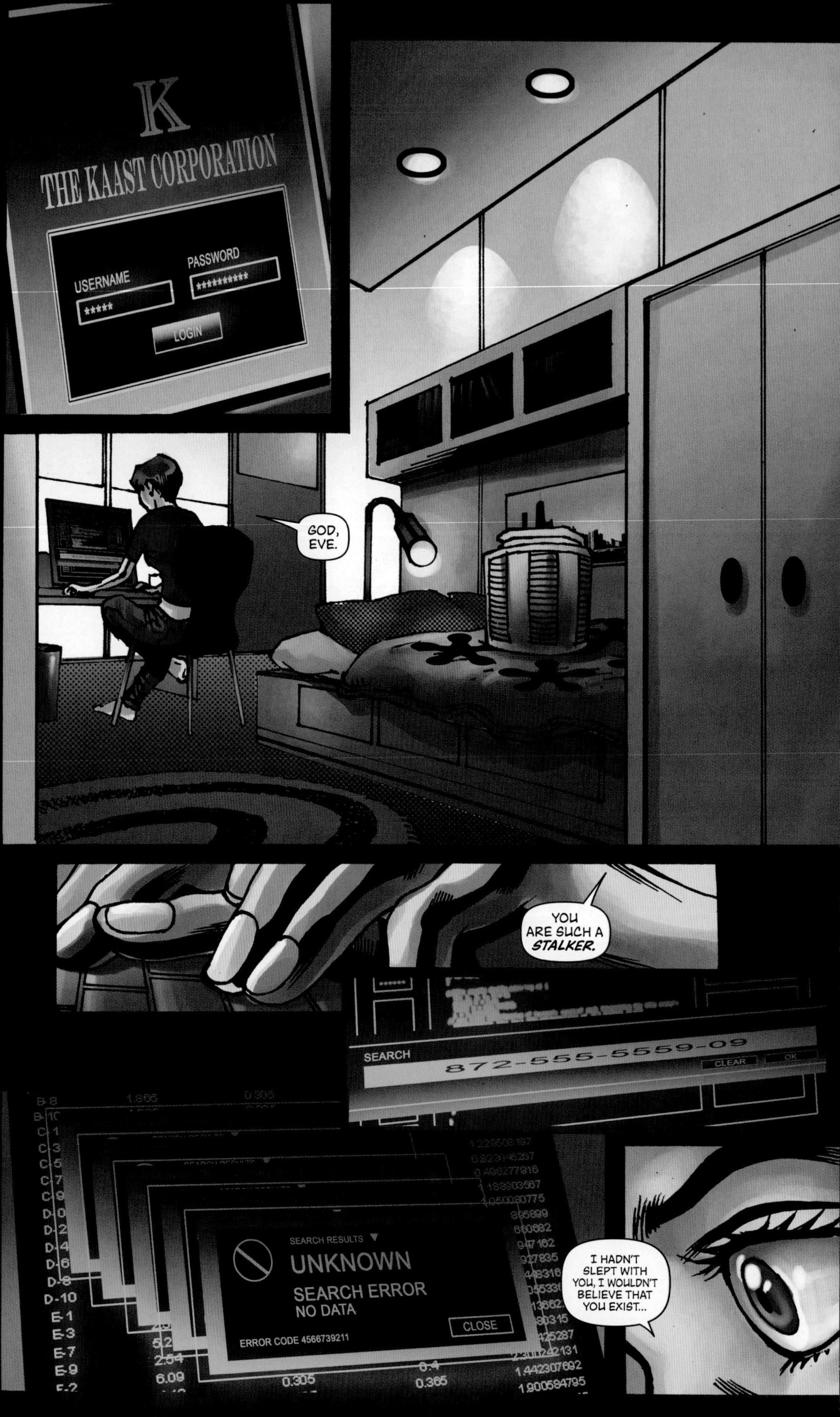
K
THE KAAST CORPORATION
USERNAME
*****
PASSWORD
****
LOGIN
GOD, EVE.
YOU ARE SUCH A STALKER.
SEARCH
872-555-5559-09
CLEAR
OK
SEARCH RESULTS
UNKNOWN
SEARCH ERROR
NO DATA
CLOSE
ERROR CODE 4566739211
I HADN'T SLEPT WITH YOU, I WOULDN'T BELIEVE THAT YOU EXIST...

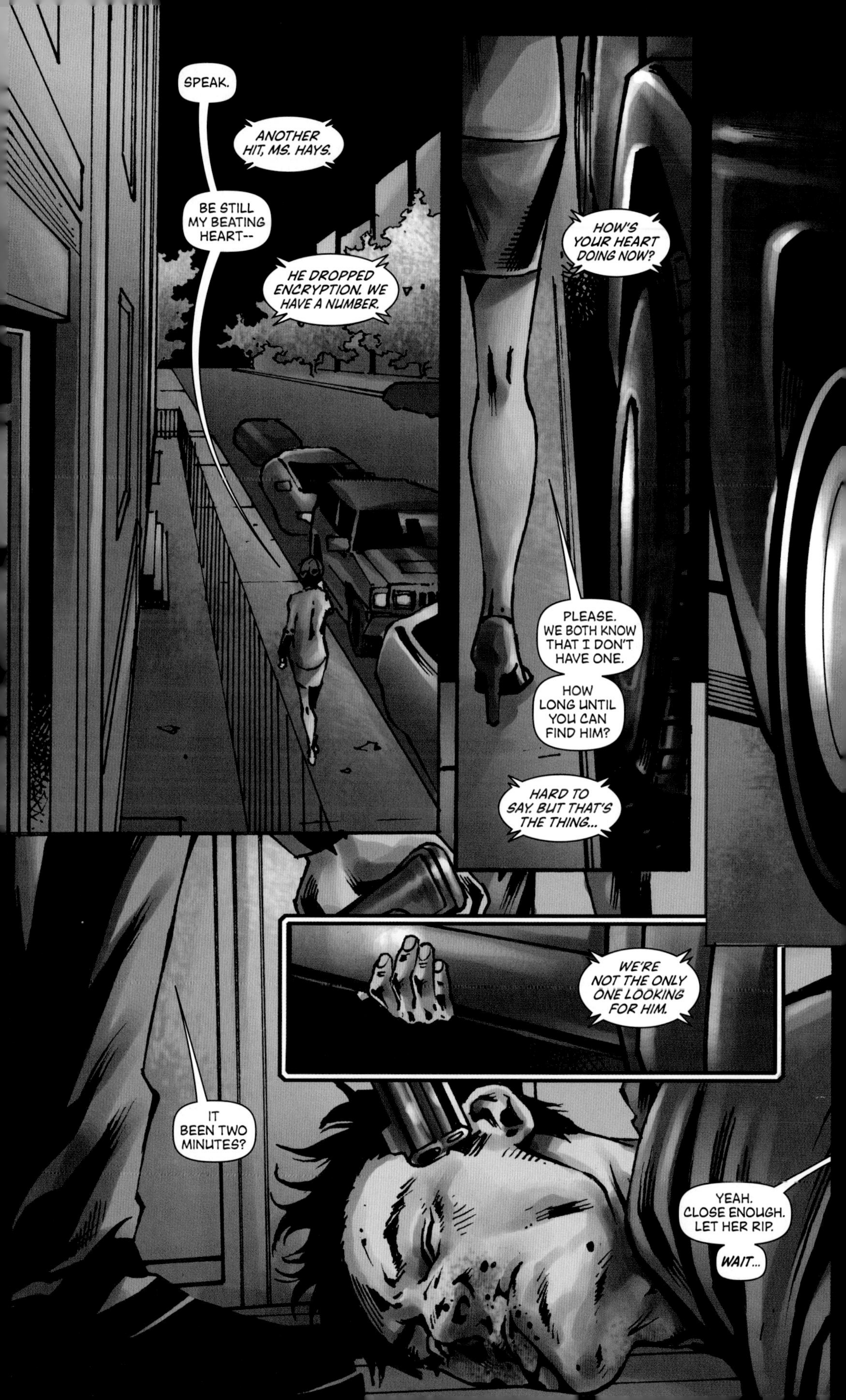
SPEAK.
ANOTHER HIT, MS. HAYS.
BE STILL MY BEATING HEART--
HE DROPPED ENCRYPTION. WE HAVE A NUMBER.
HOW'S YOUR HEART DOING NOW?
PLEASE. WE BOTH KNOW THAT I DON'T HAVE ONE.
HOW LONG UNTIL YOU CAN FIND HIM?
HARD TO SAY. BUT THAT'S THE THING...
WE'RE NOT THE ONLY ONE LOOKING FOR HIM.
IT BEEN TWO MINUTES?
YEAH. CLOSE ENOUGH. LET HER RIP.
WAIT...

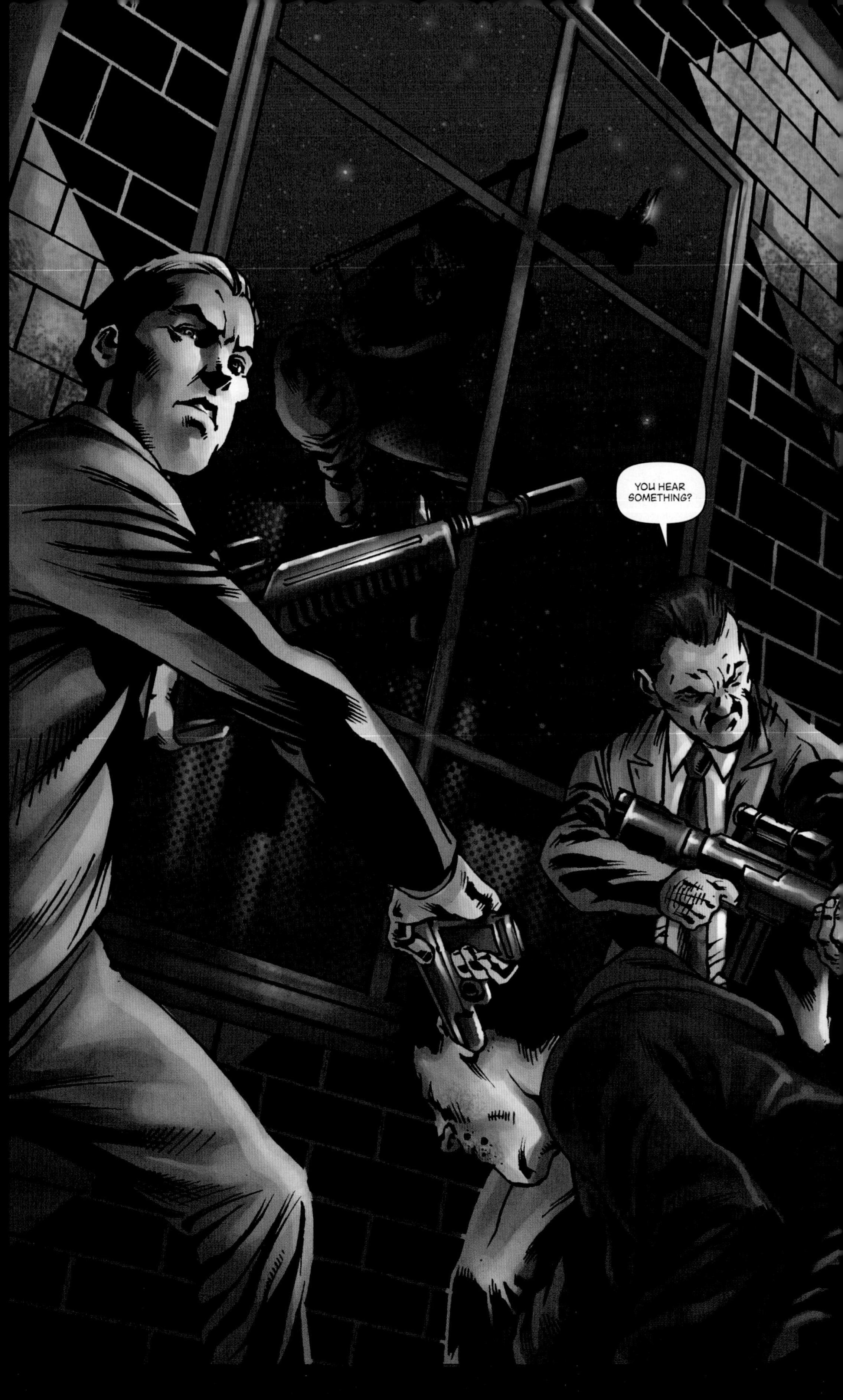
YOU HEAR SOMETHING?

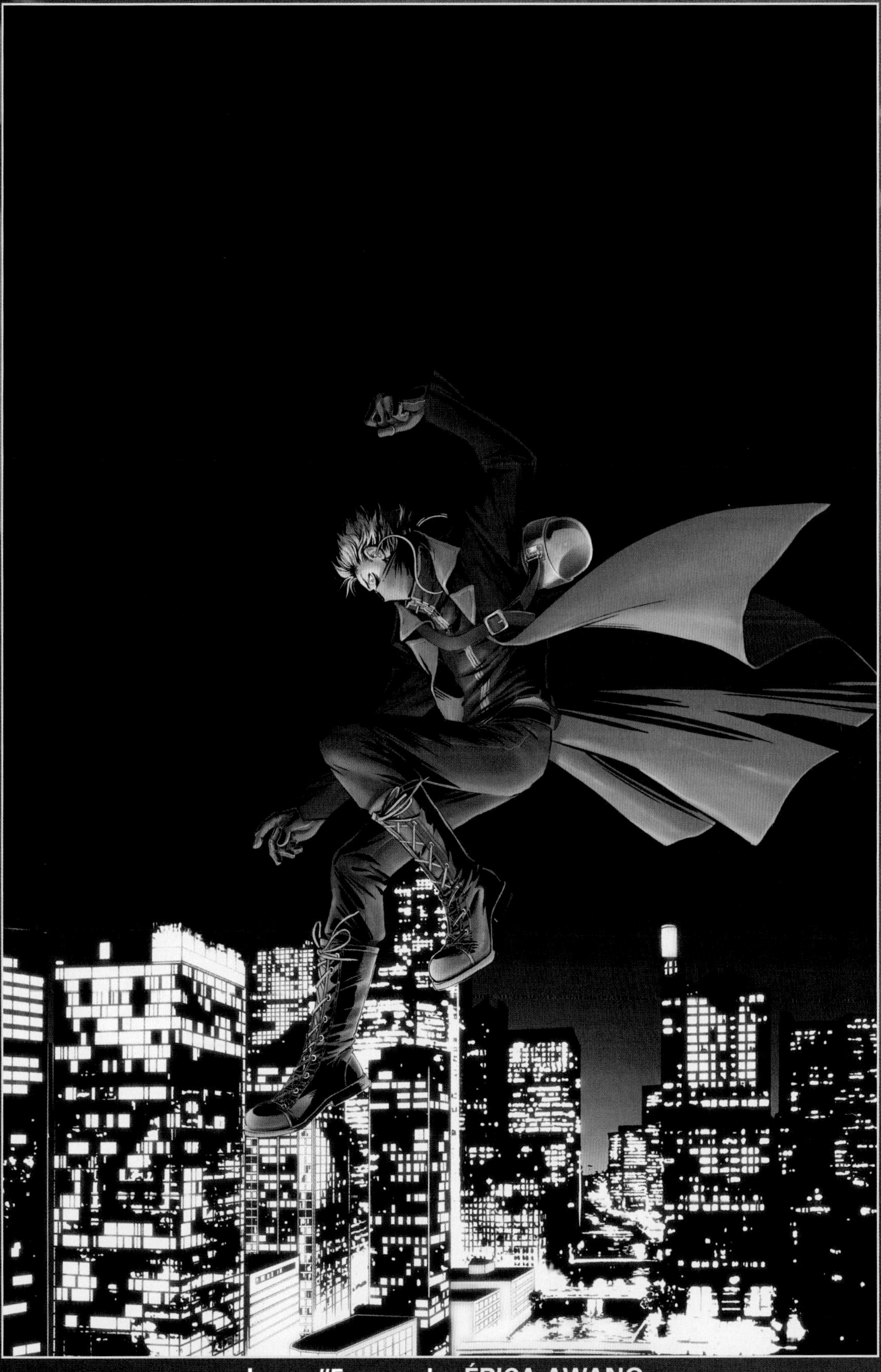

Issue #5 cover by ÉRICA AWANO

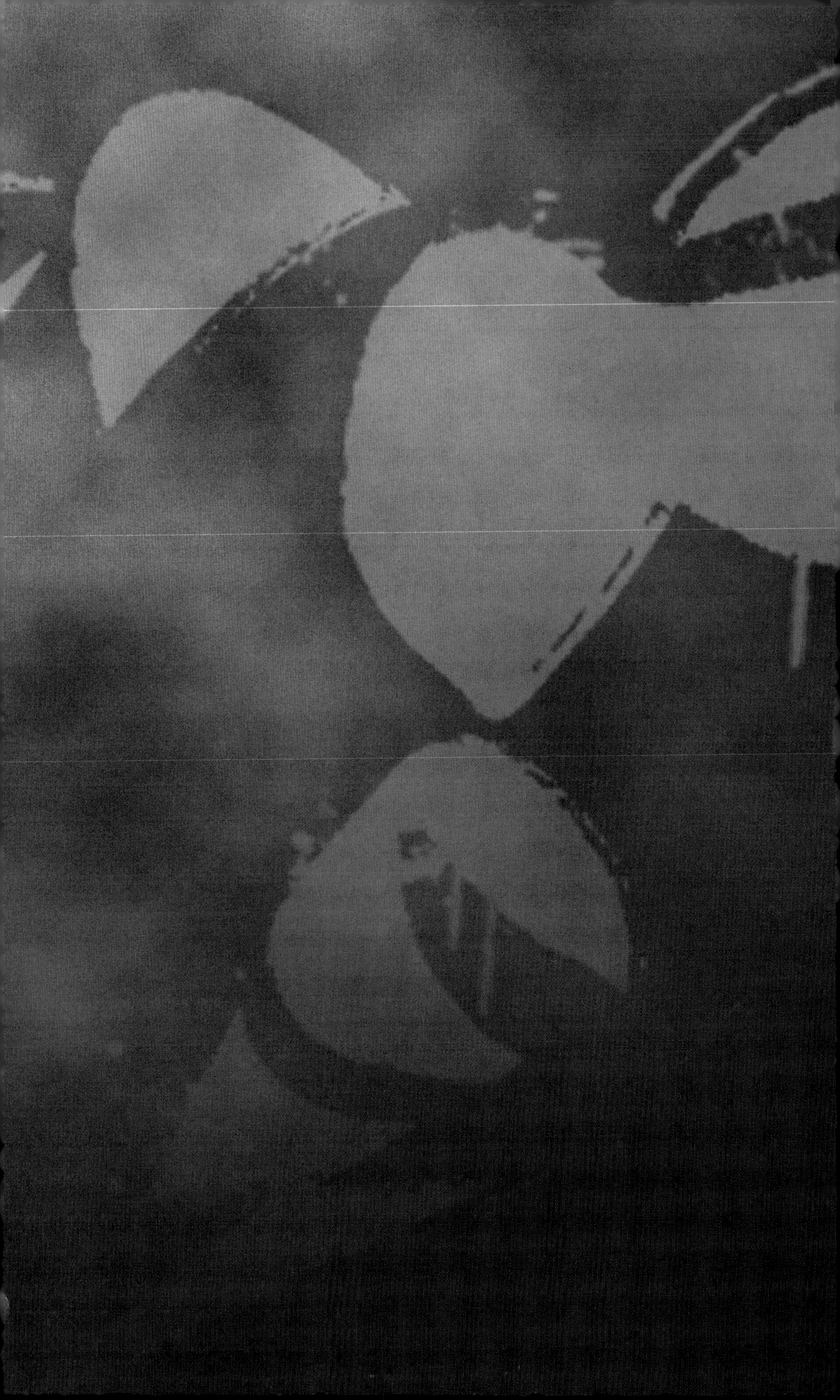

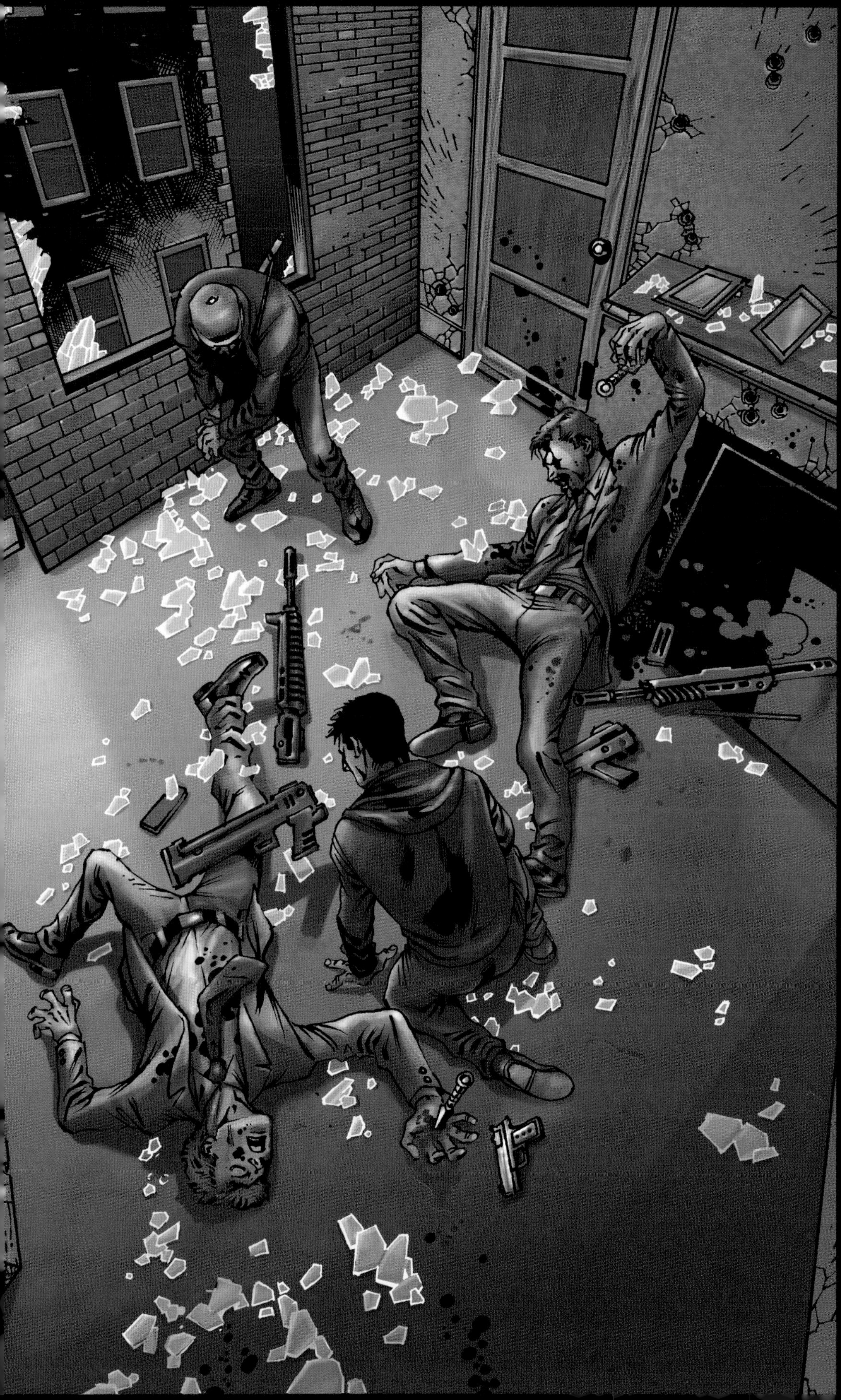

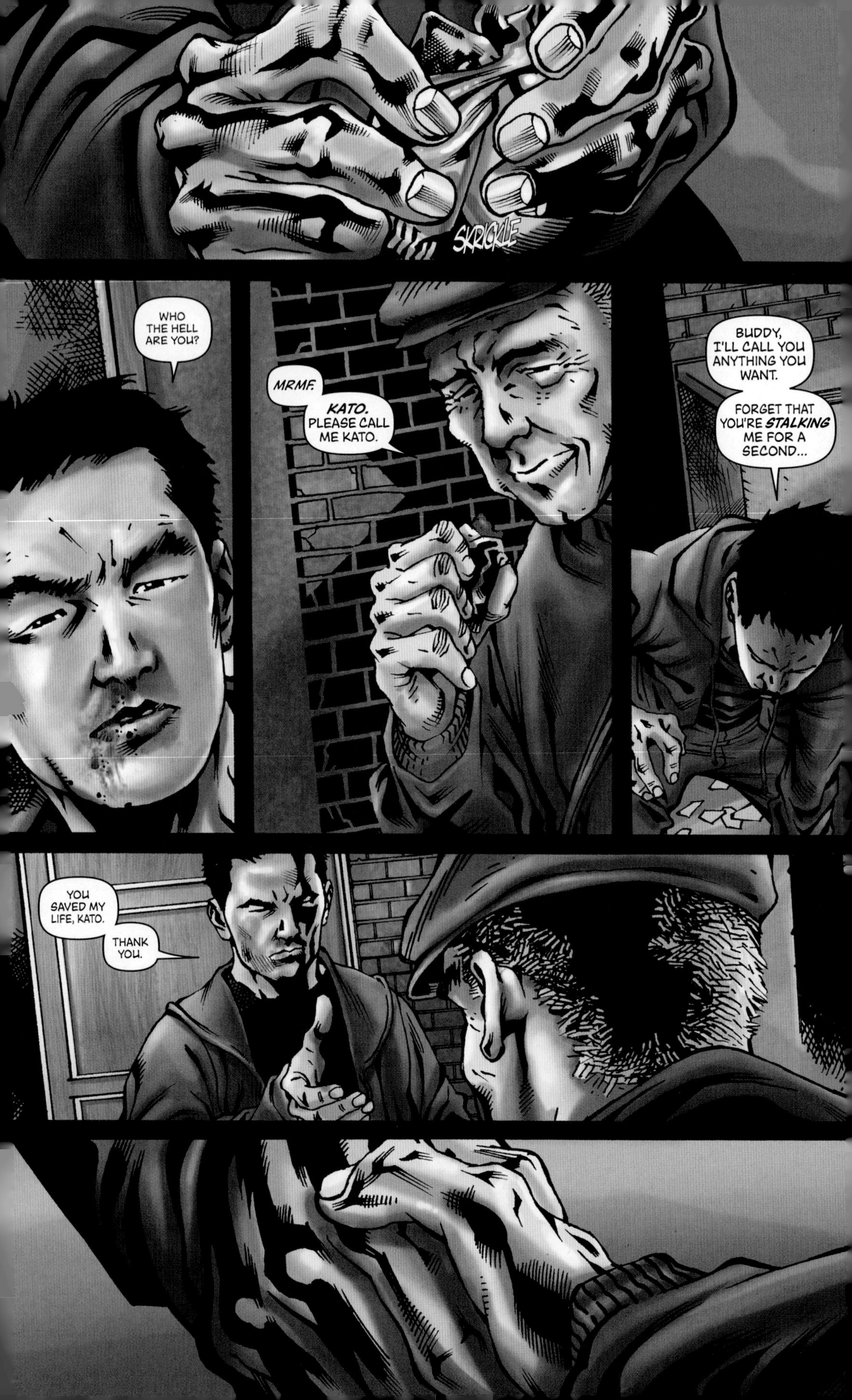
SKRICKLE
WHO THE HELL ARE YOU?
MRMF.
KATO. PLEASE CALL ME KATO.
BUDDY, I'LL CALL YOU ANYTHING YOU WANT.
FORGET THAT YOU'RE STALKING ME FOR A SECOND...
YOU SAVED MY LIFE, KATO.
THANK YOU.

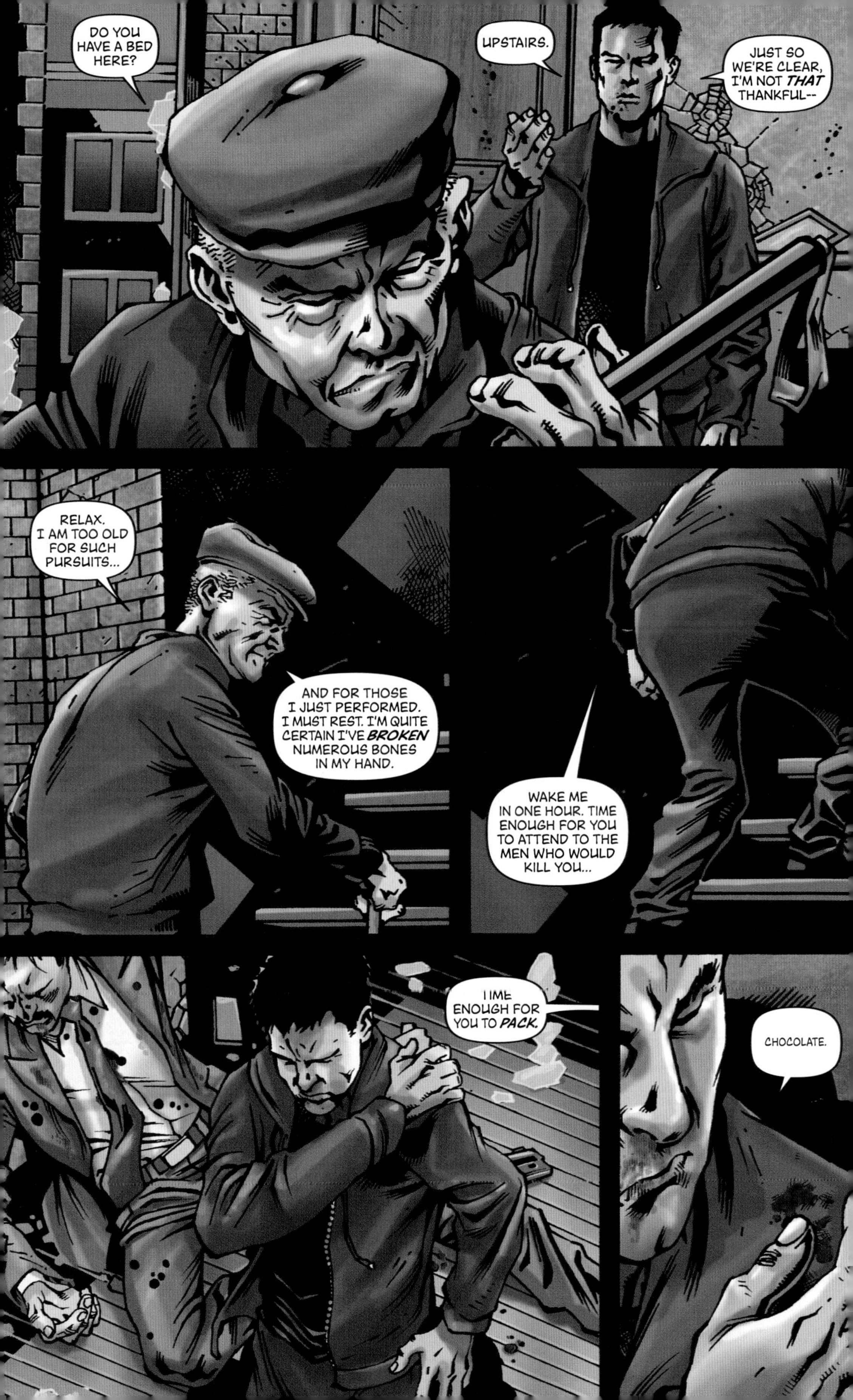
DO YOU HAVE A BED HERE?
UPSTAIRS.
JUST SO WE'RE CLEAR, I'M NOT *THAT* THANKFUL--
RELAX. I AM TOO OLD FOR SUCH PURSUITS...
AND FOR THOSE I JUST PERFORMED. I MUST REST. I'M QUITE CERTAIN I'VE *BROKEN* NUMEROUS BONES IN MY HAND.
WAKE ME IN ONE HOUR. TIME ENOUGH FOR YOU TO ATTEND TO THE MEN WHO WOULD KILL YOU...
TIME ENOUGH FOR YOU TO *PACK.*
CHOCOLATE.

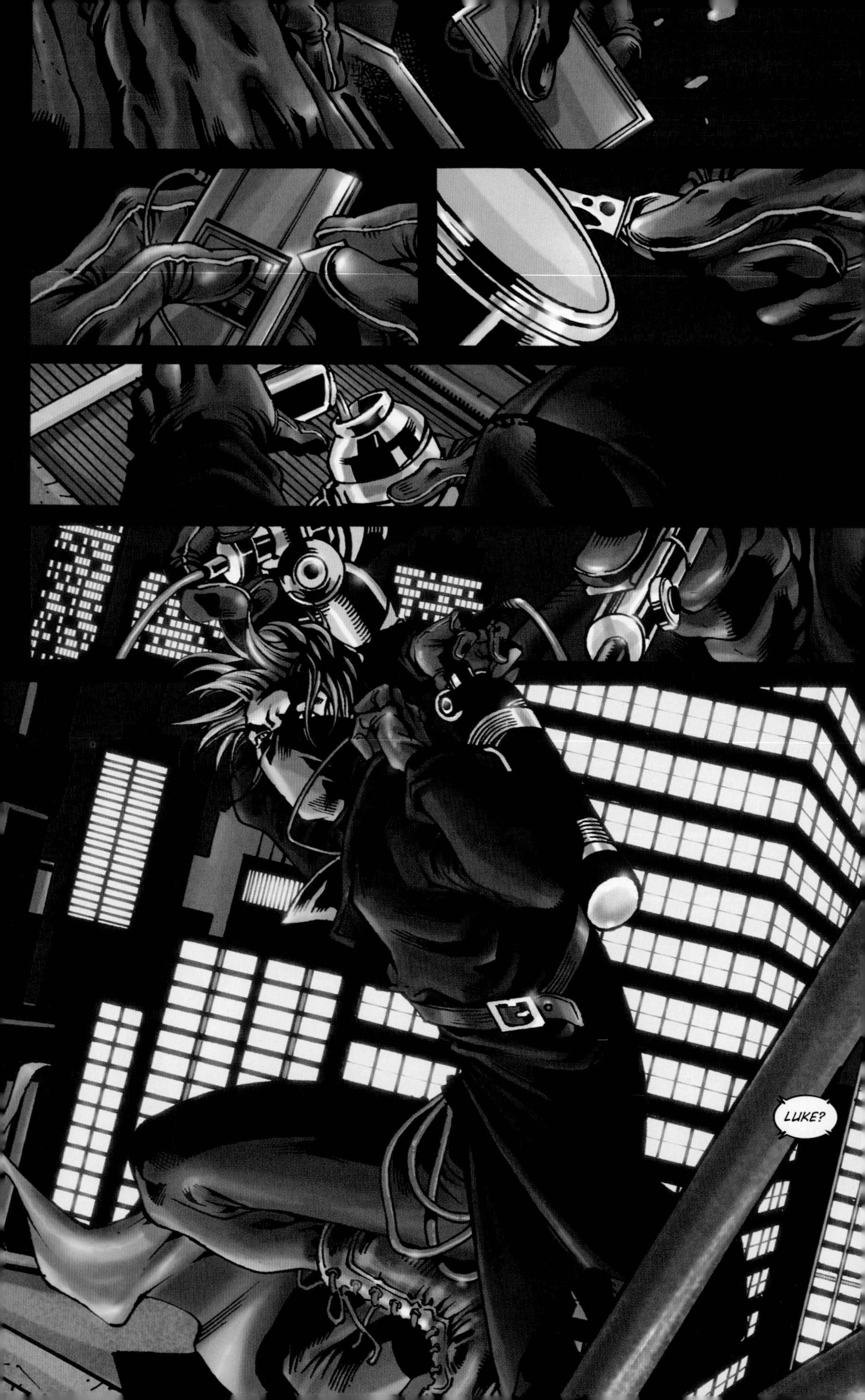
LUKE?

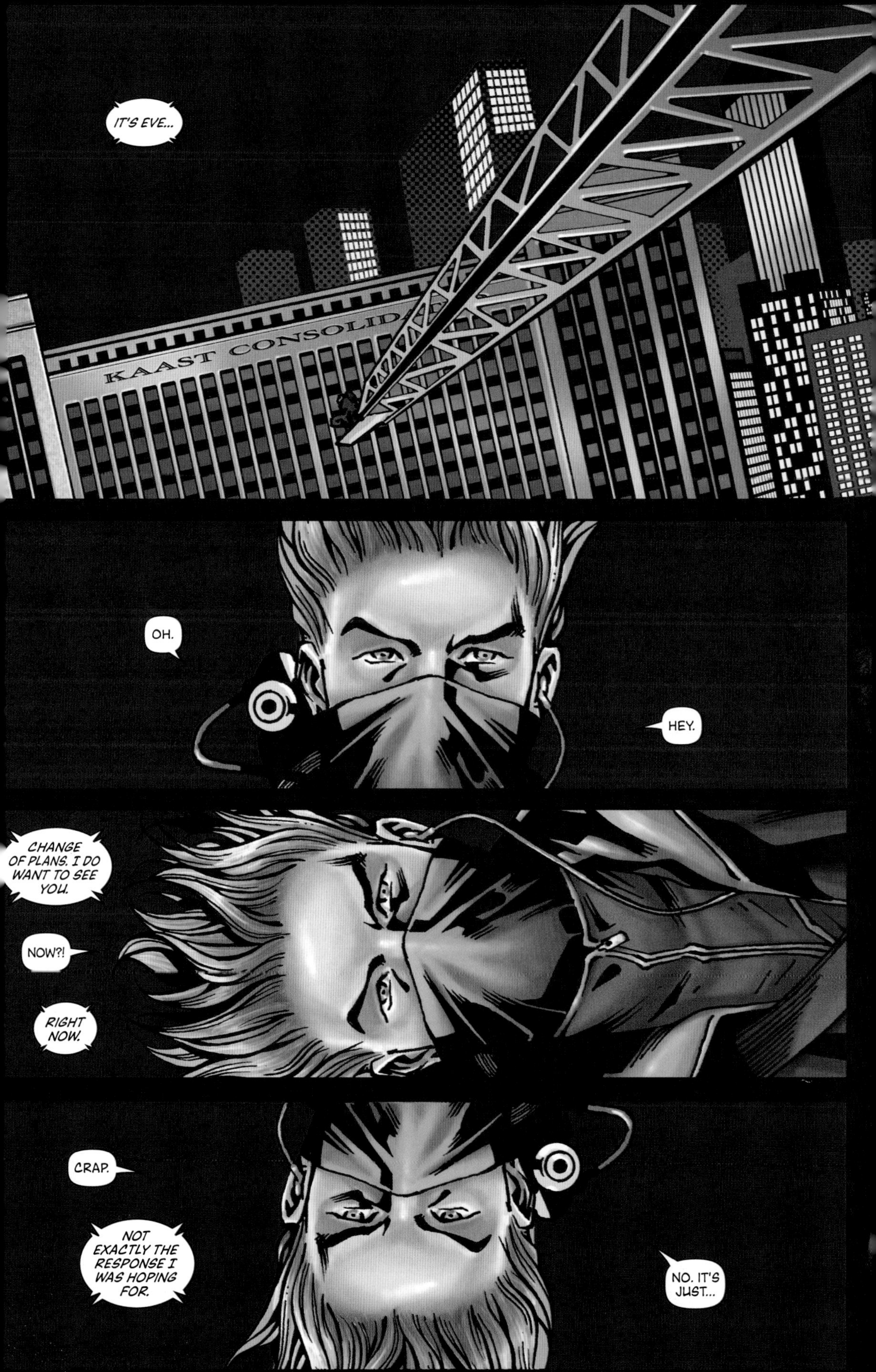
IT'S EVE...
KAAST CONSOLID
OH.
HEY.
CHANGE OF PLANS. I DO WANT TO SEE YOU.
NOW?!
RIGHT NOW.
CRAP.
NOT EXACTLY THE RESPONSE I WAS HOPING FOR.
NO. IT'S JUST...

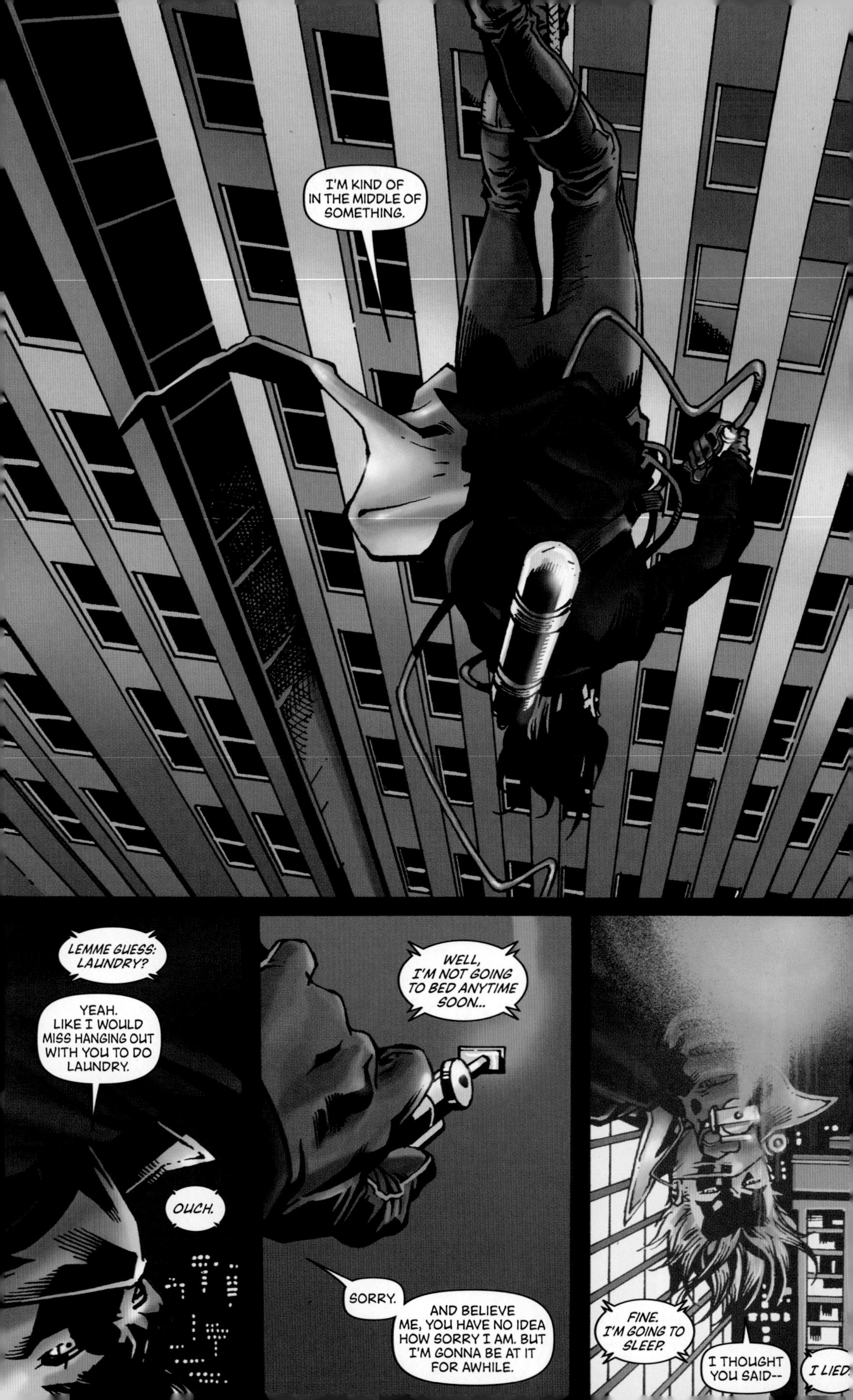

I'M KIND OF IN THE MIDDLE OF SOMETHING.
LEMME GUESS: LAUNDRY?
YEAH. LIKE I WOULD MISS HANGING OUT WITH YOU TO DO LAUNDRY.
OUCH.
WELL, I'M NOT GOING TO BED ANYTIME SOON...
SORRY.
AND BELIEVE ME, YOU HAVE NO IDEA HOW SORRY I AM. BUT I'M GONNA BE AT IT FOR AWHILE.
FINE. I'M GOING TO SLEEP.
I THOUGHT YOU SAID--
I LIED.

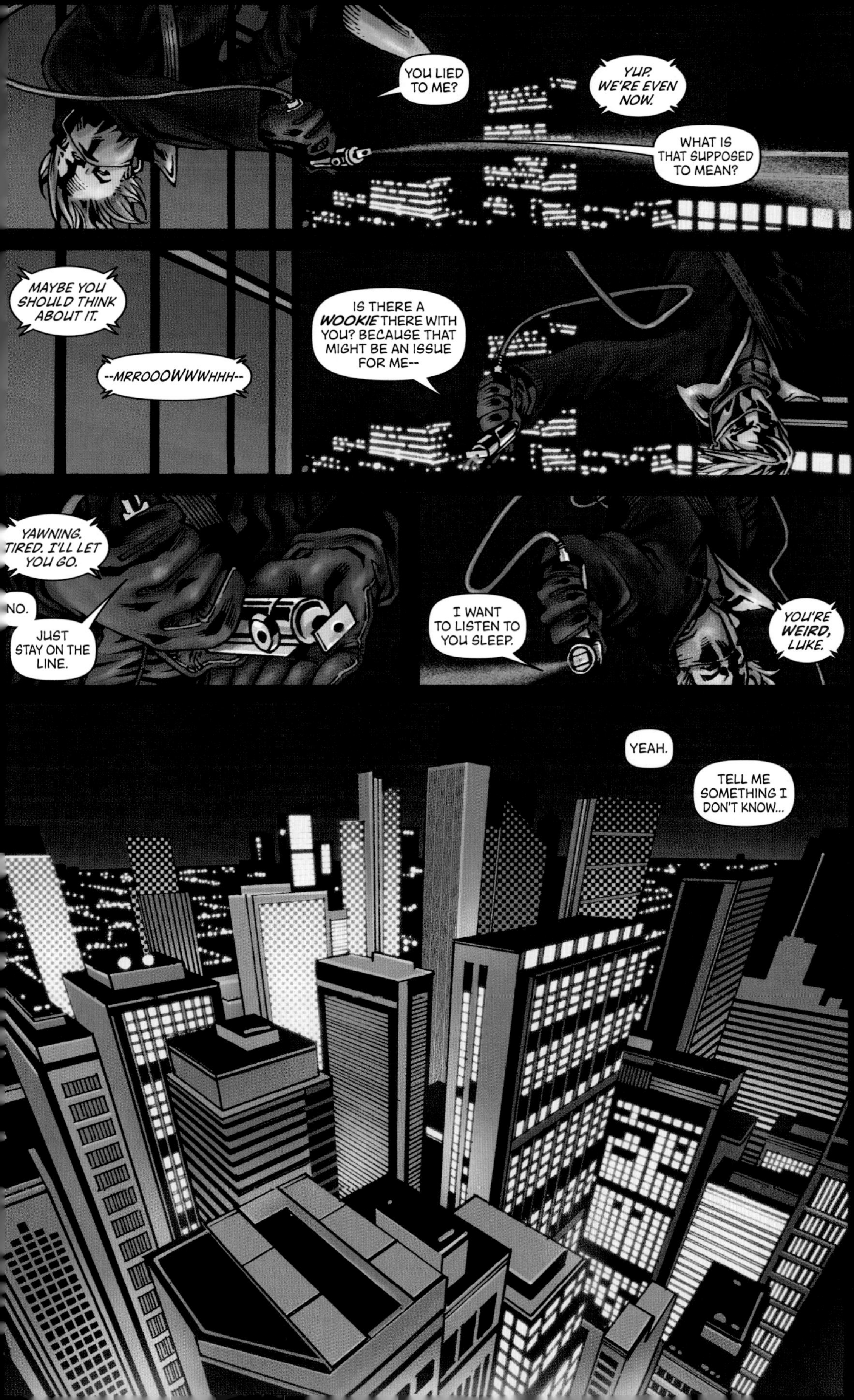
YOU LIED TO ME?
YUP. WE'RE EVEN NOW.
WHAT IS THAT SUPPOSED TO MEAN?
MAYBE YOU SHOULD THINK ABOUT IT.
--MRROOOWWWHHH--
IS THERE A WOOKIE THERE WITH YOU? BECAUSE THAT MIGHT BE AN ISSUE FOR ME--
YAWNING. TIRED. I'LL LET YOU GO.
NO.
JUST STAY ON THE LINE.
I WANT TO LISTEN TO YOU SLEEP.
YOU'RE WEIRD, LUKE.
YEAH.
TELL ME SOMETHING I DON'T KNOW...

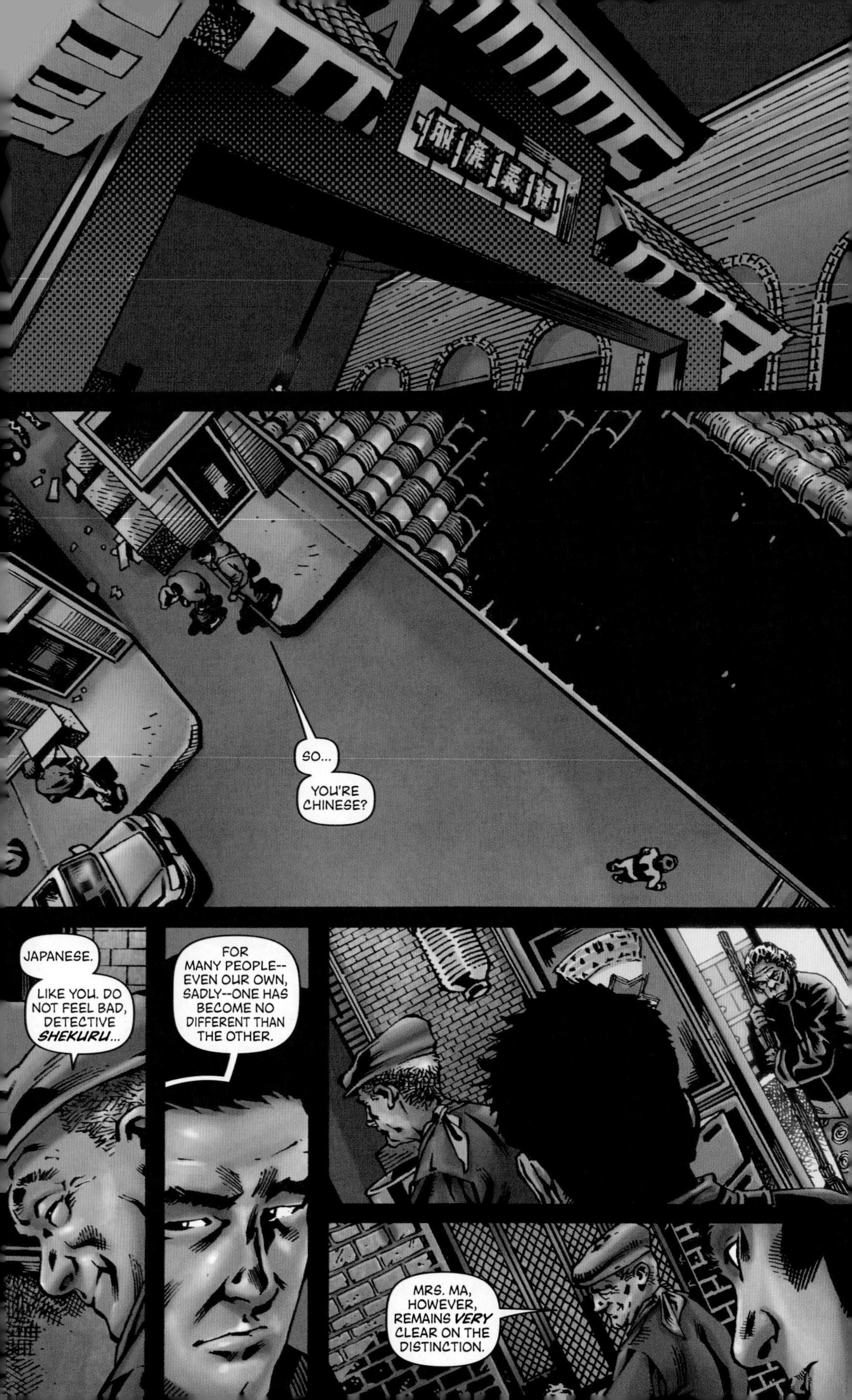
SO...
YOU'RE CHINESE?
JAPANESE.
LIKE YOU. DO NOT FEEL BAD, DETECTIVE SHEKURU...
FOR MANY PEOPLE-- EVEN OUR OWN, SADLY--ONE HAS BECOME NO DIFFERENT THAN THE OTHER.
MRS. MA, HOWEVER, REMAINS VERY CLEAR ON THE DISTINCTION.

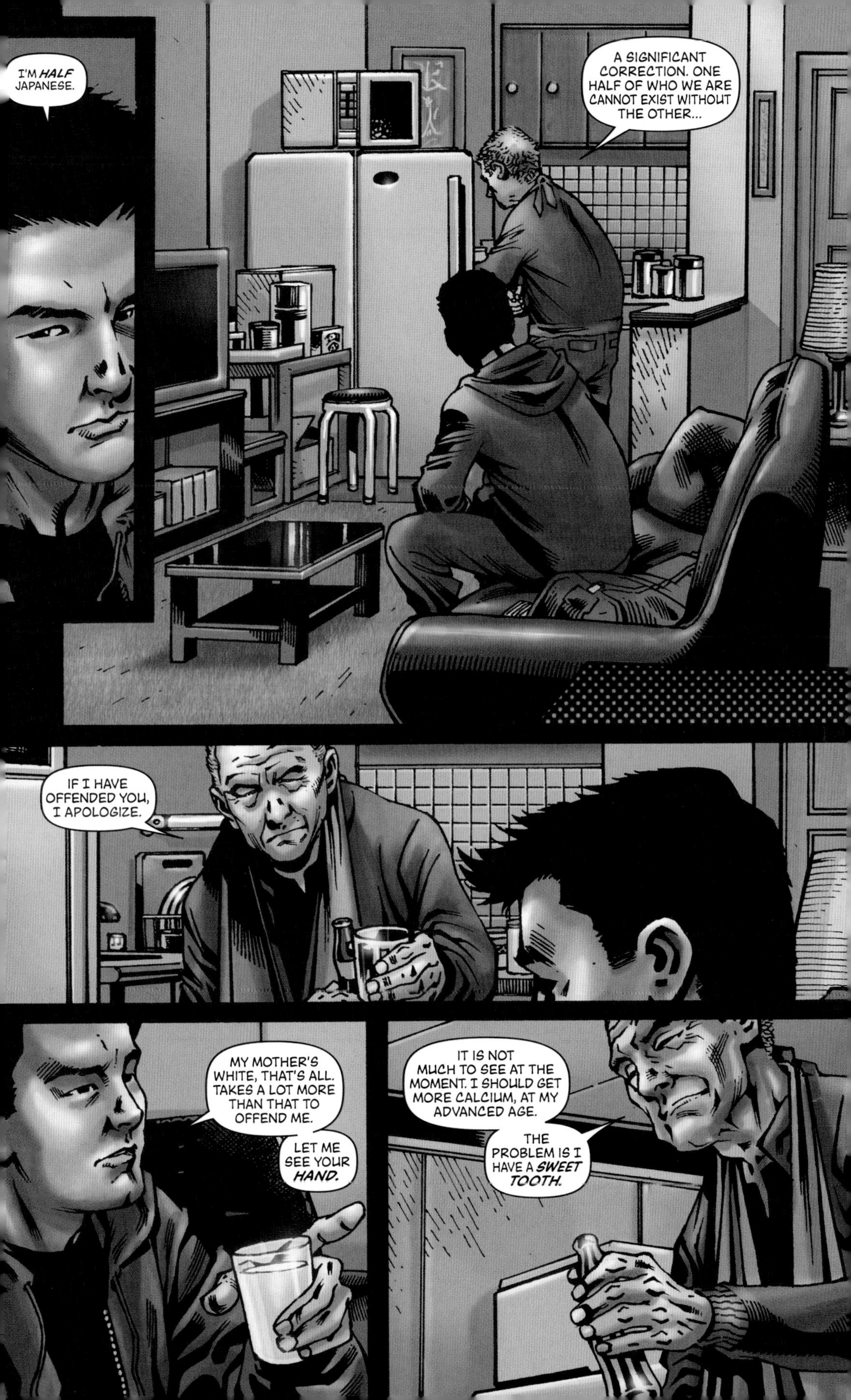
I'M HALF JAPANESE.
A SIGNIFICANT CORRECTION. ONE HALF OF WHO WE ARE CANNOT EXIST WITHOUT THE OTHER...
IF I HAVE OFFENDED YOU, I APOLOGIZE.
MY MOTHER'S WHITE, THAT'S ALL. TAKES A LOT MORE THAN THAT TO OFFEND ME.
LET ME SEE YOUR HAND.
IT IS NOT MUCH TO SEE AT THE MOMENT. I SHOULD GET MORE CALCIUM, AT MY ADVANCED AGE.
THE PROBLEM IS I HAVE A SWEET TOOTH.

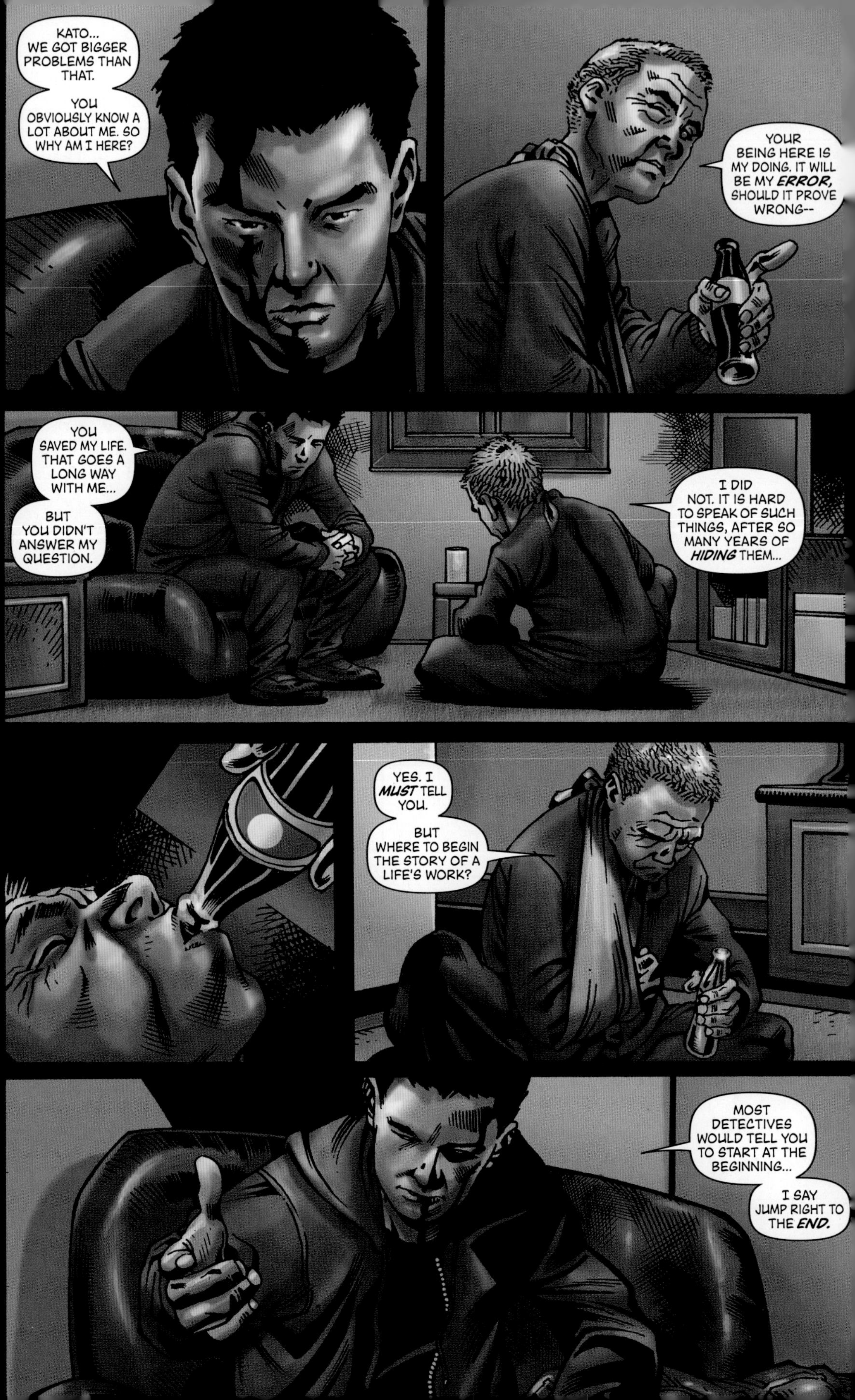
KATO... WE GOT BIGGER PROBLEMS THAN THAT.
YOU OBVIOUSLY KNOW A LOT ABOUT ME. SO WHY AM I HERE?
YOUR BEING HERE IS MY DOING. IT WILL BE MY ERROR, SHOULD IT PROVE WRONG--
YOU SAVED MY LIFE. THAT GOES A LONG WAY WITH ME...
BUT YOU DIDN'T ANSWER MY QUESTION.
I DID NOT. IT IS HARD TO SPEAK OF SUCH THINGS, AFTER SO MANY YEARS OF HIDING THEM...
YES. I MUST TELL YOU.
BUT WHERE TO BEGIN THE STORY OF A LIFE'S WORK?
MOST DETECTIVES WOULD TELL YOU TO START AT THE BEGINNING...
I SAY JUMP RIGHT TO THE END.

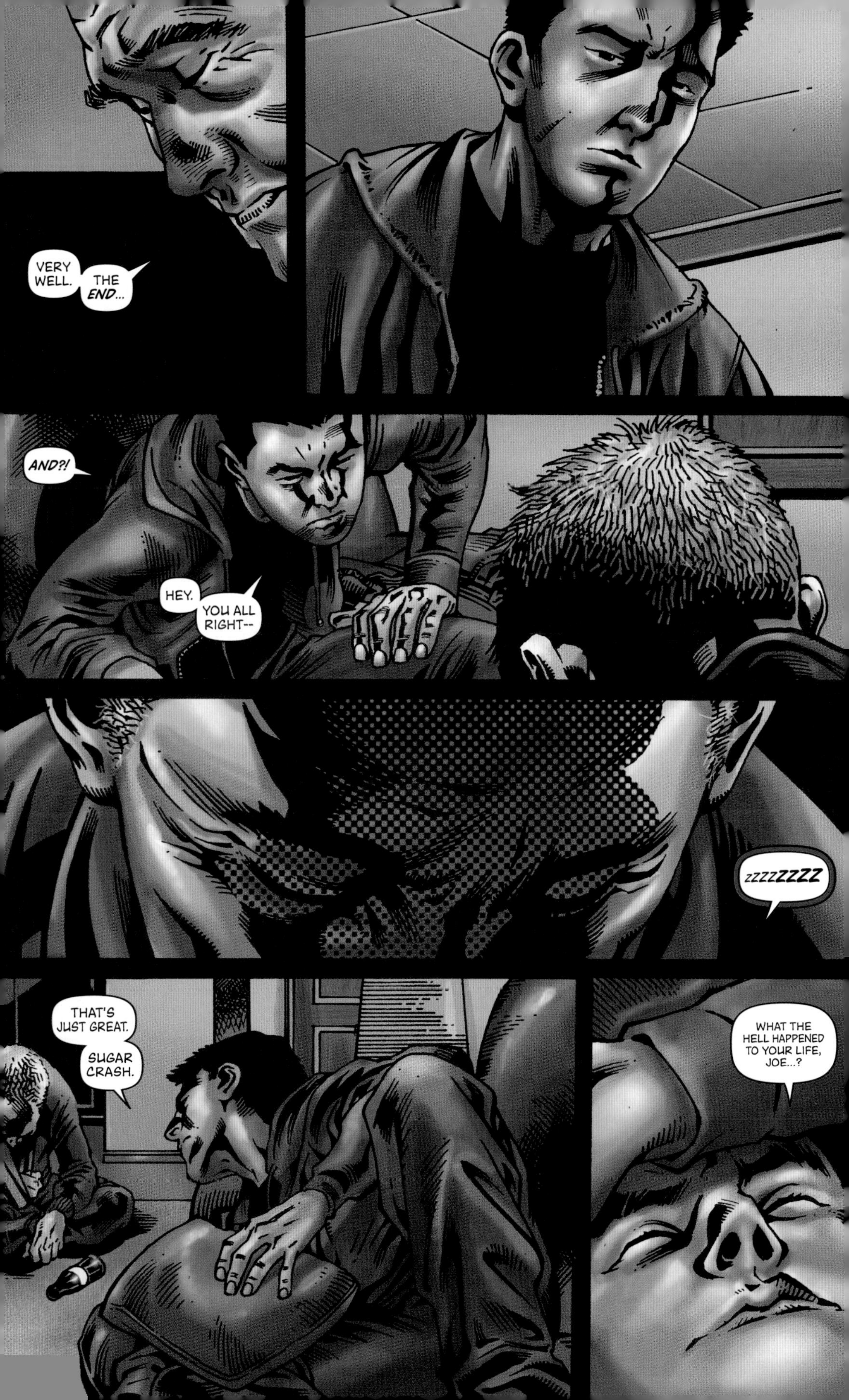
VERY WELL.
THE END...
AND?!
HEY.
YOU ALL RIGHT--
zzzzZZZZ
THAT'S JUST GREAT.
SUGAR CRASH.
WHAT THE HELL HAPPENED TO YOUR LIFE, JOE...?

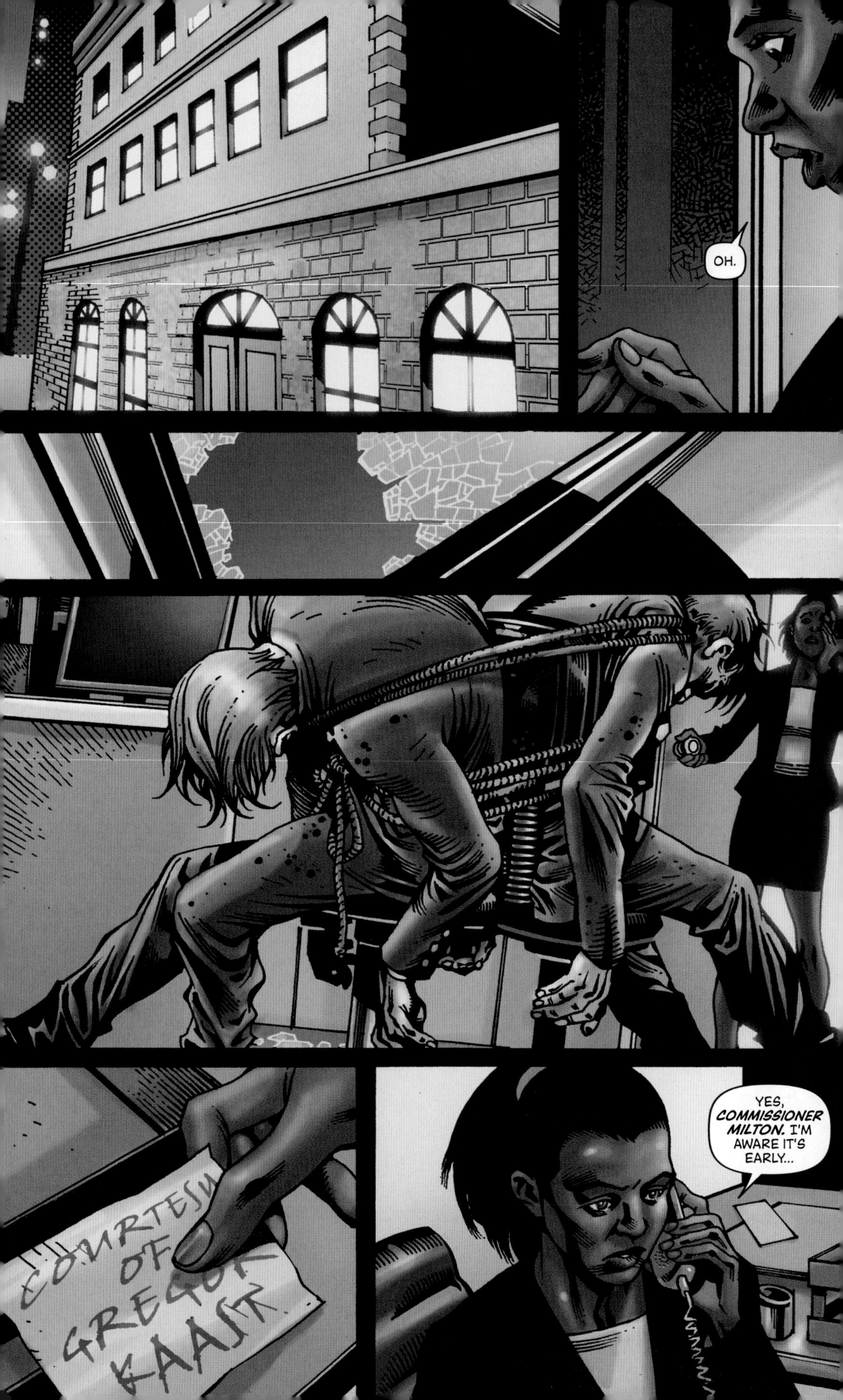
OH.
COURTESY OF GREGOR KAAST
YES, COMMISSIONER MILTON. I'M AWARE IT'S EARLY...

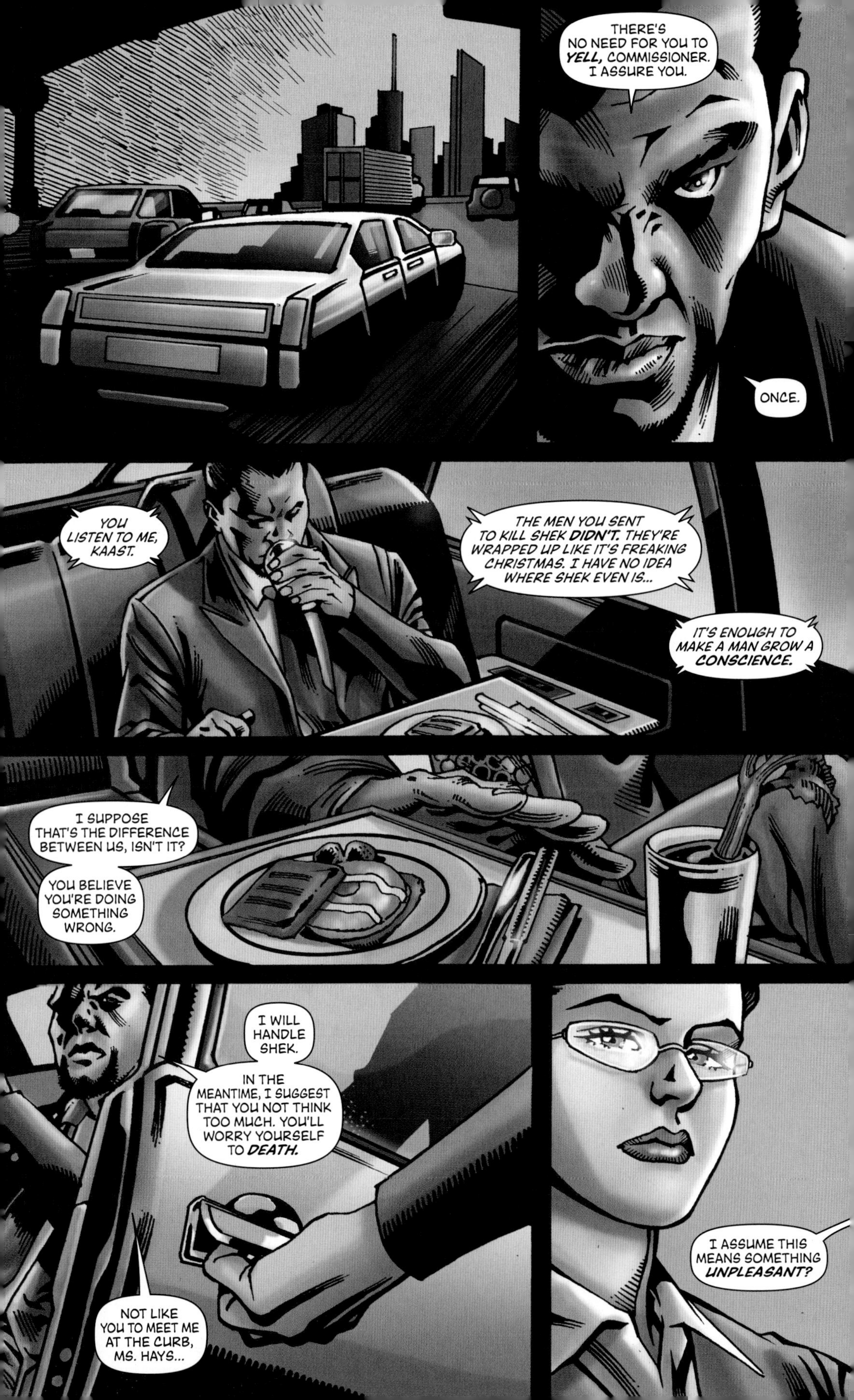
THERE'S NO NEED FOR YOU TO *YELL,* COMMISSIONER. I ASSURE YOU.
ONCE.
YOU LISTEN TO ME, KAAST.
THE MEN YOU SENT TO KILL SHEK *DIDN'T.* THEY'RE WRAPPED UP LIKE IT'S FREAKING CHRISTMAS. I HAVE NO IDEA WHERE SHEK EVEN IS...
IT'S ENOUGH TO MAKE A MAN GROW A *CONSCIENCE.*
I SUPPOSE THAT'S THE DIFFERENCE BETWEEN US, ISN'T IT?
YOU BELIEVE YOU'RE DOING SOMETHING WRONG.
I WILL HANDLE SHEK.
IN THE MEANTIME, I SUGGEST THAT YOU NOT THINK TOO MUCH. YOU'LL WORRY YOURSELF TO *DEATH.*
NOT LIKE YOU TO MEET ME AT THE CURB, MS. HAYS...
I ASSUME THIS MEANS SOMETHING *UNPLEASANT?*

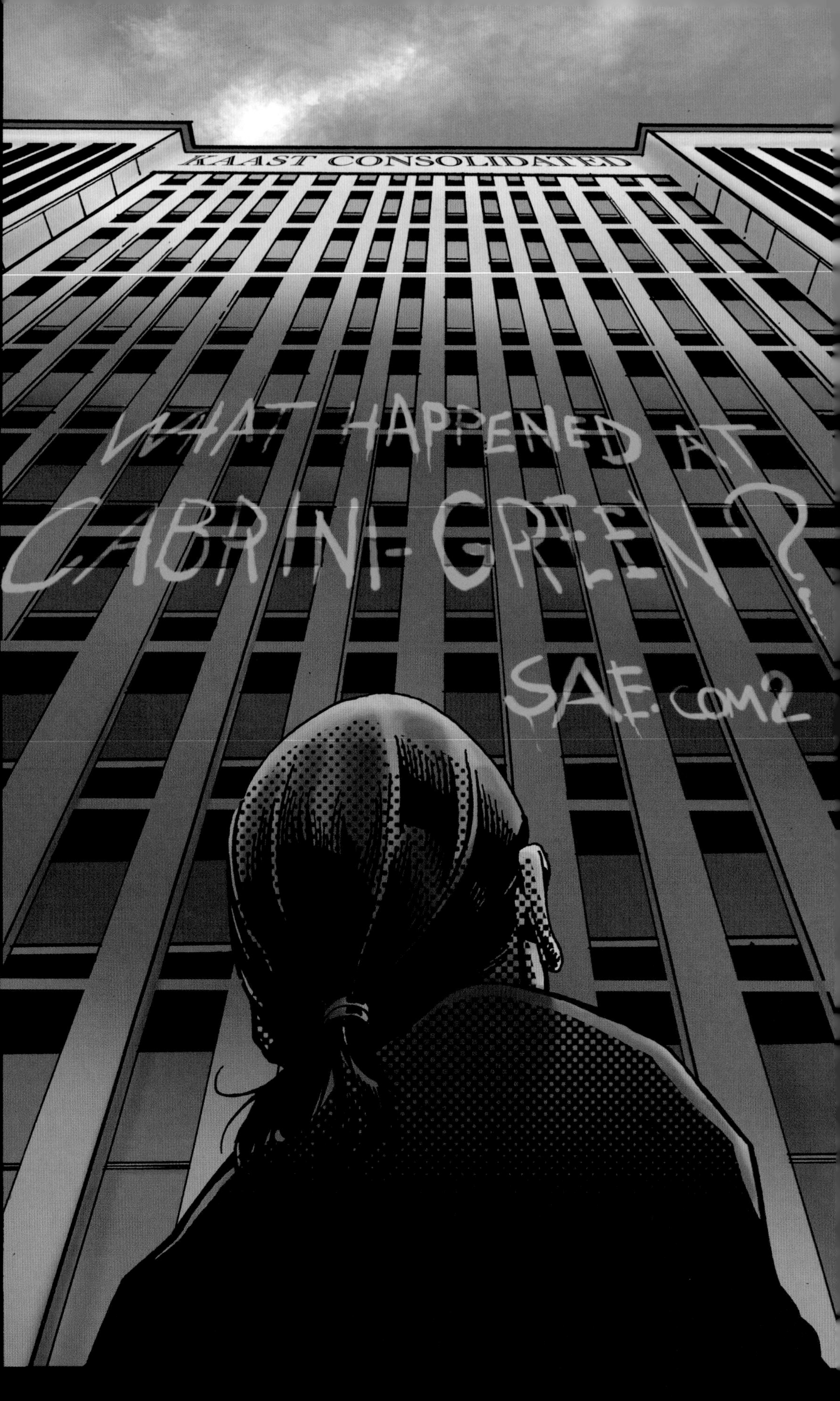
KAAST CONSOLIDATED
WHAT HAPPENED AT
CABRINI-GREEN?
SAE.COM2

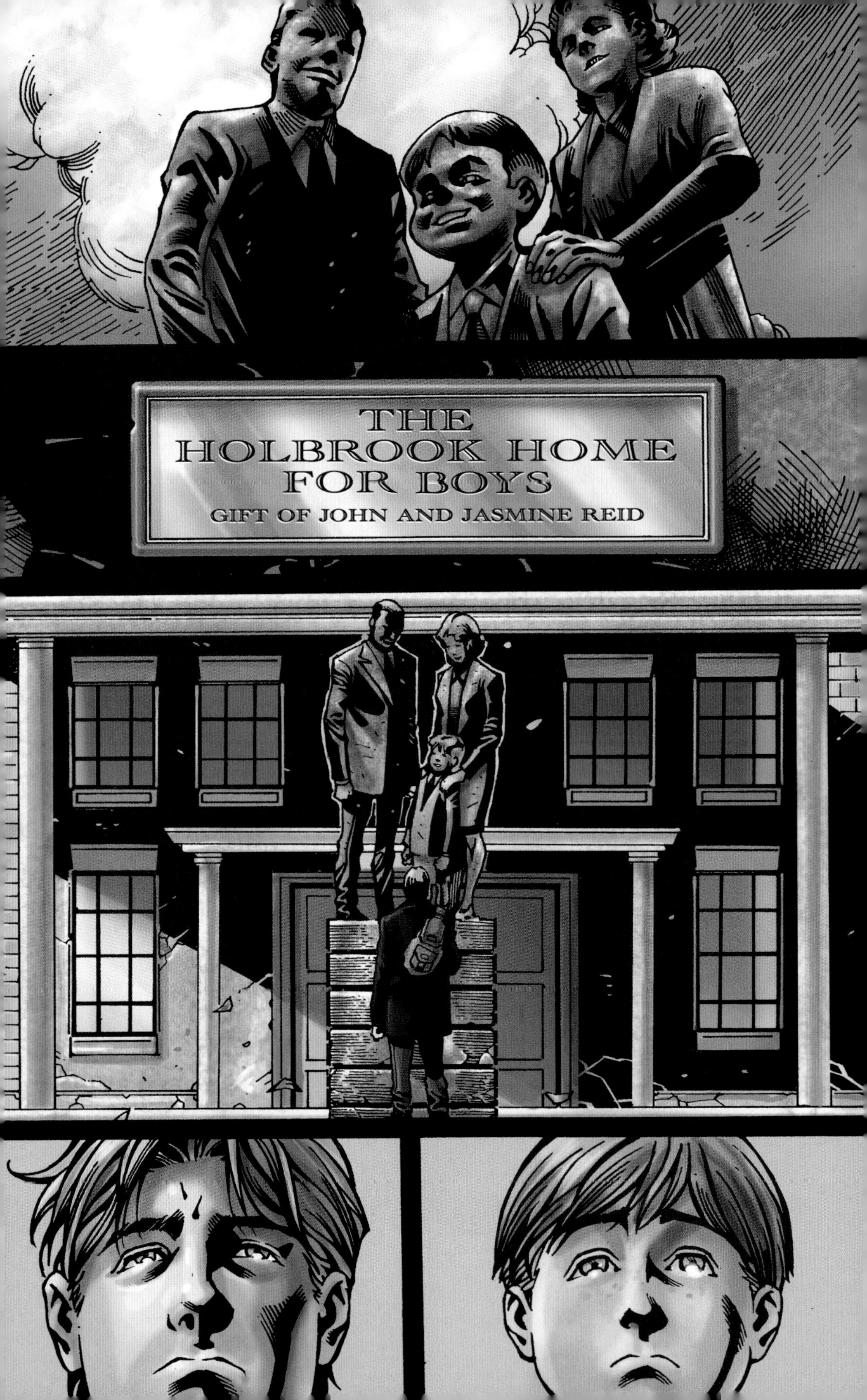
THE
HOLBROOK HOME
FOR BOYS
GIFT OF JOHN AND JASMINE REID

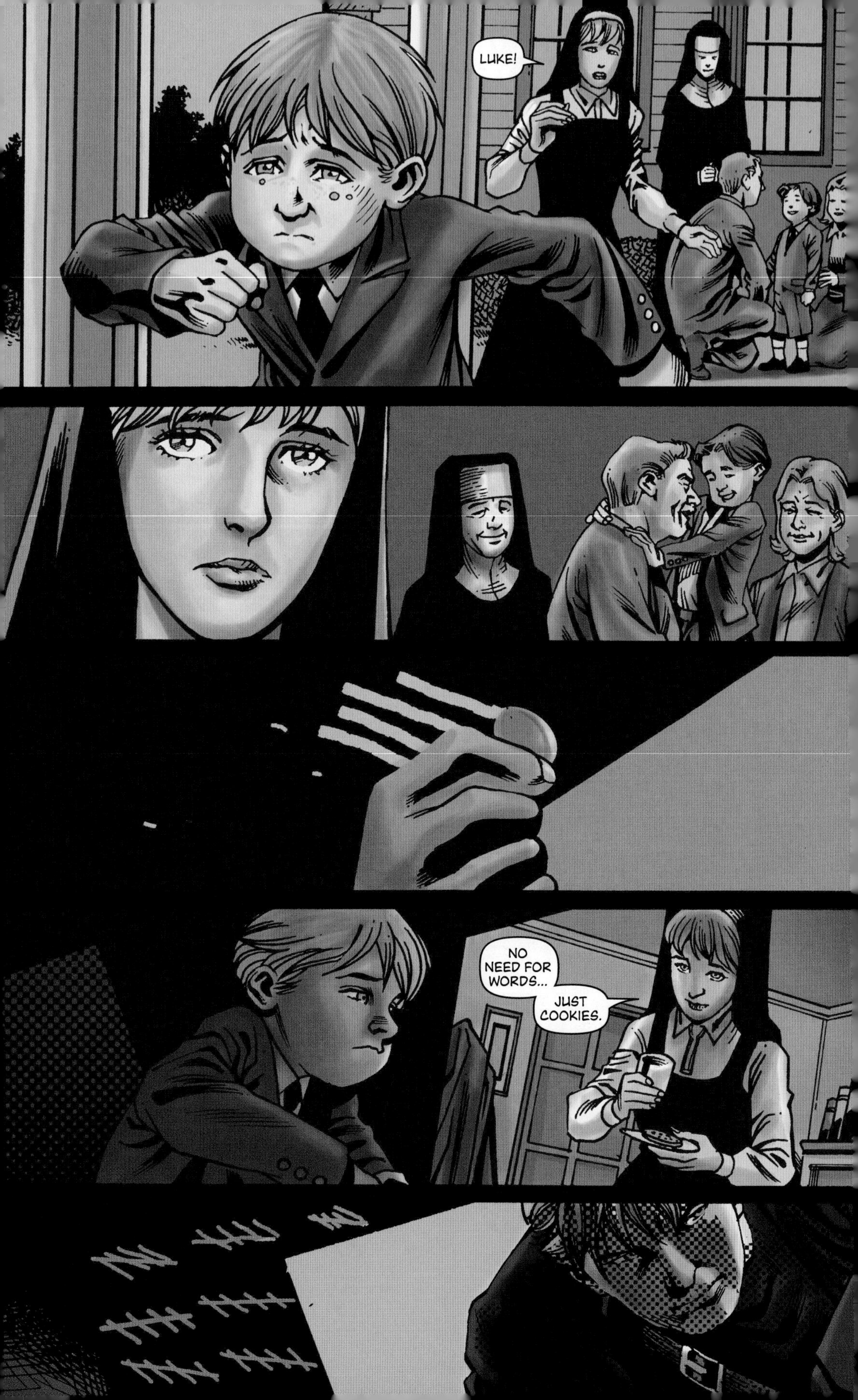
LUKE!
NO NEED FOR WORDS...
JUST COOKIES.

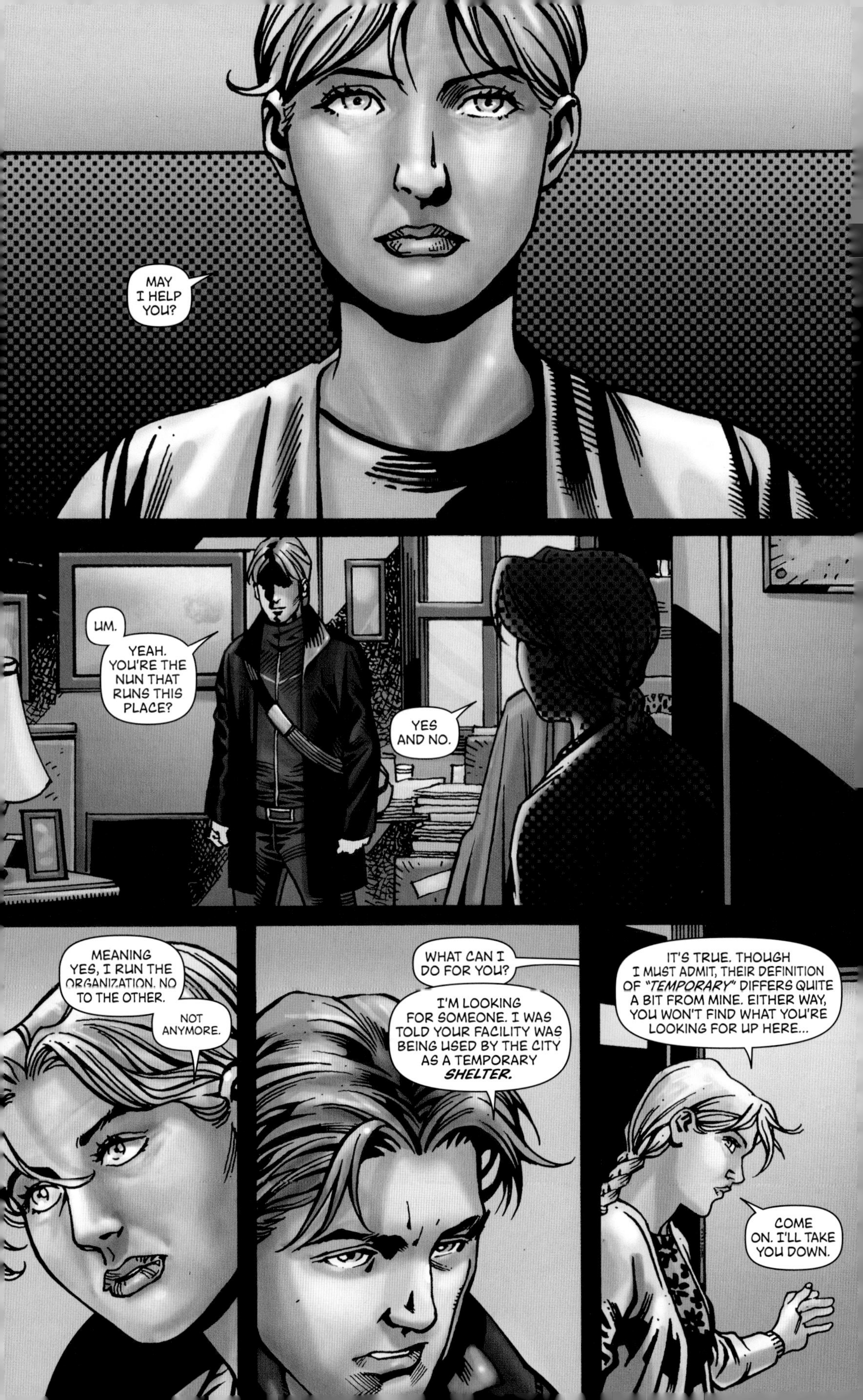

MAY I HELP YOU?
UM.
YEAH. YOU'RE THE NUN THAT RUNS THIS PLACE?
YES AND NO.
MEANING YES, I RUN THE ORGANIZATION. NO TO THE OTHER.
NOT ANYMORE.
WHAT CAN I DO FOR YOU?
I'M LOOKING FOR SOMEONE. I WAS TOLD YOUR FACILITY WAS BEING USED BY THE CITY AS A TEMPORARY SHELTER.
IT'S TRUE. THOUGH I MUST ADMIT, THEIR DEFINITION OF "TEMPORARY" DIFFERS QUITE A BIT FROM MINE. EITHER WAY, YOU WON'T FIND WHAT YOU'RE LOOKING FOR UP HERE...
COME ON. I'LL TAKE YOU DOWN.

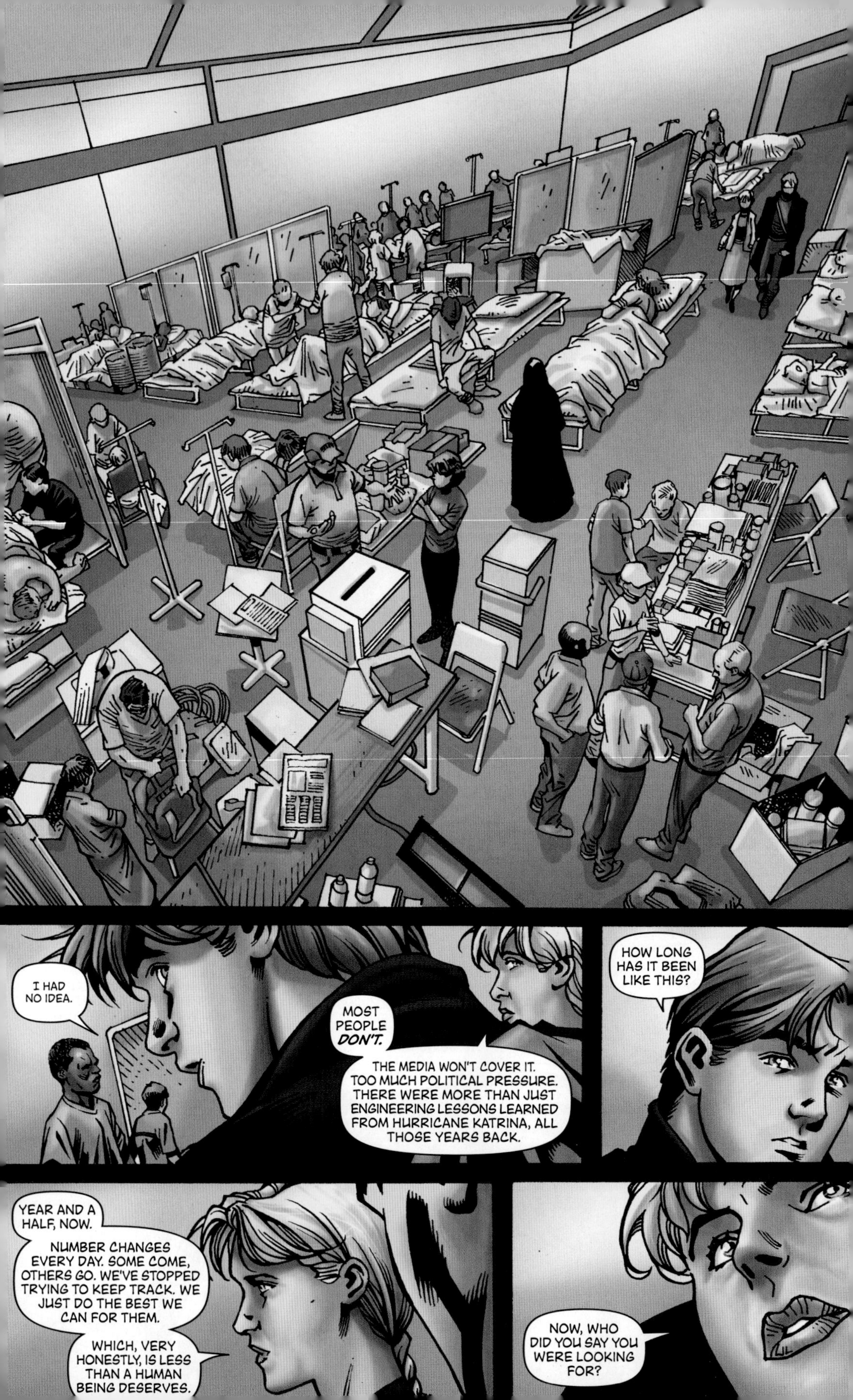
I HAD NO IDEA.
MOST PEOPLE DON'T.
THE MEDIA WON'T COVER IT. TOO MUCH POLITICAL PRESSURE. THERE WERE MORE THAN JUST ENGINEERING LESSONS LEARNED FROM HURRICANE KATRINA, ALL THOSE YEARS BACK.
HOW LONG HAS IT BEEN LIKE THIS?
YEAR AND A HALF, NOW.
NUMBER CHANGES EVERY DAY. SOME COME, OTHERS GO. WE'VE STOPPED TRYING TO KEEP TRACK. WE JUST DO THE BEST WE CAN FOR THEM.
WHICH, VERY HONESTLY, IS LESS THAN A HUMAN BEING DESERVES.
NOW, WHO DID YOU SAY YOU WERE LOOKING FOR?

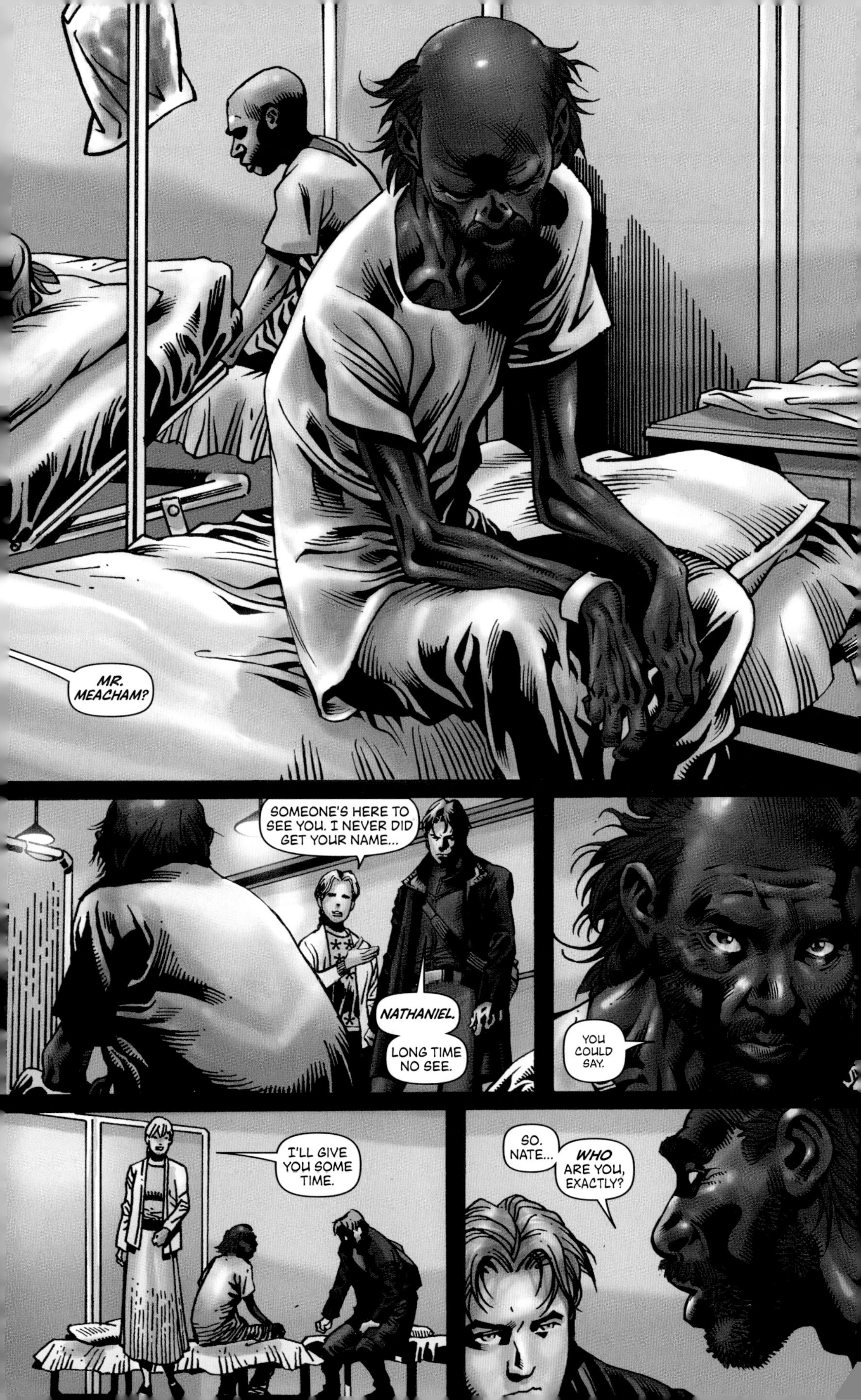
MR. MEACHAM?
SOMEONE'S HERE TO SEE YOU. I NEVER DID GET YOUR NAME...
NATHANIEL.
LONG TIME NO SEE.
YOU COULD SAY.
I'LL GIVE YOU SOME TIME.
SO. NATE...
WHO ARE YOU, EXACTLY?

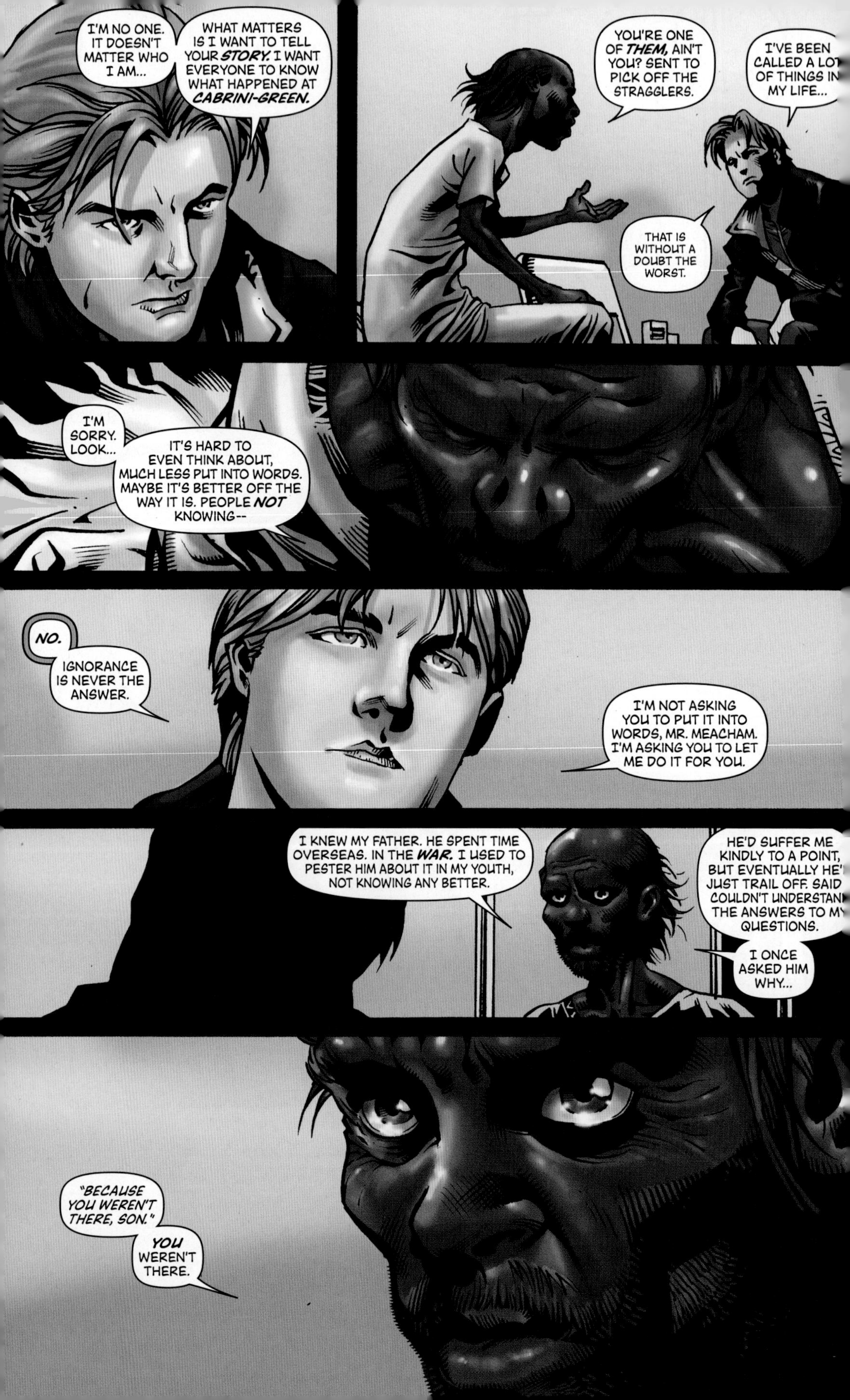
I'M NO ONE. IT DOESN'T MATTER WHO I AM...
WHAT MATTERS IS I WANT TO TELL YOUR STORY. I WANT EVERYONE TO KNOW WHAT HAPPENED AT CABRINI-GREEN.
YOU'RE ONE OF THEM, AIN'T YOU? SENT TO PICK OFF THE STRAGGLERS.
I'VE BEEN CALLED A LOT OF THINGS IN MY LIFE...
THAT IS WITHOUT A DOUBT THE WORST.
I'M SORRY. LOOK...
IT'S HARD TO EVEN THINK ABOUT, MUCH LESS PUT INTO WORDS. MAYBE IT'S BETTER OFF THE WAY IT IS. PEOPLE NOT KNOWING--
NO.
IGNORANCE IS NEVER THE ANSWER.
I'M NOT ASKING YOU TO PUT IT INTO WORDS, MR. MEACHAM. I'M ASKING YOU TO LET ME DO IT FOR YOU.
I KNEW MY FATHER. HE SPENT TIME OVERSEAS. IN THE WAR. I USED TO PESTER HIM ABOUT IT IN MY YOUTH, NOT KNOWING ANY BETTER.
HE'D SUFFER ME KINDLY TO A POINT, BUT EVENTUALLY HE' JUST TRAIL OFF. SAID COULDN'T UNDERSTAN THE ANSWERS TO M QUESTIONS.
I ONCE ASKED HIM WHY...
"BECAUSE YOU WEREN'T THERE, SON."
YOU WEREN'T THERE.

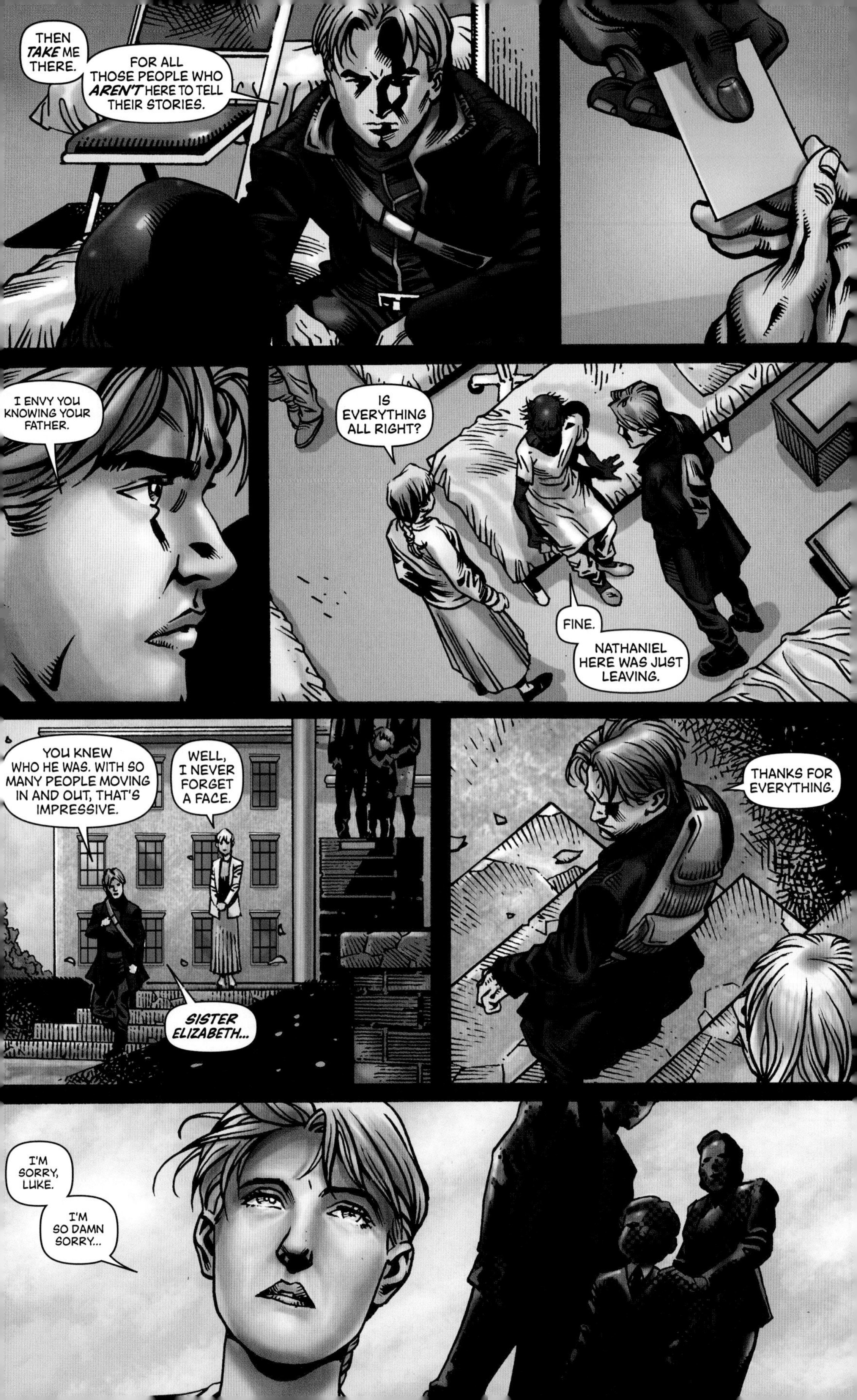
THEN *TAKE* ME THERE.
FOR ALL THOSE PEOPLE WHO *AREN'T* HERE TO TELL THEIR STORIES.
I ENVY YOU KNOWING YOUR FATHER.
IS EVERYTHING ALL RIGHT?
FINE.
NATHANIEL HERE WAS JUST LEAVING.
YOU KNEW WHO HE WAS. WITH SO MANY PEOPLE MOVING IN AND OUT, THAT'S IMPRESSIVE.
WELL, I NEVER FORGET A FACE.
SISTER ELIZABETH...
THANKS FOR EVERYTHING.
I'M SORRY, LUKE.
I'M SO DAMN SORRY...

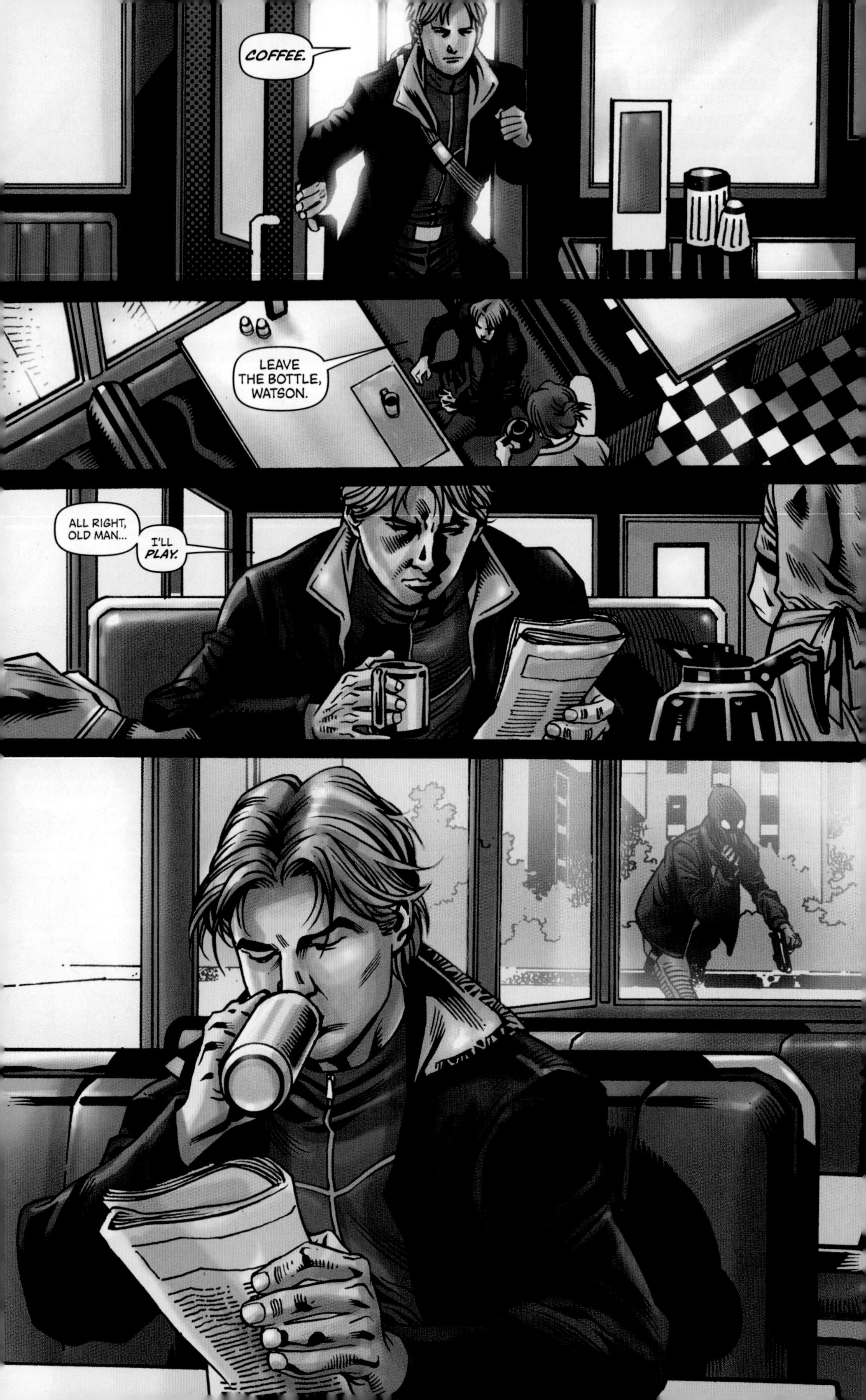
COFFEE.
LEAVE THE BOTTLE, WATSON.
ALL RIGHT, OLD MAN...
I'LL PLAY.

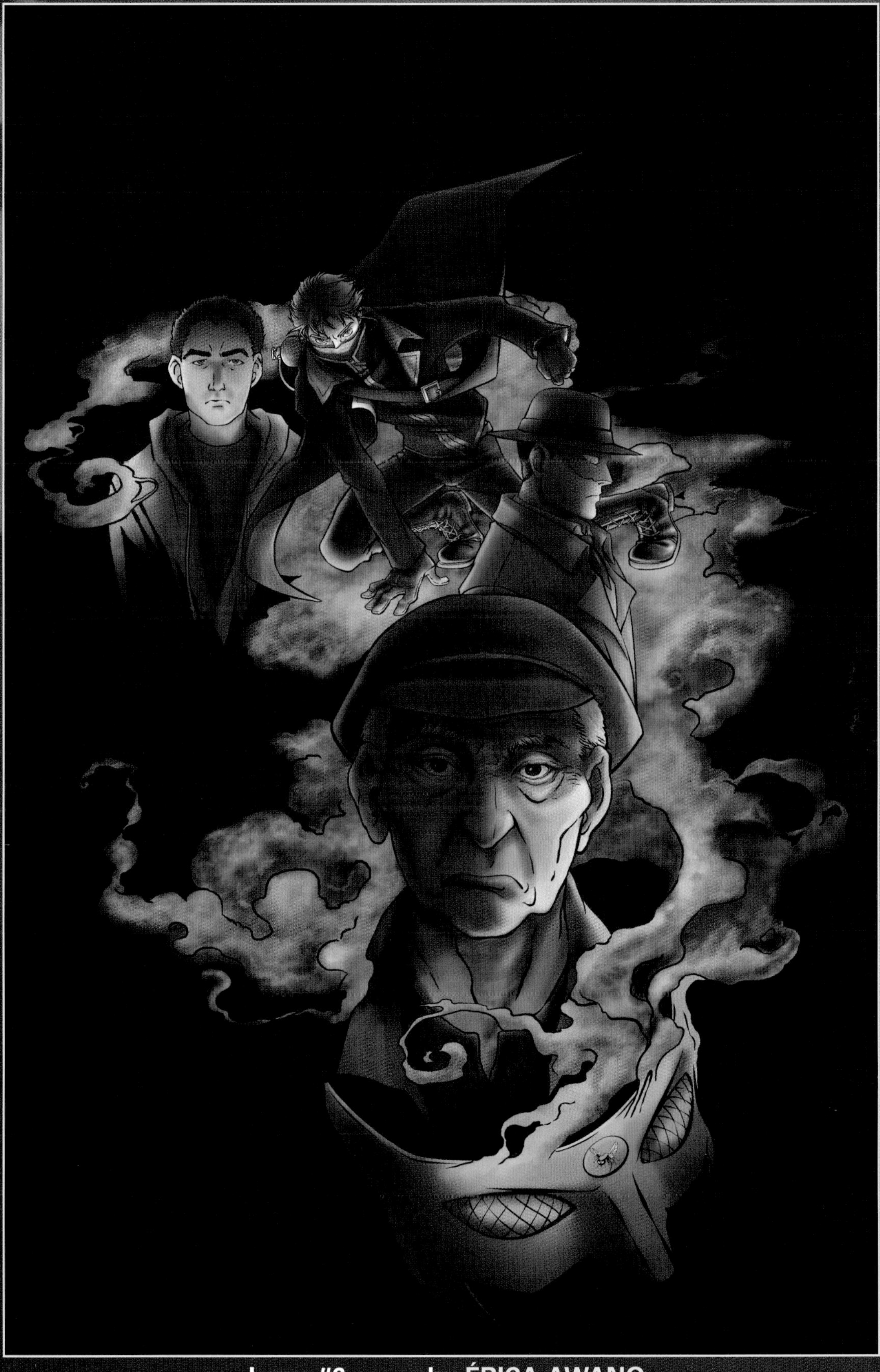

Issue #6 cover by ÉRICA AWANO

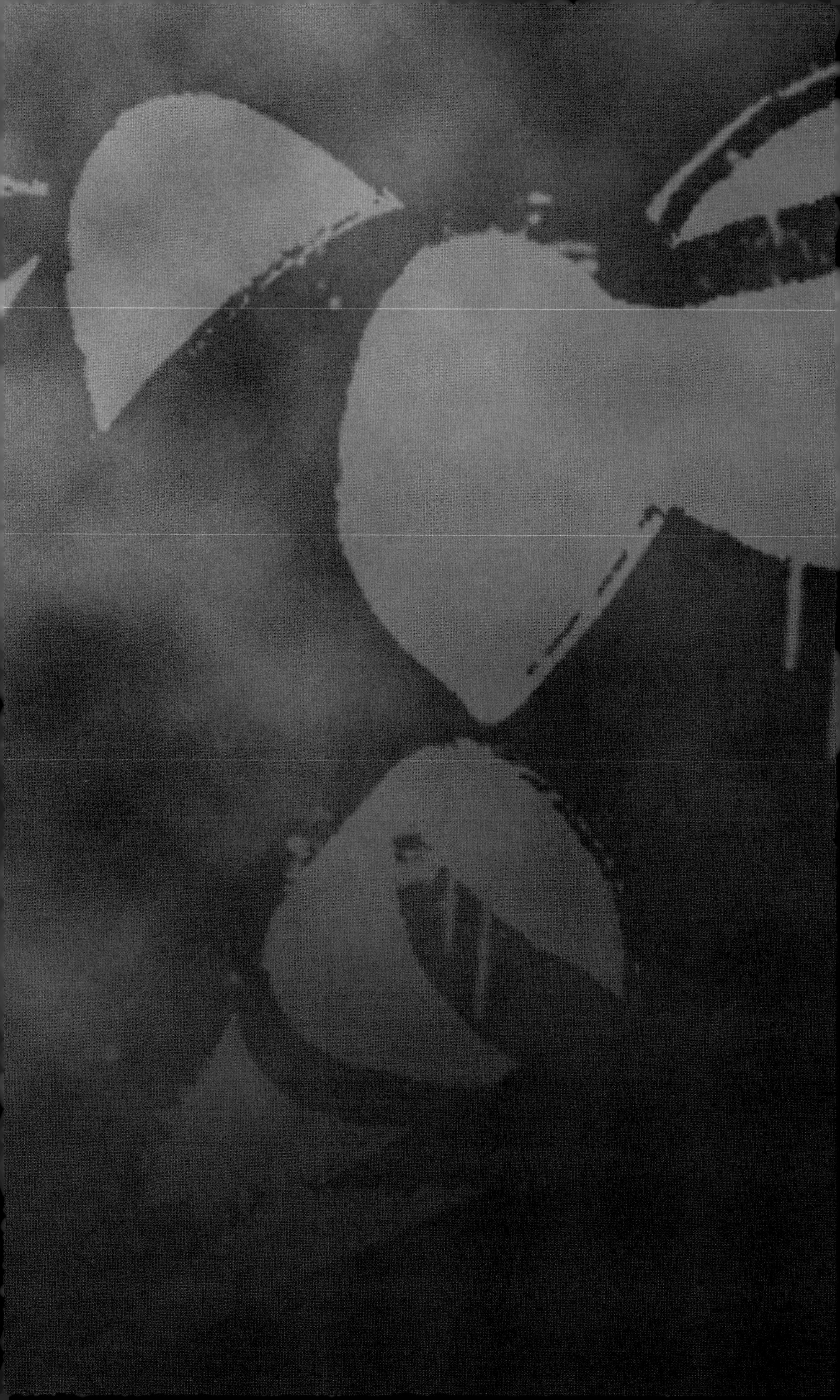

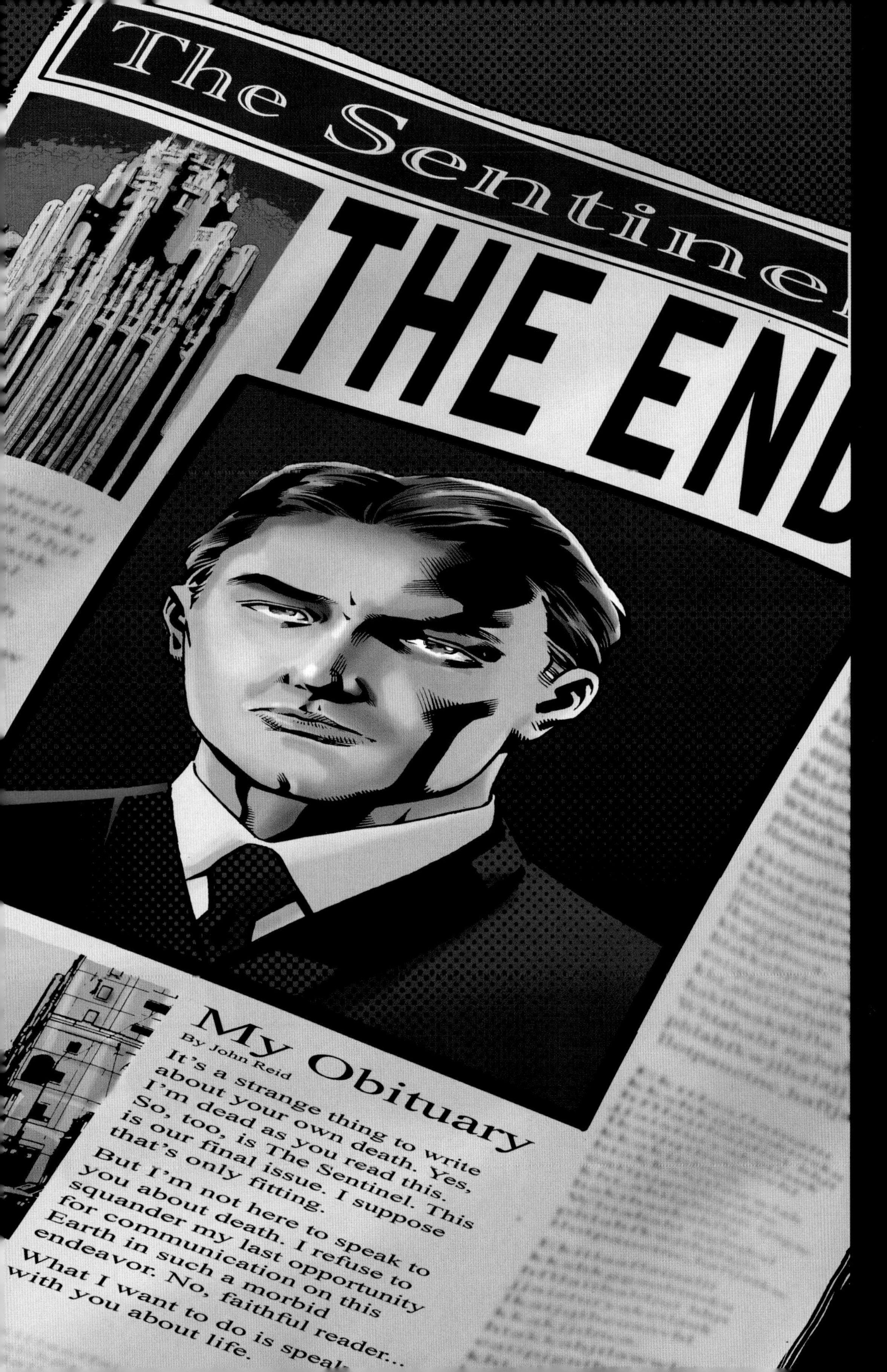

The Sentine
THE EN
My Obituary
By John Reid
It's a strange thing to write
about your own death. Yes,
I'm dead as you read this.
So, too, is The Sentinel. This
is our final issue. I suppose
that's only fitting.
But I'm not here to speak to
you about death. I refuse to
squander my last opportunity
for communication on this
Earth in such a morbid
endeavor. No, faithful reader...
What I want to do is spea
with you about life.

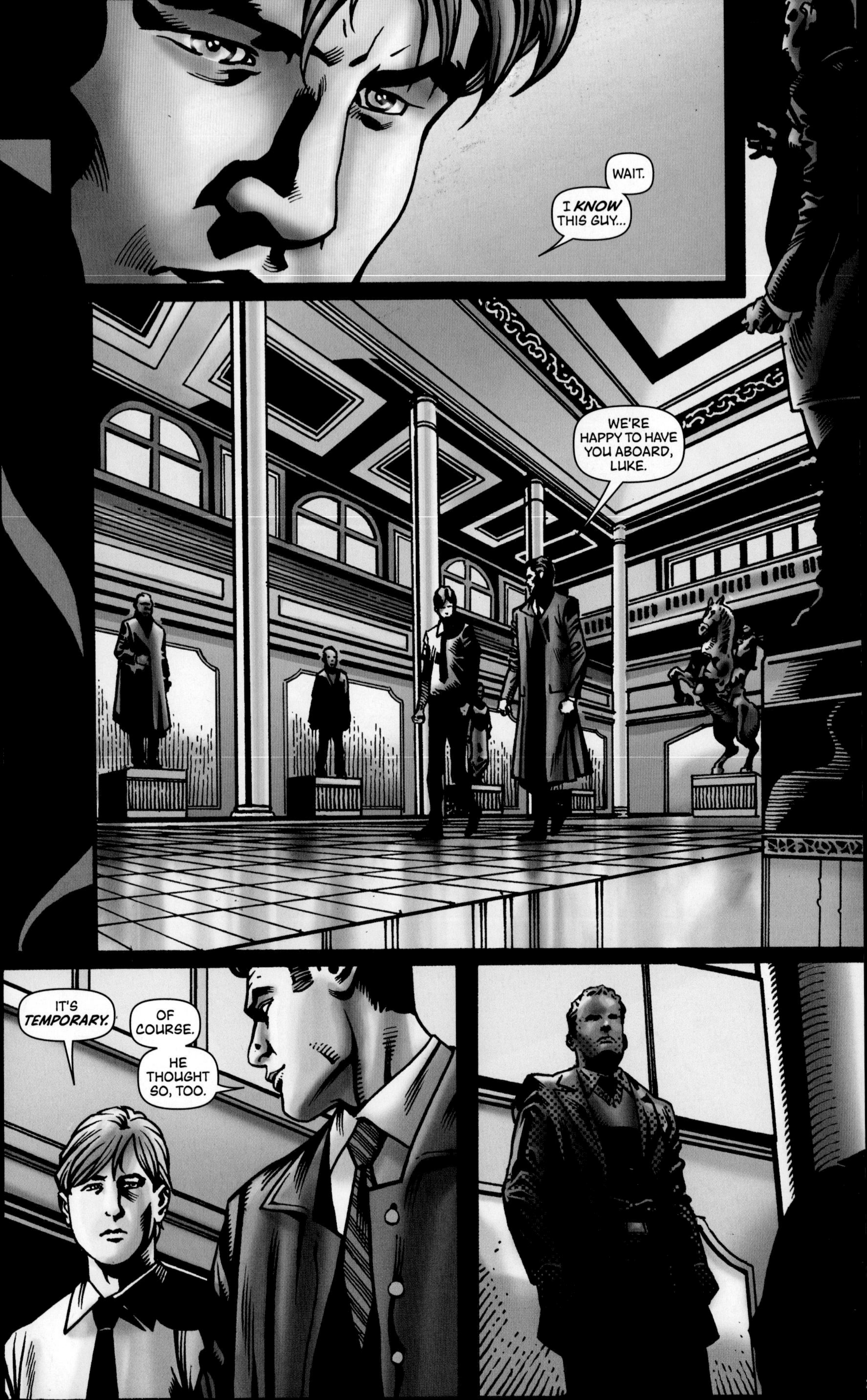
WAIT.
I *KNOW* THIS GUY...
WE'RE HAPPY TO HAVE YOU ABOARD, LUKE.
IT'S *TEMPORARY.*
OF COURSE.
HE THOUGHT SO, TOO.

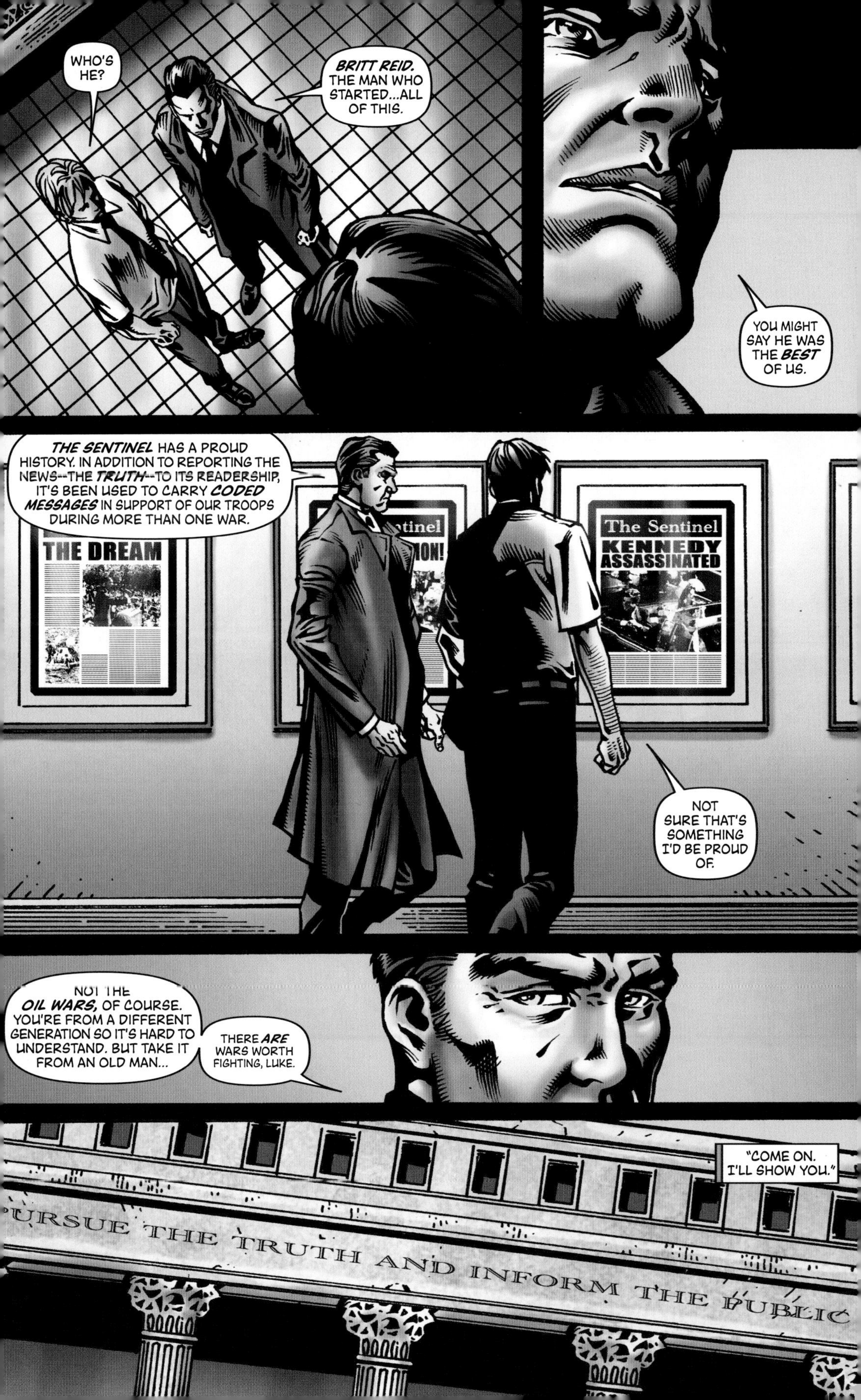
WHO'S HE?
BRITT REID. THE MAN WHO STARTED...ALL OF THIS.
YOU MIGHT SAY HE WAS THE BEST OF US.
THE SENTINEL HAS A PROUD HISTORY. IN ADDITION TO REPORTING THE NEWS--THE TRUTH--TO ITS READERSHIP, IT'S BEEN USED TO CARRY CODED MESSAGES IN SUPPORT OF OUR TROOPS DURING MORE THAN ONE WAR.
THE DREAM
The Sentinel
KENNEDY ASSASSINATED
NOT SURE THAT'S SOMETHING I'D BE PROUD OF.
NOT THE OIL WARS, OF COURSE. YOU'RE FROM A DIFFERENT GENERATION SO IT'S HARD TO UNDERSTAND. BUT TAKE IT FROM AN OLD MAN...
THERE ARE WARS WORTH FIGHTING, LUKE.
"COME ON. I'LL SHOW YOU."
PURSUE THE TRUTH AND INFORM THE PUBLIC

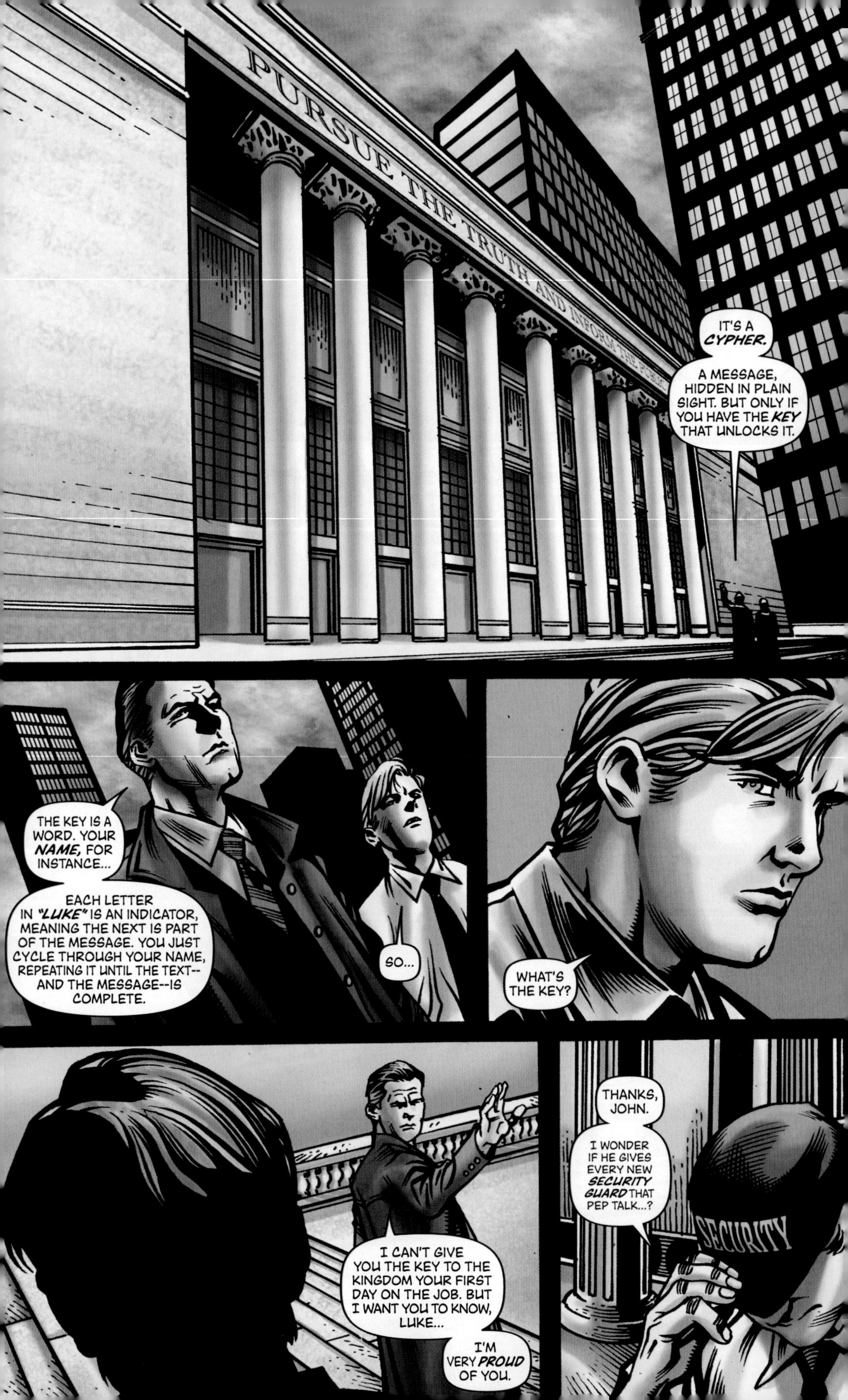
PURSUE THE TRUTH AND INFORM THE PUBLIC
IT'S A CYPHER.
A MESSAGE, HIDDEN IN PLAIN SIGHT. BUT ONLY IF YOU HAVE THE KEY THAT UNLOCKS IT.
THE KEY IS A WORD. YOUR NAME, FOR INSTANCE...
EACH LETTER IN "LUKE" IS AN INDICATOR, MEANING THE NEXT IS PART OF THE MESSAGE. YOU JUST CYCLE THROUGH YOUR NAME, REPEATING IT UNTIL THE TEXT--AND THE MESSAGE--IS COMPLETE.
SO...
WHAT'S THE KEY?
I CAN'T GIVE YOU THE KEY TO THE KINGDOM YOUR FIRST DAY ON THE JOB. BUT I WANT YOU TO KNOW, LUKE...
I'M VERY PROUD OF YOU.
THANKS, JOHN.
I WONDER IF HE GIVES EVERY NEW SECURITY GUARD THAT PEP TALK...?
SECURITY

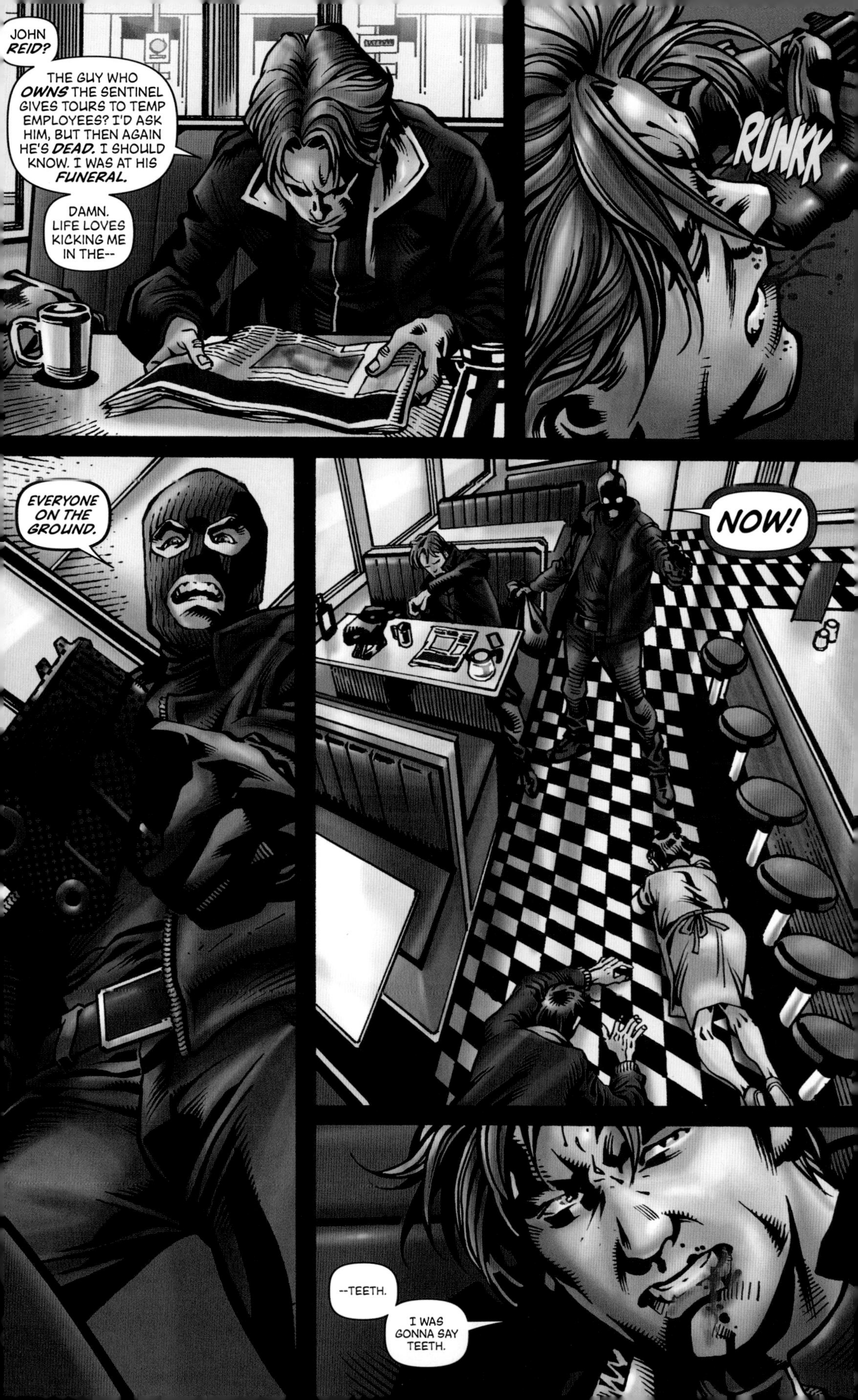
JOHN REID?
THE GUY WHO OWNS THE SENTINEL GIVES TOURS TO TEMP EMPLOYEES? I'D ASK HIM, BUT THEN AGAIN HE'S DEAD. I SHOULD KNOW. I WAS AT HIS FUNERAL.
DAMN. LIFE LOVES KICKING ME IN THE--
RUNKK
EVERYONE ON THE GROUND.
NOW!
--TEETH.
I WAS GONNA SAY TEETH.

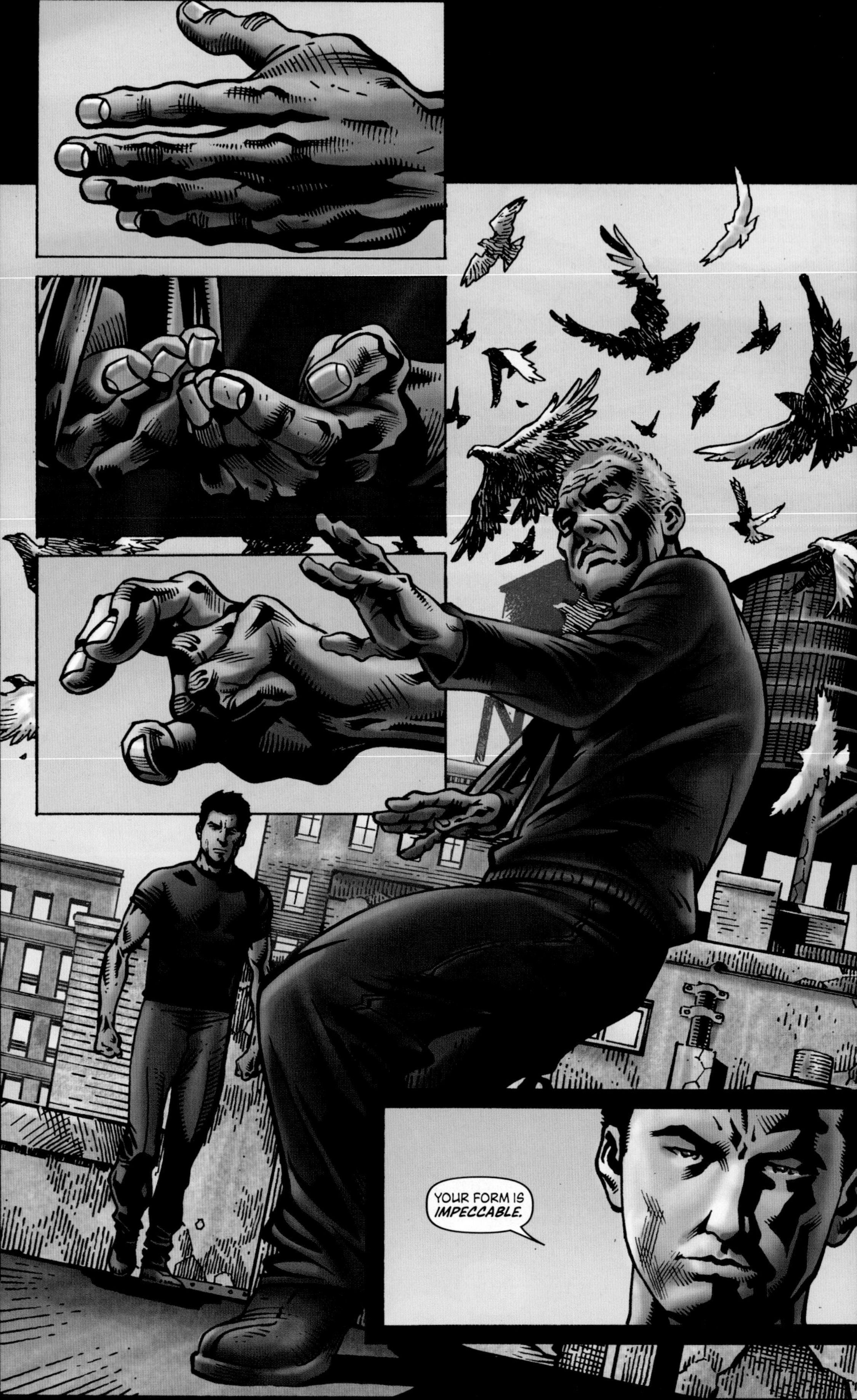
YOUR FORM IS *IMPECCABLE.*

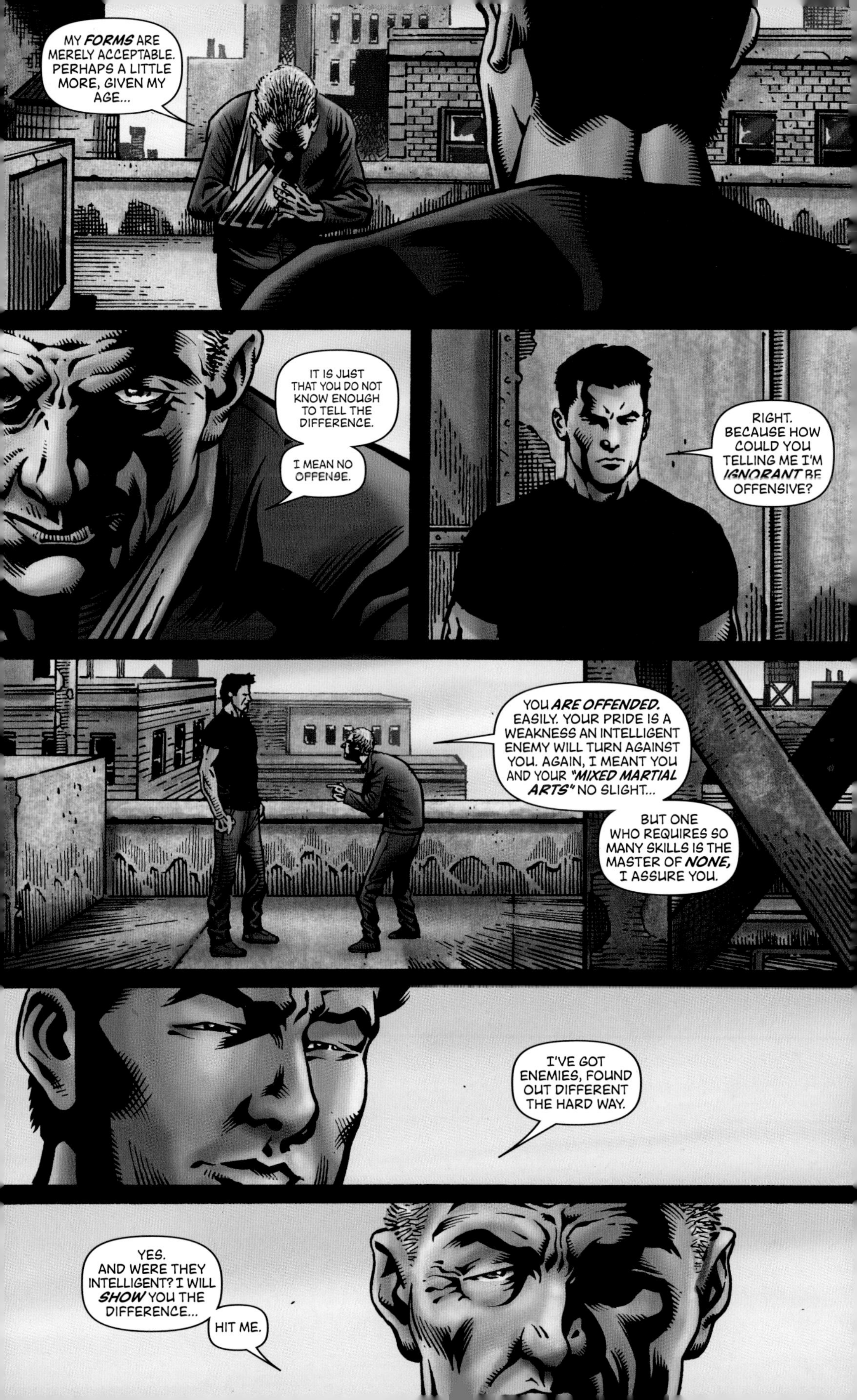

MY FORMS ARE MERELY ACCEPTABLE. PERHAPS A LITTLE MORE, GIVEN MY AGE...
IT IS JUST THAT YOU DO NOT KNOW ENOUGH TO TELL THE DIFFERENCE.
I MEAN NO OFFENSE.
RIGHT. BECAUSE HOW COULD YOU TELLING ME I'M IGNORANT BE OFFENSIVE?
YOU ARE OFFENDED. EASILY. YOUR PRIDE IS A WEAKNESS AN INTELLIGENT ENEMY WILL TURN AGAINST YOU. AGAIN, I MEANT YOU AND YOUR "MIXED MARTIAL ARTS" NO SLIGHT...
BUT ONE WHO REQUIRES SO MANY SKILLS IS THE MASTER OF NONE, I ASSURE YOU.
I'VE GOT ENEMIES, FOUND OUT DIFFERENT THE HARD WAY.
YES. AND WERE THEY INTELLIGENT? I WILL SHOW YOU THE DIFFERENCE...
HIT ME.

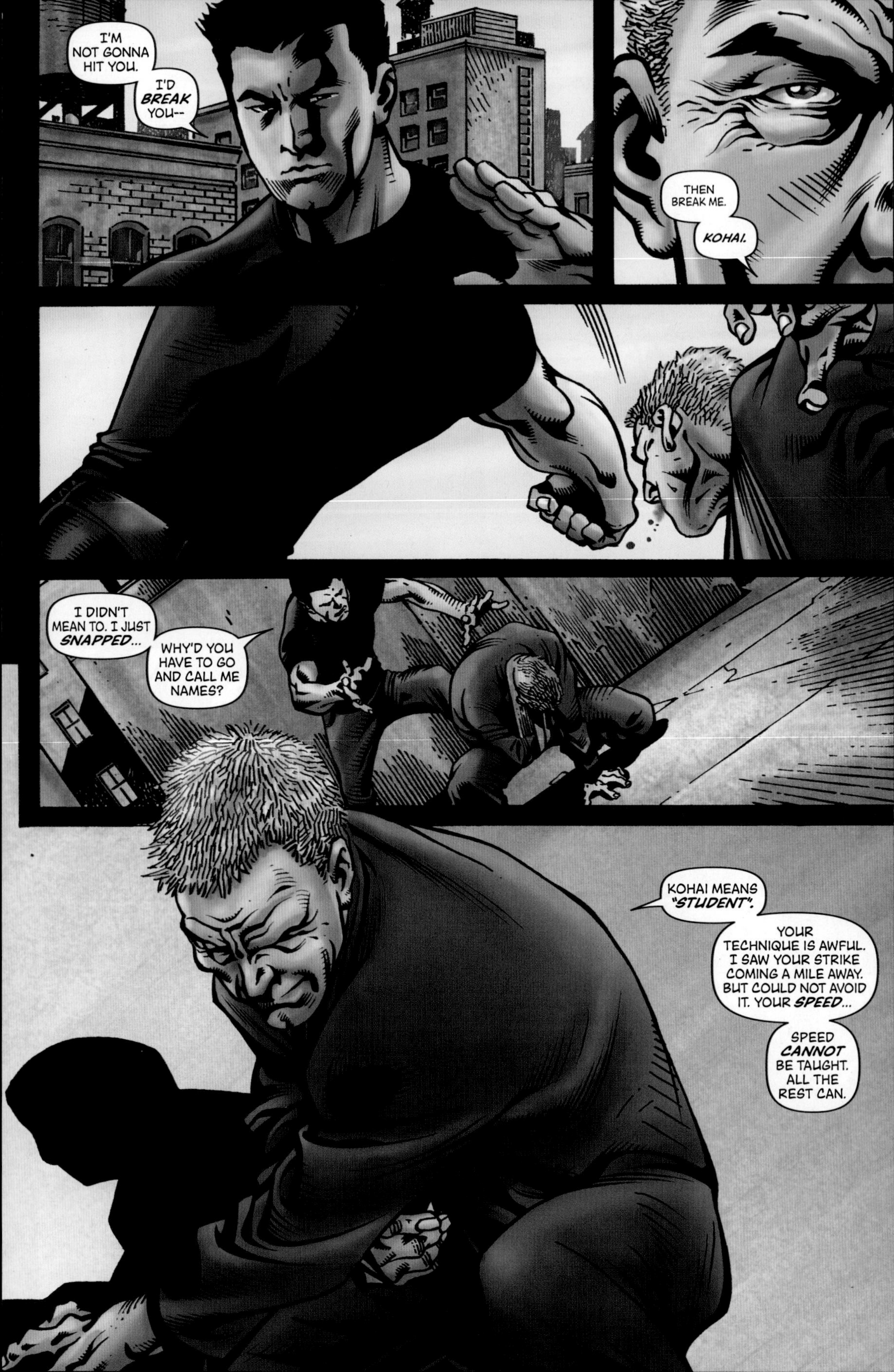
I'M NOT GONNA HIT YOU.
I'D *BREAK* YOU--
THEN BREAK ME.
KOHAI.
I DIDN'T MEAN TO. I JUST *SNAPPED*...
WHY'D YOU HAVE TO GO AND CALL ME NAMES?
KOHAI MEANS *"STUDENT"*.
YOUR TECHNIQUE IS AWFUL. I SAW YOUR STRIKE COMING A MILE AWAY. BUT COULD NOT AVOID IT. YOUR *SPEED*...
SPEED *CANNOT* BE TAUGHT. ALL THE REST CAN.

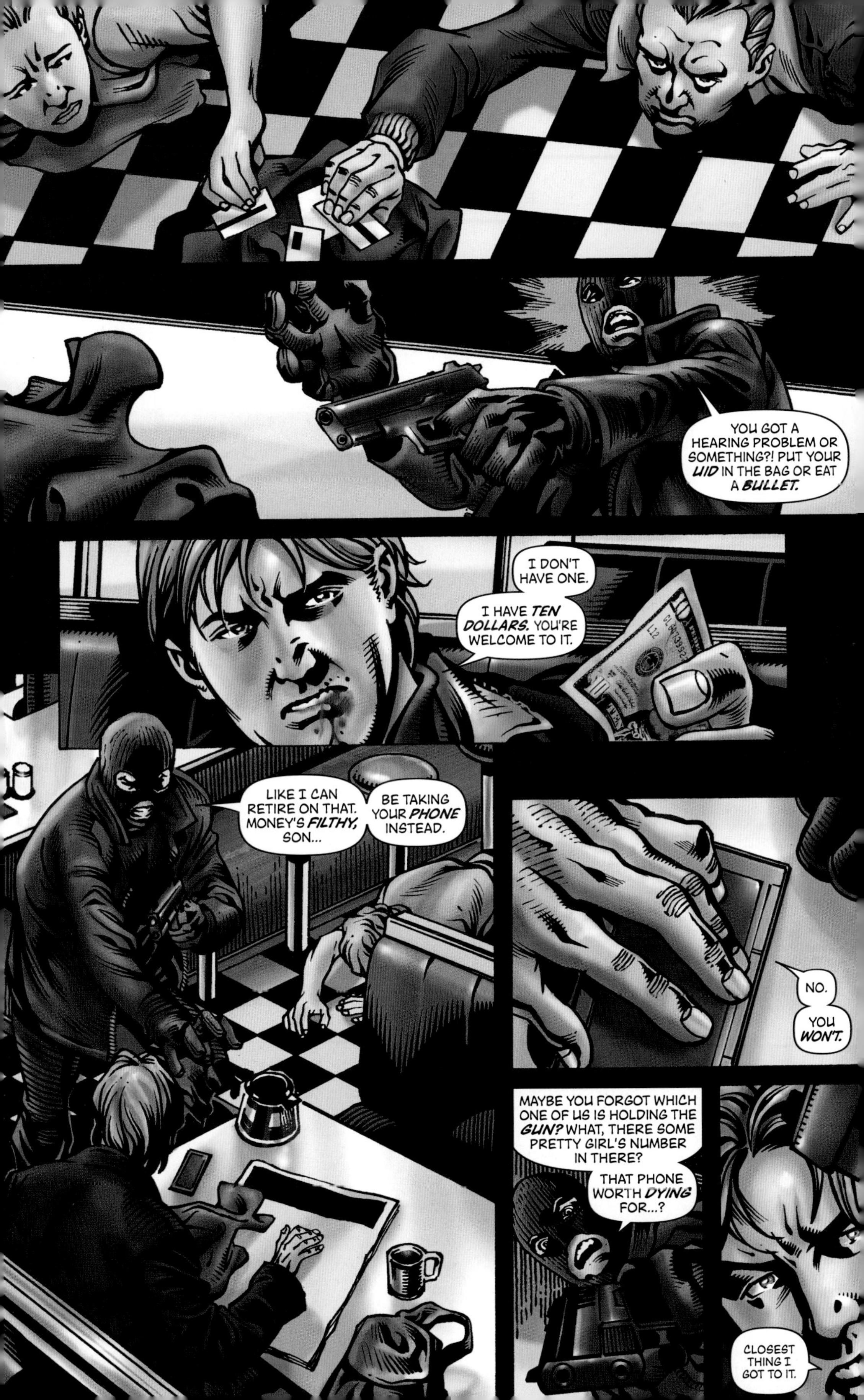
YOU GOT A HEARING PROBLEM OR SOMETHING?! PUT YOUR UID IN THE BAG OR EAT A BULLET.
I DON'T HAVE ONE.
I HAVE TEN DOLLARS. YOU'RE WELCOME TO IT.
LIKE I CAN RETIRE ON THAT. MONEY'S FILTHY, SON...
BE TAKING YOUR PHONE INSTEAD.
NO.
YOU WON'T.
MAYBE YOU FORGOT WHICH ONE OF US IS HOLDING THE GUN? WHAT, THERE SOME PRETTY GIRL'S NUMBER IN THERE?
THAT PHONE WORTH DYING FOR...?
CLOSEST THING I GOT TO IT.

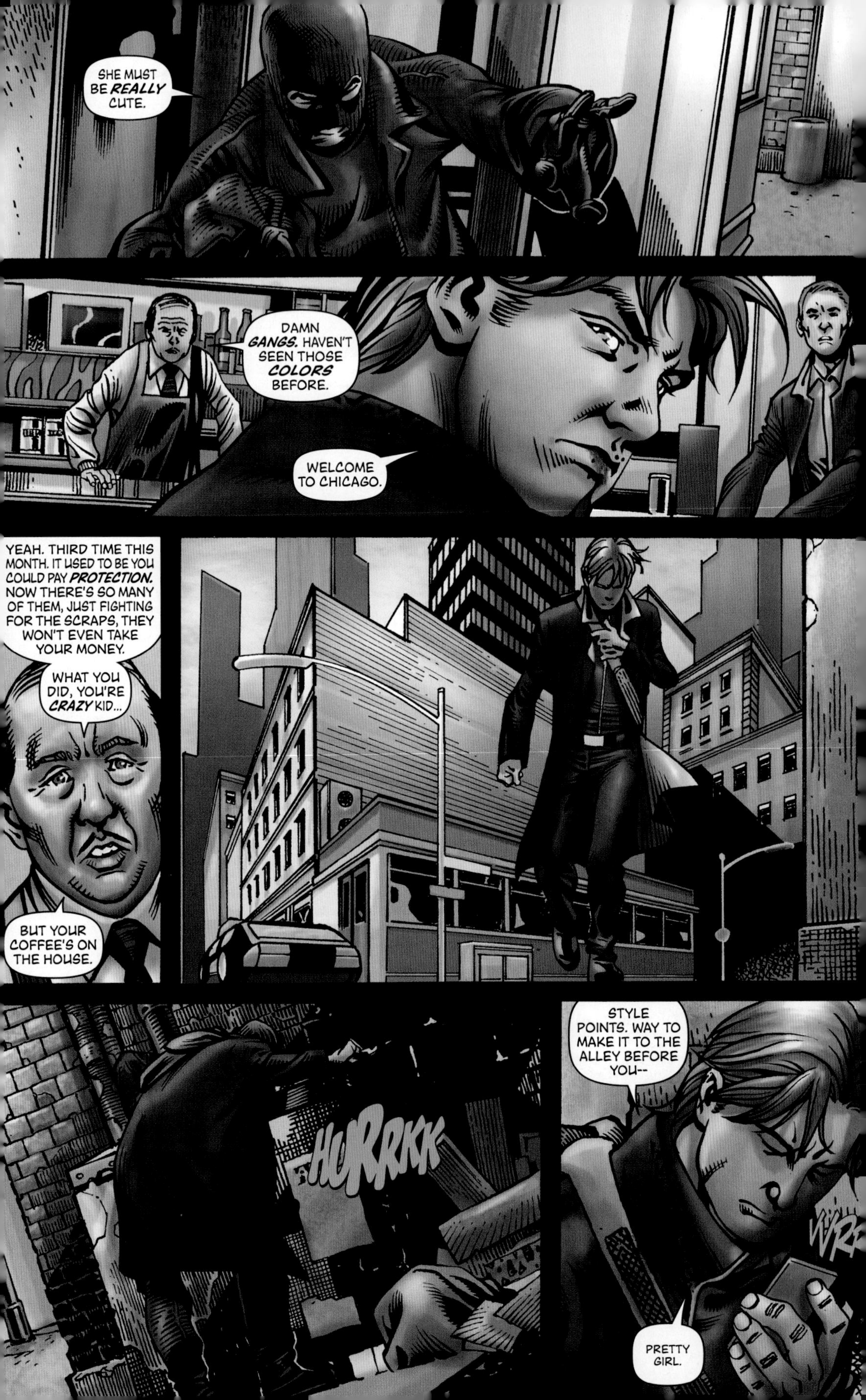
SHE MUST BE REALLY CUTE.
DAMN GANGS. HAVEN'T SEEN THOSE COLORS BEFORE.
WELCOME TO CHICAGO.
YEAH. THIRD TIME THIS MONTH. IT USED TO BE YOU COULD PAY PROTECTION. NOW THERE'S SO MANY OF THEM, JUST FIGHTING FOR THE SCRAPS, THEY WON'T EVEN TAKE YOUR MONEY.
WHAT YOU DID, YOU'RE CRAZY KID...
BUT YOUR COFFEE'S ON THE HOUSE.
HURRKK
STYLE POINTS. WAY TO MAKE IT TO THE ALLEY BEFORE YOU--
PRETTY GIRL.

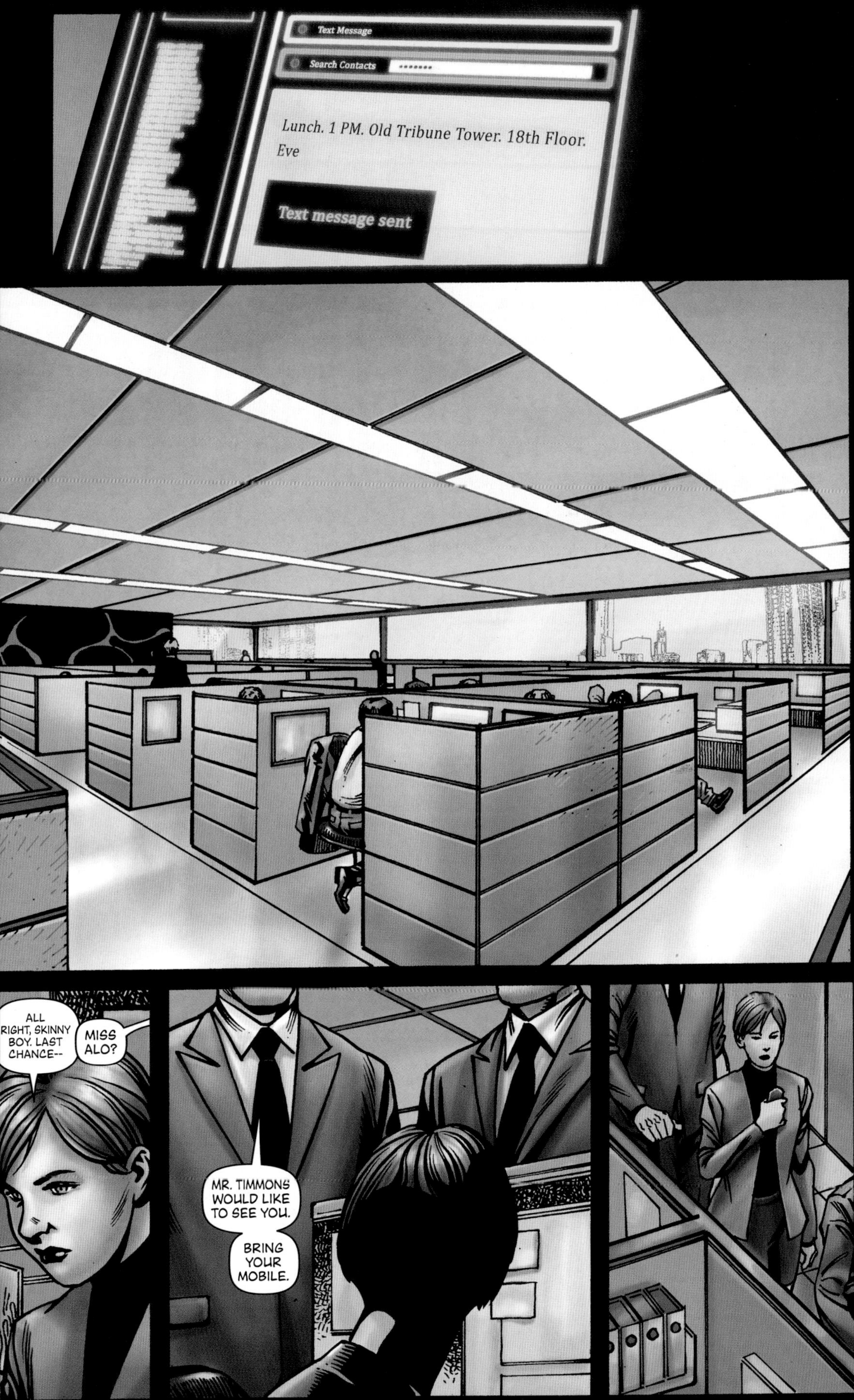
Text Message
Search Contacts
Lunch. 1 PM. Old Tribune Tower. 18th Floor.
Eve
Text message sent
ALL RIGHT, SKINNY BOY. LAST CHANCE--
MISS ALO?
MR. TIMMONS WOULD LIKE TO SEE YOU.
BRING YOUR MOBILE.

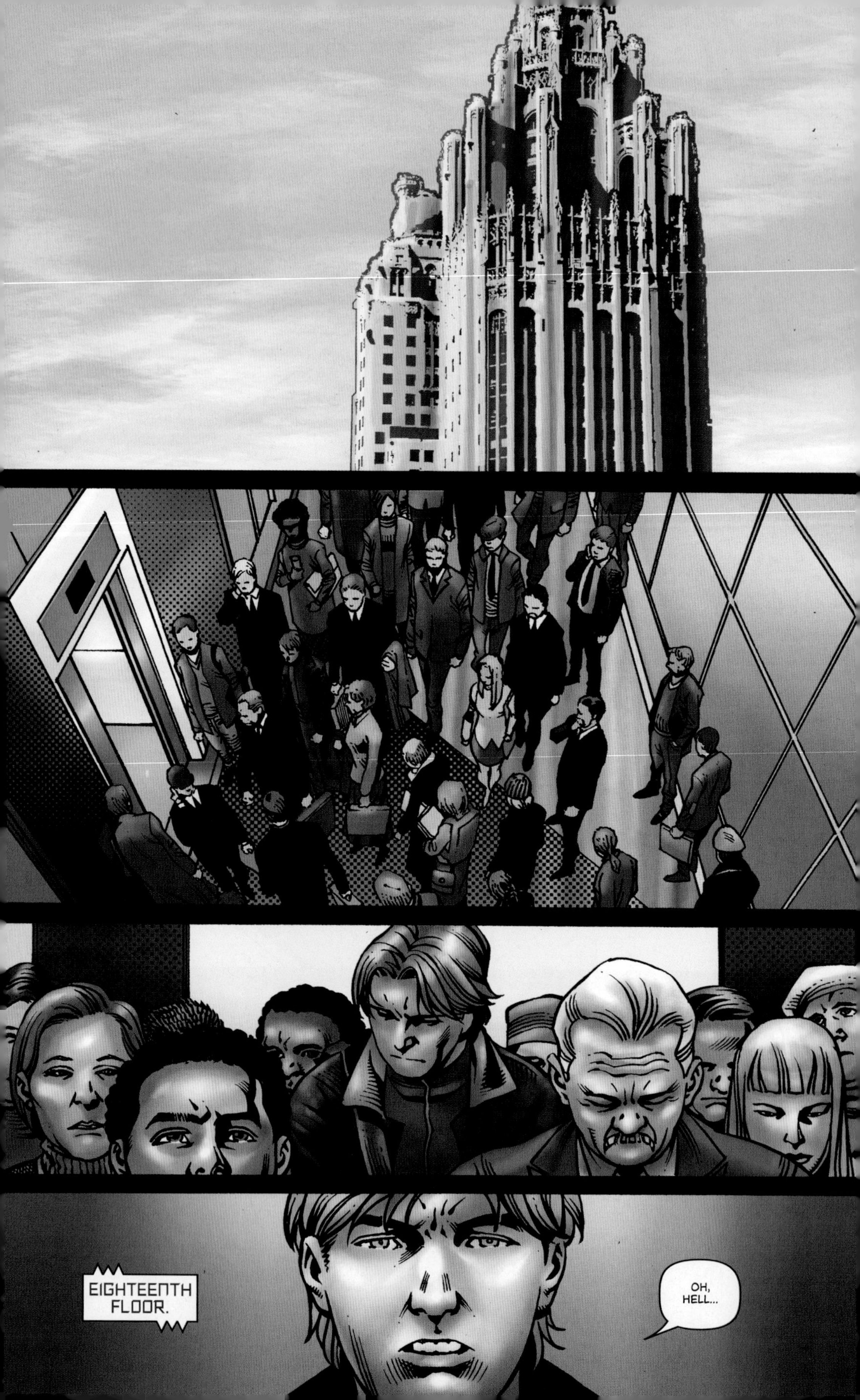
EIGHTEENTH FLOOR.
OH, HELL...

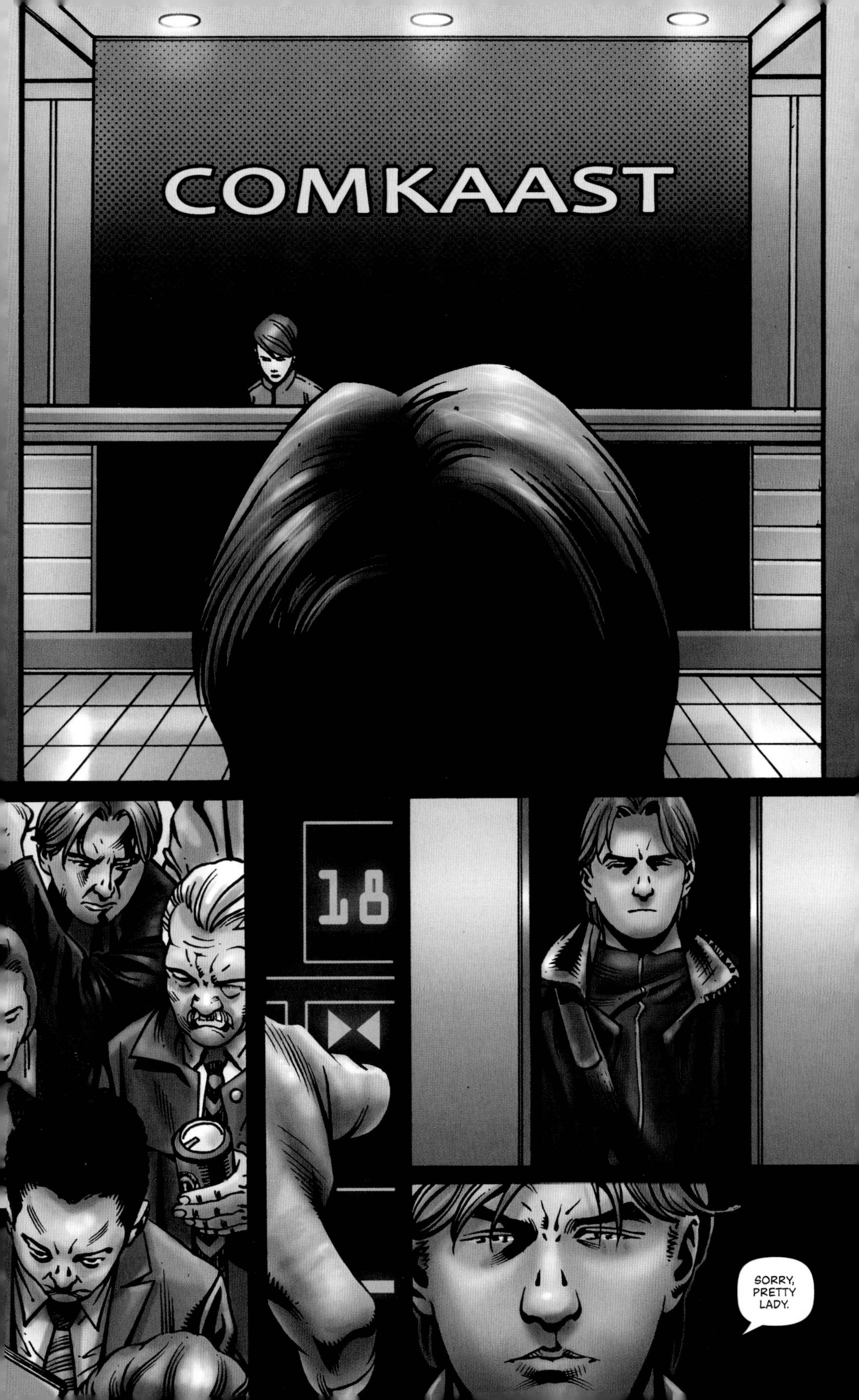
COMKAAST
18
SORRY, PRETTY LADY.

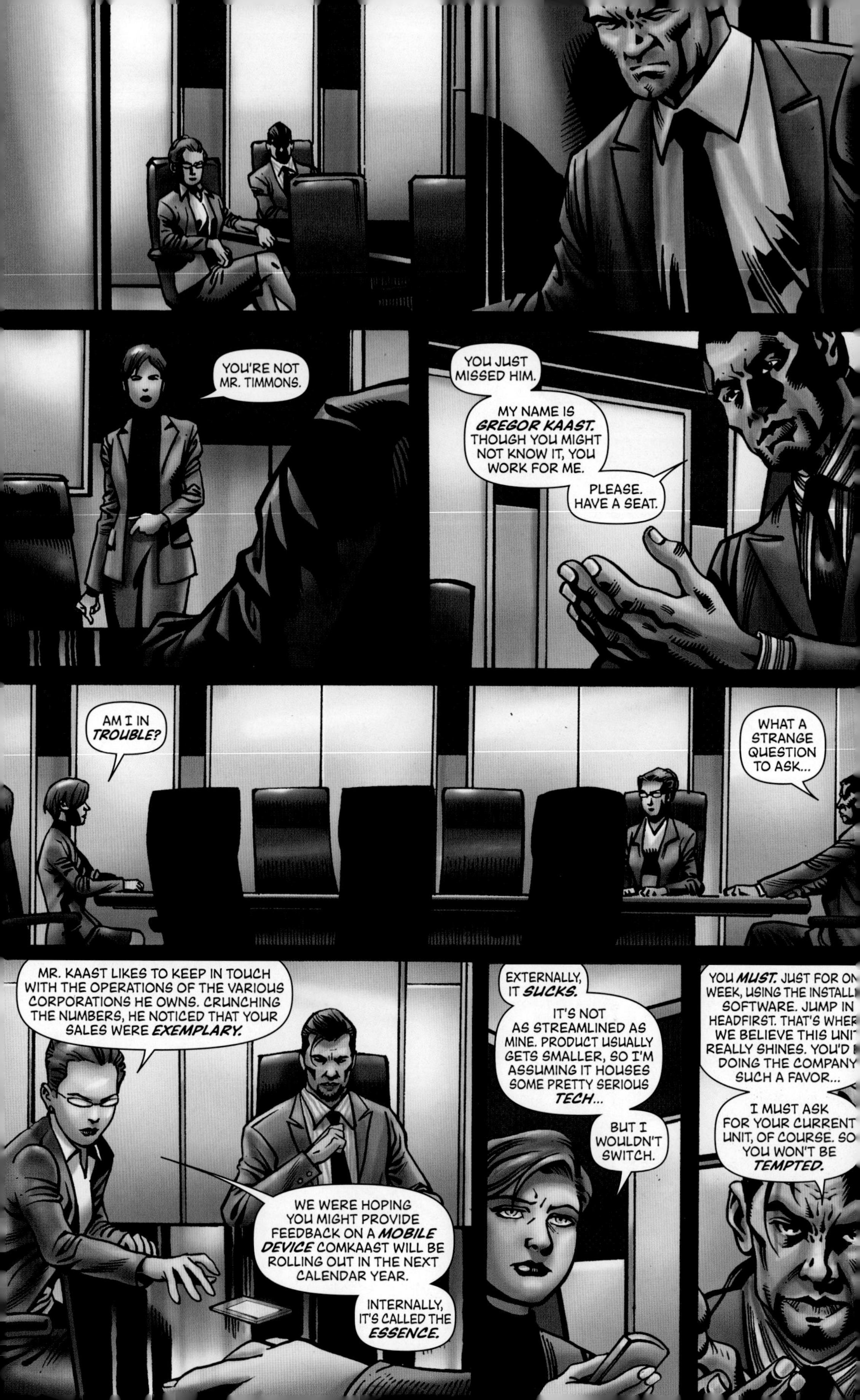
YOU'RE NOT MR. TIMMONS.
YOU JUST MISSED HIM.
MY NAME IS GREGOR KAAST. THOUGH YOU MIGHT NOT KNOW IT, YOU WORK FOR ME.
PLEASE. HAVE A SEAT.
AM I IN TROUBLE?
WHAT A STRANGE QUESTION TO ASK...
MR. KAAST LIKES TO KEEP IN TOUCH WITH THE OPERATIONS OF THE VARIOUS CORPORATIONS HE OWNS. CRUNCHING THE NUMBERS, HE NOTICED THAT YOUR SALES WERE EXEMPLARY.
WE WERE HOPING YOU MIGHT PROVIDE FEEDBACK ON A MOBILE DEVICE COMKAAST WILL BE ROLLING OUT IN THE NEXT CALENDAR YEAR.
INTERNALLY, IT'S CALLED THE ESSENCE.
EXTERNALLY, IT SUCKS.
IT'S NOT AS STREAMLINED AS MINE. PRODUCT USUALLY GETS SMALLER, SO I'M ASSUMING IT HOUSES SOME PRETTY SERIOUS TECH...
BUT I WOULDN'T SWITCH.
YOU MUST. JUST FOR ON WEEK, USING THE INSTALL SOFTWARE. JUMP IN HEADFIRST. THAT'S WHER WE BELIEVE THIS UNI REALLY SHINES. YOU'D DOING THE COMPANY SUCH A FAVOR...
I MUST ASK FOR YOUR CURRENT UNIT, OF COURSE. SO YOU WON'T BE TEMPTED.

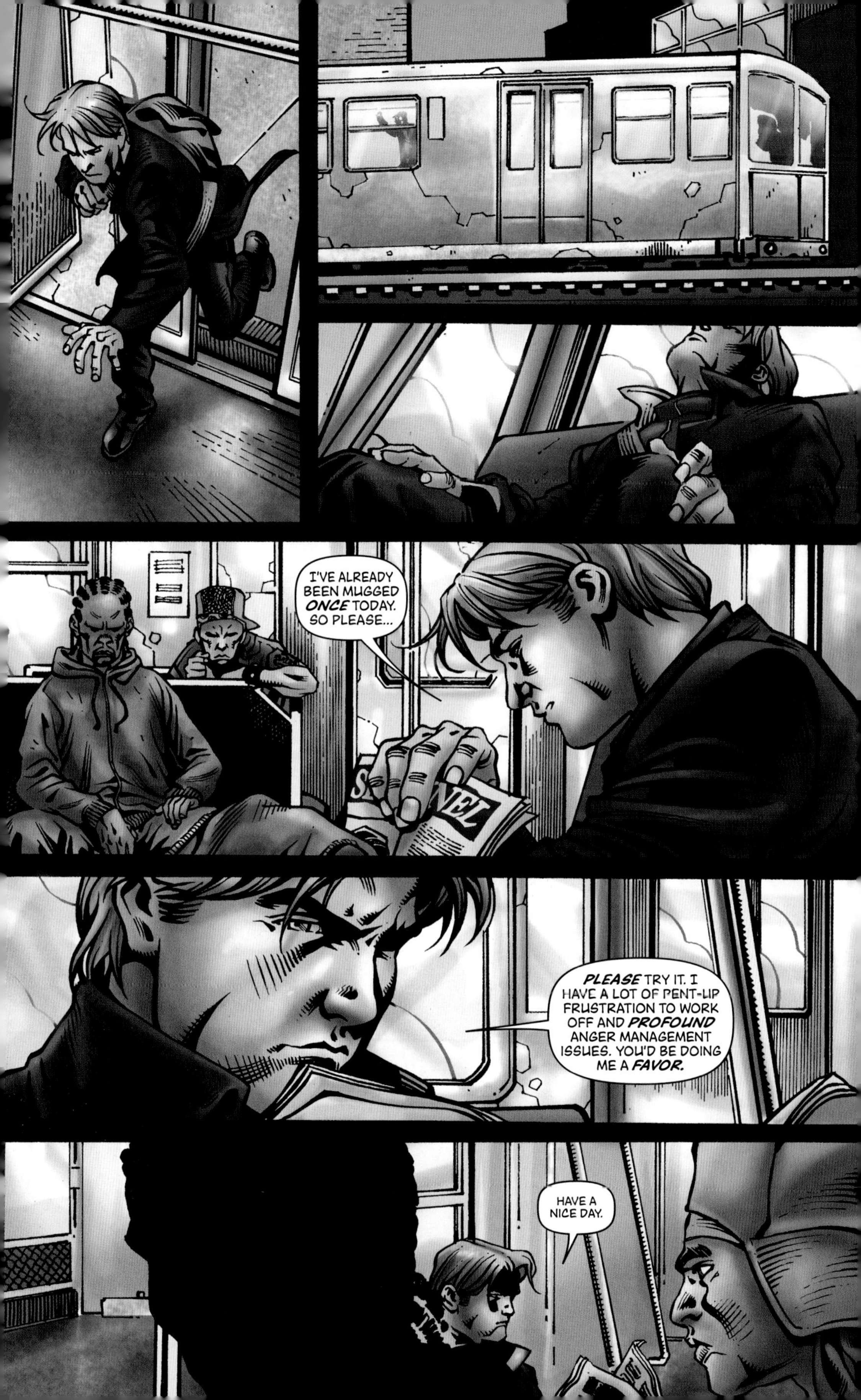
I'VE ALREADY BEEN MUGGED ONCE TODAY. SO PLEASE...
PLEASE TRY IT. I HAVE A LOT OF PENT-UP FRUSTRATION TO WORK OFF AND PROFOUND ANGER MANAGEMENT ISSUES. YOU'D BE DOING ME A FAVOR.
HAVE A NICE DAY.

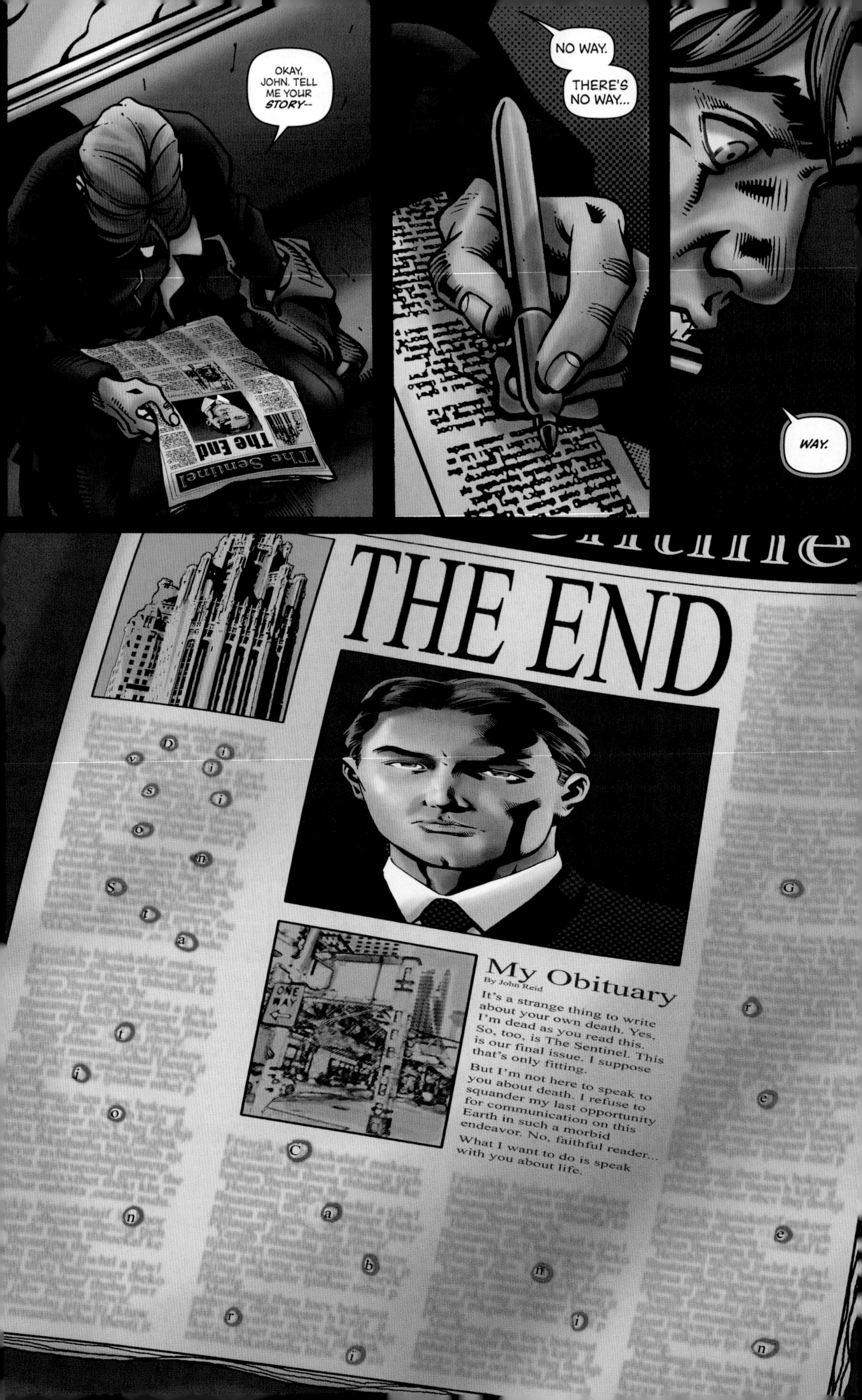
OKAY, JOHN. TELL ME YOUR *STORY*--
The Sentinel
The End
NO WAY.
THERE'S NO WAY...
WAY.
THE END
My Obituary
By John Reid
It's a strange thing to write about your own death. Yes, I'm dead as you read this. So, too, is The Sentinel. This is our final issue. I suppose that's only fitting.
But I'm not here to speak to you about death. I refuse to squander my last opportunity for communication on this Earth in such a morbid endeavor. No, faithful reader...
What I want to do is speak with you about life.
ONE WAY

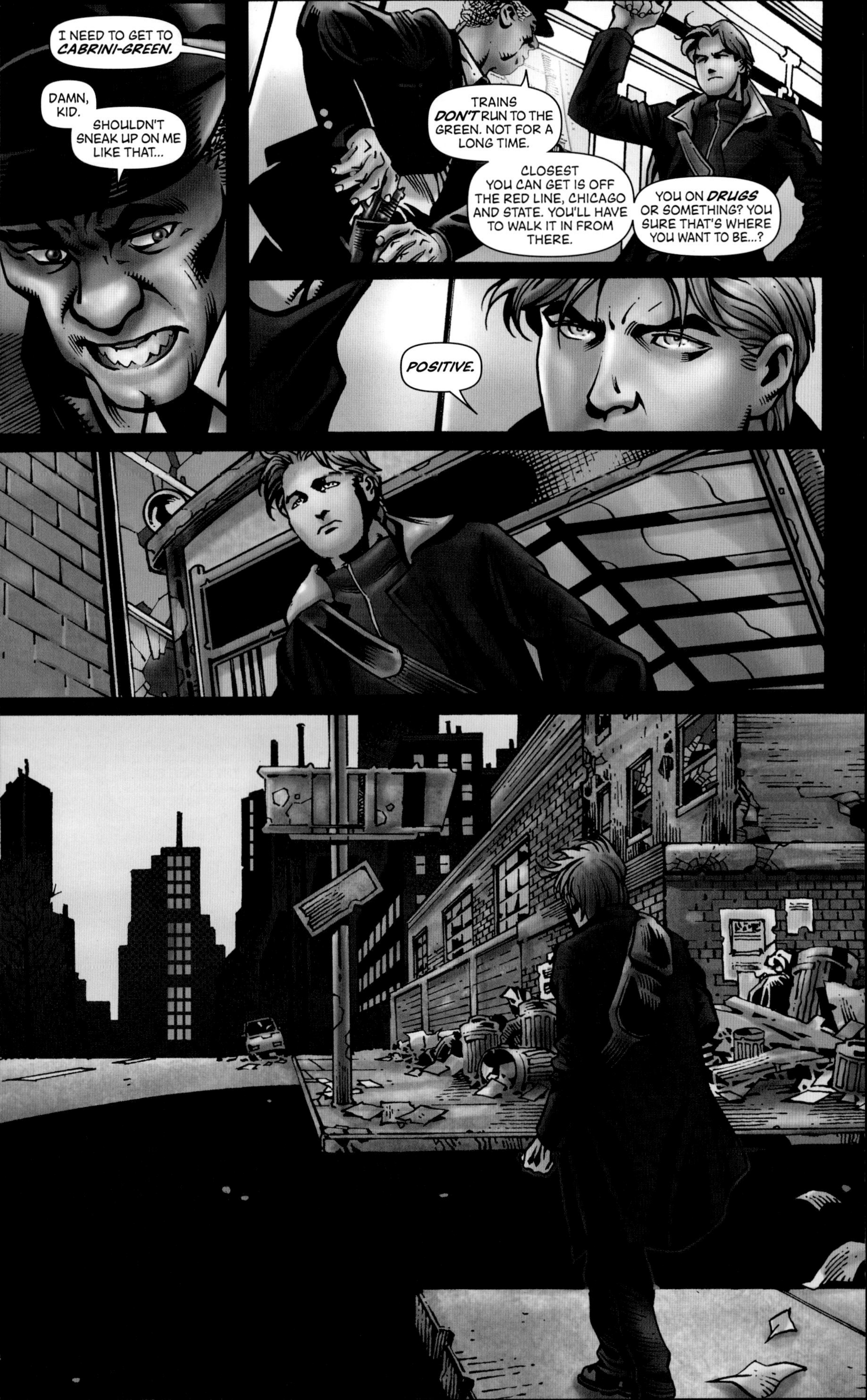
I NEED TO GET TO *CABRINI-GREEN.*
DAMN, KID.
SHOULDN'T SNEAK UP ON ME LIKE THAT...
TRAINS *DON'T* RUN TO THE GREEN. NOT FOR A LONG TIME.
CLOSEST YOU CAN GET IS OFF THE RED LINE, CHICAGO AND STATE. YOU'LL HAVE TO WALK IT IN FROM THERE.
YOU ON *DRUGS* OR SOMETHING? YOU SURE THAT'S WHERE YOU WANT TO BE...?
POSITIVE.

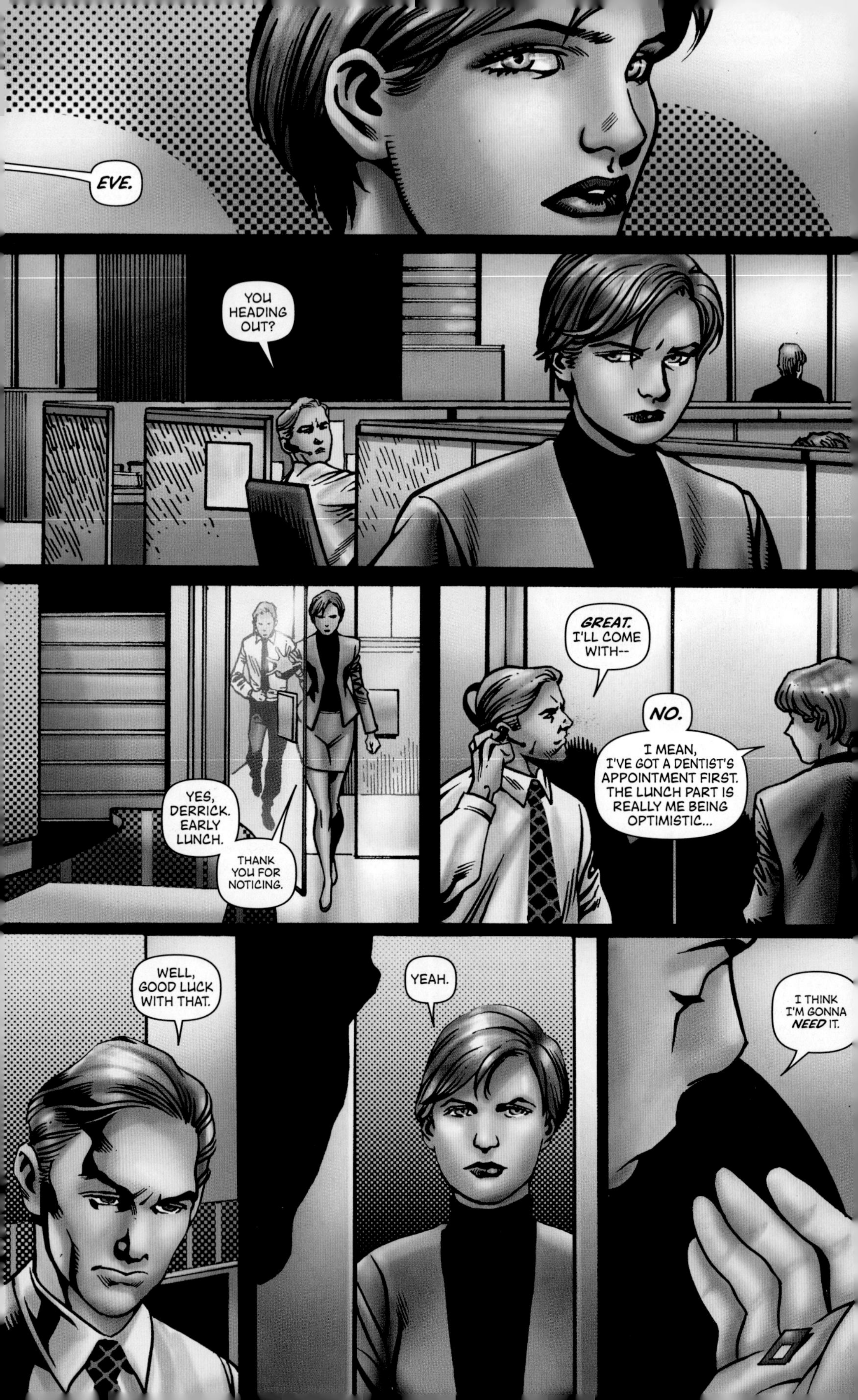
EVE.
YOU HEADING OUT?
YES, DERRICK. EARLY LUNCH.
THANK YOU FOR NOTICING.
GREAT. I'LL COME WITH--
NO.
I MEAN, I'VE GOT A DENTIST'S APPOINTMENT FIRST. THE LUNCH PART IS REALLY ME BEING OPTIMISTIC...
WELL, GOOD LUCK WITH THAT.
YEAH.
I THINK I'M GONNA NEED IT.

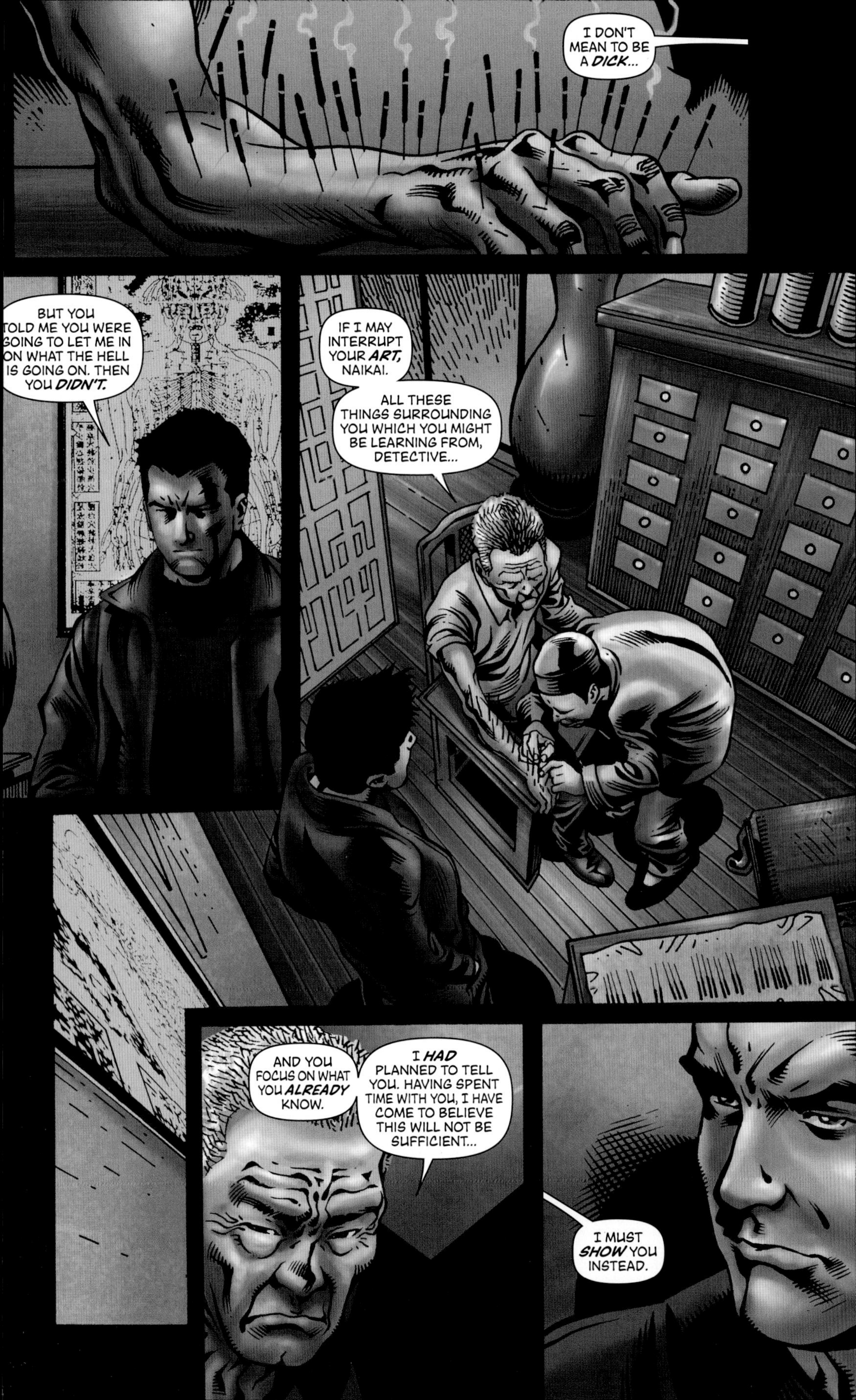
I DON'T MEAN TO BE A DICK...
BUT YOU TOLD ME YOU WERE GOING TO LET ME IN ON WHAT THE HELL IS GOING ON. THEN YOU DIDN'T.
IF I MAY INTERRUPT YOUR ART, NAIKAI.
ALL THESE THINGS SURROUNDING YOU WHICH YOU MIGHT BE LEARNING FROM, DETECTIVE...
AND YOU FOCUS ON WHAT YOU ALREADY KNOW.
I HAD PLANNED TO TELL YOU. HAVING SPENT TIME WITH YOU, I HAVE COME TO BELIEVE THIS WILL NOT BE SUFFICIENT...
I MUST SHOW YOU INSTEAD.

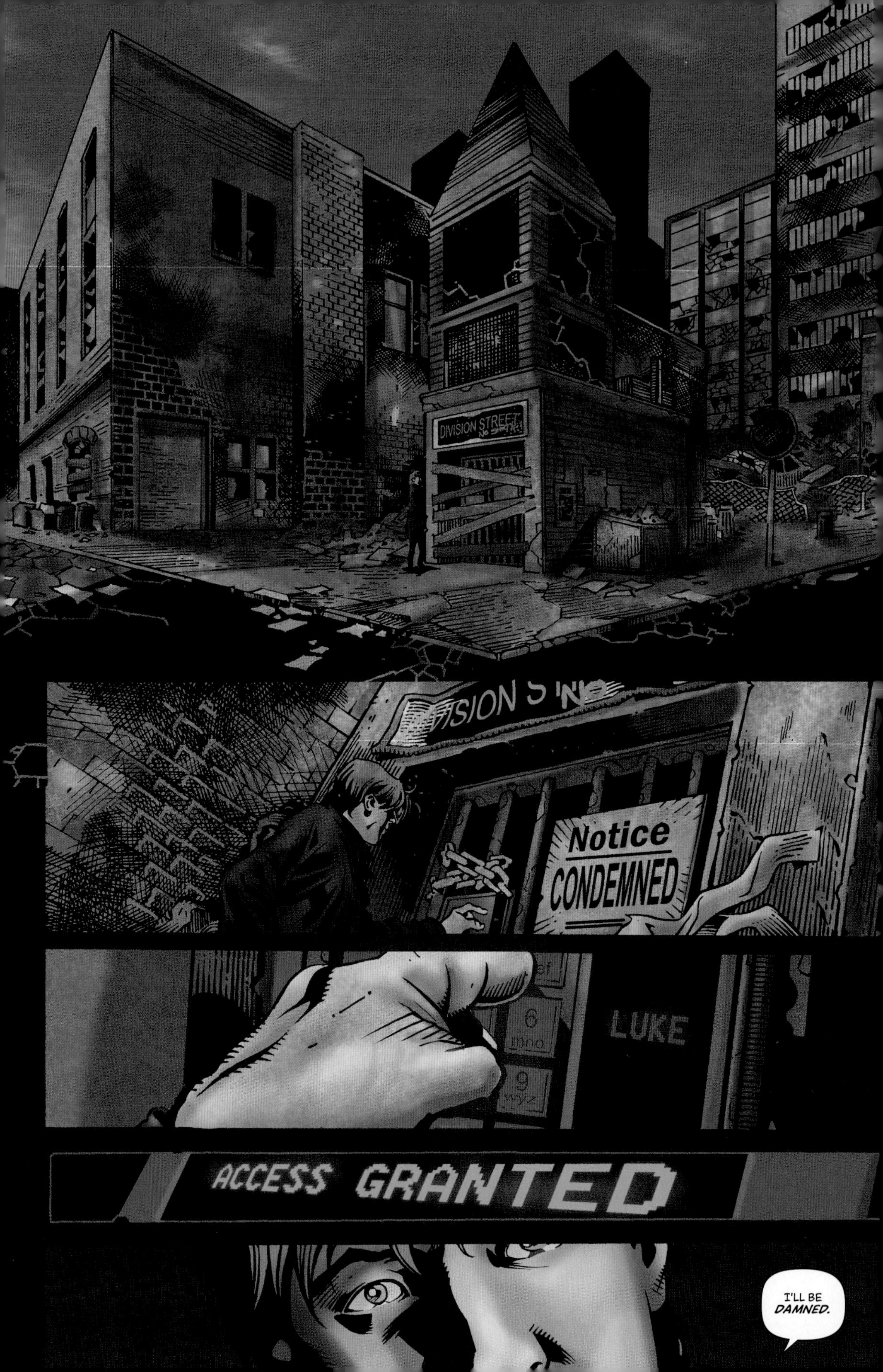
DIVISION STREET
Notice
CONDEMNED
LUKE
ACCESS GRANTED
I'LL BE *DAMNED.*

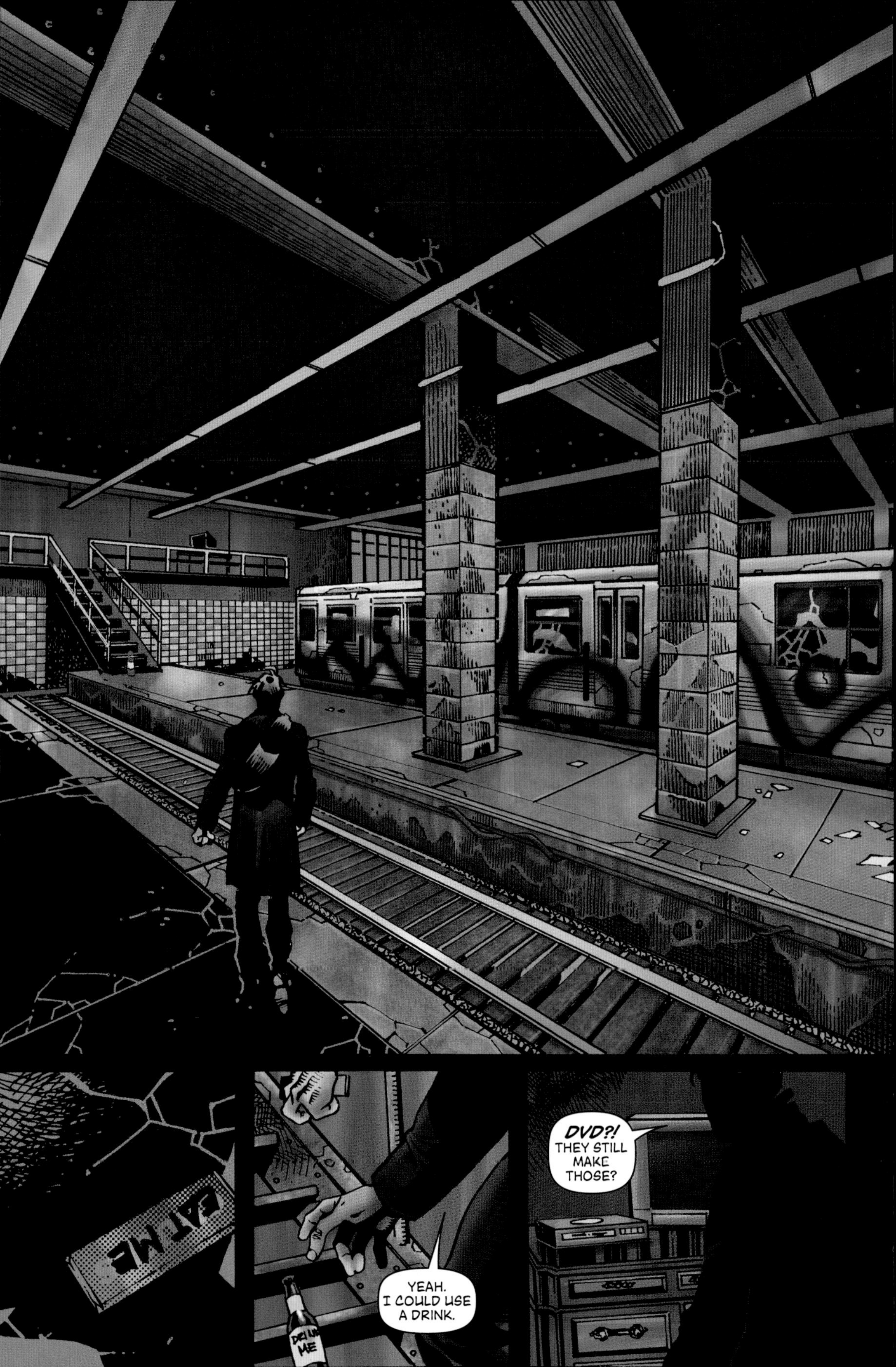
EAT ME
YEAH. I COULD USE A DRINK.
DVD?! THEY STILL MAKE THOSE?

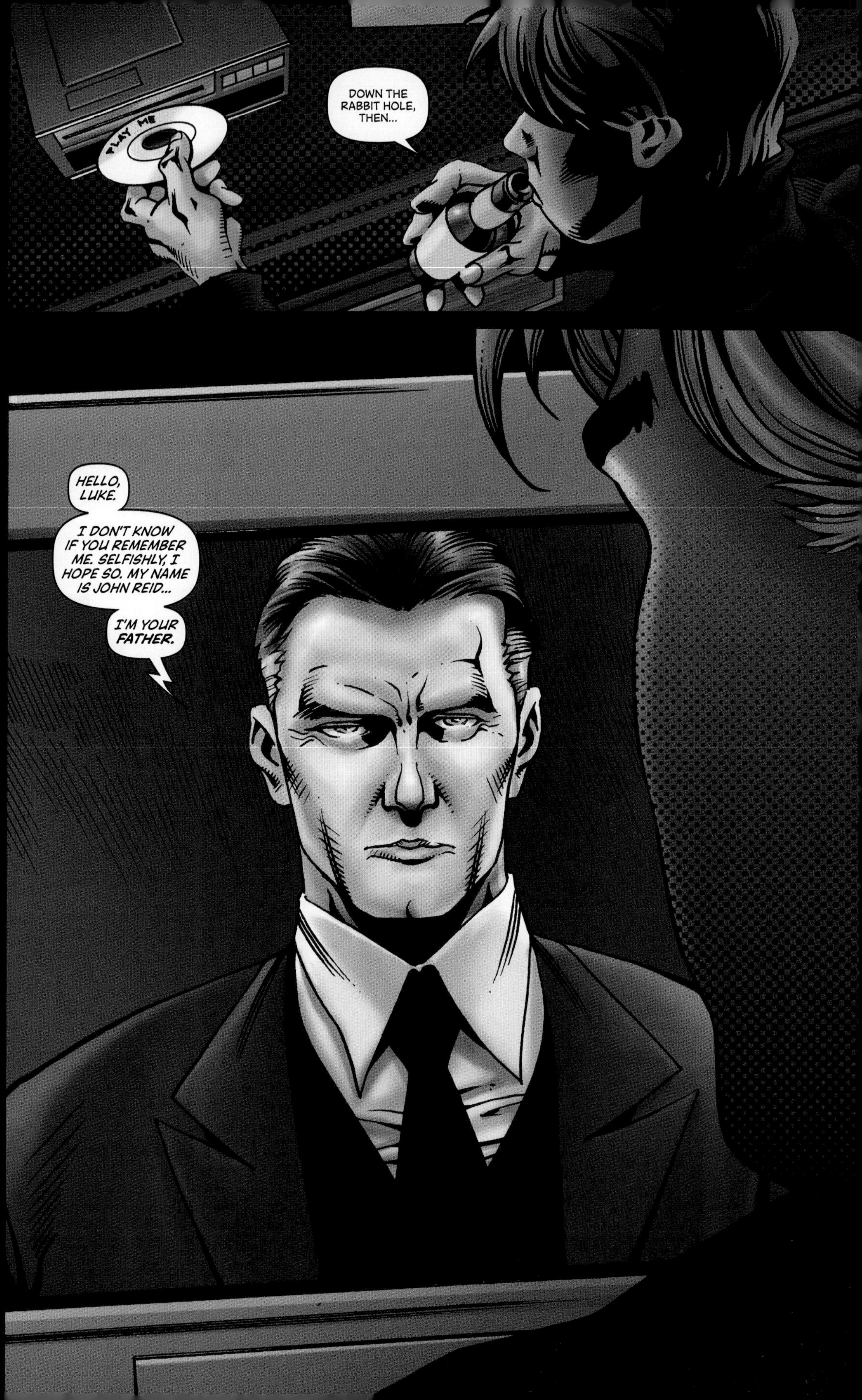
PLAY ME
DOWN THE RABBIT HOLE, THEN...
HELLO, LUKE.
I DON'T KNOW IF YOU REMEMBER ME. SELFISHLY, I HOPE SO. MY NAME IS JOHN REID...
I'M YOUR FATHER.

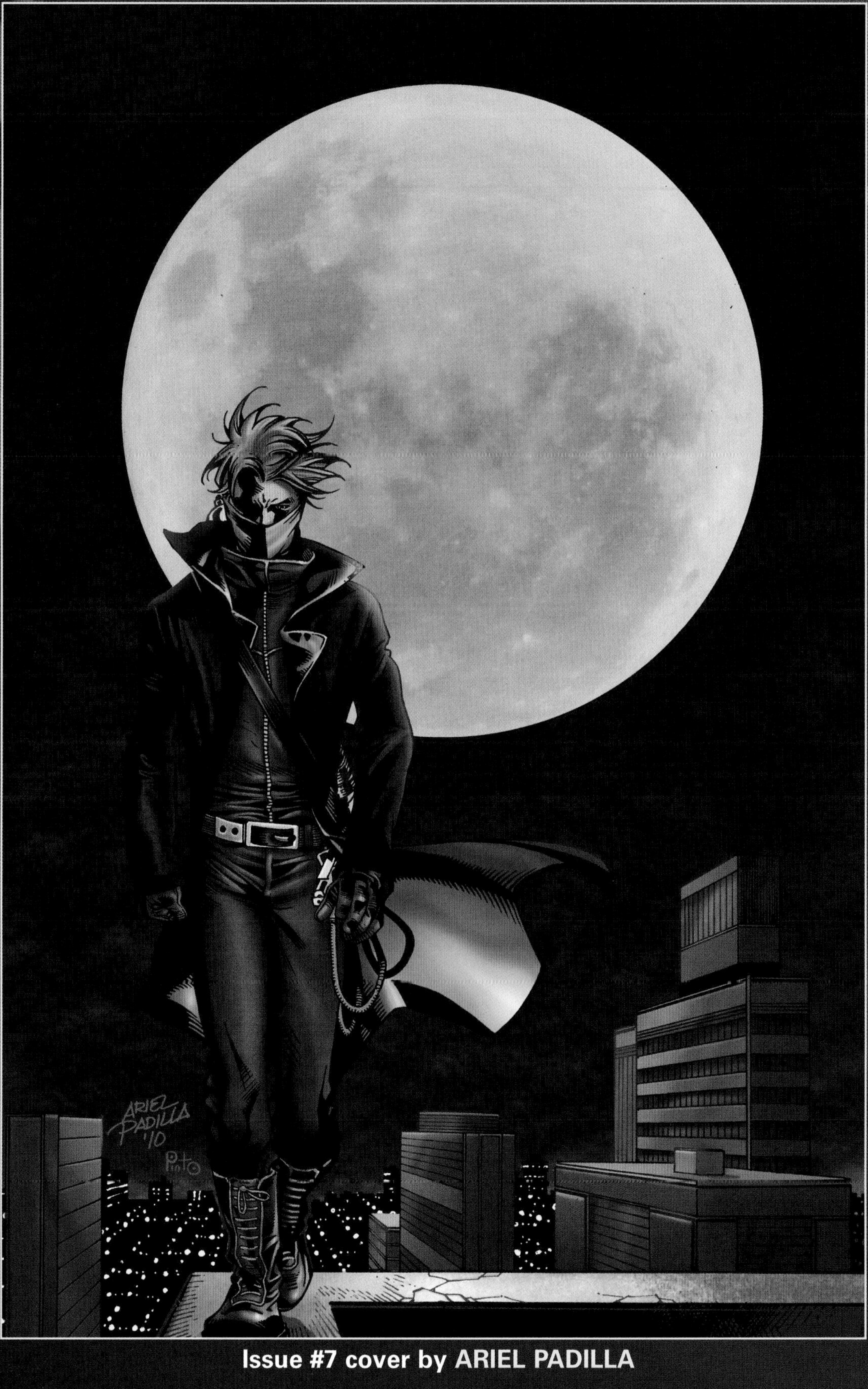
ARIEL PADILLA '10
Pinto

Issue #7 cover by ARIEL PADILLA

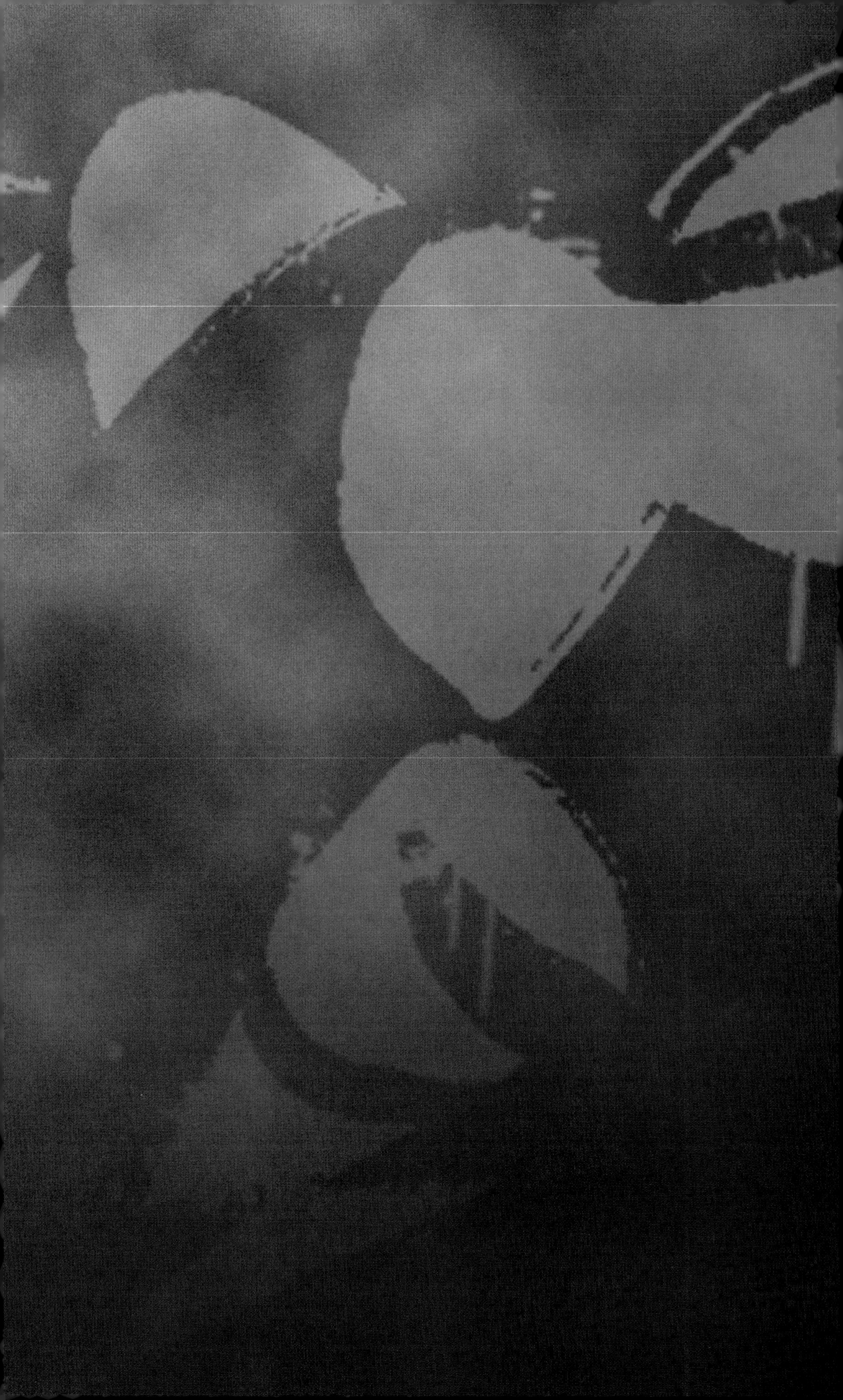

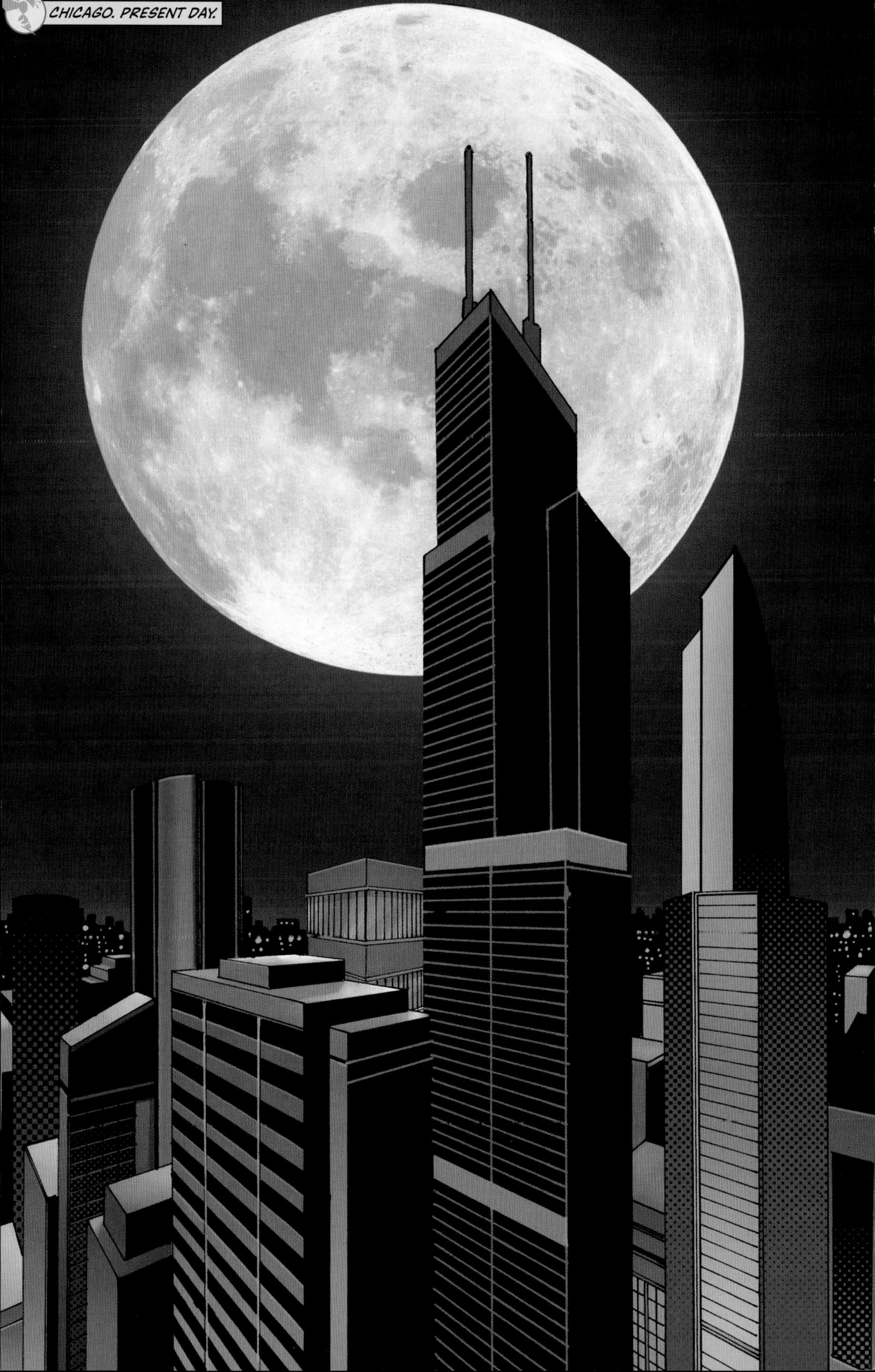
CHICAGO. PRESENT DAY.

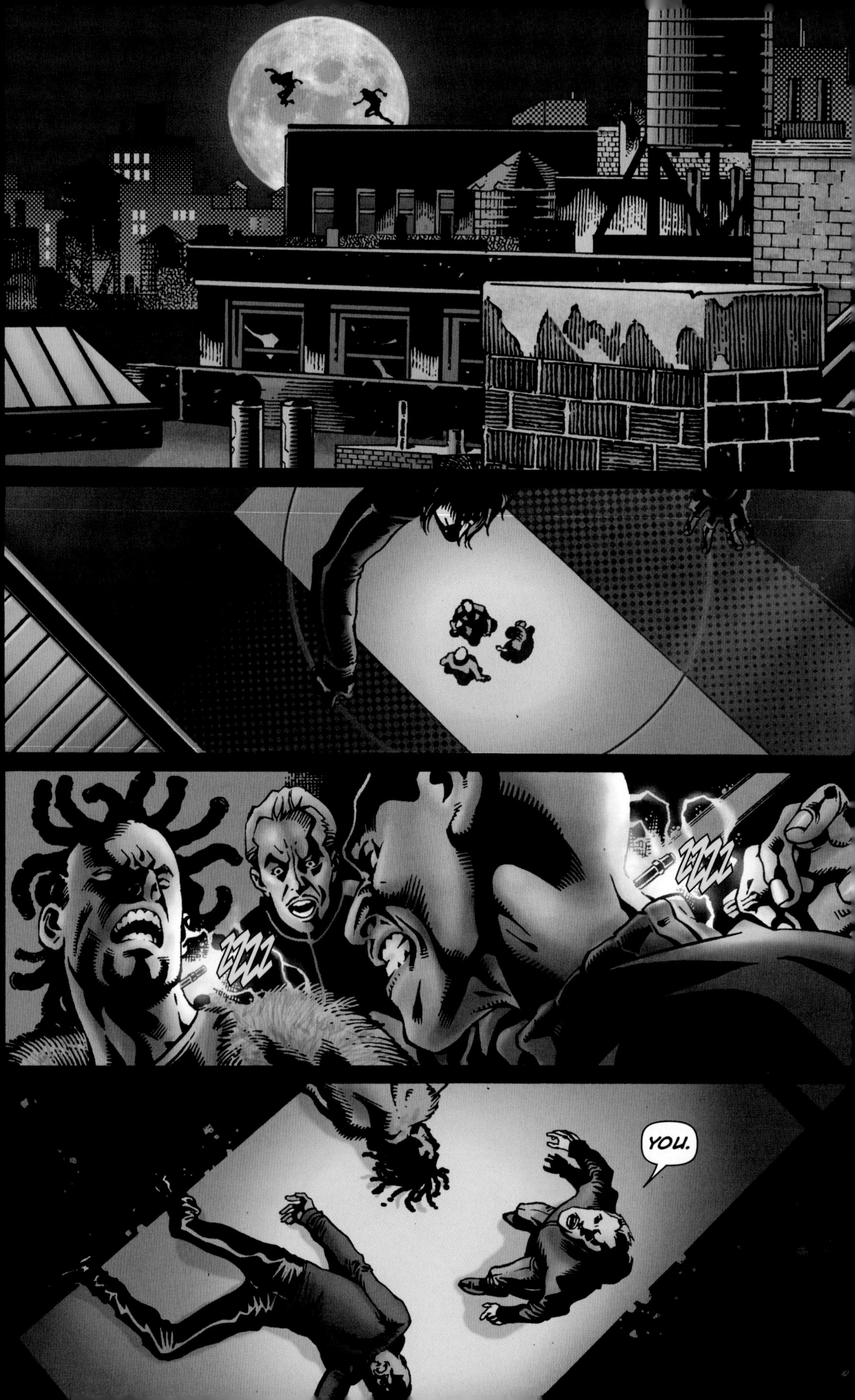
YOU.

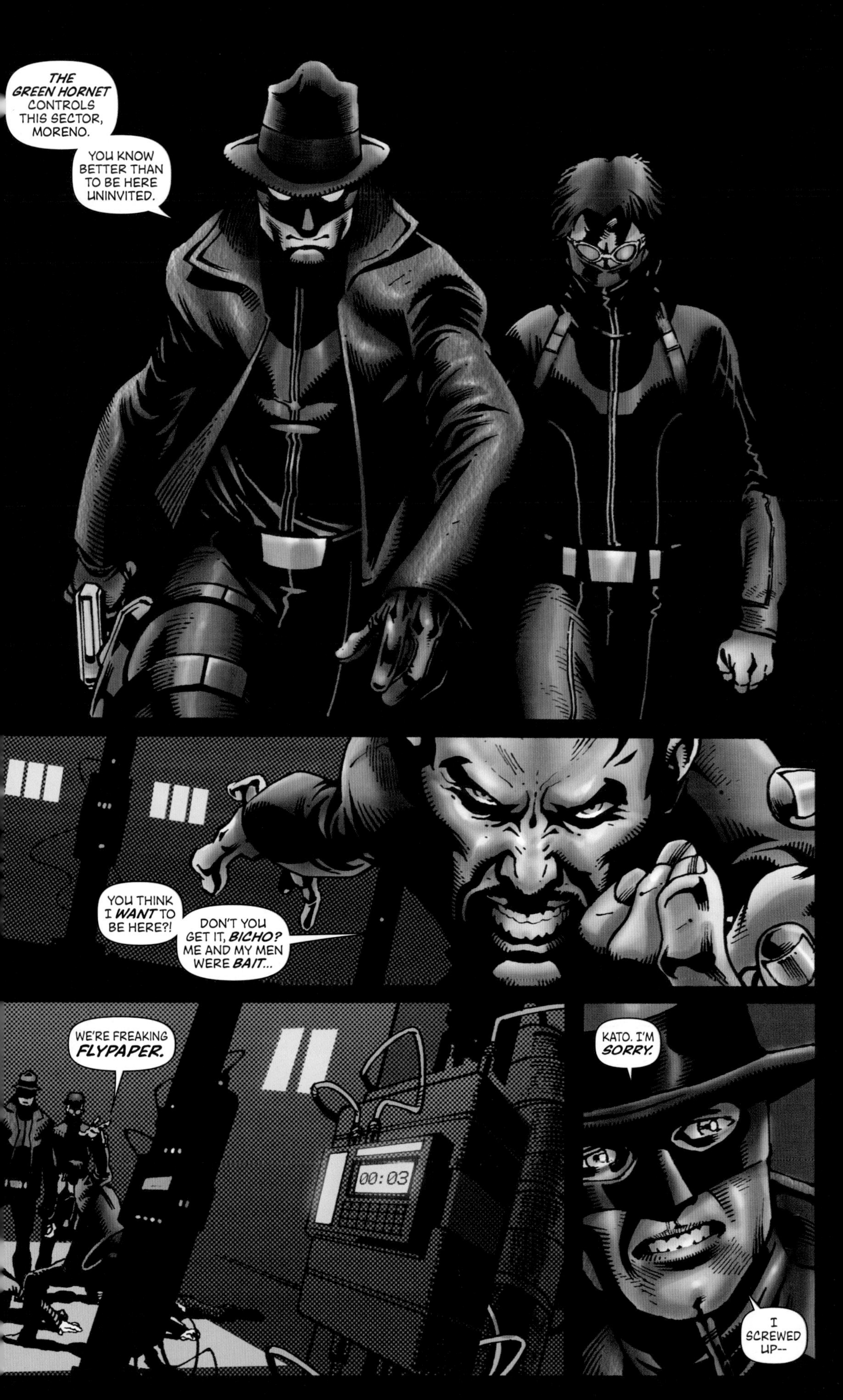
THE GREEN HORNET CONTROLS THIS SECTOR, MORENO.
YOU KNOW BETTER THAN TO BE HERE UNINVITED.
YOU THINK I WANT TO BE HERE?!
DON'T YOU GET IT, BICHO? ME AND MY MEN WERE BAIT...
WE'RE FREAKING FLYPAPER.
00:03
KATO. I'M SORRY.
I SCREWED UP--

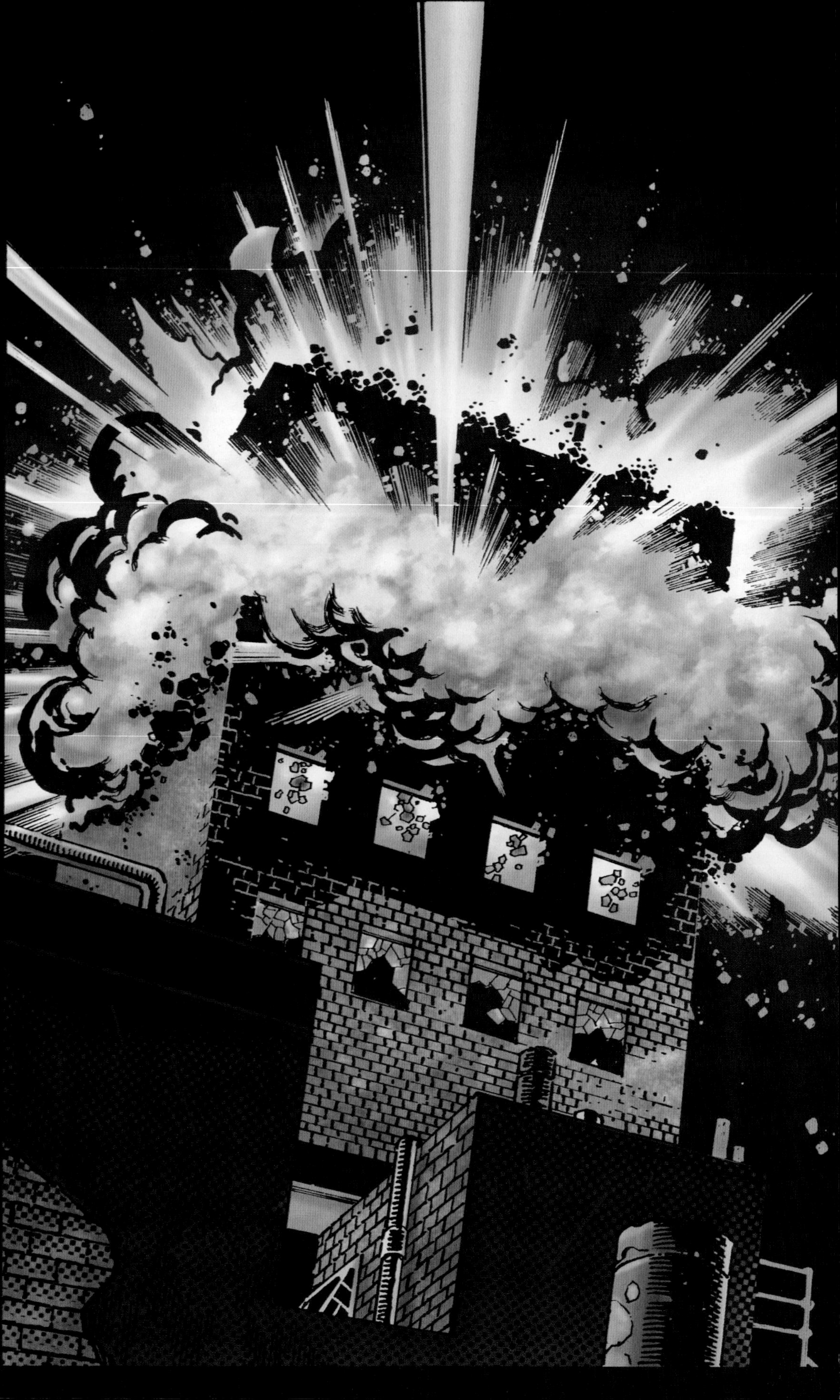

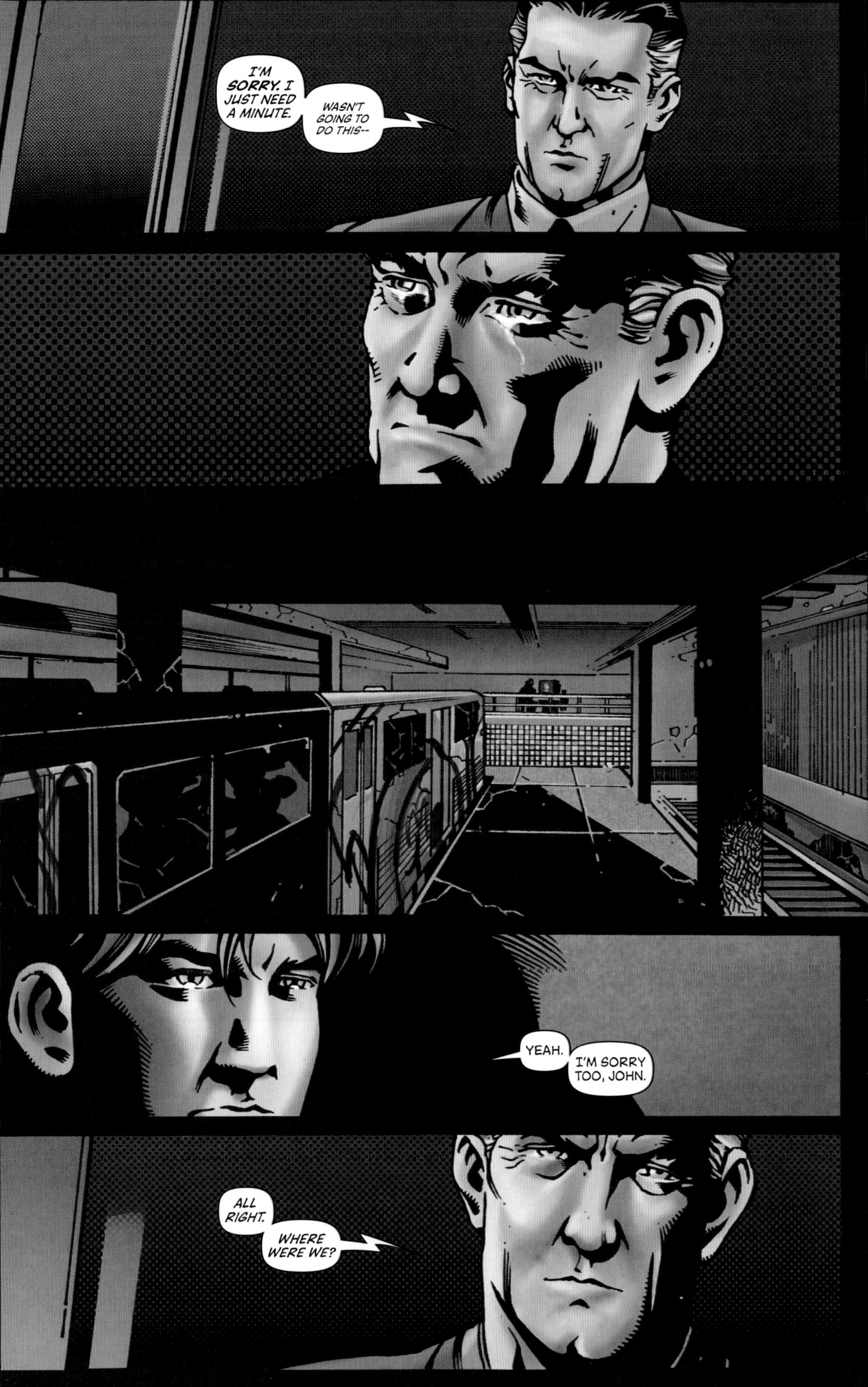
I'M SORRY. I JUST NEED A MINUTE.
WASN'T GOING TO DO THIS--
YEAH.
I'M SORRY TOO, JOHN.
ALL RIGHT.
WHERE WERE WE?

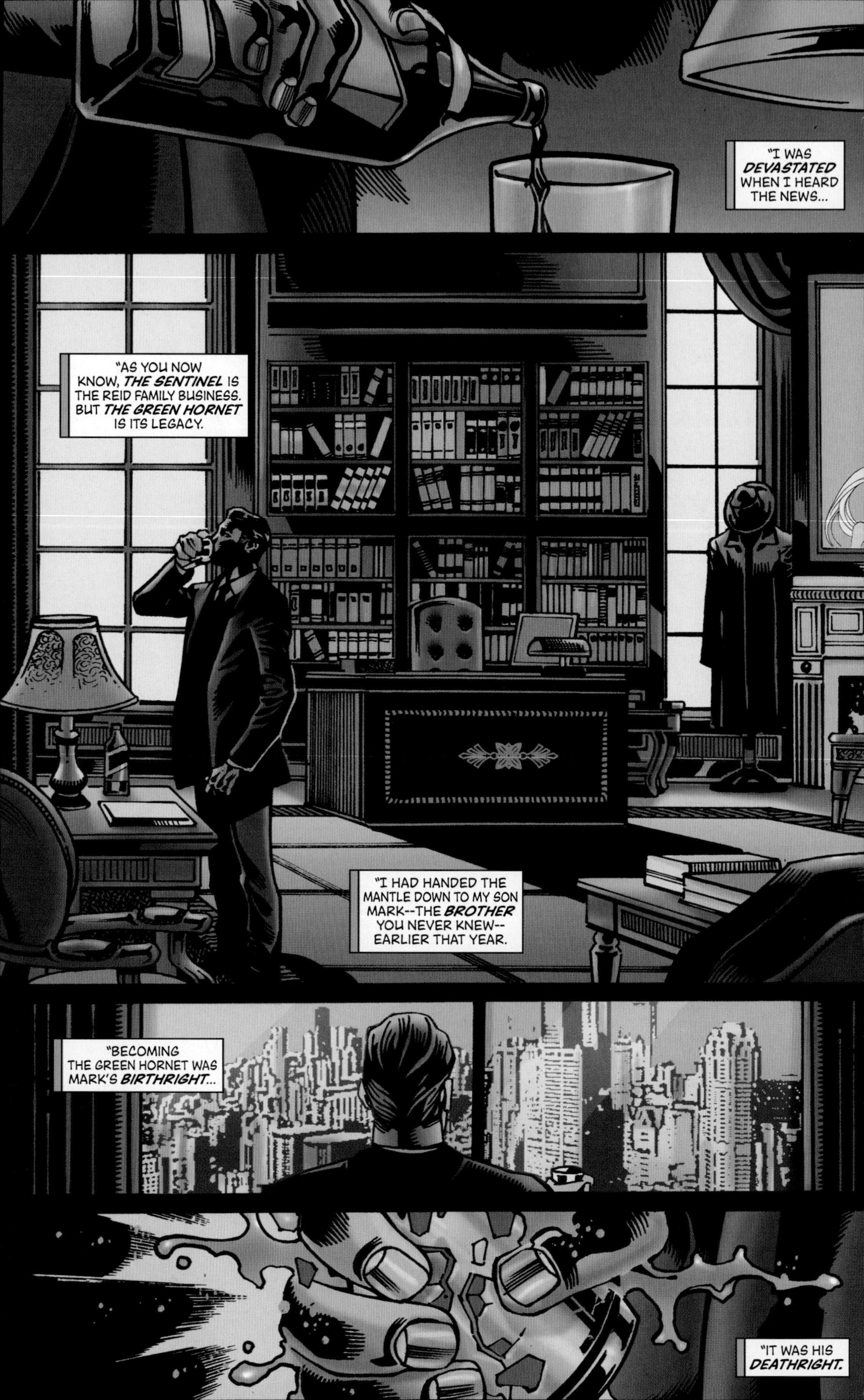
"I WAS *DEVASTATED* WHEN I HEARD THE NEWS...
"AS YOU NOW KNOW, *THE SENTINEL* IS THE REID FAMILY BUSINESS. BUT *THE GREEN HORNET* IS ITS LEGACY.
"I HAD HANDED THE MANTLE DOWN TO MY SON MARK--THE *BROTHER* YOU NEVER KNEW--EARLIER THAT YEAR.
"BECOMING THE GREEN HORNET WAS MARK'S *BIRTHRIGHT*...
"IT WAS HIS *DEATHRIGHT.*

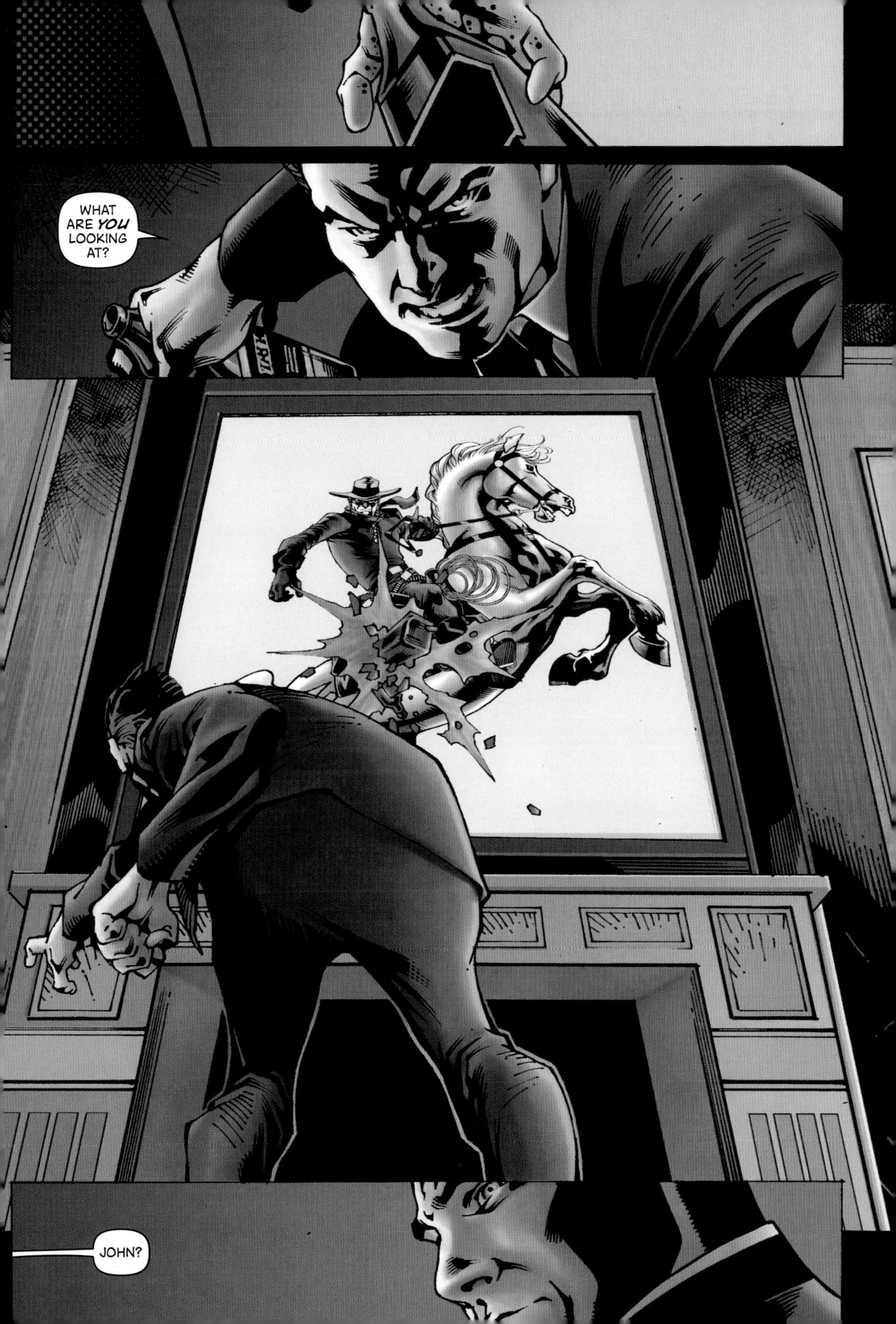

WHAT ARE *YOU* LOOKING AT?
JOHN?

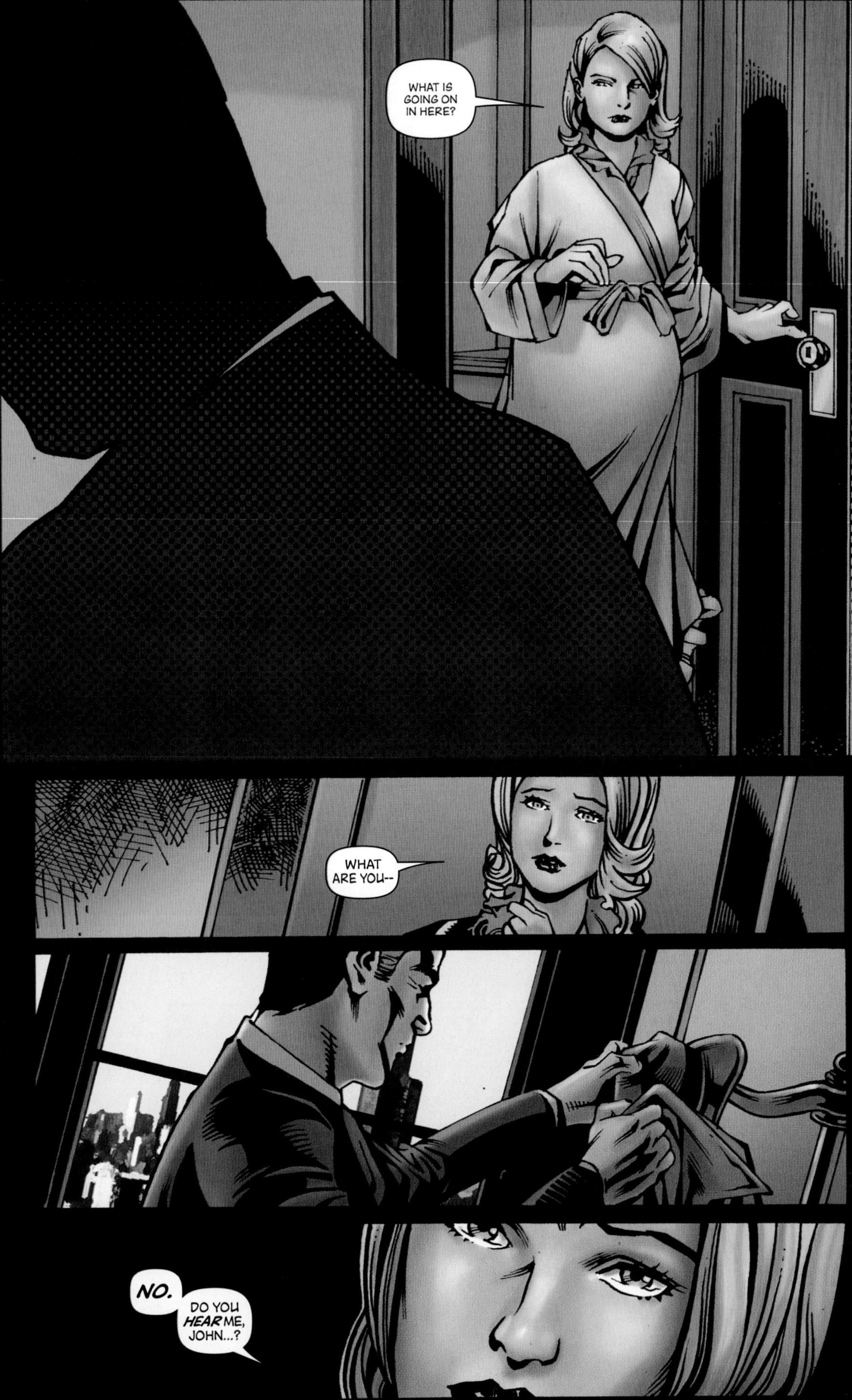
WHAT IS GOING ON IN HERE?
WHAT ARE YOU--
NO.
DO YOU HEAR ME, JOHN...?

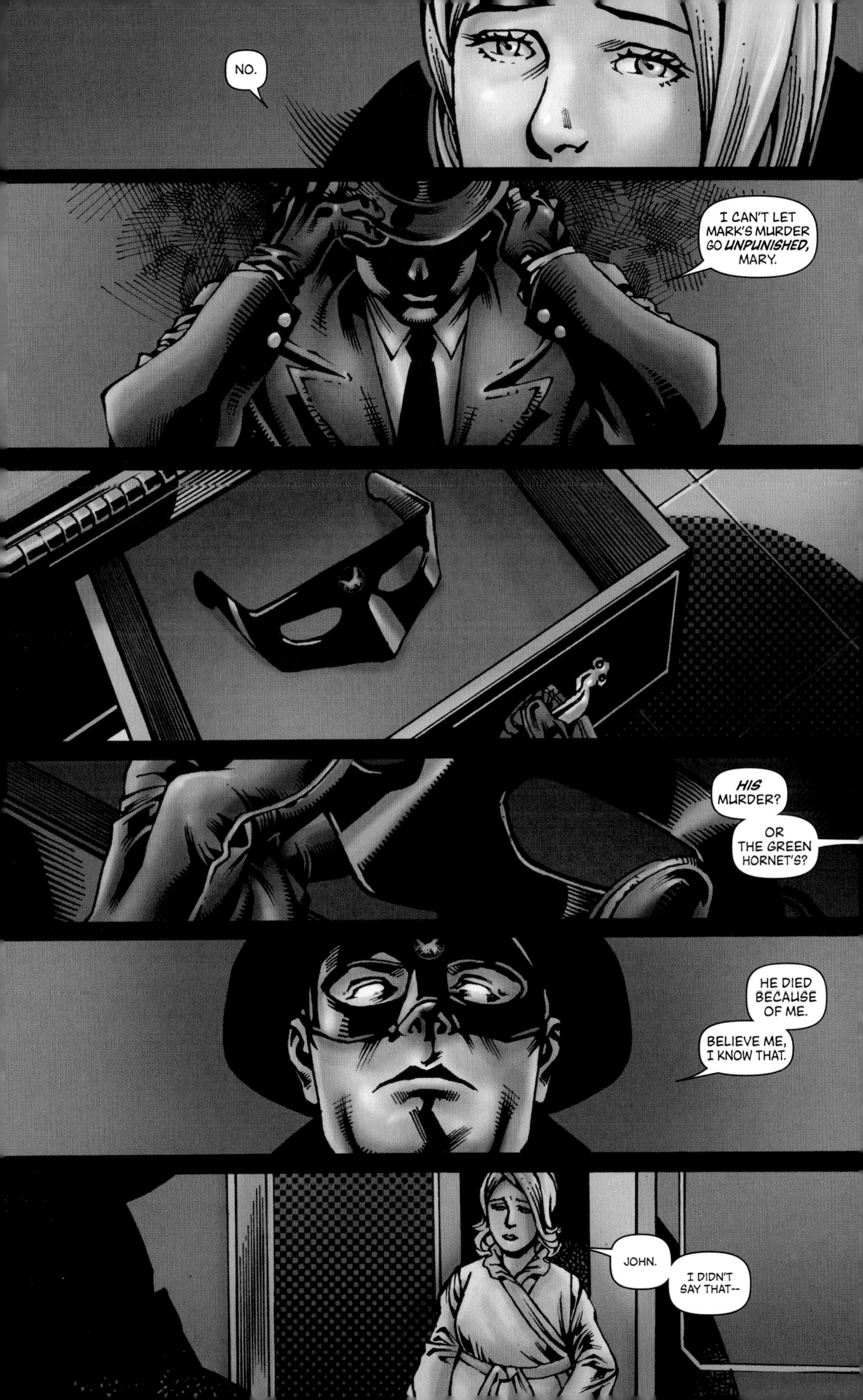
NO.
I CAN'T LET MARK'S MURDER GO *UNPUNISHED,* MARY.
HIS MURDER?
OR THE GREEN HORNET'S?
HE DIED BECAUSE OF ME.
BELIEVE ME, I KNOW THAT.
JOHN.
I DIDN'T SAY THAT--

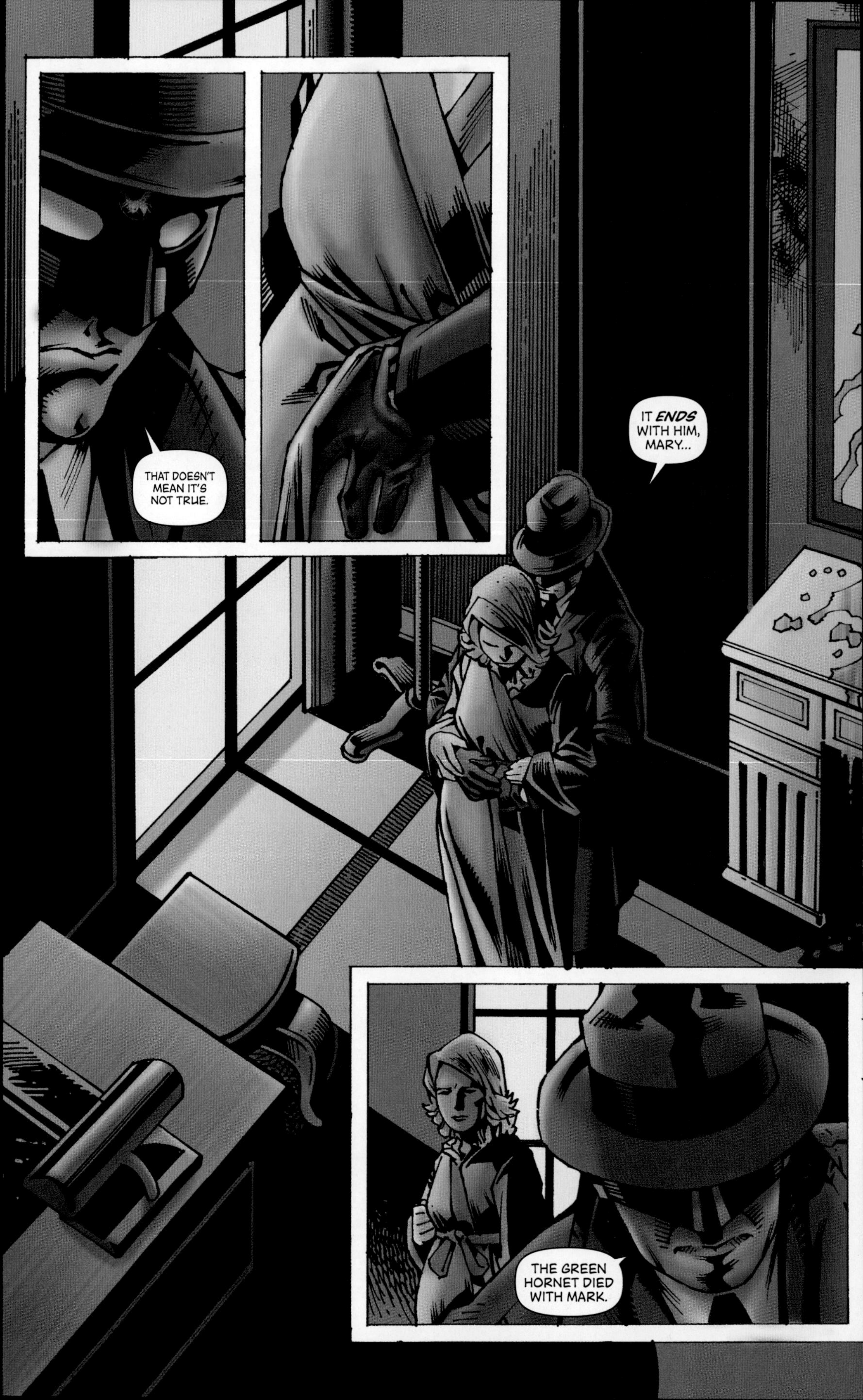
THAT DOESN'T MEAN IT'S NOT TRUE.
IT ENDS WITH HIM, MARY...
THE GREEN HORNET DIED WITH MARK.

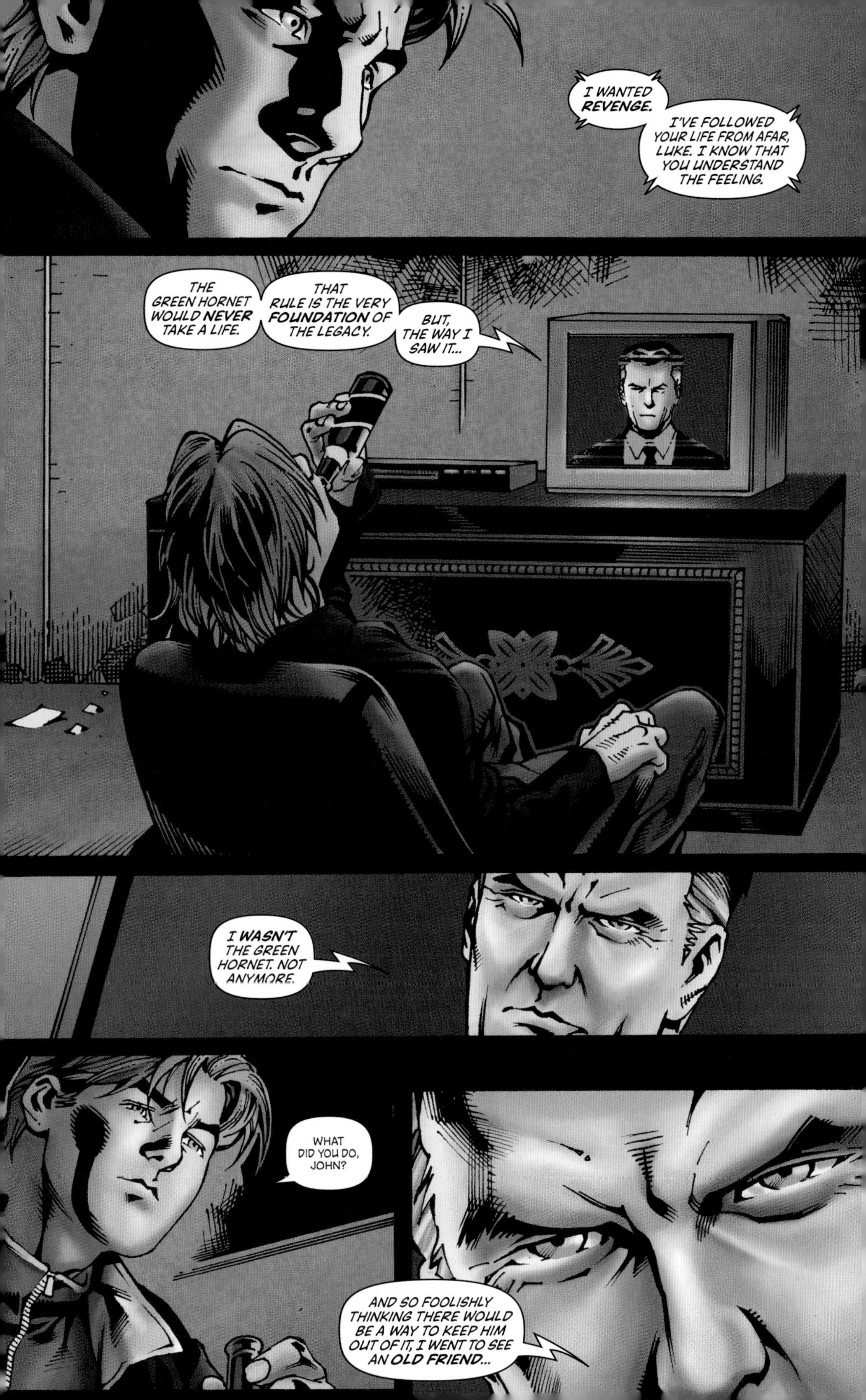
I WANTED **REVENGE.**
I'VE FOLLOWED YOUR LIFE FROM AFAR, LUKE. I KNOW THAT YOU UNDERSTAND THE FEELING.
THE GREEN HORNET WOULD **NEVER** TAKE A LIFE.
THAT RULE IS THE VERY **FOUNDATION** OF THE LEGACY.
BUT, THE WAY I SAW IT...
I **WASN'T** THE GREEN HORNET. NOT ANYMORE.
WHAT DID YOU DO, JOHN?
AND SO FOOLISHLY THINKING THERE WOULD BE A WAY TO KEEP HIM OUT OF IT, I WENT TO SEE AN **OLD FRIEND...**

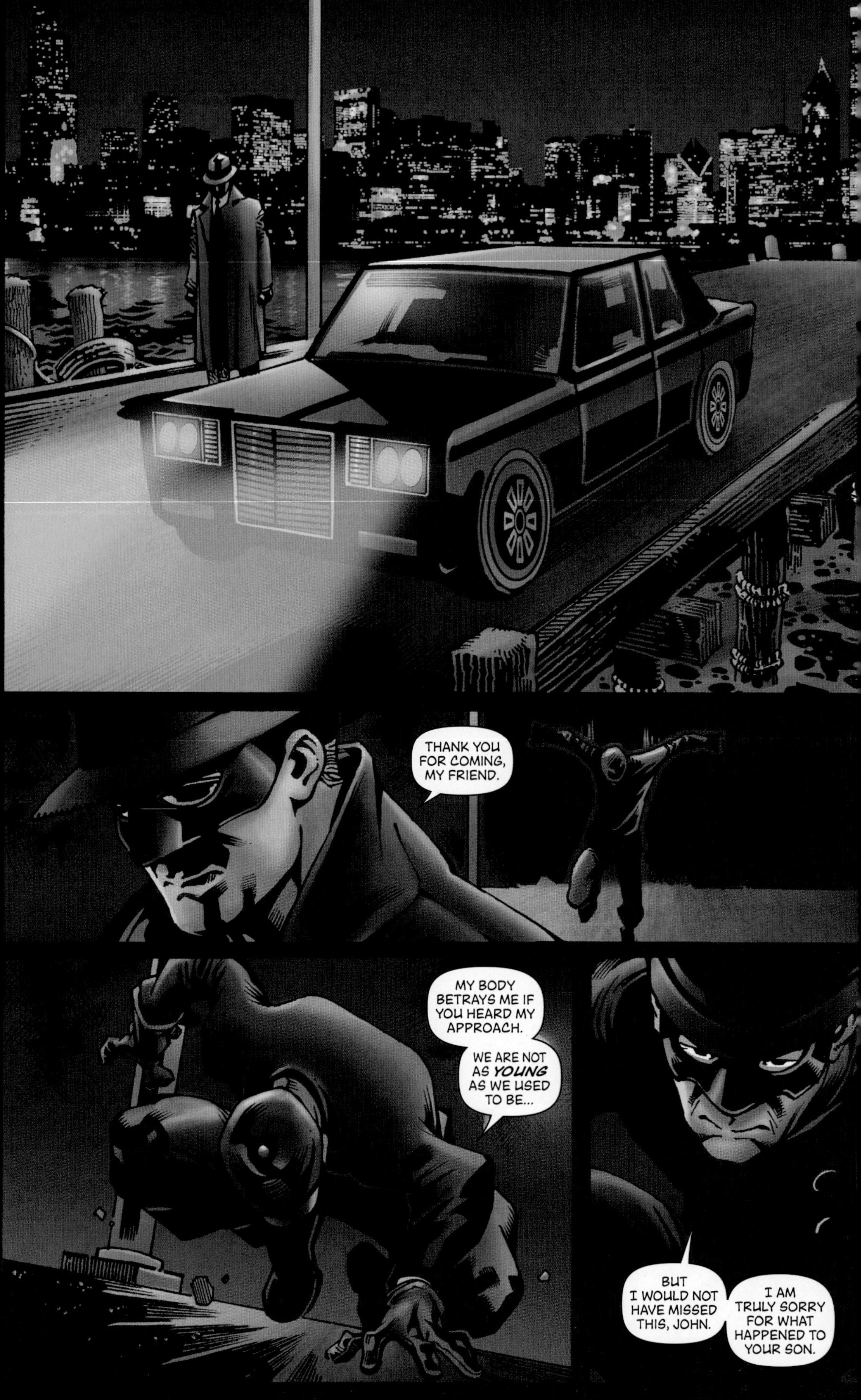
THANK YOU FOR COMING, MY FRIEND.
MY BODY BETRAYS ME IF YOU HEARD MY APPROACH.
WE ARE NOT AS *YOUNG* AS WE USED TO BE...
BUT I WOULD NOT HAVE MISSED THIS, JOHN.
I AM TRULY SORRY FOR WHAT HAPPENED TO YOUR SON.

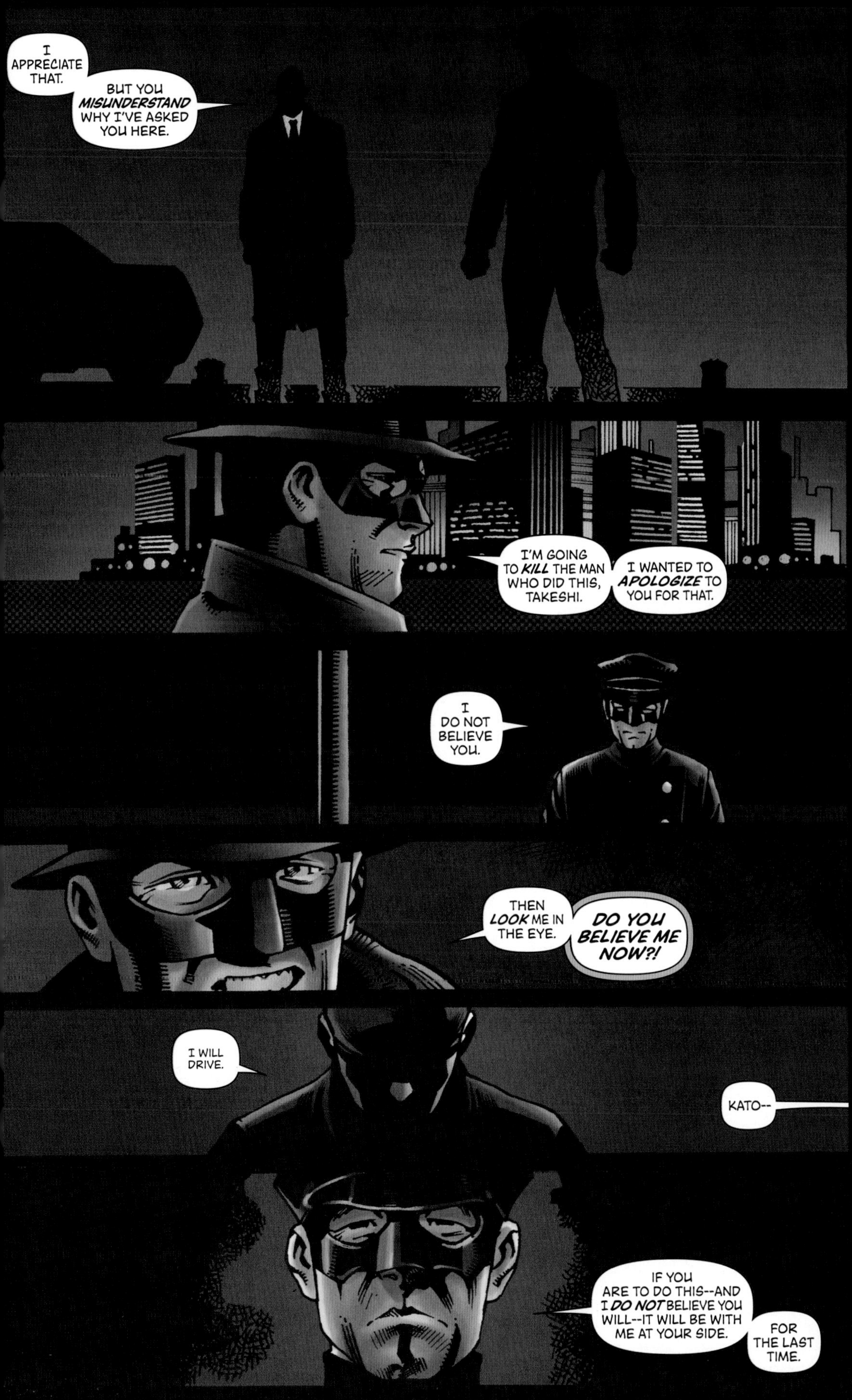
I APPRECIATE THAT.
BUT YOU MISUNDERSTAND WHY I'VE ASKED YOU HERE.
I'M GOING TO KILL THE MAN WHO DID THIS, TAKESHI.
I WANTED TO APOLOGIZE TO YOU FOR THAT.
I DO NOT BELIEVE YOU.
THEN LOOK ME IN THE EYE.
DO YOU BELIEVE ME NOW?!
I WILL DRIVE.
KATO--
IF YOU ARE TO DO THIS--AND I DO NOT BELIEVE YOU WILL--IT WILL BE WITH ME AT YOUR SIDE.
FOR THE LAST TIME.

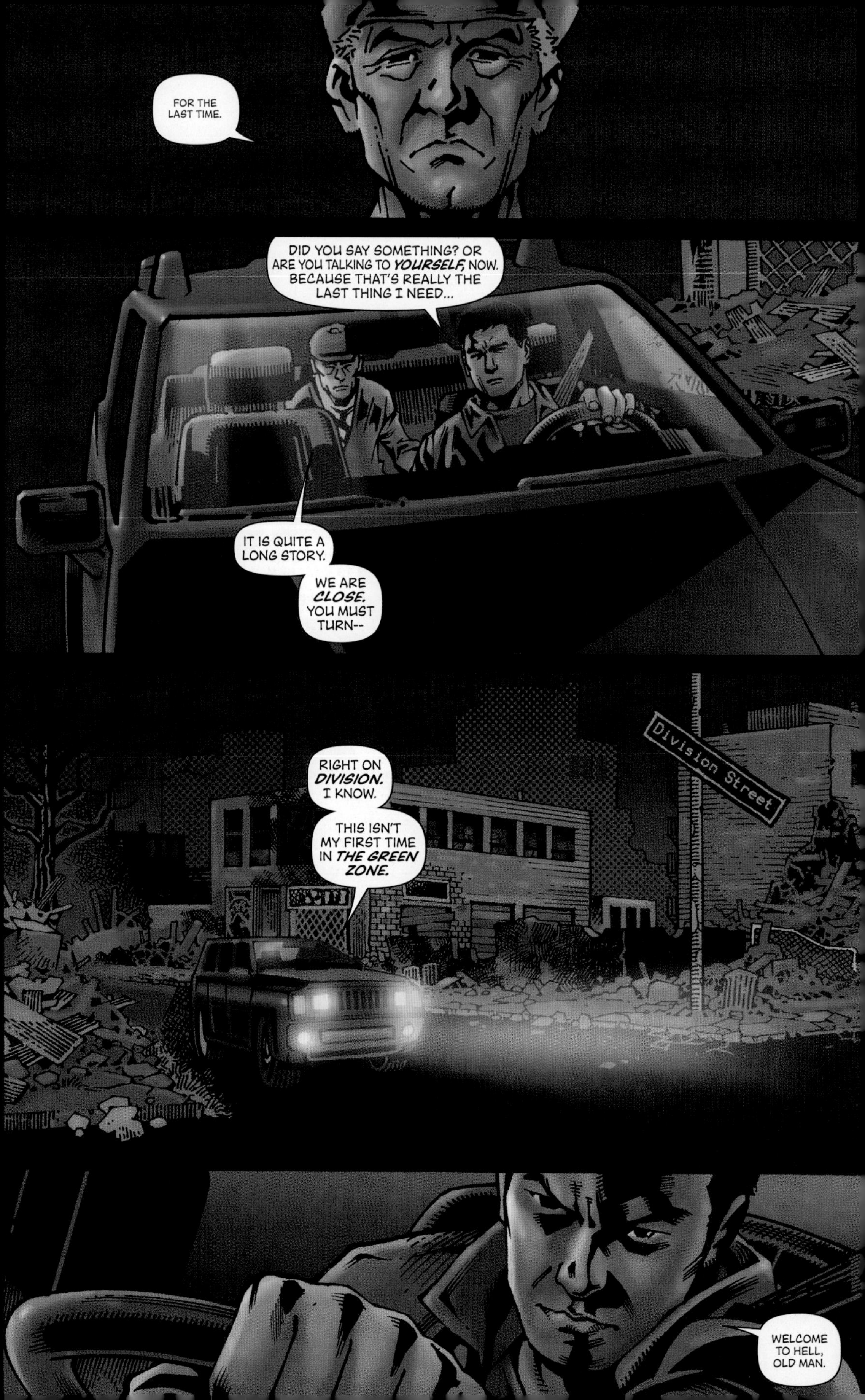
FOR THE LAST TIME.
DID YOU SAY SOMETHING? OR ARE YOU TALKING TO YOURSELF, NOW. BECAUSE THAT'S REALLY THE LAST THING I NEED...
IT IS QUITE A LONG STORY.
WE ARE CLOSE. YOU MUST TURN--
Division Street
RIGHT ON DIVISION. I KNOW.
THIS ISN'T MY FIRST TIME IN THE GREEN ZONE.
WELCOME TO HELL, OLD MAN.

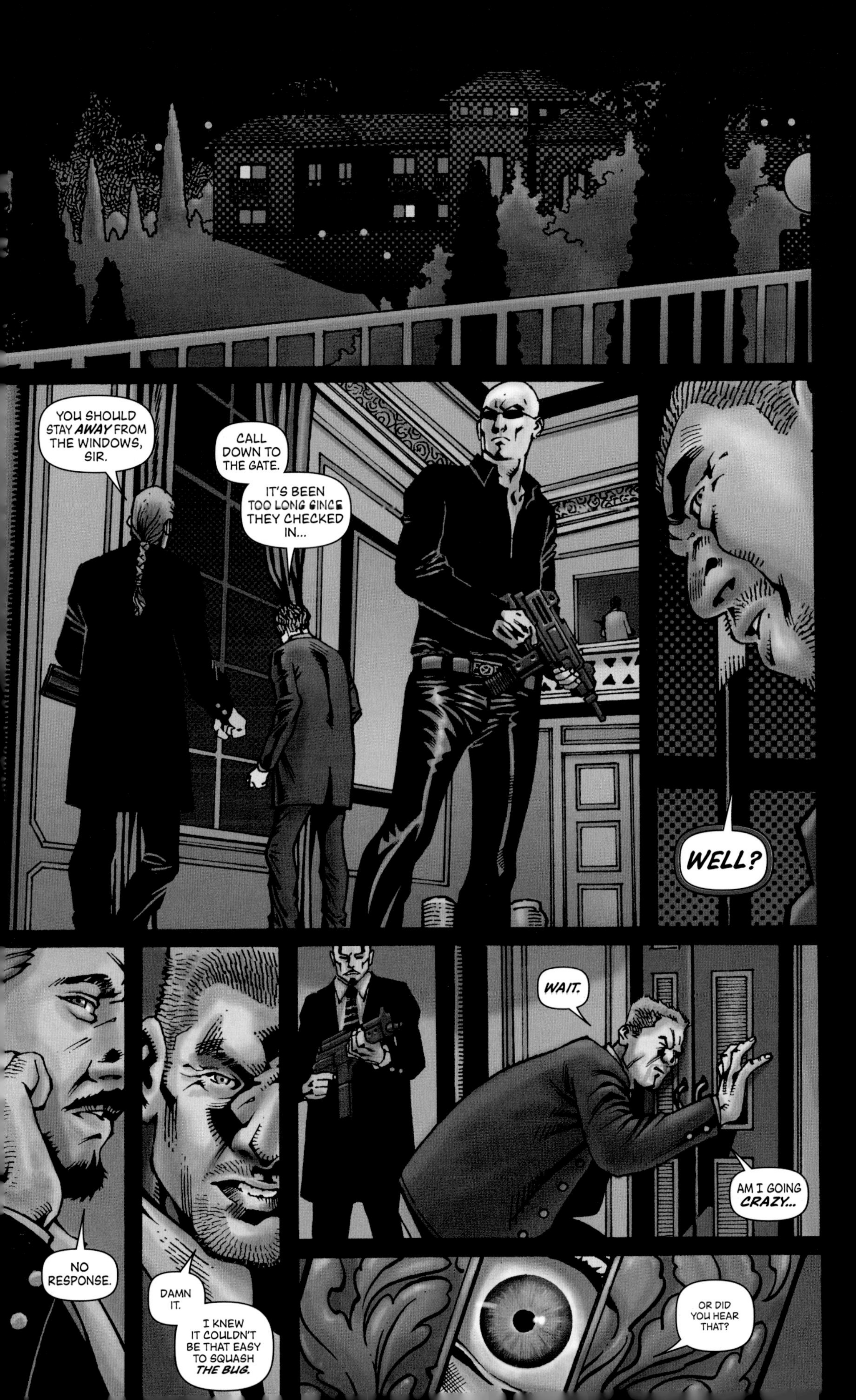
YOU SHOULD STAY AWAY FROM THE WINDOWS, SIR.
CALL DOWN TO THE GATE.
IT'S BEEN TOO LONG SINCE THEY CHECKED IN...
WELL?
NO RESPONSE.
DAMN IT.
I KNEW IT COULDN'T BE THAT EASY TO SQUASH THE BUG.
WAIT.
AM I GOING CRAZY...
OR DID YOU HEAR THAT?

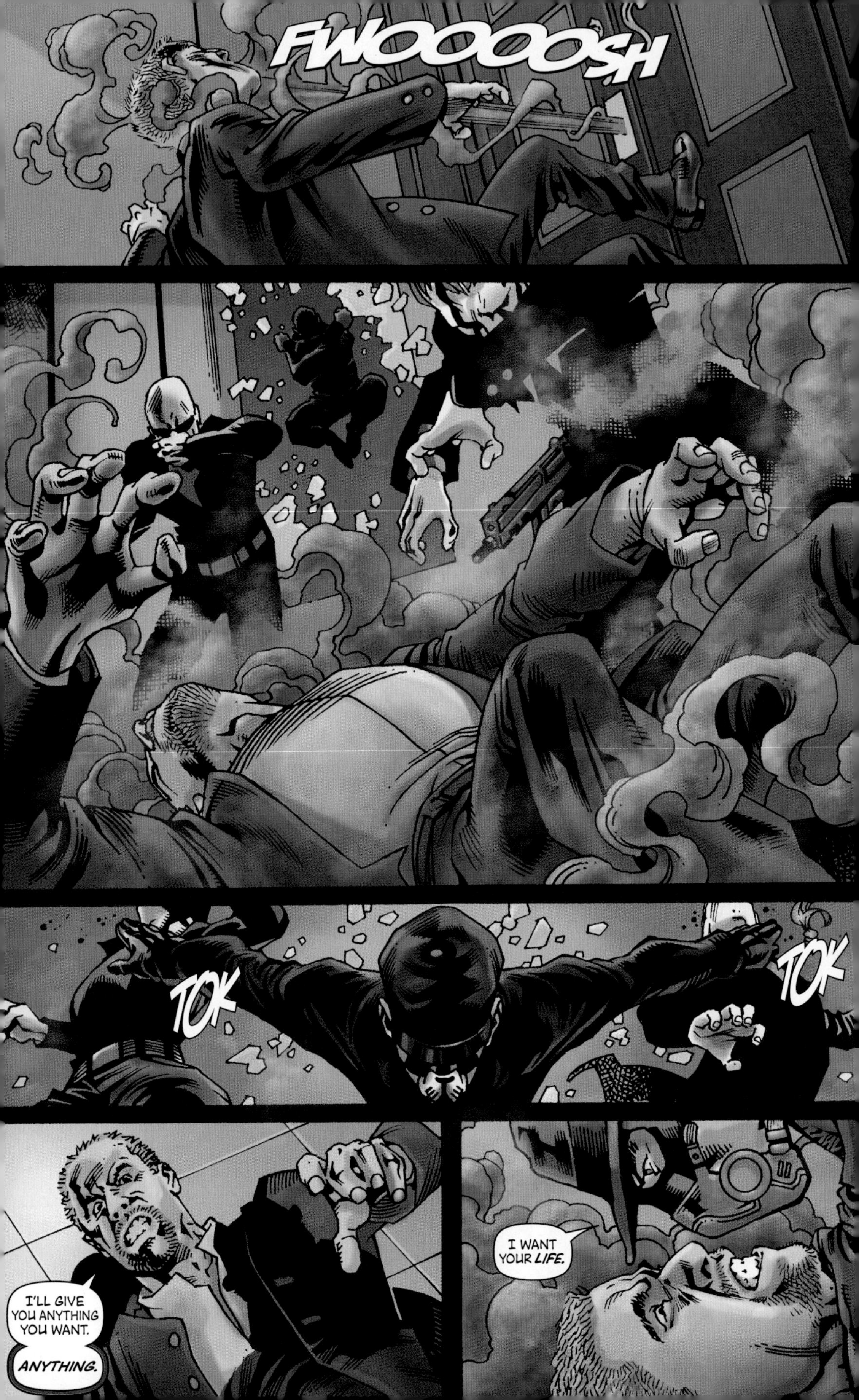
FWOOOOSH
TOK
TOK
I'LL GIVE YOU ANYTHING YOU WANT.
ANYTHING.
I WANT YOUR LIFE.

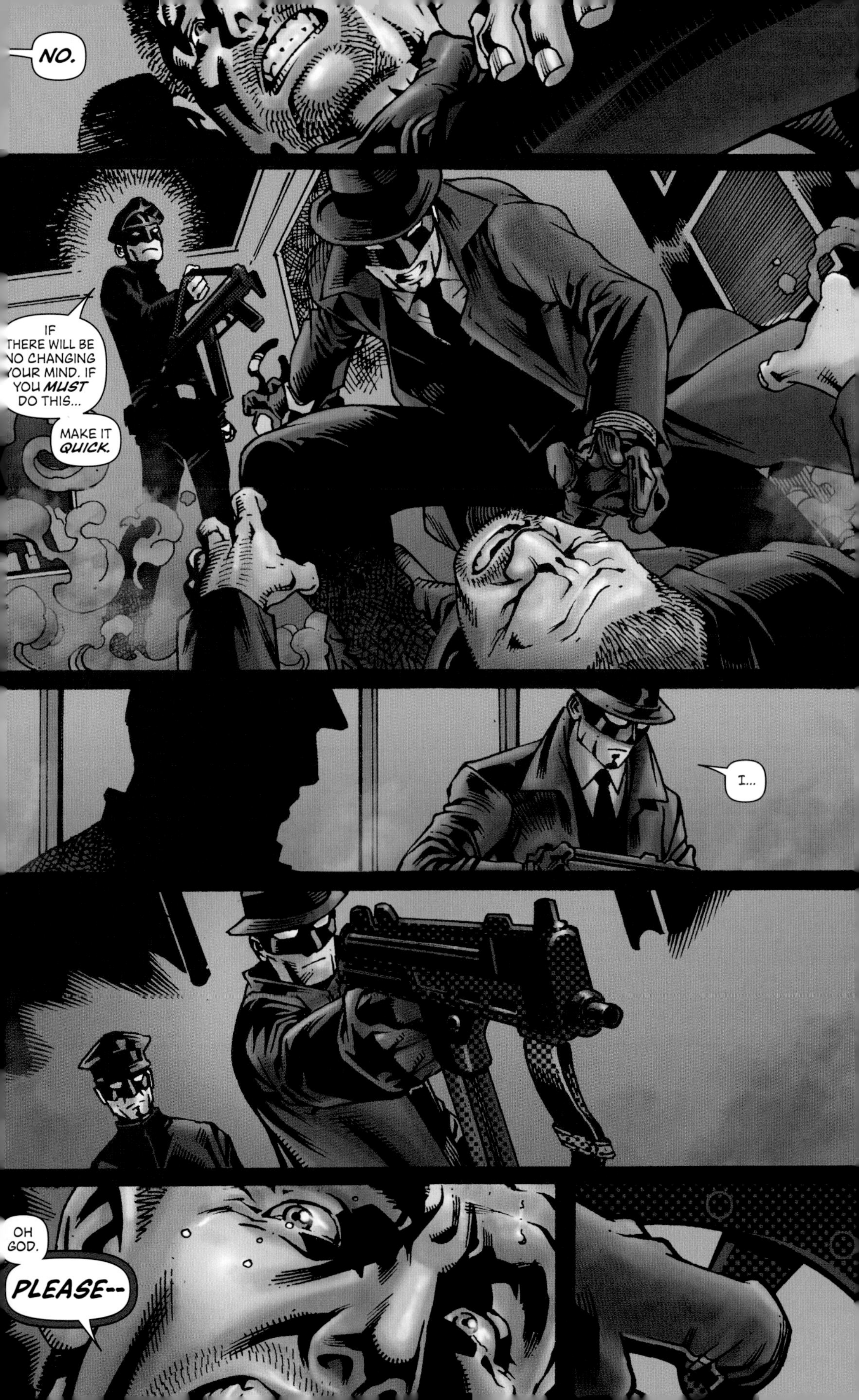
NO.
IF THERE WILL BE NO CHANGING YOUR MIND. IF YOU MUST DO THIS...
MAKE IT QUICK.
I...
OH GOD.
PLEASE--

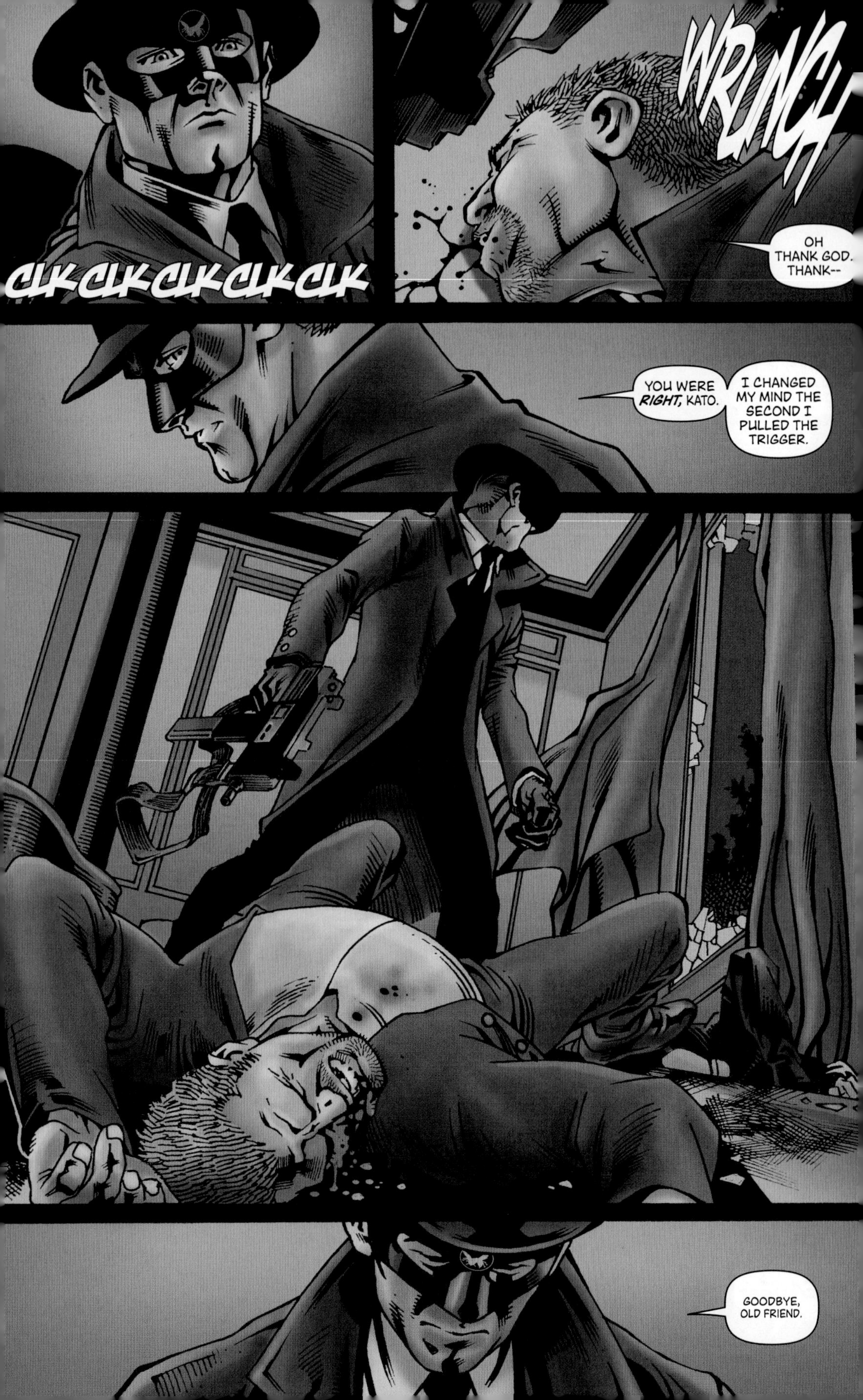
CLK CLK CLK CLK CLK
WRUNCH
OH THANK GOD. THANK--
YOU WERE *RIGHT,* KATO.
I CHANGED MY MIND THE SECOND I PULLED THE TRIGGER.
GOODBYE, OLD FRIEND.

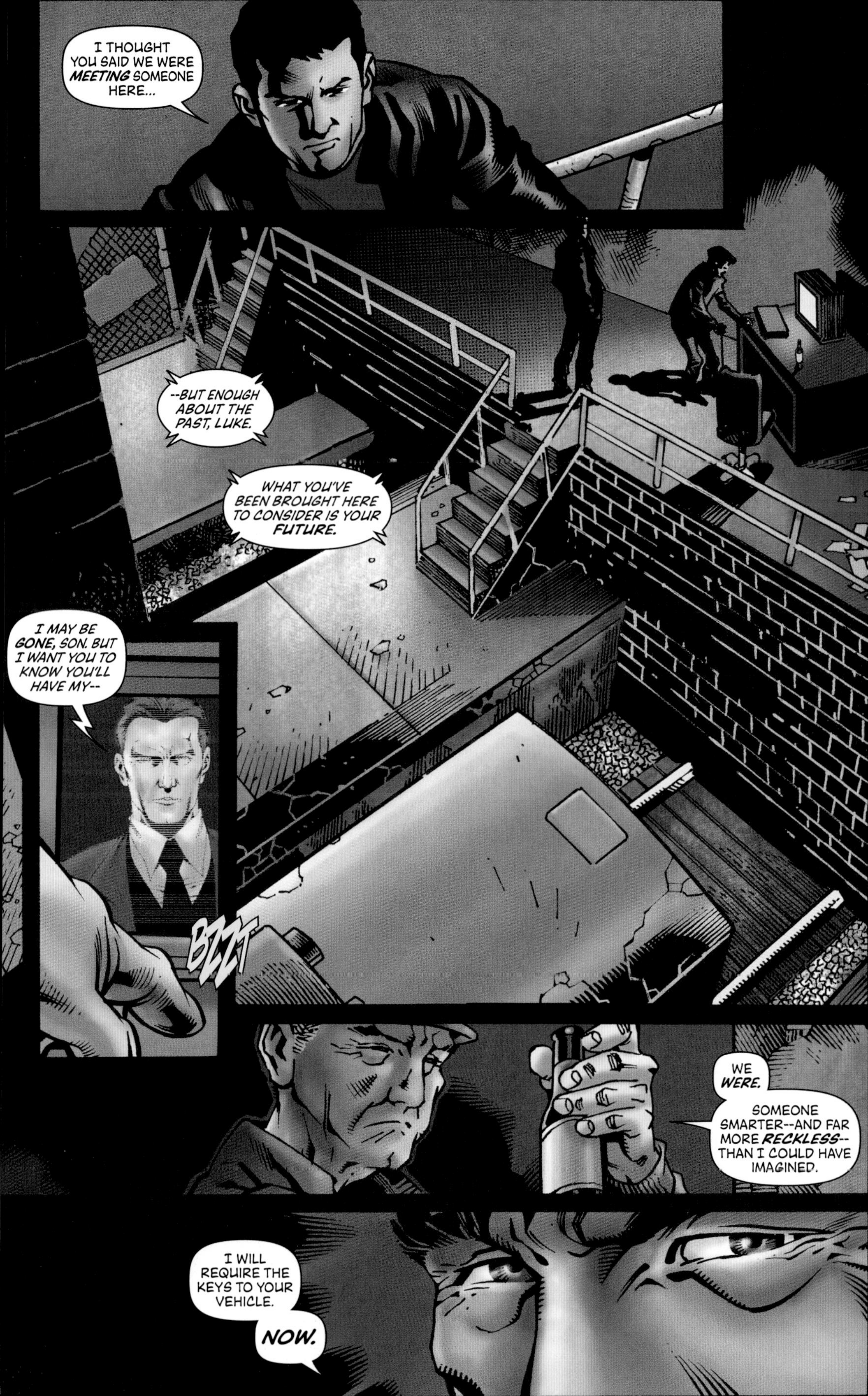
I THOUGHT YOU SAID WE WERE *MEETING* SOMEONE HERE...
--BUT ENOUGH ABOUT THE PAST, LUKE.
WHAT YOU'VE BEEN BROUGHT HERE TO CONSIDER IS YOUR *FUTURE.*
I MAY BE *GONE,* SON. BUT I WANT YOU TO KNOW YOU'LL HAVE MY--
BZZT
WE *WERE.*
SOMEONE SMARTER--AND FAR MORE *RECKLESS*--THAN I COULD HAVE IMAGINED.
I WILL REQUIRE THE KEYS TO YOUR VEHICLE.
NOW.

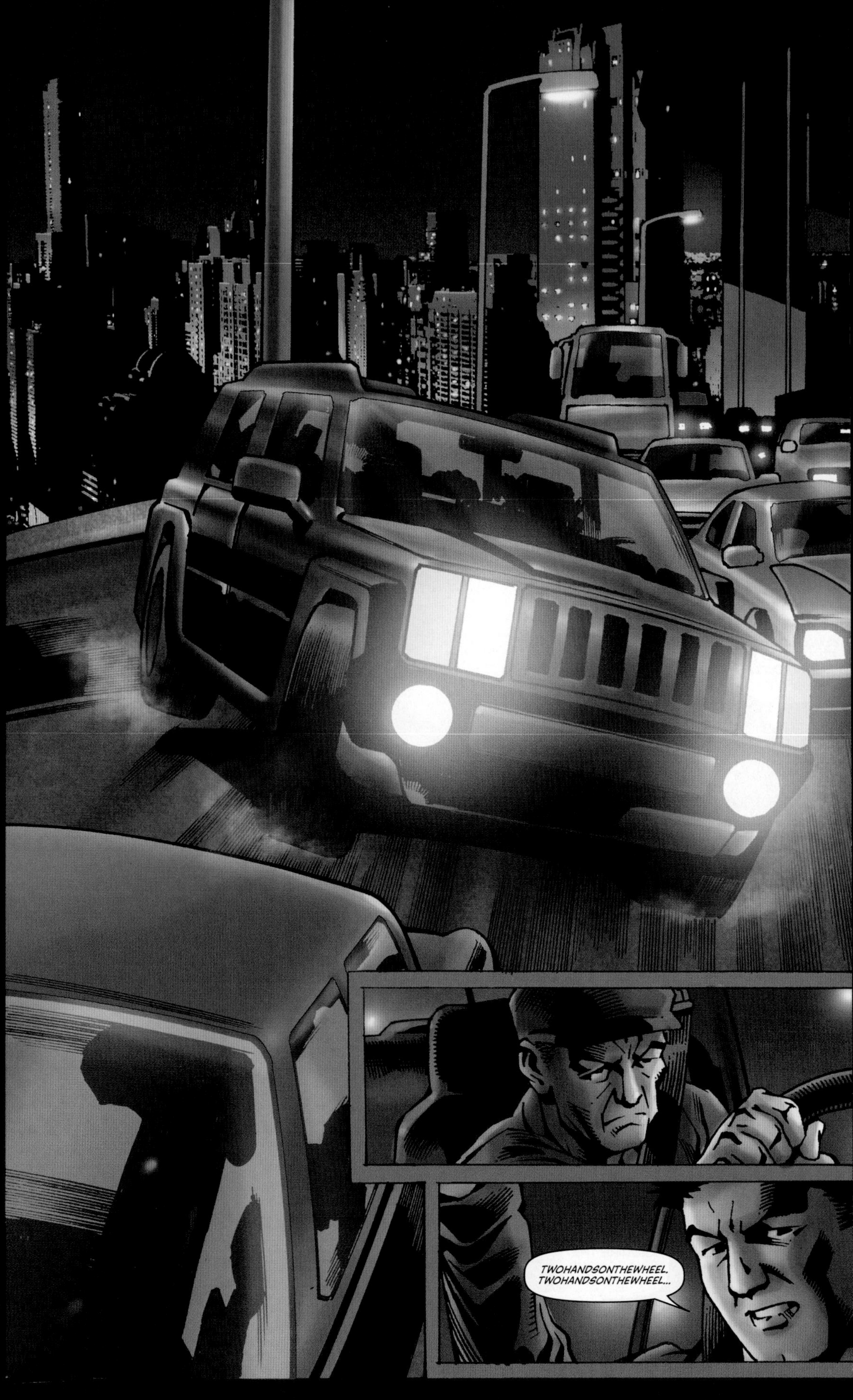
TWOHANDSONTHEWHEEL.
TWOHANDSONTHEWHEEL...

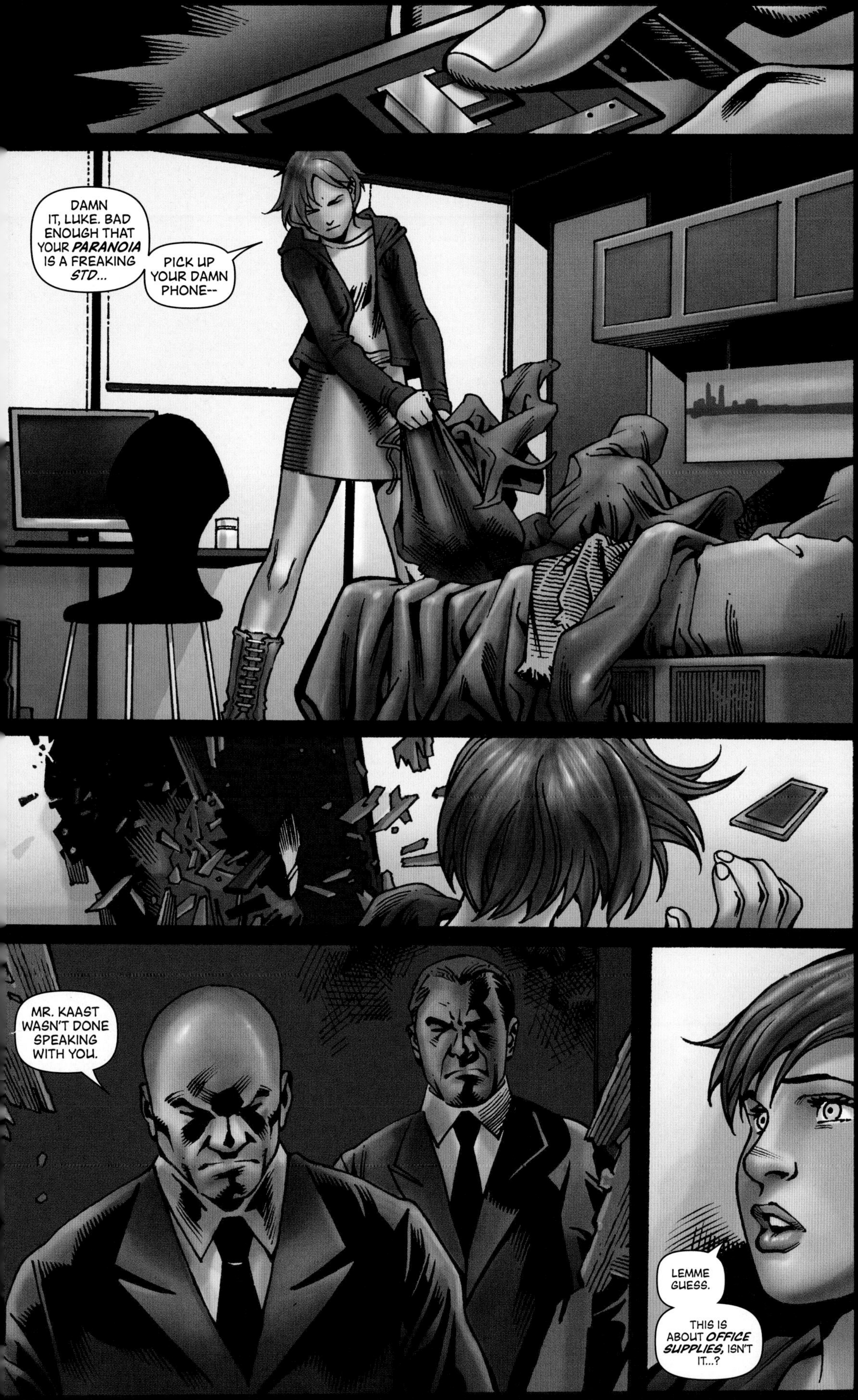
DAMN IT, LUKE. BAD ENOUGH THAT YOUR *PARANOIA* IS A FREAKING *STD*...
PICK UP YOUR DAMN PHONE--
MR. KAAST WASN'T DONE SPEAKING WITH YOU.
LEMME GUESS.
THIS IS ABOUT ***OFFICE SUPPLIES,*** ISN'T IT...?

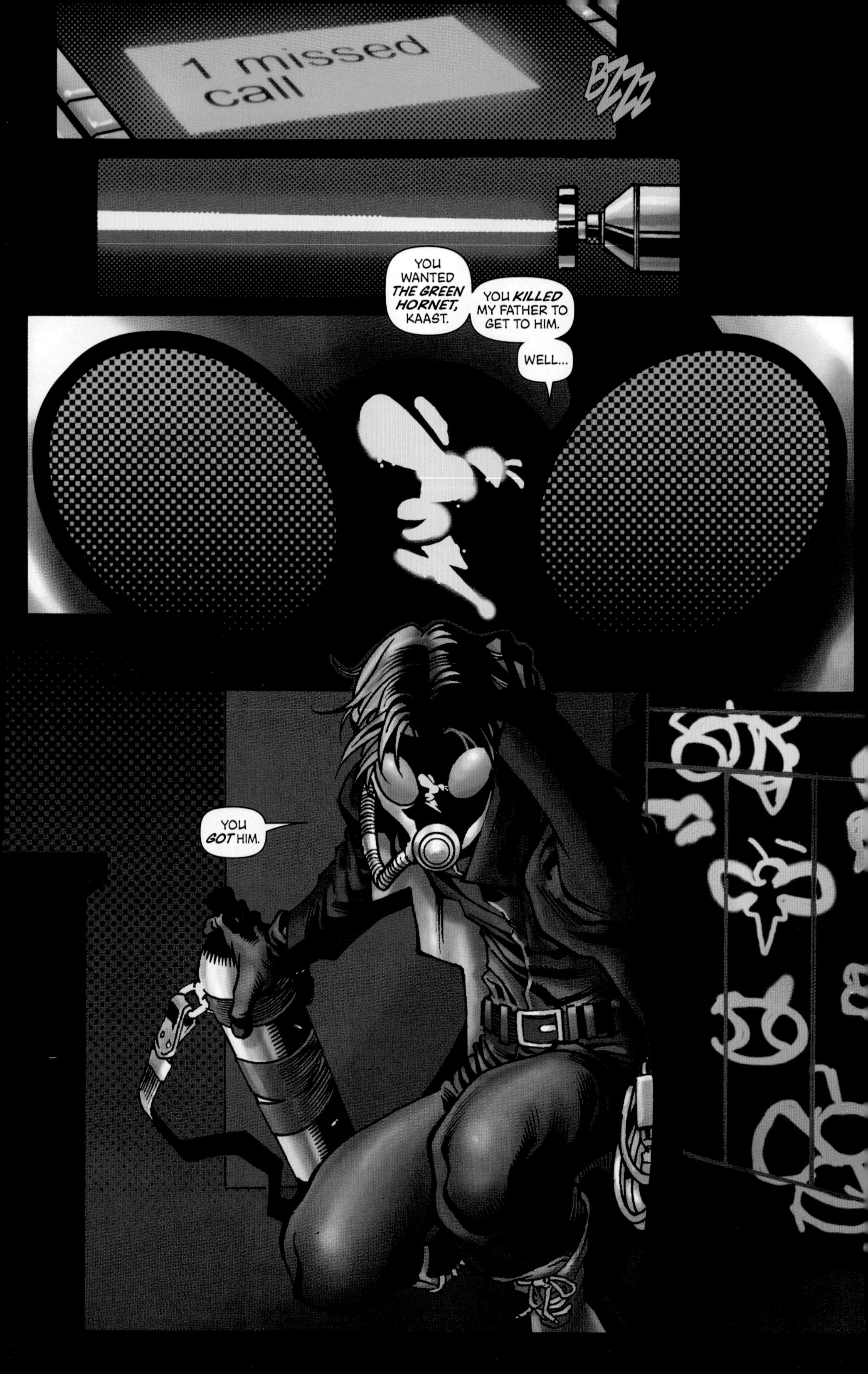
1 missed call
BZZZ
YOU WANTED *THE GREEN HORNET,* KAAST.
YOU *KILLED* MY FATHER TO GET TO HIM.
WELL...
YOU *GOT* HIM.

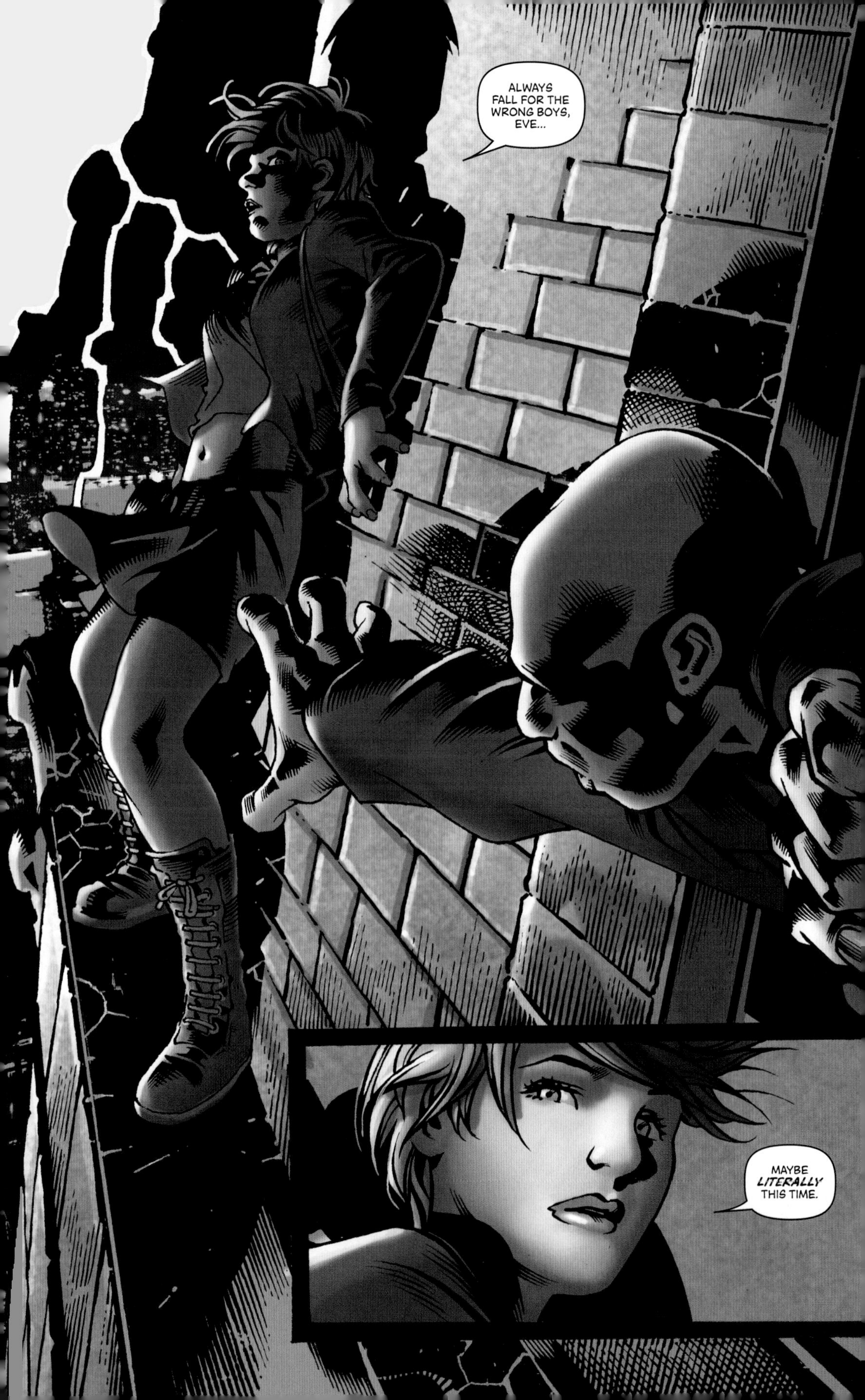
ALWAYS FALL FOR THE WRONG BOYS, EVE...
MAYBE *LITERALLY* THIS TIME.

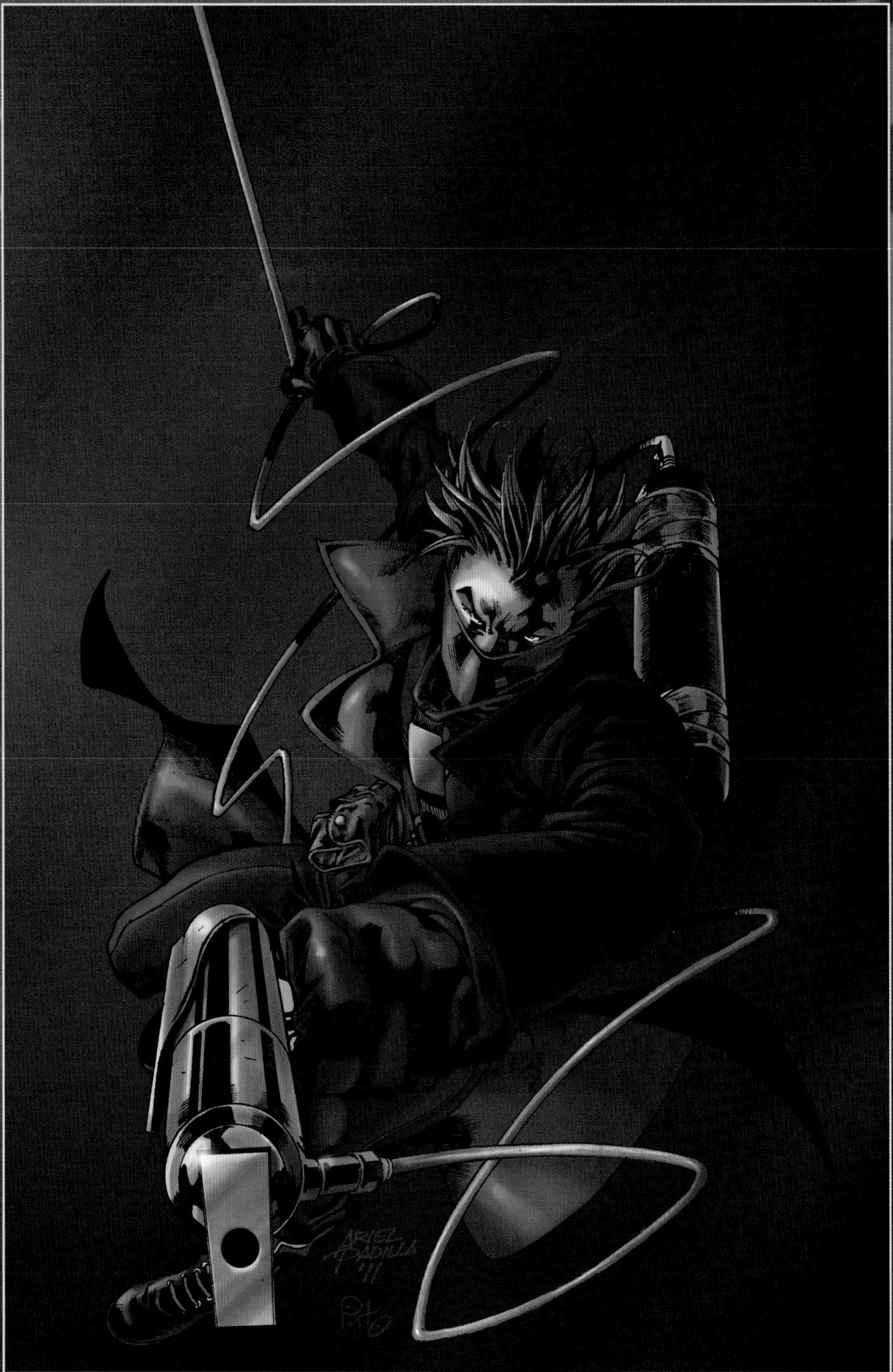

Issue #8 cover by ARIEL PADILLA

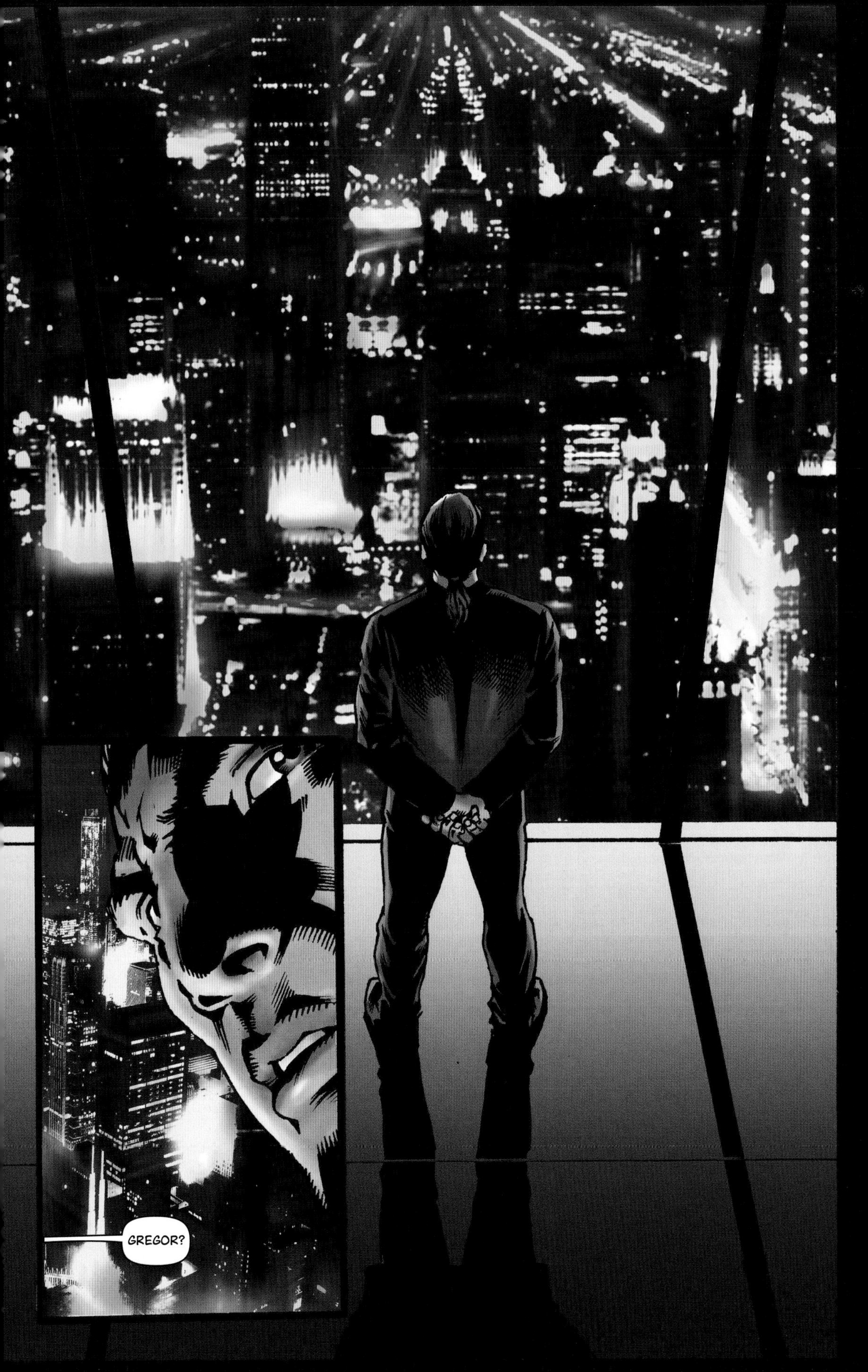
GREGOR?

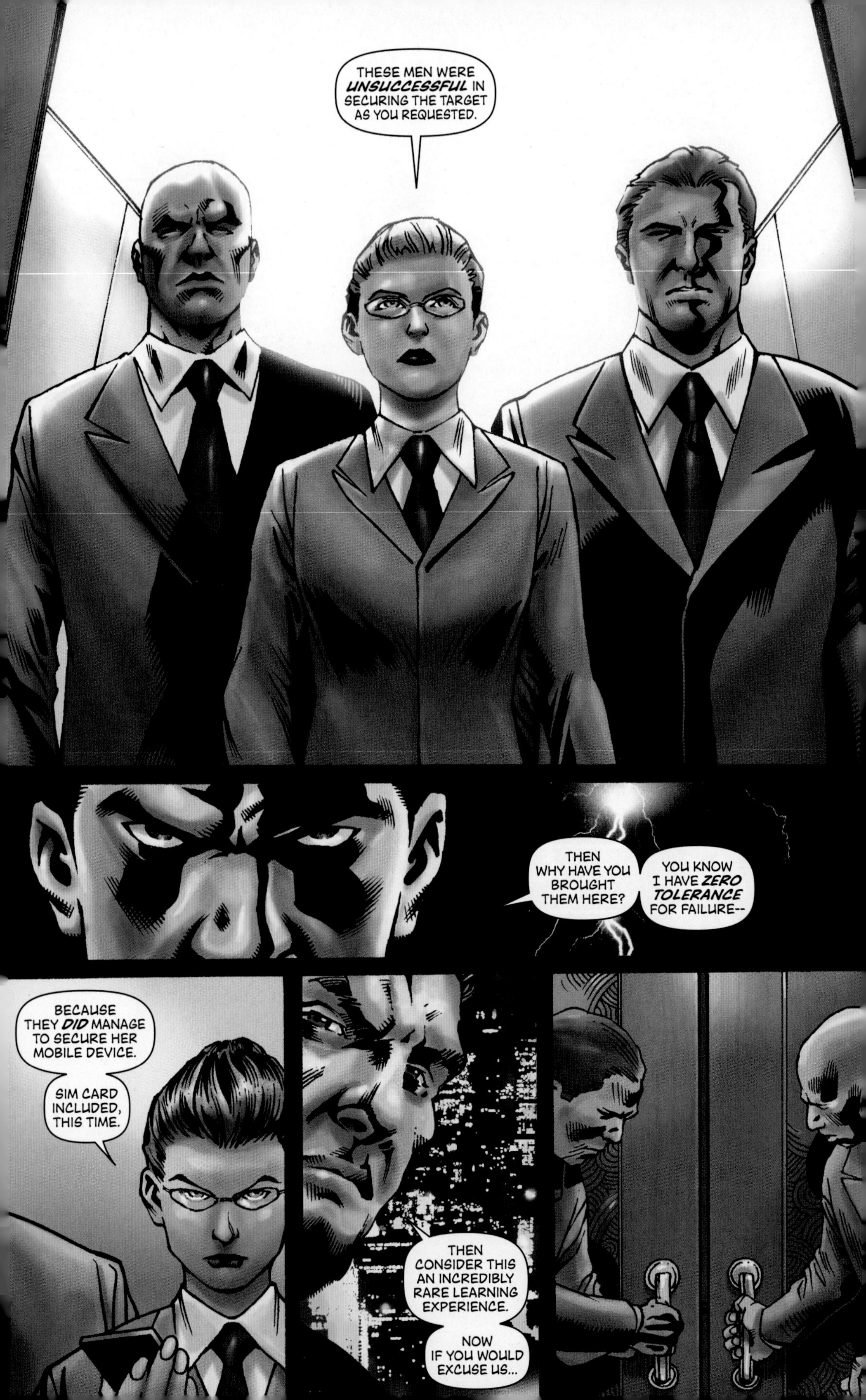
THESE MEN WERE *UNSUCCESSFUL* IN SECURING THE TARGET AS YOU REQUESTED.
THEN WHY HAVE YOU BROUGHT THEM HERE?
YOU KNOW I HAVE *ZERO TOLERANCE* FOR FAILURE--
BECAUSE THEY *DID* MANAGE TO SECURE HER MOBILE DEVICE.
SIM CARD INCLUDED, THIS TIME.
THEN CONSIDER THIS AN INCREDIBLY RARE LEARNING EXPERIENCE.
NOW IF YOU WOULD EXCUSE US...

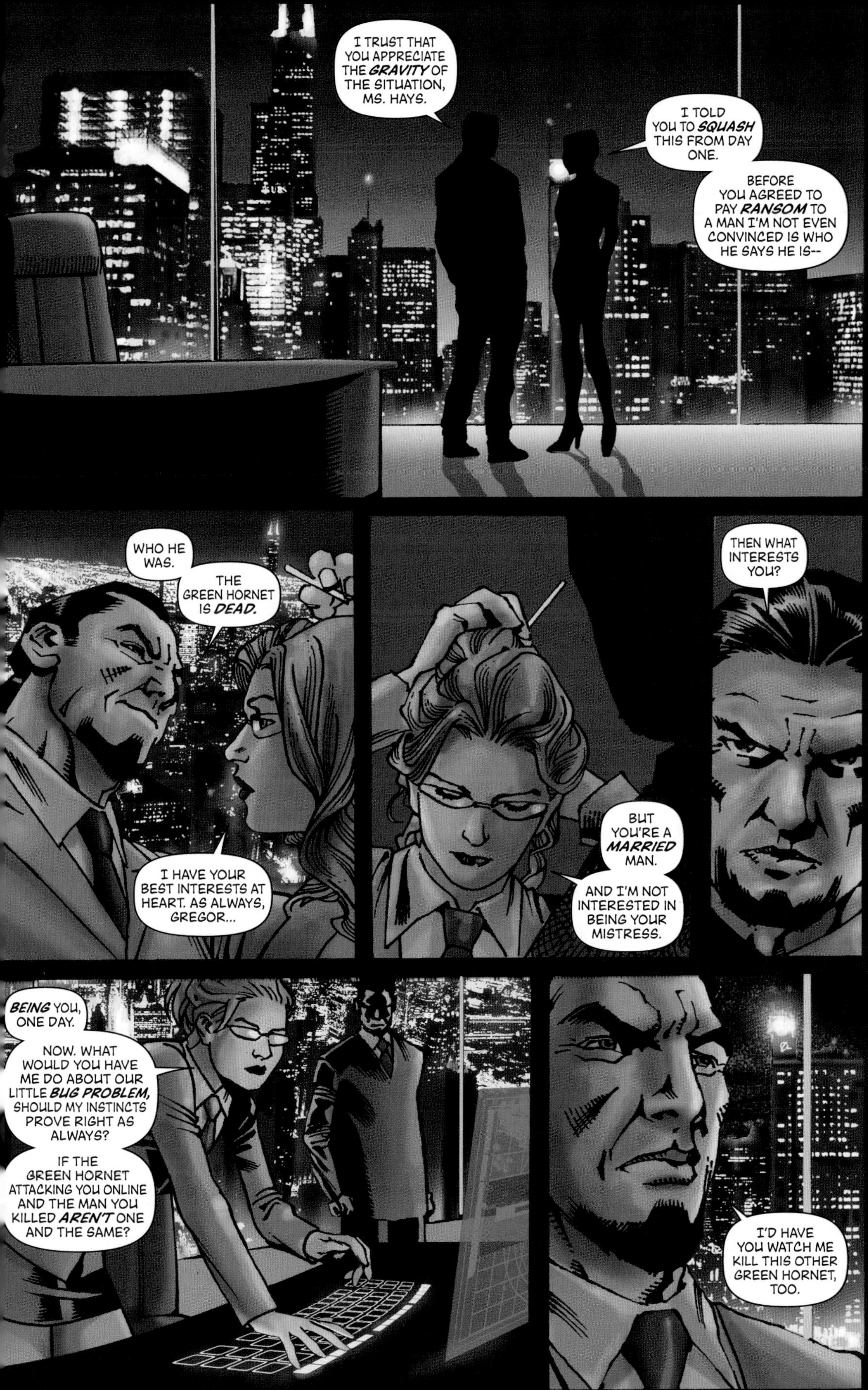
I TRUST THAT YOU APPRECIATE THE GRAVITY OF THE SITUATION, MS. HAYS.
I TOLD YOU TO SQUASH THIS FROM DAY ONE.
BEFORE YOU AGREED TO PAY RANSOM TO A MAN I'M NOT EVEN CONVINCED IS WHO HE SAYS HE IS--
WHO HE WAS.
THE GREEN HORNET IS DEAD.
I HAVE YOUR BEST INTERESTS AT HEART. AS ALWAYS, GREGOR...
BUT YOU'RE A MARRIED MAN.
AND I'M NOT INTERESTED IN BEING YOUR MISTRESS.
THEN WHAT INTERESTS YOU?
BEING YOU, ONE DAY.
NOW. WHAT WOULD YOU HAVE ME DO ABOUT OUR LITTLE BUG PROBLEM, SHOULD MY INSTINCTS PROVE RIGHT AS ALWAYS?
IF THE GREEN HORNET ATTACKING YOU ONLINE AND THE MAN YOU KILLED AREN'T ONE AND THE SAME?
I'D HAVE YOU WATCH ME KILL THIS OTHER GREEN HORNET, TOO.

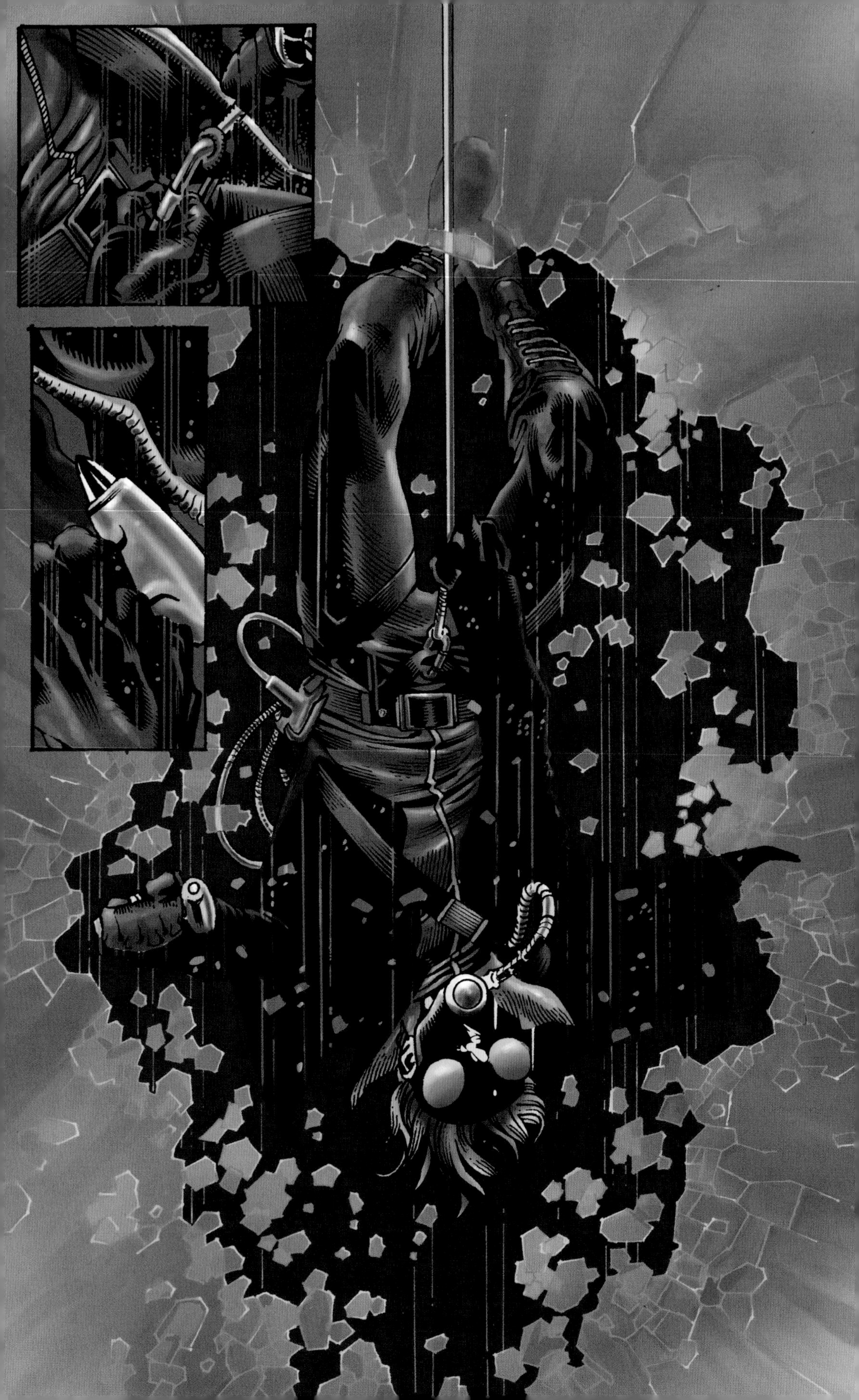

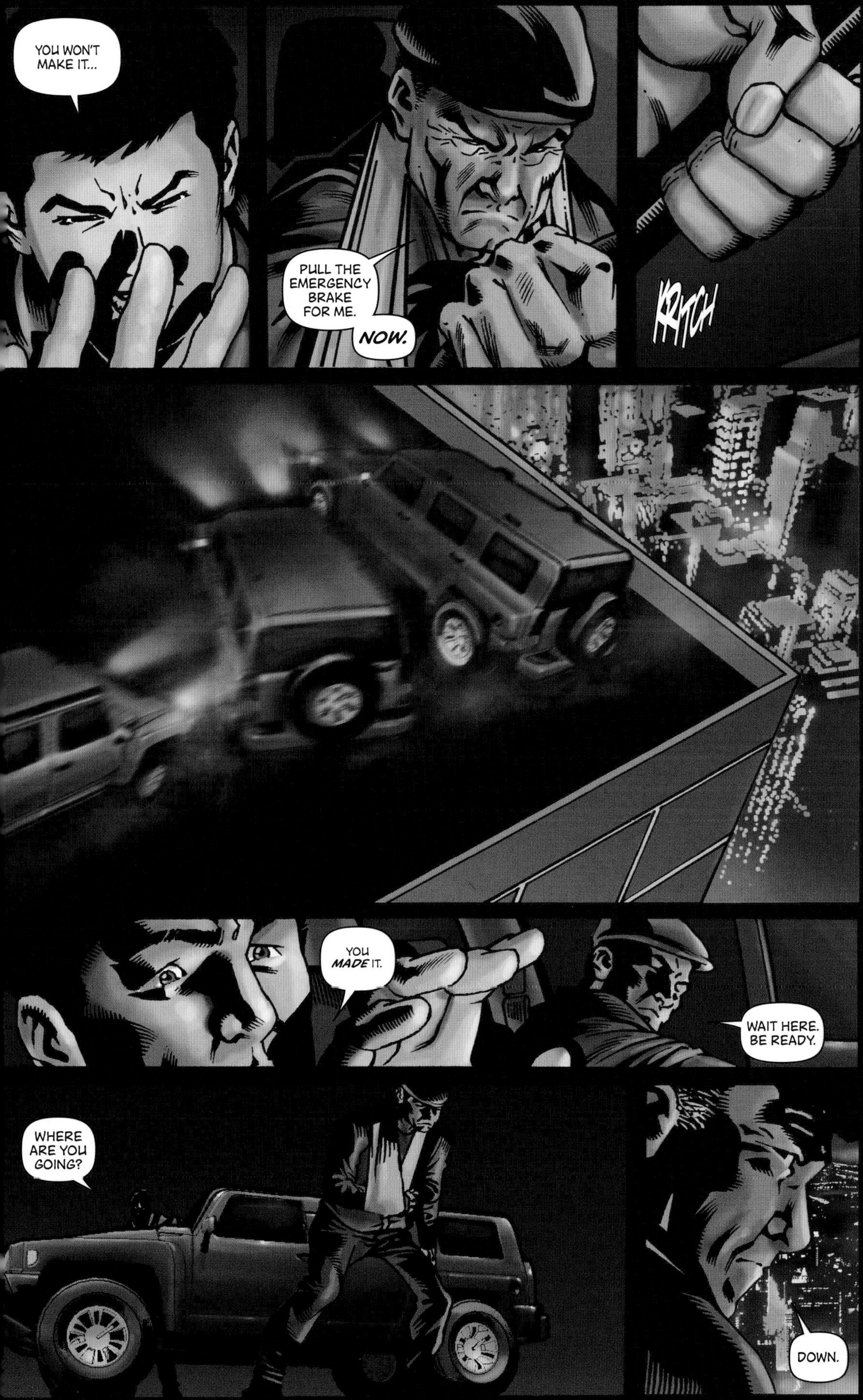
YOU WON'T MAKE IT...
PULL THE EMERGENCY BRAKE FOR ME.
NOW.
KRYCH
YOU MADE IT.
WAIT HERE. BE READY.
WHERE ARE YOU GOING?
DOWN.

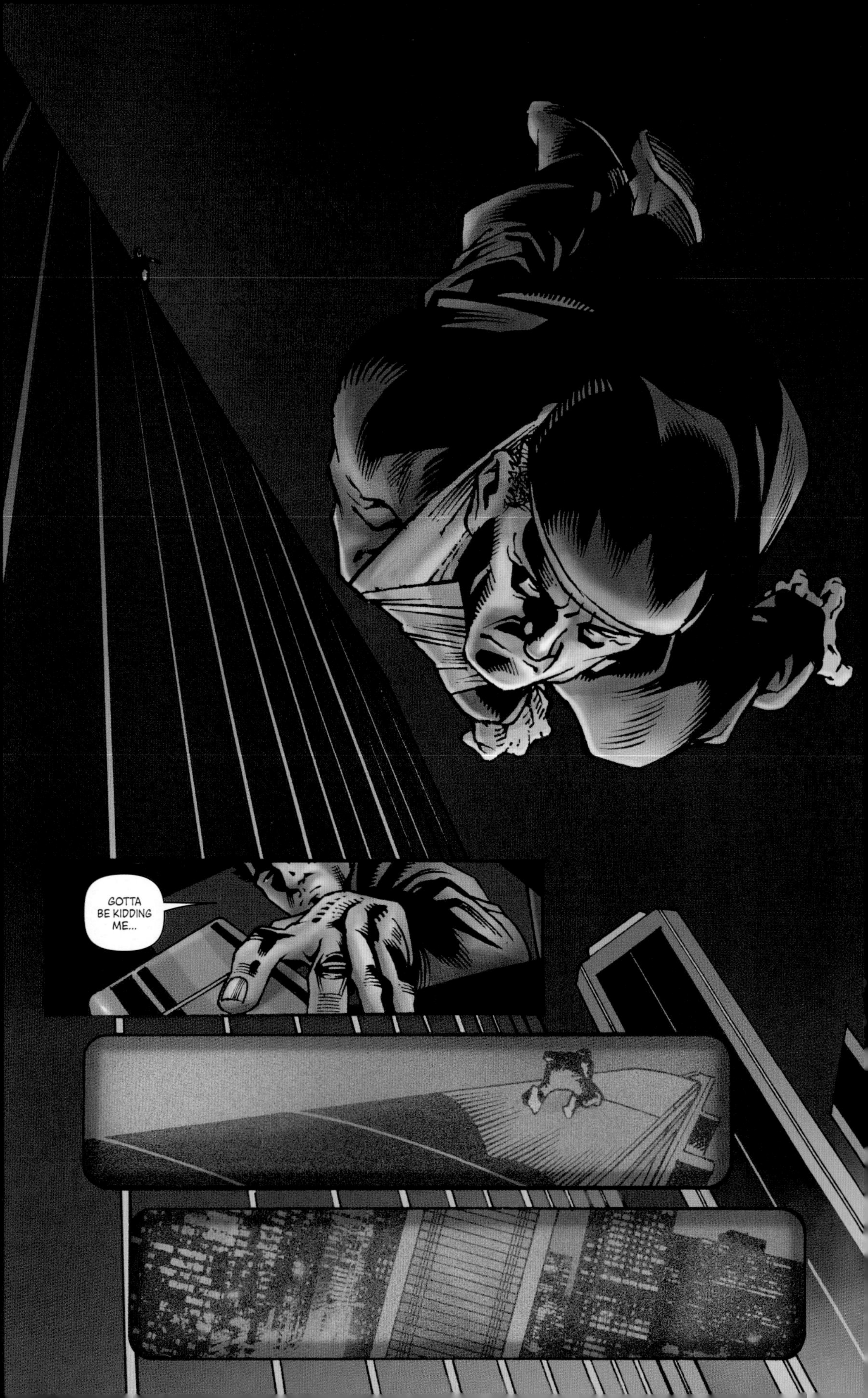
GOTTA BE KIDDING ME...

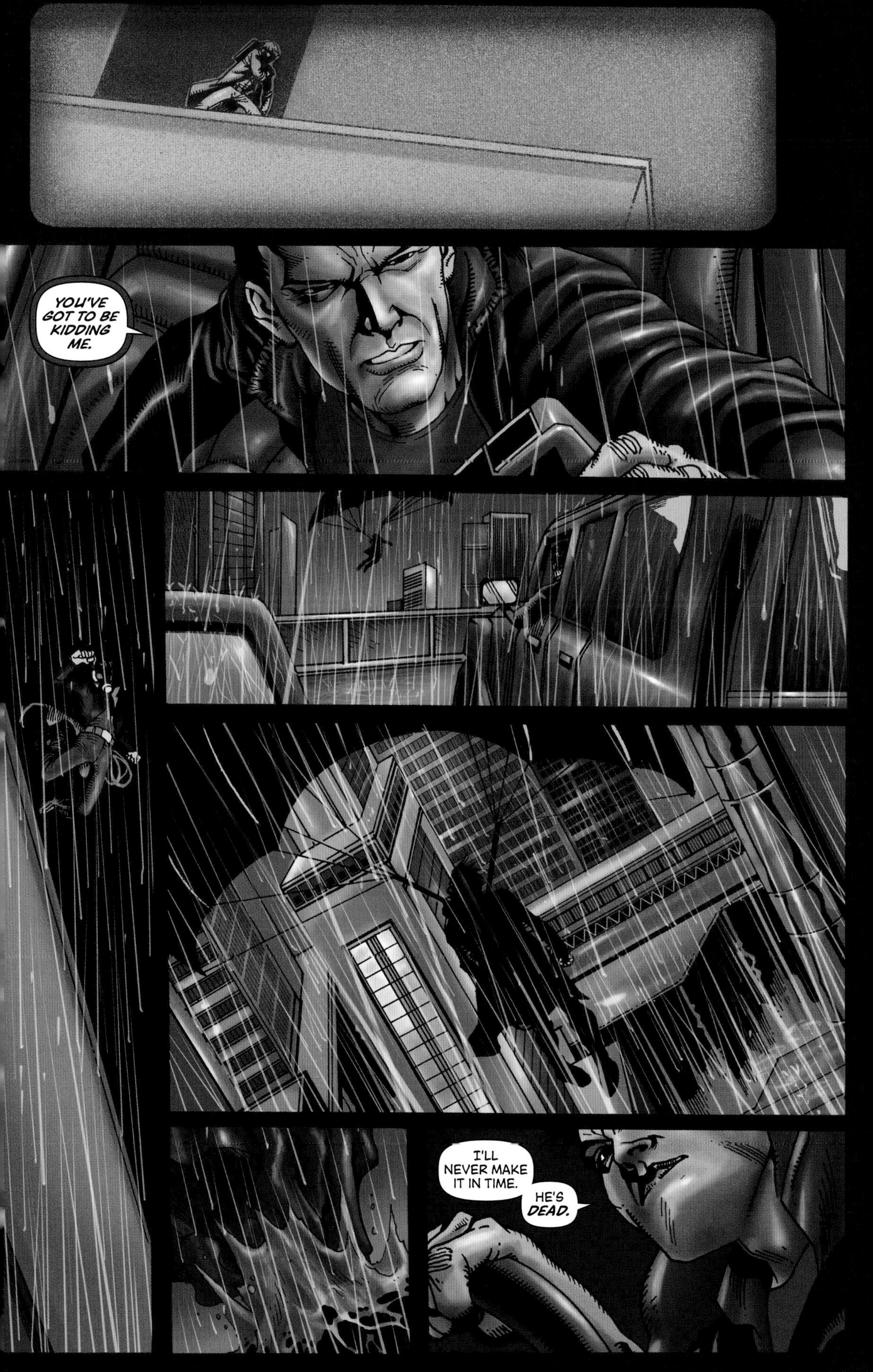
YOU'VE GOT TO BE KIDDING ME.
I'LL NEVER MAKE IT IN TIME.
HE'S DEAD.

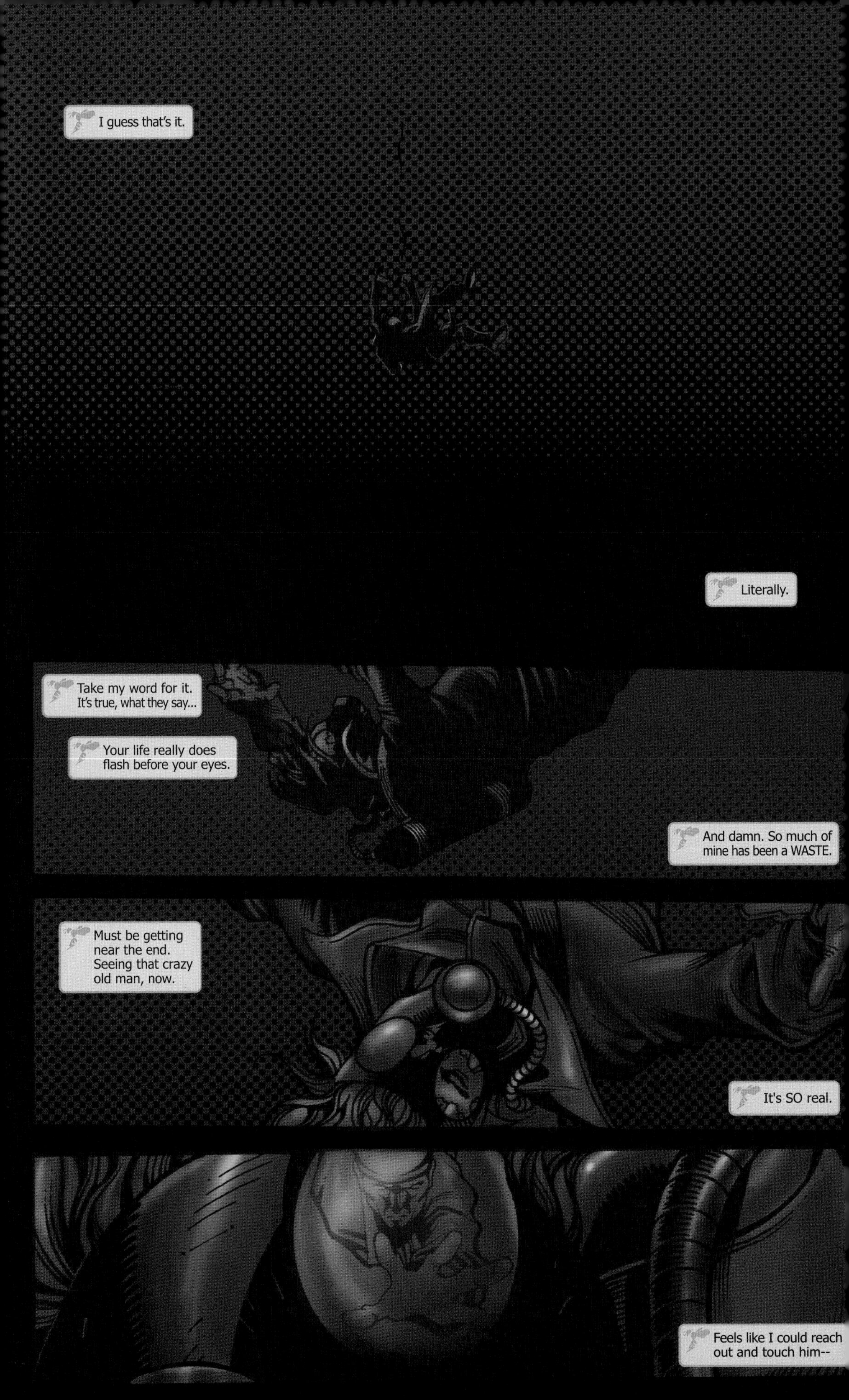

I guess that's it.
Literally.
Take my word for it. It's true, what they say...
Your life really does flash before your eyes.
And damn. So much of mine has been a WASTE.
Must be getting near the end. Seeing that crazy old man, now.
It's SO real.
Feels like I could reach out and touch him--

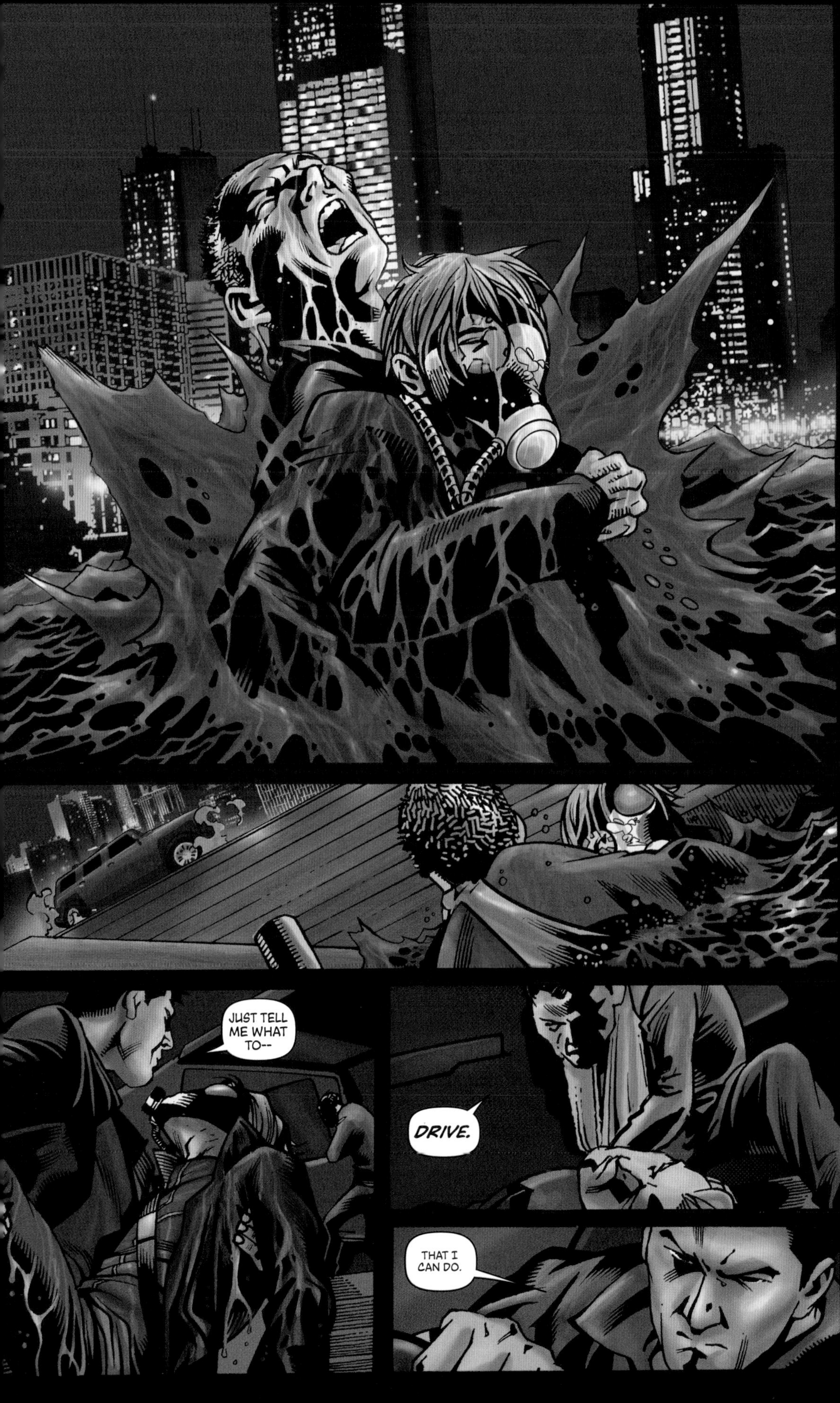

JUST TELL ME WHAT TO--
DRIVE.
THAT I CAN DO.

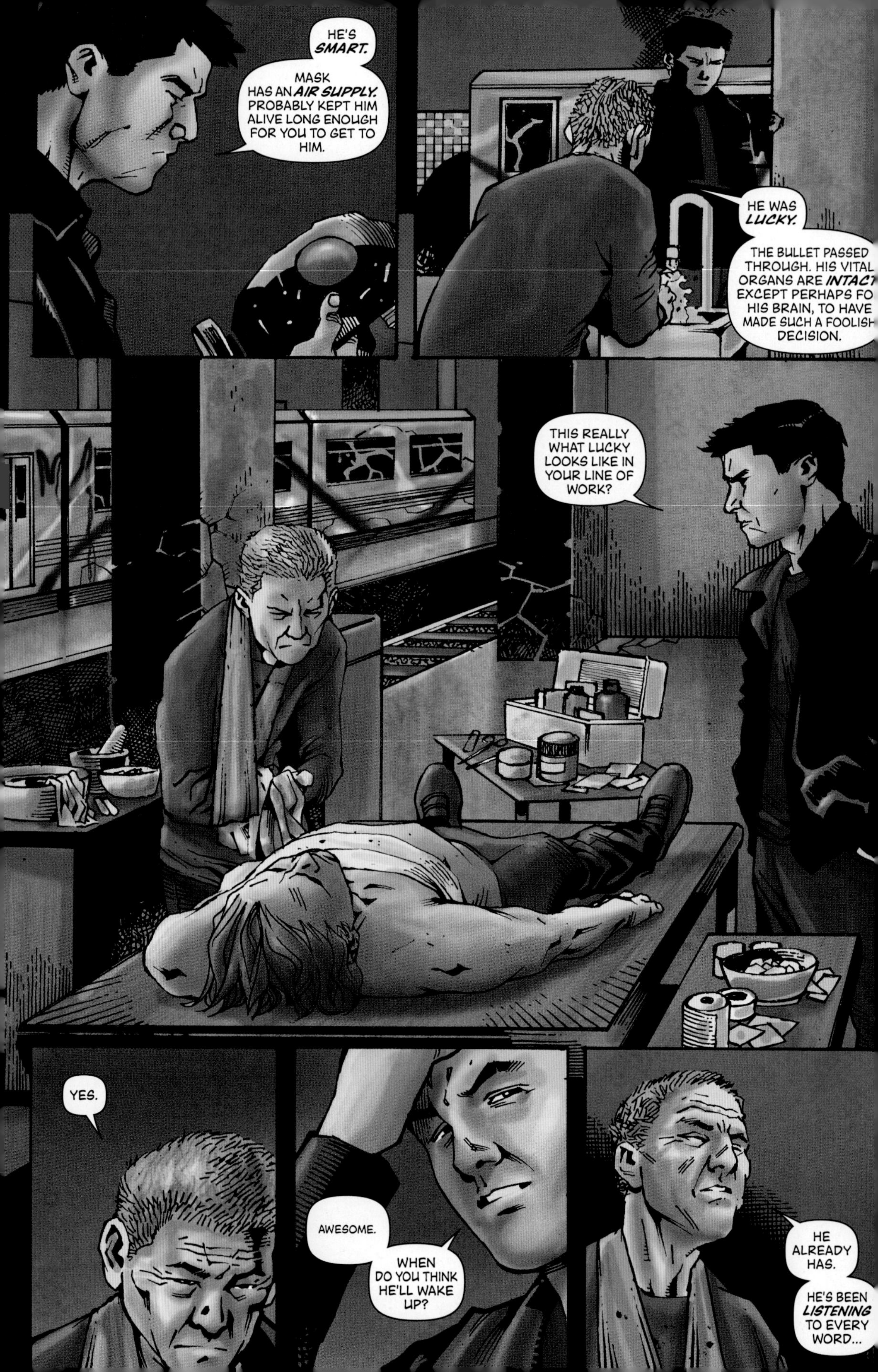
HE'S SMART.
MASK HAS AN AIR SUPPLY. PROBABLY KEPT HIM ALIVE LONG ENOUGH FOR YOU TO GET TO HIM.
HE WAS LUCKY.
THE BULLET PASSED THROUGH. HIS VITAL ORGANS ARE INTACT EXCEPT PERHAPS FO HIS BRAIN, TO HAVE MADE SUCH A FOOLISH DECISION.
THIS REALLY WHAT LUCKY LOOKS LIKE IN YOUR LINE OF WORK?
YES.
AWESOME.
WHEN DO YOU THINK HE'LL WAKE UP?
HE ALREADY HAS.
HE'S BEEN LISTENING TO EVERY WORD...

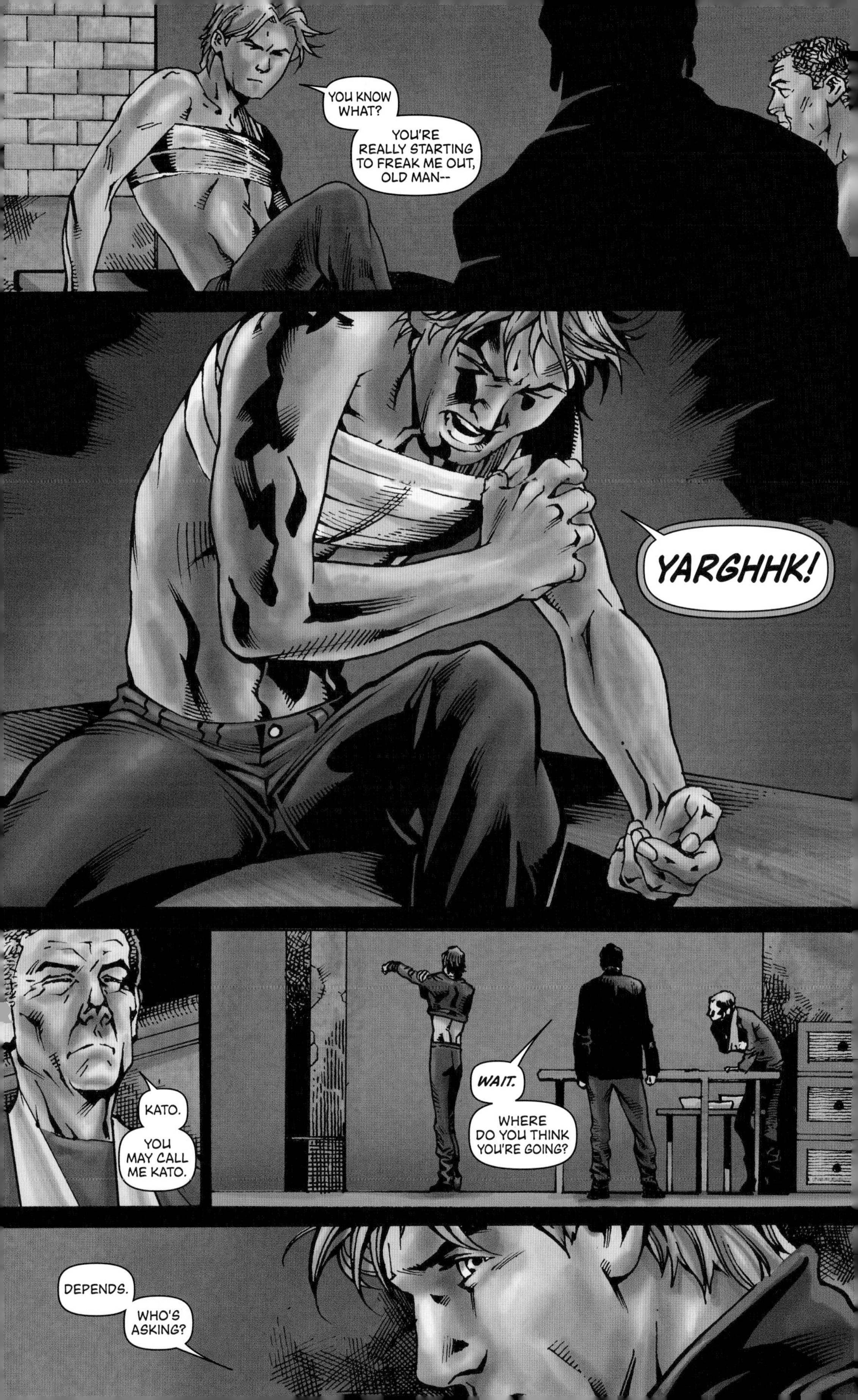
YOU KNOW WHAT?
YOU'RE REALLY STARTING TO FREAK ME OUT, OLD MAN--
YARGHHK!
KATO.
YOU MAY CALL ME KATO.
WAIT.
WHERE DO YOU THINK YOU'RE GOING?
DEPENDS.
WHO'S ASKING?

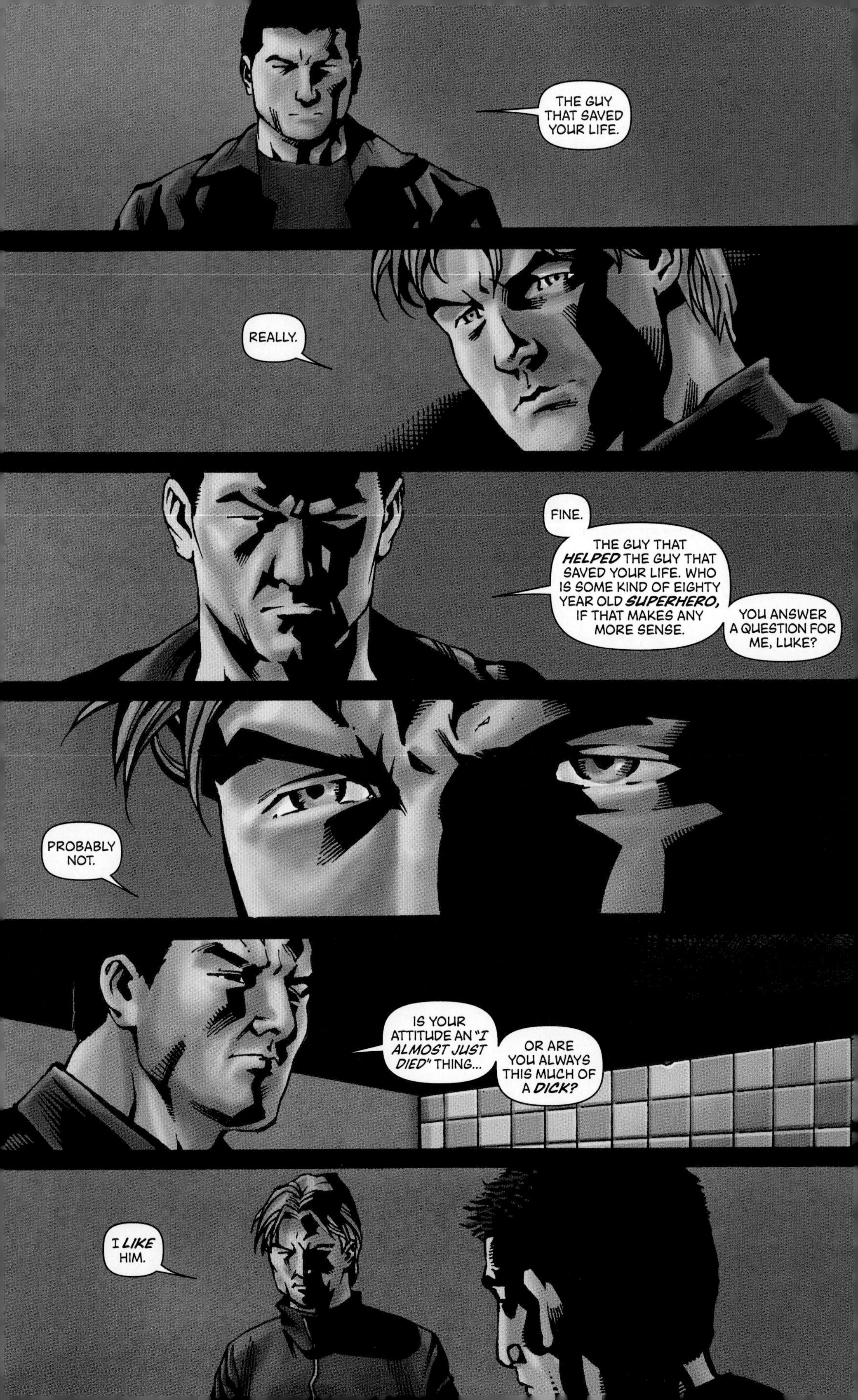
THE GUY THAT SAVED YOUR LIFE.
REALLY.
FINE.
THE GUY THAT HELPED THE GUY THAT SAVED YOUR LIFE. WHO IS SOME KIND OF EIGHTY YEAR OLD SUPERHERO, IF THAT MAKES ANY MORE SENSE.
YOU ANSWER A QUESTION FOR ME, LUKE?
PROBABLY NOT.
IS YOUR ATTITUDE AN "I ALMOST JUST DIED" THING...
OR ARE YOU ALWAYS THIS MUCH OF A DICK?
I LIKE HIM.

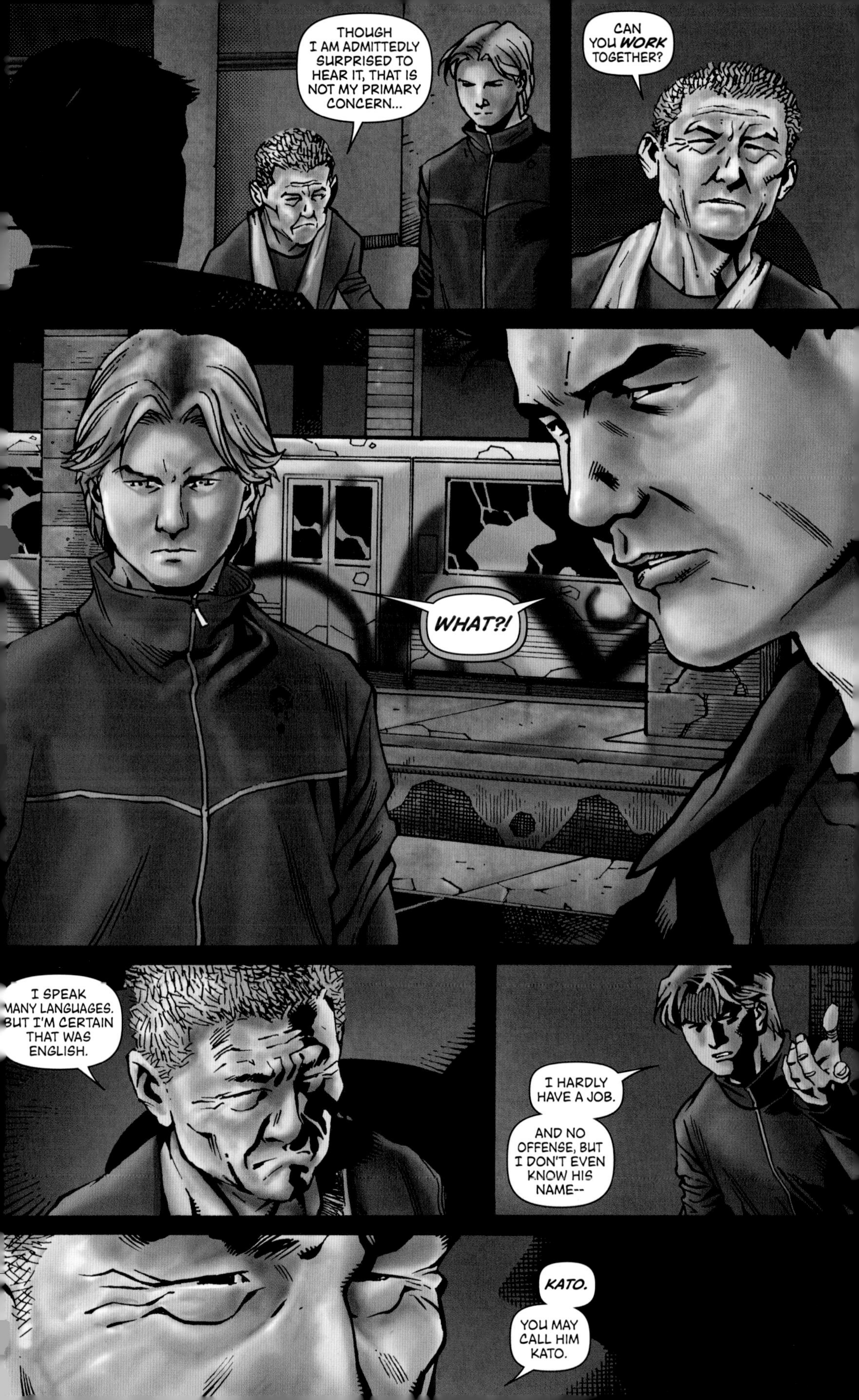
THOUGH I AM ADMITTEDLY SURPRISED TO HEAR IT, THAT IS NOT MY PRIMARY CONCERN...
CAN YOU WORK TOGETHER?
WHAT?!
I SPEAK MANY LANGUAGES. BUT I'M CERTAIN THAT WAS ENGLISH.
I HARDLY HAVE A JOB.
AND NO OFFENSE, BUT I DON'T EVEN KNOW HIS NAME--
KATO.
YOU MAY CALL HIM KATO.

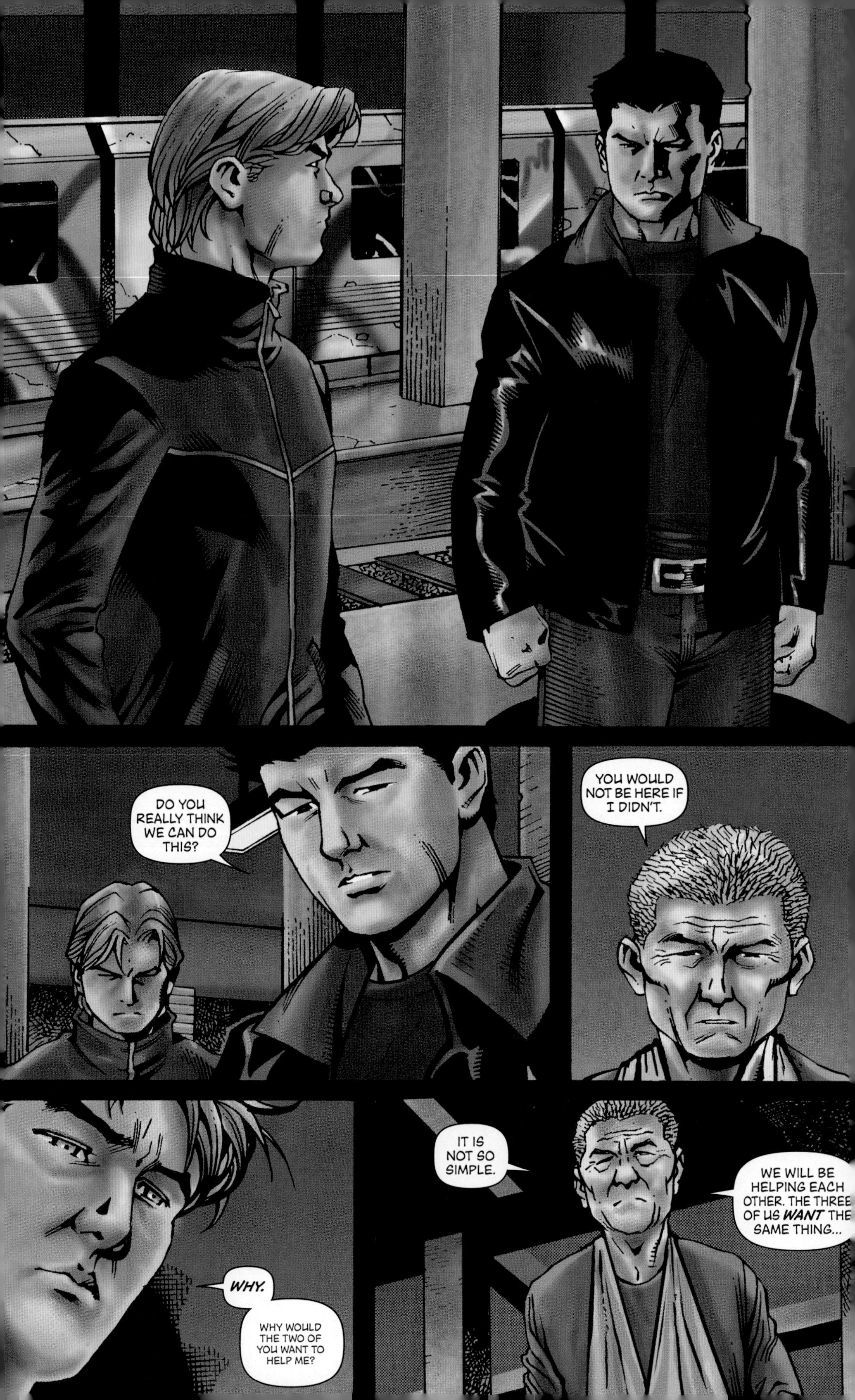

DO YOU REALLY THINK WE CAN DO THIS?
YOU WOULD NOT BE HERE IF I DIDN'T.
WHY.
WHY WOULD THE TWO OF YOU WANT TO HELP ME?
IT IS NOT SO SIMPLE.
WE WILL BE HELPING EACH OTHER. THE THREE OF US *WANT* THE SAME THING...

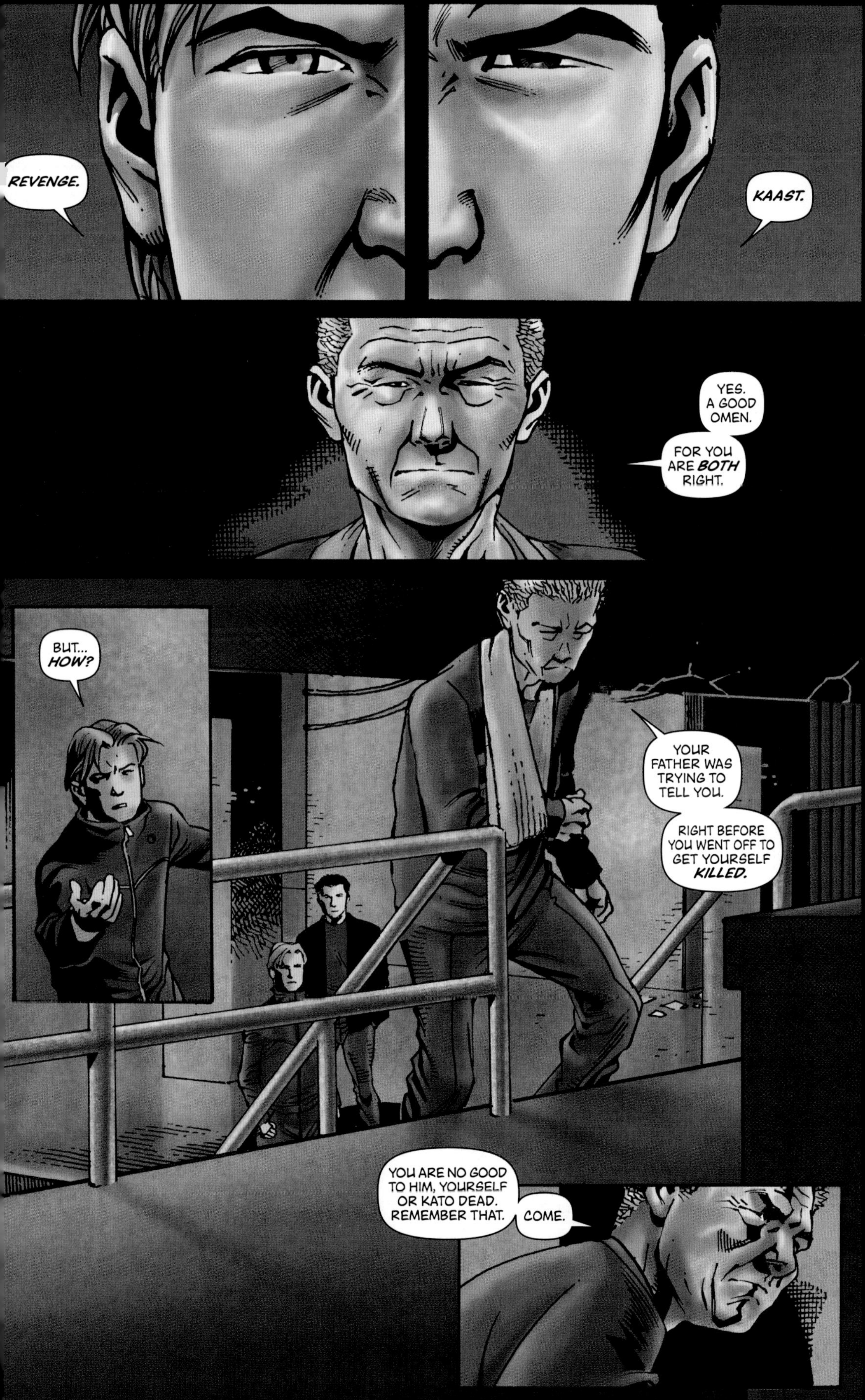
REVENGE.
KAAST.
YES. A GOOD OMEN.
FOR YOU ARE BOTH RIGHT.
BUT... HOW?
YOUR FATHER WAS TRYING TO TELL YOU.
RIGHT BEFORE YOU WENT OFF TO GET YOURSELF KILLED.
YOU ARE NO GOOD TO HIM, YOURSELF OR KATO DEAD. REMEMBER THAT.
COME.

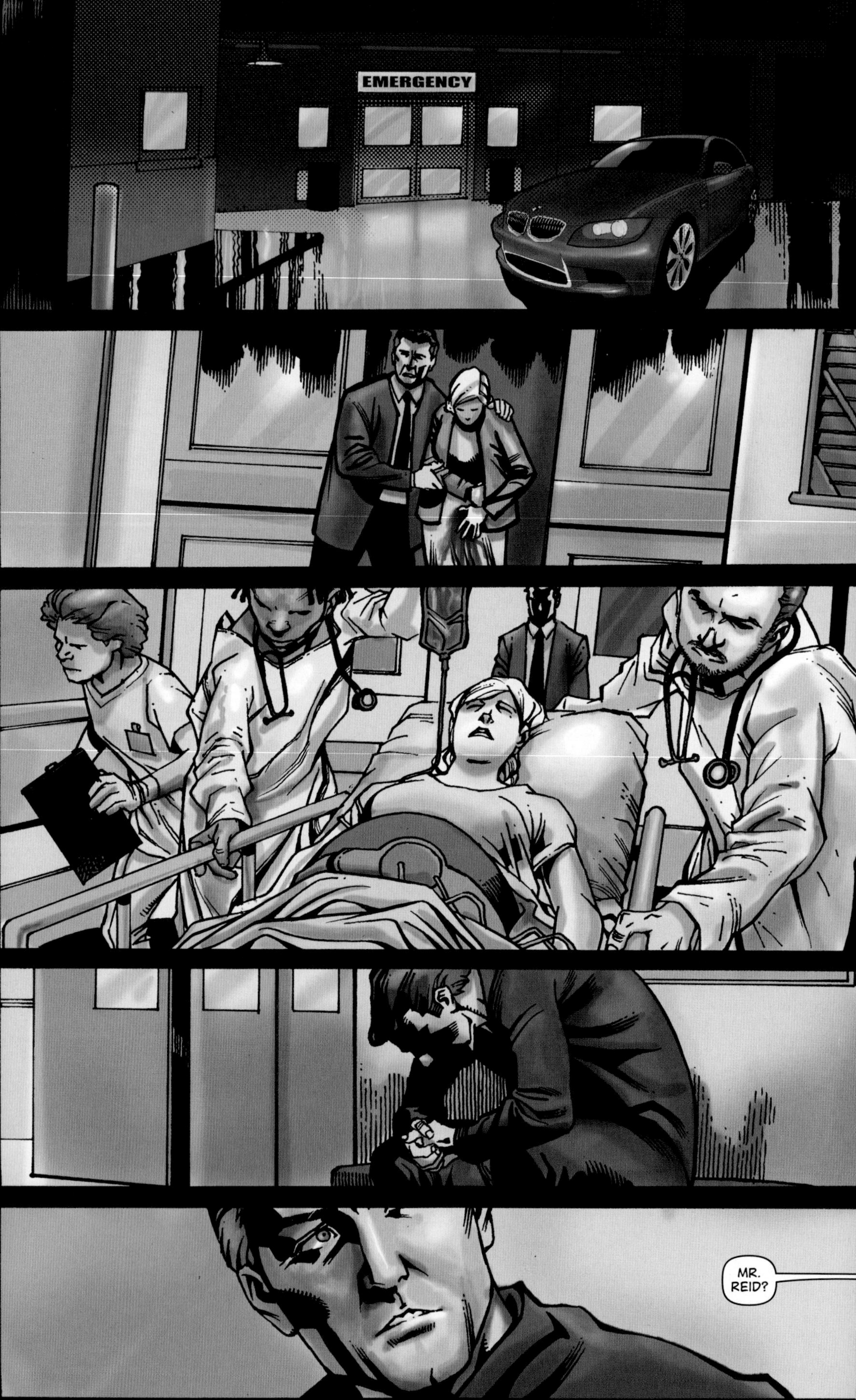
EMERGENCY
MR. REID?

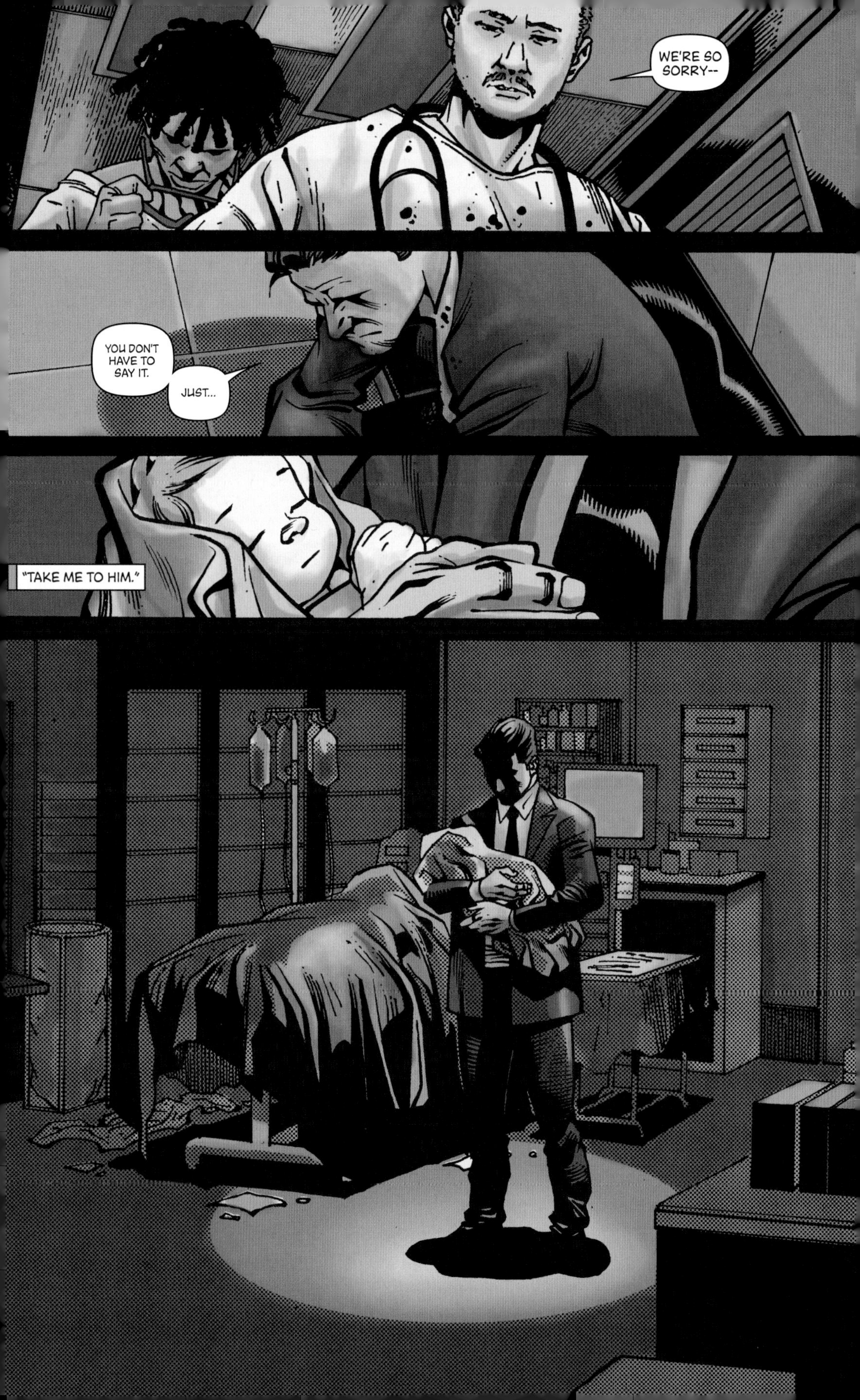
WE'RE SO SORRY--
YOU DON'T HAVE TO SAY IT.
JUST...
"TAKE ME TO HIM."

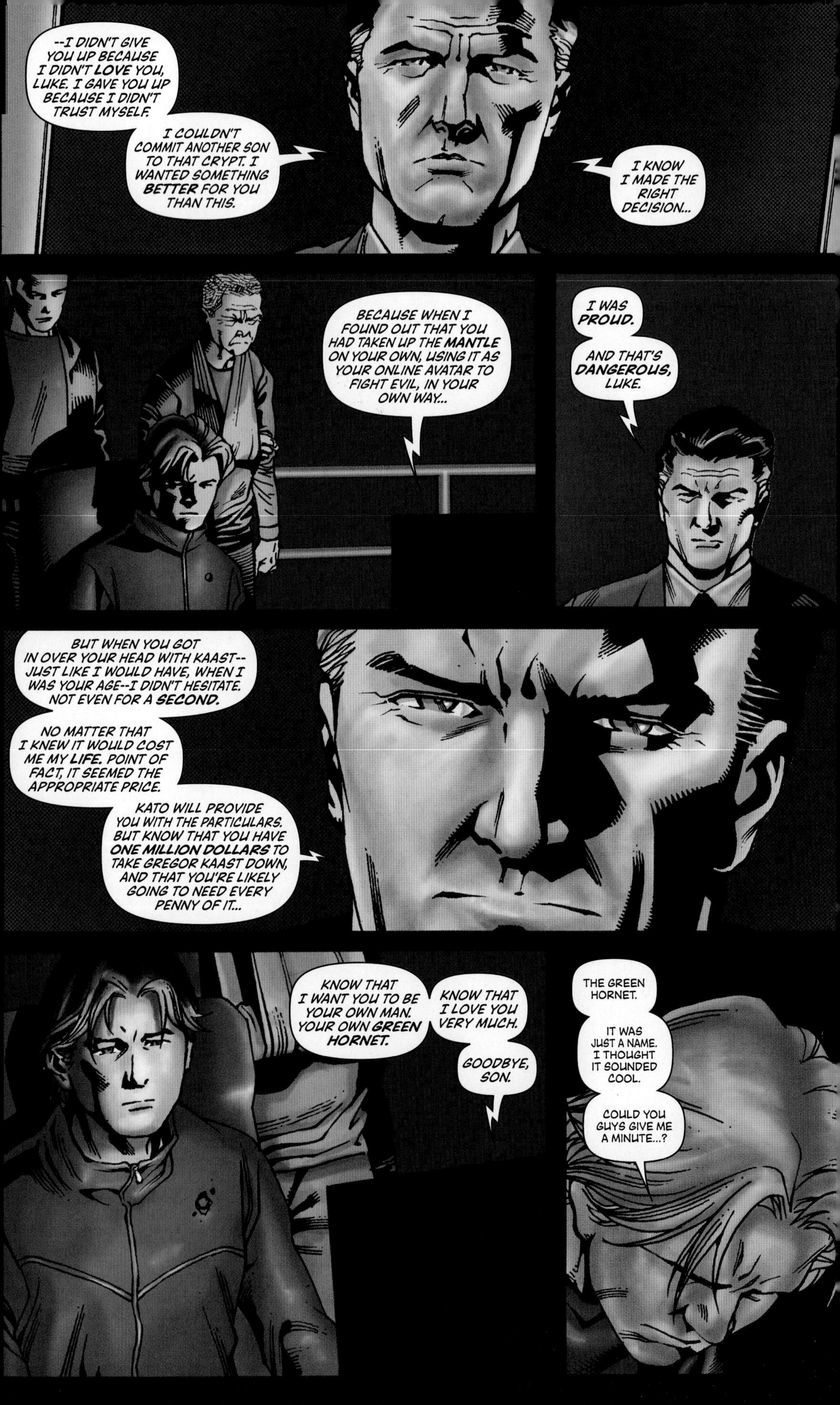
--I DIDN'T GIVE YOU UP BECAUSE I DIDN'T LOVE YOU, LUKE. I GAVE YOU UP BECAUSE I DIDN'T TRUST MYSELF.
I COULDN'T COMMIT ANOTHER SON TO THAT CRYPT. I WANTED SOMETHING BETTER FOR YOU THAN THIS.
I KNOW I MADE THE RIGHT DECISION...
BECAUSE WHEN I FOUND OUT THAT YOU HAD TAKEN UP THE MANTLE ON YOUR OWN, USING IT AS YOUR ONLINE AVATAR TO FIGHT EVIL, IN YOUR OWN WAY...
I WAS PROUD.
AND THAT'S DANGEROUS, LUKE.
BUT WHEN YOU GOT IN OVER YOUR HEAD WITH KAAST-- JUST LIKE I WOULD HAVE, WHEN I WAS YOUR AGE--I DIDN'T HESITATE. NOT EVEN FOR A SECOND.
NO MATTER THAT I KNEW IT WOULD COST ME MY LIFE. POINT OF FACT, IT SEEMED THE APPROPRIATE PRICE.
KATO WILL PROVIDE YOU WITH THE PARTICULARS. BUT KNOW THAT YOU HAVE ONE MILLION DOLLARS TO TAKE GREGOR KAAST DOWN, AND THAT YOU'RE LIKELY GOING TO NEED EVERY PENNY OF IT...
KNOW THAT I WANT YOU TO BE YOUR OWN MAN. YOUR OWN GREEN HORNET.
KNOW THAT I LOVE YOU VERY MUCH.
GOODBYE, SON.
THE GREEN HORNET.
IT WAS JUST A NAME. I THOUGHT IT SOUNDED COOL.
COULD YOU GUYS GIVE ME A MINUTE...?

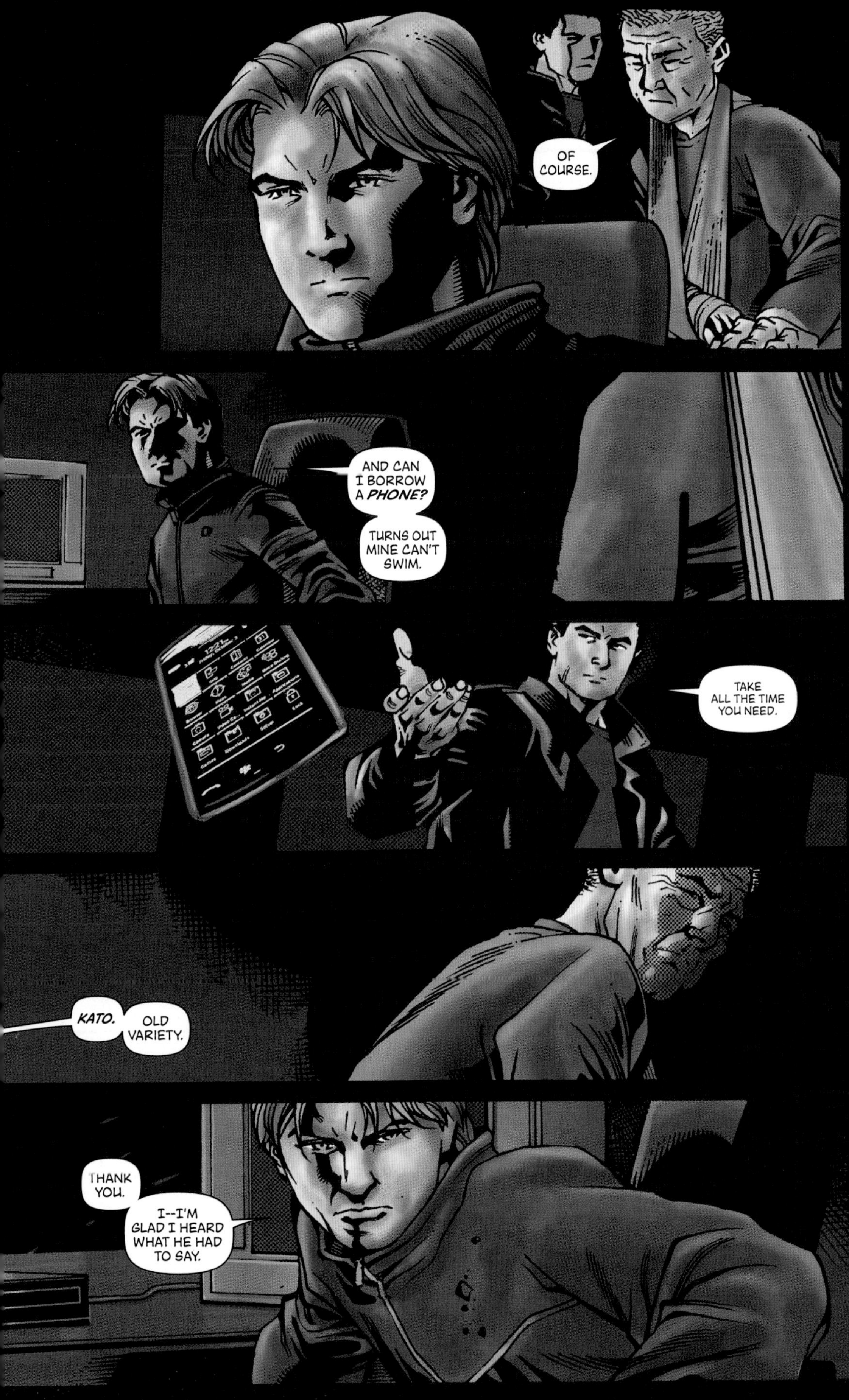
OF COURSE.
AND CAN I BORROW A *PHONE?*
TURNS OUT MINE CAN'T SWIM.
TAKE ALL THE TIME YOU NEED.
KATO.
OLD VARIETY.
THANK YOU.
I--I'M GLAD I HEARD WHAT HE HAD TO SAY.

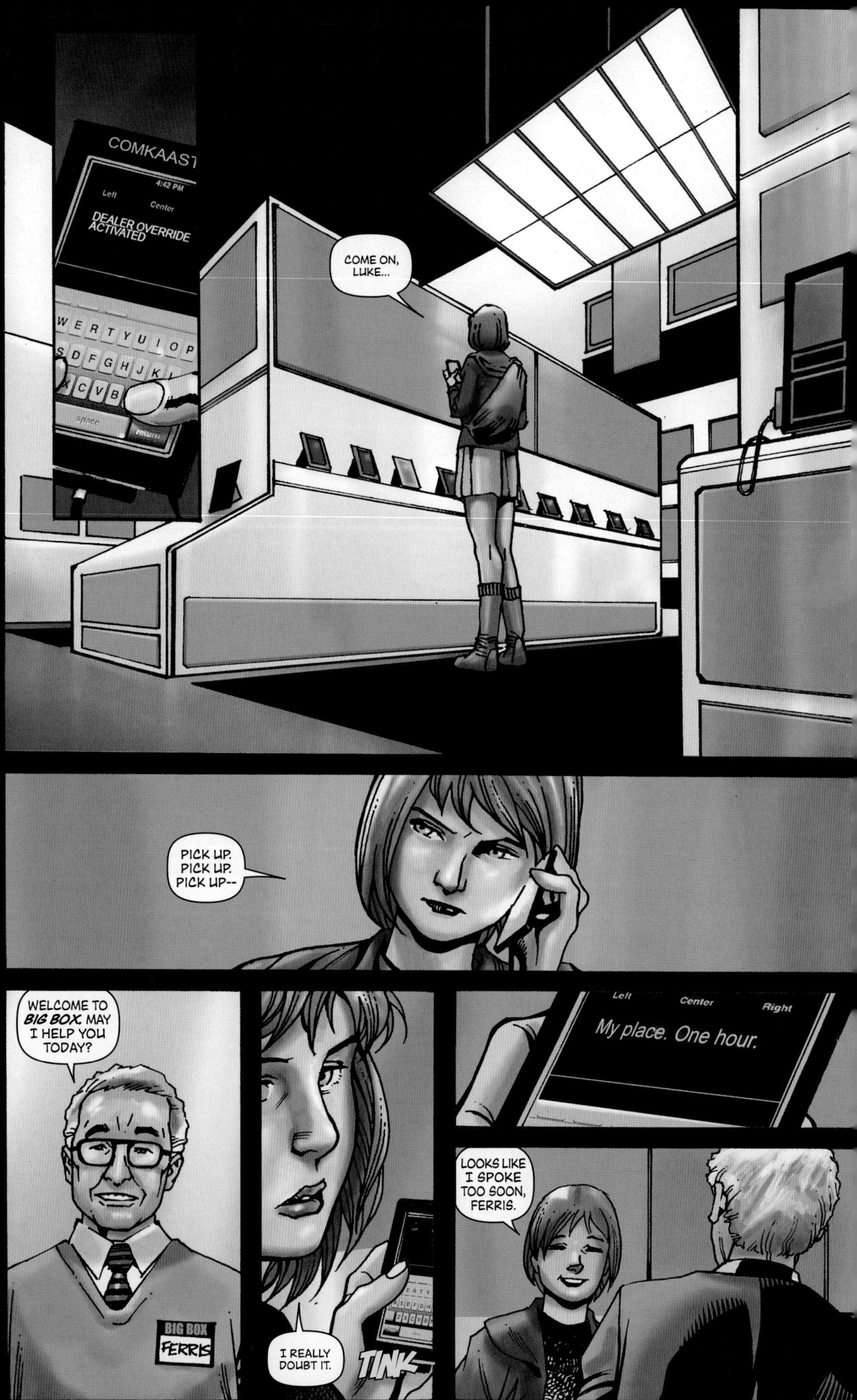

COMKAAST
4:42 PM
Left
Center
DEALER OVERRIDE ACTIVATED
COME ON, LUKE...
PICK UP. PICK UP. PICK UP--
WELCOME TO BIG BOX. MAY I HELP YOU TODAY?
BIG BOX
FERRIS
I REALLY DOUBT IT.
TINK
Left
Center
Right
My place. One hour.
LOOKS LIKE I SPOKE TOO SOON, FERRIS.

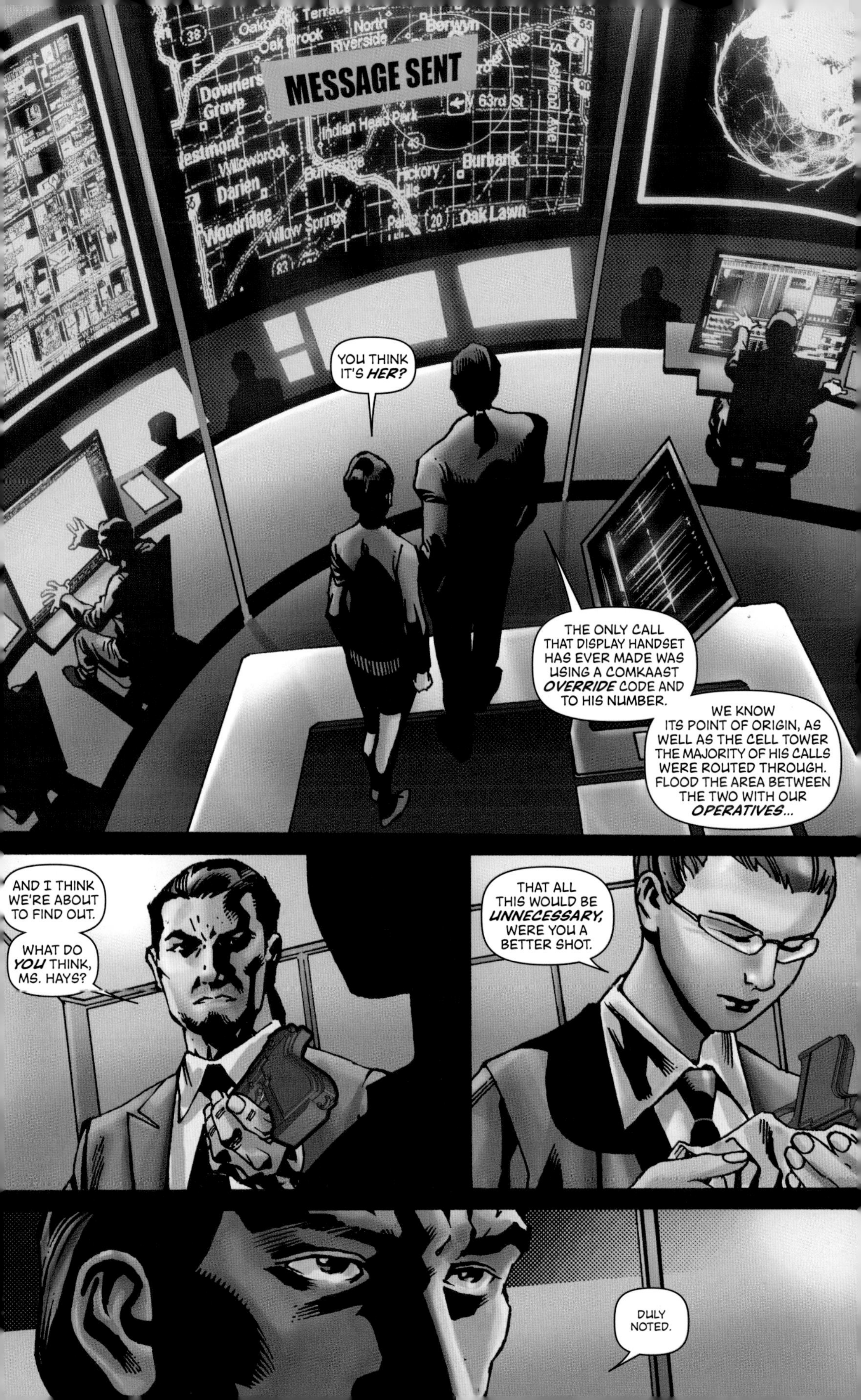
MESSAGE SENT
YOU THINK IT'S *HER?*
THE ONLY CALL THAT DISPLAY HANDSET HAS EVER MADE WAS USING A COMKAAST *OVERRIDE* CODE AND TO HIS NUMBER.
WE KNOW ITS POINT OF ORIGIN, AS WELL AS THE CELL TOWER THE MAJORITY OF HIS CALLS WERE ROUTED THROUGH. FLOOD THE AREA BETWEEN THE TWO WITH OUR *OPERATIVES...*
AND I THINK WE'RE ABOUT TO FIND OUT.
WHAT DO *YOU* THINK, MS. HAYS?
THAT ALL THIS WOULD BE *UNNECESSARY,* WERE YOU A BETTER SHOT.
DULY NOTED.

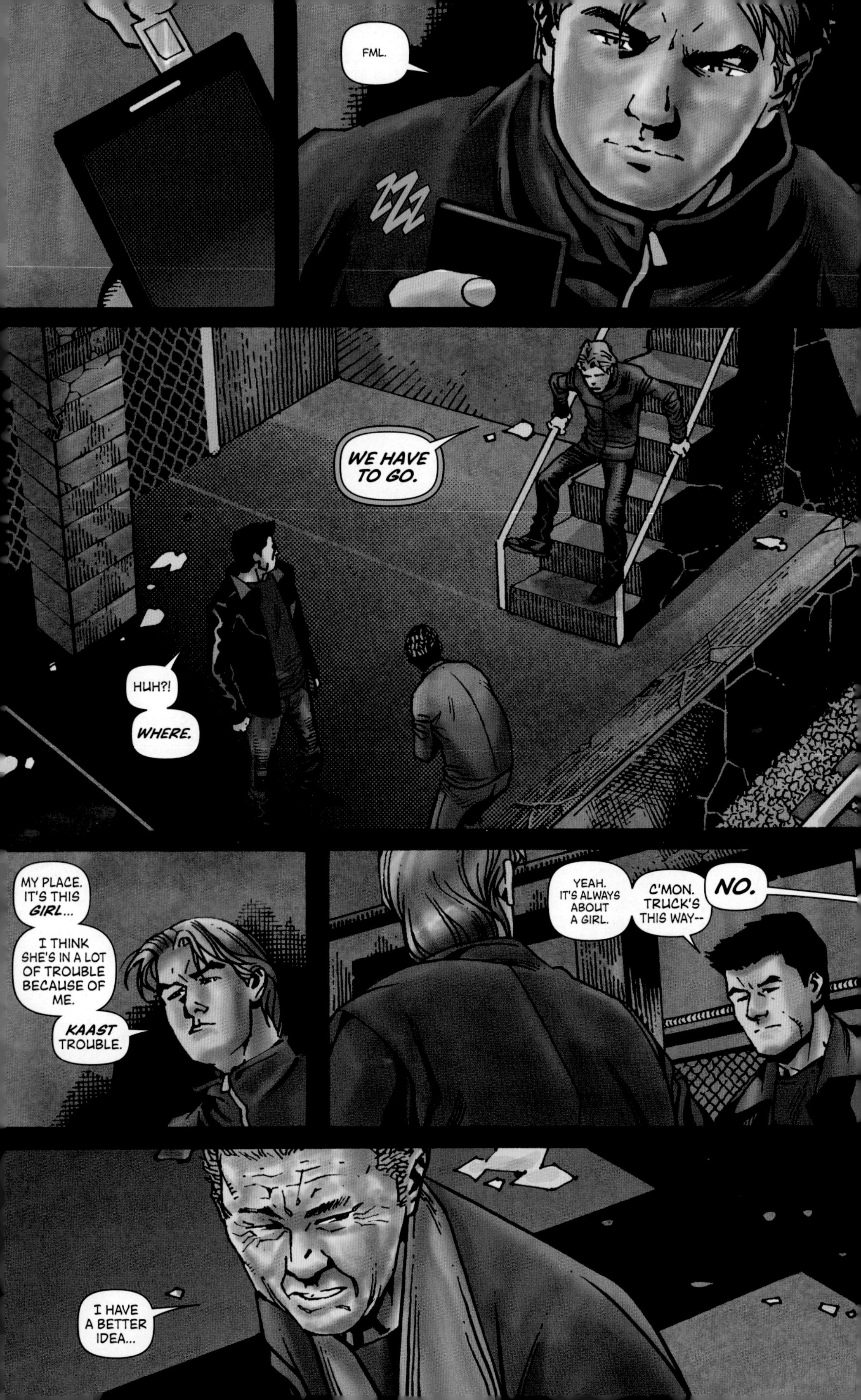
FML.
WE HAVE TO GO.
HUH?!
WHERE.
MY PLACE. IT'S THIS GIRL...
I THINK SHE'S IN A LOT OF TROUBLE BECAUSE OF ME.
KAAST TROUBLE.
YEAH. IT'S ALWAYS ABOUT A GIRL.
C'MON. TRUCK'S THIS WAY--
NO.
I HAVE A BETTER IDEA...

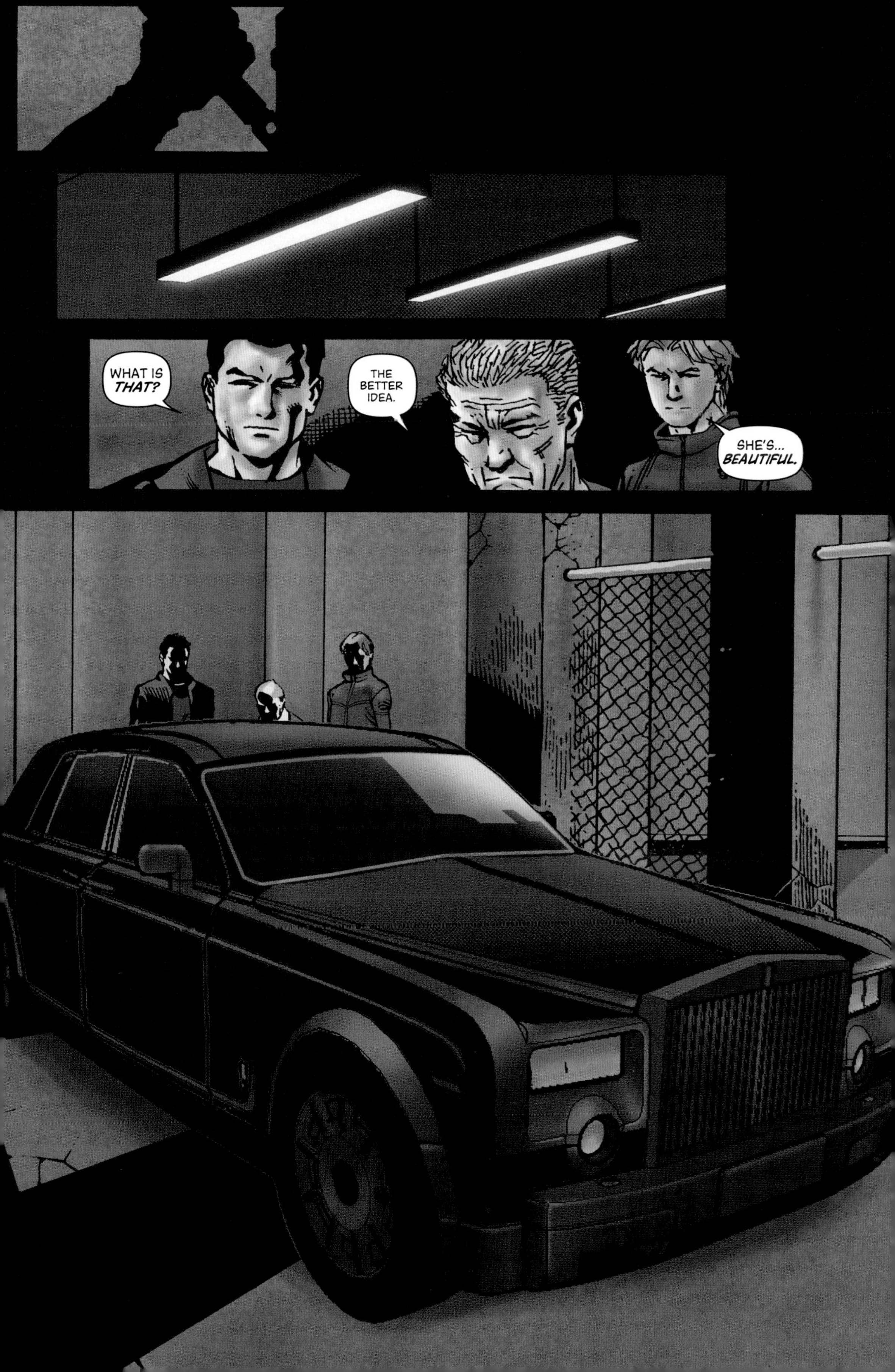
WHAT IS *THAT?*
THE BETTER IDEA.
SHE'S... *BEAUTIFUL.*

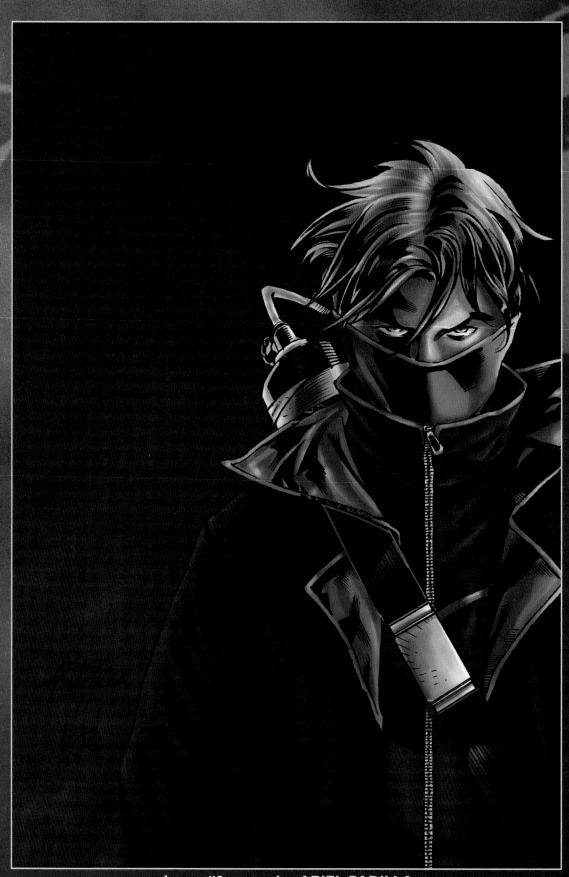

Issue #9 cover by ARIEL PADILLA

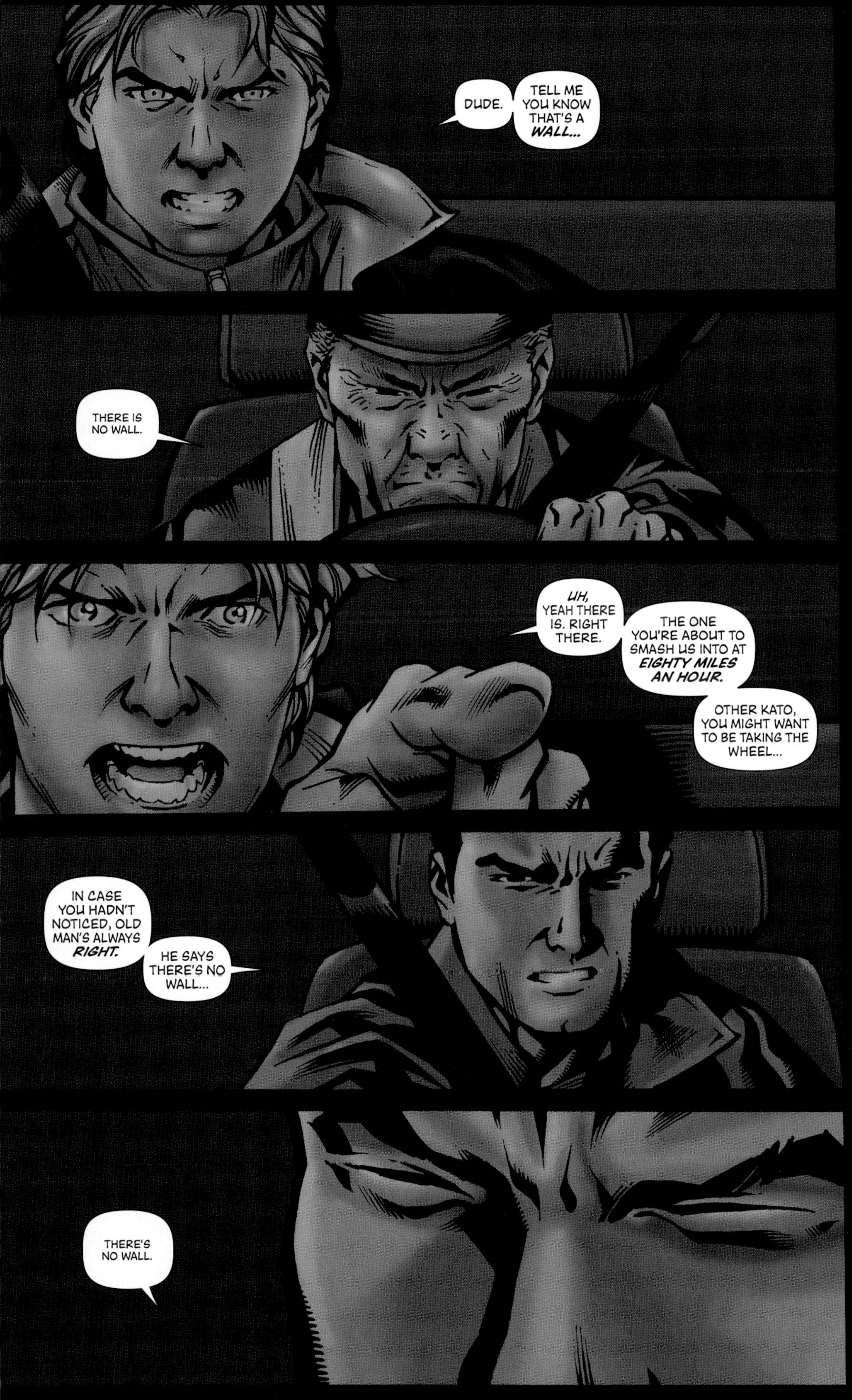
DUDE.
TELL ME YOU KNOW THAT'S A *WALL...*
THERE IS NO WALL.
UH, YEAH THERE IS. RIGHT THERE.
THE ONE YOU'RE ABOUT TO SMASH US INTO AT *EIGHTY MILES AN HOUR.*
OTHER KATO, YOU MIGHT WANT TO BE TAKING THE WHEEL...
IN CASE YOU HADN'T NOTICED, OLD MAN'S ALWAYS *RIGHT.*
HE SAYS THERE'S NO WALL...
THERE'S NO WALL.

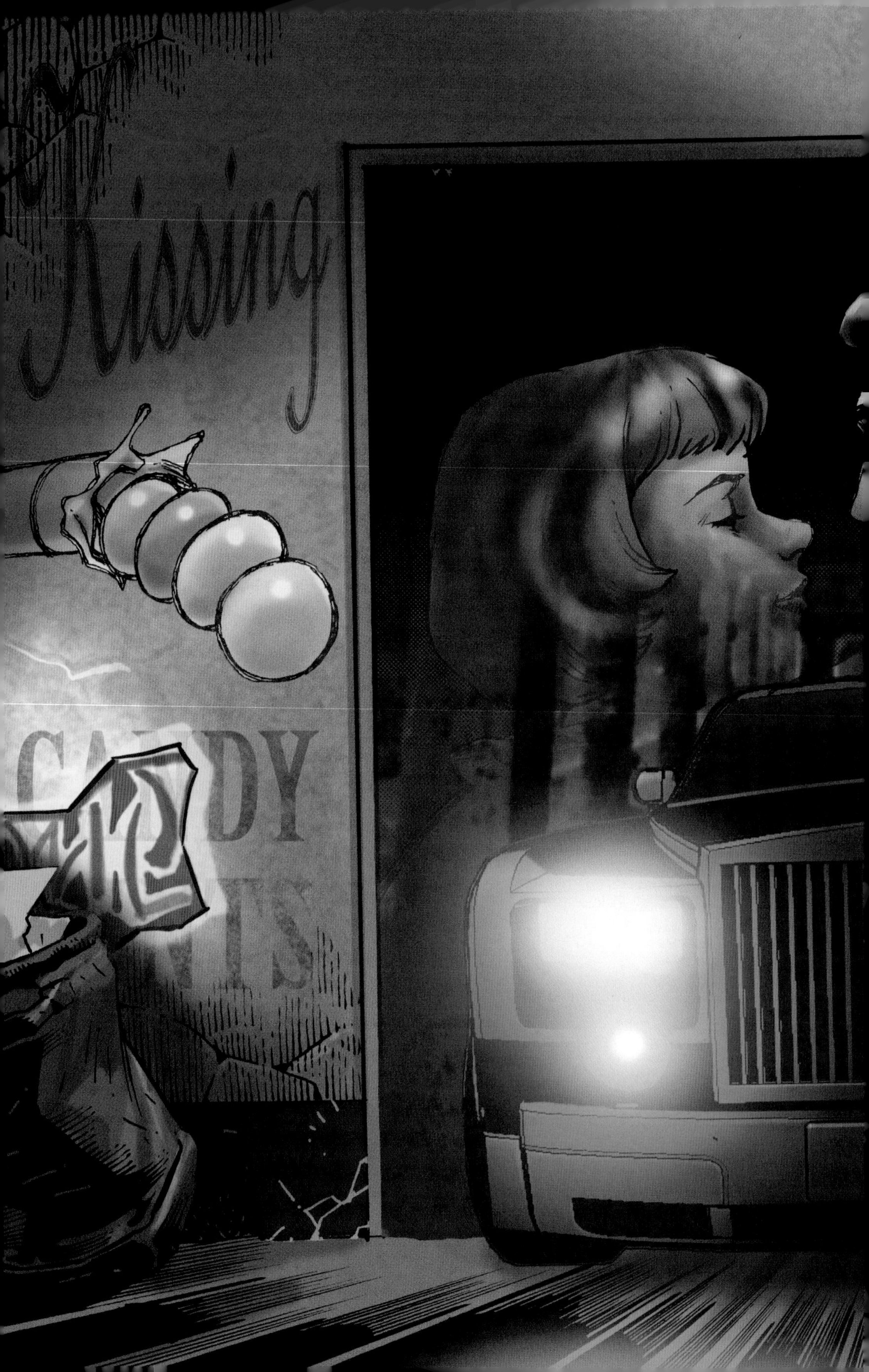
Kissing

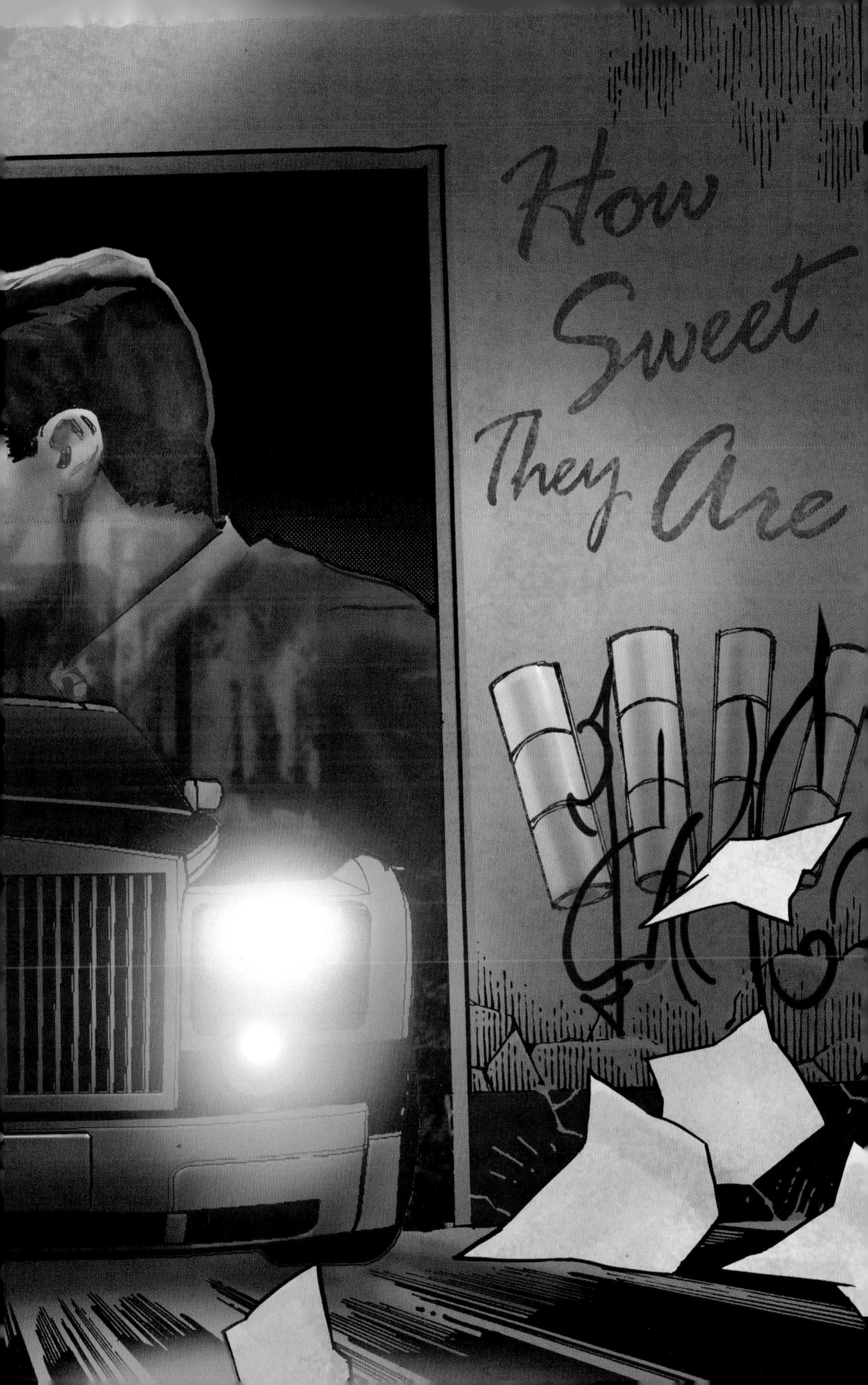
How Sweet They Are

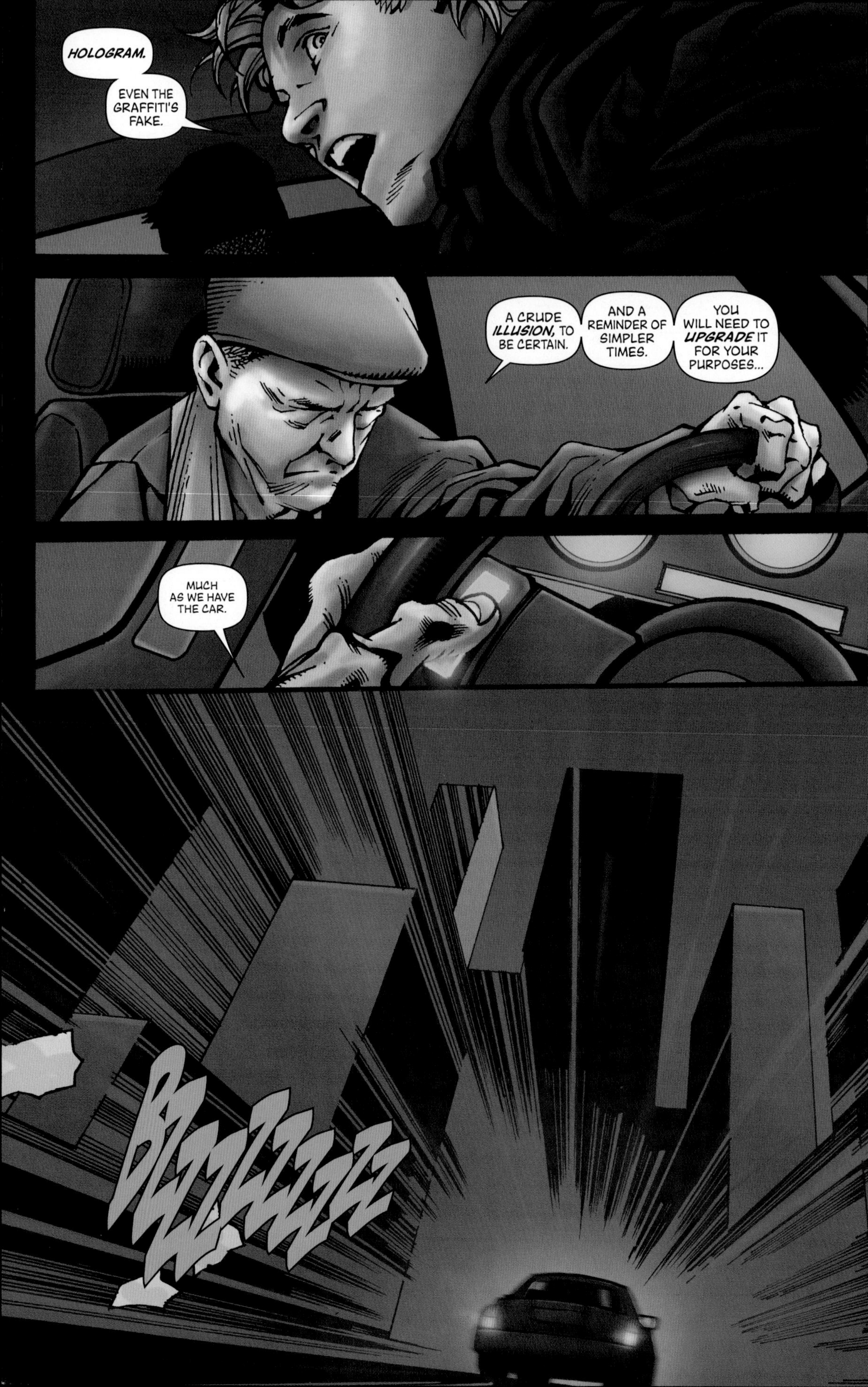

HOLOGRAM.
EVEN THE GRAFFITI'S FAKE.
A CRUDE ILLUSION, TO BE CERTAIN.
AND A REMINDER OF SIMPLER TIMES.
YOU WILL NEED TO UPGRADE IT FOR YOUR PURPOSES...
MUCH AS WE HAVE THE CAR.
BZZZZZZZ

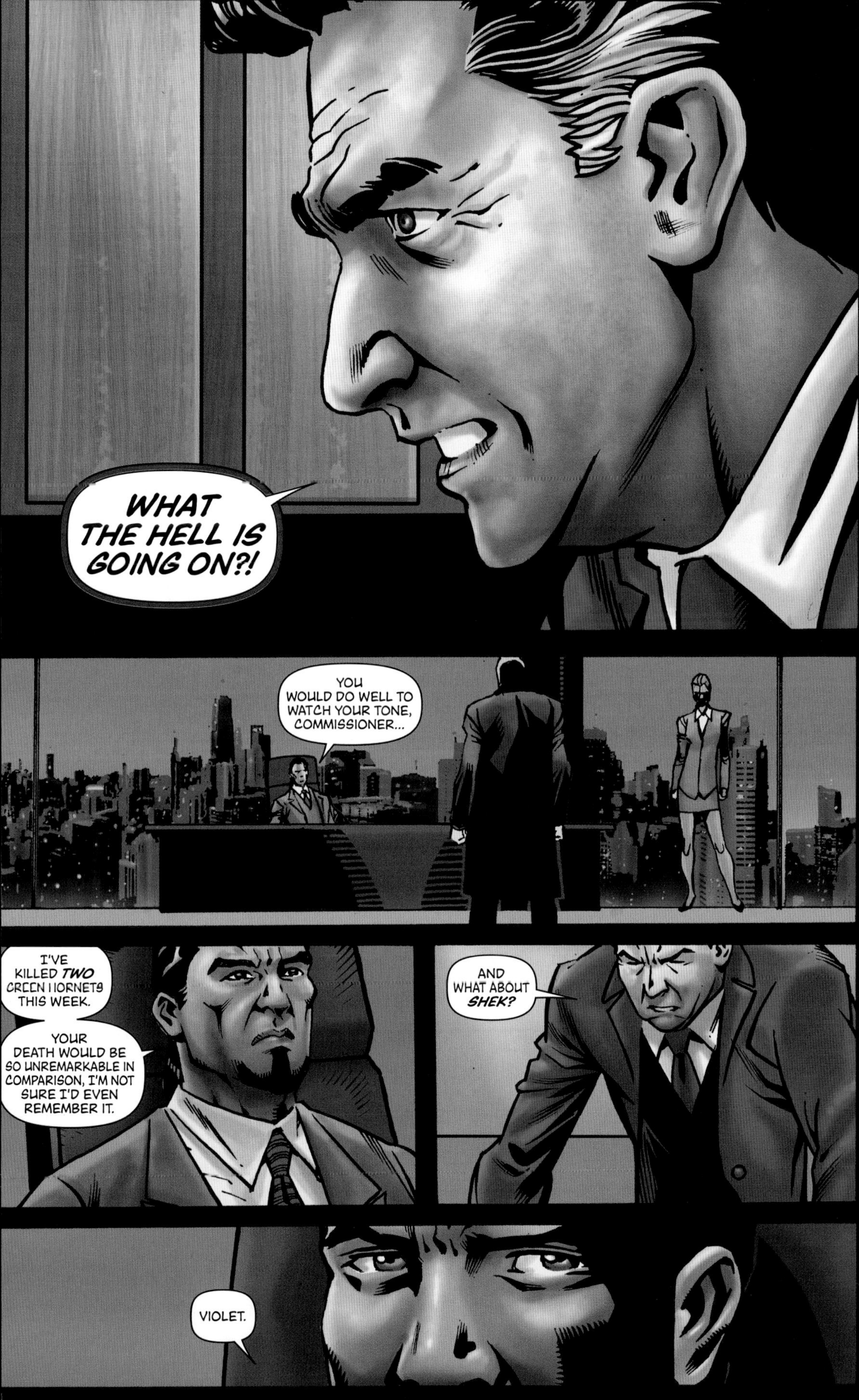
WHAT THE HELL IS GOING ON?!
YOU WOULD DO WELL TO WATCH YOUR TONE, COMMISSIONER...
I'VE KILLED *TWO* GREEN HORNETS THIS WEEK.
YOUR DEATH WOULD BE SO UNREMARKABLE IN COMPARISON, I'M NOT SURE I'D EVEN REMEMBER IT.
AND WHAT ABOUT *SHEK?*
VIOLET.

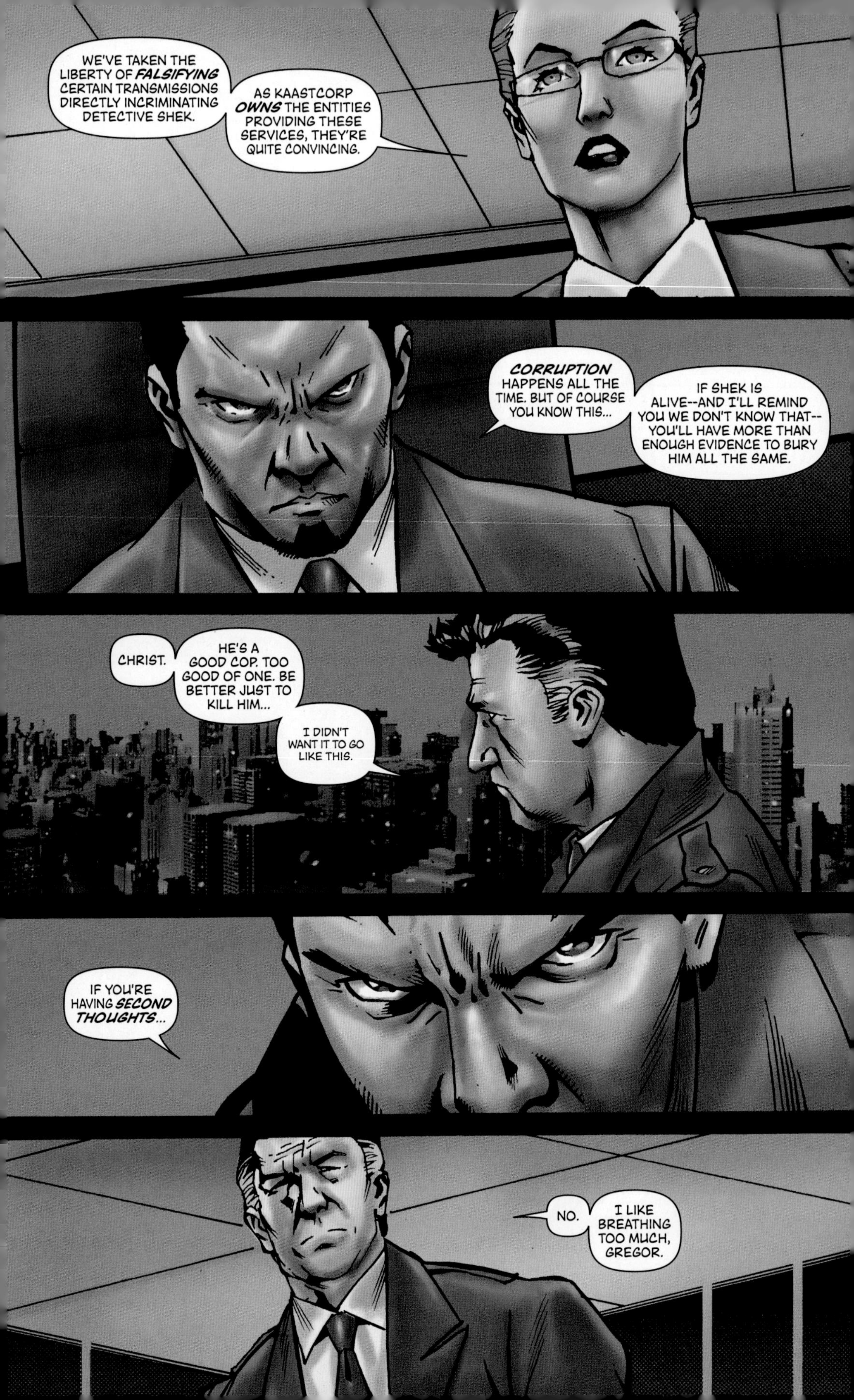

WE'VE TAKEN THE LIBERTY OF *FALSIFYING* CERTAIN TRANSMISSIONS DIRECTLY INCRIMINATING DETECTIVE SHEK.
AS KAASTCORP *OWNS* THE ENTITIES PROVIDING THESE SERVICES, THEY'RE QUITE CONVINCING.
CORRUPTION HAPPENS ALL THE TIME. BUT OF COURSE YOU KNOW THIS...
IF SHEK IS ALIVE--AND I'LL REMIND YOU WE DON'T KNOW THAT--YOU'LL HAVE MORE THAN ENOUGH EVIDENCE TO BURY HIM ALL THE SAME.
CHRIST.
HE'S A GOOD COP. TOO GOOD OF ONE. BE BETTER JUST TO KILL HIM...
I DIDN'T WANT IT TO GO LIKE THIS.
IF YOU'RE HAVING *SECOND THOUGHTS*...
NO.
I LIKE BREATHING TOO MUCH, GREGOR.

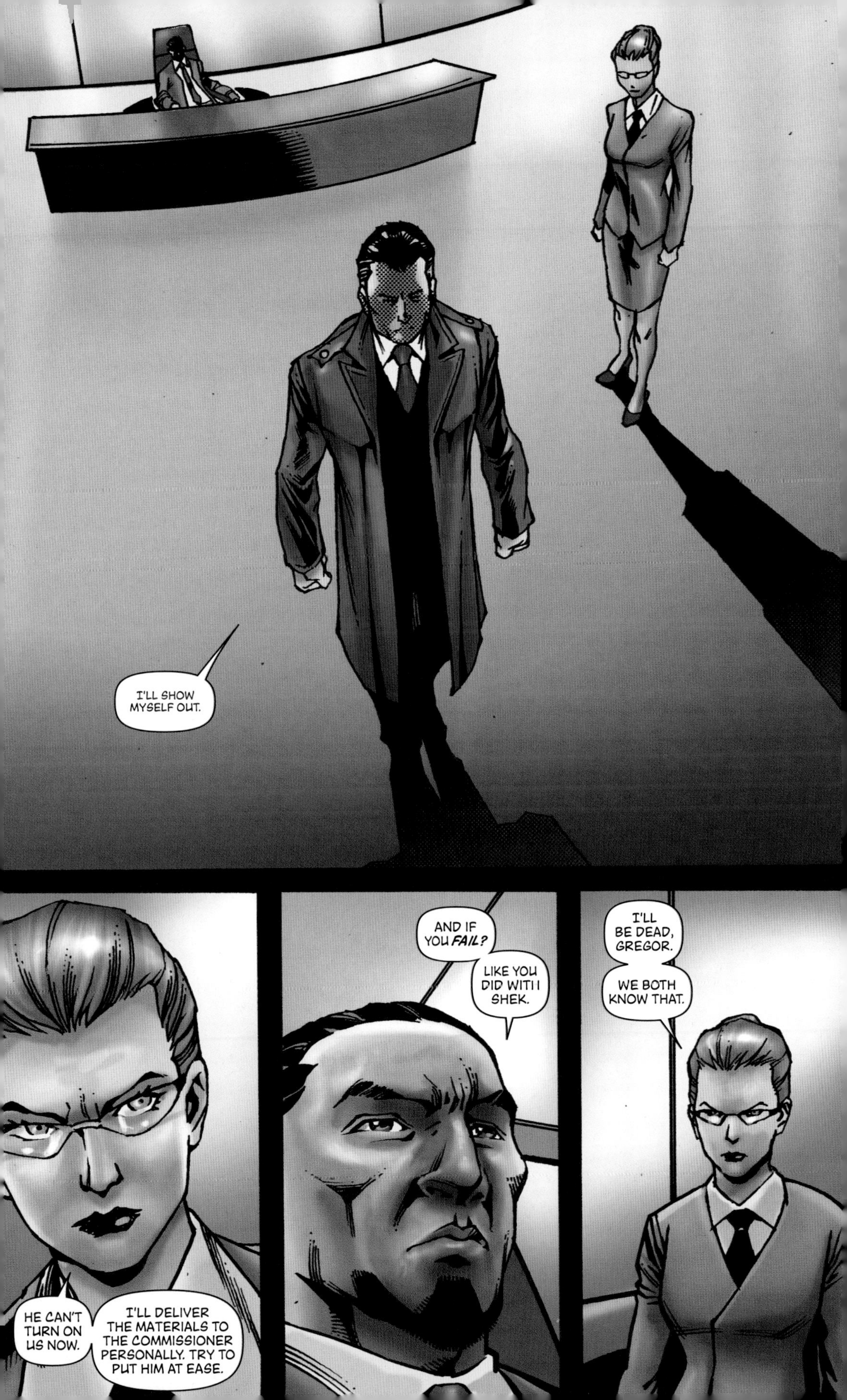
I'LL SHOW MYSELF OUT.
HE CAN'T TURN ON US NOW.
I'LL DELIVER THE MATERIALS TO THE COMMISSIONER PERSONALLY. TRY TO PUT HIM AT EASE.
AND IF YOU ***FAIL?***
LIKE YOU DID WITH SHEK.
I'LL BE DEAD, GREGOR.
WE BOTH KNOW THAT.

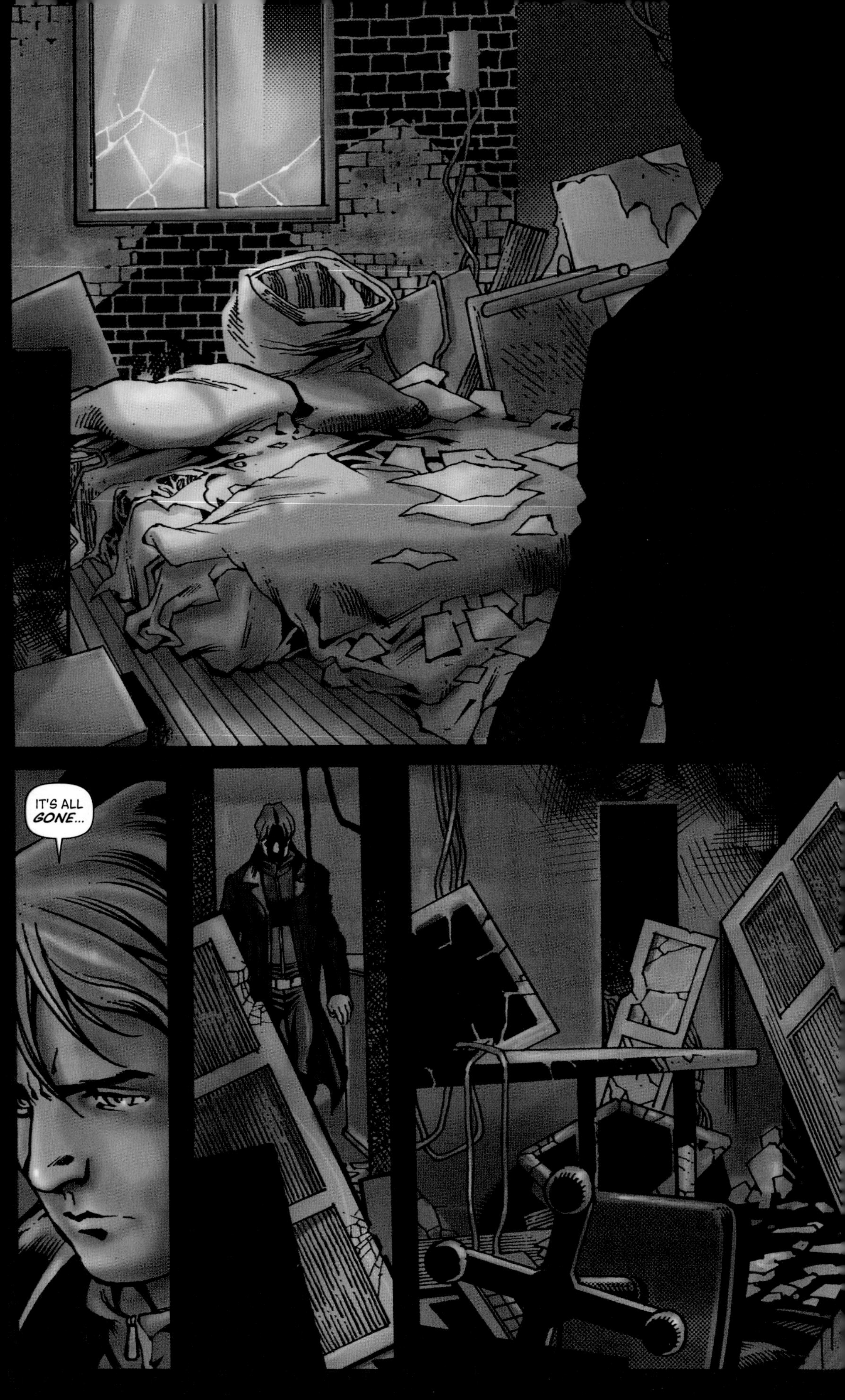
IT'S ALL GONE...

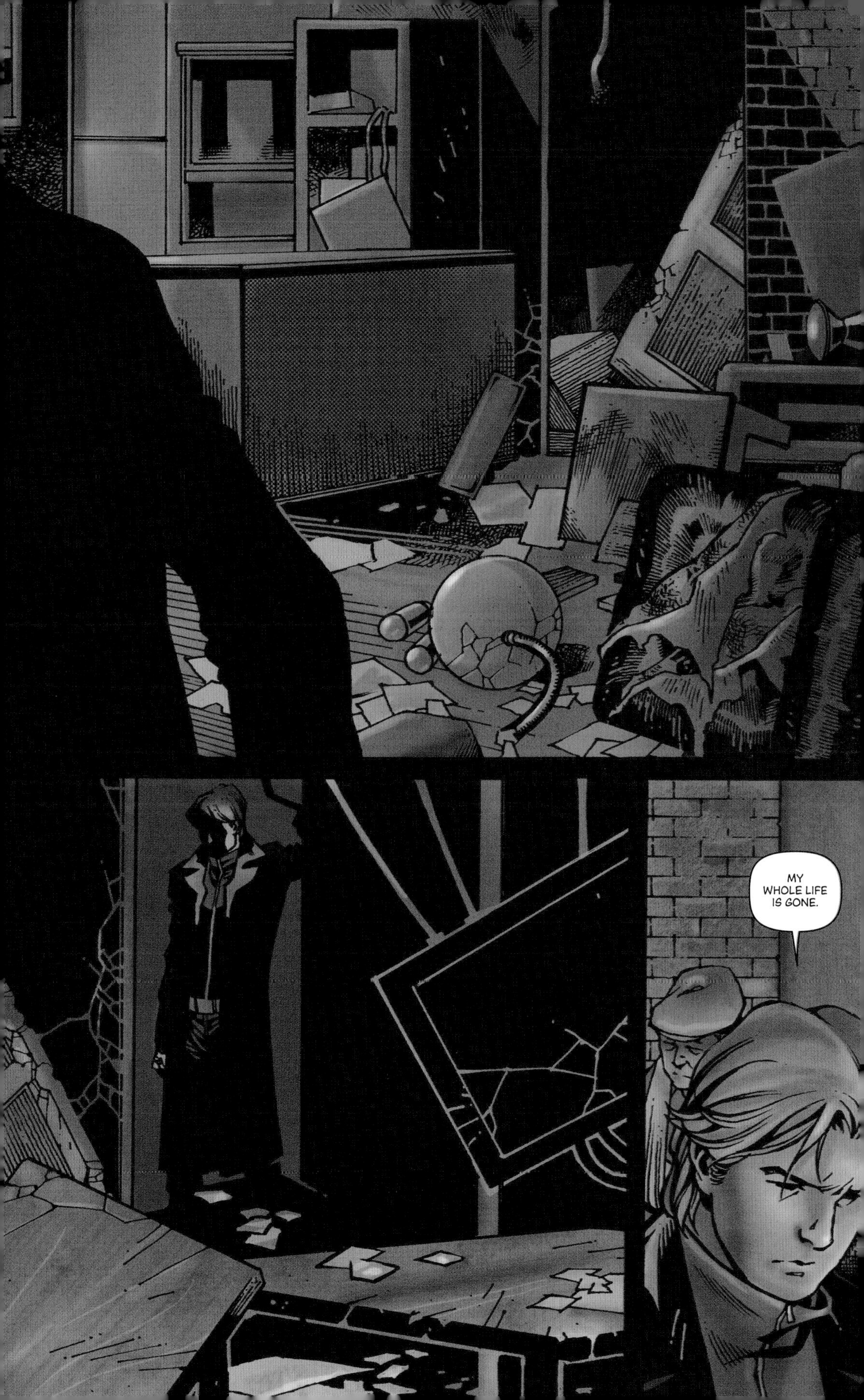
MY WHOLE LIFE IS GONE.

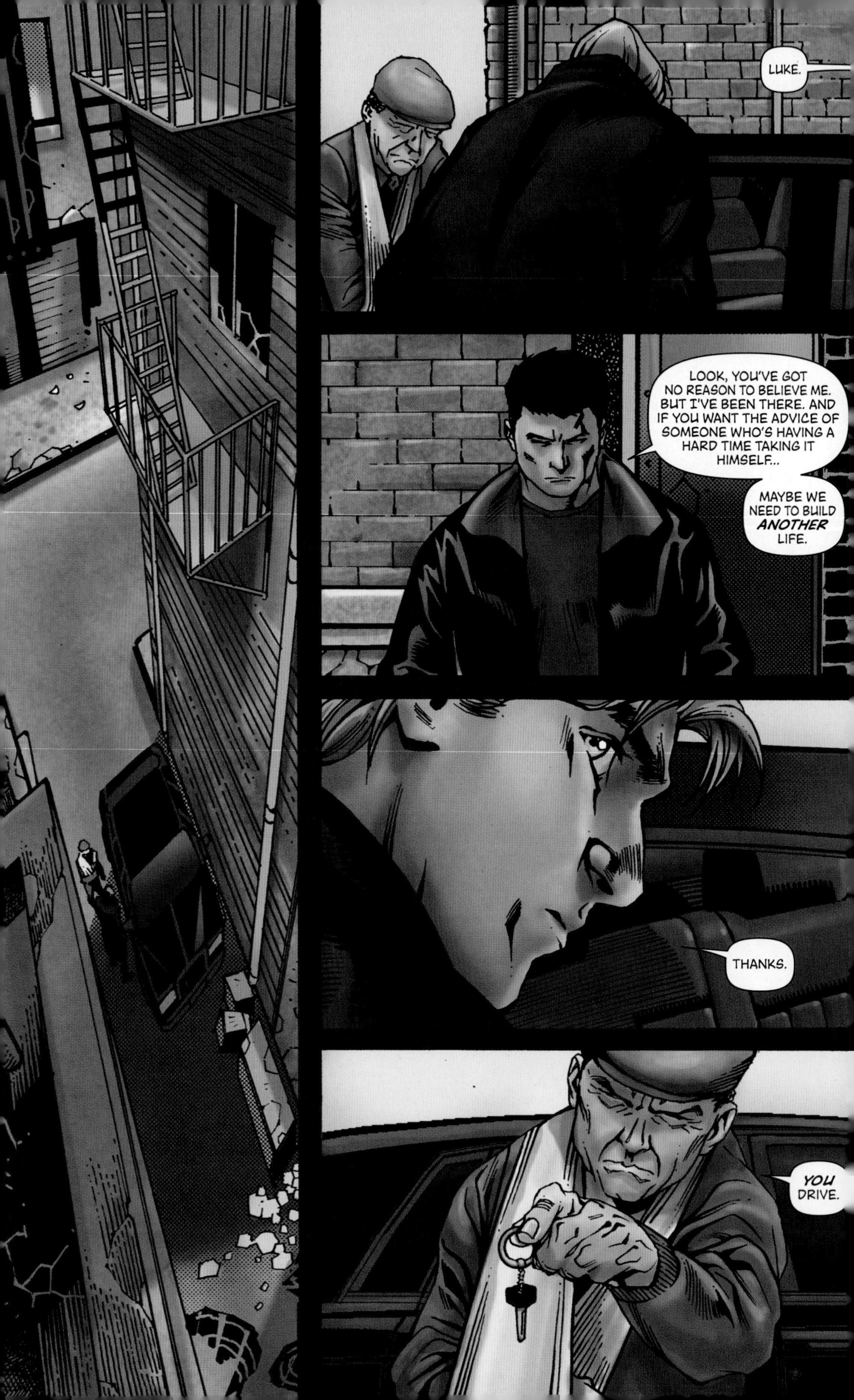
LUKE.
LOOK, YOU'VE GOT NO REASON TO BELIEVE ME. BUT I'VE BEEN THERE. AND IF YOU WANT THE ADVICE OF SOMEONE WHO'S HAVING A HARD TIME TAKING IT HIMSELF...
MAYBE WE NEED TO BUILD ***ANOTHER*** LIFE.
THANKS.
YOU DRIVE.

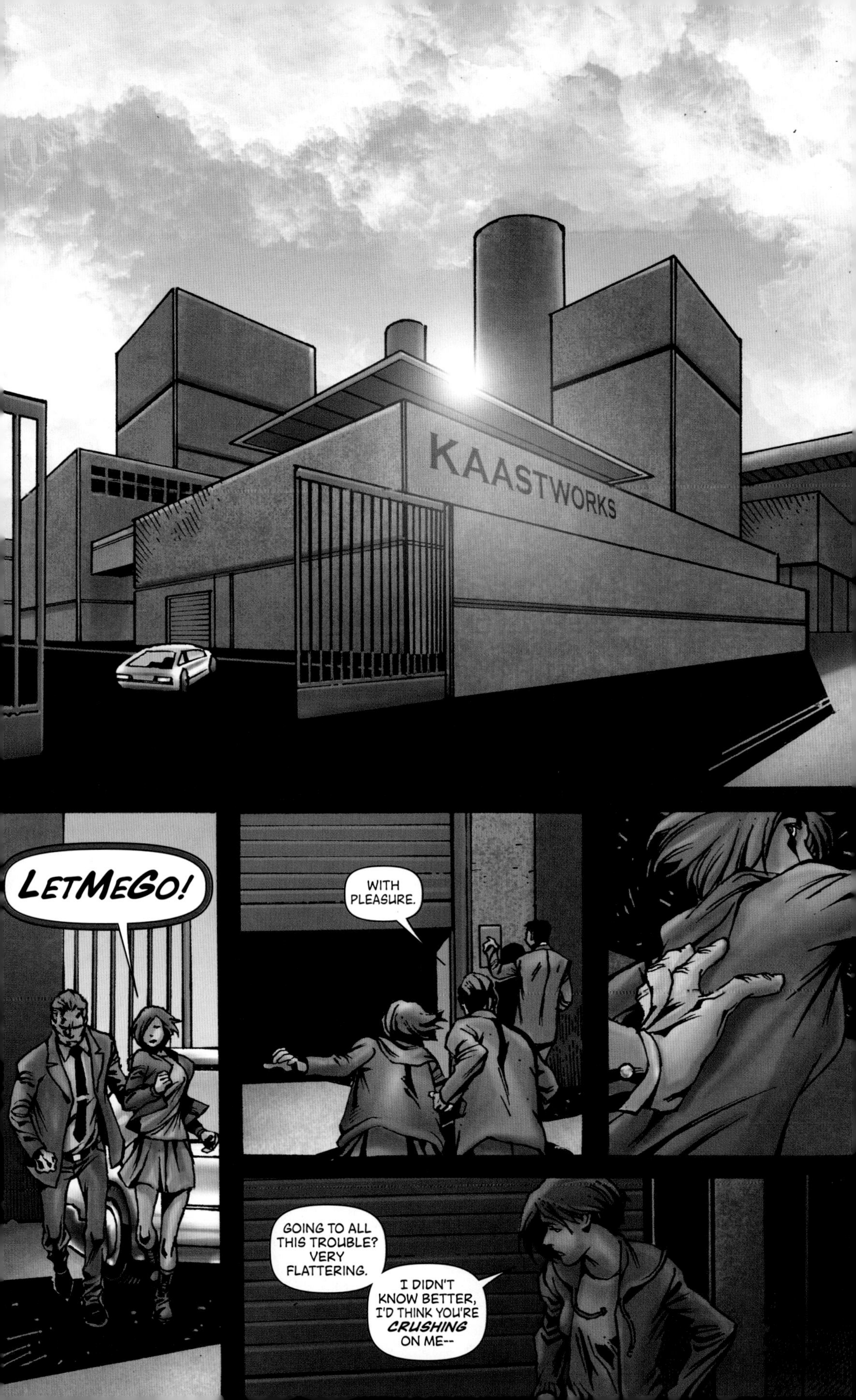
KAASTWORKS
LetMeGo!
WITH PLEASURE.
GOING TO ALL THIS TROUBLE? VERY FLATTERING.
I DIDN'T KNOW BETTER, I'D THINK YOU'RE *CRUSHING* ON ME--

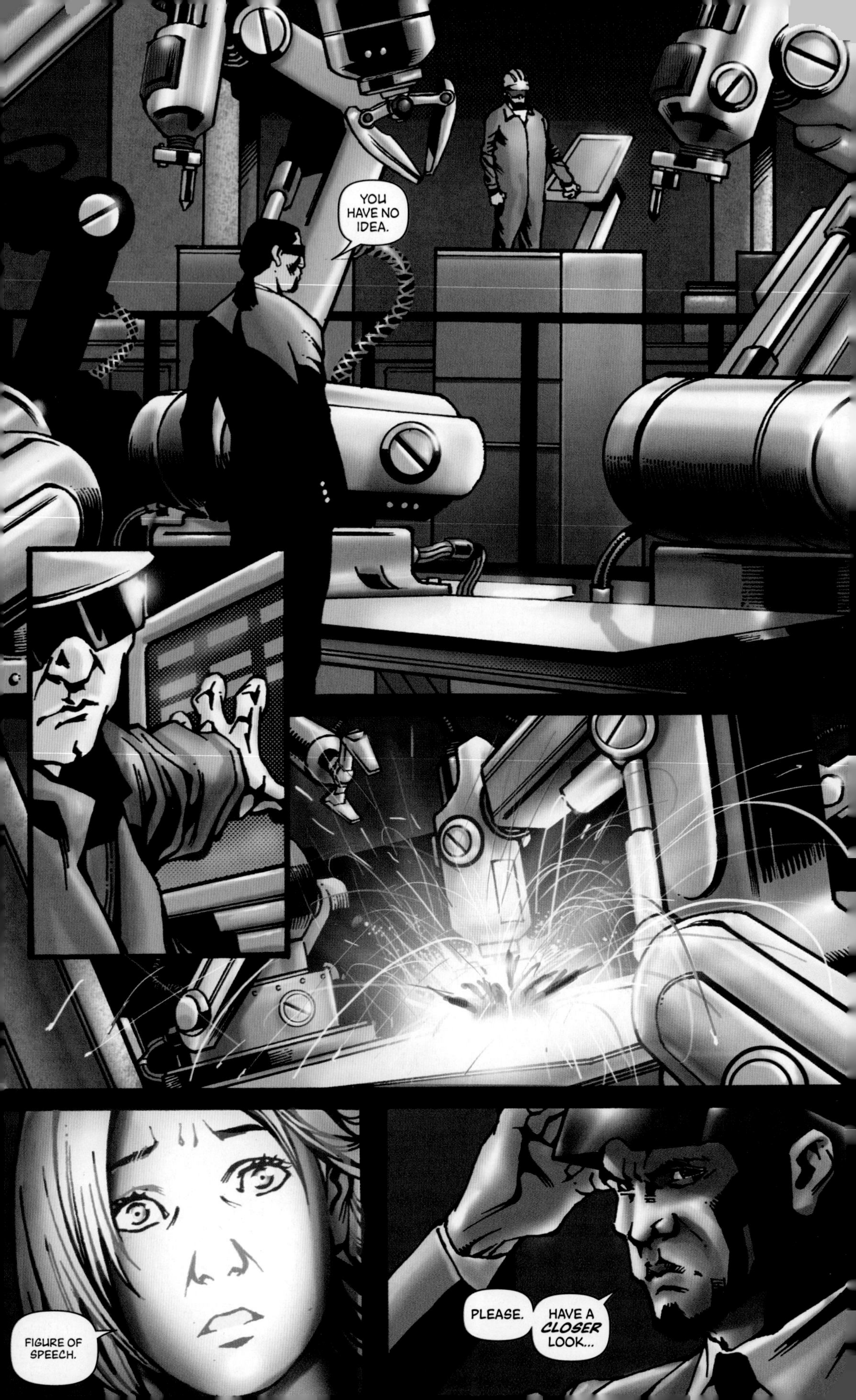
YOU HAVE NO IDEA.
FIGURE OF SPEECH.
PLEASE.
HAVE A *CLOSER* LOOK...

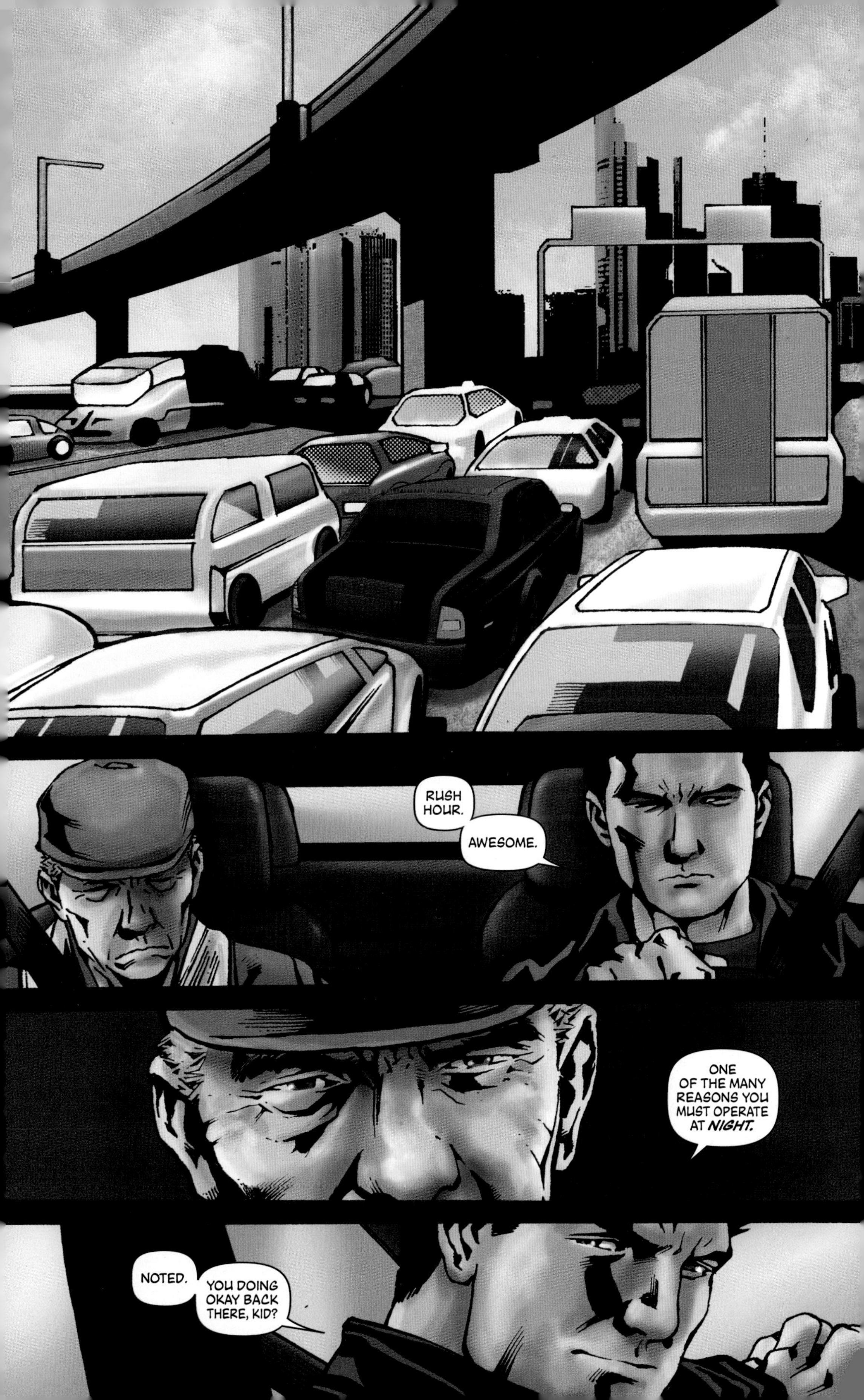

RUSH HOUR.
AWESOME.
ONE OF THE MANY REASONS YOU MUST OPERATE AT *NIGHT.*
NOTED.
YOU DOING OKAY BACK THERE, KID?

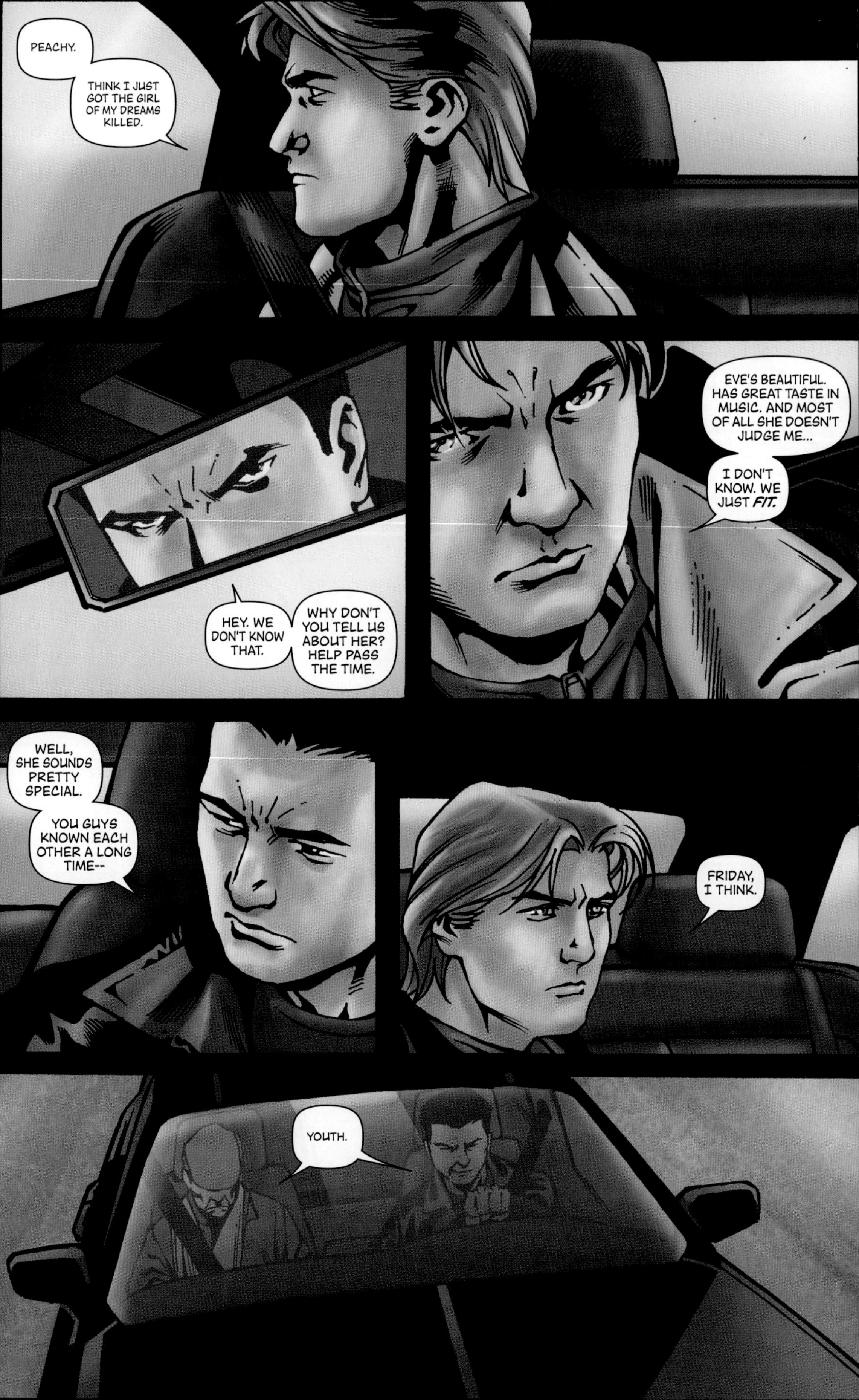
PEACHY.
THINK I JUST GOT THE GIRL OF MY DREAMS KILLED.
HEY. WE DON'T KNOW THAT.
WHY DON'T YOU TELL US ABOUT HER? HELP PASS THE TIME.
EVE'S BEAUTIFUL. HAS GREAT TASTE IN MUSIC. AND MOST OF ALL SHE DOESN'T JUDGE ME...
I DON'T KNOW. WE JUST *FIT.*
WELL, SHE SOUNDS PRETTY SPECIAL.
YOU GUYS KNOWN EACH OTHER A LONG TIME--
FRIDAY, I THINK.
YOUTH.

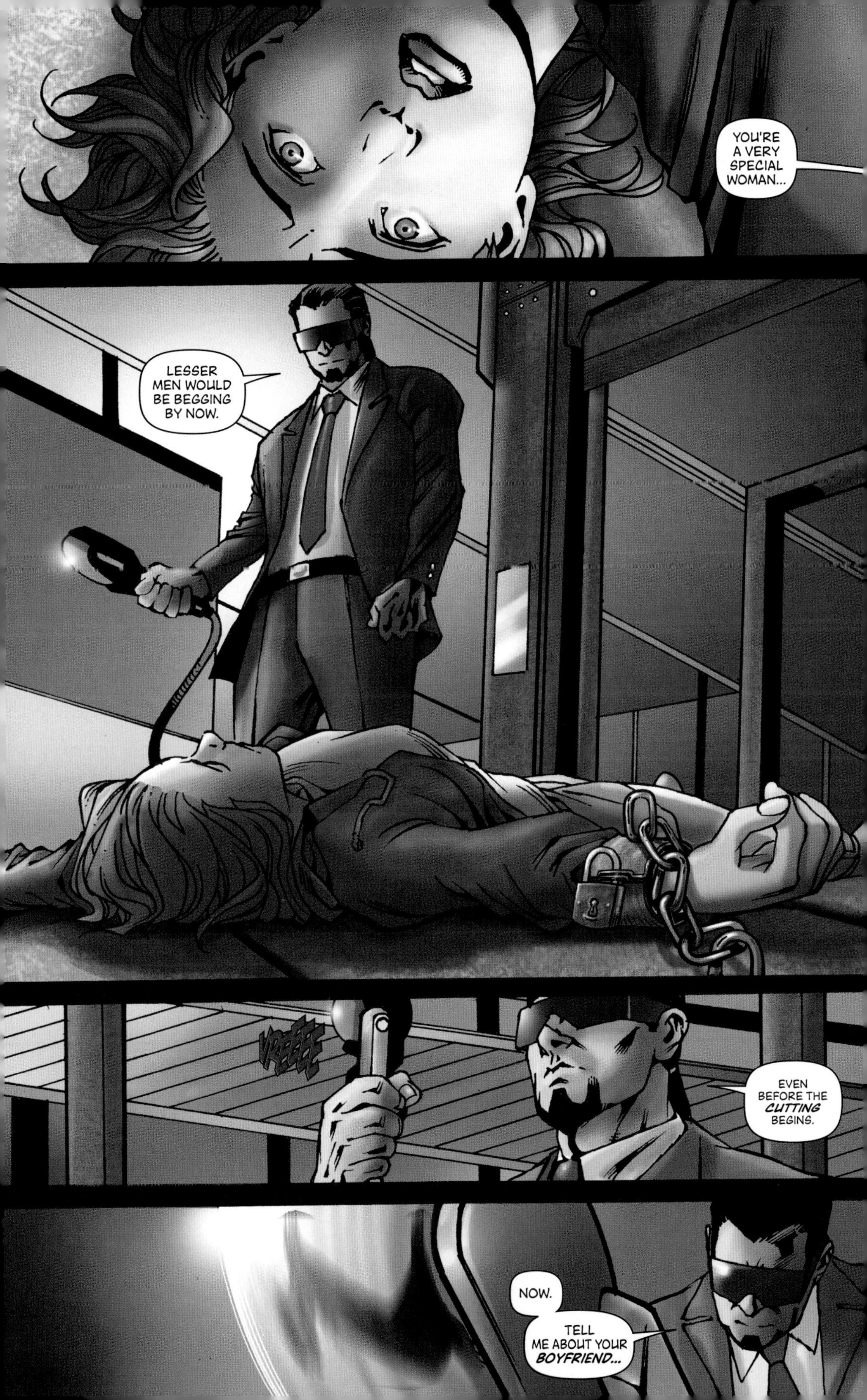
YOU'RE A VERY SPECIAL WOMAN...
LESSER MEN WOULD BE BEGGING BY NOW.
VREEEE
EVEN BEFORE THE *CUTTING* BEGINS.
NOW.
TELL ME ABOUT YOUR *BOYFRIEND...*

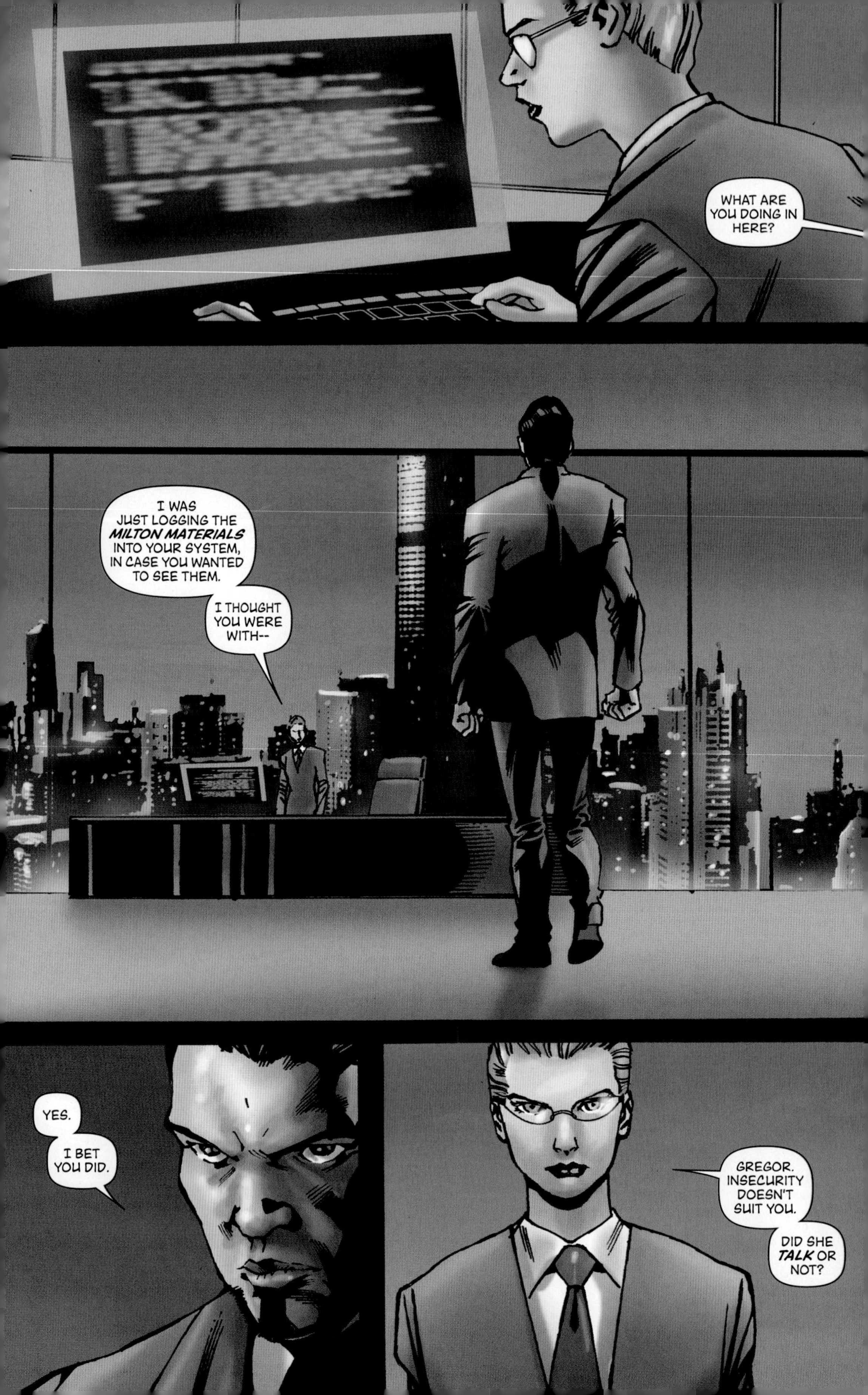
WHAT ARE YOU DOING IN HERE?
I WAS JUST LOGGING THE *MILTON MATERIALS* INTO YOUR SYSTEM, IN CASE YOU WANTED TO SEE THEM.
I THOUGHT YOU WERE WITH--
YES.
I BET YOU DID.
GREGOR. INSECURITY DOESN'T SUIT YOU.
DID SHE *TALK* OR NOT?

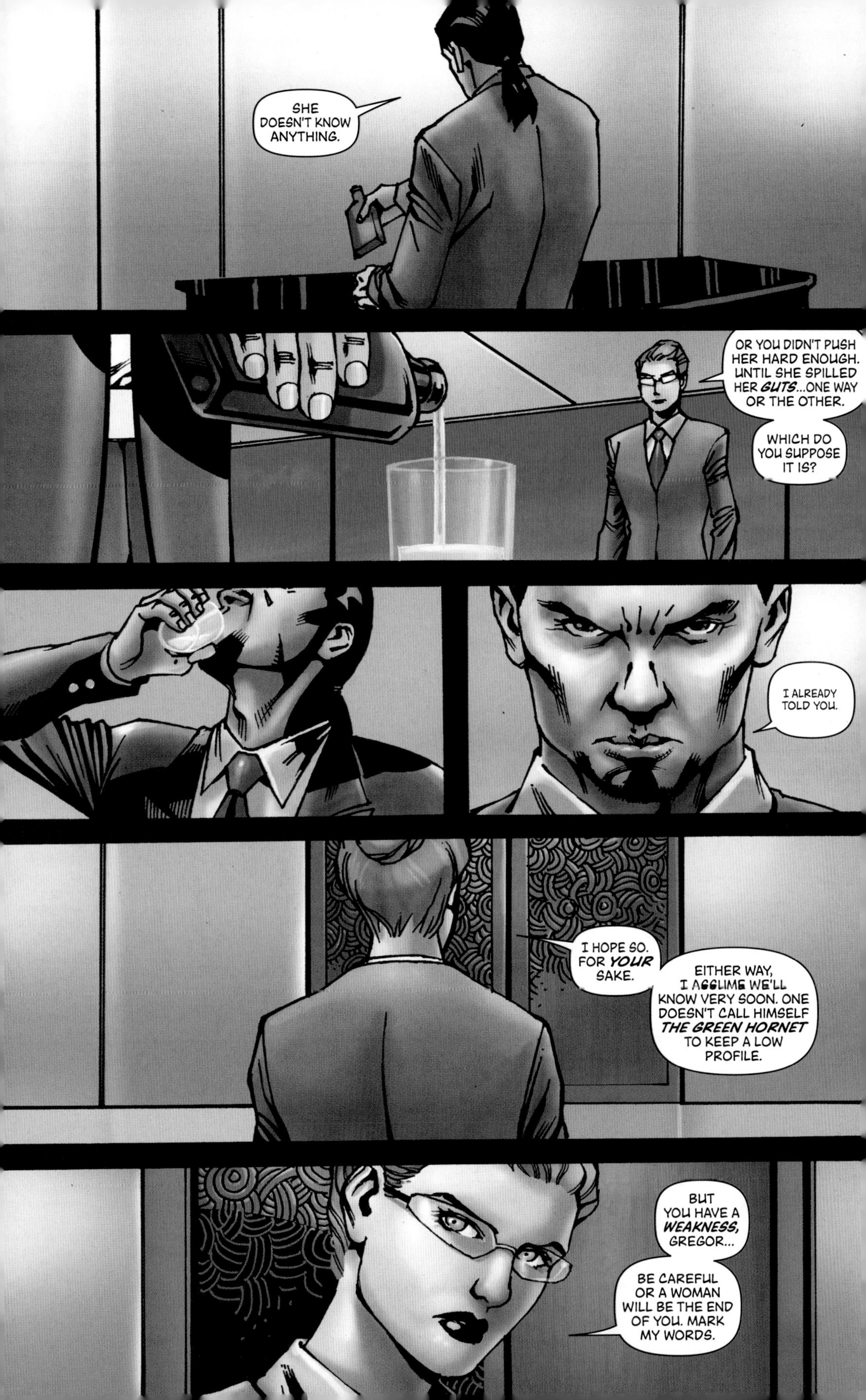
SHE DOESN'T KNOW ANYTHING.
OR YOU DIDN'T PUSH HER HARD ENOUGH. UNTIL SHE SPILLED HER GUTS...ONE WAY OR THE OTHER.
WHICH DO YOU SUPPOSE IT IS?
I ALREADY TOLD YOU.
I HOPE SO. FOR YOUR SAKE.
EITHER WAY, I ASSUME WE'LL KNOW VERY SOON. ONE DOESN'T CALL HIMSELF THE GREEN HORNET TO KEEP A LOW PROFILE.
BUT YOU HAVE A WEAKNESS, GREGOR...
BE CAREFUL OR A WOMAN WILL BE THE END OF YOU. MARK MY WORDS.

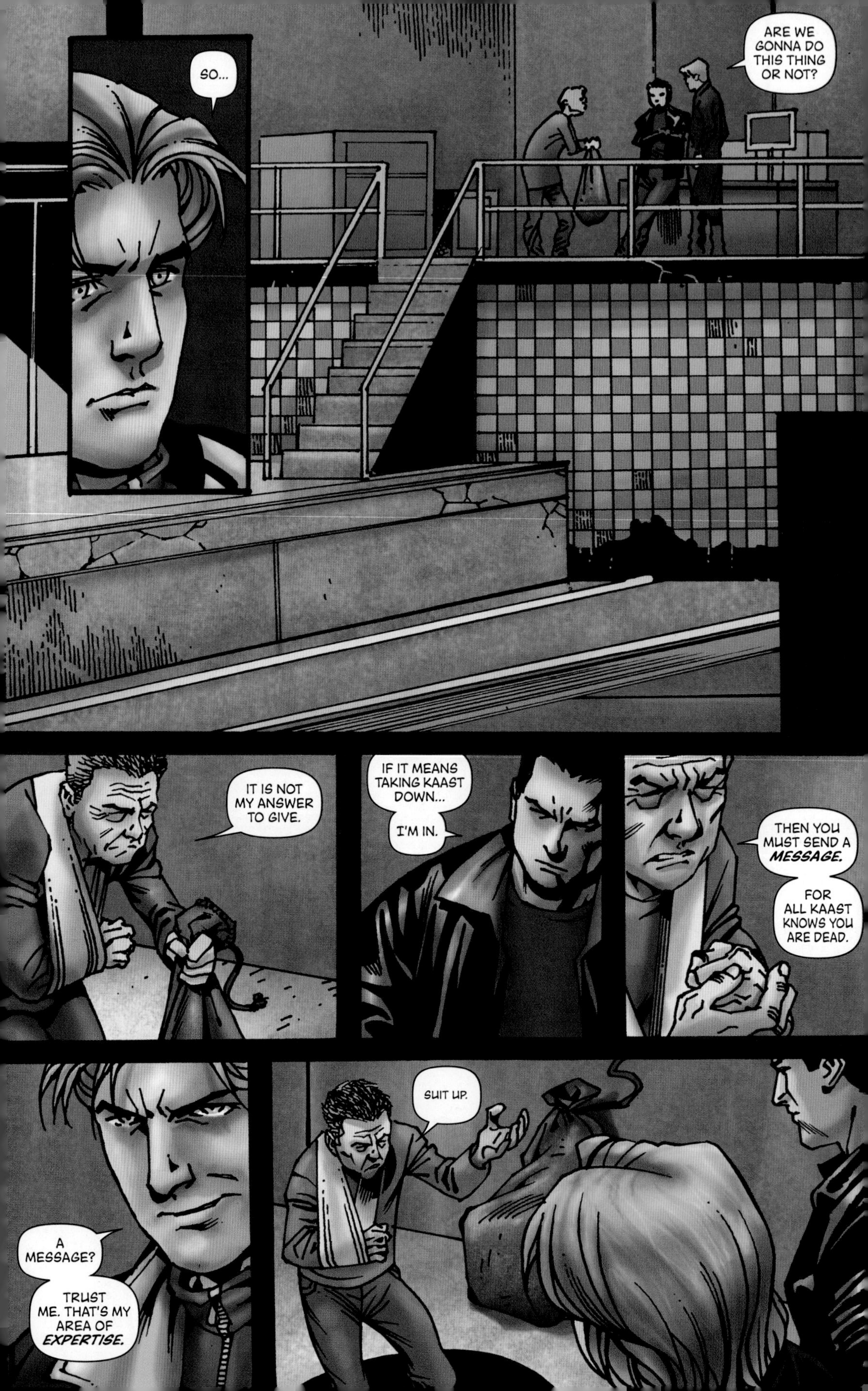
SO...
ARE WE GONNA DO THIS THING OR NOT?
IT IS NOT MY ANSWER TO GIVE.
IF IT MEANS TAKING KAAST DOWN...
I'M IN.
THEN YOU MUST SEND A *MESSAGE.*
FOR ALL KAAST KNOWS YOU ARE DEAD.
A MESSAGE?
TRUST ME. THAT'S MY AREA OF *EXPERTISE.*
SUIT UP.

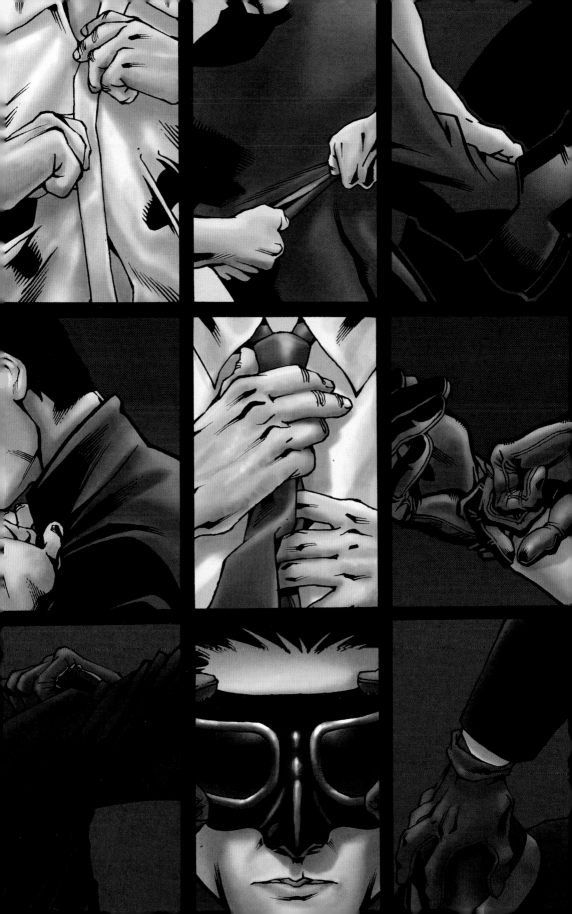

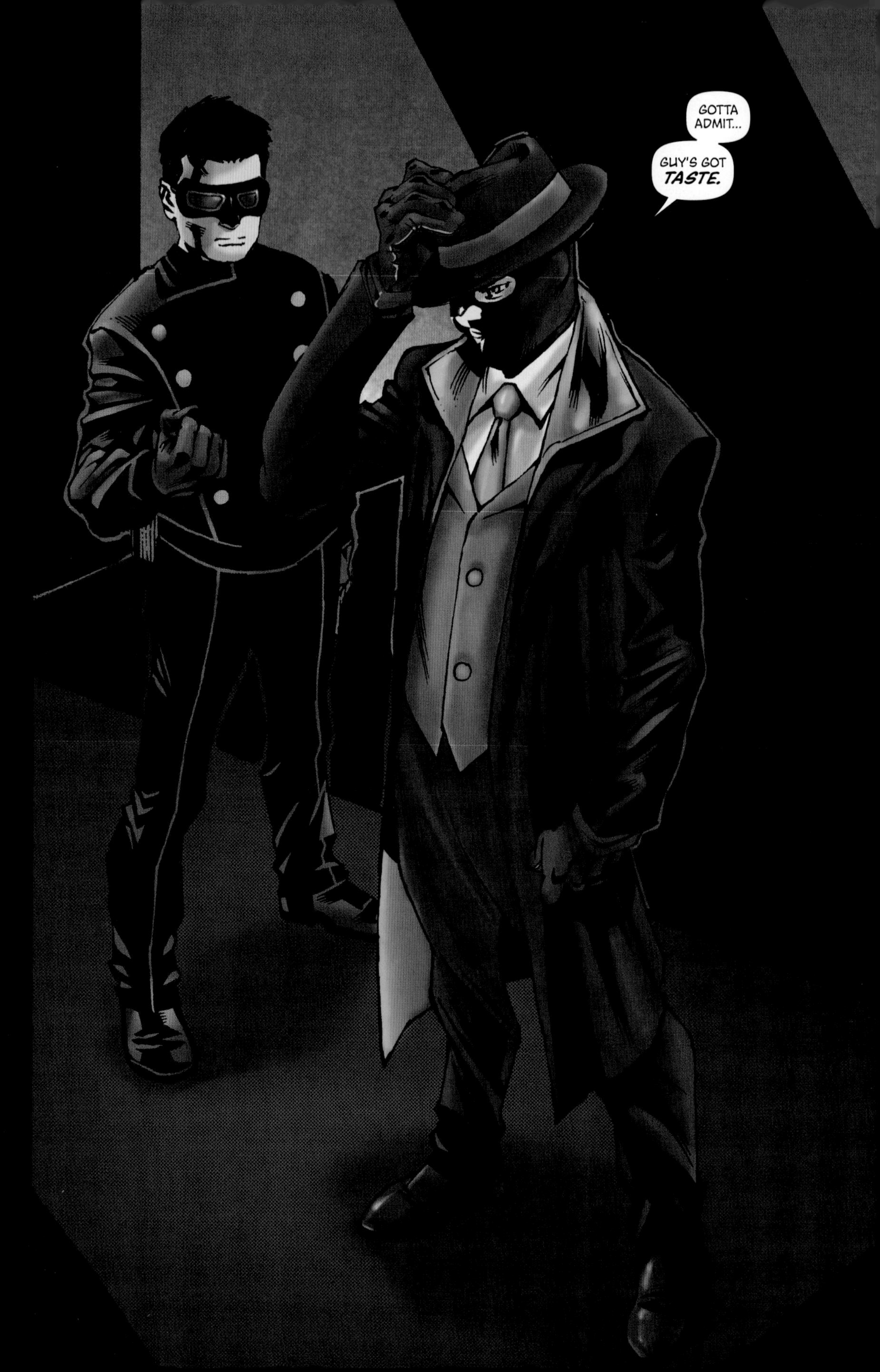
GOTTA ADMIT...
GUY'S GOT *TASTE.*

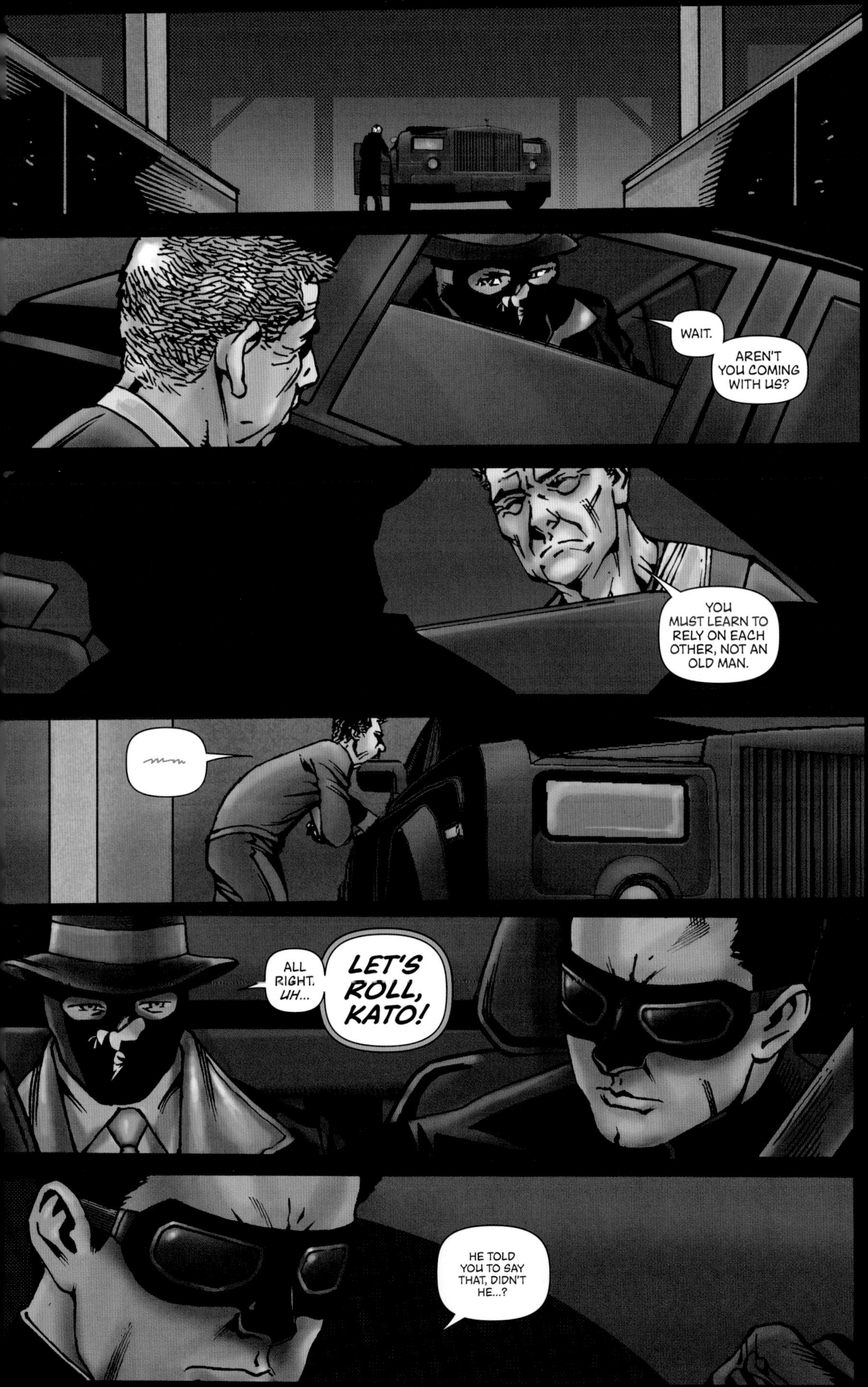
WAIT.
AREN'T YOU COMING WITH US?
YOU MUST LEARN TO RELY ON EACH OTHER, NOT AN OLD MAN.
ALL RIGHT. UH...
LET'S ROLL, KATO!
HE TOLD YOU TO SAY THAT, DIDN'T HE...?

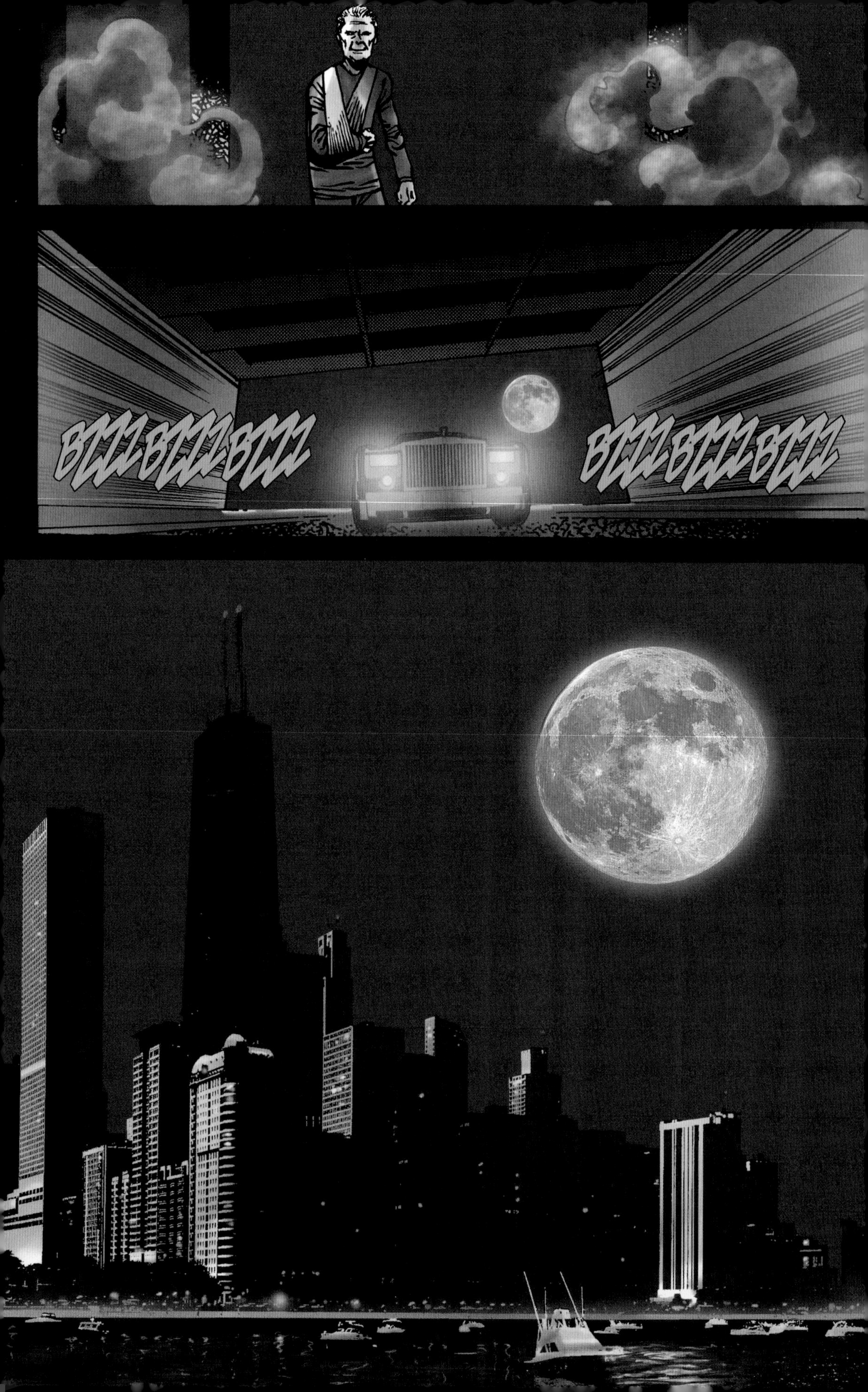
BZZZ BZZZ BZZZ
BZZZ BZZZ BZZZ

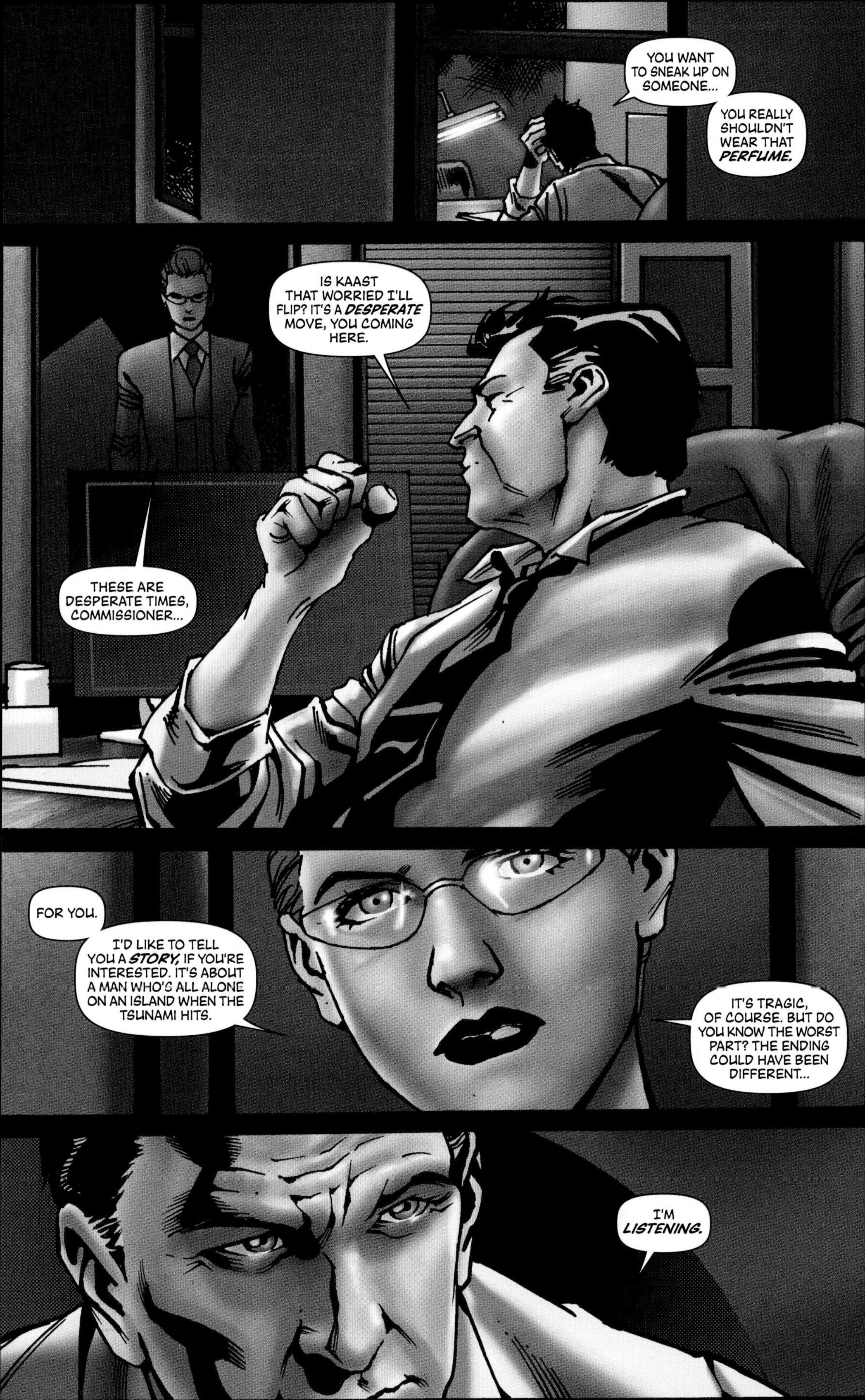
YOU WANT TO SNEAK UP ON SOMEONE...
YOU REALLY SHOULDN'T WEAR THAT PERFUME.
IS KAAST THAT WORRIED I'LL FLIP? IT'S A DESPERATE MOVE, YOU COMING HERE.
THESE ARE DESPERATE TIMES, COMMISSIONER...
FOR YOU.
I'D LIKE TO TELL YOU A STORY, IF YOU'RE INTERESTED. IT'S ABOUT A MAN WHO'S ALL ALONE ON AN ISLAND WHEN THE TSUNAMI HITS.
IT'S TRAGIC, OF COURSE. BUT DO YOU KNOW THE WORST PART? THE ENDING COULD HAVE BEEN DIFFERENT...
I'M LISTENING.

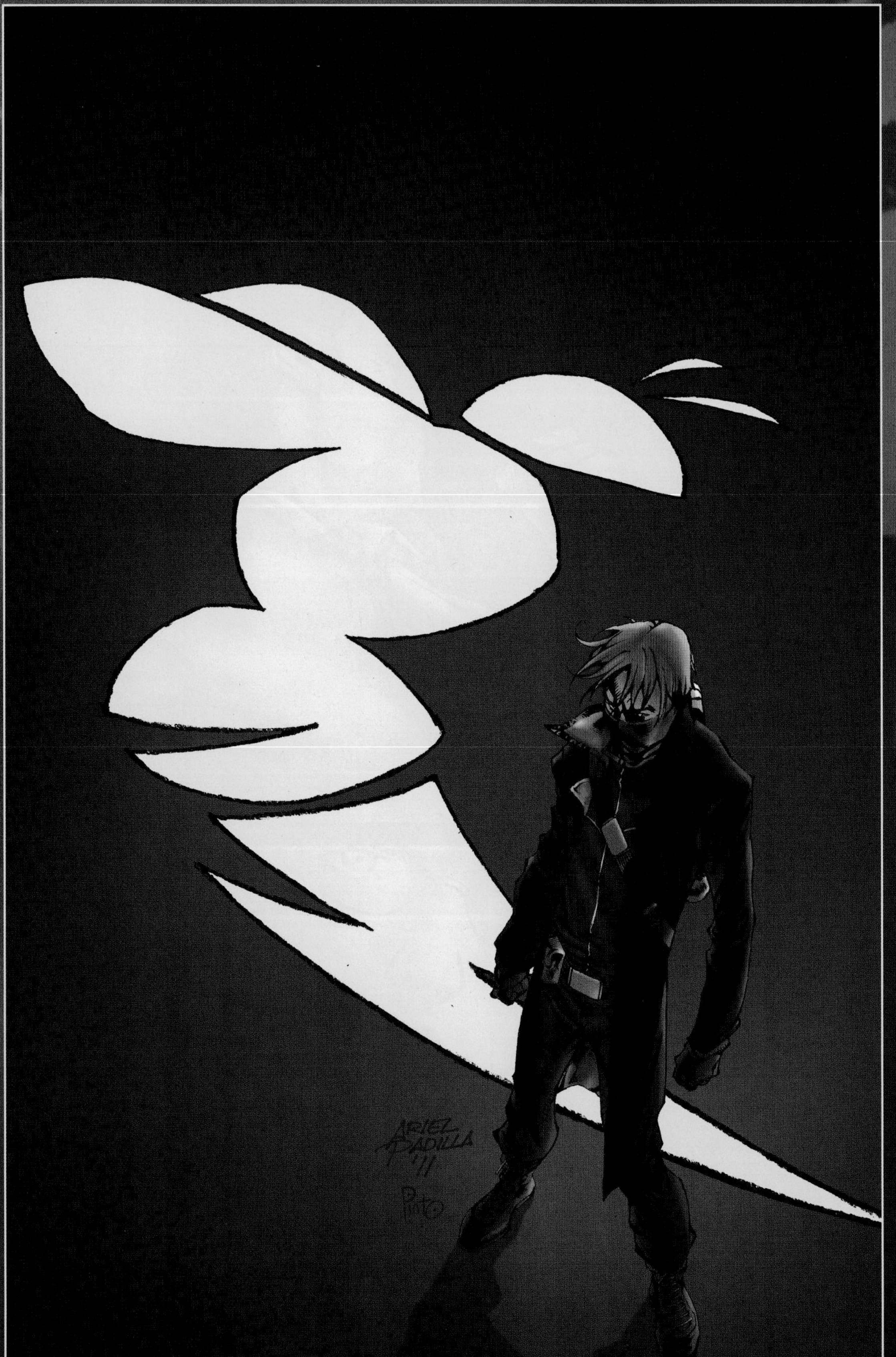

Issue #10 cover by ARIEL PADILLA

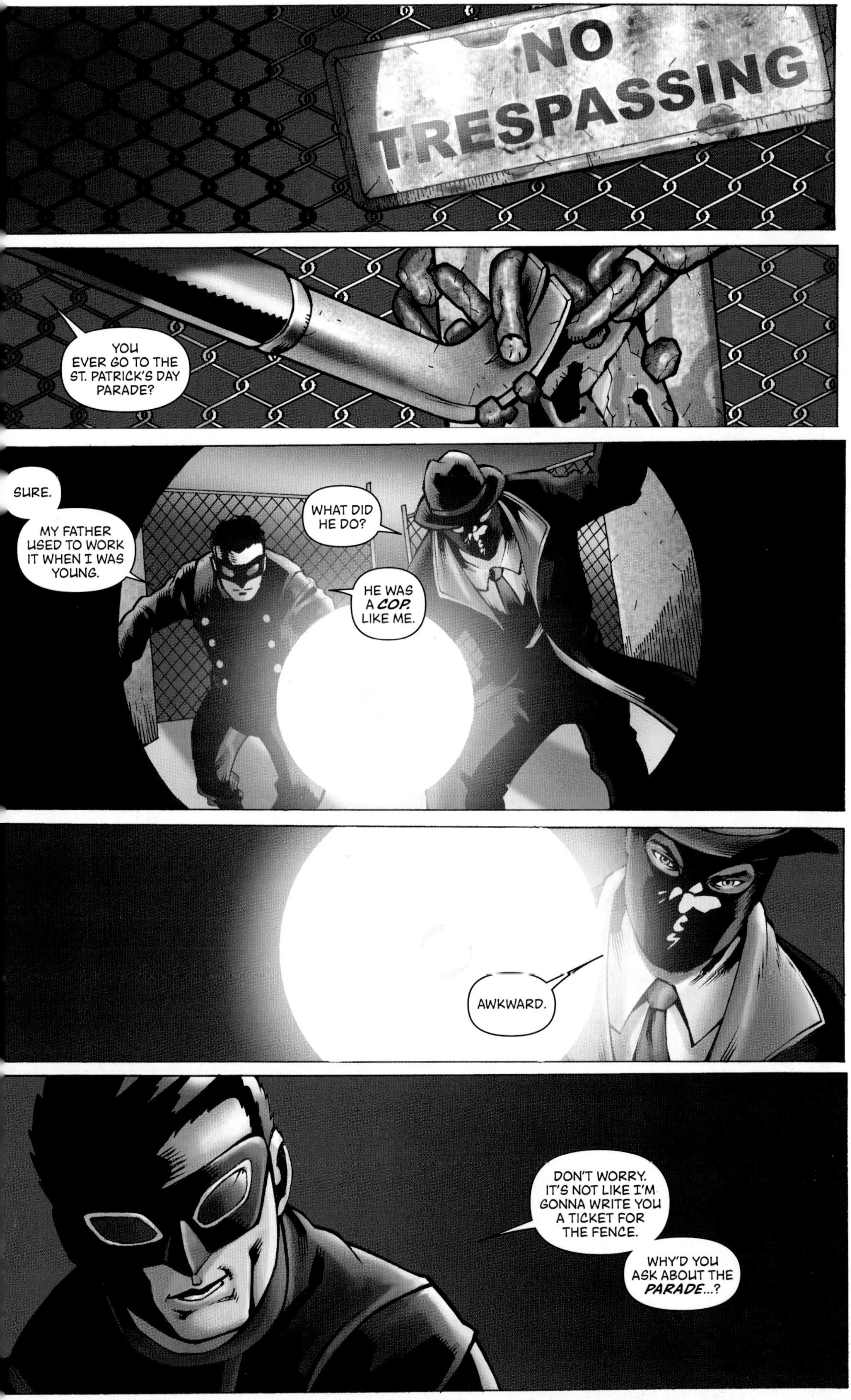
NO TRESPASSING
YOU EVER GO TO THE ST. PATRICK'S DAY PARADE?
SURE.
MY FATHER USED TO WORK IT WHEN I WAS YOUNG.
WHAT DID HE DO?
HE WAS A *COP.* LIKE ME.
AWKWARD.
DON'T WORRY. IT'S NOT LIKE I'M GONNA WRITE YOU A TICKET FOR THE FENCE.
WHY'D YOU ASK ABOUT THE *PARADE*...?

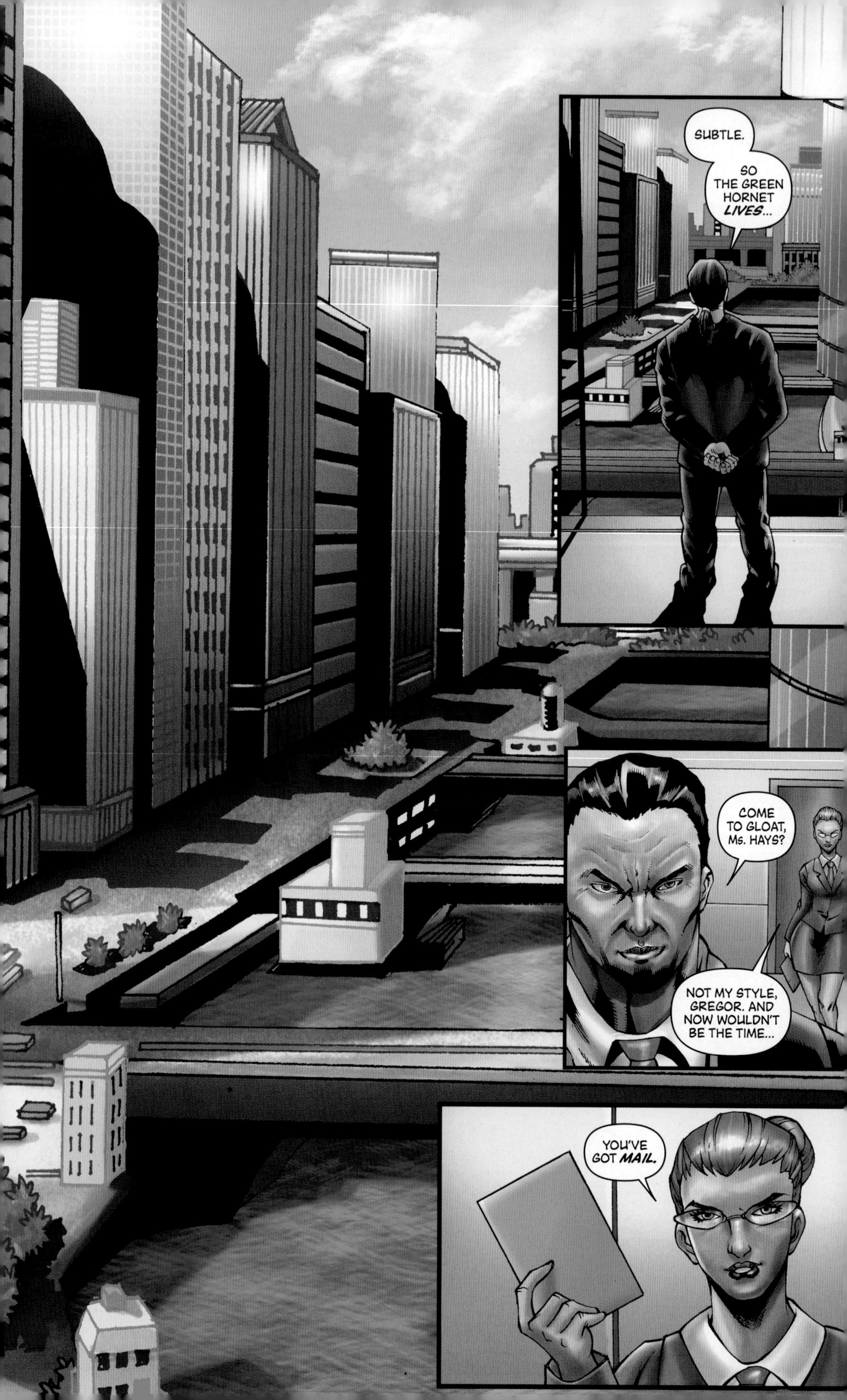
SUBTLE.
SO THE GREEN HORNET LIVES...
COME TO GLOAT, Ms. HAYS?
NOT MY STYLE, GREGOR. AND NOW WOULDN'T BE THE TIME...
YOU'VE GOT MAIL.

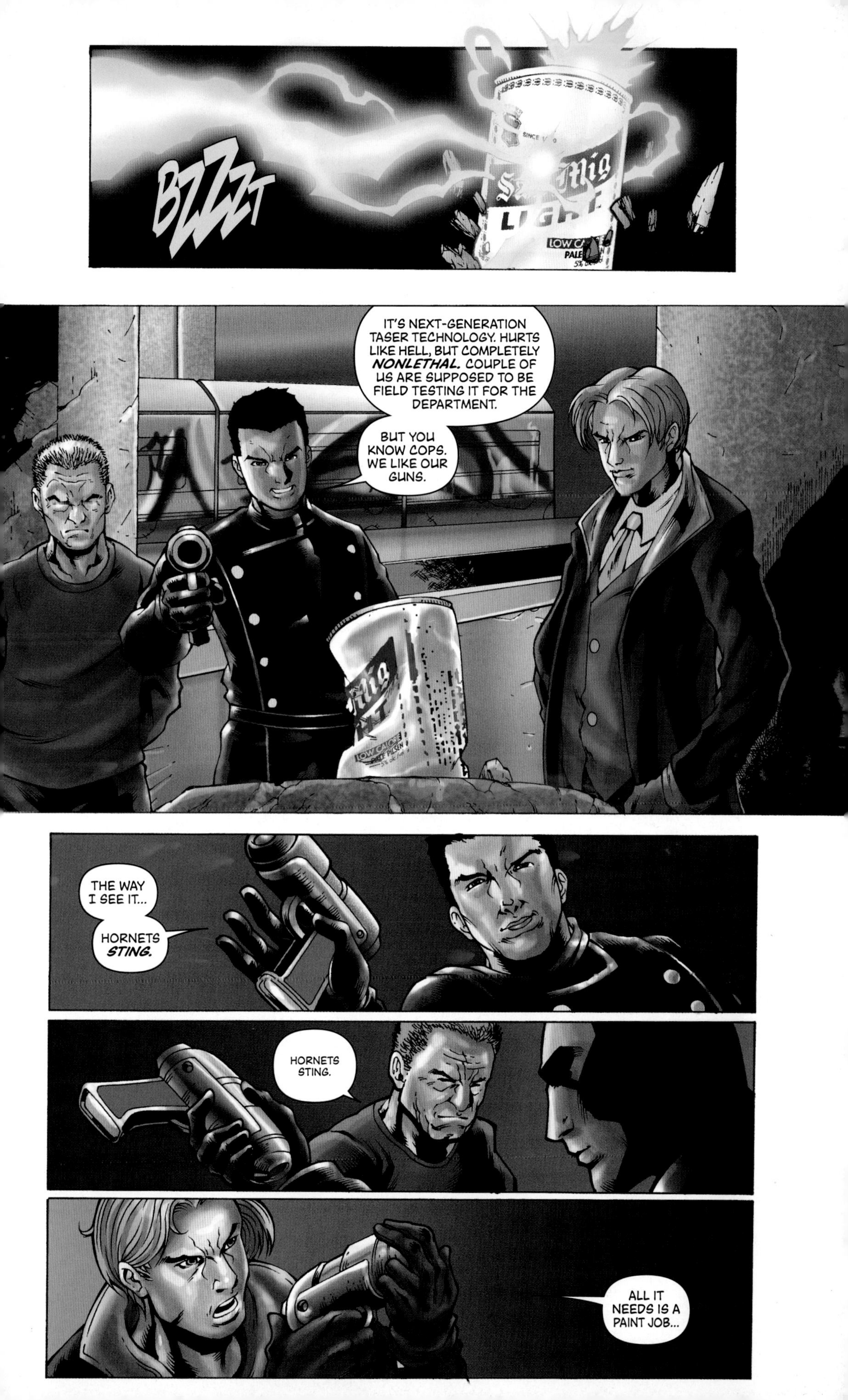
BZZZZT
IT'S NEXT-GENERATION TASER TECHNOLOGY. HURTS LIKE HELL, BUT COMPLETELY *NONLETHAL.* COUPLE OF US ARE SUPPOSED TO BE FIELD TESTING IT FOR THE DEPARTMENT.
BUT YOU KNOW COPS. WE LIKE OUR GUNS.
THE WAY I SEE IT...
HORNETS *STING.*
HORNETS STING.
ALL IT NEEDS IS A PAINT JOB...

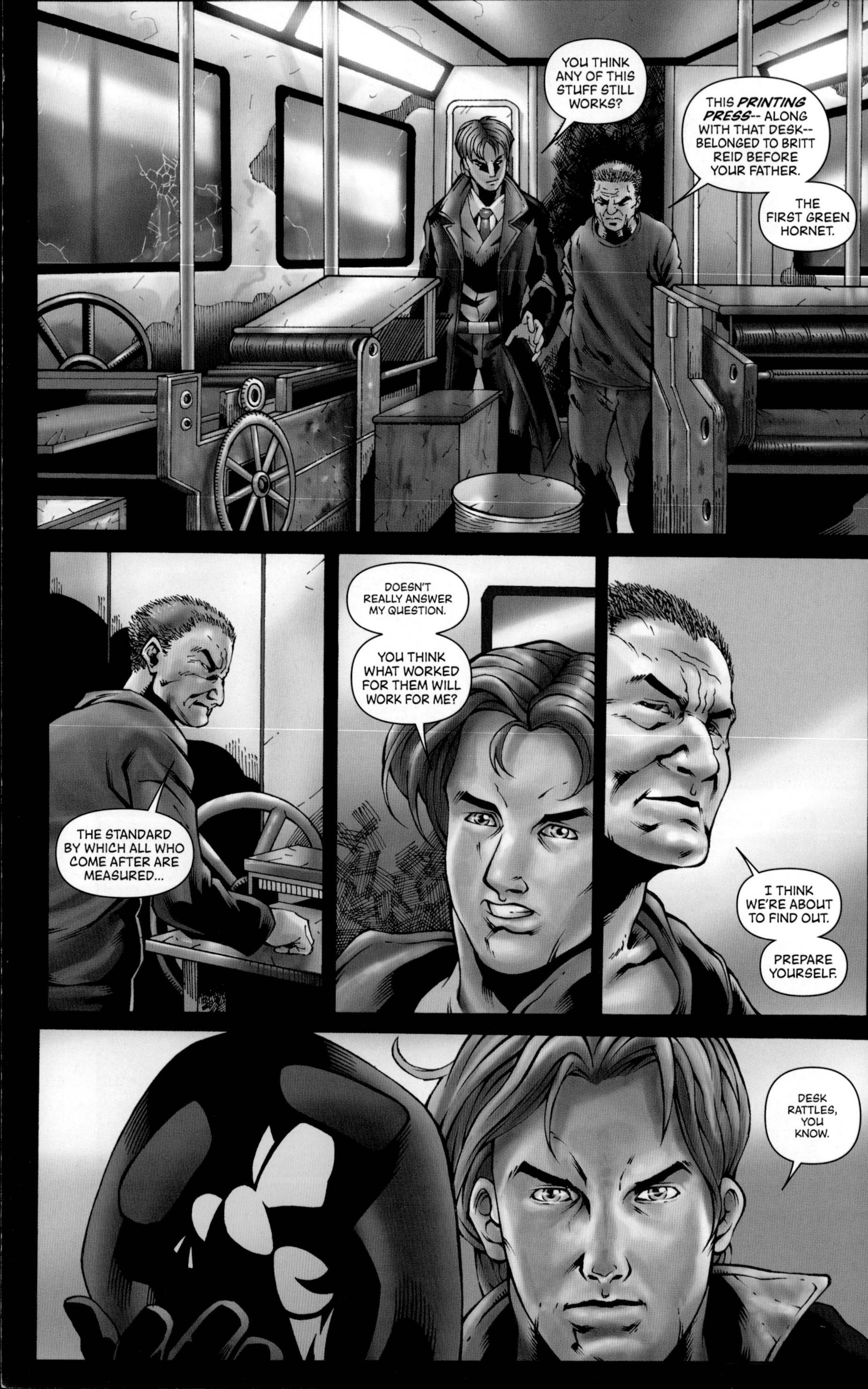
YOU THINK ANY OF THIS STUFF STILL WORKS?
THIS PRINTING PRESS-- ALONG WITH THAT DESK-- BELONGED TO BRITT REID BEFORE YOUR FATHER.
THE FIRST GREEN HORNET.
THE STANDARD BY WHICH ALL WHO COME AFTER ARE MEASURED...
DOESN'T REALLY ANSWER MY QUESTION.
YOU THINK WHAT WORKED FOR THEM WILL WORK FOR ME?
I THINK WE'RE ABOUT TO FIND OUT.
PREPARE YOURSELF.
DESK RATTLES, YOU KNOW.

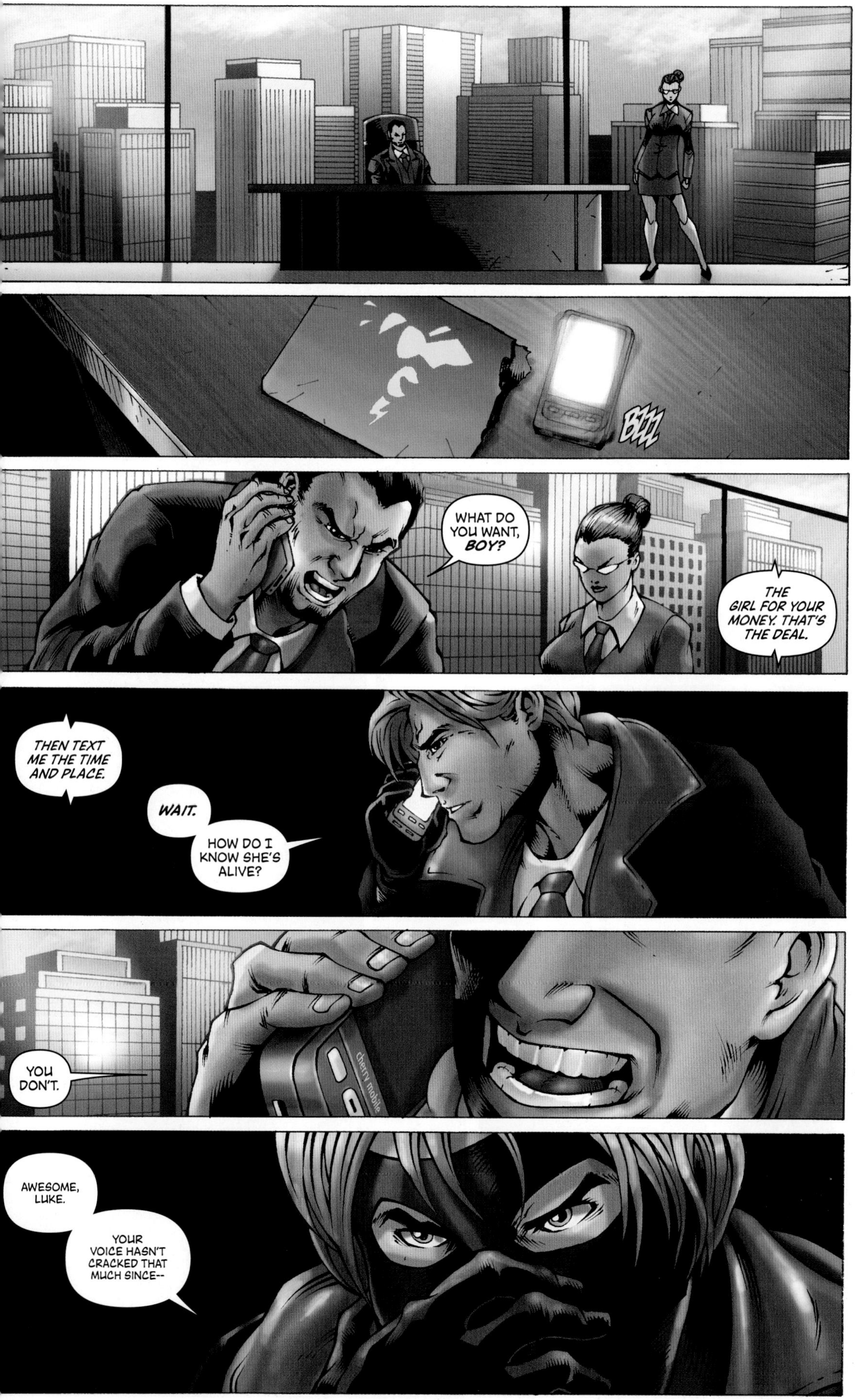
BZZZ
WHAT DO YOU WANT, *BOY?*
THE GIRL FOR YOUR MONEY. THAT'S THE DEAL.
THEN TEXT ME THE TIME AND PLACE.
WAIT.
HOW DO I KNOW SHE'S ALIVE?
YOU DON'T.
cherry mobile
AWESOME, LUKE.
YOUR VOICE HASN'T CRACKED THAT MUCH SINCE--

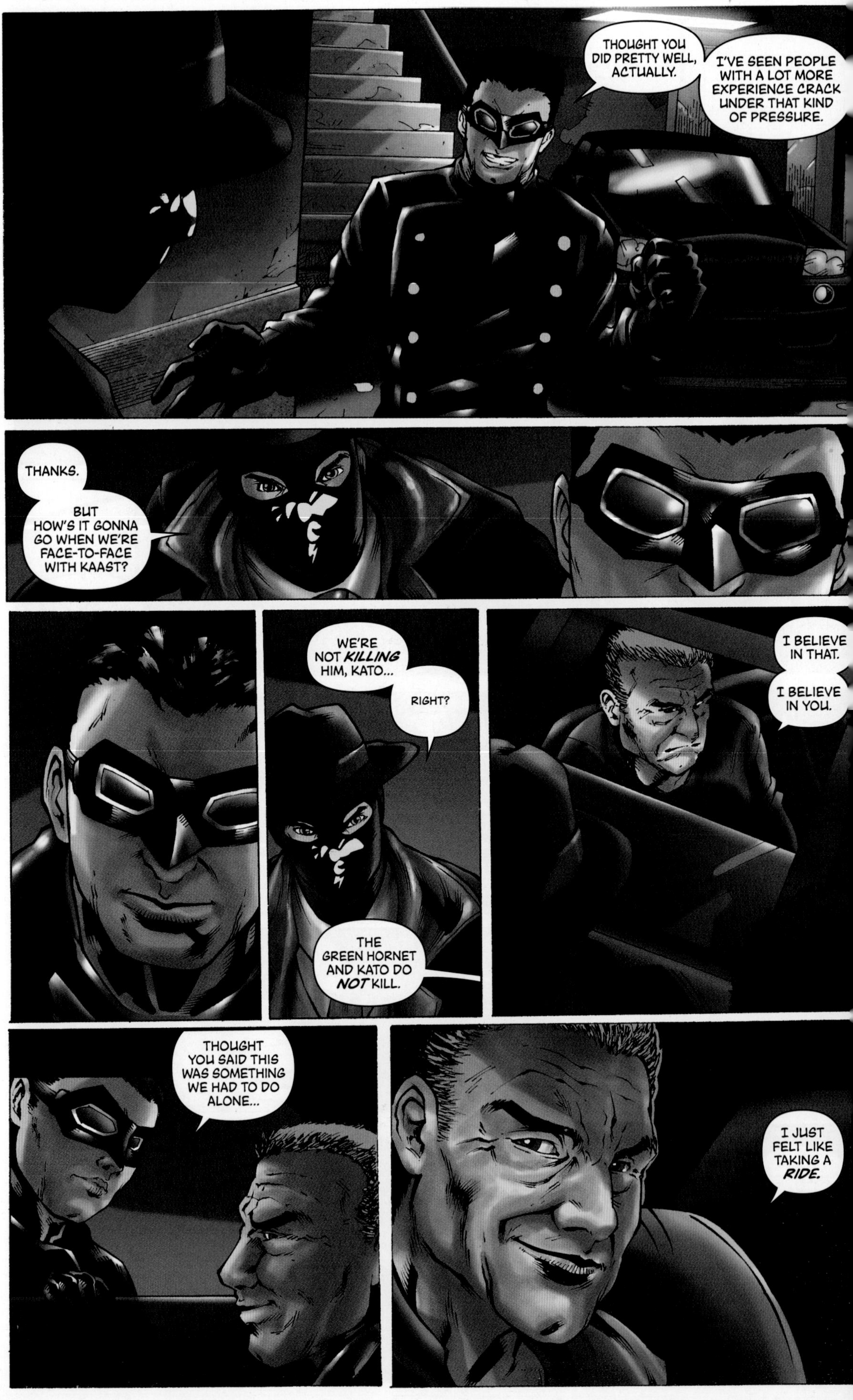
THOUGHT YOU DID PRETTY WELL, ACTUALLY.
I'VE SEEN PEOPLE WITH A LOT MORE EXPERIENCE CRACK UNDER THAT KIND OF PRESSURE.
THANKS.
BUT HOW'S IT GONNA GO WHEN WE'RE FACE-TO-FACE WITH KAAST?
WE'RE NOT *KILLING* HIM, KATO...
RIGHT?
THE GREEN HORNET AND KATO DO ***NOT*** KILL.
I BELIEVE IN THAT.
I BELIEVE IN YOU.
THOUGHT YOU SAID THIS WAS SOMETHING WE HAD TO DO ALONE...
I JUST FELT LIKE TAKING A ***RIDE.***

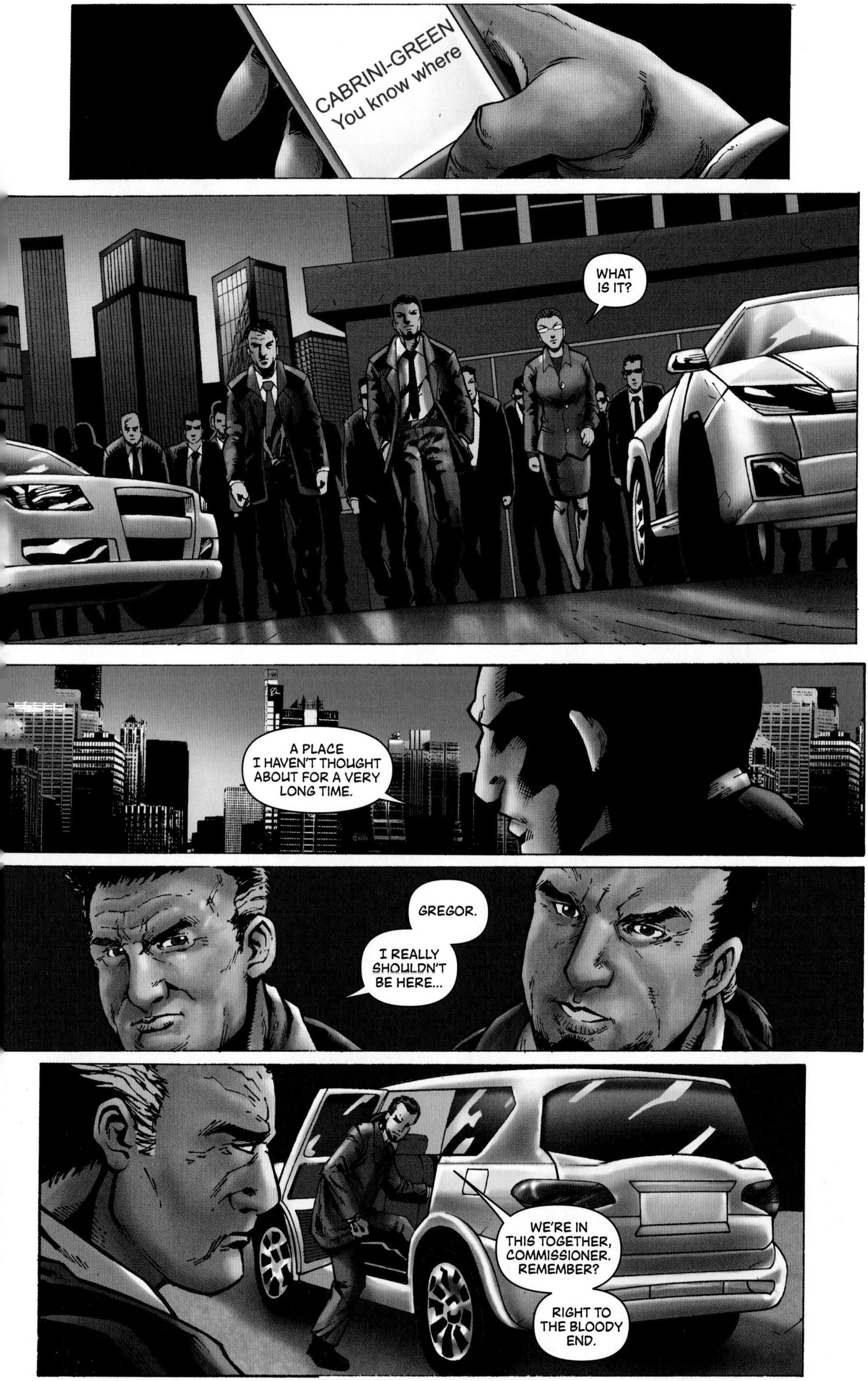
CABRINI-GREEN
You know where
WHAT IS IT?
A PLACE I HAVEN'T THOUGHT ABOUT FOR A VERY LONG TIME.
GREGOR.
I REALLY SHOULDN'T BE HERE...
WE'RE IN THIS TOGETHER, COMMISSIONER. REMEMBER?
RIGHT TO THE BLOODY END.

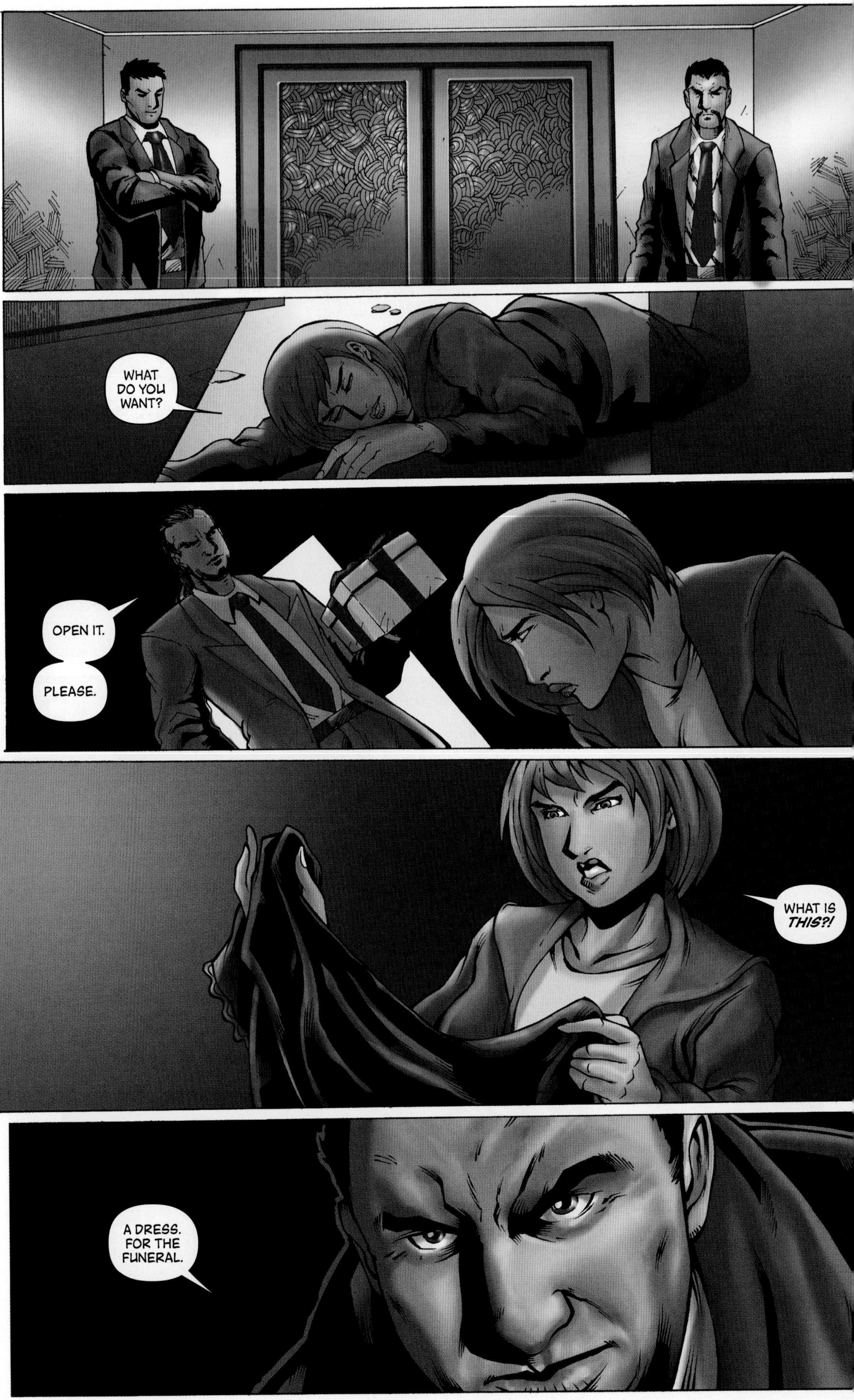
WHAT DO YOU WANT?
OPEN IT.
PLEASE.
WHAT IS *THIS?!*
A DRESS. FOR THE FUNERAL.

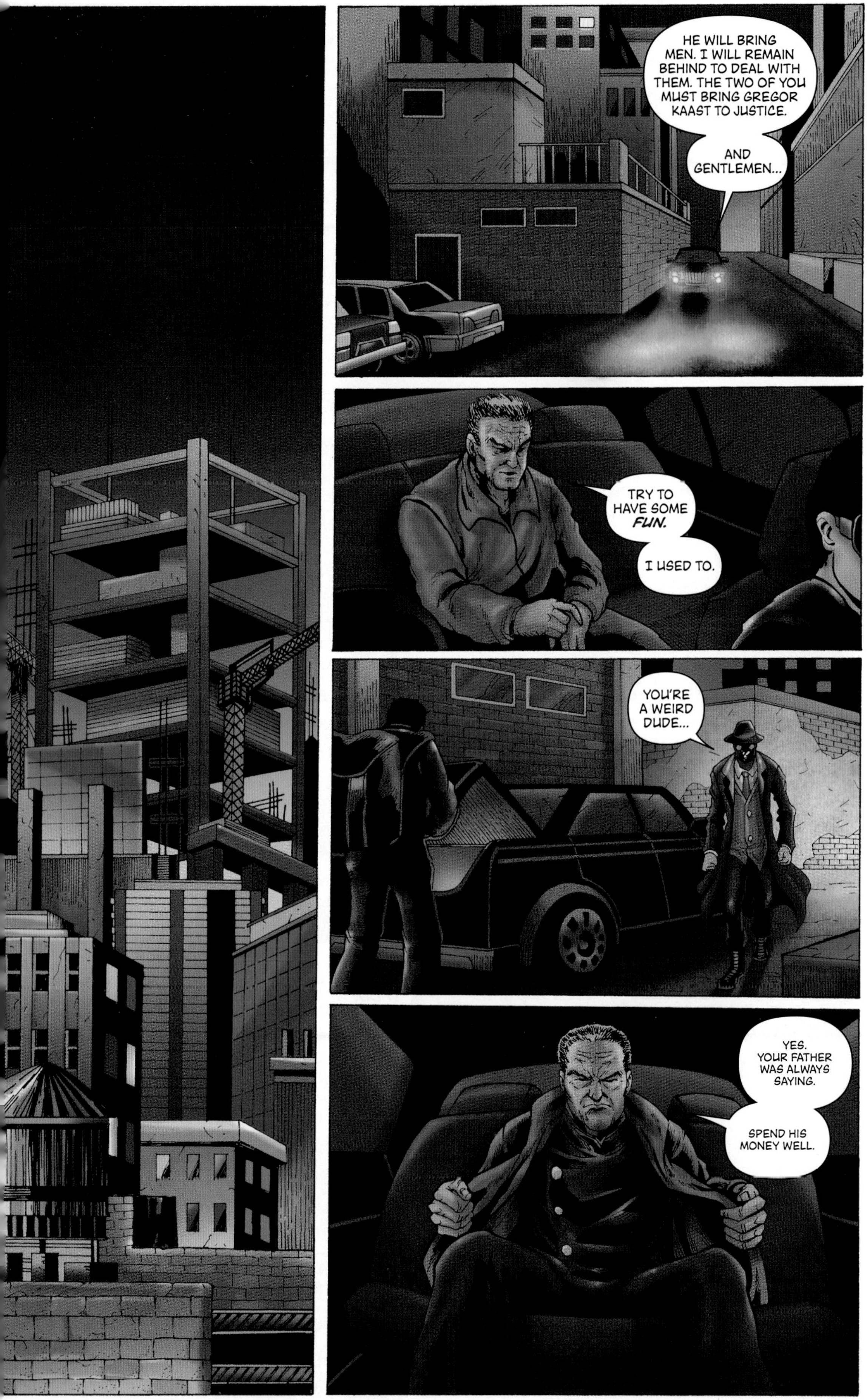
HE WILL BRING MEN. I WILL REMAIN BEHIND TO DEAL WITH THEM. THE TWO OF YOU MUST BRING GREGOR KAAST TO JUSTICE.
AND GENTLEMEN...
TRY TO HAVE SOME *FUN.*
I USED TO.
YOU'RE A WEIRD DUDE...
YES. YOUR FATHER WAS ALWAYS SAYING.
SPEND HIS MONEY WELL.

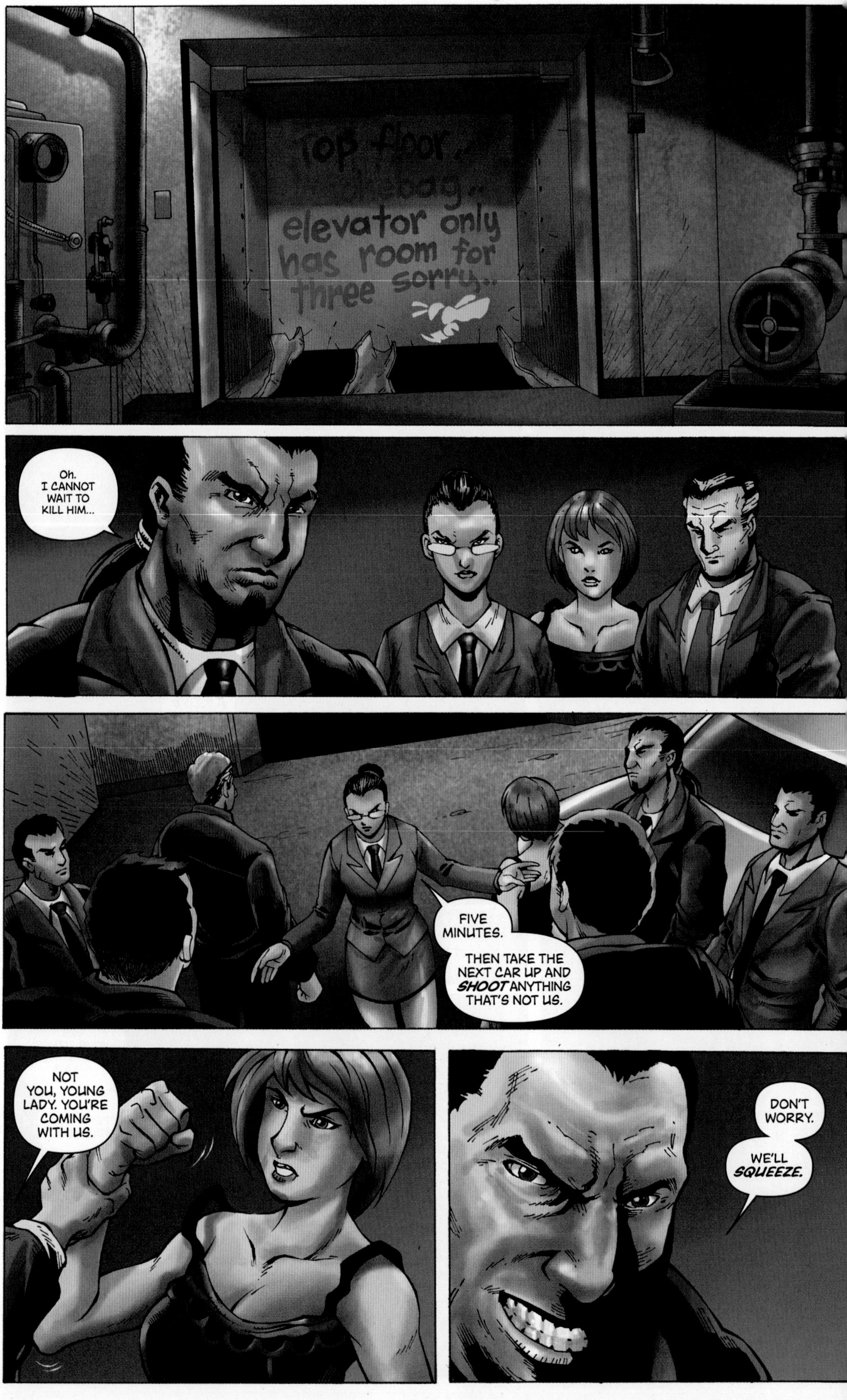
Top floor..
elevator only has room for three sorry..
Oh. I CANNOT WAIT TO KILL HIM...
FIVE MINUTES.
THEN TAKE THE NEXT CAR UP AND *SHOOT* ANYTHING THAT'S NOT US.
NOT YOU, YOUNG LADY. YOU'RE COMING WITH US.
DON'T WORRY.
WE'LL *SQUEEZE.*

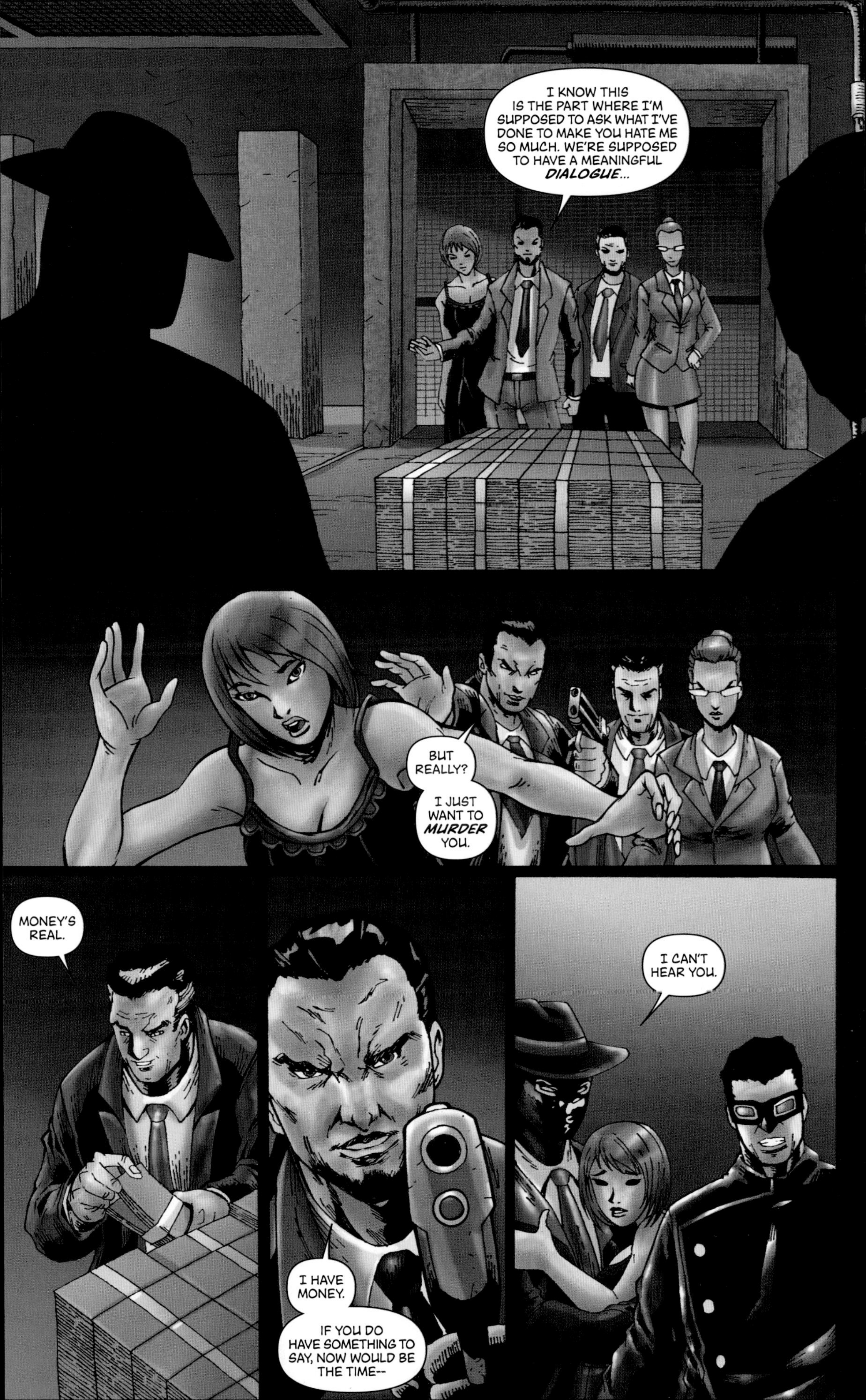
I KNOW THIS IS THE PART WHERE I'M SUPPOSED TO ASK WHAT I'VE DONE TO MAKE YOU HATE ME SO MUCH. WE'RE SUPPOSED TO HAVE A MEANINGFUL *DIALOGUE*...
BUT REALLY?
I JUST WANT TO *MURDER* YOU.
MONEY'S REAL.
I HAVE MONEY.
IF YOU DO HAVE SOMETHING TO SAY, NOW WOULD BE THE TIME--
I CAN'T HEAR YOU.

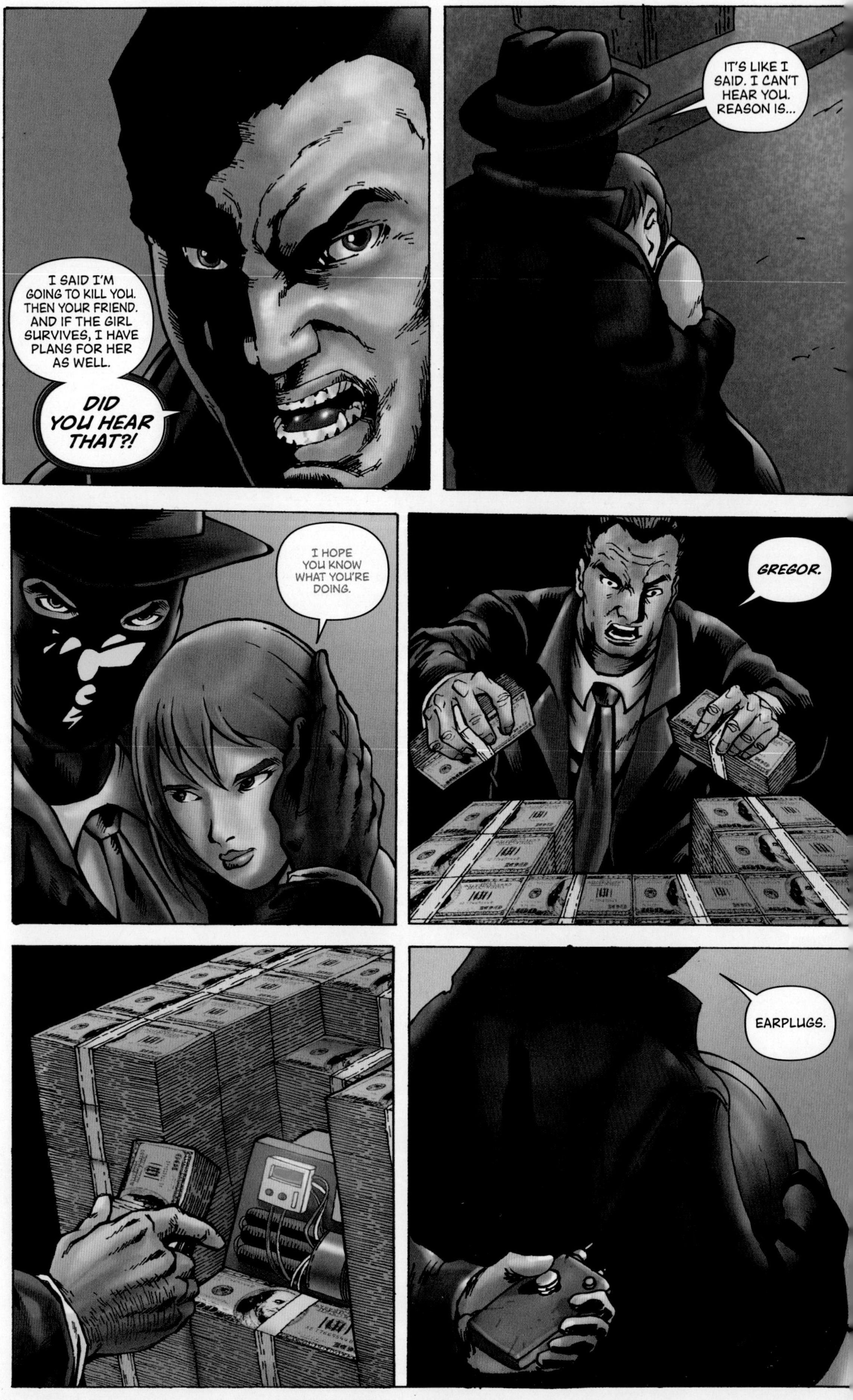
I SAID I'M GOING TO KILL YOU. THEN YOUR FRIEND. AND IF THE GIRL SURVIVES, I HAVE PLANS FOR HER AS WELL.
DID YOU HEAR THAT?!
IT'S LIKE I SAID. I CAN'T HEAR YOU. REASON IS...
I HOPE YOU KNOW WHAT YOU'RE DOING.
GREGOR.
EARPLUGS.

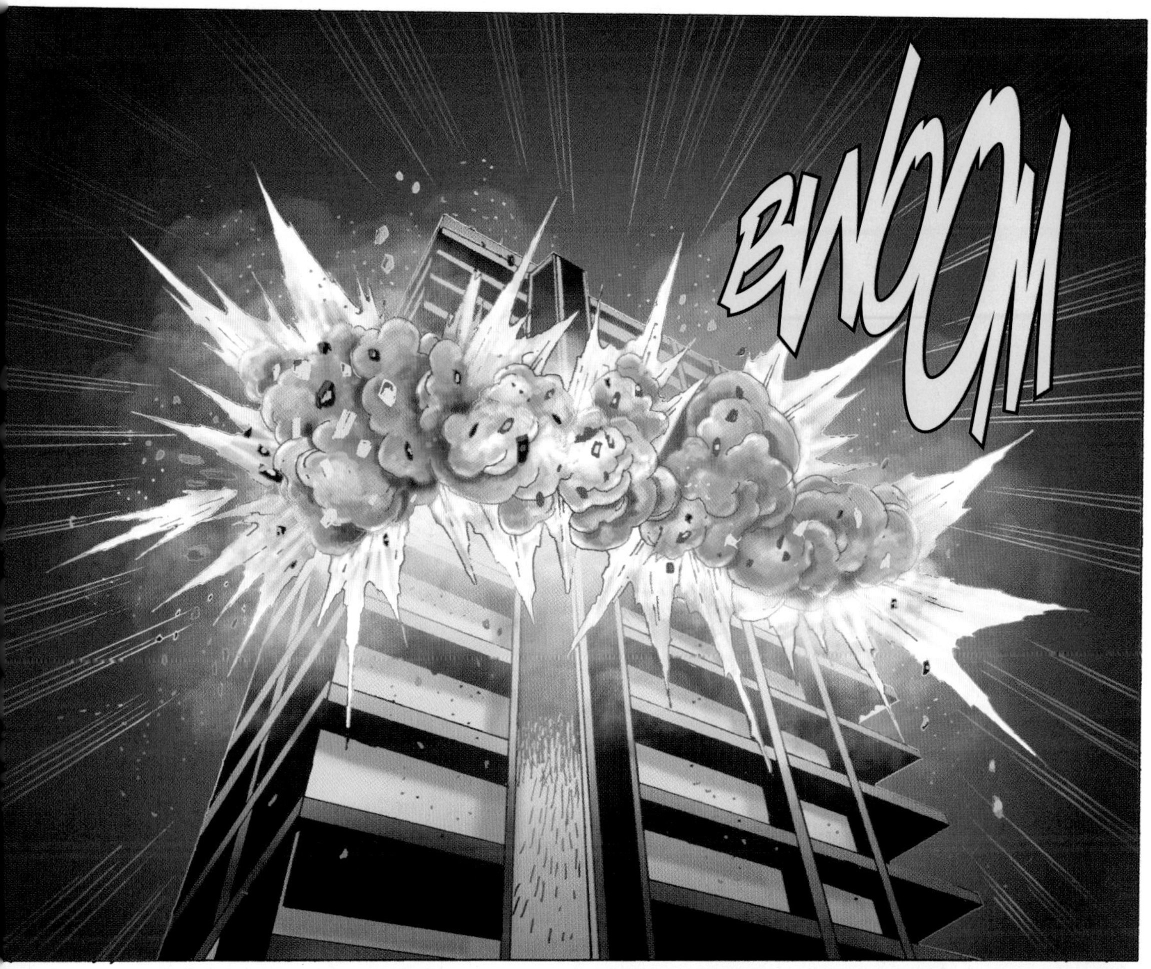
BWOOM

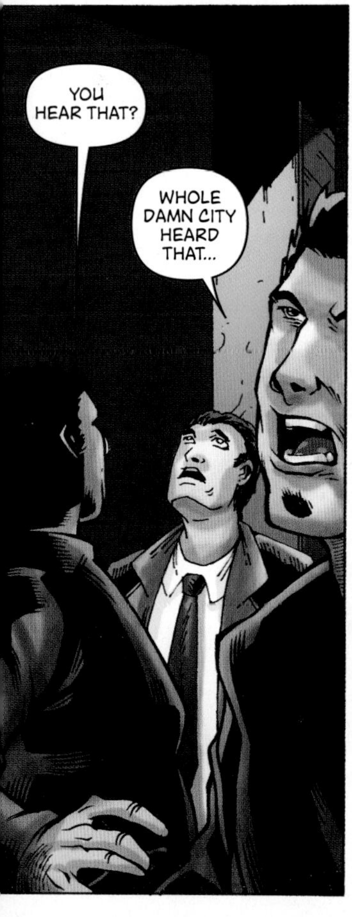
YOU HEAR THAT?
WHOLE DAMN CITY HEARD THAT...

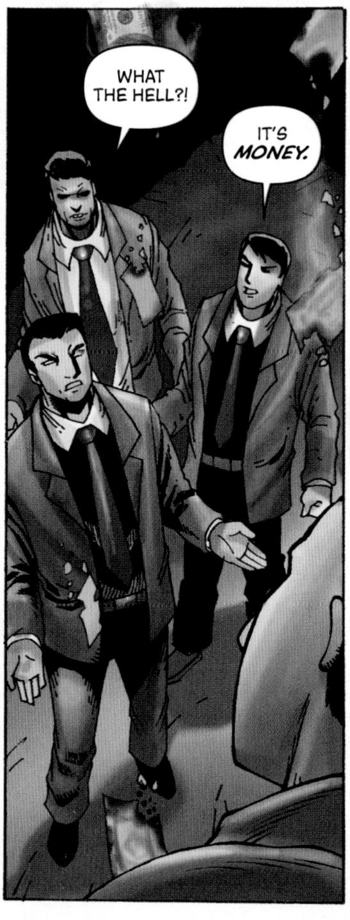
WHAT THE HELL?!
IT'S MONEY.

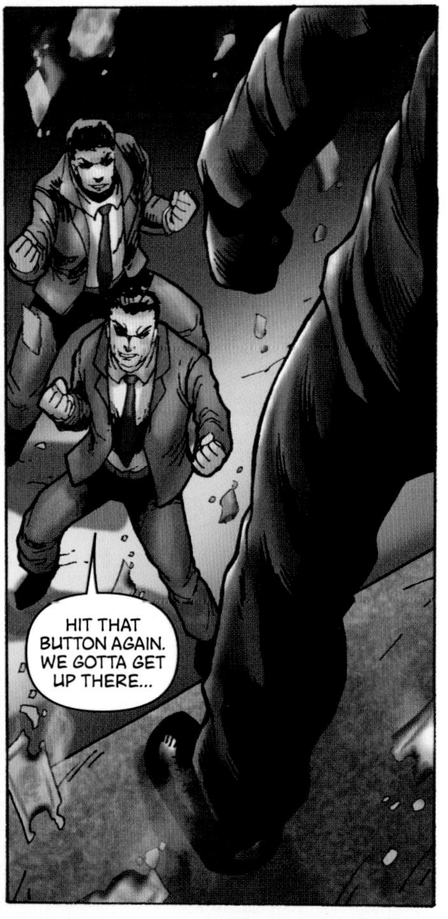
HIT THAT BUTTON AGAIN. WE GOTTA GET UP THERE...

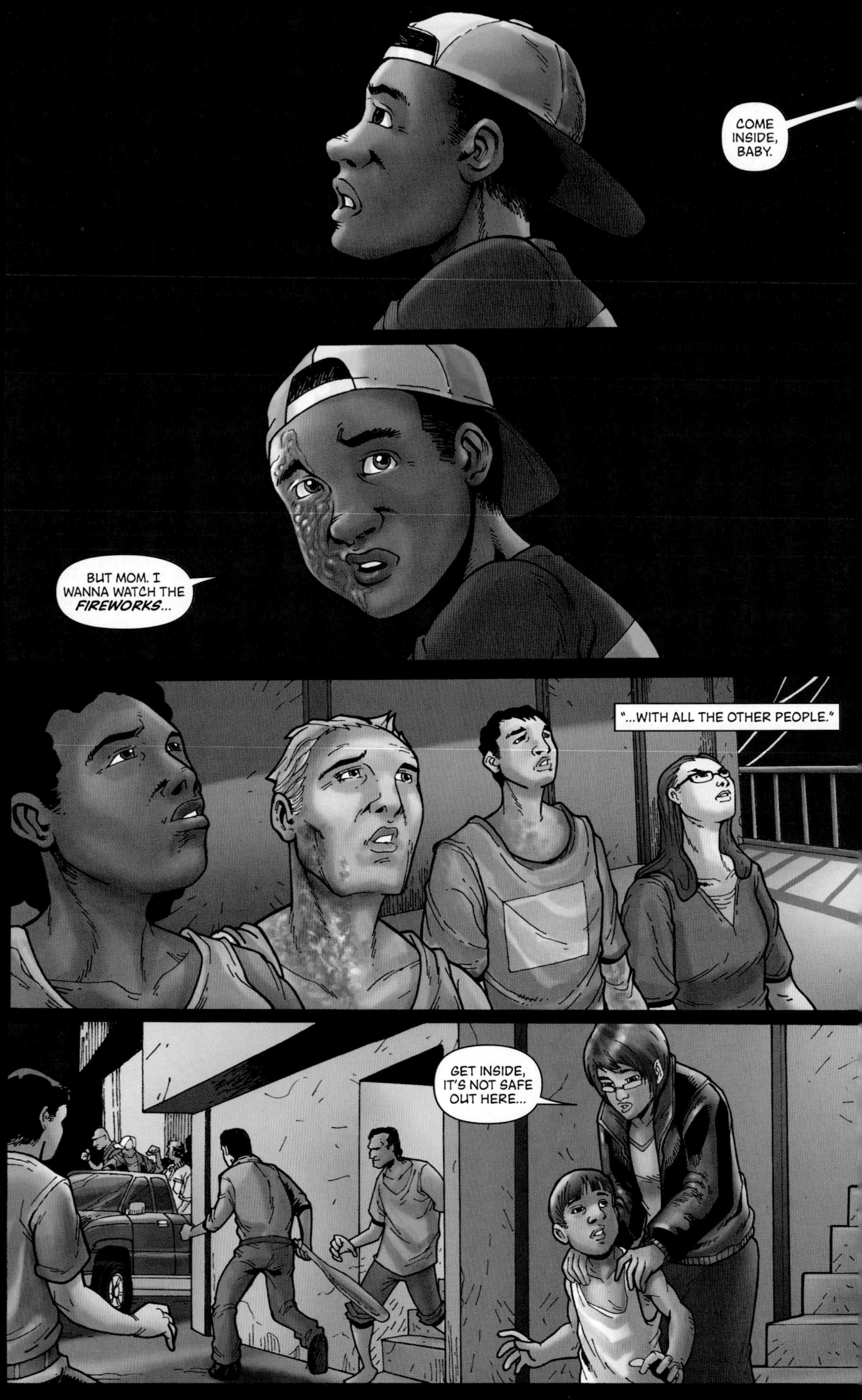
COME INSIDE, BABY.
BUT MOM. I WANNA WATCH THE *FIREWORKS*...
"...WITH ALL THE OTHER PEOPLE."
GET INSIDE, IT'S NOT SAFE OUT HERE...

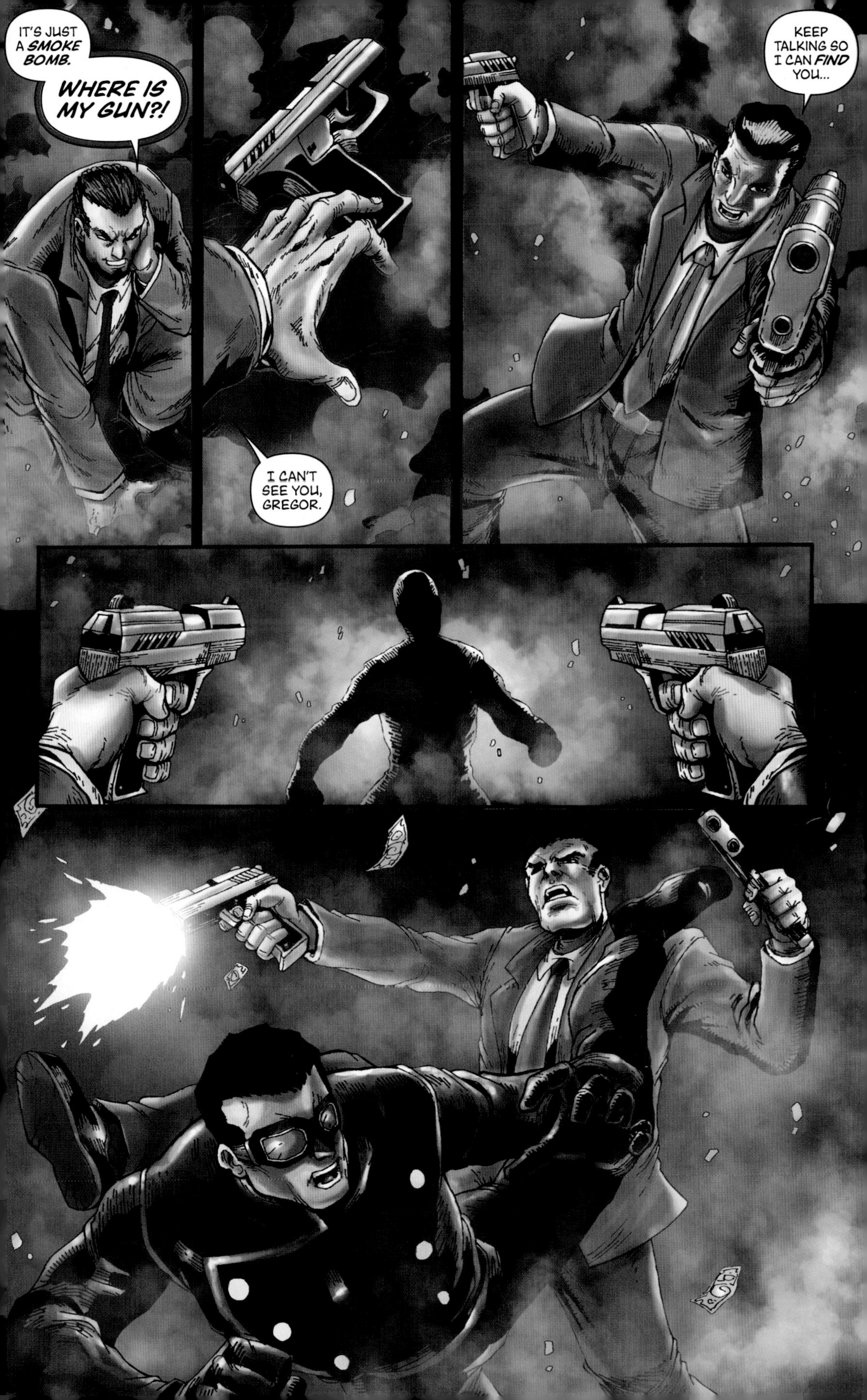
IT'S JUST A *SMOKE BOMB.*
WHERE IS MY GUN?!
I CAN'T SEE YOU, GREGOR.
KEEP TALKING SO I CAN *FIND* YOU...

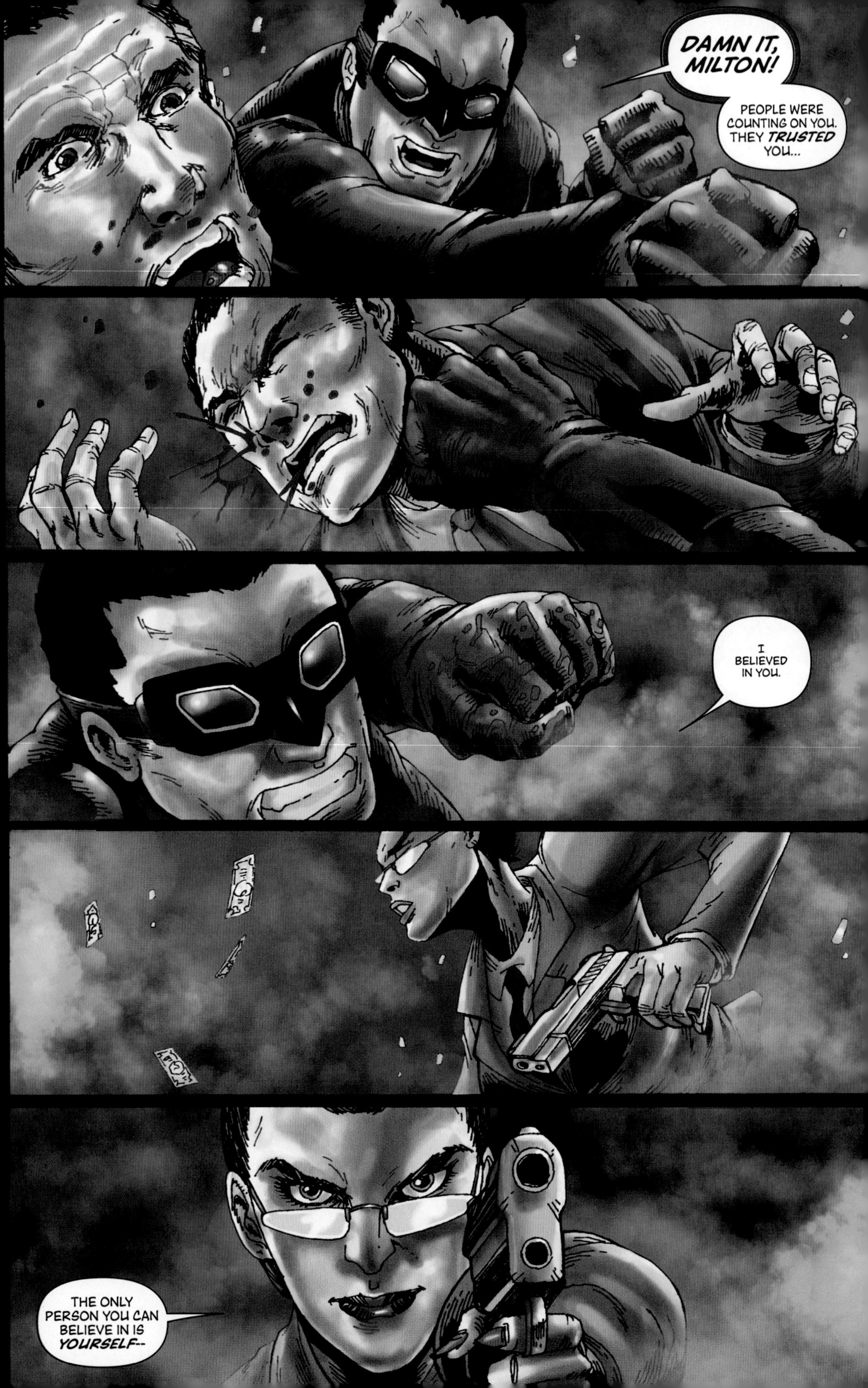
DAMN IT, MILTON!
PEOPLE WERE COUNTING ON YOU. THEY TRUSTED YOU...
I BELIEVED IN YOU.
THE ONLY PERSON YOU CAN BELIEVE IN IS YOURSELF--

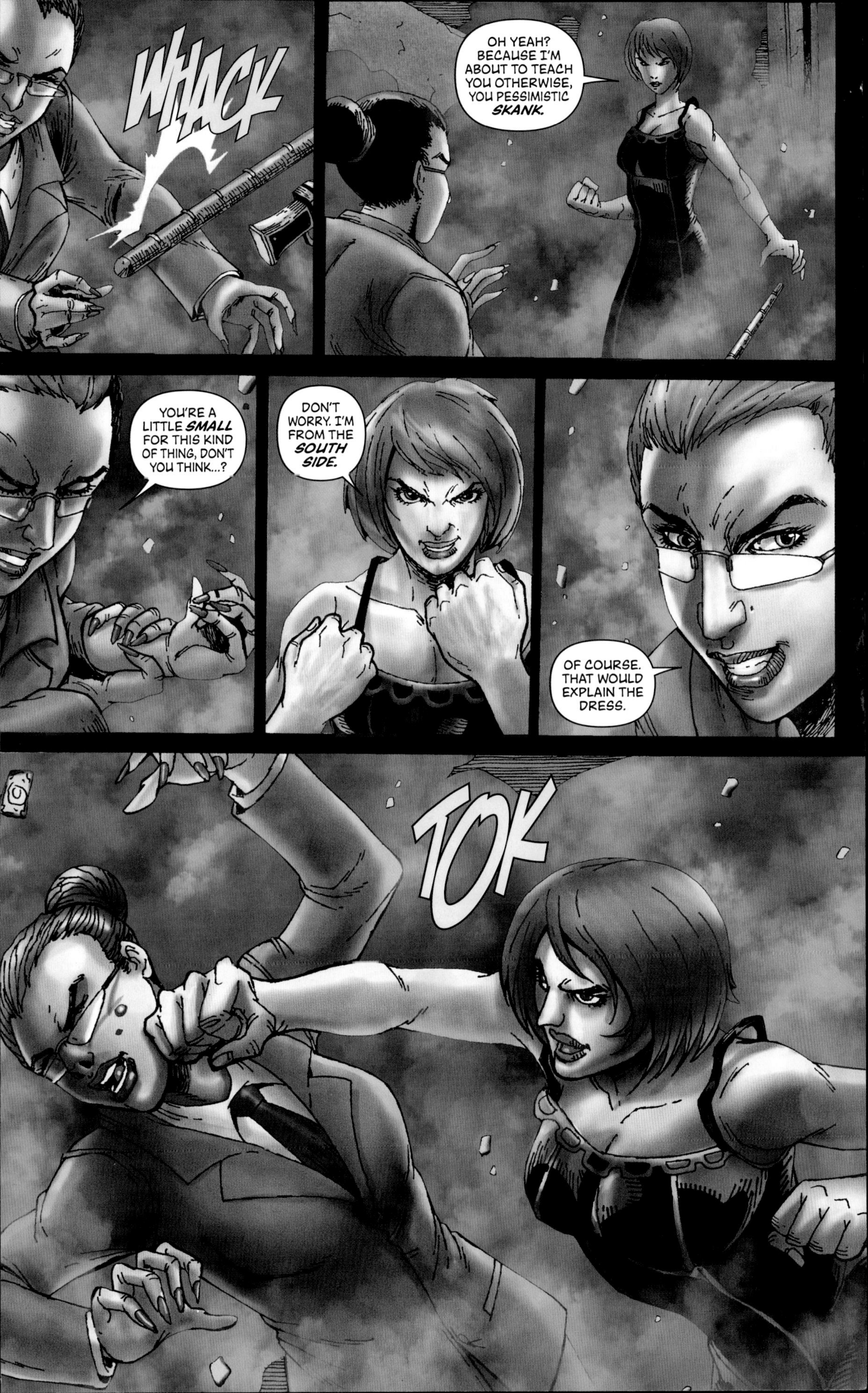
WHACK
OH YEAH? BECAUSE I'M ABOUT TO TEACH YOU OTHERWISE, YOU PESSIMISTIC SKANK.
YOU'RE A LITTLE SMALL FOR THIS KIND OF THING, DON'T YOU THINK...?
DON'T WORRY. I'M FROM THE SOUTH SIDE.
OF COURSE. THAT WOULD EXPLAIN THE DRESS.
TOK

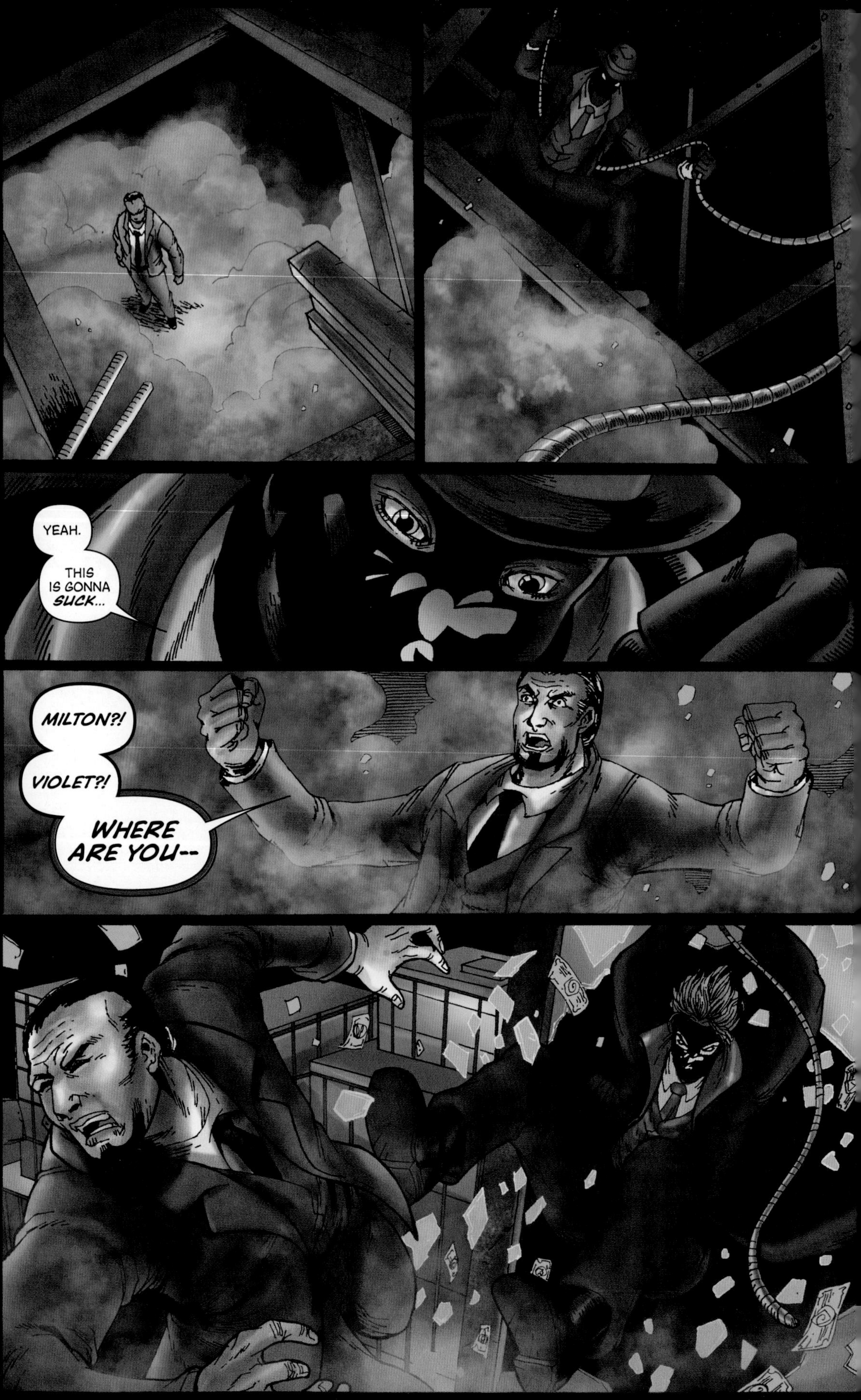
YEAH.
THIS IS GONNA SUCK...
MILTON?!
VIOLET?!
WHERE ARE YOU--

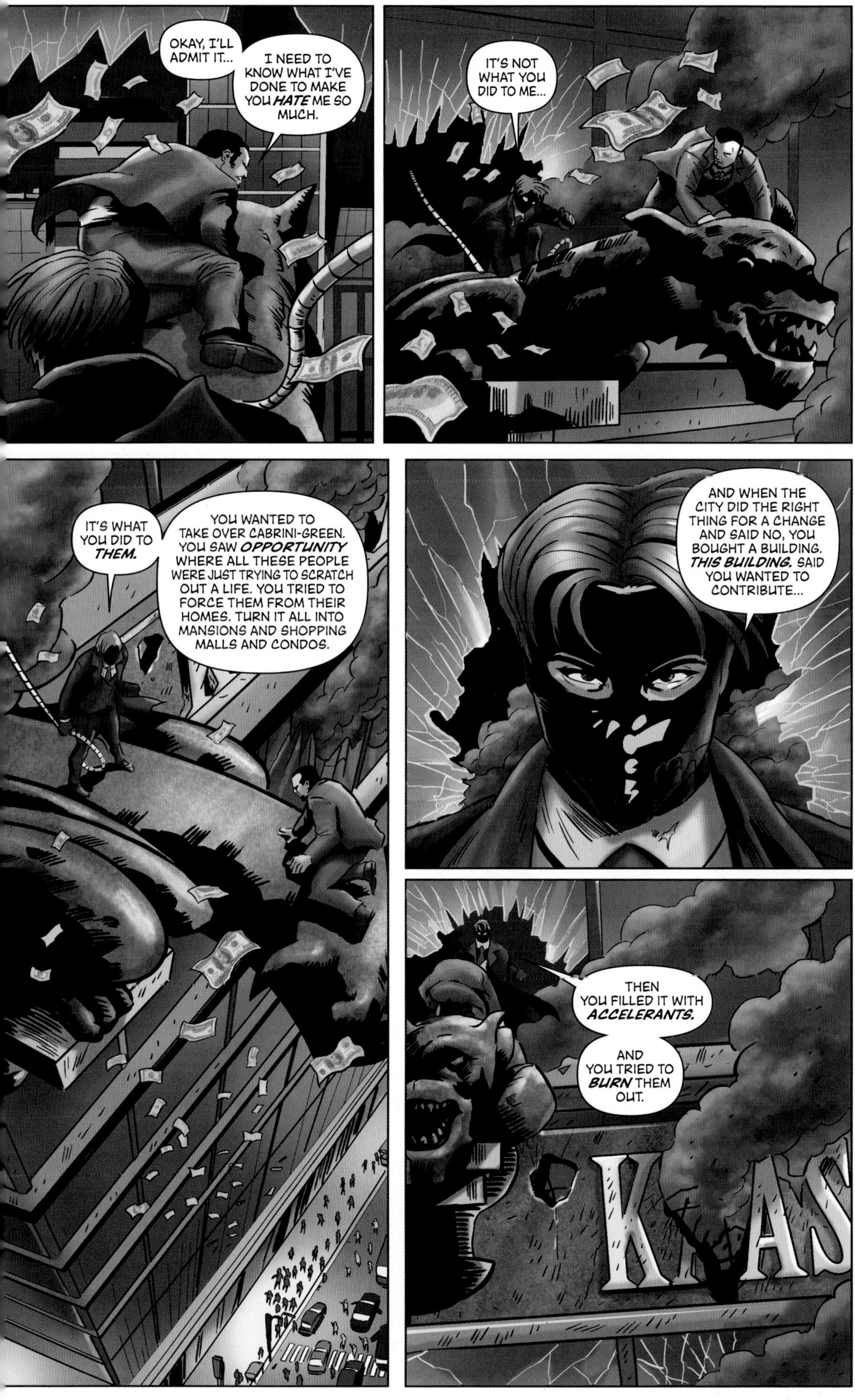
OKAY, I'LL ADMIT IT...
I NEED TO KNOW WHAT I'VE DONE TO MAKE YOU *HATE* ME SO MUCH.
IT'S NOT WHAT YOU DID TO ME...
IT'S WHAT YOU DID TO *THEM.*
YOU WANTED TO TAKE OVER CABRINI-GREEN. YOU SAW *OPPORTUNITY* WHERE ALL THESE PEOPLE WERE JUST TRYING TO SCRATCH OUT A LIFE. YOU TRIED TO FORCE THEM FROM THEIR HOMES. TURN IT ALL INTO MANSIONS AND SHOPPING MALLS AND CONDOS.
AND WHEN THE CITY DID THE RIGHT THING FOR A CHANGE AND SAID NO, YOU BOUGHT A BUILDING. *THIS BUILDING.* SAID YOU WANTED TO CONTRIBUTE...
THEN YOU FILLED IT WITH *ACCELERANTS.*
AND YOU TRIED TO *BURN* THEM OUT.

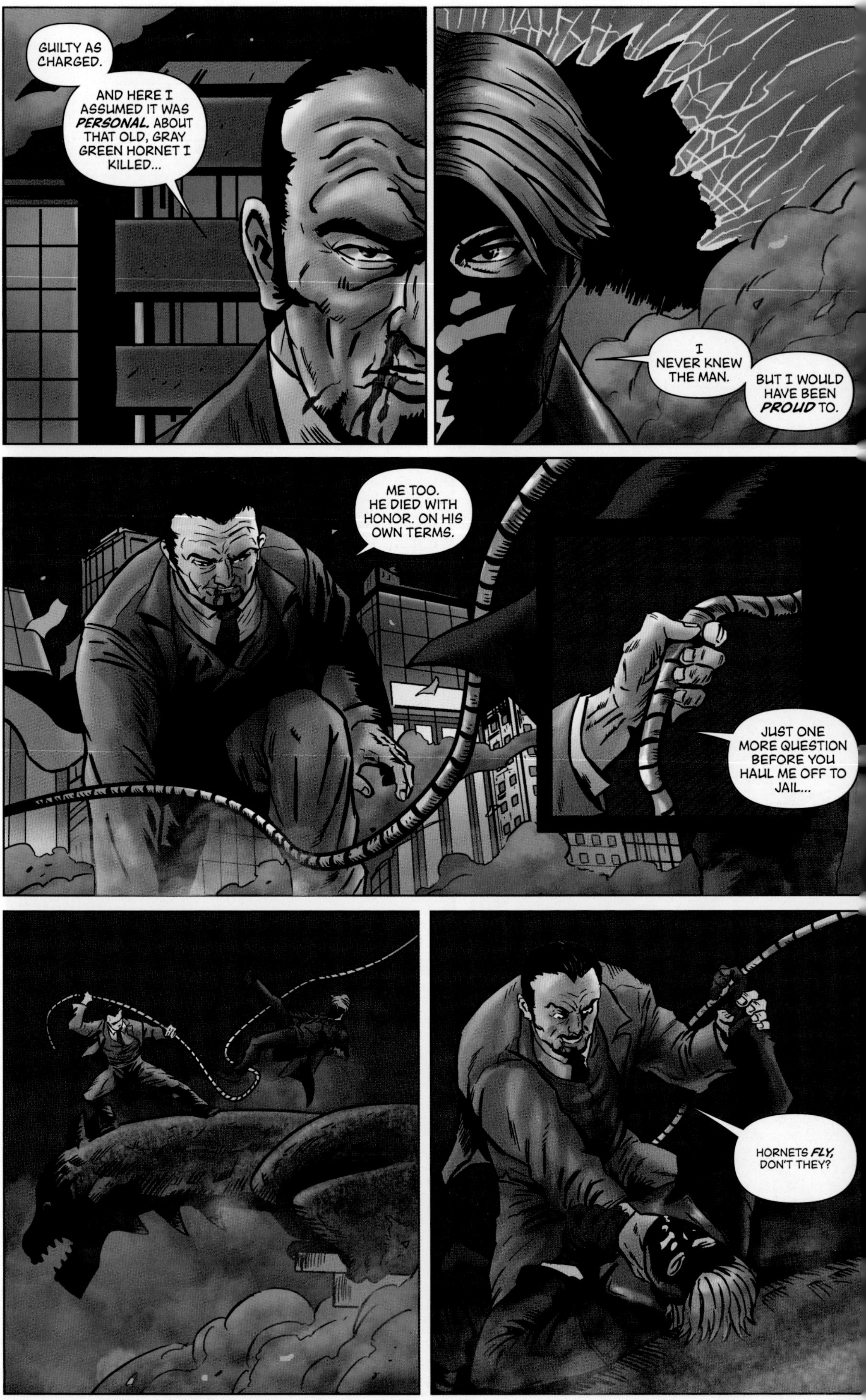
GUILTY AS CHARGED.
AND HERE I ASSUMED IT WAS *PERSONAL.* ABOUT THAT OLD, GRAY GREEN HORNET I KILLED...
I NEVER KNEW THE MAN.
BUT I WOULD HAVE BEEN *PROUD* TO.
ME TOO. HE DIED WITH HONOR. ON HIS OWN TERMS.
JUST ONE MORE QUESTION BEFORE YOU HAUL ME OFF TO JAIL...
HORNETS *FLY,* DON'T THEY?

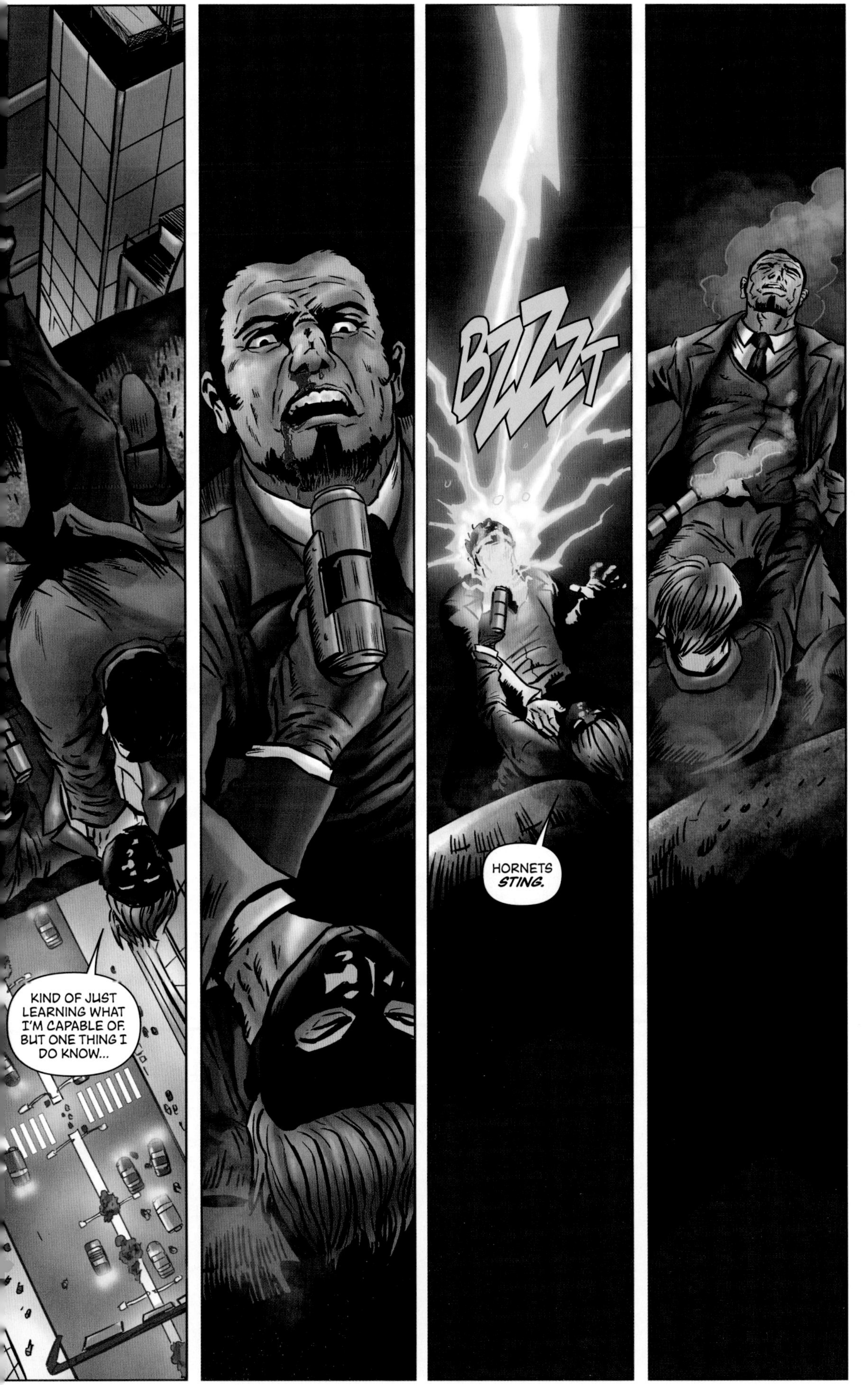
KIND OF JUST LEARNING WHAT I'M CAPABLE OF. BUT ONE THING I DO KNOW...
BZZZZT
HORNETS STING.

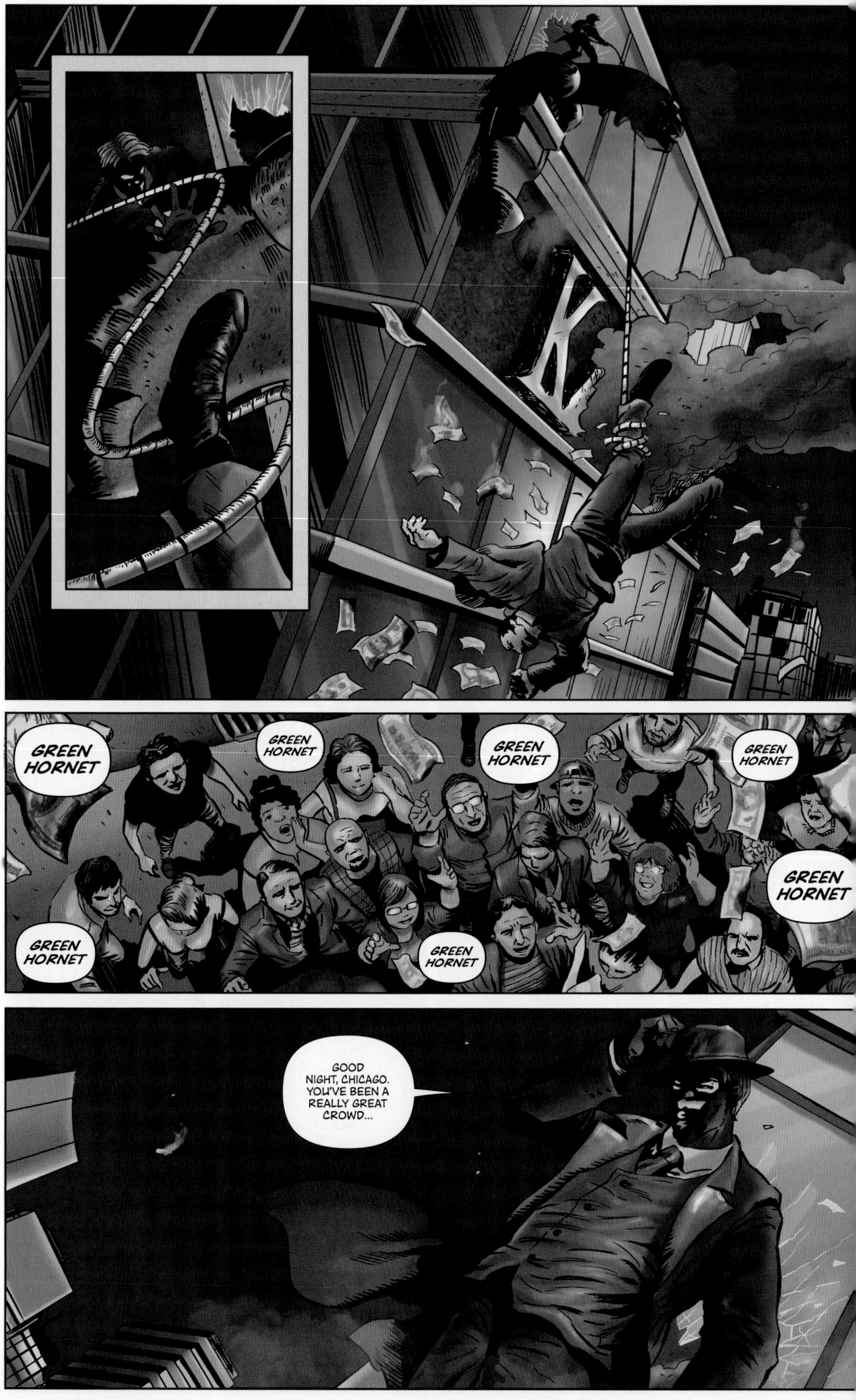
GREEN HORNET
GREEN HORNET
GREEN HORNET
GREEN HORNET
GREEN HORNET
GREEN HORNET
GREEN HORNET
GOOD NIGHT, CHICAGO. YOU'VE BEEN A REALLY GREAT CROWD...

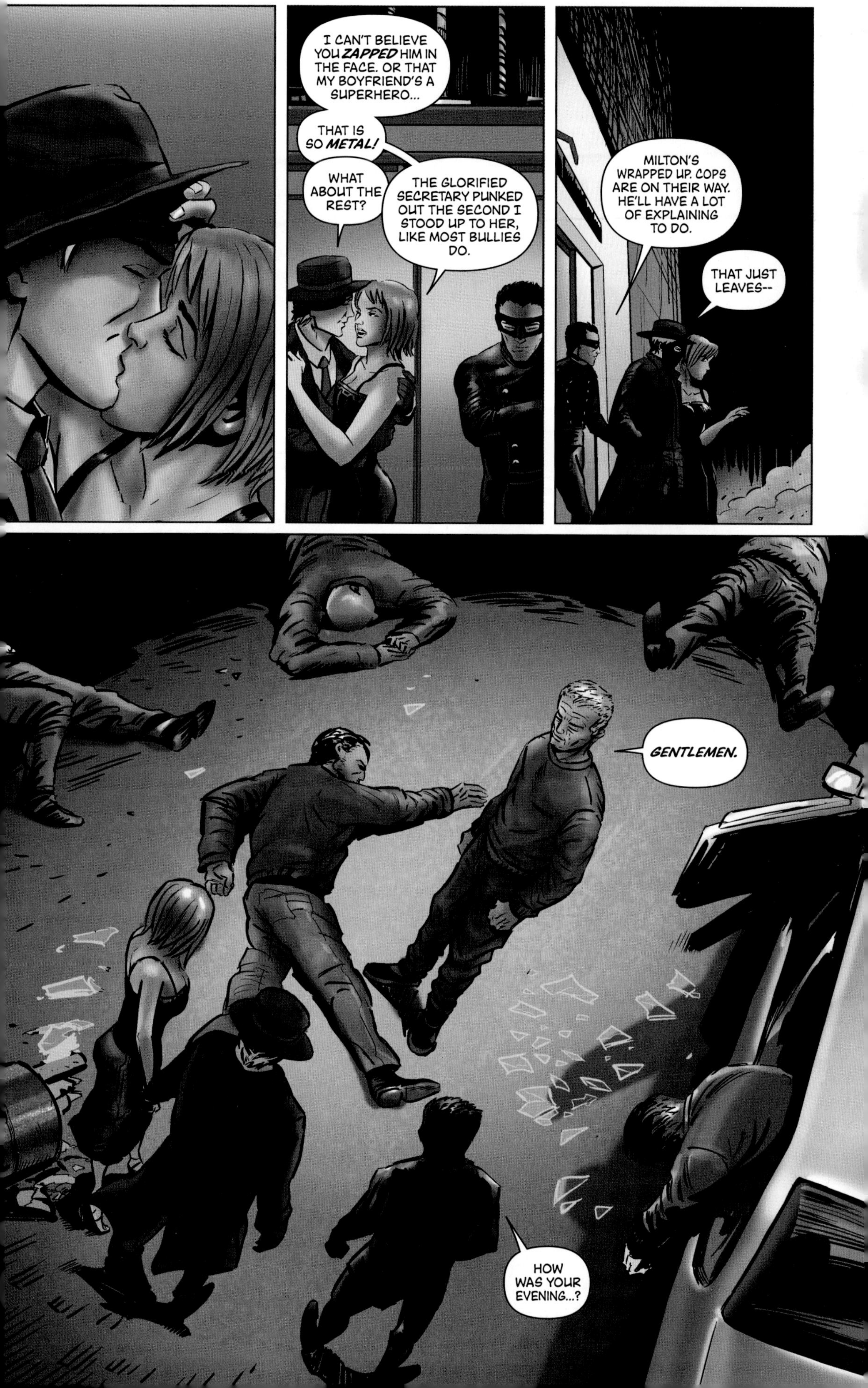
I CAN'T BELIEVE YOU ZAPPED HIM IN THE FACE. OR THAT MY BOYFRIEND'S A SUPERHERO...
THAT IS SO METAL!
WHAT ABOUT THE REST?
THE GLORIFIED SECRETARY PUNKED OUT THE SECOND I STOOD UP TO HER, LIKE MOST BULLIES DO.
MILTON'S WRAPPED UP. COPS ARE ON THEIR WAY. HE'LL HAVE A LOT OF EXPLAINING TO DO.
THAT JUST LEAVES--
GENTLEMEN.
HOW WAS YOUR EVENING...?

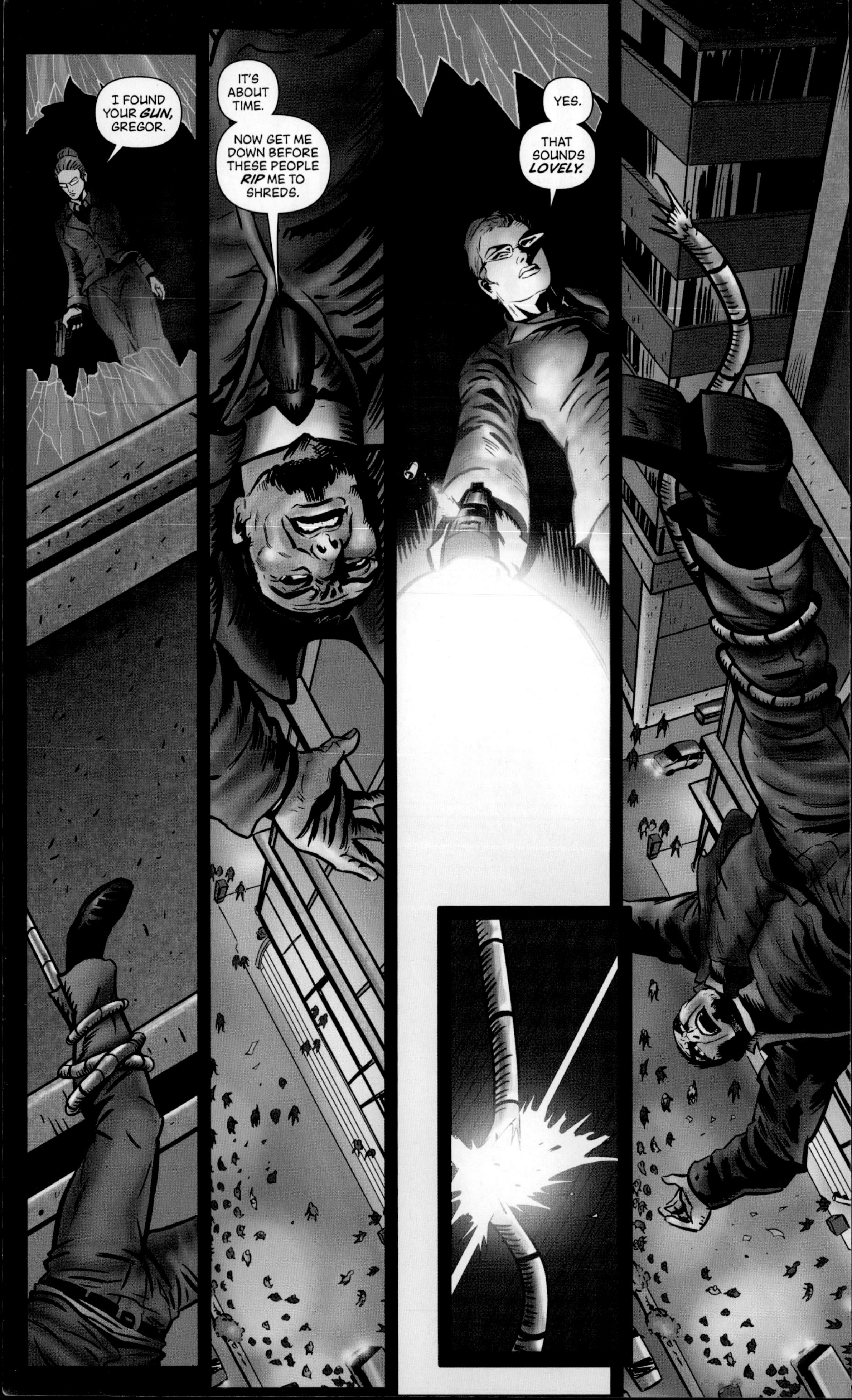
I FOUND YOUR GUN, GREGOR.
IT'S ABOUT TIME.
NOW GET ME DOWN BEFORE THESE PEOPLE RIP ME TO SHREDS.
YES.
THAT SOUNDS LOVELY.

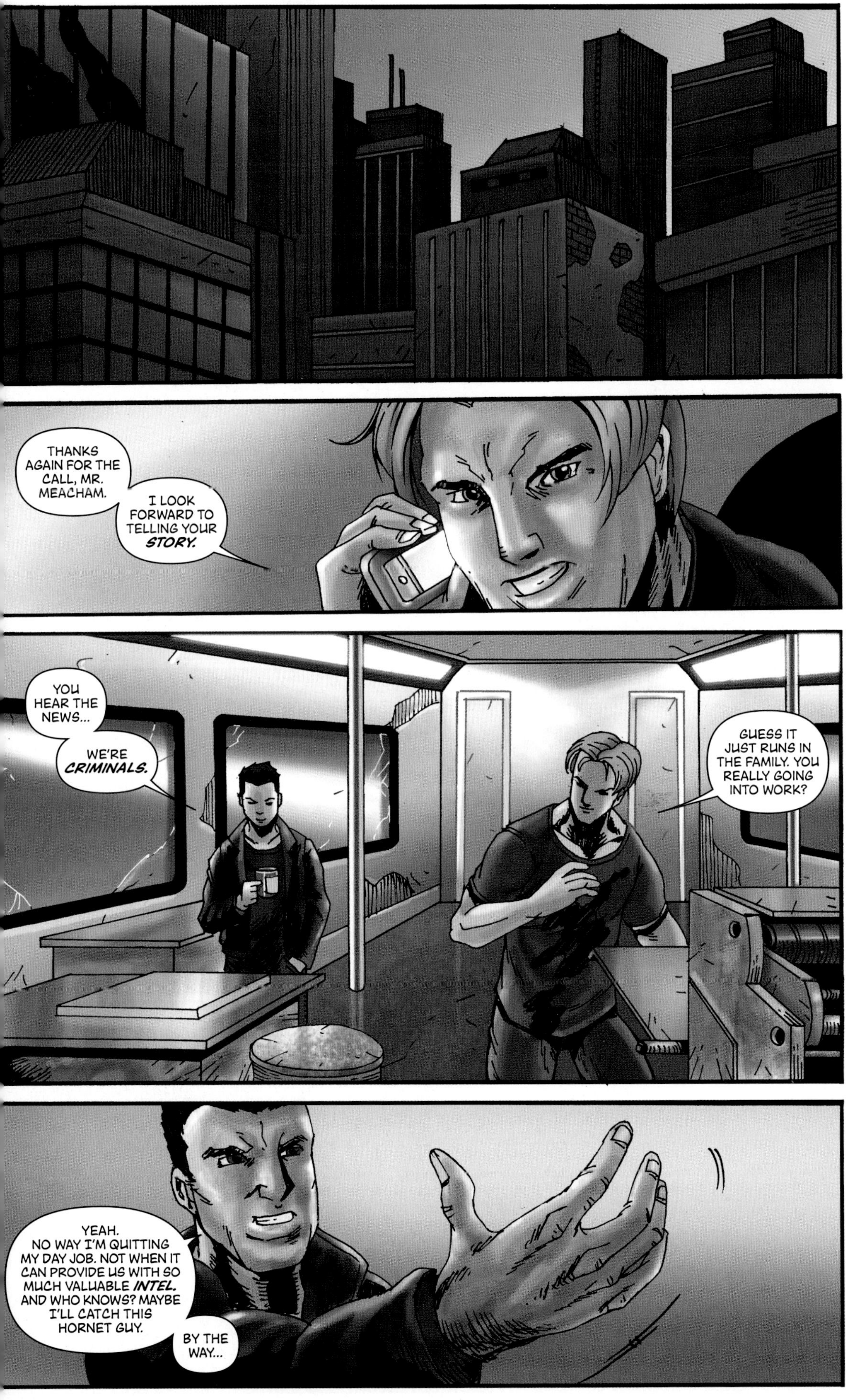
THANKS AGAIN FOR THE CALL, MR. MEACHAM.
I LOOK FORWARD TO TELLING YOUR STORY.
YOU HEAR THE NEWS...
WE'RE CRIMINALS.
GUESS IT JUST RUNS IN THE FAMILY. YOU REALLY GOING INTO WORK?
YEAH. NO WAY I'M QUITTING MY DAY JOB. NOT WHEN IT CAN PROVIDE US WITH SO MUCH VALUABLE INTEL. AND WHO KNOWS? MAYBE I'LL CATCH THIS HORNET GUY.
BY THE WAY...

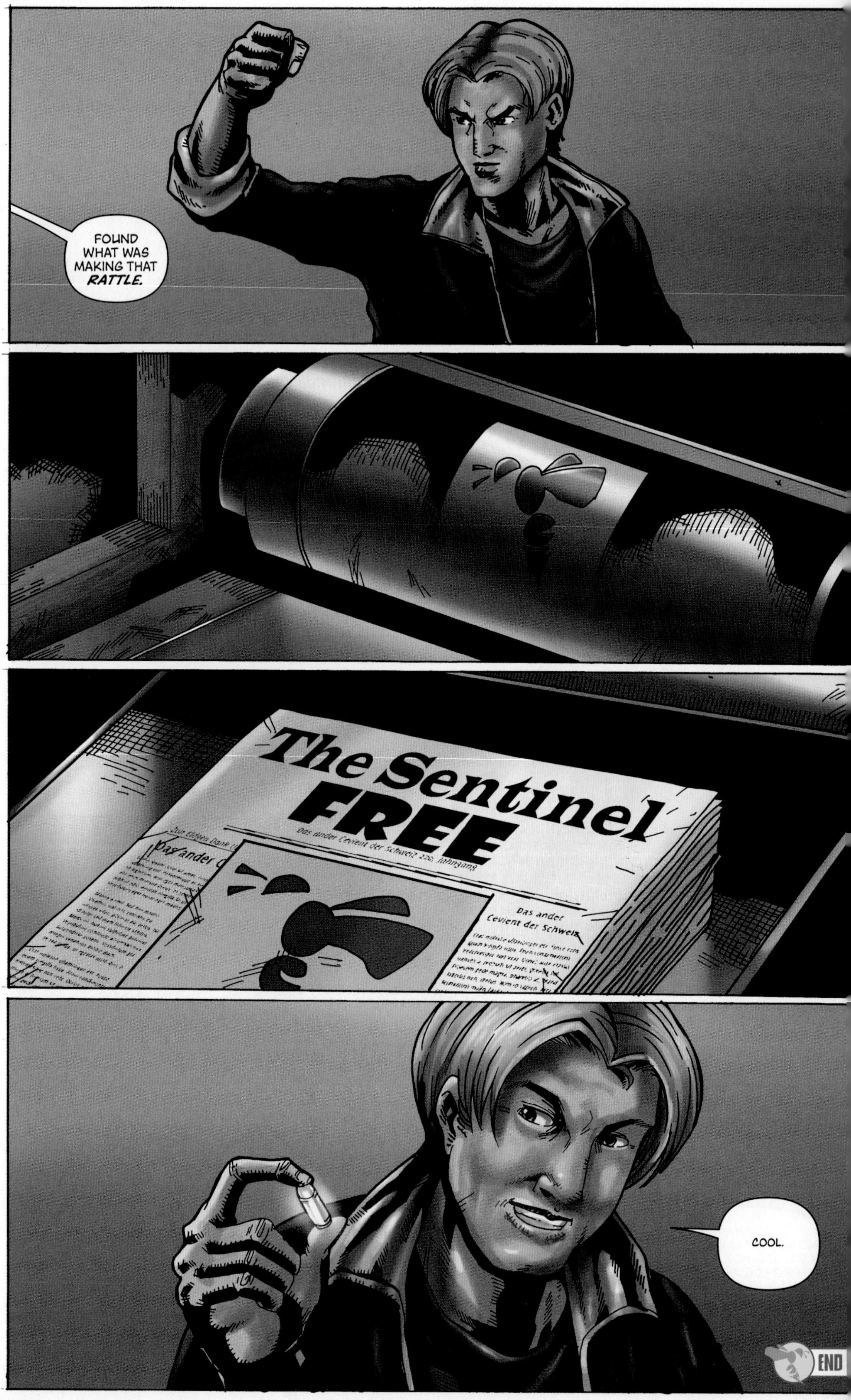
FOUND WHAT WAS MAKING THAT *RATTLE.*
The Sentinel
FREE
Das ander Cevient der Schweiz
COOL.
END

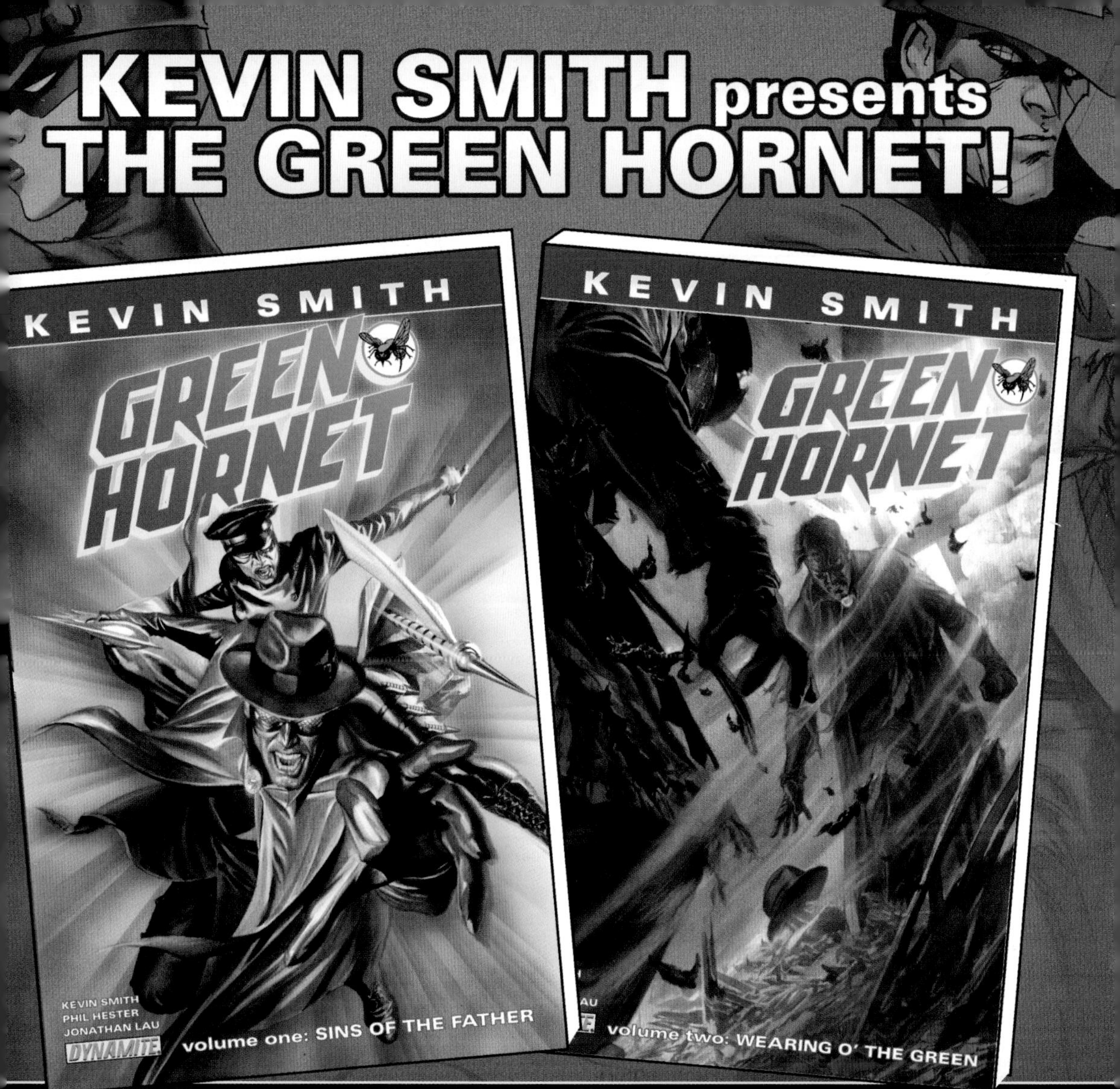
KEVIN SMITH presents
THE GREEN HORNET!
KEVIN SMITH
GREEN HORNET
KEVIN SMITH
PHIL HESTER
JONATHAN LAU
DYNAMITE
volume one: SINS OF THE FATHER
KEVIN SMITH
GREEN HORNET
volume two: WEARING O' THE GREEN

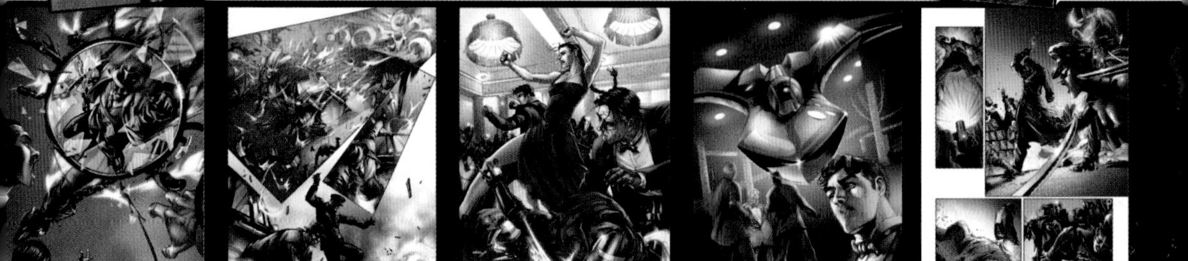

KEVIN SMITH'S GREEN HORNET

VOL. ONE: "SINS OF THE FATHER" & VOL. TWO: "WEARING O' THE GREEN"

written by **KEVIN SMITH** art by **JONATHAN LAU** covers by **ALEX ROSS**

Playboy Britt Reid Jr. has lived a frivolous life of luxury. But when a mysterious figure from the past brutally and publicly murders his father, all of that changes. Now, driven by a thirst for vengeance and guided by two generations of Katos, this one time underachiever will find those responsible and take his father's place as Century City's greatest protector – The Green Hornet! In Stores Now!

Also available: Green Hornet Vol. 3: Idols, Green Hornet Vol. 4: Red Hand, and Green Hornet Vol. 5: Outcast

DYNAMITE WWW.DYNAMITE.COM Information • Newsletters • Contests • Downloads • Forums • More

LOOK FOR THESE DYNAMITE GREATEST HITS!

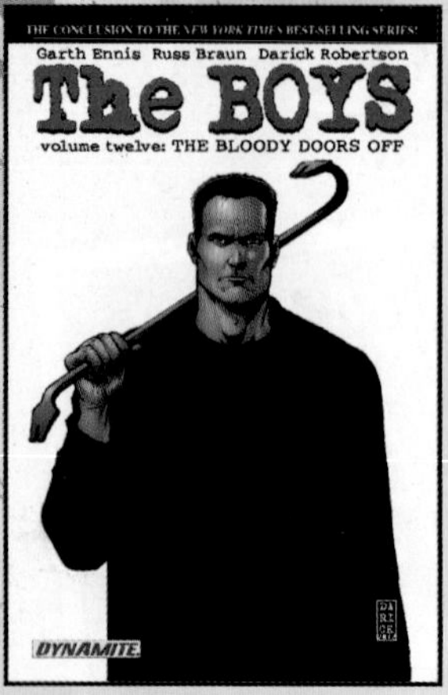
THE CONCLUSION TO THE NEW YORK TIMES BEST-SELLING SERIES!
Garth Ennis Russ Braun Darick Robertson
The BOYS
volume twelve: THE BLOODY DOORS OFF
DYNAMITE

GARTH ENNIS THE BOYS & MORE!

(Garth Ennis') Battlefields V1: The Night Witches
Ennis, Braun

(Garth Ennis') Battlefields V2: Dear Billy
Ennis, Snejbjerg

(Garth Ennis') Battlefields V3: The Tankies
Ennis, Ezquerra

(Garth Ennis') The Complete Battlefields V1
Ennis, Braun, Ezquerra, more

(Garth Ennis') Battlefields V4: Happy Valley
Ennis, Holden

(Garth Ennis') Battlefields V5: The Firefly and His Majesty
Ennis, Ezquerra

(Garth Ennis') Battlefields V6: Motherland
Ennis, Braun

(Garth Ennis') The Complete Battlefields V2
Ennis, Braun, Holden, more

The Boys V1 The Name of the Game
Ennis, Robertson

The Boys V2 Get Some
Ennis, Robertson, Snejbjerg

The Boys V3 Good For The Soul
Ennis, Robertson

The Boys V4 We Gotta Go Now
Ennis, Robertson

The Boys V5 Herogasm
Ennis, McCrea

The Boys V6 The Self-Preservation Society
Ennis, Robertson, Ezquerra

The Boys V7 The Innocents
Ennis, Robertson, Braun

The Boys V8 Highland Laddie
Ennis, McCrea

The Boys V9 The Big Ride
Ennis, Braun

The Boys V10: Butcher, Baker, Candlestickmaker
Ennis, Robertson

The Boys V11 Over the Hill With the Swords of a Thousand Men
Ennis, Braun

The Boys Definitive Edition V1
Ennis, Robertson

The Boys Definitive Edition V2
Ennis, Robertson

The Boys Definitive Edition V3
Ennis, Robertson, more

The Boys Definitive Edition V4
Ennis, Robertson, more

Dan Dare Omnibus
Ennis, Erskine

Jennifer Blood V1 A Woman's Work Is Never Done
Ennis, Batista, Baal, more

Jennifer Blood V2 Beautiful People
Ewing, Baal, more

Just A Pilgrim
Ennis, Ezquerra

The Ninjettes
Ewing, Casallos

Seven Brothers Omnibus
Ennis, Diggle, Kang, more

The Shadow V1 The Fire of Creation
Ennis, Campbell

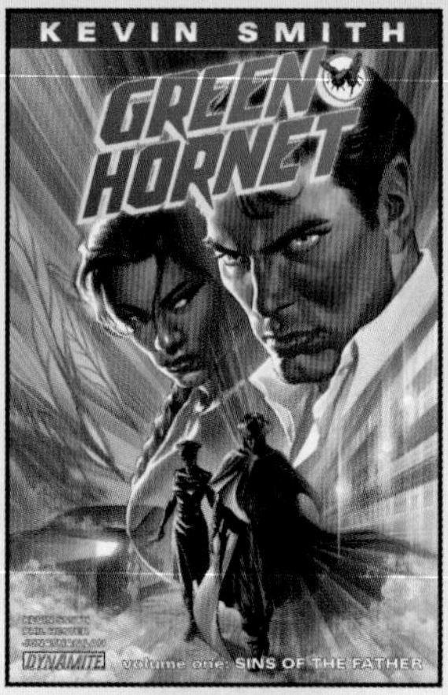
KEVIN SMITH
GREEN HORNET
DYNAMITE
volume one: SINS OF THE FATHER

GREEN HORNET KEVIN SMITH & MORE!

(Kevin Smith's) Green Hornet V1 Sins of the Father
Smith, Hester, Lau

(Kevin Smith's) Green Hornet V2 Wearing 'o the Green
Smith, Hester, Lau

Green Hornet V3 Idols
Hester, Lau

Green Hornet V4 Red Hand
Hester, Smith, Vitorino, more

Green Hornet: Blood Ties
Parks, Desjardins

The Green Hornet: Year One V1 The Sting of Justice
Wagner, Campbell

The Green Hornet: Year One V2 The Biggest of All Game
Wagner, Campbell

The Green Hornet Parallel Lives
Nitz, Raynor

The Green Hornet Golden Age Re-Mastered
Various

Kato V1 Not My Father's Daughter
Parks, Garza, Bernard

Kato V2 Living in America
Parks, Bernard

Kato Origins V1 Way of the Ninja
Nitz, Worley

Kato Origins V2 The Hellfire Club
Nitz, Worley

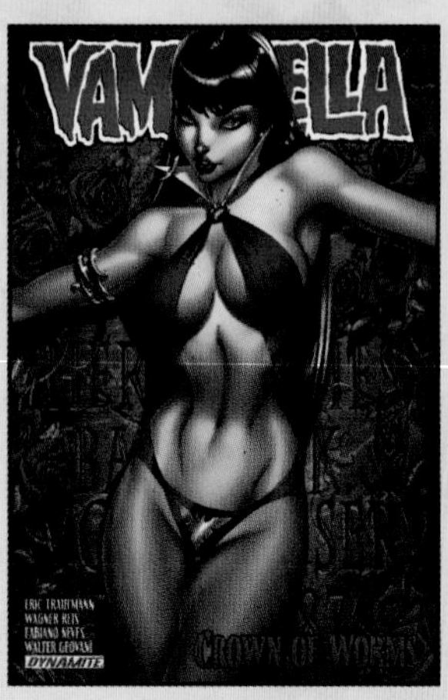
VAMPIRELLA
ERIC TRAUTMANN
WAGNER REIS
FABIANO NEVES
WALTER GEOVANI
DYNAMITE
CROWN OF WORMS

VAMPIRELLA!

Vampirella Masters Series V1 Grant Morrison & Mark Millar
Morrison, Millar, more

Vampirella Masters Series V2 Warren Ellis
Ellis, Conner Palmiotti, more

Vampi Omnibus V1
Conway, Lau

Vampirella Masters Series V3 Mark Millar
Millar, Mayhew

Vampirella Masters Series V4 Visionaries
Moore, Busiek, Loeb, more

Vampirella Masters Series V5 Kurt Busiek
Busiek, Sniegoski, more

Vampirella Masters Series V6 James Robinson
Robinson, Jusko, more

Vampirella Archives V1
Various

Vampirella Archives V2
Various

Vampirella Archives V3
Various

Vampirella Archives V4
Various

Vampirella Archives V5
Various

Vampirella V1 Crown of Worms
Trautman, Reis, Geovani

Vampirella V2 A Murder of Crows
Trautman, Neves, more

Vampirella V3 Throne of Skulls
Trautman, Malaga, more

Vampirella And The Scarlet Legion
Harris, Malaga

Vampirella vs. Dracula
Harris, Rodriguez

RED SONJA!

Adventures of Red Sonja V1
Thomas, Thorne, More

Adventures of Red Sonja V2
Thomas, Thorne, More

Adventures of Red Sonja V3
Thomas, Thorne, More

Queen Sonja V1
Ortega, Rubi

Queen Sonja V2 The Red Queen
Nelson, Herbert

Queen Sonja V3 Coming of Age
Lieberman, Rubi

Queen Sonja V4 Son of Set
Nelson, Salazar

Red Sonja She-Devil With a Sword V1
Oeming, Carey, Rubi

Red Sonja She-Devil With a Sword V2: Arrowsmiths
Oeming, Rubi, more

Red Sonja She-Devil With a Sword V3: The Rise of Kulan Gath
Oeming, Rubi, more

Red Sonja She-Devil With a Sword V4: Animals & More
Oeming, Homs, more

Red Sonja She-Devil With a Sword V5: World On Fire
Oeming, Reed, Homs

Red Sonja She-Devil With a Sword V6: Death
Marz, Ortega, Reed, more

Red Sonja She-Devil With a Sword V7: Born Again
Reed, Geovani

Red Sonja She-Devil With a Sword V8: Blood Dynasty
Reed, Geovani

Red Sonja She-Devil With a Sword V9: War Season
Trautmann, Geovani, more

Red Sonja She-Devil With a Sword V10: Machines of Empire
Trautmann, Geovani, more

Red Sonja She-Devil With a Sword Omnibus V1
Oeming, Carey, Rubi, more

Red Sonja She-Devil With a Sword Omnibus V2
Oeming, Reed, Homs, more

Red Sonja She-Devil With a Sword Omnibus V3
Reed, Geovani

Red Sonja vs. Thulsa Doom V1
David, Lieberman, Conrad

Savage Red Sonja: Queen of the Frozen Wastes
Cho, Murray, Homs

Red Sonja: Travels
Marz, Ortega, Thomas, more

Sword of Red Sonja: Doom of the Gods (Red Sonja vs. Thulsa Doom 2)
Lieberman, Antonio

Red Sonja: Wrath of the Gods
Lieberman, Geovani

Red Sonja: Revenge of the Gods
Lieberman, Sampere

Savage Tales of Red Sonja
Marz, Gage, Ortega, more

ART BOOKS!

The Art of Howard Chaykin
The Art of Painted Comics
The Art of Ramona Fradon
The Art of Red Sonja
The Art of Vampirella
The Dynamite Art of Alex Ross
George Pérez: Storyteller
The Romita Legacy